EUROPEAN ECONOMIC INTEGRATION

FRANK McDONALD

AND

STEPHEN DEARDEN

Second Edition

LONGMAN
LONDON AND NEW YORK

Addison Wesley Longman Limited
Edinburgh Gate, Harlow,
Essex CM20 2JE, England
and Associated Companies throughout the world

Published in the United States of America
by Addison Wesley Longman Publishing, New York

© Longman Group UK Limited 1992
© Longman Group Limited 1994

First published 1992
Second edition 1994
Third impression 1997

ISBN 0582 25141 9 PPR

British Library Cataloguing-in-Publication Data

A catalogue record for this book is
available from the British Library

Library of Congress Cataloging-in-Publication Data

McDonald, Frank, 1951–
    European economic integration / Frank McDonald and Steven Dearden.
-- 2nd ed.
      p.   cm.
    Includes bibliographical references and index.
    ISBN 0-582-215141-9 (pbk.)
    1. European Economic Community. 2. European Economic Community
countries--Economic policy. I. Dearden, Steven, 1950–
II. Title.
HC241.2.M227 1994
337.1'42--dc20
                                       94-28344
                                       CIP

Set by 7 in 10/12.5 Times

Produced by Longman Singapore Publishers Pte Ltd
Printed in Singapore

CONTENTS

CONTRIBUTORS

Stephen Dearden, Senior Lecturer in Economics, Manchester Metropolitan University. Chapters 9, 12 and 15.

John Gibbons, Senior Lecturer in Politics, Manchester Metropolitan University. Chapter 13.

John Hassan, Senior Lecturer in Economic History, Manchester Metropolitan University. Chapter 11.

John Kemp, Senior Lecturer in Economics, Manchester Metropolitan University. Chapter 7.

Andrei Kuznetsov, Senior Lecturer in International Business, Manchester Metropolitan University. Chapter 16 (with F. McDonald and K. Penketh).

Frank McDonald, Senior Lecturer in International Business, Manchester Metropolitan University. Introduction, and chapters 2, 3, 8 (with M. Potton), 16 (with A. Kuznetsov and K. Penketh) and 17.

Keith Penketh, Principal Lecturer in Economics, Manchester Metropolitan University. Chapters 1, 6, 14, and 16 (with F. McDonald and A. Kuznetsov).

Margaret Potton, Research Fellow in EU Studies, Manchester Metropolitan University. Chapter 8 (with F. McDonald).

Judith Tomkins, Senior Lecturer in Economics, Manchester Metropolitan University. Chapter 10 (with J. Twomey).

Heinz Josef Tüselmann, Senior Lecturer in International Business, Manchester Metropolitan University. Chapter 18.

Jim Twomey, Former Senior Lecturer in Economics, Manchester Metropolitan University, currently working as a manager in a Health Authority. Chapter 10 (with J. Tomkins).

George Zis, Professor of Economics, Manchester Metropolitan University. Chapters 4 and 5.

GLOSSARY

ACP	African, Caribbean and Pacific
ASEAN	Association of South East Asian Nations
ATC	Air traffic control
BCO	Business Co-operation Office
BL	Economic union of Belgium and Luxembourg
bn.	billion – one thousand million
BR	British Railways
BRITE	Basic Research in Industrial Technologies in Europe
BRIDGE	Biotechnology Research for Innovation and Development in Europe
CAP	Common Agricultural Policy
CCP	Common Commercial Policy
Cedefop	European Centre for the Development of Vocational Training.
CEN	Comité Européen de Normalisation (European Standards Body)
CENELEC	Comité Européen de Normalisation Electronique (European Standards Body for Electrical Equipment)
CET	Common External Tariff
CFC	Chlorofluorocarbon
CM	Common Market
COMECON	Council for Mutual Economic Assistance (also known as CMEA)
COMETT	Community Action Programme for Education and Training for Technology
COST	European Co-operation in the Field of Scientific and Technical Research
COREPER	Committee of Permanent Representatives
CSF	Community Support Framework
CTP	Common Transport Policy
CU	Customs Union
D	Germany
DELTA	Developing Learning through Technological Advance
DFI	Direct Foreign Investment
DG	Directorate General
DK	Denmark
E	Spain
EAGGF	European Agricultural Guidance and Guarantee Fund

EAP	Environmental Action Programme
EBRD	European Bank of Reconstruction and Development
EC	European Communities
ECB	European Central Bank
ECJ	European Court of Justice
ECSC	European Coal and Steel Community
ECU	European Currency Unit
EDF	European Development Fund
EEA	European Economic Area
EEIG	European Economic Interest Group
EFTA	European Free Trade Association
EIA	Environmental Impact Assessment
EIB	European Investment Bank
EMI	European Monetary Institute
EMS	European Monetary System
EMU	Economic and Monetary Union
EP	European Parliament
ERASMUS	European Community Action Scheme for the Mobility of University Students
ERDF	European Regional Development Fund
ERM	Exchange Rate Mechanism
ESCB	European System of Central Banks
ESF	European Social Fund
ESPIRIT	European Strategic Programme for Research and Development in Information Technology
ETUC	European Trade Union Confederation
EU	European Union
EURATOM	European Atomic Energy Community
EUR6	Six original members of the EU
EUR12	Twelve current members of the EU
EUREKA	European Research Cooperation Agency
EWC	European Works Council
FDR	Federal Republic of Germany (West Germany)
FTC	Fair Trade Commission (Japan)
G7	Group of seven Western industrial countries
G24	Group of 24 Western industrial countries
GATT	General Agreement on Tariffs and Trade
GEMU	German Economic and Monetary Union
GDP	Gross Domestic Product
GDR	German Democratic Republic (East Germany)
GNP	Gross National Product
GR	Greece
GSP	General System of Preferences
HGV	Heavy goods vehicle
I	Italy
IATA	International Air Transport Association
ILO	International Labour Organisation

IMF	International Monetary Fund
IMP	Integrated Mediterranean Programme
IRL	Ireland
IT	Information technology
JRC	Joint Research Centre
LDC	Less Developed Countries
LPG	German Farm Co-operatives
M	Imports
Marpol	International Convention for the Prevention of Pollution from Ships
MCA	Monetary Compensation Amount
MEP	Member of the European Parliament
MES	Minimum Efficiency Scale
MFA	Multi Fibre Arrangement
MFN	Most-favoured-nation
MITI	Ministry of International Trade and Industry (Japan)
MNC	Multinational company
MTIP	Multi-annual Transport Infrastructure Programme
NAFTA	North American Free Trade Area
NATO	North Atlantic Treaty Organisation
NIC	Newly Industrialised Country
NIP	National Indicative Programme
NL	Netherlands
NTB	Non-tariff barrier
NUTS	Nomenclature of Territorial Units
OECD	Organisation for Economic Co-operation and Development
P	Portugal
PHARE	Pologne–Hongrie: Actions pour la reconversion économique (Programme for the Reconstruction of Poland and Hungary)
PPS	Purchasing Power Standard
PSO	Public Service Obligation grant
QMV	Qualified majority voting
R&D	Research and Development
RACE	Research and Development Programme in Advanced Communications Technologies for Europe
RECHAR	Fund for the Reconversion of Coal Mining Areas
RENAVAL	Fund for the Reconversion of Shipbuilding Areas
RESIDER	Fund for the Reconversion of Steel Areas
RETEX	Fund for the Reconversion of Textile Areas
ROW	Rest of the World
RPK	Revenue passenger kilometres
RTD	Research and Technological Development
SAS	Structural Adjustment Support
SEA	Single European Act
SEM	Single European Market
SME	Small and medium sized enterprises

SPRINT	Strategic Programme for the Transnational Promotion of Innovation and Technology Transfer
STABEX	Fund for the Stabilisation of Primary Product Prices
STC	Specific Transport Instrument
STEP	Science and Technology for Environmental Protection
STRIDE	Science and Technology for Regional Innovation and Development in Europe
SYSMIN	Fund for the stabilisation of mineral prices
TACIS	Programme for Technical Assistance to the Commonwealth of Independent States
TEMPUS	Trans-European Mobility Scheme for University Studies
TEU	Twenty foot units
TIC	Transport Infrastructure Committee
TGV	Train à Grande Vitesse
UIC	Union Internationale des Chemins de Fer
UK	United Kingdom
UNCTAD	United Nations Conference on Trade and Development
UNICE	Union of Industrial and Employers' Confederations of Europe
VAT	Value Added Tax
VER	Voluntary Export Restraint
WTO	World Trade Organisation
X	Exports

PREFACE

Many changes have taken place in Europe since the first edition of this book. The deadline for the completion of the internal market has been passed and frontier controls have been removed. The Maastrict Treaty has been ratified and a detailed process and timetable to move to monetary union has been set out. This treaty also extended the scope of activities that may be subject to the laws, policies and programmes of the Community. Agreement was reached to create a European Economic Area between the members of the EU and Austria, Finland, Iceland, Norway and Sweden. These changes have had, and will continue to exercise, a considerable influence on the course of economic integration in Europe.

However, the early 1990s proved to be a difficult time for European integration programmes. The ratification process for the Maastrict Treaty revealed that there was considerable resistance to deepening the integration process. The EMS experienced a crisis which effectively resulted in the suspension of the ERM. The problem of unemployment became the dominant issue in the EU. The EU was also shown to be unable to quickly come to terms with the collapse of communism. It could be argued that the EU lost the sense of vision and purpose that it appeared to have had in the late 1980s. New problems such as recession, unemployment and resistance to deeper integration led to a questioning of the role and purpose of the EU.

In the light of these events the authors thought that a second edition should be issued to examine the implications of these changes for the process of integration.

The most significant changes have been the addition of four new chapters (Macroeconomic policy coordination in the EU, The European financial common market, Industrial policy in the EU and Transport policy) and the replacement of the chapter on German unification with a new chapter – Economic events in Germany and their impact on Europe. These new chapters add important new material which is important for the examination of the process of integration in Europe.

All the chapters have been revised and updated. In some cases these revisions have been fairly minor, for example modifying tables to make them more up-to-date and assessing the impact of recent changes. However, the Introduction has been substantially modified and extended to highlight the main events and changes that have taken place and to indicate their importance to the integration process. The chapter on European monetary union has also been substantially revised to provide an assessment of the important changes in this area. The chapter on the EU and the rest of Europe has also been considerably revised to examine the growing links between EFTA and the EU and to explore the progress that has been made in the restructuring of the economies of the former communist countries. The chapter on the European Community and the USA and Japan has been considerably revised and renamed – The Triad and the NICs. This chapter examines relationships within the Triad and with the NICs. Material on the significance of the agreement on the Uruguay Round of GATT has been added to the chapters on the Common Agricultural Policy, the External trade policy and the Triad and the NICs.

The authors hope that the additions, revisions and updating of material will increase the value of this book for students of the process of economic integration in Europe.

INTRODUCTION

Frank McDonald

The study of European Economic Integration has become a major area of interest in recent years. The moves to create a Single European Market (SEM), combined with the pressures to establish Economic and Monetary Union (EMU), have focused attention on the European Union (EU) as the key actor in this process of integration. Increasingly, the EU is becoming involved in a host of policies which affect many aspects of the economic and social activities of the member states. Agricultural matters, especially the common agricultural policy (CAP), were once the only significant policy of the EU. The increasing moves to integrate the EU have brought many other policy areas to the forefront, such as competition, social, regional, and environmental policies.

In addition to the growing importance of the EU, other factors have been at work which have increased the significance of studying economic conditions in Europe. These include the ending of the Cold War and the demise of communism in most of Central and Eastern Europe, the reunification of Germany and the collapse of the Soviet Union. These developments present a series of new problems for European integration, in particular the future relations of the countries of Central and Eastern Europe and the republics of the former Soviet Union to the Community. The EFTA countries are also being drawn closer to the EU and an agreement has been reached between the EU and most of the countries of EFTA to form a European Economic Area (EEA). The EEA allows for the creation of an area of free trade for goods, services, labour and capital between the member states of the EU and most of the EFTA countries. Austria, Finland, Norway and Sweden are due to become full members of the EU in 1995. The rest of the world is becoming more interested in and economically linked to Europe. Already the EU has an important role in the GATT and has strong links to many Third World countries through special arrangements with the African, Caribbean and Pacific countries (ACP). The USA, Japan and the NICs are also heavily involved in the European economy, both as traders and, in the cases of the USA and Japan, as sources of Direct Foreign Investment (DFI) into Europe. The origin of these developments can be traced to the rise of the European Unity movement.

The European Unity movement

A full description and analysis of the historical development of the European unity movement can be found in Nugent (1992), and a review of the main elements in this process is provided in Swann (1988). The origins of the move to achieve European unity stemmed from the desire to avoid the periodic wars between the competing nation-states of Europe. There was also some consideration of the advantages of creating a larger market in Europe to allow for the reaping of economies of scale. However, it was political factors which predominated in the early attempts to achieve European unity. Therefore, although there were economic factors behind this movement, the main objectives were political. When the first steps towards creating the EU were made, specific economic objectives were the main methods advocated to achieve European unity; they were however generally regarded as means to an end, and the end was the establishing of some kind of political union.

In the aftermath of the Second World War the countries of Europe were faced with several difficult issues. Much of the continent of Europe was severely war damaged, and a large reconstruction process was necessary. The Cold War was developing and Europe was divided into two opposing camps with the emergence of East and West Europe, with a divided Germany as the potential flashpoint for renewed conflict in Europe. Any such conflict would have been between the two new superpowers of the USA and the Soviet Union, and could have involved the use of nuclear weapons. In such circumstances it was not surprising that the Europeans should have looked for some methods to ensure that they had some voice in shaping the dramatic events which were taking place in Europe. The main obstacles to this were that Europe could not speak with one voice because it was composed of a number of sovereign nation-states and these states did not have a common view on the solutions to the problems of postwar Europe. The main powers in Europe were the USA and the Soviet Union. The UK, which was the strongest European power, was not particularly interested in becoming involved in attempts to achieve European unity. In this period the UK was interested in stability in Europe that would allow the UK to concentrate on the creation of zones of influence in the Commonwealth and with developing a 'special relationship' with the USA. Therefore, although the UK was not opposed to European unity, it was in favour of very loose inter-governmental arrangements between the countries of Europe where each country retained complete sovereignty (the right to make decisions independently of other governments or agencies) in the important areas of policy-making. Consequently, the UK was not prepared to become involved in attempts to create any supranational European agencies as they would have powers which would erode the sovereignty of the member countries. The Scandinavian countries were concerned to isolate themselves from the increasing conflicts between the superpowers, and as Europe was at the centre of these conflicts they had little desire to become involved in creating a United States of Europe which would add a third party to these conflicts. The countries of Southern Europe were hardly connected to these events. Spain and Portugal were dictatorships and were not considered to be eligible to join the democratic countries of Europe in creating new arrangements to forge European unity. Greece was in a state of political flux with the possibility that it could go communist and forge links with the Soviet Union. Indeed the main focus of attention on the countries of Southern Europe was to ensure that they were not recruited to the communist side and to enrol them in the defence coalition opposing the Soviet Union.

In the immediate postwar period Europe was divided not only into East and West, but also into those countries which favoured the creation of some kind of United States of Europe, where new agencies would be created with supranational powers which would displace many of the decision-making functions of the member countries (those who advocated this are normally called Federalists), and others who looked for some loose forms of inter-governmental co-operation. There was also division between the democratic countries of Western Europe and the dictatorships of Southern Europe. The countries of Western Europe were also faced with the economic and political dominance of the USA.

In the late 1980s all of these divisions began to crumble and the division with Southern Europe vanished. There still exist conflicts and divisions in some of these areas. The conflict between the Federalists and the Inter-governmentalists is intensifying within the EU. The USA no longer economically dominates Europe and the ending of the Cold War has reduced American political and military influence in Europe, but there is no consensus on the future role of the USA in European economic, political and military matters. Although Europe has largely ceased to be divided into different camps on the basis of ideology, in that there is general acceptance of liberal democratic forms of government with market-based allocation of resources, there is still considerable dispute as to what characteristics the new European economy should have.

In spite of these disputes there is a consensus that in economic matters the EU is the key to the development of Europe. In political and even military matters the EU, or at least institutions with strong connections to it, is seen as the way forward to allow adjustment to the new conditions which prevail in Europe. The EEC, and its precursor the European Coal and Steel Community (ECSC), always had economic objectives to the fore, and this remains true even though the EU is beginning to expand into more overtly political objectives. Indeed many of the pressures to move into political areas stem from the need to create the necessary conditions under which economic objectives such as establishing the SEM and EMU can be achieved. There are also pressures to modify the political structures to aid in the growing role that the EU plays in the world economy. The process of European economic integration is therefore at the heart of the current changes in Europe, and the EU is the key agent in this process.

The origins of the EU

The EU arose as a result of the failure of the main countries of Europe to reach agreement on how European unity should proceed. The Federalists in France and West Germany tended to win the argument for the need for some kind of supranational European agencies and Italy, Belgium, Holland and Luxembourg also tended to this conclusion. It was these six countries which started the process which ultimately led to the EU. In the UK and the Scandinavian countries the principle of inter-governmentalism was the predominant view. In matters of foreign relations and military arrangements the Cold War and the dominance of the USA and the Soviet Union resulted in the setting-up of opposing alliances in Europe. This led to the establishing of the Warsaw Pact alliance in Eastern Europe, and NATO in Western Europe, the former dominated by the Soviet Union and the latter by the USA. The early attempts to establish economic and non-military political arrangements in Western Europe were centred on the Organisation for European Economic Co-operation (OEEC), and the Council of Europe. The OEEC failed to develop because of disputes about the need for some kind of supranational decision-making powers. It eventually expanded its membership and became the Organisation for Economic Co-operation and Development (OECD). The Council of Europe was not granted any supranational powers and it still exists as a forum for inter-governmental discussion on issues of interest to Europe. The main advantage that it has is that its membership includes most European countries. It has not played any significant role in the integration of Europe.

By the early 1950s a series of inter-governmental agencies existed in Western Europe – the Council of Europe, the OEEC, and NATO. For those countries which favoured more supranational powers for European agencies these institutions did not seem to be capable of integrating Europe. The Federalists were therefore faced with no institutional frameworks from which they thought a united Europe could emerge. In 1948, Belgium, Holland and Luxembourg agreed to form a Customs Union (CU), which came to be known as Benelux. This use of specific economic means of achieving European unity was to come to the fore in the development of the EU. The main political and military issues in Western Europe were heavily influenced by NATO and the Americans, and were firmly based on inter-governmentalism. The European Federalists were therefore unable to expand their ideas into these areas. The involvement of West Germany in any attempt to form a type of supranational agency with responsibility for political and defence issues was restricted by the opposition of the Soviet Union to any German involvement in these matters, and in the immediate postwar period there was popular opposition within Western Europe to allowing Germany any such role in these areas. Consequently, the Federalists were restricted to economic matters in proposals for any supranational agency.

In those countries where Federalist views were dominant (France, Germany, Italy, Holland, Belgium, and Luxembourg: the original six), there was a desire to establish agencies with some supranational powers. This led to the setting up of the ECSC established by the Treaty of Paris signed in 1951. The motive for this was to integrate the coal and steel industries of Germany, the heart of its war machine, into an interdependent European industrial structure, thereby making war between West European countries impossible. The ECSC had a High Authority which had some supranational powers in the areas of coal and steel, but the main decision-making powers rested with the Council of Ministers. This Council was composed of the Ministers of the member states, and was therefore inter-governmental in character. Nevertheless, the ECSC was an agency which had some supranational powers, and was a kind of a cross between an inter-governmental and a supranational agency. This strange mixture was also to characterise the European Economic Community (EEC) and EURATOM, the agencies which followed the ECSC, and from which the EU arose. Consequently the origins of the EU led to an institutional structure which was focused on economic matters and is neither a pure inter-governmental nor a supranational agency, but rather is a mixture of these forms.

The setting up of the EEC and the EURATOM resulted from the Spaak committee which was first convened in 1955. The UK joined in with the original six in this committee, but withdrew when it became clear that the original six wanted new institutional forms based on the model of the ECSC, and were also seeking wide-ranging economic integration. Therefore the UK did not join with the original six when they established the EEC and EURATOM by the two Treaties of Rome, signed in 1957. Instead the UK formed EFTA in 1960 with Austria, Switzerland, Norway, Sweden, Denmark, and Portugal. The arrangements within EFTA were considerably less ambitious than the EEC. The EEC had elements of supranationality in decision-making and was committed to the establishment of a Customs Union, a Common

Market and had vaguely defined objectives to create Economic and Monetary Union (EMU), while EFTA was purely inter-governmental and was only aiming to achieve a free trade area.

By the early 1960s Europe appeared to have created a new political order which was based on the division of Europe into East and West, with the Soviet Union and the USA largely directing events in this area, and an economic order based on the EEC, EFTA and COMECON. However, the EEC was soon to emerge as the dominant economic agency in Europe.

The development of the EU

The original six experienced high growth rates in the 1960s and this was often attributed to the ambitious programme of economic integration on which the EEC had embarked. It may however have had more to do with the rapid growth of West Germany as it experienced an 'economic miracle' in the postwar reconstruction process. In this period Germany became the leading industrial power in Europe and the other members of the EEC benefited from their growing economic links with this dynamic economy. Whatever the reason for the relative success of the member states of the EEC, certain groups in the UK eventually came to regard the Community as the key to the future economic prosperity of Britain. It had become clear to key decision-makers in the UK that the Commonwealth was not a viable economic bloc and that EFTA was not big enough to provide the necessary market size to allow for the reaping of economies of scale. The EEC, with the new economic power of Germany at the centre, was deemed to be the appropriate vehicle to allow the UK to halt and then reverse its relative economic decline. It was therefore mainly economic reasons which drew the UK towards applying for membership of the EEC. The accession of the UK to the EEC was a long and difficult process because the CAP and the commitment of the EEC to a degree of supranational decision-making ran counter to long-held traditions in the UK. However, after a series of long and complex negotiations (see Swann 1988 for a survey), the UK, along with Ireland and Denmark, joined the EEC. This was to have a profound influence on the development of the EU. The EEC now included the four largest economies in Europe: Germany, France, Italy, and the UK. There was also an increase in the conflicts within the EEC as the UK had an economic and political structure which did not sit easily with that of the EEC. This became obvious with disputes about the CAP and the connected budgetary problems: these issues are discussed in Chapter 6. The regional problems of the EEC were also brought more sharply into focus as the membership of both the UK and Ireland greatly increased the number of relatively deprived regions in the Community. The impact of this on the development of the regional policy of the Community is outlined in Chapter 10.

The expansion in the membership of the EEC in 1973 was not followed by fast progress in implementing the integration programme of the Community. Indeed the 1970s was a period of considerable stagnation in the Community. The problems in adjusting to the issues raised by the enlargement were one factor in the lack of progress in developing the necessary policies and programmes to allow greater integration to take place. There were also problems raised by the OPEC oil price increases, and the instability of the international monetary system caused by the ending of the Bretton Woods system. These problems led to poor growth rates in the member states. The EEC did not manage to adopt a united approach to these issues and generally there was a pronounced lack of momentum in the Community. By the 1970s the

Community had accomplished the creation of the CU (although a large number of non-tariff barriers remained in place), but was not making much progress to create a Common Market. The CAP was the only significant common policy of the EEC and that was causing considerable problems both within the Community and with the rest of the world. In the movements towards EMU practically no progress was being made. However, this state of affairs was to change dramatically in the 1980s.

A new momentum began to arise with the second enlargement of the EEC when Greece joined in 1981, and Spain and Portugal in 1986. This led to the creation of a market of 320 million consumers, *the largest market in the world*. This enlargement resulted in few problems in incorporating these countries into the Community, in spite of the large differences in their levels of economic development as compared to the rest of the EEC. There were also movements to alter the Treaty of Rome to remove some of the constraints imposed by the cumbersome nature of the decision-making process of the Community. This led to the Single European Act (SEA) and the launching of the SEM programme: these issues are examined in Chapter 2. The launching of the EMS in 1979, and the implications of the creation of the SEM for monetary and other macro-economic policies, increased pressures for monetary integration in the EC.

By the early 1990s the EU had made considerable progress in establishing the SEM. It had also developed detailed plans for the creation of monetary union and a momentum had built up to increase Community competencies in the social, environmental and regional areas. Furthermore, issues connected to foreign and security policies and other types of political policies increased in importance. The reunification of Germany and the collapse of communism in Central and Eastern Europe swept away the postwar economic and political order of Europe. These factors lead to pressures to increase the integration programmes of the Community. Germany and France, in particular, sought to deepen the integration of the Community. To investigate the means to achieve these aims the Community established two Inter-governmental Conferences (IGCs): one on Economic and Monetary Union and the other on Political Union. The IGCs sought to build upon the changes that the SEA had brought about and to develop the ideas that had been advocated in the Delors report on Economic and Monetary Union (Commission EC 1989).

The IGC led to the negotiations on the Maastricht Treaty. The debates and arguments that emerged in the drafting of this treaty clearly indicated that there was little consensus among the member states about how 'federal' the Community should become. The UK made it clear that the concept of a federal Community was not acceptable. France and Germany were also opposed to granting significant new powers to the EP and the Commission. However, many of the smaller member states were in favour of granting more powers to these institutions. The negotiations consequently proved to be very difficult. Agreement was reached to establish monetary union but the UK and Denmark secured the right to 'opt out' of the process. The Maastricht Treaty also contained a Social Chapter as a basis for expanding EU competencies in the social policy area. However, the UK also obtained an 'opt out' from implementing any legislation that might emerge from the Social Chapter. In the areas of foreign and security policy and justice and home affairs the treaty created new structures that were separate from the existing institutions of the Community. In these fields any cooperation or coordination was to be achieved by inter-governmental procedures.

The difficulties that were encountered in ratifying the treaty further exposed the lack of consensus on the future development of the Community. A referendum on ratification, held in

Denmark in 1992, produced a 'no' verdict. This was followed by a narrow 'yes' vote in a referendum in France. In the UK the government faced considerable difficulties in processing the ratification bill through Parliament, and the ruling Conservative Party experienced a deep and damaging split over their European policy. A second referendum in Denmark, in 1993, secured a small majority for ratification. The final obstacle was a referral to the constitutional court in Germany. This followed from a claim, by a former German Commissioner, that the German government could not ratify the treaty because it did not have the right to transfer sovereignty to non-German institutional structures. The court ruled that the treaty could be ratified, but that any decision to establish monetary union would need the approval of all the major political institutions of Germany. The final irony of the ratification process was that Germany, one of the strongest supporters of the Maastricht Treaty, was the last country to ratify the treaty.

In 1992, speculative pressures began to undermine the ERM and by the end of 1993 the ERM had effectively ceased to operate as an effective mechanism for managing the exchange rate policies of the member states. By early 1993 both the UK and Italy had withdrawn from the ERM and Spain, Ireland and Portugal had experienced substantial devaluations of their currencies within the EMS. By the end of 1993 the ERM bands had been widened to +/– 15 per cent (with the exception of the Deutschmark/Guilder rate).

The Community also experienced considerable difficulties in reforming the CAP in order to satisfy the conditions for reaching agreement on the Uruguay Round of the GATT. France caused some concern by refusing to acquiesce to the reform of the CAP that had been agreed between the Community and the USA. Agreement over the reform of the CAP was necessary if the Uruguay Round of GATT was to be successfully completed. France also objected to the liberalisation of trade in television programmes and films in the GATT round. Eventually, this area had to be removed from the GATT round in order to allow agreement to be reached. However, the French stance on these issues caused considerable concern in the EU, especially in the UK, Germany and the Netherlands.

Problems such as these led to growing confusion among both governments and citizens as to the future role of the Community.

Despite these difficulties the Community reached agreement, in 1993, to establish the European Economic Area (EEA). The EEA is an area composed of the 12 member states and most of the countries of EFTA. In the EEA there exists free movement of goods, services, capital and labour, and most of the laws relating to the SEM are also accepted by the EFTA members of the EEA. The EFTA members of the EEA also contribute towards the costs of helping the poorer regions of the Community. In March 1994 agreement on conditions for membership was reached with Austria, Finland, Norway and Sweden for these countries to join the Community.

In the early 1990s progress was made to increase the help that was given to the poorer regions of the Community. The structural adjustment funds were considerably expanded and proposals on how to make best use of the 'Cohesion Fund' and the structural funds were put forward in a package of proposals commonly called Delors II. The 'Cohesion Fund' (founded on the basis of article 130 d of the Maastricht Treaty) is meant to help in the areas of the environment and trans-European networks in transport infrastructures. Delors II (Commission EC, 1992) recommended that the funds should be concentrated in Objective 1 areas; that is those regions with a per capita GDP that is less than 75 per cent of the average of the EU – Ireland, Northern Ireland, Portugal, Greece, Southern Italy, most of Spain, Corsica and the

French Overseas Departments. However, Germany and the UK, the two largest net contributors to the budget of the Community, expressed concern over the cost of the structural funds and the 'Cohesion Fund'. The prospect of some of the countries of Central and Eastern Europe joining the Community caused even more concern about the cost to the richer member states of transferring large amounts of funds to the poorer members. These concerns led to calls for the Community to concentrate on creating an effective SEM as the best method of increasing the living standards of the citizens of the Community. However, the Southern European member states and Ireland regarded the transfer of funds as a crucial component in the attempt to boost the living standards of all of the citizens of the Community. Once again dispute emerged as to the future direction of the Community.

The EU experienced a remarkable change in its fortunes in the early 1990s. It moved from being an agency making seemingly unstoppable progress towards some kind of 'federal' system to an agency that was unclear as to which direction it should take. The Community was very much a child of the Cold War and consequently a Western European club. The Community has found it difficult to develop its role in a Europe that is no longer divided into hostile blocs.

The institutional structure of the EU

The structure of the EU has been largely determined by the various Treaties that have been agreed by the member states. The Treaties of Paris (1951) and Rome (1957), as amended by the SEA (1986) and the Maastricht Treaty (1992) form the current basis of the EU.

There are six main institutions in the current structure of the EU.

1. The European Council

2. The European Commission

3. The Council of Ministers

4. The European Parliament (EP)

5. The European Court of Justice (ECJ)

6. The European Monetary Institute (EMI) to be replaced by the European System of Central Banks (ESCB)

The European Council had no treaty basis until the role of this body was recognised in the SEA. However, since 1974 the European Council (summit meetings of the heads of government of the member states) has met on a regular basis. There has been established a pattern of three European Council meetings per year, with special summits called to discuss major issues. The summits are chaired by the member state which holds the Presidency of the Council, and they are generally strongly influenced by whoever holds the Presidency. The Council is therefore very firmly an inter-governmental institution, and often reflects the interests of the country which holds the Presidency. In spite of this some of the most significant steps in the integration process have been initiated by the European Council, such as the SEA and the moves towards EMU. Indeed, no major developments in the integration process would be possible without the approval of the European Council. The European Council therefore plays a key role in the development of the EU and it is very clearly under the control of the governments of the member states. This does not mean that the EU has no significant supranational characteristics. Once the European Council decides to establish elements of supranational decision-making into Community policies or programmes, member states effectively lose sovereignty in that area. This is increasingly happening in many areas connected to the SEM, Competition Policy and the Common Commercial Policy (CCP). The European Council established the two Inter-governmental Conferences which led to the Maastricht Treaty. The European Council is therefore a necessary mechanism to allow the member states to reach agreement on the pace and direction of the integration process.

The European Commission is a cross between a civil service and an executive body. There are 17 Commissioners, two each from Germany, France, Italy, Spain, and the UK, and one from each of the other member states. The composition of the Commission will have to alter if Austria, Finland, Sweden and Norway join the EU. They are appointed by their member states, but are not responsible to them. In principle they are accountable to the EP. The President of the Commission, who is appointed by governments of the member states and approved by the EP, has considerable influence by way of a seat on the European Council, and in other economic and political forums. In its role as an administrative body it is split into 23 Directorates General (DGs), which have specific areas of responsibility (see Appendix I). The Commission is the guardian of the Treaties and is responsible for monitoring and policing EU law. It does not normally implement these laws, but usually depends on the governments of the member states to carry out this function. The Commission has the power to investigate suspected breaches of EU law by governments, companies and individuals, and can impose fines if it considers that the law has been broken. It also has powers to compel changes in the policies of national governments if it considers that they are contrary to Community law. The governments of the member states are obliged to ensure that the decisions of the Commission in these matters are implemented unless they dispute the ruling of the Commission. When this occurs the case is sent to the ECJ. The Commission therefore has supranational powers in certain areas. The day-to-day operation of EU policies and programmes, and the administrating of the Structural Funds (see Appendix II), are also under the control of the Commission. All proposals for new Community legislation must be initiated by the Commission on the basis of the Treaties, or the decisions of the European Council. A simplified version of how EU legislation proceeds is given in Appendix III. The Commission also provides help and information on Community matters to companies and organisations of various types. The operations of the Commission are largely supranational in character because it is not accountable to the control of the governments of the member states. The Commission is not, however, the body which decides if a proposal for new Community law will be accepted. The main body with this power is the Council of Ministers.

The Council of Ministers is composed of the relevant government ministers of the member states, so if the proposal is concerned with agricultural matters then the ministers of agriculture from the member states will form the Council of Ministers. Matters of a general nature are usually dealt with by the foreign ministers. The Council of Ministers has a standing committee of civil servants called the Committee of Permanent Representatives (COREPER), who do most of the groundwork on any proposed legislation. The ministers generally become involved at the end stage to settle unresolved problems, or to agree to disagree. In the latter case a proposal can be returned to the Commission for further consideration, or it can be left on the table until some sort of compromise can be reached. This means that the governments of the member states have considerable powers to prevent, delay or modify any proposal for new Community laws. Voting in the Council of Ministers can be by unanimity (e.g. taxation matters) or by qualified majority (e.g. many issues connected with the SEM). It is therefore possible for EU legislation to become Community law against the wishes of a member state. Hence the power which the governments of the member states have to control the legislative programme of the Community depends on how far they are in agreement with each other, and on the extent of qualified majority voting. It is quite clear that the decision-making system of the EU has fairly strong supranational characteristics.

The EP is an institution which is not responsible to, nor appointed by, the governments of the member states. Since 1979 the EP has been directly elected by the citizens of the Community. The quota of Members of the European Parliament (MEPs) which a country has depends on the size of the population, the larger countries having more seats than the smaller. The powers of the EP are fairly limited, except with regard to the Commission. In principle the EP can dismiss the Commissioners and can refuse to approve the budget of the EU. These powers are however too great to be used, as they would effectively make the government of the Community impossible. The EP does have some rights to allocate minor amounts in the budget (see Chapter 6), and can influence the content of proposed legislation (see Appendix III). It organises debates and investigates the activities of the Commission. It has influence on the appointment of the Commission and has the right to refuse to accept the nominations for the President of the Commission. The Council of Ministers is not accountable to the EP. Although there are loose arrangements between the political parties in the European Parliament this does not mean that they form a coherent European political party system. However, the Socialist Group in the EP, the largest grouping, has achieved considerable consensus on long-term objections. In short, the EP is not a parliament in the normal sense of the word.

The European Court of Justice (ECJ) is composed of 13 judges who are appointed by the member states. It is responsible for interpreting Community law and making judgments when there are disputes on this law. If EU law and national law conflict, then Community law must take precedence. The ECJ is the final court to which disputes on EU law can be brought, and national courts must accept and implement the judgments of the ECJ. In some respects the ECJ is the most supranational institution in the EU, for it is not accountable to any national government, and the decisions of this Court determine national law. The decisions of the ECJ are also important in the operation of the Competition Policy as the Court has established many important principles by its judgments on particular cases. Decisions of the ECJ are also important in establishing principles in the area of employment law and equal opportunities.

The Maastricht Treaty established two further institutions – the European Monetary Institute (EMI) and the European System of Central Banks (ESCB). Both of these institutions are involved in the move towards monetary union. The EMI, which began operation in 1994, will develop the procedures for strengthening cooperation between the central banks of the member states. It will also monitor the convergence of the economic and monetary conditions that are necessary to achieve monetary union. The ESCB will be composed of the heads of the central banks of the member states and the European Central Bank (ECB); in effect the ESCB is a type of federal central bank on similar lines to the Bundesbank. The ESCB will replace the EMI when (or if) the final stage of monetary union takes place. The ESCB will be responsible for the monetary policy of those member states that proceed to monetary union. The ECB will be the executive part of the bank and it will be appointed by the European Council for a period of eight years. The ESCB will be independent of national governments and the other institutions of the EU and it will have as its prime objective the pursuit of price stability.

There are three other major institutions in the Community: the Economic and Social Committee, the Court of Auditors and the Committee of the Regions. The Economic and Social Committee is a forum for pressure and interest groups to express opinions on proposed legislation. It does not have any powers other than to express opinions. The main function of the Court of Auditors is to audit the expenditure activities carried out on behalf of the Community. As these activities are often carried out by national governments, this can give it rights to investigate the practices of the governments of member states. The Court of Auditors is generally concerned with the proper use of funds and to check on fraud, rather than value for money evaluations. However, the Court of Auditors could in future be used to assess the effectiveness of Community expenditures. At present it may submit reports on the use of Community funds to the institutions of the EU and this could develop into the basis for value for money evaluations. A Committee of the Regions composed of representatives from regional and local authorities was established in 1994 in accordance with article 198a of the Maastricht Treaty. This Committee is appointed by the Council on the recommendation of the national governments of the member states. It may be consulted by the Commission and the Council on matters which affect the regions, but the Committee need not be consulted. In this respect the Committee would appear to have less power than the Economic and Social Committee. It may however issue an opinion on its own initiative.

The institutional structure of the EU is complex, with many different bodies responsible for decision-making and for the implementation, monitoring and policing of Community laws. Most of these institutions are appointed by national governments. Nevertheless, there is a degree of supranationality in these institutions, and the increased powers that the Maastricht Treaty has given to the EP (see Appendix III) combined with the possibility of an independent ESCB may enhance this supranationality.

The inclusion of the concept of subsidiarity in the Maastricht Treaty was an attempt by the EU to tackle the problems of assigning governmental competencies within the Community. Article 3b of the Maastricht Treaty states: 'The Community shall take action, in accordance with the principle of subsidiarity, only if and in so far as the objectives of the proposed action cannot be sufficiently achieved by the Member States and can therefore, by reason of the scale or effects of the proposed action, be better achieved by the Community.' The concept of subsidiarity is therefore concerned with discovering the appropriate tier structure of government. The key is to give to that level of government those functions that would be best performed at that level. The Padoa-Schioppa Report (1987) recommended that the EU should be governed at the local, regional, national or Community level depending on which tier of government could carry out the task most efficiently. This principle is analogous to the recommendations that arise from fiscal federalism (Oates 1972). These issues are examined below.

The democratic deficit

There have also been concerns about the 'democratic deficit' in the EU. Only the EP is directly elected and is therefore subject to the choice of the citizens of the Community. However, the Council of Ministers and the Commission take decisions that impinge on many of the activities of the citizens of the Community. Furthermore, the successful development of monetary union would lead to the creation of another powerful Community institution – the ESCB. The ESCB could develop into the most important economic agency in the EU, but its accountability to the citizens of the Community would be very indirect. These issues have led to pressures to expand the powers of the EP and to develop federal-type structures that are accountable to the citizens of the EU. The member states of the EU are committed by the Maastricht Treaty to examining these issues. This will be done by undertaking a review of the institutional structures of the EU; this process will begin in 1996.

The voting procedures of the Council of Ministers have also caused some problems. The Council can take decisions by unanimity, simple majority vote or qualified majority vote. The system for qualified majority voting allows the smaller member states to excercise some power in the decision-making systems of the EU. The four large member states cannot obtain a winning coalition among themselves, that is, they need the support of some of the smaller member states in order to secure a winning coalition for those decisions subject to qualified majority voting. Furthermore, a coalition of most of the smaller member states can result in a blocking vote. Normally, a blocking minority would be composed of some larger member states and a group of smaller states. This ability to use blocking minorities gives the smaller member states considerable leverage in the decision-making frameworks of the EU. This leverage arises from the process of log-rolling. Log-rolling involves the use of bargaining between parties to use strategic voting to further their objectives (see Buchanan 1978). Thus a group of smaller member states could agree to vote with some of the larger member states for issues in which they have no particular interest in return for the support of the larger member states for issues in which they do have a strong interest. For example, some of the smaller member states could support France to block a proposal deemed to be against French interests, in return for the support of France against proposals that are regarded as against the interests of the smaller member states.

Such log-rolling behaviour has both advantages and disadvantages. It allows the smaller member states to exercise some degree of power in the EU. Therefore, it helps to overcome some of the problems that may arise from the power of the larger member states. However, log-rolling can allow rejection of proposals that have net benefits for the EU. Outcomes such as this can arise when the benefits of implementing proposals are skewed towards certain member states, but these member states cannot secure a winning coalition because of strategic voting by disinterested parties who are engaged in log-rolling exercises.

The extension of the areas of decision-making that are subject to qualified majority voting has increased the problems that the EU has experienced with the voting procedures of the Council. The possible extension of the Community to include many more smaller member states may well expand opportunities for log-rolling behaviour in the EU.

The issue of qualified majority voting became one of some importance when the UK and Spain objected to the proposals to change the voting procedures in the Council in response to the expected extension of the Community to include Austria, Finland, Norway and Sweden. This issue was resolved, but further enlargement of the EU can only intensify these problems.

The economic objectives of the EU

The EU has some clearly defined economic objectives which are listed in the various Treaties. These include commitments to establish a CU, a Common Market and EMU. The Treaties also contain strong commitments to create common policies in the agriculture, transport, social, regional, environmental and technology areas. The Community can therefore be regarded as an agency seeking to promote regional economic integration. Economists such as Balassa (1961), Tinbergen (1954), and Viner (1950) developed methods to analyse regional economic integration agencies such as the EU. It is possible to use such analysis to examine the economic objectives of the EU.

The process of regional economic integration can be described by a series of four steps towards creating economic union for a group of countries:

1. A free trade area, where the member countries abolish all trade barriers between themselves, but retain the right to implement their own type and levels of protection against non-members. Free trade areas are often restricted to industrial goods and to the removal of tariffs and quotas. The EFTA countries and NAFTA are examples of such areas.

2. A Customs Union is basically a free trade area but with a common external policy, especially a common external tariff (CET). This should, in principle, avoid problems of rules of origin, i.e. the need to specify the source of the various products which have been used to make a final product to ensure that it can be classified as a good of a member country of the bloc. In a free trade area the absence of a CET means that goods could be imported into the area at a low tariff country and subsequently be exported to a high tariff member of the area. To avoid this, rules of origin regulations must be implemented.

3. A Common Market is a CU which also has free factor movement therefore a Common Market has free movement of goods, services, capital, and labour. The EU is in the process of creating such an area.

4. Economic Union is rather more difficult to define: it can mean a Common Market with unified monetary and fiscal policies. A more strict definition would include a system with unified or harmonised economic and social policies in all areas which affect economic activity, and these could include competition, labour and industrial relations, environmental, and other policies. It is also not clear what the term unified or harmonised means. Generally, unified means under the control of one government agency to cover the whole bloc, while harmonised refers to agreements between several government agencies to try and ensure that their policies do not conflict. Such harmonised policies can be backed by legal restrictions on implementing policies or laws which could hinder free movement, or by loose inter-governmental agreements to try to achieve policy consistency. The attempts by the EU to define its long-term objective of Economic Union reflect this confusion on what this term means. Often Economic Union is considered to be the same as Monetary Union. However, this is just part, although a crucial part, of the more general Economic and Monetary Union (EMU).

The Community has therefore some economic objectives which can readily be defined (the CU and a Common Market). The objective of EMU is less easily defined; however, the conditions necessary for Monetary Union have been specified in the Maastricht Treaty. The implementation of the CU and a CM means not only negative integration (the removal of barriers to trade) but also positive integration (the implementation of policies and the creation of institutional frameworks to allow these blocs to operate effectively). Negative integration does not normally cause many problems of definition; however, positive integration is rather more difficult to define. The creation of the SEM has highlighted these problems. Disputes are arising over the need for Community involvement in areas such as labour and industrial relations, taxation systems and the environment. While there is agreement on the need for some Community involvement in areas such as competition policy, there are disputes on the stage at which the Community should take over from the national governments. In many areas the case is being argued for loose inter-governmental harmonisation, rather than for legally binding harmonisation or unified policies. These arguments are complicated by the overtly political objectives of the Community to create Political Union and the increasing pressure for the EU to redistribute resources to allow the poorer member states to develop. Such political and redistribution factors may well be necessary to allow the economic objectives to be realised. As was discussed above, the EU was founded to pursue economic objectives, but these have always had political overtones.

Political union

The EU has had a long-standing commitment to European Political Cooperation (EPC). This was restricted to a series of meetings of the foreign ministers of the member states to discuss, and where possible to reach common positions on issues relating to foreign relations and security matters. This was necessary in areas relating to trade as the EU has a great influence in the external economic relations of the member states. There have also been attempts to arrive at common positions on matters concerned with the prevention of terrorism, relations with the former Soviet Union and Eastern Europe and on the security of Europe in the light of the ending of the Cold War. The Community has sought to reach a common position on the Gulf war, and to act collectively in response to the civil war in the former Yugoslavia.

These attempts to act collectively have not been very successful, especially with regard to the Gulf war. During this crisis the Community could do little more than reflect the differences in the interests of the member states. The attempts by the Community to act in the civil war in the former Yugoslavia were hampered by the reluctance to become involved militarily to provide a peace keeping force, and by the failure of the member states to reach agreement on anything other than a minimum intervention by imposing trade embargoes and providing the means for the various parties to negotiate cease-fires with a view to arranging a lasting peace. The disappointment caused by this failure to reach effective common positions has resulted in increased calls for a radical restructuring of the political integration programme of the EU.

The SEA had rather vague statements on the need for closer cooperation on foreign and security matters. There has been considerable pressure to move beyond such statements towards a clearer policy on political union. The Maastricht Treaty envisages a Community with a single currency, and with an increasing role for the EU in social policy. The commitment to establishing a stronger political union has also been increased by the Treaty. In particular, the member states have agreed to use inter-governmental procedures based on general guidelines from the European Council with the Council of Ministers taking policy decisions. Joint actions (or positions) may be adopted by unanimous decision of the Council of Ministers, and in some cases qualified majority voting could be used. These procedures cover two of the three 'pillars' of the EU (the other 'pillar' being the EC). The two new 'pillars' are: foreign and security issues; justice, home affairs and immigration. The Treaty envisages the creation of a common defence policy based on the expansion of the Western European Union (WEU). The WEU is charged with the task of collaborating with NATO to create a coherent policy on European defence. The Commission and the EP will only have a very limited role to play in these areas. It is not clear how these 'pillars' will operate, and there is reason to doubt how effective the EU can be in these areas given the wide disparities in the views that the member states take in these policy fields.

The political and institutional nature of the Community is becoming more supranational. This prospect has caused some alarm among some politicians and decision-makers, particularly in the UK. The possible emergence of what would be some sort of federal Europe brings with it the prospect of national governments being little more than regional assemblies, with their legislative programmes constrained by the growing integration of markets which will lead to common or harmonised policies in many areas. Moves towards a common monetary policy would also curtail the taxation and expenditure plans of national governments. If many aspects of foreign policy and security and justice and affairs were determined by majority voting at the Council of Ministers, the characteristics of national governments would indeed begin to resemble those of regional or local government. There are doubts as to the feasibility of common foreign and security policies among countries with quite diverse perceptions of what constitutes sensible policies in these areas.

In spite of such reservations there are strong forces at work to enhance the political integration of the EU. In international trade matters the Community is already more important than the member states in negotiations with other countries, and with the GATT. Movement towards EMU will also require a Community voice in organisations such as the IMF and the G7 group of countries. Many issues of foreign policy and security matters are connected to international trade and financial flows, and the growing economic integration of the EU will increasingly require a measure of consistency by the member states in these areas. The Gulf war and the crisis in the former Yugoslavia are matters of economic as well as political importance. A trading body of the size of the EU, which has significant trade with many countries, is likely to face considerable political issues connected to its trading activities. If the Community fails to devise methods of resolving internal differences between the member states on these issues the policy frameworks will be set by others, notably the USA. The policies of the USA on the Middle East, or other areas of regional conflict or political instability, may not be the policies which are most beneficial to the EU. These American-led policies have a strong, if somewhat diffuse, impact on the stability of political systems in the world, and this has effects on the world economy. The Community is therefore faced with continuing to accept American leadership in these matters, or with creating a programme of political integration to complement the economic programme.

The loss of sovereignty (the ability of a state to determine its own policies independently of other governments) is already undermined by the dominance of the Americans in matters connected to global political and security issues. The real question is whether the Community is in a position to achieve a degree of political integration sufficient to allow a more independent line to be pursued. This would perhaps require a common and effective European foreign policy and security arrangements, and a European defence force. In these circumstances the Europeans could exercise a significant counterbalancing force if American policies were considered to be against European interests. Such an outcome would involve a radical revision of the foreign and security policies of the member states, and may not be feasible unless all the major member states come to regard this as a viable and desirable goal.

In political matters more directly connected to the economic integration programme the need for some change to the policies and political arrangements of the Community is widely accepted, except in some sections of the Conservative Party in the UK. The granting of new powers for the EU to act in the social area; in education, training and employment conditions, may be necessary to overcome fears that the more competitive conditions induced by the SEM will result in a downward spiral in social and working conditions. There are also growing pressures to grant new competences to Community institutions in industrial, and research and development policies to help in the restructuring of the economy of the EU induced by the creation of the SEM and moves towards EMU. The removal of frontier controls may require a common policy on immigration into the member states as entry into one country would effectively result in access to all EU countries. This would have implications for the policing arrangements of all member states, and could lead to Community border police.

Some member states seem to want more policy-making to be decided at Community level, while wishing to keep important decisions in the domain of the Council of Ministers, but with the Commission and the EP having more influence in the decision-making process. In the future it is possible that many of the policies which govern economic activity will be decided at Community level by majority voting. An outcome such as this will ultimately lead to changes to the political structure of the EU to ensure that decisions can be effectively made, and to give the system some kind of legitimacy and accountability. The implication is that the Community will evolve into some kind of a federal system.

The main challenges facing the EU

The EU faces a series of challenges to the development of its integration programmes. Two main issues may be identified:

1. the high levels of unemployment that have afflicted the EU in the 1990s;

2. the difficulties of implementing the principle of subsidiarity.

Unemployment

In the early 1990s the member states had an average rate of unemployment that was some 3 to 4 per cent higher than that of the USA and approximately 8 per cent higher than that of Japan. The recession that afflicted continental Europe in 1993 led to an increase in the gap in these unemployment figures. Thus by the end of 1993, the unemployment rate in the USA was some 6 per cent lower than that in the EU and the Japanese rate was about 10 per cent lower. Only the UK experienced a fall in unemployment in this period. The unemployment rate in Spain rose to nearly 24 per cent.

In the 1990s unemployment has clearly been a more serious problem for the EU than for the USA and Japan. It is apparent that both the Americans and the Japanese seem better able to deal with the problems of unemployment that emerged in the developed economies in the 1990s. The USA seems to be able to generate more jobs from growth than do the Europeans, while the Japanese seem to be more able to retain employment levels in the face of pressures on jobs resulting from recession and structural change.

Concern over unemployment led to a reappraisal of policies to counter unemployment. At the Edinburgh meeting of the European Council in 1992, an initiative was put forward to coordinate macroeconomic policies to help boost non-inflationary growth in the EU. The prime objective of this initiative was to lower unemployment. However, this initiative envisaged only a small boost to the economy of the EU and it was largely based on an aggregation of existing public expenditure plans by the member states (the Edinburgh initiative is examined in Chapter 3).

The debate on the appropriateness of using the Social Chapter of the Maastricht Treaty to improve working conditions was also brought into question (the Social Chapter is analysed in Chapter 9). The UK government consistently argued that to use EU legislation to improve working conditions would result in higher non-wage costs (and possible wage costs) of hiring labour and that this would inevitably lead to higher unemployment. The implications of increasing the non-wage costs (or wage costs) of hiring labour are that either such increases are compensated for by higher productivity, or EU-based producers become less competitive. In the latter case the EU would have to protect its industries and/or seek to use depreciation of the currencies of the member states (relative to main trading partners) in order to defend the competitive position of EU-based companies. Outcomes such as these are not attractive because of the problems that would be caused to trading relations, in particular with the USA, Japan and the NICs (these issues are discussed in Chapter 17). Such actions could also harm the allocation of resources within the EU by encouraging production and consumption from high cost European sources when lower cost supplies are available from outside the EU. The long-term position of the EU could also be harmed by such policies because they could encourage European producers to maintain production in areas where they do not have comparative advantage. Chapters 1 and 2 provide examinations of the benefits, in terms of resource allocation, of liberalising trade. One of the main fears of those who oppose the Social Chapter is that it could lead to the EU moving away from a fairly pro-free trade position to a more protectionist stance. This issue is examined in Chapter 17.

In 1993 the Commission published a White Paper on Growth, Competitiveness and Employment (Commission EC 1993). The White Paper set a target of 15 million new jobs in the EU by the year 2000. To achieve this objective the EU is encouraged to pursue policies that will deliver non-inflationary growth, create more jobs from growth and improve the global competitiveness of EU-based companies.

In order to ensure that the growth is non-inflationary, the White Paper argued that the member states should not expand their public sector deficits; the Commission maintained rather that it is important for macroeconomic stability that the current high levels of these deficits should be reduced. This objective is also connected to the plan for the convergence of the economies of the member states in preparation for monetary union (see Chapters 3 and 4). The White Paper therefore did not favour Keynesian type aggregate demand management measures to boost growth rates in order to reduce unemployment.

However, the White Paper regarded the development of trans-European networks as an important component in the creation of a competitive high growth economy. The Commission therefore argued for an investment in these networks of some ECU 20 billion per year, from 1994 to 1999. The financing of these investments is not, however, to be achieved by expansion of the public deficits of the member states, but rather funding is to be found from existing EU funds and EIB financing together with the issue of about ECU 8 billion 'Union Bonds' by the Commission. The latter would give the Commission the right to borrow on financial markets and to re-route the funds to trans-European network investments. Such borrowing rights would give the Commission the right to operate a budget deficit and thus would constitute a radical change in the powers of the Commission. Although the White Paper did not advocate macroeconomic policy coordination as a method of boosting growth, it proposed greater cooperation with regard to the composition of public expenditures and it also recommended granting the Commission powers that would give it some minor fiscal policy leverage with respect to public expenditures.

To encourage the creation of more jobs from growth, the White Paper recommended that the structural problems that have led to unemployment should be addressed. Thus the Commission advocated encouragement of new fast growing industries such as information technology, telecommunications services and equipment and biotechnology. This would seem to indicate an increased role for Industrial Policy in the EU (see Chapter 8).

The problems caused by high non-wage costs were also considered to be a significant obstacle to the creation of jobs, and the White Paper recommended that labour market regulations should be compatible with labour market flexibility. Nevertheless, the Commission made it clear that it did not wish to see a deterioration in working conditions and in the rights of employees. In particular, the White Paper recommended that steps should be taken to avoid the creation of large amounts of low paid and low skilled jobs. However, the White Paper advocated that part-time working should be encouraged and that work-sharing might also contribute to the solution of finding ways to lower the unemployment rate. The Commission also recommended the use of government help to lower the costs to companies of hiring the long-term unemployed and young people (these groups make up the bulk of the unemployed in most member states).

The White Paper regarded the creation and maintenance of an open economy for the EU as a crucial requirement for promoting an efficient and dynamic economy. The use of protectionist policies was therefore not advocated as a solution to the high levels of unemployment in Europe. The Commission also maintained that large fluctuations in exchange rates were not conducive to stable and growing world trade. Thus, the White Paper did not advocate the use of depreciation of currencies as a viable solution to the unemployment problem. However, it recommended that the EU adopt a more rapid commercial defence in the new GATT structures that were agreed in the Uruguay Round. This may mean that the Commission's commitment to free trade is not very strong, because the EU has used its Common Commercial Policy in ways that suggest protectionist behaviour (see Chapters 14–17).

The White Paper provided a clear statement that unemployment was the major economic problem facing the EU. However, it did not provide any significantly new proposals as to how to solve this problem.

For those who favour an EU based on an open trading system with the rest of the world, these proposals were welcome. However, some of the recommendations of the White Paper were less welcome, for example the indications of a need for a more interventionist Industrial

Policy and the possibility of a stronger use of the Common Commercial Policy to protect EU industries that faced 'unfair competition'. The indiciations that the Commission is still committed to using the Social Chapter to improve working conditions by use of laws that may increase the non-wage costs of hiring labour was also not welcomed by free-traders. The free traders regard the creation of an open and competitive economy as the best method to boost productivity and thereby to tackle the unemployment problem. According to this view, the role of the EU in helping to find solutions to the problem of unemployment is mainly connected to the creation of an effective SEM and the development of an open economy with the rest of the world. Employment may also be generated by the creation of monetary union to eliminate the barriers to free trade (within the EU) caused by exchange rate fluctuations and the transaction costs that result from the existence of different currencies. In the long run it is also possible that monetary union could lead to benefits arising from higher rates of non-inflationary growth and from a more efficient allocation of capital (see Chapters 4 and 5).

The EU faces considerable difficulties in reconciling the opposing views as to the best methods of reducing unemployment in Europe. The free traders advocate liberalisation of markets, in particular labour markets, and an opening up of Community markets to foreign trade and investments (see Chapter 17 for discussion on the role of foreign investments in promoting an efficient and dynamic economy in Europe). The free traders are also reluctant to commit significant funds to Industrial Policy initiatives that seek to identify new and expanding industries: on the whole they would favour the use of market forces to promote the creation of new jobs. The interventionists are keen to promote active government involvement in the encouragement of new industries and to use the law to improve living and working conditions. Indeed, the debate is not unlike the debates that take place within any modern advanced economy between right wing (or pro-market forces) groups and left wing (or interventionist) groups.

In the context of the EU it is often assumed that the UK is the only country that stands firmly in the pro-market group. However, in terms of opposition to the use of Keynesian demand management policies the UK is supported by Germany and the Netherlands. Indeed, no member state appears to be strongly in favour of an expansion of aggregate demand that might risk the resurgence of inflation. With regard to Industrial Policy, the UK, Germany and the Netherlands have generally been reluctant to pursue government policies that seek to identify future industries that have strong growth potential. In the field of Social Policy the UK does seem to stand out in its opposition to the need for new laws to promote improve-ments in working conditions. However, most of the employers' organisations in Europe have major reservations about the Social Chapter, and in Germany there is considerable concern about any new legislation that might increase the non-wage costs (or wage costs) of hiring labour.

It seems that there is no strong consensus in the Community as to how to tackle the problem of unemployment. It is also clear that the Conservative Government in the UK is not the only objector to the use of interventionist social and industrial policies as solutions to this problem. The White Paper reflected this confusion, and it appeared to be advocating solutions that are closer to the views of the Conservative Government of the UK than, for example, the views of the Socialist parties of France or Spain, or indeed the UK.

There does seem to be a large measure of agreement among the member states that there is a need for better education and training policies that would enhance the productivity potential of labour. However, the concept of subsidiarity casts doubt as to whether these policy areas should be significantly subject to EU policies.

The principle of subsidiarity

The principle of subsidiarity requires that the EU undertakes only those policies that it would be most efficient in governing. The main issue, if this principle is to be connected to efficiency considerations, is to identify those national policies that have significant spill-over effects into other countries.

If the market fails to deliver an optimal allocation of resources, because of externalities or monopoly power, there is a clear case for government action to seek to improve the allocation of resources. Therefore, a case can be made for government policies in areas such as R&D expenditures, education and training, environmental standards and public health. The case for such intervention depends on the existence of the external effects of these activities (i.e. the benefits and/or costs of these activities affect other agents as well as the producers and/or consumers of such activities). Similarly, the case for government action to create and maintain a competitive environment is a clear requirement for an efficient allocation of resources in a market-based economy.

However, the existence of a rationale for government policies within a country does not necessarily mean that there are good reasons for supranational policies in these areas. Only if national policies have significant spill-overs to other countries do sound reasons exist for supranational policies in these areas. This can be analysed by use of a pay-off matrix. In Figure I.1 the matrix illustrates the pay-off for two countries from the various options that are available for some policy, for example, help with R&D expenditures.

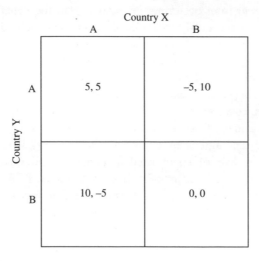

Figure I.1 Subsidiarity and policy spill-overs

In case A the country provides help to its companies to cover the external benefits of R&D payments, while in case B the country does not provide help in the R&D area. If both countries adopt policy A they reap benefits shown by pay-offs of 5 each, shown by the outcome in the top left-hand corner of the matrix. If they both adopt policy B, they end up at the bottom right-hand corner with pay-offs of zero. However, if country X adopts policy A and country Y opts for policy B the pay-offs will be 10 for country Y and –5 for country X, shown in the bottom left-hand corner. In this situation country X meets the cost of helping with R&D expenditures, while country Y benefits from these expenditures without incurring any expenditures. In other words, country Y benefits from the spill-over effects of the R&D policy of country X. The outcomes of country X adopting B and country Y choosing A are shown in the top right-hand corner of the matrix. In this situation the outcome for each country depends on the choices made by the other country. The two countries are interdependent because of the spill-overs that arise from their policies. If both countries are averse to risk with regard to the costs of policy mistakes, they will both choose policy B (leading to the outcome illustrated in the bottom right-hand corner). This outcome is preferable to policy A because it avoids the risk of a negative outcome. However, if the countries coordinate their policies, to ensure that both countries adopt policy A, they reap the pay-offs shown in the top left-hand corner of the matrix. This is a more desirable outcome than the non-cooperative outcome shown in the bottom right-hand corner of the matrix.

Consequently, taking account of the policy decision of other countries makes sense only if countries are interdependent with respect to the outcomes of policy actions, that is, they must experience spill-overs. However, the existence of such spill-overs does not mean that common policies are sensible. In some cases coordination of policies to take account of spill-over effects is all that is required. Furthermore, the existence of spill-overs is not a sufficient reason for coordination. If the costs of coordination are greater than the benefits of taking into account spill-over effects, it is not efficient to coordinate policies. Thus in the example above, if the costs of reaching agreement on coordination exceeded 5, the countries would be better off not seeking to reach agreement to coordinate policies. In these circumstances it would be better to find methods of internalising the spill-over effects. This could be done by taking action to prevent spill-over from occurring, i.e. retaining all the benefits of the policy within the country. If this proves too costly to achieve, the countries could form one government agency to deal with the policy that is creating the spill-over effects, i.e. adopt a common policy. This analysis suggests that good reasons for common policies in the EU may arise when the costs of reaching coordinated agreements, or preventing spill-overs, are high. In other areas it may be better to seek to coordinate policies, and where there are no (or insignificant) spill-overs, countries should adopt policies independently from other countries.

However, the allocation of government competencies using such criteria requires considerable knowledge (and agreement among affected parties) about the extent and size of spill-overs and about the cost of coordinated or common policy solutions. Also, it is not obvious that the EU is always the appropriate agency to be used for coordinated or common policies. In cases where spill-overs extend beyond the frontiers of the EU, or where the spill-overs affect only parts of the EU, it may be more efficient to have other governmental agencies to determine policies. In these circumstances an agency to find the most efficient solution may be useful. The EU could provide the institutional framework to determine such solutions for the member states. The EU could provide the means to determine whether there should be coordinated policies, common policies for all the Community, common policies that are operative for part of the Community, and policies (coordinated or common) that extend beyond its frontiers.

In such a scenario the EU would assess the costs and benefits of assigning governmental competencies and would seek to find the best solution. However, this would require a federal-type constitution for the EU with clear rules on the powers of the federal government relative to those of the member states. This analysis suggests that the principle of subsidiarity can work efficiently only if the EU develops a federal system of government with a constitution backed by an independent court. In other words, the EU would need to become a federal state not dissimilar to the USA or Germany. Attempts to implement the subsidiarity principle in the present governmental system of the EU are likely (at best) to lead to a good deal of confusion or (at worst) to an inefficient and problematical system for determining governmental competencies.

Most of the chapters in this book contain material that is concerned with these problems of efficient government in the EU.

Conclusion

The EU has achieved a remarkable degree of integration among its member states in the postwar period. It has extended its membership to include the largest economies in Europe and it has become one of the most important economic blocs in the world. In the mid to late 1980s it experienced a surge in implementing its integration programmes, particularly with the SEM programme and the moves towards monetary union. However, in the 1990s the EU has experienced a series of problems that have cast doubt on its future development. The end of the Cold War and the collapse of communism did not provide an easy opportunity for the EU to expand its membership, while also deepening its integration programmes. The problems encountered in ratifying the Maastricht Treaty illustrated the difficulties of convincing the citizens of the EU that further integration was in their interests. The crisis in the EMS and the return to floating exchange rates by some member states has also been a disappointment for those who looked to a deepening of the integration programmes of the EU. The growing problem of unemployment in Europe has also made it very difficult for the EU to press on with its integration programmes. The pressures for the EU to become more involved in transferring income from its richer to its poorer regions have also grown and they have added to the difficulties of reaching agreement among the member states on the appropriate development of the EU.

Nevertheless, the EU remains at the heart of the process of constructing economic and political frameworks in Europe. Only a few politicians in the British Conservative Party are in favour of a fundamental downgrading of the EU, such that it would become little more than a free trading area. The EU is likely to expand to include most of the countries of EFTA and possibly some of the countries of Central and Eastern Europe. In world terms the EU plays a major part in global economic arrangements and it may increase its role in political frameworks. The pressures to develop federal types of government in the EU are also growing, and if monetary union proceeds these pressures will continue to grow. Nevertheless, the EU is likely to encounter considerable difficulties in finding solutions to the economic and political problems that it faces.

This book seeks to address these issues and in particular to examine the economic background to these problems.

Appendix I The Directorates General

The Commission of the EU is split into 23 Directorates General (DGs), who have responsibility for both the day-to-day administration of Community operations and the framing of proposals for new laws.

The current DGs are:

DGI	External Economic Relations
DGIA	External Political Relations
DGII	Economic and Financial Affairs
DGIII	Industry
DGIV	Competition
DGV	Employment, Industrial Relations and Social Affairs
DGVI	Agriculture
DGVII	Transport
DGVIII	Development
DGIX	Personnel and Administration
DGX	Audiovisual Media, Information, Communication and Culture
DGXI	Environment, Civil Protection and Nuclear Safety
DGXII	Science, Research and Development
DGXIII	Telecommunications, Information Market and Exploitation of Research
DGXIV	Fisheries
DGXV	Internal Markets and Financial Services
DGXVI	Regional Policies
DGXVII	Energy Policies
DGXVIII	Credits and Investments
DGXIX	The Budget
DGXX	Financial Control
DGXXI	Customs and Indirect Taxation
DGXXII	(Has been abolished)
DGXXIII	Enterprise Policy, Distributive Trades, Tourism, and Cooperatives

There are also two Task Forces: Task Force for Human Resources, Education, Training and Youth; Enlargement Task Force, and a Consumer Policy service.

Appendix II The Structural Funds

The Community has four main Funds to aid in structural adjustment.

EAGGF	European Agricultural Guidance and Guarantee Fund (Guidance section). This is to provide aid to restructuring agricultural systems and processes.
EDF	European Development Fund. A fund to provide development assistance to ACP countries.
ERDF	European Regional Development Fund. This fund is to aid in the adjustment of the regions of the Community to the integration programmes of the EU.
ESF	European Social Fund. A fund to help disadvantaged groups within the member states.

The European Investment Bank (EIB) can also provide loans to help in projects which will aid the member states to adjust to the integration process.

Appendix III The legislative process of the EU

The legislative process of the Community is complex, what follows is a simplified outline of this process (for a fuller treatment see Nugent 1992). The EU has four main methods of making law or of influencing economic and social activity within the Community. These are:

1. regulations; these are binding and have direct effect in the member states;

2. directives; these must be incorporated into the law of the member states in accordance with their national legislative practices;

3. decisions; these are decisions of the Commission applied to governments, companies, and individuals and they must be complied with;

4. recommendations and opinions; these have no legal standing.

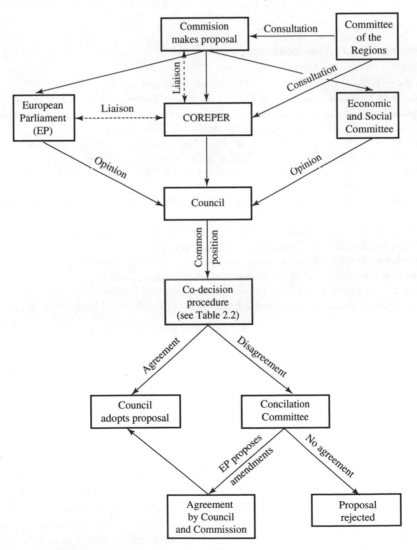

Figure I.2 The co-decision procedure

In practice most Community law-making is done by issuing directives. The use of regulations and decisions is mainly used to govern or amend policies which have already been agreed. The method of issuing directives involves a series of protracted discussions and negotiations between the Commission, the EP and the Council of Ministers. Since the Maastricht Treaty this is primarily done via the co-decision procedure.

The Maastricht Treaty gives the EP new powers of co-decision with the Council. In the event of a disagreement between the Council and the EP over a proposal for a new EU law, a Conciliation Committee is convened. This Committee is composed of equal numbers from the Council and the EP. The Committee is empowered to seek a compromise to allow for the approval of the proposal. This co-decision process applies to proposals relating to the SEM, R&D, trans-European networks, health and consumer affairs and training and education policies. The co-decision procedure is illustrated in Figure I.2. The EP may also request the Commission to submit proposals in areas where it deems a need for new legislation.

References and further reading

Balassa B 1961 *The Theory of Economic Integration*, Allen and Unwin, London.

Buchanan J M 1978 *The Economics of Politics*, Institute of Economic Affairs, London.

Commission EC 1989 *Report on Economic and Monetary Union in the European Community*, Office for Official Publications of the European Communities, Luxembourg.

Commission EC 1990 *European Unification: The Origins and Growth of the European Community*, Office for Official Publications of the European Communities, Luxembourg.

Commission EC 1992 *From the Single Act to Maastricht and Beyond: The Means to Match our Ambitions*, COM(92) 2000, Brussels.

Commission EC 1993 *White Paper on Growth, Competitiveness and Employment*, COM(93) 700 Final, Brussels.

Nugent N 1992 *The Government and Politics of the European Community*, Macmillan, London.

Oates W E 1972 *Fiscal Federalism*, Harcourt Brace, New York.

Padoa-Schioppa T 1987 *Efficiency, Equity and Stability*, Cambridge University Press.

Swann D 1988 *The Economics of the Common Market*, Penguin, London.

Tinbergen J 1954 *International Economic Integration*, Elsevier, London.

Viner J 1950 *The Customs Issue*, Carnegie Endowment for International Peace, New York.

Note

The European Union

The European Union (EU) is the term which is used to cover the EC, the foreign and security and the home affairs and justice arrangements of the member states. The use of the term EU began in November 1993 in response to the ratification of the Maastricht Treaty. The EU is therefore a wider term than the EC as the EU includes areas which are outside of the competences of the institutions of the EC, for example issues connected to immigration, justice and foreign affairs. The book normally uses the term EU rather than EC.

CHAPTER 1

The Customs Union

Keith Penketh

Introduction

One of the major methods of achieving a regional economic bloc is to create a Customs Union (CU). A CU arises when countries join together to abolish all restrictions on trade between themselves while maintaining a common external tariff on imports into the Union. The formation of a CU certainly breaches the principle of universal free trade because it practices discrimination against non-members. However, it reduces trade barriers between members of the CU and generally stimulates inter-bloc trade and reduces the share of trade with countries which are not in the Union. As such a CU is an aid to the economic integration of its members, but may be harmful to the liberalisation of trade on a global basis. In 1948 the Netherlands, Belgium and Luxembourg formed Benelux which was a CU in industrial goods. This method of integration was extended with the foundation of the ECSC in 1951, to establish a CU for coal and steel products between Benelux, France, Germany and Italy. When the EEC was established in 1957 the objective of creating a CU was clearly spelt out in the Treaty of Rome. Until the 1980s when the moves to create the SEM began to assume major importance, the formation of a CU was the main method used by the EU to integrate the economies of the member states. The CU of the EU therefore forms a central and fundamental position in the economic integration of the Community. With the enlargement of the EC, firstly by the accession of the UK, Ireland and Denmark in 1973, followed by Greece in 1981, and Spain and Portugal in 1986, the CU of the EC became the largest regional trading bloc in the world. It is from this position that the EU is seeking to move on to deeper integration by the creation of the SEM and the movement towards EMU.

The Customs Union of the EU

A CU reduces tariffs to zero on intra-union trade, but on extra-union trade a Common External Tariff (CET) is adopted. It is the CET which distinguishes a CU from a free-trade area. With the latter form of regional economics association, nation states are free to adopt their own tariff levels on goods imported from the rest of the world. It is often claimed that a CU represents a movement towards freer trade. However, participation in a CU does not necessarily represent a freer trading regime for all participating countries. There are two reasons for this. Firstly, as a consequence of averaging tariff levels to calculate the CET, some countries' post-union tariff levels (namely the CET) will be higher than pre-union tariff levels. Secondly, as adjustments to the CET are not made following the entry of new members, there may be cases where a CET is significantly above pre-union tariff rates. Agriculture in the UK is an example. Imported largely duty free into the UK before accession, agricultural products were subject to a variable levy under CAP after accession. This is hardly a characteristic of freer trade in goods. Whether membership of a CU is from the single country viewpoint a step in the direction of freer trade depends on the tariff levels which prevail before and after joining a CU.

Any decision in favour of participating in a CU depends on the ultimate objectives of economic policy, namely what it is that countries are attempting to maximise. Although it may be clear what countries are attempting to maximise – real income for example – there is no consistency as to the correct approach to adopt in evaluating the attainment of this objective. Broadly, two approaches can be discussed: the traditional approach and the direct cost approach.

The traditional approach

This approach may be termed the static welfare approach to the analysis of customs unions, and was developed by Viner (1950), Meade (1955) and Lipsey (1970). Originally presented in terms of partial equilibrium analysis, it has been extended in two principal directions. Firstly general equilibrium analysis was used to study the effects of CU formation, and secondly it was extended to embrace more than two goods (Collier 1979). The traditional approach is concerned almost exclusively with the role of countries as importers. Viner was able to analyse and illustrate that the formation of a CU was not necessarily advantageous to individual countries, to the union as a whole, or indeed to the world as a whole. In his analysis Viner developed the concepts of 'trade creation' and 'trade diversion'. Although concerned initially with resource allocation effects, the concepts of trade creation and trade diversion were used to represent advantageous and disadvantageous welfare shifts in trading patterns. Using partial equilibrium analysis, and assuming that a non-member country is considering participation in an existing CU, an analytical evaluation of the welfare effects is possible using the traditional concepts of producer and consumer surplus. If CU formation results in a shift in domestic consumption away from relatively high cost domestic production to relatively low cost partner production, or rest of world production, or both, then trade creation is said to arise. A full scheme of possible outcomes is documented in Collier (1979).

One possibility arises when a relatively small country in international trade participates in a union which has a 'large' share of world trade. For a given commodity the union producers' export supply curves and those of the rest of the world are below the equilibrium price for the good in the domestic economy. Prior to the CU all external suppliers are excluded from the domestic market by a prohibitive tariff. After participation in the CU, and the adoption by the CU of a CET against non-members equal to that applied by the domestic economy before the union, the commodity will be imported from the union partner. Domestic production as a source of domestic consumption has been displaced by partner country production. This switch from high cost domestic production to lower cost partner production is termed 'trade creation'. It is depicted in Figure 1.1.

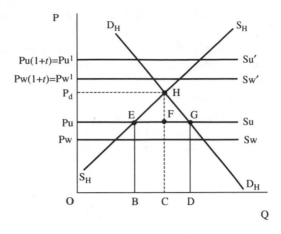

Figure 1.1 Trade creation

D_H and S_H represent the home demand and supply curves for the good. PuSu and PwSw are the CU and rest of the world supply curves. However, prior to membership of the union both external producers are excluded from the home market by the imposition of a tariff which moves their import supply curves above the equilibrium price in the domestic economy. The home country is self-sufficient at an equilibrium price of OP_d and quantity of OC. Upon membership of the union the common external tariff does not apply to the union partner, but obviously applies to the rest of the world. The union partner's supply curve now reverts to PuSu and supplies imports of BD to the home country. Domestic supply falls from OC to OB, but domestic demand rises from OC to OD. The resource cost of producing BC of the good has fallen from BCHE to BCFE, a saving of EFH. This is beneficial in terms both of union welfare and world welfare. The home country has clearly gained, for although producers' surplus has fallen by PuEHPd, consumers' surplus has risen by PuGHPd. Assuming that these surpluses are equally weighted, the net gain to the home economy is HEG. Now clearly the gain would have been larger had the home economy formed the union with the rest of the world. More realistically, of course, had a policy of free trade been pursued rather than membership of a discriminatory trading regime, the gain would appear to be maximised. However in terms of welfare gain, participation in the union is obviously a step in the right direction, because there is a gain from free trade. Nevertheless, free trade with all trading partners would lead to greater welfare gains.

Viner (1950) provided a framework for the analysis of changes in trade patterns when participation in a union results in a switch from a low cost source of supply to a higher cost source of supply. He called this 'trade diversion'. Before the union was formed the tariff against all outsiders was not prohibitive, and the home country's imports came from the lowest cost source, namely the rest of the world. However, after participation in the union, tariffs against the union partners' exports were abolished. To domestic consumers imports of this commodity from union partners were cheaper than those from the rest of the world. Although the rest of the world was the lowest cost source of supply, it was not the lowest priced source of supply in the domestic economy. Appropriate analysis of trade diversion is again dependent on the nature of the countries described by the model. Either countries are small in world trade or they are large. In respect of trade in some commodities the home country may be classified as small and the union partner and the rest of the world large. In this case the last two groups of countries present infinitely elastic import supply curves to the domestic economy. Alternatively, for certain traded goods the home and partner countries may be classified as small compared to the rest of the world. In this case upward sloping supply curves are a feature of both home and partner supply curves but not the rest of the world. It is also possible that the home country union partners and the rest of world could be classified as small. Clearly there are a variety of possibilities. Here the focus is on one of the possibilities, where the home country is small and the partner country and the rest of the world large.

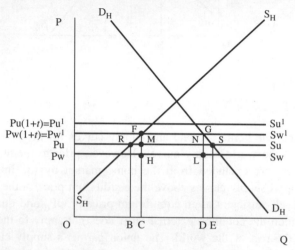

Figure 1.2 Trade diversion: home country small; partner country and rest of world large

Refer to Figure 1.2, which provides an analysis of trade diversion. Prior to participation in a union and with a tariff level t on potential partner and rest of world supplies, the lowest priced source of import supply is the rest of the world Pw^1Sw^1. Domestic production is OC and imports CD. Tariff proceeds FGLH go to the government of the home economy. The home country joins a union whose external tariff is identical to that of the home country prior to participation. Domestic production falls to OB but domestic consumption rises to OE; BE imports now come from the union partner at a tariff-free price of OPu. Trade diversion has arisen. The cost of the original quantity of imports CD has risen by HLNM. There is a loss of tariff revenue to the domestic government of FGLH. Additionally, producers' surplus has fallen by $PuPw^1RF$, but consumers' surplus has risen by $PuPw^1GS$. The gain in consumers' surplus minus the loss in producers' surplus is equal to RFGS. Part of this, namely FGNM, is part of the lost tariff revenue and consequently this reduces the gain of RFGS to the areas RFM and SGN. The other part HLNM (the amount of trade diversion) may be compared with the two triangles RFM and SGN. Clearly here there is a net trade diversionary loss. The extent of this loss will be the greater the bigger the gap between world prices and union prices.

When trade diversion arises, higher cost supplies from the union partner displace lower cost supplies from the rest of the world (ROW). This switch in the source of supply arises because although imports from the union partner are more costly than imports from outside the CU, after CU membership they are cheaper to domestic consumers and producers. Imports from the union partner are not subject to the CET, whereas imports from the ROW are subject to the CET. The cost of the imported good (excluding the tariff imposition) is the focus for terms of trade changes. Clearly (see Figure 1.2) import prices rise (from OPw to OPu) after CU formation. The deterioration in the domestic country's terms of trade is the essence of trade diversion. However, a cheapening of the import to domestic residents occurs now that tariff-free partner country imports replace tariff-laden ROW imports. Of course on diverted trade the government does not derive tariff revenue. When the change in surpluses of the three groups – consumers, producers and government – are collectively considered, there is an overall loss resulting from trade diversion in the example depicted by Figure 1.2.

This type of analysis can be made more sophisticated and sometimes more realistic by introducing alternative assumptions relating to country size. For instance, the home and partner country can be assumed to be small, and the rest of the world large. In this circumstance the supply curve of both the home and partner countries slopes upwards and different consequences arise when a CU is formed. Hence a small country has no power to change the terms of trade by changing its trading policy because it confronts an infinitely elastic supply of imports. This is not the case with a large country. In this case a change in trade policy can have a substantial effect on its terms of trade. A large country faces an upward sloping supply of imports and therefore the more it imports, the higher it raises import prices and hence changes the terms of trade.

The dynamic effects of CUs

The concepts of trade creation and diversion are concerned with the allocation of resources in a static framework, i.e. a system with a given set of factors of production and a fixed technology. It is also normally assumed that there is a perfectly competitive market structure and no potential to reap economies of scale. However, the change in trade patterns induced by the creation of a CU could result in alterations to the competitive environment and give rise to opportunities to reap economies of scale. These dynamic factors may well have a stronger impact on members of a CU than the static effects of trade creation and diversion. Here the focus will be on three of the so-called dynamic effects (these factors are also discussed in Chapter 2).

1. Monopoly power.
   The removal of tariffs can reduce monopoly power within the home country by increasing the possible sources of supply. This can result in higher outputs, lower prices and the reduction of monopoly profits. It is also possible that non-price competition, in terms of quality of products, can be stimulated by the creation of a CU.

2. Efficiency gains.
   This relates to possible gains in technical efficiency arising from an increase in competition. The productivity of existing resources is alleged to rise in response to the threat to established markets provoked by tariff-free trade between union partners. This can result because of reductions in overmanning and improvements in other types of slack management procedures. However, Pelkmans (1984) reminds us that the technical efficiency gains are by no means automatic as a result of greater competition in integrated markets. Participants may swim faster or indeed may sink; much depends on the willingness and abilities of firms to adjust to the increase in competition.

3.   Economies of scale.
    Although a CU may have implications for both internal and external economies of scale, the emphasis is normally placed on the technical aspects of internal economies. Whenever a CU is formed it is likely that some industries will flourish in certain countries as the market widens. This can occur if plants are operating at less than minimum efficiency scale (see Chapter 2). In these circumstances the increase in output made possible by the CU would lead to a reduction in the unit cost of production. A higher scale of output may also provide the opportunity to introduce new techniques of production which would be uneconomic at lower scales of output. The market in the countries of the CU may come to be dominated by producers in one of them. The more enterprising economies experience a gain while industries located in less enterprising countries languish.

The direct cost approach

Studies that use this approach have ranged from attempts to estimate the effects of membership on the balance of payments as a whole to a more narrow focus on the balance of commodity trade. They have one feature in common, namely an attempt to discover what the condition of, say, the balance of trade would have been had the country in question not participated in the CU. Once this 'anti-monde' is defined and calculated, the difference between actual trade and 'anti-monde' trade is ascribed to union membership. The main problem with this type of analysis is that there are so many different 'anti-mondes' to choose between (Winters 1987). Also, as the years between initial membership and the present day extend, a time must come when the accuracy of any 'anti-monde' is open to serious doubt. One of the last serious attempts to derive an attributable cost of membership of a CU was undertaken by Grinols (1984) for the UK. Since then, information on this front has been hard to locate. It is also the case that most of the studies of this type have been concerned with the effects on the UK of membership.

In order to estimate the costs of membership of a regional trading bloc as a whole, membership dues and integration induced trade flows must be included in the calculations. If, however, concern is more narrowly focused only on the effects of the CU then the consequences for the balance of trade are the major concern. With this approach any movement in the direction of a trade deficit is identified as a cost, and conversely a gain is associated with the development of a surplus. Generally it is the total trade associated with a CU which should be investigated. However, policies of positive integration such as the CAP, which impinge on trading relationships, can blur the CU issue and can incline us to exclude a particular class of trade. Hence trade in agricultural products in the EU may be excluded because strictly it is the operation of the CAP which largely determines trade in agricultural products.

Prospective members are concerned with the total effects on their international accounts of joining the CU. Hence the British government adopted a broader approach to membership of the EU than a basic CU framework would dictate (British Government White Paper 1971). In consequence the central objective of governmental concern prior to membership was the balance of payments. However, after the event several attempts have been made to estimate the direct cost of participating in the EU. These studies highlight the balance of trade in manufactures (European Free Trade Association 1972, Kreinin 1969, Resnick and Truman 1971, Williamson and Bottrill 1971).

Balance of trade effects of membership

In terms of the allocation of resources the Vinerian concepts of trade creation and diversion are respectively welfare enhancing and welfare reducing. Full realisation of benefit with regard to trade creation is conditional on the existence of traditional classical assumptions, namely that resources are mobile nationally but immobile internationally. Given the existence of resource mobility in a single country, the exploitation of comparative advantage is possible. Without it, the gain is smaller and confined to the consumption benefit of cheaper imports. If the criterion for the evaluation of gain or loss is not in terms of either the 'maximisation of productive efficiency' or the 'optimisation of consumption', but rather in terms of the impact of membership of a regional trading bloc on the balance of trade, then it is difficult to identify trade creation with a benefit arising from a switch between the domestic supplier and the union partner. Trade creation induces a rise in imports and hence induces a deterioration in the balance of trade.

Trade diversion involves a switch between third country and union suppliers at worsened terms of trade (see Figure 1.2: PuSu replaces PwSw). The good imported from the union partner is now tariff-free and lower in price to domestic consumers than the tariff-laden import from the rest of the world. There is a so-called unfavourable movement in the domestic economy's terms of trade. The effect on the balance of trade is also adverse because not only is the initial volume of imports more costly, but also, because the price of imports in the domestic market has fallen, cutbacks in domestic production and increases in domestic consumption simply stimulate more imports.

If the focus of attention were to dwell solely upon imports, a potential or existing member would hardly relish CU membership on a balance of trade basis. In reality, the focus for the aggregate balance is of course on both imports and exports. Clearly trade creation experienced by union members on the import side results in an equivalent rise in exports of other union members. For the CU as a whole there is no change in the balance of trade as the changes of the individual members balance out. However, individual members could be faced with a deterioration in their balance of trade if the trade creation effect were to increase imports more than exports.

With trade diversion, the preferred tariff-laden imports from third countries are replaced by tariff-free imports from within the CU. These are cheaper to consumers, but more costly than those from countries outside the union. Clearly for the union as a whole trade diversion improves the balance of trade, because union exports to union partners replace third country exports to union partners. For each individual country in the union, however, the balance of trade deteriorates on the import side. Imports are cheaper to consumers and hence a rise in the volume of imports is to be expected, as the cost of the goods excluding the tariff has risen but the domestic price of the goods including the CET has fallen. The terms of trade in these goods has worsened and the trade balance will inevitably deteriorate. However, there will also be 'export trade diversion' when a union country supplies a partner country in place of the imports from third countries. This improves the balance of trade for those countries that supply other member countries with such diverted imports.

The integration induced effects on the trade balance cannot be confined to the standard Vinerian concepts. Both static and dynamic effects arise. There are other effects additional to the Vinerian concepts of 'trade creation' and 'trade diversion' which impinge on the trade accounts. When the EEC was established, the CET was defined in terms of an average of the tariffs of the original six members. This meant that for some countries the CET was lower than national tariffs. Of itself, this served to stimulate rest of the world exports into these countries. Increased trade with third countries due to this effect and also perhaps the induced trade following from the increase in growth stimulated by the creating of the CU have been called 'external trade creation'. Alternatively, where the level of the CET was higher than pre-existing national tariffs this would stimulate a rise in home sales: this is termed 'trade suppression' and would lead to an improvement in the balance of trade of such union members. Dynamic effects can also arise from economies of scale, and other factors induced by the formation of the CU. An industry inside the bloc may have a comparative advantage and benefits may be reaped from internal economies of scale, learning effects, and inducements to alter production processes. Lower cost production and prices would follow, and this would help to expand an area of manufacture within EU markets and also would serve to enhance the market for such goods in the rest of the world.

Estimates of the effect of integration on trade

Numerous studies have attempted to estimate the effects of membership on a country joining the EU. Some studies have dwelt solely on the CU aspect of membership, with a focus on manufacturing industry. Other studies have cast a wider net to embrace other elements in the balance of payments (Featherstone, Moore and Rhodes 1979). Other major studies by Kreinin (1969, 1972), Resnick and Truman (1971), Williamson and Bottrill (1971), the European Free Trade Association (1972) and Balassa (1987) are indicated in the references at the end of this chapter.

An 'anti-monde' analysis is used to try and establish and quantify the effects of integration. It is normally assumed that a given variable would have remained constant in the absence of integration. What is termed 'residual imputation' is used to establish the integration effect by deducting the 'anti-monde' result from the actual result. Balassa's (1987) 'anti-monde' was derived using the assumption that the income elasticity of demand would have remained constant had it not been for the effect of economic integration. With regard to the UK, a recent test by Winters using the 'Almost Ideal Demand System' led to the conclusion that the British trade balance had worsened by £3.1 billion and UK output had fallen by 1.5 per cent resulting from joining the CU of the EU (Winters 1987).

It is not the purpose of this chapter to provide a comprehensive survey of the empirical work undertaken on this topic. However, a flavour of recent procedures and problems can be had by examining two contributions. A work similar to Resnick and Truman (1971) was developed by Jacquemin and Sapir (1988). This takes a 'Constant Share Approach' to some balance of trade effects of membership.

Given the variety of forces influencing a country's trade and domestic consumption after the formation of a CU, there is much diversity of outcome. It is not sufficient, for example, to establish that for a given country inside the union exports and/or imports rise after integration. In absolute terms this may simply represent trends in a growing economy. It is more appropriate to focus on the proportions by which domestic consumption is served by domestic production, partner country and rest of world imports. For instance, if the proportion of domestic consumption that came from domestic production rose then this may have resulted from 'trade suppression', or the existence of dynamic effects producing lower prices in an industry exhibiting comparative advantage within the integrated area. The use of share analysis is a way of investigating the impact of integration on a country's trade. The technique involves estimating apparent consumption by deducting exports from domestic production and adding imports from union and non-union sources. Each element of the consumption aggregate is then expressed as a proportion of the total. Table 1.1 indicates the range of possibilities after foreign trade is subject to disturbances resulting from membership of a CU.

Table 1.1 Change in shares

Direction of change in apparent consumption

Case	P – X	Mp	Mrow
A	↑	↑	↓
B	↑	↓	↑
C	↑	↓	↓
D	↓	↑	↑
E	↓	↓	↑
F	↓	↑	↓

Key : P = production
        X = exports
        Mp = imports from partner country
        Mrow = imports from rest of world

Jacquemin and Sapir use share analysis to study the effect of integration on a country's trade over time. Their interest is focused on revealed changes in integration effects over time, as indicated by a domestic share of apparent domestic consumption (P–X), a partner share of apparent domestic consumption (Mp), and a rest of the world share of apparent domestic consumption (Mrow).

Cases D, E and F (Table 1.1) show that since integration the country under observation has experienced a decline in its share of domestic production in apparent consumption and also a rise in partner and/or rest of the world share. Where both partner and ROW shares have risen it cannot be claimed that the effects of integration have been to reduce dependence on non-partner countries. Clearly here is a case of both internal and external trade creation. With case F, the share of imports from the partner country has risen, but the share of both domestic production and imports from non-partner countries have declined. This suggests that the forces both of trade creation and of trade diversion have been at work. That is, those commodities subject to trade creation result in a cutback in the share of domestic production, but those commodities subject to trade diversion result in a diminution of the share of extra trade. In cases A, B and C the share of domestic production in apparent consumption has risen, which may result from trade diversion. Imports from the partner country or imports from the rest of the world, or both, have declined in case C.

Unfortunately, figures which can be derived as a result of this exercise are not free from influences on trade that may have arisen irrespective of the process of integration. In other words, any increases or decreases cannot be solely attributed to the effects of economic integration. The data capture movements of relative prices and incomes which may have little to do with the effect of economic integration on trade, but rather follow from changes in policies or other factors. Hence share analysis is hardly a refined tool to use to examine the effects of CU.

An alternative approach is offered by Grinols (1984). Basically, Grinols poses the question 'how much do individuals need in the UK at a new set of prices to be no worse off than before?' His attention is therefore focused on Britain's welfare and not confined simply to the balance of trade. To determine whether Britain's welfare from membership has risen or fallen he draws attention to the value:

$$(T - p_1 z_0) + S_1$$

T   = actual transfer in £ from UK to EU

$p_1 z_0$ = value of pre-membership trade at post-membership prices

S_1 = increase in profits from domestic production at post-membership prices relative to pre-membership production levels + the saving at post-membership prices from the substitution by consumers of cheaper goods.

The focus is on three aggregates when a judgement is made as to whether a country is paying an 'appropriate' amount for membership of the EU. The first is the actual transfer itself (T). This is the payment or receipt which arises from the way in which the EU budget is financed and disbursed. The second aggregate $(p_1 z_0)$ is the increase in the cost of purchasing Britain's 1972 trade quantities at post-membership prices. In fact the resulting terms of trade loss from membership on the pre-entry trade quantities was estimated on average at 2.3 per cent of GDP. If in addition to a negative $(p_1 z_0)$ there arises a negative (T) then an overall income deficit exists. However, there may be dividends in production and consumption measured by (S_1), which, if positive, help to reduce the overall size of the income deficit.

Grinols defines the dividend in production as 'the profits of British post-entry production less the profits which would have been earned using 1972 pre-existing production levels.' The dividend in consumption is defined as 'the cost of 1972 pre-entry consumption less the minimum cost of purchasing an equally desirable bundle at post-entry prices.' Both are estimated as positive for the UK between 1973 and 1979. Their effect is to reduce the average loss arising for the UK from membership of the EU. Between 1973 and 1979 the loss is estimated at 1.9 per cent of GDP. The conclusion one is driven to from these studies is that Britain has suffered a significant real income loss from membership.

The current position

It is perhaps not surprising that estimates of the gains and losses to the UK from EU membership appear to have dried up, and the other member states have not engaged in large-scale studies to assess the costs and benefits of membership of the CU. As the years since joining the EU increase, confidence in the accuracy of figures describing an anti-monde must decline. It becomes increasingly difficult to establish what effect would have arisen without integration and hence to calculate the value of the integration effect. Consequently, more rough and ready calculations might serve to provide an assessment of the current situation with regard to UK membership of the EU (see Dearden 1986).

The state of a country's trading balance on a geographical basis may direct our attention to the condition of the trade balance with the rest of the world. This is more likely to occur when there is an obvious contrast between the balance on intra-trade (trade within the EU) and the balance on extra-trade (EU trade with outside countries). The so-called 'direct cost approach' in the estimation of the effects of a CU dwelt on the trading balance of the integrated area. It is not uncommon to attribute the entire outcome of the regional trading balance to the effects of economic integration. For example, the division of the UK's balance on visible trade between the EU and the rest of the world provides this kind of contrast (Table 1.2).

Table 1.2 UK visible balance of trade with the EU and ROW (£m.)

	1982	1983	1984	1985	1986	1987	1988	1989	1990	1991	1992
EU	−1 320	−2 844	−3 466	−2 561	−8 859	−9 657	−13 762	−15 397	−9 896	−878	−3 657
ROW	−3 231	1 307	−1 870	−784	−700	−1 925	−7 718	−9 286	−8 913	−9 406	−9 749
Total	1 911	−1 537	−5 336	−3 345	−9 559	−11 582	−21 480	−24 683	18 809	−10 284	−13 406

EU figures for all years relate to the eleven.
Source: calculated from Table 2.2 UK Balance of Payments Pink Book 1993

A noticeable feature of Table 1.2 is the difference between the visible trade balance with the EU and that with the rest of the world. Up to 1990, the visible deficit of the UK with the EU was larger than that with the rest of the world. Indeed, in the first six years of the series, the deficit was much greater. However, since 1991 the position has changed, with the size of the deficit between the UK and the rest of the world exceeding that between the UK and the EU.

Even when narrowly conceived, the figures do not focus solely on the CU effect of membership, but also embrace other effects of membership such as the outcome for visible trade of the CAP. It is customary therefore to focus on a narrower trade related concept than the balance of visible trade to distinguish the CU effect of membership. Trade in such goods as energy supplies, for instance oil, is not part of the CU effect of membership. We are left with trade in manufactured goods, and it is to this trade on an intra- and extra-basis that we now turn. In Table 1.3 figures for the trade balance in manufactured goods are given on an intra- and extra-basis for the four major industrial countries in the EU.

Certain features merit particular comment. Firstly, the strength of Germany's balance on both an intra- and an extra-area basis is very pronounced. Secondly, the stability of Italy's balance on an intra-basis and a modest growth of surplus on an extra-basis is evident. Perhaps surprisingly, the country which on balance has experienced the largest deficit in trade on a manufacturing basis with the EU is France. Until recently, the deficits of France on an intra-area basis have been offset by surpluses on an extra-area basis.

However, the statistics on intra-trade are not wholly attributable to a country's membership of the EU. Other factors such as changes in relative prices and incomes that may not be significantly influenced by the formation of a CU can obscure the effects of a CU on trade. A simple procedure used some years ago by Kreinin (1969) consists of normalising intra-trade statistics. Here normalisation is undertaken by utilising trends in extra-trade. Normalisation is done by taking the average rate of growth exhibited by the extra-area trading balances. The proposition is that had these four countries remained outside the EU, their intra-trade in manufactures would have developed in the same way as their extra-trade. Hence we can predict the development of intra-trade had these countries not joined the CU. The difference between the actual intra-trade and the normalised intra-trade is then described as the CU effect

Table 1.3 Trade balance in manufactured goods (SITC V–VIII) of four EU industrial countries (ECUm.)

		Intra-trade		
Year	Germany	France	Italy	United Kingdom
1980	15 403	−7 835	1 091	−1 918
1981	17 928	−9 478	1 838	−5 851
1982	24 794	−14 454	4 211	−6 607
1983	22 383	−13 079	7 132	−14 129
1984	26 710	−13 538	4 578	−15 007
1985	29 754	−14 473	4 510	−17 087
1986	35 653	−18 179	6 477	−16 711
1987	40 165	−19 648	4 824	−16 329
1988	46 160	−18 458	6 685	−18 816
1989	53 115	−19 451	30 190	22 813
1990	39 899	−20 527	6 303	−14 627
1991	20 476	−16 038	7 041	−4 918
1992	24 312	−15 390	4 739	−7 691

		Extra-trade		
Year	Germany	France	Italy	United Kingdom
1980	28 909	11 935	11 787	12 258
1981	35 970	15 727	19 319	11 671
1982	42 883	15 891	19 385	11 232
1983	42 429	18 045	22 182	4 770
1984	47 417	22 046	24 938	3 791
1985	55 068	22 381	26 554	5 830
1986	53 023	16 160	22 150	2 504
1987	47 995	12 441	18 192	437
1988	44 605	11 447	16 612	−5 987
1989	44 968	13 262	19 041	−8 853
1990	29 745	11 527	19 389	−2 797
1991	27 855	10 022	17 654	−5 868
1992	30 037	14 329	18 774	−6 893

Source : Eurostat Statistical Yearbook: External Trade 1990–1993

on trade. These calculations for the four countries in question appear in Table 1.4. The figures in Table 1.4 using the Kreinin method constitute the 'anti-monde' for trade in manufactured goods of the four countries indicated.

Table 1.4 Calculated intra-trade in manufactured goods based on average rate of growth of extra-trade (ECUm.)

Year	Germany	France	Italy	United Kingdom[1]
1981	19 165	−10 324	1 788	−3 701
1982	22 848	−10 432	1 794	−5 484
1983	22 606	−11 846	2 053	−7 267
1984	25 264	−14 473	2 308	−9 050
1985	29 340	−14 693	2 485	−10 833
1986	28 251	−10 609	2 050	−12 616
1987	25 572	−8 167	1 684	−14 399
1988	23 765	−7 515	1 538	−16 182
1989	23 959	−8 706	1 762	−17 965
1990	15 848	−7 567	1 795	−19 748
1991	14 841	−6 579	1 634	−21 531
1992	16 004	−9 406	1 737	−23 314

[1] In this model intra-trade is assumed to decline by an absolute amount each year given by the estimated equation $EX = 14182 - 1783t$, where EX = extra-trade and t = time.

All that remains is to normalise the actual trade figures in Table 1.3, using the 'anti-monde' figures in Table 1.4. The results are given in Table 1.5.

Table 1.5 Estimated customs union effect on trade in manufactured goods (ECUm.)

Year	Germany	France	Italy	United Kingdom
1981	− 1237	846	50	−2 150
1982	1 945	−4 112	2 416	−3 123
1983	−223	−1 232	5 079	−6 862
1984	1 445	934	2 270	−5 957
1985	413	220	2 052	−6 254
1986	7 401	−7 570	4 426	−4 095
1987	14 592	−11 480	3 140	−2 930
1988	22 394	−10 943	5 147	−2 634
1989	29 155	−10 745	28 427	−4 848
1990	24 050	−12 960	4 508	+5 121
1991	5 635	−9 459	5 407	+16 613
1992	8 308	−5 983	3 001	+15 623

As expected, the calculations indicate that the CU has significantly strengthened the manufactured trade balance of Germany and of Italy. It has significantly weakened the trading balance of France and the UK. Since 1990, however, because the calculated deficit for the UK is in excess of the actual deficit on intra-trade, the CU effect for the UK is shown to be positive! Additionally, the deficit for France since the mid-1980s is shown to be in excess of that for the UK.

Estimates of this kind, although more refined than the raw trade statistics, can only be tentative. In the first place the division of trade between intra- and extra-trade is not affected only by economic integration. The normalisation technique is not independent of the process of economic integration and to that extent it is not analytically clean. Furthermore, it would be remarkable if changes in relative prices and incomes were identical between the two areas. To the extent that they are not, the CU effect is clearly picking up other influences.

Unfortunately the statement of Kreinin made some years ago remains true: 'there exists no wholly satisfactory way of measuring the effect of a customs union or free trade area on trade flows. International transactions are governed by many factors, and it is difficult to isolate the influences exercised by regional integration.' (Kreinin 1972)

References

Balassa B 1987 *Trade Creation and Diversion in the European Common Market*, The Manchester School, vol. XLII, No. 2, pp. 93–125.

British Government White Paper 1971 *The United Kingdom and the European Communities*, cmnd 4715.

Collier P 1979 The welfare effects of a customs union: an anatomy, *Economic Journal*, 89, pp. 84–95.

Dearden S 1986 EEC membership and the United Kingdom's trade in manufactured goods, *National Westminster Bank Quarterly Review*.

European Free Trade Association 1972 *The Trade Effects of EFTA and the EEC 1959–1967*, Geneva.

Featherstone M, Moore B and **Rhodes J** 1979 EEC membership and UK Trade in Manufactures, *Cambridge Journal of Economics*, 3, 399–407.

Grinols E L 1984 A thorn in the lion's paw. Has Britain paid too much for common market membership? *Journal of International Economics*, 16, pp. 271–293.

Jacquemin A and **Sapir A** 1988 European integration or world integration?, *Weltwirtschaftliches Archiv*, 124, 1, pp. 121–145.

Kreinin M E 1969 Trade creation and diversion by the EEC and EFTA, *Economia Internazionale*, vol. 22, pp. 1–43.

Kreinin M E 1972 Effects of the EEC on Imports of Manufactures, *Economic Journal*, 82, pp. 897–920.

Lipsey R G 1970 *The Theory of Customs Unions: General Equilibrium Analysis*, Weidenfeld and Nicolson, London.

Marques Mendes A J 1988 *Economic Integration and Growth in Europe*, Croom Helm, London.

Meade J E 1955 *The Theory of Customs Unions*, North Holland, Amsterdam.

Pelkmans J 1984 *Market Integration in the European Community*, Martinus Nijhoff, The Hague.

Resnick S A and **Truman E M** 1971 An empirical examination of bilateral trade in Western Europe, *Journal of International Economics*, 3, pp. 305–335.

Viner J 1950 *The Customs Union Issue*, Carnegie Endowment for International Peace, New York.

Williamson J and **Bottrill A** 1971 The impact of customs unions on trade in manufactures, *Oxford Economic Papers*, 23, pp. 323–51.

Winters A 1987 Britain in Europe: a survey of quantitative trade studies, *Journal of Common Market Studies*, 25, pp. 315–335.

CHAPTER 2

The Single European Market

Frank McDonald

The Treaty of Rome and the SEM

The concept of the Single European Market (SEM) has become one of the most studied and debated topics of recent years. It is known by many names: the SEM, the Internal Market, the 1992 Programme. It might be thought that the concept is a new one. However, all of these terms are simply alternative names for a Common Market. The concept of a Common Market is not new; the term arose in the 1950s, to describe an area where there exists free movement of goods, services, capital and labour. A Common Market is therefore an area with a Customs Union, plus free movement of factors of production. The move to establish an SEM is simply a programme to enable the EU to create a Common Market. The EU has been committed to establishing a Common Market since the Treaty of Rome was signed in 1957. Article 3 of the Treaty of Rome contains the following provisions: 'the elimination, as between member states, of customs duties and quantitative restrictions on the import and export of goods, and all other measures having equivalent effect; the abolition, as between member states, of obstacles to freedom of movement for persons, services and capital'. Article 8 calls for the Common Market to be progressively established over a period of 12 years. That is to say the Common Market should have been established between the original six members by 1969. Obviously this did not happen according to plan. The CU was achieved by the original six members in 1968. The creation of the Common Market has proved to be a more difficult objective to achieve.

Before agreement was reached to establish the SEM by the end of 1992, there had been very little progress towards establishing the Common Market. The main problem was the difficulty of reaching agreement about eliminating the many non-tariff barriers (NTBs) which hindered free movement. A range of NTBs based on diverse national rules, regulations, taxation, and subsidies governed the movement of goods, services, capital, and labour. Consequently, frontier controls were necessary to ensure that cross-frontier trade in goods adhered to the various national requirements. Cross-frontier trade in some service sectors was basically rendered impossible by different national rules and regulations. Capital movements were restricted by the use of capital and exchange controls imposed by some member states. Labour mobility was hampered by differences in professional qualifications, and by labour and social security laws and regulations. Prior to the agreement on the SEA, the EU had attempted to eliminate these NTBs by creating a set of European laws and regulations to govern all aspects of economic activity. This resulted in attempts to determine European standards for a large range of products. Member states could, however, veto any proposal which they thought was detrimental to their economies, therefore very little progress to harmonise to common European standards took place. This tendency to protect national interests meant that little progress was made to eliminate the barriers to the free movement of services, capital and labour. Hence the EU did not take any significant steps towards establishing the Common Market, despite the fact that the Treaty of Rome clearly committed the member states to achieving this objective.

The origins of the SEM programme

In the 1980s a process was begun which greatly accelerated the progress towards creating a Common Market. In this period the member states were experiencing lower growth rates and higher unemployment than the USA and Japan. The Japanese were successfully entering many of the most sensitive markets in the EU (e.g. cars, consumer electronic equipment, computing equipment), and the NICs were becoming an increasing threat to many of the industries of the member states. The leading high technology companies tended to be American or Japanese, and many European companies were unable to maintain a presence in these markets. Within the EU continuing conflict over the CAP and associated budgetary problems (see Chapter 6) had diverted the EU from making progress on establishing the Common Market. A view emerged that the EU was stuck in a rut, and was losing its vision and direction.

In spite of these problems there were also signs of the EU making some progress. The EMS, founded in 1979, had not collapsed as had been predicted in many quarters, rather it had achieved some success in stabilising exchange rate fluctuations and in helping to promote convergence of inflation rates. Greece joined the EU in 1981, and Spain and Portugal joined in 1986 creating a potential market of 320 million consumers. An ECJ ruling in 1978 – the Cassis de Dijon case – established the principle of mutual recognition. In this case the ECJ ruled that Germany could not ban the importing of Cassis de Dijon (a French alcoholic beverage) on the grounds that it did not conform to German rules and regulations governing the sale of alcoholic beverages. The ECJ established that goods which adhered to the national rules and regulations in the member state in which they were produced should be able to be sold in any member state without need to adhere to the rules and regulations governing the production and sale of the goods in the importing member state. This principle provided an escape route from the long process of establishing common European rules and regulations for all goods. This process could be replaced by the mutual recognition of each other's rules and regulations. The use of mutual recognition was accepted by the EU when the 'New approach to technical harmonisation' was adopted in 1985. The acceptance of the concept of mutual recognition was a major step in the process of removing NTBs caused by differences in rules and regulations. Harmonisation could be limited to essential requirements in order for health and public safety considerations to be accounted for, and to ensure technical compatibility of products. The combination of these factors contributed to the idea that the EU still had potential to be a dynamic body in Europe and the world.

In 1983, at the Stuttgart summit, there was an acknowledgement of the need to take new initiatives to restore some dynamism into the activities of the EU. This took the form of a Solemn Declaration of European Union. There was a growing feeling that the failure to establish the Common Market (now called the Internal Market) within the EU resulted in major handicaps for EU companies. There was a strong opinion that EU firms faced considerable disadvantages compared to American and Japanese firms. It was noted that American firms had a domestic market of over 200 million consumers, and Japanese firms had a market of 100 million. If the EU were to become a single market it would have a domestic market of 320 million consumers, making it the largest market in the world.

In 1984 the European Parliament issued a draft treaty on European Union. This called for political and economic change, in particular the creation of an internal market and the reform of decision-making procedures of the EU to make them more democratic, or at least more accountable to the European Parliament. At the Fontainebleau summit of 1984, two committees, the Adonnino and the Dooge, were set up. Both of these committees called for institutional change, and the Dooge called for the creation of an Internal Market. In 1985 there was published the White Paper, 'Completing the Internal Market', which called for a programme of legislation to be implemented to create an Internal Market by the end of 1992. At the Milan summit of 1985 all these moves came to a head, and an Inter-governmental Conference was set up to discuss European Union. This resulted in agreement on the SEA which was approved by all member states in 1986, and implemented in 1987. The SEA was a compromise between those countries such as France and Germany that wanted a new Treaty on European Union, and the UK and Denmark which did not want a new Treaty, but simply the implementation of the White Paper in order to create an SEM. The SEA was basically a limited set of changes to the Treaty of Rome which allowed for majority voting in the Council of Ministers in areas connected to establishing the Internal Market, and also had some rather vague references to EMU, Political Union and other policy areas such as the environment. The main thrust of the SEA was to establish the SEM by 31 December 1992. When the SEA was approved it was considered to be a poor substitute for a new Treaty on European Union, but given the opposition of the UK and Denmark it was the best that could be achieved. However, the SEA resulted in a dramatic increase in the activities of the EU, and it led to a chain of events which focused attention on the EU as being one of the most successful and dynamic economic agencies in the world. At the heart of the 1992 programme was Article 13 of the SEA: 'The internal market shall comprise an area without internal frontiers in which the free movement of goods, persons, services and capital is ensured in accordance with the provisions of this Treaty'.

This was simply a reformulation of the original commitment, in the Treaty of Rome, to establish a Common Market. The major difference was that there was the political will, and a detailed programme with a practical method of implementation, to achieve this objective. The EU had finally adopted a comprehensive programme to establish a Common Market. Basically this programme involved the removal of all legal barriers to the free movement of goods, services, capital and labour. The theoretical basis for this rests on economic models which predict that there are net welfare gains available from removing these barriers.

The theory of free movement

Traditional economic theory suggests that there are benefits to be reaped from creating free movement. Using simple partial equilibrium analysis, and assuming perfectly competitive markets, it can be shown that there are net welfare gains to be had from eliminating NTBs and thereby allowing free movement to take place. Much of the analysis which follows is based on the models used in Emerson *et al.* (1988).

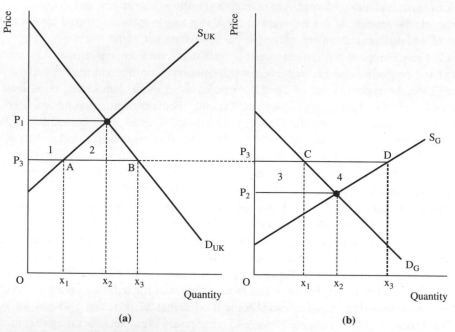

Figure 2.1 Reaping comparative advantage

In Figure 2.1 the case of reaping comparative advantage is examined. This analysis may be used to investigate trade in both goods and services.

In Figure 2.1(a) the demand and supply conditions for a good in the UK are depicted; Figure 2.1(b) shows market conditions in Germany. The lower equilibrium price in Germany shows that it has a comparative advantage in producing this good. Suppose that trade is prevented by the imposition of an NTB such as rules and regulations which prevent the selling of this German good in the UK. When the NTB is removed the UK would import the good from Germany. This would result in the price increasing in Germany and falling in the UK. When the price reached the level where imports into the UK were equal to exports from Germany, a new equilibrium price would have been established, i.e. at P_3 where UK imports (AB) = German exports (CD). This results in a rise in consumer surplus in the UK equal to the areas 1 + 2. The area 1 is a transfer of producer surplus to consumers; it is not a net welfare gain as it is transferred from producers in the UK to consumers in the UK. The remaining consumer surplus gain of area 2 represents the net welfare gain to the UK. The areas 3 + 4 represent the gain in producer surplus in Germany. Area 3 is a transfer of consumer surplus to German producers from German consumers. The net gain in Germany is therefore represented by area 4. There is a net gain to both countries equivalent to areas 2 + 4. These gains in producer and consumer surpluses can be considered as increases in real incomes to consumers and producers. However, this involves a change in the distribution of income. Consumers in the UK gain real incomes via lower prices, while consumers in Germany suffer a decline in real income. Similarly, producers in the UK suffer a loss of real income due to lower prices, but producers in Germany experience a gain. This highlights an important implication of establishing the SEM: although there might be net gains to be reaped, this does not mean that all participants in the process experience benefits. The analysis also indicates that a good deal of income redistribution is likely to occur in the process of creating the SEM. However, the net welfare gains represent increases in real incomes in the EU, and it is these real income increases which lie at the heart of the benefits of creating the SEM.

Benefits can also accrue from removing NTBs even if there is no comparative advantage to be reaped. This can occur when the market environment is not competitive and when the removal of NTBs results in an increase in competition. The extreme case would be when the removal of NTBs led to a domestic monopoly becoming a perfectly competitive market. This would result in a net gain equal to the deadweight loss of the monopoly (see Chapter 7 for an analytical exposition of this deadweight loss). Such an outcome is most unlikely in any real world situation. What is more likely is some increase in competition within an imperfectly competitive market. This will result in downward pressure on prices as domestic firms face foreign competition. This is examined in Figure 2.2.

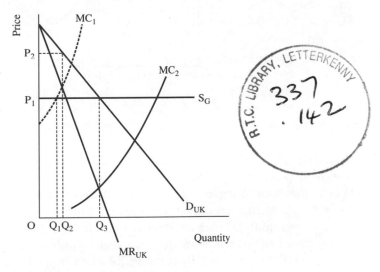

Figure 2.2 Effects of external competition on a domestic monopolist

If the UK had a domestic monopolist totally protected by an NTB, then price would be P_2 and output Q_2 if the monopolist faced the marginal cost curve shown by MC_1. Assuming a perfectly elastic supply of this good from Germany, the ruling market price in the absence of the NTB would be P_1 and the total demand in the UK would be Q_3. If the NTB were removed the price in the UK would fall to P_1, and the monopolist would be constrained to this price. The monopolist would have to adjust output to Q_1 and the gap in satisfying market demand in the UK at this price would be met by imports from Germany of $Q_1 - Q_3$. There would be benefits in the UK from a lower price and higher output provided that the domestic monopolist's marginal cost curve lay above MC_2. A paper by Jacquemin (1982) shows that this disciplinary effect from foreign competition can also work in oligopolistic markets. Hence, the creation of the SEM could lead to benefits from increasing the competitive structure of the EU economy.

This disciplinary effect of free movement can also set in motion factors which reduce production costs and stimulate improvements in the non-price characteristics of goods and services. This argument rests on increased competition reducing X-inefficiency, and stimulating research and development (R&D) and innovation to reduce production costs and improve non-price characteristics. A possible scenario is depicted in Figure 2.3.

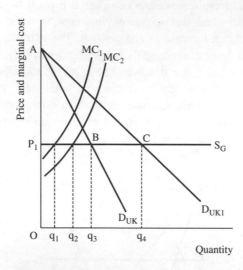

Figure 2.3 Effects of reducing X inefficiency and improvements in non-price factors

This situation is similar to Figure 2.2, i.e. a UK monopolist constrained to the price P_1 because of imports from Germany. If this increase in competition is also accompanied by R&D and innovation to improve the non-price characteristics of this good, the demand curve shifts to D_{UK1}. Consumer surplus is increased from P_1AB before the improvements in non-price factors, to P_1AC after the improvements. Initially, the increase in demand in the UK is met by increased imports from Germany, that is, imports rise from q_1-q_3 to q_1-q_4. If, however, the UK firm responds by reducing X-inefficiency, this could shift the marginal cost to MC_2 and allow the UK firm to increase its share of the market from q_1 to q_2. If the UK firm reduced X-inefficiency without any increase in the non-price characteristics of the good, the result would be that the UK firm would increase market share and its producer surplus. There would be no benefit in terms of increased consumer surplus. This implies that reductions in X-inefficiency do not necessarily lead to net welfare improvements for consumers. Only if the lowering of production costs results in lower prices will there be any benefits to consumers.

A further benefit from eliminating NTBs may arise if it is possible to reap economies of scale. This is illustrated in Figure 2.4. This assumes that firms always set price equal to average costs because they are constrained by the level of competition to making only normal profits. If the NTBs mean that firms face restriction on exports, they can be constrained from reaping economies of scale because they cannot expand their output beyond the limits imposed by their domestic market.

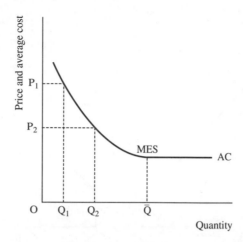

Figure 2.4 Effects of economies of scale

The level of output constrained by the NTB is Q_1, and this results in a price of P_1. If the NTB is removed, the firm could increase exports and thereby expand output to Q_2 which would reduce price to P_2. This outcome is dependent on the level of competition being sufficient to ensure that firms are constrained to making normal profits, and that they are therefore forced to reduce price when costs are lowered. Such an outcome is possible if there exist contestable markets, so that firms can easily enter an industry when profits rise, and exit when they fall (see McDonald 1987). It is also necessary for the firm to be operating at above minimum efficiency scale (MES), the low point of the average cost curve. If the firm is operating at MES, the opportunity to expand output will not result in lower costs. Learning effects may also help to reduce costs and thereby prices. These effects arise when expansion of output allows firms to learn how to produce more output using the same inputs.

Establishing free movement of capital and labour can also be shown to lead to net welfare gains. In Figure 2.5, the effects of barriers to free movement of labour are examined, assuming perfect mobility of labour, i.e. no transaction costs or cultural barriers to movement, and that the only barrier is a legal prohibition on UK workers migrating to Germany. The situation prior to the establishing of free movement of labour would be a wage of W_1 and employment at E in the UK. In Germany the wage would be W_2 and employment at B. When the barrier was lifted a new equilibrium wage would emerge of W_3. At this wage the number of migrant workers from the UK is equal to the inflow to Germany. Employment in the UK would fall to D, with DF of migrant workers. This reduces the supply of labour in the UK to S_{UK-m}, the supply of labour in the UK minus migrants. Employment of German workers would fall to A, with AC of migrant workers from the UK. This leads to gains and losses of economic rent (area above the supply curve of labour, and below the wage line) for labour. Workers in Germany lose an amount equal to area 1, while workers who remain in the UK gain higher wages leading to economic rent equal to area 3. Migrant workers from the UK would gain the areas 4 + 5. Employers also make gains and losses (the areas below the

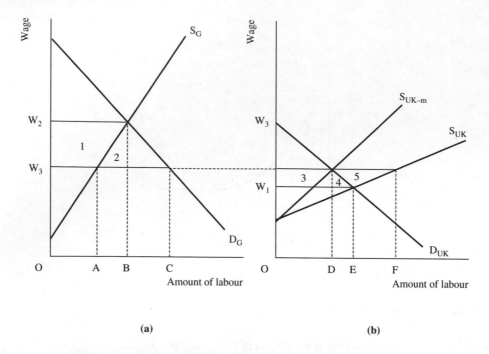

Figure 2.5 Effects of free movement of labour: (a) Germany; (b) UK

demand for labour and above the wage line). In Germany employers gain area 2 from the employment of migrant workers, while in the UK employers lose an amount equivalent to the areas 3 + 4. The areas 1 + 3 + 4 are transfers, area 1 from German workers to German employers, and areas 3 + 4 from UK employers to UK workers. This leaves areas 2 and 5 as net welfare gains of allowing free movement of labour.

Removal of barriers to capital mobility can also lead to net welfare gains. In a perfectly competitive market system, with a fixed stock of capital, and no capital mobility the situation is as depicted in Figure 2.6.

The stock of capital in the UK is given by K_1 and in Germany by K_3. The marginal productivity of capital is shown by M_{UK} and M_G. The marginal productivity of capital in Germany is higher than in the UK, therefore the rate of return to capital in Germany (r_3) is higher than in the UK (r_1). In the UK capital receives a total reward equal to the areas 4 + 5, while labour receives 1 + 2 + 3. In Germany the total return to capital is shown by areas 8 + 9, and area 6 is the payment to labour. If the barriers to capital mobility are removed, capital will flow from the UK to obtain the higher rate of return available in Germany. This will continue until the rate of return is equal in both countries, i.e. at r_2. This results in an export of capital from the UK of K_1–K_2, corresponding to the capital stock increase in Germany of K_3–K_4. This reduces total product in the UK to an amount equal to areas 1 + 2 + 4. However, the exported capital results in a transfer of profits to the UK from Germany, equal to area 10. In Germany national product is increased by areas 7 + 10, leading to a net welfare gain to Germany equivalent to area 7. The shaded part of area 10 is equal to the higher return to UK **capital** from being invested in Germany. In Figure 2.6 this area is twice the size of area 3.

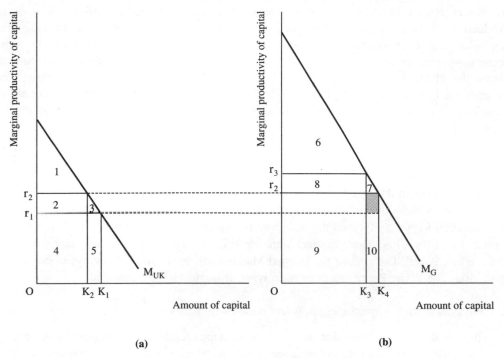

Figure 2.6 Effects of free movement of capital: (a) UK; (b) Germany

Hence the net loss of areas 3 + 5 to the UK is more than compensated for by the remittance of profits from Germany, as area 10 is greater than areas 3 + 5. So the net welfare gains of allowing free movement of capital are equal to area 7 plus half the shaded area. There are however, distribution effects to labour resulting from capital mobility. Labour's share in the UK falls by areas 2 + 3, while in Germany it rises by areas 7 + 8.

The above analysis assumes that capital movements arise only from differences in productivity. However, capital movements may result as a by-product of companies transferring technology and know-how. This results not only in a shift along the marginal productivity of labour curves, but in shifts in the positions of the curves. Capital flows are also influenced by uncertainty, and the influence of different monetary and exchange rate policies. The establishment of EMU would eliminate many of the distortions to capital movements caused by differences in the macro-economic policies of the member states. Hence, the creation of a single capital market in the EU would seem to require EMU, if capital mobility is to be driven by reasons of efficiency in the allocation of resources.

The theory of free movement implies that the removal of NTBs offers the potential for reaping net welfare gains. These arise from comparative advantage opportunities, increasing competition (including X-inefficiency and non-price effects), reaping economies of scale and from increased returns to capital and labour. These gains cannot however be acquired without changing the distribution of income. The removal of NTBs implies that some consumers, workers and companies will gain, while others will lose. The overall effect is deemed to be beneficial as net gains are reaped, and the efficiency of the allocation of resources is improved. The theory also indicates that reconstruction of the economy will occur as free movement results in changes in the location of capital and labour, and in methods of production. It is normally assumed that this reconstruction will not result in long-term unemployment of resources, or worse, permanent under-utilisation of resources in some sectors. We will return to question this assumption after an examination of the programme to create the SEM. A major study – The Costs of Non-Europe – was established to try and estimate the benefits of creating the SEM. Forms of analysis somewhat similar to those above were used to estimate the net gains. This study has come to be known as the Cecchini Report (see Cecchini (1988) and Emerson *et al.* (1988) for summaries of this report).

The Cecchini Report

The Cecchini Report established the main barriers which were to be removed by implementing Article 13 of the SEA. These barriers were identified by references to those outlined in the 1985 White Paper, 'Completing the Internal Market', and by a series of surveys of businesses in the EU. The White Paper lists three main types of barriers to be eliminated.

1.   Physical barriers – frontier controls and customs formalities.

2.   Technical barriers – restriction on economic activities resulting from national rules and regulations. These include technical specifications which hinder or prevent trade in goods; rules and regulations governing services which hinder non-domestic companies from trading across frontiers; discriminatory public procurement rules which limit tendering for government contracts to domestic companies, and legal obstacles faced by foreign companies seeking to set up subsidiaries in other member states.

3.   Fiscal barriers – the need to adjust VAT and excise duties as goods cross EU frontiers. This is necessary as member states operate different coverage, and levy different rates of VAT and excise duties.

The Cecchini Report reclassifies these barriers in order to estimate the benefits of removing these NTBs. Hence five main barriers were defined by Cecchini: tariffs, quotas, cost-increasing barriers, market-entry restrictions, and market-distorting activities practised by governments.

Tariffs and quotas had largely been eliminated by the CU, but some remained, in particular VERs relating to cars and electronic equipment, and quotas on textiles connected to the MFA. These were national quotas and they were removed or harmonised to allow frontier controls to be eliminated. The bulk of the benefits arise from eliminating the remaining barriers. Cost-increasing barriers include customs formalities such as VAT and excise duty assessments, verification of technical regulations, and also costs incurred by companies in adhering to different technical regulations. These can include modification to products, changes to packaging, etc. Market-entry restrictions include prohibiting or restricting access by foreign companies to the services sector, and rules and regulations which prevent foreign firms from bidding for public procurement contracts. Market-distorting activities arise from state aids such as subsidies, tax concessions, and other financial help given to domestic companies.

Table 2.1 Estimates of the benefits of removing barriers to create the SEM

	ECU (bn.)		as % of the GDP of the EC	
	(a)	(b)	(a)	(b)
Stage I Barriers affecting trade (frontier controls)	8	9	0.2	0.3
Stage II Barriers affecting production (technical and regulatory rules)	57	71	2.0	2.4
Stage III Barriers preventing the reaping of economies of scale	60	61	2.0	2.1
Stage IV Barriers which allow X-inefficiency and monopoly rents to exist	46	46	1.6	1.6
Total benefits	171	187	5.8	6.4

Notes :
(1) (a) Low estimates (b) High estimates
(2) For the EU6 plus the UK
(3) At 1985 prices

Source : Based on the Cecchini Report 'Costs of non-Europe'

Using this taxonomy of barriers, estimates of the benefits of removing them were made. This was generally done for the EU as a whole; few attempts were made to estimate the redistribution effects of removing these trade barriers. These estimates were based on a four-stage assessment of the effects of creating free movement. Stage I is connected to the benefits from removing barriers affecting trade, i.e. frontier controls. Stage II benefits arise from the removal of technical and regulatory rules which increase the costs of companies. The reaping of economies of scale provide the benefits in Stage III. Finally, Stage IV estimates gains from increased competition leading to reductions in X-inefficiency and monopoly rents. The magnitude of these gains is outlined in Table 2.1.

There is some dispute as to whether the Cecchini Report attempted to quantify the impact of increased competition on levels of X-inefficiency. In Emerson *et al.* (1988) the tables indicate that estimates of gains from reductions in X-inefficiency were included in the Cecchini study; however, Smith (in Dyker, 1992) maintains that the Cecchini estimates do not include any effects that arise from reductions in X-inefficiency.

These benefits result from large-scale changes affecting a wide variety of industries (see Table 2.2). Studies on the impact of the SEM on various industries are provided in Mayes (1991) and Dyker (1992).

Table 2.2 Benefits from creating the SEM by sector – the top ten

		ECU (bn.)
(1)	Electrical goods	19.7
(2)	Motor vehicles	17.8
(3)	Chemicals	15.2
(4)	Mechanical engineering	14.0
(5)	Credit and insurance	11.7
(6)	Food (excluding meat and dairy products)	7.6
(7)	Building and civil engineering	7.2
(8)	Office machinery	6.9
(9)	Transport	6.1
(10)	Wholesaling and retailing	5.3

Notes :
(a) For the EU6 plus the UK
(b) At 1985 prices
(c) Based on the high estimates

Source : Based on the Cecchini Report 'Costs of non-Europe'

These benefits were held to stem from three separate but connected effects of removing the barriers to free movement. These were the effects of: (a) reducing frontier controls; (b) reducing market entry barriers; (c) reducing cost-increasing barriers. Effect (a) results from the reduction in the cost of frontier formalities, that is delays at frontiers and administration costs of dealing with customs forms. The removal of these would have a small but direct effect by increasing trade between EU countries and would lead to secondary effects of lower prices and incentives to increase investment. Effect (b) arises when barriers are of such a high level as to prevent any entry into the market. Such barriers are common in public procurement where standards and rules and regulations can prevent entry by non-national firms. They are also obstacles to the free movement of labour and capital. The removal of such barriers would increase market entry which would directly lead to an increase in competition, and thereby to reductions in X-inefficiency and monopoly pricing practices. There would also be stimulation of investment to reap economies of scale, and to rationalise production and distribution systems. Effect (c) brings benefits by reducing costs incurred by different technical standards for goods, and by removing the barriers caused by the variety of rules and regulations governing key business and consumer services such as financial, legal, accounting, and transport services. The removal of these barriers would lead to a direct lowering of costs by reducing the price of imported goods and services. There would also be secondary effects which would increase the degree of competition and the level of investment. The combined effects of these changes would be to increase the GDP of the EU as illustrated in Figure 2.7.

The bulk of the benefits are seen to derive from the effects of increased competition and lower costs which lead to lower prices, and also stimulate investment. New market opportunities allow for increased economies of scale, and the rationalisation of artificially segmented markets. The increase in competition allows for considerable improvements in the effective use of inputs, and reductions in the anti-competitive practices of companies. This process is further aided by reductions in the costs of business and consumer services made possible by the liberalisation of the service sector. The creation of the SEM is seen by

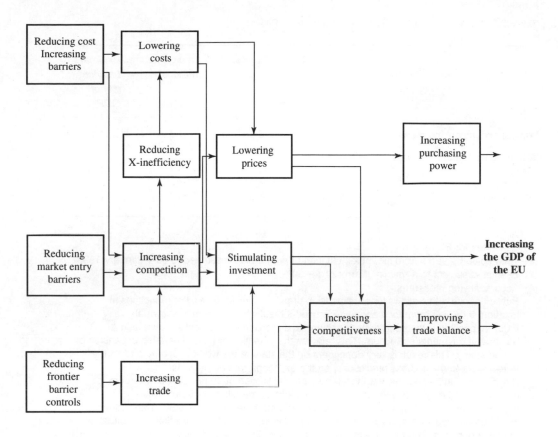

Figure 2.7 How the SEM increases the GDP of the EU

Cecchini as a programme which boosts the effectiveness of the supply-side of the economy. This improvement in the supply-side leads to an increase in aggregate demand by increasing real purchasing power, increasing investment, and improving the competitiveness of the EU relative to the rest of the world. These changes to the supply-side also lead to improvements in public sector budgetary positions, because of reductions in the costs of public procurement, and the growth of GDP which increases taxation revenues. This could allow for the consideration of a policy of expansion of the economy led by government expenditure. Such an expansion could help with temporary unemployment problems associated with the reconstruction of the economy, which is induced by the creation of the SEM. These supply-side changes improve the productive potential of the economy and enhance the ability to reach higher levels of non-inflationary growth. Such government-led expansion of aggregate demand would need to be coordinated to avoid problems of inconsistent growth levels. The Cecchini Report does not have much to say on this issue, but the implication of such a policy is that monetary policies would need to be coordinated to prevent the growth of monetary instability. Cecchini estimated these accompanying macro-economic policies to have very significant effects on the overall benefits of creating the SEM (see Table 2.3).

Table 2.3 Macro-economic benefits of creating the SEM

	GDP (%)	Prices (%)	Employment (millions)	External balance (%) of GDP
Without accompanying measures	4.5	−6.1	1.8	1.0
With accompanying measures				
Public finance	7.5	−4.3	5.7	−0.5
External position	6.5	−4.9	4.4	0.0
Disinflation	7.0	−4.5	5.0	−0.2

Notes :
(1) Estimates for EU12
(2) Time scale 6+ years from full implementation of programme (assumed to be 1 January 1993)
(3) Estimates subject to a margin of error of +/− 30%
(4) Accompanying measures:
   Public finance − this allows for an expansion of public investment and/or reductions in taxation; if the full room for manoeuvre is used it results in the benefits shown above.
   External position − the benefits here assume that the Community seeks to maintain a balance of payments equilibrium. This reduces the potential for government-led expansion of the economy. This result is very dependent on the state of the world economy and, in the model used to make these predictions, on the exchange rate of the dollar.
   Disinflation − this assumes that there would be a utilisation of 30 per cent of the room for expansion of the economy which would be brought by the fall in prices and the improvements in public finances which follow from the creation of the SEM. This option would protect the external balance and would allow for a significant disinflationary effect on the level of prices, and also create more employment than the previous option.

Source : Cecchini Report 'Costs of non-Europe'

The growth effects of the creation of the SEM have been considered by Baldwin (1989). The Cecchini Report estimate of the additional growth available from the SEM programme concentrates on the improvement in the efficiency of factors of production. Baldwin investigates the effect of this improvement in efficiency on the investment function. Using a constant returns to scale (or moderately increasing returns to scale) production function, Baldwin shows how the SEM programme can lead to an increase in the trend growth rate of investment. This effect arises from the increase in savings that results from the improvement of the efficiency of factors of production. This 'Baldwin' effect should lead to a permanent rise in the trend growth rate of the EU.

The SEM programme could lead to other efficiency gains and inducements to increase investment. The expansion of output arising from the SEM programme may give rise to learning effects that could stimulate output growth. The increase in market size and the more competitive environment may also lead to incentives to undertake innovative investments to aid in the process of defending or increasing the market share of companies. Finally, the creation of the SEM has led to a growth in DFI. This process may lead to an increase in investment and to the transfer of new and more productive techniques of production. This issue is examined in Chapter 17. The end effect of such processes should be to boost the trend rate of growth of the EU.

Nevertheless, the SEM also has the potential to reduce investment in some sectors within the EU. Those sectors in the member states that are not able to adjust to the more competitive environment may find a decline in investment as capital moves to those regions of the EU that offer the highest returns. Further, the rise of DFI from countries such as Japan may lead to a decline in investment from European companies as they fail to compete with the new vibrant Japanese companies that operate within the EU. In short, it is not certain that all regions and sectors within the EU will experience improvements in productivity and increases in investment levels. However, the case that the EU as a whole should experience an improvement in its trend rate of growth is fairly strong.

Criticism of the Cecchini Report

This rather rosy picture has been subjected to a great deal of criticism. This criticism may be classified under four main headings:

1. the assumption that the legislative programme would be completed by 1992;

2. inadequacies in the legislative programme;

3. the view that NTBs are the main obstacles to free movement;

4. failure to investigate the impact of the removal of fiscal barriers.

The Cecchini Report estimates assumed that all the necessary legislation would be approved and implemented by 1 January 1993. This was generally held to be wildly optimistic, and in some quarters, an impossible timescale. This issue is discussed below in the section on the position post-1992.

Criticism was also levelled at possible inadequacies in the legislative programme. In many sectors worries exist over the sufficiency of the mutual recognition approach. This was highlighted by the BSE (mad cow disease) scare where mutual recognition of health standards for food was called into question by some EU members. This resulted in the imposition of controls on the import of British beef by some member states, although this was contrary to EU law on free movement. Worries also exist over mutual recognition of testing and certification procedures, as there is concern that some member states may not have adequate facilities and experience to ensure that these procedures are carried out with appropriate attention to important details. Similar concerns exist over the regulatory systems of control for financial services. A strong case is being made for expanding the scope of selective harmonisation of essential requirements to ensure that minimum standards apply in these areas. Problems relating to the policing of legislation are also considered to be inadequately dealt with. For example, the legislation to open up public procurement systems is making good progress. However, policing this legislation and investigating breaches of tendering rules is an enormous task, as there exist thousands of government agencies in the EU with the power to issue and process procurement tenders. The record of some EU members in implementing existing EU legislation is not good (see Butt Philip 1989). The extension of EU legislation brought about by the creation of the SEM is likely to intensify conflicts between member states on these issues. In the past such conflicts have often led to implicit, and sometimes explicit, breaking of EU law relating to free movement.

The first two criticisms revolve around the adequacy of the programme in terms of its ability to meet the timetable for the legislative programme, and of the effective scope and implementation of legislation. The third criticism is more fundamental. It brings into question whether NTBs are a significant barrier in many sectors of the economy.

The reaping of benefits from removing NTBs is crucially dependent on fundamental reconstruction in many industries. This largely depends on achieving economies of scale, and integrating activities by firms to overcome fragmented markets. This implies that many European firms are too small. There is, according to Neuburger (1989), no strong evidence to suggest that this is the case. Some industries do seem to be rather small relative to the size of the EU market, thus there are ten manufacturers of electricity-generating equipment in the EU and only two in the USA (Curzon-Price 1988). Many of these industries seem to be heavily involved in the public procurement sector, and the benefits of increased size could be limited to companies with large interests in this area.

Strong criticisms are also voiced about the benefits to be reaped from economies of scale. The Cecchini Report finds evidence that many plants in Europe operate at less than MES. The benefits of reaping economies of scale depend on how far costs fall as output levels are increased. This is determined by the gradient of the average cost curve, and by the degree to which plants are operating at less than MES. In Figure 2.8 two alternative average cost curves are shown.

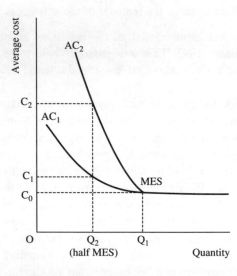

Figure 2.8 MES and the gradient of the average cost curve

The figure shows that the cost disadvantage of operating at half MES depends on the gradient of the average cost curve. A study using engineering estimates of costs was made by Pratten for the Cecchini Report, and this study found evidence of cost advantages from increasing output levels in some industries (see Table 2.4).

Table 2.4 The potential for the creation of the SEM to allow for the reaping of economies of scale (by industrial branch)

NACE code	Branch	Cost gradient at half MES	Comments
35	Motor vehicles	6–9%	large EOS possible in production and development costs
36	Other transport equipment	8–20%	very variable possibilities for reaping EOS, depends on which part of the branch is considered
25	Chemical industry	2.5–15%	large EOS possible in production costs and in R&D costs in pharmaceuticals
26	Man-made fibres	5–10%	EOS in general
32	Mechanical engineering	3–10%	EOS in production costs
47	Paper, printing and publishing	8–36%	large EOS in paper mills and printing books
41 & 42	Food	3.5–21%	large EOS in production costs and in marketing and distribution costs

Notes :
(1) MES – minimum efficiency scale; EOS – economies of scale
(2) Cost gradient at half MES measures the cost disadvantages of operating at half of MES, e.g. in NACE branch 25 – chemical industry – cost disadvantage of between 2.5 and 15 per cent can be incurred by operating at 50 per cent of the optimal level of production. These NACE divisions are at a high level of aggregation and some plants operate at more than half MES. The comments column therefore gives some indication of where the main EOS may be achieved within that branch.
(3) Because of the high level of aggregation and the limitations of using the MES approach to estimate the potential for reaping EOS, Pratten considers that these estimates are subject to a considerable degree of ambiguity.

Source : Based on a study by Pratten for the EC Commission

This evidence is disputed by many economists. Neuburger (1989) and Cutler *et al.* (1989) point out that the concept of MES is based on traditional engineering methods of estimating cost conditions. However, these normally assume production processes based on a single plant producing one good, whereas in modern production methods output is often manufactured in a complex set of multi-plant, and multi-product operations and some of these plants are quite small. Evidence from successful Japanese companies has suggested that production costs are often closely connected to management practices and operations, rather than the scale of operations within plants. Consequently, there is a need for considerable caution about using concepts such as MES as a firm guide to assess potential economies of scale. In spite of these problems of estimating economies of scale, the Cecchini Report does use MES calculations to estimate the benefits of removing NTBs, and these scale benefits form a very large part of the benefits of creating the SEM. A study by Caballero and Lyons (in Winters and Venables, 1991) found little evidence that the SEM would provide significant internal economies of scale. However, this study discovered that significant external economies of scale could be reaped by the creation of the SEM. These externality effects lead to cost reductions arising from: industry specialisation leading to, for example, a larger pool of trained labour; the spread of technical knowledge within an industry; improvements in infrastructures and other economies from conglomeration within an industry. The study estimated that if realistic estimates were made for both internal and external economies the figure for gains from economies of scale would be 47 billion ECU. This is some 14 billion ECU lower than the Cecchini estimate.

There is also a view (see for example Quelch *et al.* 1991) that market segmentation is often caused by cultural and regional factors leading to different qualities and specifications being demanded for goods and services. Such differences could mean that homogeneous products could not be effectively marketed on a Pan-European basis. There are also trading barriers such as a lack of detailed marketing and distribution and other sorts of business information, which could restrict the ability of companies to conduct cross-frontier operations. Therefore, simply to remove NTBs does not mean that increased trade and the rationalisation of production processes will necessarily follow. Many of the industries which are most able to operate on a European-wide basis are probably already doing so. In industries such as car production many companies such as Ford, General Motors and Volkswagen are already Pan-European in their operations; this is also true in areas such as food processing and many types of consumer durables. It is unlikely that these sorts of companies will be able to benefit greatly from increased economies of scale/size as a result of the creation of the SEM. The main benefits for such companies are likely to arise from reductions in costs caused by the emergence of common European standards.

The major sector to be affected by the removal of NTBs could well be small to medium-sized companies. The reduction of trading costs which will result from the creation of the SEM could lead to many such companies expanding into cross-frontier trading activities. Many of these companies may also benefit from economies of scale as they expand into such activities.

In the service sector there is also evidence that the removal of NTBs will not, at least in the near future, have significant effects on the bulk of retail financial services (Bank of England 1989). This follows from the goodwill and experience which existing national firms possess. In financial services there is also an issue of customer credibility for unknown foreign firms seeking business in other EU countries.

Free movement of labour is likely to be hindered by cultural, linguistic, and social security differences (see Turner 1989). Generally, economic factors such as unemployment rates, trade and capital flows seem to be the main determinants of labour mobility. These factors along with demographic trends and recent events in Central and Eastern Europe are likely to have more influence on labour mobility than the legislation programme to allow for free movement of labour. However, Gasiorek *et al.* (in Winters and Venables, 1991) using a general equilibrium model, found evidence that the creation of the SEM would lead to increased demand for highly skilled labour in France, Germany and the UK.

Differences in national taxation systems can result in price distortions which may result in obstacles to the reaping of comparative advantage. If goods were exported with VAT and excise duties which prevail in the exporting country, with no adjustment at borders, the price of such goods in the importing country would reflect the rates of tax levied in the supplying country. In cases where there were significant differences in taxation systems, in terms of coverage (goods and services liability to tax) and tax rates, the price of traded goods would be subject to tax-induced distortions. This problem did not occur in any major way in the EU before the SEM programme because exports were subject to zero rating for VAT and excise duties when they crossed frontiers. In order to operate this system of tax adjustment it was necessary to have frontier controls to check the claims for refunds of VAT when goods were exported at zero rate and to ensure goods subject to excise duties were indeed exported and therefore were no longer subject to such duties. The problem of cross-border shopping (buying goods in member states with lower rates of VAT and/or excise duties) was controlled by specifying limits on personal imports and policing this by frontier controls. However, the removal of frontier controls made this system of adjustment for taxation differences impossible to operate.

The White Paper proposed to eliminate these fiscal barriers by ending the zero rating of VAT on exports and by introducing a system of bonded warehouses with a marking procedure for goods subject to excise duties, so that these goods could be legally sold only in the country which imposed the excise duty. Importers would pay VAT at the rate imposed by the exporting country, then they would reclaim the VAT they had paid from their national taxation authorities when they sold the goods. This system would have required an international clearing-house arrangement because some countries in the EU are net importers and/or have lower than average rates of VAT. In these circumstances such countries would refund more VAT on imports than they would receive from VAT on exports. In order to allow this system to operate it was deemed necessary to harmonise both the coverage and rates of indirect tax. This was seen to be necessary to avoid problems of cross-border shopping both by personal visits to countries with lower rates of indirect tax and by the use of mail ordering from such countries. This harmonisation of indirect taxation would have resulted in significant changes to the taxation revenues in some of the member states and also large-scale shifts in demand patterns. The latter effect would have been very pronounced in the UK because of high excise duties on alcoholic beverages and exemptions or zero VAT rates for many goods and services. The main implications of adopting the proposal to harmonise indirect taxation systems are highlighted in Chapter 3.

The case that the removal of NTBs leads to a fundamental reconstruction of the economy of the EU may have been overestimated by the Cecchini Report. There probably will be significant changes in some sectors, particularly those connected to public procurement, and for small to medium-sized firms where economies of scale can be reaped. In many sectors, large-scale reconstruction may be limited by failure to reach agreement on the necessary legislation, or by the problems of implementing such legislation. Cultural and trading barriers to free movement will also restrict this reconstruction process. The initial effects of creating the SEM are likely to be relatively small for much of the economic base of the EU. The main effect of the 1992 programme may well turn out to be psychological, that is to turn the attention of producers in the EU, and other developed economies, towards the European market and to encourage them to gather information on the markets of Europe. This effect may also induce a European sense of identity among the citizens of the member states, and this could have implications for some of the cultural barriers to free movement. The 1992 programme has achieved a measure of success in this area as there has been a pronounced shift in attitudes towards Europe. This could do much to remove many of the cultural and trading barriers to free movement. In this scenario the reconstruction of the economic base of the EU is effectively driven by changes in attitudes. Learning about the cultural, marketing and distribution characteristics of such a diverse market as the EU is likely to involve considerable use of the resources and effort of companies, consequently this process is likely to take a long time. Changes in the attitudes of the citizens of the EU are likely to be an even longer process. However, the implications of any such change could be quite large. It is possible that some of the biggest changes from the creation of the SEM could arise from placing companies, institutions and citizens on learning curves.

Further criticisms of the Cecchini Report

The Cecchini Report has also been criticised because certain key issues are said to have been omitted or insufficient attention was paid to important implications of creating the SEM. Four main factors may be identified:

1. the effects on member states;
2. the effects caused by the redistribution of income;
3. the importance of institutional arrangements;
4. the external effects of creating the SEM.

Although the Cecchini Report provided some estimates of the likely changes in prices in the member states, there has not been much investigation of the implications of these changes for income in the poorer regions of the EU. It has been argued that lower productivity countries such as the Southern European states, Ireland and the UK could suffer from the creation of the SEM. This would occur as more efficient companies in the rest of the EU displaced domestic companies in these countries. Some commentators consider that this is likely in the UK because of long-run problems with the manufacturing sector (Burkitt and Baimbridge 1989 and Cutler *et al*. 1989). It is thought that the UK could not cope with the increase in price and non-price competition which the SEM would bring about. This would lead to balance of payments problems, or in the event of the establishment of EMU, the progressive impoverishment of the UK until it became a poor region of the EU. However, Pelkmans and Winters (1988) thought that the UK was likely to experience net gains from the creation of the SEM, especially in high-tech industries and in many service sectors. Discussion on the impact of the SEM on the regions of the EU is provided in Vickerman (1992). The publication of a study (Commission EC 1990a) has extended the Cecchini Report by investigating the effects of the creation of the SEM on specific industries in the member states. This study finds evidence for net benefits for all the member states. Many of these benefits depend on the growth of intra-industry between the developed countries of the EU, and a progressive shift towards such trade in the developing member states such as Spain, Portugal and Greece. With regard to these countries, the study finds that it is important that they do not attempt to keep their existing inter-industry specialisation as many of them are in low value added and labour-intensive sectors, and therefore face strong competition from the LDCs. The Commission is reluctant to grant protection to these industries as it would harm the LDCs (see Chapter 15), and would not help in the attempts to improve the productivity of the EU economy. The growth of intra-industry is deemed to require a considerable amount of Europeanisation of the activities of companies by merger and acquisition, and DFI. This would induce '...true European firms with regard to such factors as capitalisation, operational management or in terms of the nationality of their directors. Efforts to enhance labour mobility and to remove legal and fiscal obstacles are necessary conditions for the success of this scenario.' To help the less developed member states to adjust to this process the study recommends greater use of the structural funds. The methodological problems of this study to assess the impact of the SEM on the member states are basically the same as those which seek to estimate the effects of the creation of the CU (see Chapter 1).

The redistribution effects of creating the SEM are also largely ignored by the Cecchini Report. The Report does imply that the reconstruction process will give rise to a temporary increase in unemployment. This follows from the redistribution effects, which are outlined above, of allowing free movement. However, the temporary nature of this unemployment is disputed by Cutler et al. (1989) and Grahl and Teague (1990), who lay some stress on the effects that increased competition has on labour. These include downward pressure not only on wages, but also on employment conditions. Hence, the development of 'Social Europe' by imposing high minimum employment standards is crucial if large sections of labour are not to suffer losses from the creation of the SEM. Free movement of capital may well reinforce these effects because capital movements are deemed to be mainly determined by technological and market operation reasons, rather than by simple rate of return calculations. In this scenario, capital flows tend towards areas with high technology and high productivity. Such movements could add to the downward spiral which the poorer productivity countries would experience from the SEM programme. To avoid such effects it is considered necessary for the EU to engage in coordinated macro-economic policy of a Keynesian type. This policy would be used to stimulate aggregate demand to reduce the unemployment caused by these structural changes. The use of regional, social, and technology policies is also advocated to aid in the restructuring process. The Cecchini Report did highlight potential benefits from coordinated expansion of aggregate demand, but this was rather vague and was not envisaged at the kind of level being advocated by the supporters of such Keynesian policies. For economists who regard the pursuit of price and monetary stability as the key economic objective, Keynesian-type expansion of aggregate demand would not be acceptable. The growing integration in monetary matters (see Chapter 4), places greater emphasis on member states pursuing consistent macro-economic policy. The power of Germany in the EMS, and in any future moves towards EMU, would probably allow the Germans to veto any EU moves to adopt Keynesian-type expansion of the economy. However, increasing use of the structural funds and institutional arrangements to aid the market process may be more likely to be acceptable to all the member states, as the success of Germany and Japan (who practise considerable intervention in their economies) has indicated the benefits of using such policies. Since the Maastricht Treaty a new fund – the Cohesion Fund – has been prepared to help the poorer regions of the EU. A report commonly called 'Delors II' has recommended that this fund should be concentrated on the poorest member states (Commission EC, 1992b).

There are theoretical models which suggest that effective markets depend on legal and institutional factors as well as the operation of the price mechanism. In Pelkmans and Winters (1988) and Padoa-Schioppa (1987) there is discussion of the importance of appropriate institutional and legal frameworks in the areas of competition, regional, social, and technology policies if the European market is to be beneficial to all parties. The Sutherland Report

(Commission EC 1992a) also raises the need for institutional and legal changes if the SEM is to be effectively implemented and governed.

The importance of information and transaction costs to the working of modern economies is highlighted by Grahl and Teague (1990). They maintain that these factors require markets to be backed by a set of institutional and cultural frameworks to correct for the inadequacies of the market, in particular the need for non-market based contracts and arrangements between economic agents. Such arrangements are important in long-term exchanges where information and transaction costs are high. There are examples of these arrangements in relations between highly skilled workers and employers, where it is quite common for wage and employment levels to be determined not by current market conditions, but by mutual agreement between the parties. In product markets characterised by complex production processes long-term supply contracts or subcontracts are commonly used to try and lower these costs. Indeed, many vertical mergers are justified on the basis of internalising such information and transaction costs with the hope of reducing such costs. These factors imply that not only the setting-up of institutions' arrangements, but also the growth of common cultural attitudes to the conducting of business activities, are a necessary component in the establishing of an effective SEM.

The neglect of the external effects of creating the SEM is a pronounced feature not only of the Cecchini Report, but also of most of the literature on the SEM. Some of the American literature on the SEM does concern itself with this issue, e.g. Belous and Hartley (1990) and Brainard and Perry (1989). Belous and Hartley are concerned that the growth of regional trading blocs, such as the EU, is harming the growth of free trade in the world as a whole. This results from the trade diversion effects (see Chapter 1) of eliminating trade barriers within a subset of the world, rather than from use of the multilateral methods of the GATT. The development of the NAFTA between the USA, Canada and Mexico has further strengthened the move towards regional trading blocs. These harmful effects can also be exacerbated by the adoption of increased protectionist measures by trading blocs against non-bloc countries. While Belous and Hartley are reasonably satisfied that the creation of the SEM will not result in high levels of trade diversion, at least for the USA, they are less sure about the possibility of the growth of protectionist policies connected to the SEM (see chapters 14 and 16). In the study by Brainard and Perry, this fear is also expressed by Dornbusch, who argues that the increased pressures of competition induced by the SEM will lead to calls by the lower productivity member states to increase the levels of external protection to allow them to maintain their threatened industrial structures. These pressures could be increased if the creation of the SEM is accompanied by the imposition of high minimum standards in the social and environmental fields, as this would put further competitive pressures on the low productivity member states. The adoption of the Social Chapter in the Maastricht Treaty provides some evidence that such pressures are at work. However, Dornbusch also considers that the creation of the SEM will stimulate world trade. This would be caused by the expansionary effect on the GDP of the EU which would follow from the implementation of the SEM, and would lead to an increase in the imports of the EU. It is possible that this expansionary effect could be stronger than the contractionary effect on world trade caused by the trade diversionary effects of the SEM. Given that the best solution of achieving SEM-type trade liberalisation on a global basis is not possible because of very large economic and political problems, the second best SEM programme may not be harmful to world trade provided that an expansion in world trade takes place as a result of this programme.

The position post-1992

The SEM programme was due to be completed by 1 January 1993. On this date frontier controls were abolished and by this date most of the proposed legislative changes had been adopted by the Council. However, in some areas, some major pieces of legislation have not yet been adopted. Awareness campaigns have brought the challenges and opportunities of the SEM to the attention of companies. Many companies have responded to this by constructing new strategic plans and some have altered their operational activities and organisational structures by the use of mergers, acquisitions and strategic alliances and by changing their production, marketing and distribution systems. However, the legislative programme is not yet complete and a report by the Commission – the Sutherland Report; Commission 1992a – suggests that there may have to be another raft of new legislation before the legal conditions are right for the effective operation of the SEM. Fiscal barriers have not been fully eliminated and the wave of company restructuring which took place was connected to a wide range of factors: the SEM programme may have played only a small part in this process.

The legislative programme

The legislative programme relating to financial services had not been fully implemented by the deadline. The legislation to allow cross-frontier trade in life insurance services did not come into effect until June 1994, and EU-wide trade in investment services will not come into effect until at least 1996. Legislation was also awaiting approval in the areas of transport services and in the new technologies services sector. The legislation relating to the free movement of capital was incomplete, especially with regard to funds held by institutions for retirement provision. The legislation connected to the free movement of labour was also not fully implemented, particularly with regard to comparability of vocational qualifications. The position with regard to company law and taxation, intellectual property, public procurement, veterinary and plant health controls and the new EU standards policy was somewhat similar (see Duffy 1992). The Commission is involved in a process of consolidating legislation to ensure that conflicting and inconsistent laws and regulations do not lead to problems with free movement. The completion of the legislative programme for the SEM is therefore likely to take up a considerable amount of the time of the institutions of the EU. This process could extend to the end of the century. See Commission EC (1993a, 1993b, 1993c).

The Sutherland Report

This report found that by 1 January 1992, some 264 of the 282 pieces of legislation proposed in the White Paper had been adopted by the Council. However, only 194 directives had been implemented into the national laws of the member states and just 79 had been implemented in all member states. Concern was also expressed about the knowledge of these new laws, especially among SMEs and consumers. This has led to fears that the new laws will not be adhered to because of this lack of understanding. If the laws are not effectively understood and implemented it will be very difficult for mutual recognition of technical regulations to be widely accepted. Such a situation would undermine the expected change in trade flows and therefore the restructuring process would be limited because of the relatively small changes in intra-EU trade and in the competitive environment.

The report also expressed the view that more legislation was required if the SEM was to operate effectively, particularly in the areas of consumer protection and public procurement. Consumers are unlikely to buy goods and services from companies in other member states when their rights, if products fail to meet acceptable standards, are not clearly specified. These concerns are likely to be most evident in the purchase of services and in manufactured goods with complex technical characteristics and/or where health and safety aspects are important. Concern was also expressed about how effective the laws on public procurement will be in the absence of effective monitoring and policing systems.

The Sutherland Report indicated that there were some shortcomings in the legislative programme and in the effectiveness of the implementation of this programme. The report also considered that there are significant problems with regard to the understanding by companies and consumers of the content and importance of the SEM legislation. To ensure the smooth operation of the SEM new EU laws were deemed to be required, especially in the areas of mutual recognition, consumer protection and public procurement. The report also called for the creation of a new partnership between the Commission and the governments of the member states to allow for the smooth operation of the SEM. This partnership was to be constructed in the light of the concept of subsidiarity. The Sutherland Report considered that the SEM would not operate in a smooth and effective manner unless these legislative and institutional changes were made.

The removal of fiscal barriers

In the field of the harmonisation of indirect taxation the White Paper had proposed that VAT and excise duties on intra-EU sales should move to the 'origin principle', that is, tax is paid in the country of the goods' origin. To enable this system to operate it was proposed that the goods subject to indirect taxation should be uniform in all member states and that the rates of such tax should be contained within specified bands.

The member states could not agree on this proposal and a provisional indirect taxation system was introduced. This system is based on the existing 'destination principle', i.e. tax is paid in the country where the good is finally consumed, with goods being exported at zero rate of VAT and no excise duties. The Commission intends to replace this agreement by the end of 1997 with an 'origin principle' based system.

The legislative programme with respect to the taxation of companies was also not completed by the deadline, for example directives on the taxation of interest and royalty payments, and arrangements for taking losses into account, were not implemented. There are no plans to harmonise rates of company taxation in the legislative programme of the EU. However, differences in rates of company taxation could lead to distortions in the location and financial transfer decisions of companies. Presumably the EU is depending on market forces to put pressure on the member states to harmonise such tax rates.

The restructuring of companies

That there have been significant changes in the strategies and organisational structures of many companies since the SEM programme began to be implemented is beyond question. Many companies have become more European-orientated in their production, marketing and distribution activities. The SEM programme has also stimulated foreign direct investment into the EU, particularly from Japan. This issue is examined in Chapter 17.

A report in the *Financial Times* on 17 September 1993 indicated that cross-border merger and acquisition activities in the EU had increased from $23.1 bn. in 1991 to $42.0 bn. in 1992. However, in the first half of 1993 the volume of such cross-border merger and acquisition activities had reached only $12.3 bn. The recession may have played an important part in the decline in merger and acquisition activities. However, it is not clear how important the creation of the SEM has been as an incentive for merger and acquisition activities.

The need to respond to changes in global competitiveness has also stimulated such activities. Reasons such as this seem to have been important in the merger and acquisition activities of European-based companies in the food processing industry, such as Nestlé, Unilever and BSN. They seem to have been influenced not only by the SEM but also by the need to compete in global terms with large American companies, such as Mars, Philip Morris, Campbell and Kellogg in the branded food products market. Attempts to rationalise in static or declining markets have also been important in promoting strategic alliances such as the joint-venture between ICI and Enchem – the European Vinyls Corporation (EVC). This joint-venture is for the purpose of producing and marketing PVC products. This market is suffering from over-capacity and static demand. The EVC joint-venture is primarily concerned with tackling these problems. It therefore has little direct connection to the SEM programme. The fear that deregulation may lead to an increasingly competitive market has also induced some companies to enter into mergers or joint-ventures. This can be most clearly seen in the airline sector, for example British Airways acquired the French carrier TAT, and KLM, SAS, Swissair and Austrian Airlines have sought to establish a strategic alliance. The telecommunications services sector has also witnessed a growth in mergers and strategic alliances in response to the forthcoming privatisation of state-owned companies and the moves by the Commission to deregulate this industry.

It is very difficult to ascertain whether the reorganisations of company structures that have taken place since the SEM programme began are due to this programme or to other factors. The report in the *Financial Times* indicated that a series of consolidations is taking place within Europe and that the SEM is an important factor in stimulating such merger, acquisition and strategic alliance activities. However, the privatisation programmes in Germany, France, Italy and the UK, the deregulation of the air travel and telecommunication services industries and the increasingly global competition in many markets may be at least as important in this consolidation process. These issues are explored by Halliburton and Hünerberg (1993), and Harris and McDonald (1993).

The SEM programme has moved the EU to a position where a common market among the member states is very nearly complete. However, some barriers and distortions to the effective working of the SEM still exist and these may impede the process of free movement. The Sutherland Report has raised doubts about the effectiveness of EU laws on free movement. Distortions caused by the failure to harmonise fiscal systems within the EU may also limit the effectiveness of the SEM. It is also not clear if the restructuring of the operational and organisational structures of companies was primarily due to the SEM programme or to other factors such as deregulation and the pressures of global competition.

Conclusions

The creation of the SEM has without doubt major economic and political implications. It is possible that the Cecchini Report has overestimated some of these benefits. However, if fundamental changes in business attitudes and government policies are induced by the creation of the SEM, these could lead to larger changes in the economy of the EU than are suggested by Cecchini. The spill-over effects of creating the SEM in areas such as EMU and external economic relations greatly enhance the implications of the SEM. The linkages of the SEM to competition, regional, agricultural, and environmental policies also have significant implications. These spill-over effects of creating the SEM are examined in the following chapters.

References and further reading

Baldwin R E 1989 The Growth Effects of 1992, *Economic Policy*, Vol. 2, pp. 247–281.

Bank of England 1989 *The Single European Market: Survey of the UK Financial Services Industry*, London.

Belous R S and **Hartley R S** 1990 *The Growth of Regional Trading Blocs in the Global Economy*, National Planning Association, Washington DC.

Brainard W C and **Perry G L** 1989 Brookings Papers on Economic Activity, No 2, Washington DC.

Burkitt B and **Baimbridge M** 1989 *What 1992 Really Means: Single Market or Double Cross*, British anti-Common Market Campaign, Bradford.

Butt Philip A 1989 Implementing the European internal market: problems and prospects, RIIA, Discussion Paper No 5, London.

Cecchini P 1988 *The European Challenge: 1992 The Benefits of a Single Market*, Wildwood House, Aldershot.

Commission EC 1985 *Completing the Internal Market: The White Paper*, Office for Official Publications of the European Communities, Luxembourg.

Commission EC 1990a European Economy, Special Edition: *The Impact of the Internal Market by Industrial Sector: The Challenge for the Member States*, Office for Official Publications of the European Communities, Luxembourg.

Commission EC 1990b *Taxation in the Single Market*, Office for Official Publications of the European Communities, Luxembourg.

Commission EC 1990c *Consumer Policy in the Single Market*, Office for Official Publications of the European Communities, Luxembourg.

Commission EC 1992a *The Internal Market after 1992*, Office for the Official Publications of the European Communities, Luxembourg.

Commission EC 1992b *From the Single Act to Maastricht and Beyond: The means to match our ambitions*, Office for the Official Publications of the EC, Luxembourg.

Commission EC 1993a *Reinforcing the Effectiveness of the Internal Market*, Com (93) 256 Final, Brussels.

Commission EC 1993b *Management of the Mutual Recognition of National Rules after 1992*, Com (93) 669 Final, Brussels.

Commission EC 1993c *Making the Most of the Internal Market*, Com (93) 632 Final, Brussels.

Curzon-Price V 1988 *1992: Europe's Last Change?* IEA, London.

Cutler T, Haslem C, Williams J and **Williams K** 1989 *1992 – The Struggle for Europe*, BERG, Oxford.

Dahrendorf R, Hoskyns J, Curzon-Price V, Roberts B, Woods G, Davis E and **Sealy L** 1989 *Whose Europe?* IEA, London.

Davis E, Kay J and **Smales C** 1989 *1992: Myths and Realities*, London Business School, London.

Duffy P 1992 *The Single Market: UK Implementation Guide*, Longman, London.

Dyker D (ed.) 1992 *The European Economy*, Longman, London.

Emerson M, Aujean M, Catinat M and **Jacquemin A** 1988 *The Economics of 1992*, Oxford University Press, Oxford.

Financial Times 1993 International Mergers and Acquisitions, 17 September.

Geroski P A 1988 *1992 and European Industrial Structure in the Twenty-First Century*, London Business School, London.

Gordon I and **Thirlwall A** 1989 *European Factor Mobility*, Macmillan, London.

Grahl J and **Teague P** 1990 *1992: The Big Market*, Lawrence and Wishart, London.

Halliburton C and **Hünerberg R** (eds) 1993 *European Marketing*, Addison-Wesley, Wokingham.

Harris P and **McDonald F** (eds) 1993 *European Business and Marketing*, Paul Chapman, London.

Jacquemin A 1982 Imperfect market structure and international trade – some recent research, *Kyklos*, Vol. 35, pp. 75–93.

Jacquemin A and **Sapir A** 1990 *The European Internal Market*, Oxford University Press.

Mayes D (ed.) 1991 *The European Challenge: Industry's Response to the 1992 Programme*, Harvester Wheatsheaf, London.

McDonald F 1987 Contestable markets a new ideal model? *Economics*, Vol. 23, pp. 183–186.

Neuburger H 1989 *The Economics of 1992*, Socialist Group of the European Parliament, London.

Nielsen J V, Heinrich H and **Hansen J D** 1991 *An Economic Analysis of the EC*, McGraw-Hill, Maidenhead.

Padoa-Schioppa T 1987 *Europe in the 1990s: Efficiency, Stability and Equity*, Oxford University Press.

Pelkmans J and **Winters A** 1988 *Europe's Domestic Market*, Routledge, London.

Quelch J A, Buzzell R D and **Salama E R** 1991 *The Marketing Challenge of Europe 1992*, Addison Wesley, Reading.

Turner I (ed.) 1989 *The Living Market*, Sanders and Sidney, London.

Vickerman R W 1992 *The Single European Market*, Harvester Wheatsheaf, London.

Winters L A and **Venables A** (eds) 1991 *European Integration: Trade and Industry*, Cambridge University Press.

CHAPTER 3

Macro-economic policy coordination in the EU

Frank McDonald

Introduction

Article 2 of the Treaty of Rome specifies that the main objective of economic integration is to boost the living standards of all the citizens of the member states. In general, the treaty advocates micro-economic policies as the main method to achieve this goal. Initially, therefore, the Community concentrated on the creation of the CU and the CM together with intervention in the agriculture sector as the main means of achieving the prime objective of boosting living standards. As the EU developed the issue of redistribution to achieve the prime objective began to assume a more important role, especially with the growth of the structural funds. However, macro-economic policies did not appear to have any significant role in helping to achieve the prime objective. Article 104 of the Treaty of Rome defines the major macro-economic objectives as price and exchange rate stability, equilibrium in the balance of payments and the maintenance of a high level of employment. Articles 105 and 107 call for cooperation between the member states with regard to monetary and exchange rate policies. Nevertheless, the Treaty of Rome is not very specific with regard to macro-economic policies. Consequently, the Community was not very active in the area of macro-economic policies in the 1960s.

In 1970 the EEC adopted the Werner Plan which set the goal, to be accomplished by 1980, of monetary union. This attempt at creating monetary union was not successful. However, problems caused by exchange rate fluctuations led in 1979 to the creation of the EMS. The EMS was initially less ambitious than the Werner Plan as the EMS sought to create a 'zone of monetary stability' rather than monetary union. Chapter 4 provides more information on these schemes. The SEM programme increased the pressure for the EU to become more involved in macro-economic policy issues. The free movement of goods, services and capital were considered to be hampered if member states could rapidly alter their competitive position by the depreciation of their currency. Furthermore, the existence of separate currencies and fluctuating exchange rates could hamper the development of a single European financial services market. In the early 1990s the EMS appeared to be relatively successful and when Portugal and the UK joined the ERM in 1990 all member states, except Greece, were fully participating in the EMS. Even countries which were not members, such as Austria, Sweden and Norway had pegged their currencies to the ECU. Consequently, the pressure to develop macro-economic policies within the EU became very strong. These pressures culminated, in

1992, in the Maastricht Treaty which included a detailed plan for establishing monetary union. This plan required coordination of macro-economic policies in the areas of exchange rates, monetary policy, interest rates and fiscal policy, the end goal being a common monetary policy and a single currency. The Maastricht Treaty therefore commits the member states to establish a series of macro-economic cooperation and coordination schemes with the end goal of creating a common policy in what is perhaps the most important area of macro-economic policy. The issues connected to the convergence of policies to create monetary union are discussed in this chapter. The main focus is on the rationale for cooperation and coordination and the problems associated with coordination in the key macro-economic areas of monetary and fiscal policies.

Cooperation, coordination and harmonisation

Cooperation can be defined as a system for exchanging information on policy targets (goals) and instruments (means of obtaining goals). Such exchange of information can then be used to amend or confirm policy targets and instruments. For example, if a country is considering changes to its monetary policy, cooperation systems can help to verify whether or not the proposed changes will be compatible with the policies of its main partners. Such cooperation could lead to amendments in targets and/or instruments to make the policy changes more consistent with those of the main partners. Cooperation can also be used to help judge the best time to alter policy instruments. Cooperation agreements require little in the way of formal arrangements. In general all that is required are systems that allow for an effective exchange of information.

Coordination involves the specification of a set of targets and instruments and an established procedure for implementing the instruments to achieve the agreed target. In cases where this process involves a comprehensive system for setting *common* targets and instruments the policy can be regarded as being harmonised. Thus the CET is a harmonised instrument to achieve a *common* target, i.e. a uniform level of protection for all goods entering the EU. If the set of targets and instruments are not fixed and participating members can adjust or withdraw from the agreed targets and instruments then the process can be described as coordination. For example, in the mid-1980s the degree of flexibility in the ERM (when there were frequent realignments) meant that instruments were not fixed and hence in this period the ERM could be described as a coordination scheme. However, in the early 1990s the ERM became more fixed with regard to instruments and it began to adopt the characteristics of a harmonisation system. Therefore, it is sometimes not clear at what stage systems move from being coordination to harmonised systems.

Dependency and interdependence

The creation of cooperation and coordination schemes only makes sense in situations where countries are either dependent or interdependent with regard to economic policies. In cases where economic policies have no effect other than in the country that implements these policies there can be no benefit from cooperation or coordination. However, given the amount of trade in goods and services and the movement of capital between many countries, situations of dependence and interdependence often arise from the spill-over effects of national economic policies. Thus, if Germany implements a monetary policy with a target of achieving low inflation using the instrument of high interest rates, the policy is likely to spill over to countries with strong trading and financial links with Germany. In some cases, where the country is small relative to Germany, a situation of dependence may emerge. That is, the spill-over effect in terms of the effects on monetary and fiscal policies and thereby on the growth of trade and income will be primarily from Germany to the smaller countries. Such countries may be dependent on Germany's policy decisions with respect to their main economic policies. Monetary policy in Denmark and the Netherlands may fall into this category. Larger economies may be affected by German macro-economic policy spill-overs but the macro-economic policies of these countries may also affect Germany. For example, the macro-economic policies of France, Italy and the UK that affect their growth rates will impact on German exports to these countries. In such cases interdependence can be said to exist. However, it is possible for one country to exercise more influence by the spill-over of their macro-economic policies on its partners than the policies of the other countries can exert on the larger economy. Germany would appear to occupy this position with regard to spill-over effects within Europe. These issues are discussed in Chapter 18.

The process of interdependence is therefore complex. It is difficult to distinguish between dependence on larger partners and interdependence but with more powerful spill-over effects coming from the larger economy. In cases where there exists dependence (large dominant countries can have power over the macro-economic policies of smaller countries), hegemony can arise. Thus to a large extent the monetary policy of the Netherlands is, in the main, decided by the Bundesbank. The Bundesbank also exercises considerable influence over the monetary policies of all members of the EU. Problems of achieving cooperation or coordination can arise in cases when there exists dependency or where interdependence is based on weak spill-overs from smaller to larger economies. These problems arise from the difficulties of arriving at mutually beneficial outcomes in circumstances when there exists a powerful partner. The crisis in the ERM in 1992 and 1993 illustrated the problems that can arise when a powerful economy exercises a strong influence in a coordination scheme.

Coordination of monetary policies

The main incentive to become involved in monetary policy coordination systems stems from the effects of monetary policy on exchange rates. For example, if a country expands its money supply at a time when its main partners are pursuing tight monetary policies, an interest rate differential will arise and funds will flow from the low interest rate country to the partners who now have higher interest rates. This could lead to an appreciation of the currencies of the partner countries. In these circumstances a loss of competitiveness for those countries that experience appreciation of their currencies can occur. To prevent such a loss of competitiveness the partner countries may expand their money supplies in order to reduce the interest rate differential and thereby prevent the appreciation of their currencies. However, the monetary expansion necessary to lower interest rates can lead to problems with inflation. Monetary policy coordination can be used to prevent such outcomes. Any system of fixed exchange rates is likely to require some degree of monetary policy coordination if destabilising interest differentials are to be avoided.

Monetary policy, in a fixed exchange rate system, has two general targets: (*a*) the exchange rate target; (*b*) the level of economic activity. In general the main instrument used to achieve these targets is the interest rate. Therefore, interest rates must be kept at a level that will maintain a differential between national rates and those of the partners in the fixed exchange rate scheme. If such a differential is not maintained, pressure will be exerted on the fixed exchange rate system, as funds flow from low to high interest rate countries. Those countries with a record of high inflation and regular devaluation of their currencies may have to maintain a higher interest rate than countries with a better record in these areas. Even countries with a good record in these areas may have to maintain a differential on their interest rates relative to the country with the best record. Thus the Netherlands maintains an interest differential with respect to German interest rates. This differential is necessary because the Netherlands devalued its currency relative to the Deutschmark in 1987. The Deutschmark has never been devalued and the financial markets therefore suspect that the Guilder could be devalued again. Consequently, the markets require a premium to compensate for the risk of a devaluation of the Guilder. Failure to maintain this differential can lead to speculative pressures on exchange parities because the markets fear that the countries with poorer records in terms of inflation and devaluation may resort to policies which generate inflation and that would lead such countries to devalue their currency.

The interest rate also affects consumption and investment decisions and thereby the level of economic activity. As most countries have targets for economic activity (in line with preferences for inflation and unemployment), the interest rate instrument is also concerned with achieving the target level of economic activity.

If it is assumed that two countries are interdependent with respect to their interest rate policy, and that they are in a fixed exchange rate system; then coordination of monetary policies may be mutually beneficial for these countries. If it is further assumed that country A or B acts as if the other country will not respond to changes in its interest rates, it is possible to devise reaction functions which trace out the optimal rate of interest for each country as a function of the interest rate in the other country. The reaction functions for two such countries are illustrated in Figure 3.1.

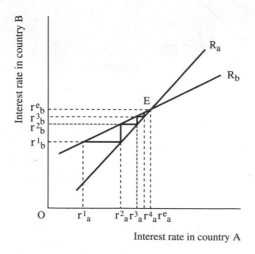

Figure 3.1 An uncoordinated outcome

For country A, an interest rate of r^1_a leads to an optimal level of economic activity and an interest rate differential with country B that allows the exchange rate target to be met. If from this position country B increases its interest rate, this will reduce the interest rate differential and thereby put pressure on the target exchange rate. Country A will respond to this by increasing its interest rate. However, given the target level of economic activity, country A will be reluctant to adjust its interest rate by the same proportion as that of country B. The degree by which countries A and B adjust in response to changes in the partner country's interest rate determines the slope of the reaction functions. If these countries were to pursue independent monetary policy an uncoordinated equilibrium outline would occur at point E, with interest rates at r^e_a and r^e_b respectively. This outcome arises from the adjustment along the reaction functions, i.e. at r^1_a country B responds with r^1_b, leading to a response from country A of r^2_a, and so on until point E is reached.

In this situation a limited role could arise for a cooperation solution whereby information was shared on target rates of economic activity and on the timing and size of any interest rate changes. This could help speed up the process of arriving at the equilibrium outcome.

However, in these circumstances it is possible that a coordinated system could generate a mutually beneficial outcome which would be different from that illustrated at point E. Suppose that both countries prefer, for purposes of economic activity, a lower rate of interest than that which prevails at point E. It is possible, in these circumstances, that a coordinated system for monetary policies would lead to a better result. This possibility is examined in Figure 3.2.

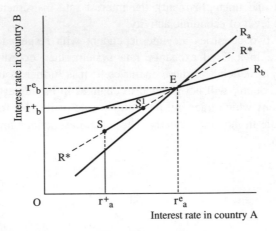

Figure 3.2 A coordinated outcome

The preferred rates of interest are assumed to be at r^+_a and r^+_b, i.e. both countries prefer lower interest rates. The line R*R* traces the locus of points where the interest rate differential between the two countries is constant. Hence, R*R* traces all points where the exchange rate target is fulfilled. In these circumstances any point between S and S^1 illustrates the interest rate combinations that are preferable to the outcome at E (in terms of the target for economic activity) but still allow the target exchange rate to be met. The closer to S, the more beneficial the result would be for country A. Hence, bargaining power becomes important in terms of the share of benefits between the two countries that result from coordinated outcomes. Nevertheless, provided both countries prefer a lower rate of interest than r^e_a and r^e_b, a coordinated system is preferable to an uncoordinated one.

However, in cases where only one country prefers a lower rate of interest than that which prevails at E, a coordinated outcome is not obviously beneficial. For example, if country A wants a higher and country B a lower rate of interest than that which prevails at point E, a coordinated outcome would require some compensation for the country that is made worse off as a result of agreement to move interest rates from those given at point E. Problems such as these can arise in cases of asymmetric shocks, i.e. when the conditions which cause a deviation from target levels of economic activity affect only one of the countries (or where the shock affects the countries to different degrees). In such circumstances the pressures to adjust interest rates may become of such a magnitude that they force the abandonment of the coordinated system. Such an outcome happened when the asymmetric shock to the German economy (caused by unification) ultimately led to a dislocation of the coordination scheme of the EMS.

It would appear either that coordination of monetary policies requires the absence of significant asymmetric shocks or there must be compensation schemes such that losers can be persuaded to remain in the coordination system. Significantly different preferences for levels of economic activity are also likely to cause problems for countries seeking to coordinate their monetary policies. The problems of coordination arising from the movement towards monetary union in the EU may also lead to considerable difficulties, especially as the Maastricht Treaty calls for strong convergence of interest rates, exchange rates and inflation rates (see Chapter 4 for details of the convergence criteria). To achieve such convergence it is likely that the member states will have to develop coordination schemes for monetary policies. This could become problematic if asymmetric shocks or large differences in preferences with regard to levels of economic activity become pronounced.

Coordination of fiscal policies

Fiscal policy interdependence arises when the effects of fiscal expansion or contraction spill over to other countries. If a country engages in fiscal expansion of its economy the subsequent increase in aggregate demand will stimulate an increase in imports and this will lead to a stimulus to aggregate demand in those countries that supply the imports. These spill-over effects can be significant among countries that have high levels of trade with each other. Fiscal policy also affects interest rates because of the implications for money markets (and therefore interest rates) of government borrowing. A fiscal expansion in a country can put upward pressure on the interest rate because of the increased demand for funds to finance the budget deficit; such increases in interest rates can spill over to partner countries and lead to rises in the interest rates in those countries. Such fiscal policy spill-over can therefore affect exchange rates and monetary policies in partner countries due to the induced rise in their interest rates caused by the fiscal expansion in the partner country. These fiscal spill-overs can become important if partner countries are seeking to establish strong monetary policy coordination or where they are seeking to create monetary union. Problems can arise if the budget deficits become unsustainable in the sense that they can be financed only by recourse to monetary expansion. In these circumstances fiscal policy spill-overs could destabilise the monetary coordination systems or in the case of monetary union lead to conflict between the central bank of the monetary union and the governments of the members of the union. The potentially destabilising effects caused by such fiscal policy spill-overs lead some economists to advocate systems of fiscal policy coordination in order to pave the way for monetary union (see Giovannini and Spaventa 1991). The Delors Report on economic and monetary union also considered that monetary union would require fiscal policy coordination (Commission EC 1989).

Coordination of fiscal polices could also help in creating more effective counter-cyclical policies for countries that experience significant fiscal spill-overs. The benefits of coordination would follow from the intelligent use of spill-over effects. Coordination schemes require the coordination of fiscal polices such that they work in the same direction as partner countries. In principle such coordination could reduce the magnitude of any fiscal expansion/contraction necessary to counteract slumps/booms. In such schemes the fiscal expansion/contraction in any one country would take into account the spill-over effects that would arise from the fiscal policy actions of partner countries.

Before the Maastricht Treaty, the fiscal policies of the member states were only marginally affected by their membership. A sharing of information on general policy direction has been established among the member states. However, normally no detailed exchange of information took place. There are also some EU rules relating to indirect taxation and to the taxation of companies and capital.

However, the relative neglect of fiscal policy began to change with the SEM programme. The SEM programme required some harmonisation of indirect taxes and some firmer rules regarding the taxation of companies and capital. Nevertheless, member states retained a considerable degree of discretion with regard to the tax base and tax rates, even in the indirect taxation area. The EU has had little effect on direct taxation, apart from some new rules with regard to the appropriate base for company and capital taxation (see Commission EC 1992a and 1992b). The SEM programme had no direct impact on the right of member states to take decisions with regard to the composition or size of public expenditures. Consequently, fiscal policy in the member states was largely free from any pressures to coordinate policies, and cooperation was limited to exchange of information on the fiscal stance that member states intended to adopt.

The Maastricht Treaty has, however, changed this situation. The commitment to move towards monetary union included a commitment to setting constraints on public borrowing to GDP ratios and also to limiting budget deficits (see Chapter 4). Article 104c of the Maastricht Treaty requires the Commission to monitor 'the development of the budgetary situation and of the stock of government debt in the Member States with a view to identifying gross errors'. The Commission will inform the Council of any member state with 'an excessive deficit', and the Council may publish a report on what it considers to be appropriate actions that the member state should take to reduce this excessive deficit. The EU is therefore moving towards the creation of what might be regarded as a strong cooperation (or weak coordination) system for the fiscal policies of the member states. Such efforts to constrain the fiscal policies of the member states are considered to be crucial if unsustainable budget deficits are to be avoided.

The Growth Initiative agreed at the Edinburgh meeting of the European Council in December 1992 further boosted the drive towards fiscal policy coordination among the member states. This Initiative arose from a desire to combat the rising levels of unemployment in the EU. The Edinburgh summit proposed a mild fiscal expansion, backed by 'supply-side' measures, to help the recovery from the recession which was affecting Europe in the early 1990s. The key elements in the Initiative were:

1.   a commitment by the member states to undertake additional public expenditures on infrastructure projects amounting to some ECU 6 bn.;

2. a temporary lending facility of ECU 5 bn. from the EIB;

3. a European Investment Fund (EIF) with capital of ECU 2 bn. to facilitate investments in trans-European networks;

4. a host of 'supply-side' measures to aid SMEs, R&D projects and job evaluation and labour training schemes;

5. the use of the Cohesion Fund of ECU 1.3 bn. to boost aggregate demand in the poorer member states.

In principle this appears to be a significant fiscal package. However, it was largely composed of existing programmes and the main new fund, the EIF, has experienced considerable difficulties in getting started. In short, the Growth Initiative was primarily an attempt to draw attention to what were, on the whole, existing public expenditure packages. The main objective may well have been to try and boost the sagging expectations of consumers and businesses about the willingness of governments to tackle the recession. However, during this period most European governments were still following tight monetary policies as a result of the restrictions imposed by the EMS. At the time of the Edinburgh summit the ERM was still in operation although there was significant speculation against the French franc. The slight stimulus arising from the Growth Initiative was perhaps marginalised by the effects of the tight monetary policy being followed by Germany, which was constraining the ability of many member states to expand their economies. Somewhat ironically, the first major attempt at fiscal policy coordination to boost aggregate demand coincided with the break-up of the monetary policy coordination system of the EMS, which was exerting strong contractionary pressure on the level of aggregate demand.

Nevertheless, the Edinburgh Growth Initiative was significant in that agreement was reached to attempt to use fiscal policy coordination for counter-cyclical purposes. There have also been attempts by the Commission and the EP to boost the budget of the EU via large scale expansion of the structural funds and the cohesion fund. Although the EU is obliged to balance its budget, it is seeking to redistribute income from richer to poorer member states. If this led to net transfers of income to groups with higher marginal propensities to consume, the end effect would be fiscal policy led expansion of aggregate demand. For the EU budget to have significant effects on aggregate demand the EU would need to have the power to operate budget deficits and surpluses and probably the power to levy taxes directly. This implies a federal type of constitution for the EU.

The EU has begun to move towards fiscal policy coordination, and the move towards monetary union could enhance this development among those member states that proceed with the plan to create monetary union. The Maastricht Treaty seems to envisage fiscal policy coordination as an important ingredient in the progress towards monetary union. The use of fiscal policy coordination as a counter-cyclical measure may also evolve from the Growth Initiative. The development of the SEM may lead to further restrictions (and some harmonisation) of the taxation policies of the member states. In the longer term the EU may develop into a large scale redistributor of income within the Community by use of the structural funds and the Cohesion fund. This could have significant fiscal effects.

Problems with coordination systems

Several difficulties arise in determining stable coordination systems even when the outcome is regarded as being mutually beneficial. Three main problems can be identified: (*a*) the costs of reaching and maintaining agreements; (*b*) the divergent views on what are appropriate targets and instruments; (*c*) the credibility of the coordination system.

The costs, in terms of negotiation time, information gathering and the setting of acceptable targets and instruments, can be significant. As the number of partners in the system grow, so do the costs of reaching agreement. This has implications for the EU if it is to be enlarged to include a number of other European countries. It is also costly to ensure that parties to the agreement abide by the rules of the system. These costs are likely to grow as the number of member states increases, and can be greatly increased if there are disagreements as to the appropriate targets and instruments for the coordination system.

In the context of the EU the main areas of contention are over the appropriate target level of inflation given the high levels of unemployment in the member states. However, if fiscal policy coordination systems were to develop in the EU, a range of other disputes over targets and instruments would be likely to emerge. If there exist divergent views on appropriate instruments and targets, there may well arise a problem of credibility for the coordination scheme. In essence, the divergent views on the appropriateness of adopting tight monetary policy in the EMS in the early 1990s was a significant factor in the credibility problem that the ERM faced. This led currency speculators to test the commitment of the member states to maintaining the parities of the ERM. Certainly the credibility of monetary policy coordination systems appears to be of crucial importance.

Other problems arise over the issue of whether coordination systems should be rules-based or discretionary. Rules-based systems require the setting of a set of rules that constrain the policies of all the parties to the system. The alternative is to have discretionary systems that allow for jointly agreed policies which can be changed as circumstances alter. Rules-based systems have advantages where there exists consensus on targets and instruments and on the methods of implementation to achieve agreed targets. The disadvantage of rules-based systems is that governments have little autonomy to alter policies in the face of unexpected shocks to their economies. This can be particularly serious when shocks are asymmetric. Discretionary systems are advantageous when it is difficult to reach a consensus and where partners in the system face asymmetric shocks. However, such systems are likely to evolve into loose agreements and they can degenerate into little more than cooperation schemes.

It is clear that some member states, particularly Germany, are very much in favour of rules-based approaches to monetary policy coordination, while other member states, such as France, appear to favour a more discretionary approach. Indeed for some member states the attraction of monetary union in the EU is that it would allow some freedom from the current monetary situation which is dominated by a rules-based Bundesbank. Difficulties with regard to these issues could prove to be a substantial obstacle to the development of macro-economic coordination systems in the EU.

Conclusions

Macro-economic policy cooperation and coordination systems are evolving in the EU. The creation of the SEM, moves towards monetary union and the desire to tackle the high level of unemployment in Europe are all contributing to the pressure to develop macro-economic cooperation and coordination systems in the EU. However, the crisis in the EMS and the difficulties of establishing effective fiscal policy coordination systems illustrate the problems that the EU faces in determining stable and effective agreements in the macro-economic area.

References and further reading

Baldassarri M and **Roberti P** 1994 *Fiscal Problems in the Single Market Europe*, Macmillan, London.
Commission EC 1989 *Report on Economic and Monetary Union in the European Community*, Office for the Official Publications of the EC, Luxembourg.
Commission EC 1990 *One Market, One Money*, European Economy No. 44, Office for the Official Publications of the EC, Luxembourg.
Commission EC 1992a *Completing the Internal Market*, Vol. 2, The Elimination of Frontier Controls, Office for the Official Publications of the EC, Luxembourg.
Commission EC 1992b *Completing the Internal Market*, Vol. 3, Conditions for Business Cooperation, Office for the Official Publications of the EC, Luxembourg.
Commission EC 1993 *The Edinburgh Growth Initiative, Background Paper*, London Office of the Commission.
Eastwood R K 1992 in Dyker D (ed.), *The European Economy*, Longman, London.
Giovannini A and **Spaventa L** 1991 in Atkinson A B and Brunetta R (eds), *Economics for the New Europe*, Macmillan, London.
Morley R 1988 *The Macroeconomics of Open Economies*, Edward Elgar, Aldershot.
Nielsen J U, Heinrich H and **Hansen J D** 1992, *An Economic Analysis of the EC*, McGraw-Hill, Maidenhead.

CHAPTER 4

European monetary union: the case for complete monetary integration

George Zis

Introduction

The EU has embarked on a path inexorably leading to the eventual replacement of member countries' currencies with a single European currency. The Maastricht Treaty, which came into force on 1 November 1993, stipulates that, at the latest, the monetary union will be in place on 1 January 1999, even if only a minority of the EU countries qualify or wish to be members of it. Therefore, the precise nature and length of the transition period to Europe's monetary unification have yet to be determined, while agreement on the political and economic structures required for the Union's monetary union to be durable is unlikely to be reached before the mid-1990s. Be that as it may, there now exists a *political* consensus in favour of the complete monetary integration of the Union. When, on the weekend of 31 July–1 August 1993 the EU member countries decided against the suspension of the EMS, the option favoured by the UK, as the solution to the turmoil which had engulfed the system since September 1992, they signalled their political determination to proceed with the creation of a European currency union. Alternative forms of monetary union, involving less than complete integration and the retention of national currencies, have been rejected as incompatible with the objectives of the Single European Act. A single European currency is a necessary condition for the creation of a single European market.

Is the objective of a European monetary union feasible? What are the expected benefits from the introduction of a single European currency? Are the costs of replacing EU member countries' currencies significant? What are the policy implications for member states of a single European currency? What are the conditions that must be satisfied if the European monetary union is to survive? Why was the EMS, after more than 13 years of spectacularly successful functioning, unable to cope with the speculative pressures that gathered momentum during the summer of 1992 and persisted well into 1993, raising doubts as to whether the system could in fact play the role envisaged for it during the transition period to monetary union? Is it likely that all EU member countries will be in a position to join the currency union by 1999? These are some of the questions which this chapter seeks to address.

First, a definition of monetary union will be presented. Then, alternate forms of monetary union will be discussed. The next section will be devoted to an outline of the background to the current debate on European monetary union. This will be followed by an evaluation of the arguments for and against the replacement of EU member countries' currencies with a single

European currency. The policy and institutional implications of the current plans will then be considered. Finally, some conclusions will be presented.

Monetary union: definition

A group of countries may be perceived to constitute a monetary union if they experience identical rates of interest and inflation. That is, the definition of monetary union describes a set of monetary characteristics which implicitly involves the *'as if' assumption* that there exists a single currency throughout the union. It follows, therefore, that a monetary union is compatible with member countries retaining their national currencies. For the 'as if' assumption to be satisfied it is necessary, but not sufficient, that: (a) there be no restrictions to the movement of capital across the union; (b) member countries' financial sectors be perfectly integrated.

Note that if national currencies are not replaced by a single union currency and the 'as if' assumption is met, then intra-union exchange rates will be fixed even if they are not *de jure* fixed.

Monetary union: alternative types

Vaubel (1988) identifies a number of alternative sets of monetary arrangements which are in theory consistent with our definition of monetary union. First, there is the case of *currency union*, the type of monetary union preferred by the EU, which involves member countries adopting a single currency. A currency union cannot exist without perfect capital mobility across the union and a fully integrated financial sector. It follows, therefore, that the creation of a currency union must be preceded by the removal of all impediments to the movement of capital across the member states and the construction of a common legal structure which will facilitate the complete integration of national financial sectors. Furthermore, in a currency union there can exist only one independent supplier of the union currency which will be responsible for the union's monetary and exchange rate policies. Any other set of institutional arrangements which would allow member countries to retain a measure of monetary autonomy, however limited, would serve only to subvert the union's credibility and, therefore, its durability.

Second, an *exchange rate union* involves the irrevocable fixity of intra-union exchange rates and the free movement of capital across the union. In contrast to a currency union, an exchange rate union does not require the establishment of a union central bank. National central banks continue to be responsible for the supply of their respective currencies and their exchange rates. It would appear, then, that in an exchange rate union member countries enjoy a higher degree of monetary autonomy than in a currency union. However, the national monetary sovereignty identified with an exchange rate union is illusory rather than real. The member country that chooses to exercise its monetary autonomy, and pursues a monetary policy independently of its partner union members, sooner or later will be forced to effect an exchange rate change. That is, membership of an exchange rate union is incompatible with the pursuit of an independent monetary policy. It follows, therefore, that the constraint imposed on the conduct of national monetary policies by the irrevocable fixity of intra-union exchange rates implies that there is no real difference between a currency union and an exchange rate union in terms of the degree of monetary autonomy enjoyed by the union member countries. On the other hand, these two types of monetary union are sharply different in one highly significant respect. In a currency union, by definition, there are no intra-union exchange rates. Therefore, exchange rate uncertainty is confined to the exchange rates of the union currency against the currencies of the countries outside the union. In contrast, in an exchange rate union there inevitably exists a degree of uncertainty, however limited, regarding intra-union exchange rates. The concept of irrevocably fixed exchange rates, by its nature, can never be fully credible. Whatever the policies and commitments of a country's past and current governments may be, it is not possible to exclude the possibility that some future government will alter the 'irrevocably fixed' exchange rates of its currency, or impose restrictions on the movement of capital and, thus, secede from the exchange rate union.

Third, Vaubel (1988) defines a *free intercirculation union* as involving the free movement of member countries' currencies throughout the union. Intra-union exchange rates need not be *de jure* fixed. However, if all union currencies are to survive in the long run, member countries cannot pursue monetary policies independently of each other. The currency competition implied by this type of monetary union will result in the persistently deviant currencies being driven out of circulation. As no government would risk the political cost of its currency disappearing, a free intercirculation union would tend to encourage convergent monetary policies among the member countries. The inherent discipline of this type of monetary union could theoretically result in common rates of interest and inflation and, therefore, *de facto* fixed exchange rates.

Finally, the fourth type of monetary union discussed by Vaubel (1988) is the *parallel currency union*. Member countries retain their respective currencies but there exists a parallel currency which circulates side by side with the national currencies. This type of union resembles the free intercirculation union in terms of the currency competition associated with it. In the latter, a member country's currency competes with the currencies of all the other union member countries. In a parallel currency union, a member country's currency competes with the parallel currency. Similarly, a parallel currency union shares certain features with a currency union. Both involve a common currency circulating throughout the union and both require the establishment of a union monetary authority with responsibility for issuing the union's currency.

As already stated, the EU has decided in favour of a currency union. British proposals for a free intercirculation union and a parallel currency union were firmly rejected by the other EC member countries. Indeed, these proposals were perceived as a British attempt to delay, if not to subvert, the process towards the creation of a European Monetary Union. But how was it that the EU opted for a currency union?

Why a currency union for Europe?

The turmoil in foreign exchange markets of the late 1960s was perceived by the EEC member countries as placing in jeopardy the successes achieved in establishing a customs union and the common agricultural policy. It was believed that fixity of exchange rates was necessary for the consolidation and development of these achievements. Thus the EU adopted in 1970 the Werner Plan which envisaged the creation of a European monetary union through 'the irrevocable fixing of parities and the total liberalisation of capital movements' by 1980. The Werner Plan placed emphasis on the fixity of exchange rates and complete freedom of capital movements. It did not consider in any detail the relative merits of a currency union. The introduction of a single European currency was viewed as potentially having a 'psychological effect' of some, but not decisive, usefulness. The Werner Plan assumed that the IMF international monetary system would survive and, therefore, provide the background against which intra-EU exchange rates would be irrevocably fixed and intra-EU capital movements be completely liberalised. The collapse of the IMF system in March 1973 and the first oil price shock of 1973–74 resulted in the EU member countries' abandoning the implementation of the Werner Plan. The process of European integration entered a period of stagnation which lasted until the European Monetary System (EMS) came into being in March 1979.

Following the collapse of the IMF system, countries abstained from systematic interventions in foreign exchange markets in defence of particular parities. The ensuing behaviour of exchange rates sharply contradicted the predictions of those who had argued in favour of flexible exchange rates. Exchange rate changes turned out to be large and unpredictable rather than small and predictable. The post-1973 exchange rate changes, more often than not, did not offset inflation rate differentials, as was anticipated by advocates of exchange rate flexibility. Indeed, on numerous occasions high inflation countries' currencies were revalued rather than devalued. The outcome of this behaviour of nominal exchange rates was that *real* exchange rate changes, or changes in countries' competitiveness, were large and unpredictable. An illustration of the economic damage that flexible exchange rates can inflict is provided by the experience of the UK during 1979–81. The British rate of inflation was significantly higher than the inflation rates of its main competitors, yet sterling was revalued by nearly 25 per cent. British goods became increasingly uncompetitive and the country's manufacturing sector suffered a severe contraction. The experience of the 1970s further demonstrated that the principal argument in favour of flexible exchange rates was ill-founded. It had been argued that exchange rate flexibility allowed the individual country to determine its own monetary policy and, therefore, choose its preferred rate of inflation. It was alleged that exchange rate changes would reflect money supply growth rate differentials and, consequently, exchange rate flexibility would insulate countries from external nominal shocks. But countries attempting to control their inflation rates through the pursuit of independent monetary policies discovered that exchange flexibility hindered rather than facilitated their attempts to effect lasting reductions in inflation.

Disenchantment with exchange rate flexibility and the recognition that inflation cannot be controlled through uncoordinated monetary policies generated the political will in France and Germany to press for the formation of a regional monetary system. With the agreement of the other EU countries, except the UK, the EMS came into existence in March 1979. The creation of the system was interpreted by Bilson (1979) as: '... the first step back from the rugged individualism and national self-interest that lay behind the formal acceptance of flexible exchange rates at the Jamaica meetings of the International Monetary Fund in January 1976.'

The objective of the EMS was defined to be the creation of 'a zone of monetary stability in Europe' through 'monetary cooperation' among the EU member countries. The choice of this particular objective was not accidental. It was preferred to the objective of monetary union because the failure of the Werner Plan had demonstrated the dangers inherent in setting ambitious goals. It is also important to consider the concept of 'monetary stability'. First, monetary stability has two dimensions: a price and an exchange rate dimension. Second, stability does not imply fixity or constancy. Stability, in this context, is measured by the predictability of inflation and exchange rates. That is, the EMS was not envisaged as a system of fixed exchange rates. Instead, its objective was to reduce exchange rate volatility and thus promote a greater degree of exchange rate predictability. Simultaneously, it aimed at the permanent reduction of inflation rates in the EU as the means of promoting price predictability. It is an empirical fact that the higher the rate of inflation is, the more unpredictable it will be. In brief then, the EMS was set the twin objectives of reducing the volatility of intra-EU exchange rates and of effecting a permanent reduction in member countries' inflation rates.

The EMS has been successful in:

(a) reducing exchange rate unpredictability

(b) inducing a reduction of, and an increasing degree of convergence among member countries' inflation rates

(c) generating, as a result of (a) and (b), a greater degree of real exchange rate predictability

(d) encouraging lower and more convergent national money supply growth rates

(e) reducing the variability of national inflation, money supply growth and interest rates.

But perhaps the most significant achievement of the EMS was to demonstrate the economic benefits that can be reaped through economic cooperation. It is arguable that the success of the EMS provided a major stimulus in the formulation and subsequent ratification of the Single European Act. The system provided a strong impetus to the process of European integration. But with it came the recognition that the ability of the system to facilitate this process is limited. There emerged a consensus that the EMS could not provide the monetary framework required for the creation of the single European market. Thus the Single European Act commits the signatory countries to the objective of monetary union. In the spring of 1989 the Delors *Report on Economic and Monetary Union in the European Community* was published. It recommends a three-stage process for the formation of monetary union. Although the Report could be interpreted as advocating an exchange rate union, it in fact recommended a currency union. The Maastricht Treaty adopted the Report's proposals that member countries' currencies be replaced by a single European currency and that a European Central Bank, with responsibility for the Community's monetary and exchange rate policies, be established. The Delors Report refrained from making the case for monetary union. What, then, are the benefits and costs of monetary union? The next section addresses this question by discussing the relative merits of a currency union over an exchange rate union.

The benefits of a European currency union

Gros (1989) observes that while a currency union involves perfect monetary integration among the member countries, this is not necessarily the case with an exchange rate union. He draws attention to the experience of Germany and the Netherlands. The latter has fixed the exchange rate of its currency against the German mark since 1983 and has systematically adjusted its monetary policy to policy changes in Germany. There are no restrictions to capital movements between the two countries, while there exists a high degree of integration of the real sectors of their economies. It could be argued, therefore, that the conditions for an exchange rate union between Germany and the Netherlands are satisfied and, consequently, should observe the *de facto* monetary union of the two countries. However, this is not the case. Dutch interest rates have been persistently higher than Germany's until recently. Fixity of exchange rates and complete freedom of capital movements between the two countries have not resulted in the guilder and the mark becoming perfect substitutes. Exchange rate uncertainty persists and is reflected in the observed interest rate differential. It follows, then, that in an exchange rate union, in contrast to a currency union, monetary integration may not be complete and the conditions for the creation of monetary union may not be satisfied because of the persistence of uncertainty regarding intra-union exchange rates. This uncertainty, by definition, does not exist in a currency union.

The creation of a currency union, by eliminating exchange rate uncertainty, can be expected to result in a more efficient allocation of resources in the union in a variety of ways. First, the elimination of exchange rate uncertainty will enhance the efficiency of the price mechanism as a resource allocator. Volatile and unpredictable exchange rates result in difficulties in interpreting the market's signals. Economic agents cannot be certain whether observed changes in relative prices are ephemeral or permanent. Therefore, they are slow to respond to market changes as reflected by movements in relative prices. Resources are misallocated and unemployment is higher than it would otherwise be. A currency union is likely to lead to a reduction in member countries' natural rate of unemployment.

Second, the elimination of exchange rate uncertainty will stimulate the manufacturing sectors of member countries. Unpredictable and volatile exchange rates are an incentive for resources to be shifted towards the non-traded goods sector which is not exposed to international competition and is largely unaffected by sizeable and unanticipated exchange rate changes. The creation of a currency union by encouraging a shift of resources back to the manufacturing sectors is likely to result in an increase in the average productivity growth rate of member countries and, again, in a decline in their respective natural rates of unemployment.

Third, the elimination of exchange rate uncertainty will stimulate competitive forces in the union. The cost of exchange rate risk management does not vary significantly with firm size. Exchange rate uncertainty places at a special disadvantage small and medium-sized firms. The creation of a currency union removes this disadvantage. Fourth, the elimination of exchange rate uncertainty is likely to yield benefits in terms of higher growth rates of intra-union trade and investment.

The conclusion that a currency union is superior to an exchange rate union does not, however, rest only on the relative merits of the two forms of monetary union in terms of exchange rate uncertainty. In an exchange rate union, the existence of national currencies necessarily implies that economic agents have to bear exchange rate related costs with respect to intra-union transactions. In a currency union these transactions costs are eliminated.

Further, in a currency union no government of a member country can manipulate the money supply growth rate for electoral purposes. As already stated, a necessary feature of a currency union is the existence of a union monetary authority responsible for the union's monetary policy. In contrast, in an exchange rate union, member countries' governments retain responsibility for the supply growth rate of their respective currencies and are able, therefore, to manipulate their monetary policy in the short-run in pursuit of popularity gains with the electorate. But such manipulation of the money supply growth rate is a source of inflationary pressures. A currency union, by eliminating the political business cycle, can be said to possess anti-inflation properties which are not necessarily present in an exchange rate union.

The above considerations suggest that the gains in resource allocation efficiency that would follow the replacement of EU member countries' currencies with a single European currency exceed those which could be expected to follow the 'irrevocable' fixing of intra-EU exchange rates. The Maastricht Treaty provision for the creation of a European currency union is consistent with the objectives of the Single European Act. The 1992 programme aims at the improvement of resource allocation in the EU through the removal of barriers to the movement of goods, services, capital and labour. The ultimate goal is the complete integration of the Union and the creation of a single European market. Such an objective would be ill-founded if the process of integration did not aim also at the Union's complete monetary integration which can only be achieved through the establishment of a European currency union. As an exchange rate union, an intercirculation union or a parallel currency union would not necessarily lead to the Union's complete monetary integration, these forms of monetary union are inconsistent with the objectives of the Single European Act. Be that as it may, what are the alleged costs involved in the creation of a European currency union?

The 'costs' of a European currency union

Opponents of the creation of a European currency union, to be found mainly in the UK, have directed a variety of criticisms, not always of an economic nature, against the EU decision to proceed with the implementation of the principal proposals of the Delors Plan. Some have concentrated on emphasising the implications of member countries no longer being able to employ monetary and exchange rate policies in pursuit of domestic economic objectives.

Even the most ardent advocates of exchange rate flexibility no longer maintain that it is feasible for a country to pursue independent policy objectives in isolation from the rest of the world. The UK experience since 1979 does not provide convincing evidence in support of the thesis that monetary policies determined at the national level and with disregard for policies in the country's main economic partners can yield significant benefits. Indeed, the UK experiment with the naive version of Friedmanite monetarism gives rise to serious doubts as to whether in fact a country can control its money supply growth rate, even under flexible exchange rates. The UK government of the 1980s was less than successful in meeting its monetary targets. Its failure was such that figures for the monetary variable to be controlled, £M3, are no longer published. It may be argued, however, that the lack of success experienced by the UK in the 1980s with its attempts to control the money supply growth rate was due to special factors and should not be employed against the search for ways of formulating an effective monetary policy at the national level. Whatever the merits of this line of reasoning, it ignores a significant development in economic agents' behaviour. The internationalisation of the financial and money markets and the technological revolution in telecommunications have resulted in economic agents increasingly holding diversified currency portfolios. The implication of this trend is that even if a country could control the money supply growth rate it would not be able to control the domestic long-run inflation rate. Only international monetary policies can ensure the control of inflation. In brief, then, EU countries currently enjoy only a limited degree of monetary autonomy and this applies only to the very short run. The benefits of this are dubious, especially as it is often used for electoral purposes with destabilising inflationary effects for the domestic economy. Therefore, the cost of the European currency union in terms of loss of monetary autonomy by the member countries is, at most, negligible.

The second set of criticisms against the creation of a European currency union draws attention to the circumstances when an exchange rate change is the appropriate policy response. Accordingly, it is maintained that the loss of exchange rate policy involves a significant cost for EU member countries.

For a high inflation country, the ability to occasionally devalue its currency is important and its exercise can yield benefits. However, the relevance of this observation when assessing the case for a European currency union is less than obvious. In such a union, there will exist a single union inflation rate, common to all member countries. There will exist no inflation rate differentials which could justify exchange rate changes, if they were available.

Similarly, the case for exchange rate changes in response to inflation rate differentials during the transition period to the establishment of the European currency union is less than convincing. As already noted, a principal objective of the EMS was to induce a reduction in member countries' inflation rates. The system has achieved this objective and in the process has established its anti-inflation credentials. Its success is partly explained by the fact that the intra-EMS exchange rate realignments that were effected until September 1992 were deliberately confined to magnitudes which did not fully offset inflation rate differentials. Thus, high inflation member countries were penalised and the EMS acquired the credibility which ensured its survival. If the exchange rate policy instrument were now to be made available for member countries to use more frequently and liberally, the anti-inflation properties of the EMS would be undermined and the gains achieved by member countries in the control of inflation would be dissipated.

Theory suggests that an exchange rate change may be the appropriate response to a country-specific shock. Again, though the validity of this proposition is beyond dispute, its relevance to the debate on the desirability or otherwise of the European currency union is less than obvious. Such is the degree of integration among the EU member economies that it is difficult to envisage a country-specific shock.

Exchange rate changes have at times been suggested as a justifiable response to productivity growth rate differentials. However, there is no empirical evidence to suggest that exchange rate changes have a systematic or durable impact on productivity growth rates.

Devaluation has often been perceived as an appropriate measure for countries running high and persistent balance of payments current account deficits. In the case of the EU member countries during the transition period to monetary union, exchange rate changes as a means of correcting current account deficits would not appear to be a desirable response. For such changes to be successful, they would need to be so large that they would undermine price stability in the Union. Note, however, that with the establishment of the European currency union, no member country will have a balance of payments problem. An incipient current account deficit which persists will manifest itself as a regional problem. Thus member countries may gradually become depressed areas of the Union. The Delors Committee recognised this potential threat to the cohesion of the Union and, accordingly, urged member countries to develop well defined regional policies, with sufficient funds made available to prevent the development of sharp regional disparities.

It can be argued, therefore, that the loss of exchange rate changes as a policy instrument does not involve a cost sufficiently significant to constitute a convincing argument against the creation of the European currency union. Indeed, this would appear to have been the judgement of the EU member countries. There was no intra-EMS exchange rate realignment between January 1987 and September 1992. That there was no realignment for over five years suggests that the member countries themselves no longer regarded exchange rate policy as an effective policy instrument.

Some critics of the Delors Plan and the Maastricht Treaty have maintained that while the creation of a European currency union may reap net benefits for a number of EU member countries, for others membership of such a union will be positively harmful, at least for the foreseeable future. They draw attention to the reliance of governments in countries such as Greece, Spain, Italy and Portugal on the inflation tax for a significant component of their revenues. These countries' fiscal systems are so inefficient, it is argued, that their governments have little option but to actively employ the inflation tax. For them high inflation is acceptable. The replacement of national currencies with a single European currency would deprive these countries' respective monetary authorities of the right to issue money and with it the revenues which currently accrue to their governments through monetary creation, while at the same time they would not be able to offset this loss through the use of other taxes. Therefore, it is suggested, membership of the European currency union and reducing inflation in preparation for such membership will have an undesirable impact on these countries.

The implications of this judgement are difficult to accept. It suggests that the benefits of an inefficient fiscal system exceed the costs of high inflation rates. It is an argument against fiscal reform in these countries. Yet they have all recognised the urgent need for such a reform, quite independently of the arguments for and against membership of the European currency union, but their governments have lacked the political will to proceed with the necessary changes to their fiscal systems. Indeed, an externally 'imposed' reform would be welcome, as it would be politically more acceptable than a reform initiated solely through domestic pressures. Be that as it may, all four countries are actively seeking to reduce their inflation rates, with Italy being particularly successful. That is, the permanent reduction of inflation is accorded a higher priority than the size of revenues associated with monetary creation. A decreasing reliance on the inflation tax can be discerned in all four countries. It follows, therefore, that the cost associated with membership of the European currency union in terms of lost revenues for these countries is unlikely to be significant. It is not surprising, then, that this particular set of objections to the implementation of the Maastricht Treaty received little attention even in the countries likely to be most affected. In brief, the case for the European currency union is well-founded. The case against is less than convincing.

The Maastricht Treaty

The extensive debate and intensive negotiations which followed the publication of the Delors Plan eventually led to the Maastricht Treaty agreed upon by EC member countries in December 1991. The Treaty addresses a number of issues which the Delors Plan either failed to consider or opted not to consider. The latter recommended a three stage process towards the creation of the European currency union but refrained from suggesting a timetable for the completion of the process and the formation of the union. It simply stated that the process should begin on 1 July 1990. The Maastricht Treaty, in line with the Delors Plan, provides for a three stage process leading to the complete monetary unification of the EU, but it also stipulates a well defined timetable for the establishment of the monetary union. It sets 1 January 1994 as the date for the commencement of the second stage. Further, it stipulates that during 1996 the European Council will determine whether a majority of EU member countries qualify for union membership and, if this is the case, will set a date for the union to become operational. Thus the earliest date for the establishment of the currency union is 1 January 1997. If there is no such majority at that time, then the union will come into effect on 1 January 1999, even if only a minority of member states satisfy the membership conditions. It follows, therefore, that no member country can veto the establishment of the currency union. But even more significant is the implication that the Maastricht Treaty is perfectly consistent with the emergence of a 'two-speed' Europe, if that is the outcome of either economic conditions or the political wishes of one or more member states. The Maastricht Treaty allows both the UK and Denmark to opt out of the monetary union even if they satisfy the membership conditions.

The Delors Plan had recommended that the second stage should be used to increase economic policy convergence among the EU member countries. In addition to increased monetary convergence, the Delors Plan identified the need for member states to adopt fiscal policies which would facilitate the establishment and enhance the potential durability of the monetary union. However, primarily for political reasons, it refrained from specifying the degree of convergence that had to be achieved prior to the start of the third and final stage. For this omission the Delors Plan was criticised, particularly in Germany. It was questioned whether the second stage was necessary. The Maastricht Treaty rectified this weakness of the Delors Plan by specifying the criteria of convergence that had to be satisfied for a country to qualify for membership of the currency union. According to the Treaty an EU member state must satisfy the following conditions:

1. its inflation rate must be no more that 1.5 per cent above the average of the lowest three inflation rates in the EMS;

2. its long-term interest rates must be no more that 2 per cent above the average of the lowest three member countries' rates;

3. it must have maintained its exchange rate within the narrow band of fluctuation of the Exchange Rate Mechanism (ERM) of the EMS for at least two years, without a realignment;

4. its budget deficit must be no larger than 3 per cent of GDP;

5. its National Debt must not exceed 60 per cent of GDP.

These convergence criteria can be judged to be stringent, particularly in their implications for the fiscal policies that need to be pursued during the transition period towards the establishment of the monetary union. Whether this degree of stringency is necessary and whether the implied level of monetary and fiscal convergence is politically feasible within the timescale prescribed by the Maastricht Treaty are issues that will be discussed later.

The European Monetary Institute (EMI), established at the start of the second stage on 1 January 1994, is expected to play a significant role in the preparation for the beginning of the third stage in 1997 or 1999. The EMI is not perceived as an institution which will evolve into the Union's Central Bank through the gradual transfer to it of the functions currently discharged by member countries' Central Banks. The latter remain responsible for national monetary policies for the duration of the second stage. The Institute's responsibilities have been defined to include the administration of the EMS, the promotion of an ever increasing convergence of member states' national monetary policies and the preparation of the procedures and instruments that the European Central Bank (ECB) will use once the third stage begins in 1997 or 1999. At the end of the second stage the EMI will cease to exist and the ECB at the head of the European System of Central Banks (ESCB) will come into existence and assume responsibility for the Union's monetary policy. The ESCB will also play a significant role in the determination of the Union's exchange rate policy towards non-union countries.

The Maastricht Treaty unambiguously specifies that the principal objective for the ECB is to maintain price stability in the EU. To facilitate the achievement of this objective the Treaty guarantees the constitutional independence of the ECB from both member states' and the Union's institutions. Equally significantly, the Treaty, by assigning a specific role in the conduct of the Union's exchange rate policy to the ECB, not only provides a framework for consistent policy decision-making but also minimises the likelihood that the ECB attempts to ensure price stability will be frustrated by economic developments external to the Union.

In brief, the Maastricht Treaty provides the foundations for the complete monetary integration of the EU. When it was agreed in December 1991 there was little doubt that the Treaty would be implemented and the currency union would come into being in 1997 or 1999. This confidence did not ignore the likely difficulties that member countries would encounter in their attempt to satisfy the convergence criteria set out in the Treaty. It rested on the spectacular success of the EMS and the perceived political commitment of member states to the objective of a genuine single European market. The UK's objections were not taken seriously. However, this is no longer the case. The turmoil which engulfed the EMS in the summer of 1992 and persisted until August 1993 has generated a high degree of scepticism as to whether the EU will in fact proceed to complete its monetary integration through the full implementation of the Maastricht Treaty.

The EMS in turmoil

The Franco-German initiative to establish the EMS in March 1979 was political in nature. It was conceived as the monetary dimension of a more general attempt to assert the identity of Europe. There was growing disenchantment with the USA's political leadership and economic policies. Individually France, Germany or any of the other EEC member countries could exert little, if any, influence on international economic and political developments. The conduct of the Cold War, as determined by the USA and the Soviet Union, severely limited the ability of EU member countries to act unilaterally, but collectively they had the potential to play an independent role in the conflict between East and West. That is, the Franco-German alliance as the engine of European integration emerged and developed against the international political background dictated by the Cold War. Europe was to seek its independence of the USA but this was to be an independence constrained by the objective of containing, if not reversing, the international influence of the Soviet Union.

It was the political commitment of member countries to the success of the EMS which ensured that the system survived a series of political changes and economic shocks during the 1980s. As already noted, the EMS was highly successful in inducing a reduction in member countries' inflation rates and a sharp decrease in the volatility of intra-EMS exchange rates. Between March 1979 and March 1984 there were seven realignments of intra-EMS exchange rates. In January 1987 the eleventh realignment was effected. This was subsequently judged to have been unnecessary. However, the intra EMS exchange rates established in January 1987 came under no pressure until the summer of 1992.

Prior to September 1992 the EMS successfully accommodated a series of policy initiatives by EU member states. In June 1989 Spain joined the system's ERM and on 1 January 1990, Italy adopted the mechanism's narrow band of fluctuation. During the first half of 1990, Italy and France dismantled all remaining controls on capital movements and in October of that year the UK finally joined the ERM. When the UK's example was followed by Portugal in April 1992 and with Sweden, Norway and Finland all unilaterally pegging their currencies to the ECU, in anticipation of becoming full members of the EU, it appeared that the process of the Union's monetary unification was gathering momentum and that the EMS had evolved into an institution of sufficient resilience to cope with the inevitable strains of the transition period towards the creation of the currency union. But suddenly the EMS was revealed to be inadequately equipped to deal with sustained speculative pressures. These pressures emerged and grew in intensity following the rejection of the Maastricht Treaty by Denmark in a referendum on 2 June 1992. The Italian lira and sterling were the currencies that were subjected to the most severe pressure. On 13 September the lira was devalued and four days later dropped out of the ERM. On 16 September the UK government announced the withdrawal of sterling from the ERM. On 17 September the Spanish peseta was devalued. In November the peseta and the Portuguese escudo were devalued. In January 1993 the Irish punt was devalued and in May the peseta and the escudo were again devalued. These exchange rate changes did not restore confidence in the ability of member countries to defend the new parities. The French franc came under particularly severe speculative pressures. Finally during the weekend 31 July–1 August 1993 member states' Finance Ministers decided to widen the fluctuation band of the ERM to 15 per cent on either side of the central parity but left existing parities unchanged. Quite amazingly, the widening of the permitted band of fluctuation was not followed by a collapse of the French franc. Up to the end of 1993 its devaluation relative to the lowest permissible value under the original mode of operation of the EMS never exceeded 3 per cent.

Why were the speculative pressures so intense that eventually the EMS member countries were forced to suspend an exchange rate arrangement which had proved highly successful for more than 13 years? Economic developments within the EU cannot adequately explain the timing, the intensity or the persistence of the speculative pressures which ultimately resulted in the temporary introduction of the +/– 15 per cent band of fluctuation. The outcome of the 1992 Danish referendum and the reactions to it, particularly in the UK, raised serious doubts as to whether there continued to exist sufficient political commitment to the objective of economic and monetary union for member countries' governments to proceed with the full implementation of the Maastricht Treaty. It may be argued that it was not just a coincidence that Italy and the UK were the first to come under pressure when foreign exchange market speculation gathered momentum during the summer of 1992. In Italy the rule of law had effectively collapsed and the country's political system and structures were rapidly disintegrating. Credible policy decision-making was no longer feasible. A reduction in the huge budget deficit was not likely to be effected by governments that lacked authority. Thus, not surprising, the Italian lira was the first target for speculators.

In the UK, the result of the 1992 Danish referendum exposed how deeply divided the government party was in its attitudes towards the objectives of the Maastricht Treaty. A sizeable minority of the governing Conservative party proclaimed its total opposition to stages two and three of the envisaged process towards economic and monetary union and pronounced the Treaty as dead, forcing the government to revise the timetable for the discussion of the Treaty in the British Parliament. Inevitably, the government's political commitment to the objectives of the Maastricht Treaty came under suspicion. This was expressed by rapidly increasing speculative pressures against sterling which were intensified by the government's incompetent management of the British economy. The more British Ministers declared that sterling was not going to be devalued, the less they were believed. The history of Britain's attitudes towards Europe's attempts to promote economic integration inspired no confidence in the government's intentions, especially as the exchange rate at which the UK chose to enter the ERM, against the advice of its partners, was not thought to be sustainable. In the event, when the speculative pressures could no longer be contained, the British government chose to withdraw sterling from the ERM rather than devalue its currency within the EMS.

The end of the Cold War implied that EU member countries were no longer subject to the political constraints dictated by the objective of containing the Soviet Union and its Eastern European socialist allies. There emerged increasing evidence that Germany intended to use its new freedom to seek an international political role independently of the EU. Inevitably, tensions in its relations with France developed. These had sufficiently escalated by the summer of 1993 that France and Germany appeared no longer to share the same objectives, or, at best, not to attach the same priority to the implementation of the Maastricht Treaty. Increasing doubts as to whether the Franco-German alliance would be the driving force in the completion of the EU's monetary integration generated speculative pressures against the French franc. These became so intense during July 1993 that eventually the EMS member countries were forced to widen the band of fluctuation of the ERM. There is no economic explanation of why the French franc came under such severe pressure in foreign exchange markets. Under no economic criterion can it be argued that the French franc was overvalued relative to the German mark. The foreign exchange market turbulence of the summer of 1993 reflected a crisis of confidence in EU member countries' political commitment to the full implementation of the Maastricht Treaty rather than developments in the fundamentals of intra-EMS exchange rates.

The perception of a weakening political commitment to the objective of monetary union was partly encouraged by the emergence of conflicting pressures on EU member countries' monetary policies. Germany had tightened its monetary policy in response to the inflationary pressures which had been generated by the economic policies that had accompanied the country's unification. But as Germany concentrated on reducing its rate of inflation, to the exclusion of any other economic objective, the other EU member countries were becoming increasingly concerned with the recessionary tendencies in their economies. The required response to the deepening recession was the easing of their monetary policies. But a reduction of their interest rates, given Germany's monetary policy, was incompatible with their ERM exchange rate commitments. Only if Germany were to reduce its interest rates could the rest of the EU member countries proceed to effect interest rate reductions without undermining the functioning of the ERM. However, Germany was not prepared to compromise its attempts to reduce its rate of inflation in order to enable the other EU member countries to respond to their growing domestic economic difficulties. The decline of German interest rates which started in September 1992 was far too slow to allow significant interest rate reductions in the rest of the EU. A policy conflict had emerged. The political climate that had been created following the result of the 1992 Danish referendum encouraged the markets to believe that member states' governments would be forced to give priority to the needs of countering the deepening recession rather than to the exchange rate obligations implied by their ERM membership. Thus speculative pressures persisted and became particularly intense during the summer of 1993, until the remaining ERM member countries decided during the weekend 31 July–1 August 1993 to widen the mechanism's band of fluctuation.

It is beyond dispute that the divergence in policy objectives that emerged between Germany, which sought to reduce its rate of inflation, and the rest of the ERM member countries, which came under increasing pressures to ease their monetary policies in response to the deepening recession, did contribute to the severity of the turmoil which engulfed the ERM. Nor can it be disputed that the mark should have been revalued against all the other ERM currencies following Germany's unification. Be that as it may, it is simply not evident that any reduction in German interest rates could have prevented the Italian lira from dropping out of the ERM. Nor is it clear that the UK could have maintained sterling's exchange rate even if German rates of interest had been reduced more significantly. The question, however, is whether the withdrawal of sterling and the lira from the ERM, the series of intra-EMS exchange rate realignments since September 1992 and the temporary widening of the mechanism's band of fluctuation imply that the process towards the complete monetary integration of the EU has now come to a halt and that the implementation of the Maastricht Treaty is unlikely to be effected. Or, in other words, are the costs of satisfying the convergence criteria likely to be so high as to force the EU member countries either to abandon or, at best, to delay the creation of the economic and monetary union?

Whither economic and monetary union?

A number of responses to the foreign exchange turbulence of July 1993 were considered. One 'solution', particularly favoured by the UK, was to suspend the ERM. The other EU member countries firmly rejected this option and, instead, decided in favour of the temporary widening of the mechanism's band of fluctuation while leaving intra-EMS exchange rates unchanged. That is, it was recognised that there was no economic case for a devaluation of the French franc. But more significantly, the decision to persist with the ERM and the prevailing central parities can be interpreted as a signal of member countries' continuing political commitment to the objective of monetary union even if the transition path to the union were to be different from that prescribed by the Maastricht Treaty.

At the end of 1993 no EU member country satisfied all the convergence criteria. There continues to exist a high degree of convergence among member countries' inflation and long-run interest rates. The only exception is Greece, whose inflation and long-run interest rates differ sharply from the Union's average values. It may, therefore, be argued that given the convergence of inflation and long-run interest rates, the narrowing of the band of fluctuation back to its original width is feasible and could be effected by the end of 1994. The EMI could facilitate this development, particularly if it succeeded in introducing more rigorous mechanisms for the support of existing intra-EMS exchange rates. The EMI could promote even further monetary convergence by encouraging member countries to focus increasingly on Union-wide monetary aggregates. In brief, for the majority of EU member countries, rapid progress towards satisfying the inflation, interest rate and exchange rate criteria is feasible and need not involve politically unacceptable costs.

Compliance with the fiscal criteria specified in the Maastricht Treaty is potentially more difficult. At the end of 1993 no member country's budget deficit was below 3 per cent of its GDP. The recession had induced sharp increases in member states' budget deficits and national debt/GDP ratios were increasing throughout the Union. If member governments were to reduce their expenditures and increase their tax revenues so as to comply with the fiscal convergence criteria within the timetable prescribed by the Maastricht Treaty, they would simply stifle the recovery of their economics. No government could entertain the adoption of fiscal policies that would perpetuate the recent increases in unemployment in the Union. However, the Treaty's fiscal criteria need not be an obstacle to the resumption of progress towards the creation of the currency union. It must be emphasized that the Maastricht Treaty regards these criteria as guidelines rather than rigidly defined conditions that a country must satisfy before it qualifies for membership of the currency union. The Treaty explicitly indicates that a budget deficit greater than 3 per cent of GDP could be tolerated if it were the outcome of exceptional circumstances or if it were on a declining trend. Similarly, the Treaty indicates that a country need not be disqualified from membership of the currency union if its national debt/GDP ratio is greater than 60 per cent but steadily declining. That is, clear evidence that a country is steadily moving towards the fiscal criteria of the Treaty would be sufficient for that country to be considered for membership of the union. However, even a liberal interpretation of the fiscal criteria potentially involves transition costs that for some member countries are likely to be politically unacceptable.

What, then, are the prospects for the complete monetary integration of the EU? It is difficult to conceive the economic and political conditions that would enable all Union countries to become members of the currency union by 1999. On the other hand, it is almost certain that a number of member countries will proceed with the full implementation of the Maastricht Treaty. That is, the emergence of a 'two-speed' Europe now appears to be inevitable. At least France, Germany, the Netherlands, Belgium and Luxembourg could proceed to form a monetary union. Economic conditions could support such a development, while in all these countries there continues to exist a political consensus in favour of monetary unification. It is not difficult to envisage Ireland and Denmark joining this group of countries. On the other hand, Italy wishes to be among the first countries to join the monetary union, but it is not easy to envisage how its political crisis could be resolved sufficiently rapidly to allow this. Similarly, it is unlikely that there will exist in the UK the political consensus that would allow the country to join the monetary union even by 1999. The case of Spain is difficult to assess, but there can be little doubt that Portugal and, especially, Greece would need a substantially longer transition period before being in a position to join the monetary union. The emergence of a 'two-speed' Europe would not be without cost and would certainly be resisted, particularly by the member countries which would be excluded from moving on the fast lane.

Conclusion

The decision to proceed to a currency union and accordingly revise the Rome Treaty was reached on political grounds, just as was the case with the signing of the original Treaty of Rome, the creation of the EMS and the ratification of the Single European Act. The end of the Cold War has resulted in a new international political environment in which the pressures on and incentives for the EU member countries to act collectively are less well defined than they were previously. The crisis which followed the 1992 Danish referendum reflected the doubts that had emerged as to whether EU member countries continued to be committed to the objective of monetary union rather than an inherent weakness of the EMS. The EU has no alternative but to proceed with the establishment of the currency union even if this can be achieved only on the basis of a 'two-speed' Europe.

References and further reading

Artis M 1992 The Maastricht Road to Monetary Union, *Journal of Common Market Studies*, Vol. XXX, No. 3, pp. 299–309.

Bilson G F O 1979 Why the Deutschmark could trouble the EMS, *Euromoney*.

Delors J 1989 *Report on economic and monetary union in the European Community*, Committee for the Study of Economic and Monetary Union, Office for Official Publications of the European Communities, Luxembourg.

Gros D 1989 Paradigms for the Monetary Union of Europe, *Journal of Common Market Studies*, Vol. XXVII, No.3, pp. 219–230.

Gros D and **Thygesen N** 1992 *European Monetary Integration: From the European Monetary System towards Monetary Union*, Longman, London.

Thygesen N 1993 Towards Monetary Union in Europe – Reforms of the EMS in the Perspective of Monetary Union, *Journal of Common Market Studies*, Vol. 31, No. 4, pp. 447–472.

Vaubel R 1988 Monetary Integration Theory in G Zis *et al.*, *International Economics*, Longman, London.

CHAPTER 5

The European financial common market: progress and prospects

George Zis

Introduction

The ever-increasing international capital mobility, which originated with the emergence and rapid growth of the Eurodollar market, has implied that international financial integration has been developing for over three decades. However, this process of integration has been uneven. As it was the outcome of market forces, rather than the result of international agreement, it inevitably reflected the institutional structures associated with the Bretton Woods international monetary system and economic conditions prevailing in the major economies at particular periods of time. Thus, for example, capital mobility within the EU did not develop at the same pace as capital mobility between the US and EU member countries. The uncoordinated nature of the market-led international financial integration resulted in policy problems which varied in severity from country to country. The growth of the Eurocurrency markets, for example, raised issues of whether or not these markets ought to be controlled. And, if they were to be controlled, how was this to be achieved? Similarly, as capital became internationally more mobile, the effectiveness of exchange controls was rapidly eroded. The scope for independent national monetary policies was, therefore, reduced. It may, then, be argued that the financial integration of the EU, largely the outcome of international developments, would have continued to develop even in the absence of special initiatives by EU member countries aimed at the creation of a European financial common market. But if the EU were to adopt a passive stance and allow the process of financial integration to be determined by international and market forces, then the completion, consolidation and development of the internal market would become highly problematic.

Given the size of EU member countries' financial sectors, the concept of a single European market which does not involve the creation of a financial common market is meaningless. Also, the complete financial integration of the EU is necessary if the benefits of establishing a unified market in goods and services are to be maximised. At the same time the creation of a European single financial market cannot be effected independently of international financial developments. That is, EU initiatives must conform with the liberalisation of trade in financial services as prescribed by the successful Uruguay Round negotiations of the General Agreement on Tariffs and Trade (GATT). Similarly, the regulation of financial institutions in EU member countries must build on the international initiatives to harmonise capital requirements across countries and to establish home country supervision of banks and securities firms.

It is therefore not surprising that the creation of a single European financial market featured prominently in the 1985 White Paper. Accordingly, the Single European Act commits the EU member countries to the elimination of all barriers to the trade in financial services within the Union. The expectation is that the removal of these impediments will yield important benefits by enhancing the efficiency of member countries' financial sectors through increased competition. Further, improved efficiency will enable EU member countries' financial institutions to compete more effectively with institutions of non-member countries, especially American and Japanese. Thus a number of EU directives have been adopted. However, although significant progress has so far been achieved, the formation of a European financial common market is far from complete.

In what follows, first, the anticipated gains associated with the establishment of a single European financial market will be considered. Second, the progress towards the removal of capital controls will be assessed. Third, the policy implications of perfect capital mobility will be discussed. The next three sections will be devoted to issues relating to banking, insurance and securities markets. Finally, some conclusions will be presented.

The benefits of completing the internal financial market

Table 5.1 presents data on the size of EU member countries' financial sectors. These, as well as subsequent, figures were used in the estimation of the potential benefits of implementing the 1992 programme. Table 5.1 demonstrates the significance of EU member countries' financial sectors, independently of their contribution to the functioning of the markets for the products of the rest of the economy.

Table 5.1 Economic dimensions of the financial services sector (1985)

	Gross value-added as % of GDP	Employment as % of total employment	Compensation of employers as % of total for economy
Belgium	5.7	3.8	6.3
Germany	5.4	3.0	4.4
Spain	6.4	2.8	6.7
France	4.3	2.8	3.8
Italy	4.9	1.8	5.6
Luxembourg	14.9	5.7	12.2
Netherlands	5.2	3.7	4.9
UK	11.8	3.7	8.5

Source : Emerson (1988:99) *The Economics of 1992*, Oxford University Press

Estimates of the potential benefits of creating a single European financial market have rested on an assessment of the impact on the prices of banking, insurance and brokerage services of the removal of all barriers to the trade in these services. These prices exhibit a high degree of divergence. The expectation is that the establishment of a financial common market will induce price reductions and a convergence towards the lowest prices. For the study of the cost of absence of financial integration the prices for 16 financial services were considered: seven banking services, five insurance services and four brokering services. The average of the four lowest prices for each service was defined as the price which would emerge if trade in these services were completely liberalised. Comparing, then, this theoretical price with that observed, an estimate of the potential price reductions in eight of the EU member countries was derived. However, for a variety of reasons the law of one price cannot be expected to hold for all financial products. Thus, the difference between the actual price of each service and the average of the lowest four prices for each particular service was adjusted. It was assumed that the creation of the single European financial market will reduce the difference between actual price and the average of the lowest four prices by half. These were judged to be the likely price reductions to follow the creation of a financial common market with a margin of plus/minus 5 percentage points. The resultant estimates are presented in Table 5.2.

Table 5.2 Estimates of potential and indicative price reductions %

	Potential price reductions (%)							
	Belgium	Germany	Spain	France	Italy	Luxembourg	Netherlands	UK
Banking	15	33	34	25	18	16	10	18
Insurance	31	10	32	24	51	37	1	4
Securities	52	11	44	23	33	9	18	12
Total	23	25	34	24	29	17	9	13
	Indicative price reductions (%): all financial services							
Range	6–16	5–15	16–26	7–17	9–19	3–13	0–9	2–12
Centre of range	11	10	21	12	14	8	4	7

Source: Emerson (1988:105) *The Economics of 1992*, Oxford University Press

These figures demonstrate prevailing price divergences across the eight EU member countries and, therefore, the differences in terms of price reductions that can be expected to follow the completion of the internal financial market. It is also worth noting that there exist large differences not only among the countries considered but also among the sub-sectors of the financial services industry in each country. The methodology employed in the estimation of the gains from completing the internal financial market has been criticised. It has been argued, with justification, that the anticipated gains have been exaggerated. Be that as it may, there can be no doubt that the establishment of the single European financial market will yield significant economic benefits to the EU member countries.

Capital controls

A necessary condition for the completion of the internal financial market is the elimination of all barriers to the movement of capital within the EU. The retention of exchange controls is incompatible with measures specifically aimed to enhance the Union's financial integration.

Consider the case of Greece. It continues to operate exchange controls while it allows foreign banks to open branches in Greece on the same basis as in their home countries. This implies that the effectiveness of exchange controls is significantly reduced. Inter-branch operations provide a means of evading the exchange controls, but if Greece were to take measures to strengthen these controls, then it would be depriving itself of the benefits associated with the integration of its financial sector with those of its partners in the EU. In other words, the benefits of an integrated European financial market can be maximised only if capital flows are completely liberalised.

The liberalisation of capital flows within the EU proceeded at a slow and uneven pace during the 1960s and 1970s. The use of exchange controls differed among the EU member countries. Germany and the Netherlands imposed controls on the inflows of capital during the 1970s, but in 1981 they removed all restrictions on capital movements. The UK abolished all exchange controls in 1979. Belgium and Luxembourg made no significant use of controls on capital movements but operated a system of dual exchange rates. On the other hand, Denmark, France, Italy, Ireland, Portugal, Greece and Spain all had in place exchange control structures aimed at restricting capital movements. As already noted, the effectiveness of these controls was steadily eroded over time. By the mid-1980s they could provide only very short-term protection when foreign exchange market pressures developed.

The process of liberalisation of capital movements was accelerated following the adoption of the second directive on capital movements in June 1988. This directive was in line with the provisions of the Single European Act. It set July 1990 as the date by which all EC member countries except Greece and Portugal were to remove all restrictions on capital movements. This deadline was met by all EC member countries, with Spain and Ireland effectively removing their exchange controls. Greece and Portugal have been allowed a longer period of adjustment. They are scheduled to remove their restrictions on capital movements by the end of 1995. They have both made sufficient progress so far that they are likely to meet the 1995 deadline. Belgium and Luxembourg abolished their dual exchange rate system in March 1990.

The progress achieved was temporarily reversed following the September 1992 turmoil in the European Monetary System (EMS). The intensity of speculative pressures forced Spain and Ireland to reintroduce capital controls. These, however, were dismantled during 1993. In brief, then, there now effectively exists freedom of capital movements within the EU. However, this achievement has serious implications for economic policy-making in EU member countries.

Policy implications

Freedom of capital movements implies that economic agents can hold diversified asset portfolios. Further, it allows economic agents to adjust the composition of their portfolios rapidly and at a relatively low cost. The importance of this implication of almost perfect mobility derives from the fact that assets are imperfect substitutes. If there were perfect asset substitutability, then economic agents in, say, Britain would be indifferent as to whether they held British or, say, French bonds. However, so long as EU member countries retain their currencies and, therefore, intra-EU exchange rates exist, perfect asset substitutability is not, by definition, possible. Exchange rate uncertainty ensures that assets remain imperfect substitutes.

In the presence of imperfect asset substitutability, perfect capital mobility among countries is sustainable only if these countries engage in a high degree of policy coordination. If divergent economic policies were pursued, then economic agents would tend to exploit the freedom of capital movements to continually change the composition of their asset portfolios. But such adjustments to portfolio compositions would involve large flows of capital among countries. This, in turn, would generate foreign exchange market crises. If the countries involved operated fixed exchange rates, speculative pressures could force them to abandon the given parities of their currencies. This is what partly occurred during the 1992 EMS crisis. If, on the other hand, the countries among which capital moved freely operated flexible exchange rates, then divergent economic policies, by inducing changes in the preferred compositions of asset portfolios, would lead to sharp fluctuations of exchange rates.

The EU is engaged in the construction of the internal market. A high degree of volatility in intra-EU exchange rates would frustrate the completion, consolidation and development of the single European market. Erratic and unpredictable exchange rates would impede the efficient allocation of resources in the Union. Therefore, exchange rate flexibility cannot provide the monetary conditions necessary for the creation of the single European market. But if exchange rate predictability is a principal ingredient in the establishment of the internal market and perfect capital mobility a necessary condition for the creation of a financial common market, then the question arises as to how the EU can ensure the full implementation of the 1992 programme. There is general agreement on the need for EU member countries to coordinate their economic policies. This, however, is not sufficient to ensure exchange rate predictability. Countries' governments have an incentive to cheat and refrain from pursuing announced policies. Thus, there exists scope for volatile exchange rate expectations. In turn, the potential for destabilising capital flows has been enhanced by the abolition of exchange controls. This line of argument leads to the proposition that only when EU member countries' currencies are replaced by a single European currency will the completion of the European financial common market be feasible. In other words, it can be maintained that the logic of the objectives of the 1992 programme dictates that the EU proceed with the full implementation of the Maastricht Treaty and establish the monetary union among the member countries by, at the latest, January 1999.

Banking

The Second Banking Coordination Directive, the Own Funds Directive and the Solvency Ratio Directive, all of which came into force on 1 January 1993 provide the legal framework for progress towards the creation of an integrated EU banking sector.

The second Banking Coordination Directive establishes the right of any bank which is licensed in any EU member country to open branches throughout the Union without needing permission from the member country in which the branch is to be located. Further, it is not required to hold separate capital for the branch. The directive establishes the principle of home-country supervision. The bank, including its branches in other countries, is subject to the supervisory regulations in force in the home country. However, the host country has the right to determine the liquidity of the branch as well as to regulate the risk borne by the branch in the domestic markets.

The Second Banking Coordination Directive is implemented through national laws. All EU member countries have now put in place the necessary legislation. These laws define the responsibilities of the national regulatory authorities and reflect member countries' applications of the principle of home-country supervision. Thus Britain has the right, for example, to exclude banks authorised in other EU member countries if they fail to maintain adequate liquidity. However, although the national enabling laws reflect member countries' particular applications of the principle of home country supervision, they do not discriminate against banks wishing to operate in EU member countries other than those in which they are located.

The Own Funds Directive provides a definition of the minimum capital for banks which is to be applied to all EU member countries. Differences in the definition of own funds, which determined the capital adequacy of banks, were a source of distortion in terms of the competitiveness of banks. The directive, by defining what resources of a bank qualify as capital, ensures a degree of harmonisation necessary for maintaining confidence in the ability of EU member countries' banks to compete without endangering their credibility. Related to the Own Funds Directive is the Solvency Ratio Directive. The latter specifies minimum ratios of capital to risk-weighted assets. Further, the Large Exposure Directive limits a bank's credit exposure to any single borrower to a maximum of 25 per cent of its capital.

The legal framework now in place, by facilitating cross-border activities, is likely to result in significant changes in EU member countries' banking systems. Nationally determined regulatory structures had the effect of countries' banking systems acting as oligopolies. Independently of whether or not it was the intention of national authorities, the effect of national regulatory structures was to protect banks from foreign competition. Now, however, any country's banking system will not be closed to banks from other member countries. Thus, there is the expectation that under the threat of increased competition banks throughout the EU will become more efficient. Progress towards the completion of the internal financial market may provide an incentive for banks to merge or to seek expansion through acquisitions or the establishment of an increasing number of branches. It is difficult to predict whether mergers and acquisitions will occur to a significant extent following the removal of restrictions on cross-border financial activities by banks. It will largely depend on whether economies of scale exist. The available empirical evidence does not provide unambiguous support to the hypothesis that mergers and acquisitions will yield benefits in terms of economies of scale.

It has been suggested that one of the effects of the Second Banking Coordination Directive may be to favour the expansion of universal banking, which allows banks to engage in a wide range of activities and feature prominently in securities markets. Banks that are permitted to compete across a wide variety of transactions are likely to enjoy a competitive advantage over banks that are restricted to deposit taking and commercial lending. UK banks are an example of the latter, while German banks are an example of universal banks. According to the Second Banking Coordination Directive, banks are allowed to engage only in the activities for which they have home authorisation. In other words, German banks can engage in all the activities for which they have secured the approval of the German authorities throughout the EU. On the other hand, British banks are not allowed to engage in activities other than those which they have authorisation to carry out in the UK. Whether and to what extent British banks will suffer a competitive disadvantage are issues that can not easily be assessed. Ultimately the survival of any bank will depend on its efficiency.

In brief, there now exists a legal framework consistent with the objective to create an integrated European banking sector. However, although competition among banks is certain to intensify it is difficult to predict how EU member countries' banking systems will evolve.

Further, the integration of national banking systems will not be completed until member countries' fiscal policies are harmonised.

Insurance

The prospects for an integrated EU market in insurance products in the foreseeable future are not as promising as in the case of banking. The adoption of a series of directives during the 1970s and 1980s has failed to generate a sustained momentum towards the integration of the EU member countries' insurance markets. The only exception is the trade in reinsurance services which has effectively been fully liberalised. Countries have erected complex legal structures that protect their domestic insurance markets from external competition. The UK operates the most liberal regime among the EU member countries. A variety of legal requirements has been employed to prevent, or at least minimise, competition by foreign insurance companies. For example, home country authorisation is not sufficient for insurance companies to trade in some EU member countries. The cost implied by the requirement of host country authorisation acts, in many cases, as a disincentive for foreign insurance companies to attempt to penetrate the insurance markets of these countries. Similarly, other EU member countries do not allow insurance contracts that do not involve the domestic currency. The barriers to cross-border insurance trade are usually justified in terms of consumer protection. Be that as it may, the complexity of the national legal structures that regulate national insurance markets and the significant differences among these structures combine to result in a series of obstacles to the process of creating an integrated EU insurance market.

A principal feature of the insurance industry is the heterogeneity of the services that it supplies. This feature partly explains why the process of integration has been so slow to develop. For example, there is the distinction between non-life insurance and life insurance and that between large and mass risks. The importance of such differences in the character of insurance services is reflected in the provisions of the directives that have been adopted. Thus the Second Non-Life Insurance Directive which came into force in 1990 enables insurance companies to operate freely within the EU in respect of large risks on the basis of the principle of home country regulation. On the other hand, the directive prescribes host country control for mass risks. There are similar differences in the provisions of the Second Life Assurance Directive. If an economic agent seeks life assurance from a company based in a country other than its location of residence, then the principle of home control applies. But if it is the insurance company that takes the initiative for the transaction, then the regulations in force in the country in which the economic agent resides apply.

Initiatives are under way to eliminate existing anomalies and introduce the principle of mutual recognition for all insurance services, as has already occurred in the case of the banking sector. The establishment of home country control and authorization as the basis for intra-EU trade in insurance products is a necessary condition for the creation of an integrated European insurance market.

Securities markets

The emergence of a European financial common market requires the development of an

EU-wide securities market. The Investment Services Directive, adopted in 1992 and due to come into force in 1996, provides the framework for the eventual creation of a single EU securities market. Prior to this directive a series of directives had been adopted aimed at the harmonisation of national rules seeking to protect investors, the improvement of market information and the easing of restrictions on the simultaneous listing of stocks on EU member countries' stock exchanges. However, there continued to exist significant impediments to the issuing and trading of securities across national markets. But pressures for harmonisation have been accumulating as a result of far-reaching technological improvements in communications, extensive product innovations and the radical deregulation of securities markets. The 1987 'Big Bang' in the UK, which involved a fundamental change in the structure of the Stock Exchange and was made possible by technological advances, had significant ripple effects throughout the EU, forcing other member countries to introduce reforms to protect their institutions' competitiveness. Member countries' fears over the potential erosion of competitiveness of their stock exchanges if trade were to be fully liberalised are a major reason for the slow progress achieved so far towards the integration of national securities markets.

The expectation now is that the adoption of the Investment Services Directive will weaken member countries' resistance to the objective of creating an internal securities market. The Directive rests on the same principles as the Second Banking Coordination Directive, that is, those of mutual recognition and home country control. The Directive establishes the right of investment firms to operate throughout the EU. They are obliged to notify the host country of their intention to trade in the domestic market, but do not need host country authorization. The supervision of these investment firms rests with the home country, but they have to provide information to the host country if they are required to do so. The directive covers a wide range of activities such as brokerage, dealing as principal, underwriting and market making. The directive is supplemented with the Capital Adequacy Directive which specifies minimum capital requirements for authorised securities firms. This directive also applies to the securities trading activities of banks. The process towards a single EU securities market is partly impeded by organisational differences in member countries' stock exchanges. On the one hand, there is the British Stock Exchange which functions on the basis of specialist dealers making markets in securities. The alternative model of organisation is that associated with the Paris Bourse, which involves economic agents submitting bid and offer prices which are then related to bid and offer prices by other economic agents so that transactions are effected. The differences between the two forms of organisation are significant enough to raise the question as to which one is the more efficient. The British Stock Exchange has dominated trade in securities. This, however, is not necessarily only a reflection of its relative efficiency. It is partly the outcome of London being an international financial centre. But if, for example, the future European Central Bank were to be located in, say, Frankfurt, London's position in the financial world would be seriously undermined. In that event, it would not be surprising if the British Stock Exchange were to lose at least some of its international prominence. In other words, the fact that the British Stock Exchange occupies a leading position is not sufficient evidence that its organisational form is necessarily more efficient than alternative arrangements for trading in securities. The Investment Services Directive is agnostic as to the relative efficiency of alternative forms of organisation, with its provisions being neutral vis-à-vis the different models of securities trading currently in place in EU member countries.

Conclusions

The price differences for similar financial products among EU member countries, employed in the estimation of the potential gains to be reaped through the creation of the European financial common market, are a measure of the degree of fragmentation of the EU financial sector. Although it is not realistic to expect that the prices of financial services will converge towards the average of the lowest four prices for each service, and the projected benefits of price convergence are therefore not likely to be as large as predicted, there can be no doubt that the opening of member countries' financial markets will yield significant benefits. EU member countries' financial sectors will inevitably be exposed to greater competitive pressures as trade in financial products across national borders increases and as domestic financial markets are penetrated by other member countries' financial institutions. There may also be gains through the exploitation of economies of scale, with financial institutions either merging or acquiring other financial firms. However, the process of financial integration is likely to be slow. The various measures that have already been introduced are not sufficient to induce the acceleration of the pace of financial integration. The removal of barriers to the trade in financial services is necessary but not sufficient to accelerate the creation of the internal financial market. With the exception of a few financial products, fully integrated markets for most services cannot be expected in the foreseeable future. This is not to minimise the importance of the directives that have been adopted in respect of the various sub-sectors of the financial industry. What it does imply is that the establishment of mutual recognition and home country control for supervisory purposes, although necessary, is not sufficient for progress to be made towards the completion of the internal financial market.

As emphasized, only with the complete monetary integration of the EU through the replacement of member countries' currencies with a single European currency will the creation of the financial common market be feasible. However, the prospects for the full implementation of the Maastricht Treaty are not as promising as they were at the time of the signing of the Treaty. The 1992 and 1993 crises of the European Monetary System cannot be explained simply in economic terms. The foreign exchange market turmoil largely reflected a crisis of confidence in member countries' political commitment to the objective of monetary unification. In the circumstances, the most probable outcome is the emergence of a 'two-speed' Europe. If that were to occur, the peripheral countries would at least occasionally be under pressure to reintroduce capital controls. Such impediments to the free movement of capital, especially if measures were taken to ensure their effectiveness, would reverse the process of financial integration across the EU. It can therefore be concluded that whether or not a European financial common market is created will ultimately depend on member countries' political commitment to proceeding with the full implementation of the Maastricht Treaty.

Further reading

Emerson M 1988 *The Economics of 1992*, Oxford University Press.
Henderson R 1993 *European Finance*, McGraw-Hill, London.

CHAPTER 6

The budget of the European Union

Keith Penketh

Introduction

Membership of an economic community requires the acceptance of a financial obligation to fund the objectives of the organisation, whether they consist of the limited objectives of a regional trading group or the more extensive objectives of an economic union. Clearly, the expenditures undertaken by a regional trading regime require a lower level of funding than those of an organisation that adopts positive policies which add to the range of expenditures. Conversely, the benefits which accrue from a fully-fledged economic union are by definition more numerous than those which result from membership of a regional trading group. Failure to benefit from some union policies need not preclude membership if advantages accrue from other union policies. In terms of funding, however, policies are not equally weighted. It is clear that certain policies have a limited call on union expenditure, while other policies are a heavy burden on expenditure. The discriminatory trading practices of the EU provide an illustration of this. One may contrast the effects upon the budget of the trade policy of the EU with respect to manufactured goods and to agricultural products. The former is basically a source of revenue, while the latter is overwhelmingly a source of expenditure. Consequently, different policies have different effects on the EU budget, and therefore on the implications of the budget for member states.

The principal item of budgetary expenditure has been agriculture. The proportion of the budget absorbed by EAGGF (Guarantee) expenditure was 58.6 per cent of total expenditure in 1991. Expenditure related to agriculture, while officially justified according to a number of criteria (Coleman 1983), is certainly protectionist in effect. One reason for the predominance of agriculture in EU total expenditure is simply the size and nature of the EU budget relative to member states' budgets. In 1991 the EU budget was around 4 per cent of the value of member states' budgets, and the EU budget encompassed a much narrower range of expenditures than national budgets. Because of the substantial omission from the EU budget of expenditure on social security, law and order, education and defence, other items of expenditure within the EU budget are naturally highlighted when comparisons are made. However, matters are set to change (see Table 6.2 below).

The EU budget is not a device for fiscal fine-tuning. Article 199 of the Treaty of Rome specifies that EU expenditure and revenue should be in balance. Naturally shortfalls and overruns occur when one year is compared with the next. A shortfall in one year is, however, matched by increased revenue in another to rectify any imbalance in the previous year. This is not to suggest that, because the budget is not used for fine tuning, it is devoid of fiscal impact. The saving and production propensities of those who are taxed and those who are recipients of EU expenditure are unlikely to be the same. Therefore the EU budget will have implications for the allocation of resources in the member states. Moreover, the principle of *juste retour* does not pervade the budget. This principle, which seeks to balance a nation's contributions to and receipts from the budget, is not in evidence. Some members are in a net surplus position whilst others are in net deficit. There is fiscal impact on an inter-country basis and in aggregate the impact of the budget is probably positive, but is likely to be small. In terms of the 1991 budget the relative significance of items of expenditure and revenue is given in Table 6.1.

Table 6.1 Payments made by sector and actual own resources, 1991

Structure of payments: main areas (%)		Actual own resources (%)	
EAGGF (guarantee)	58.6	VAT resources	59.4
Structural operations	25.8	Customs duties	24.1
Administration	4.7	GNP-based resources	14.1
Cooperation	4.1	Agricultural levies	3.1
Research	2.9	Sugar and isoglucose levies	2.2
Repayments	2.5	Costs incurred in collecting own resources	–2.9
Other	1.4		

Source : Adapted from Official Journal C330 Volume 35, 15 December 1992. Court of Auditors: Annual Report concerning the Financial Year 1991

The principal problems of the EU budget

There are a range of problems that allegedly beset the EU budget. Some of them are related to the expenditure side of the budget, others to the revenue side. Indeed, a glance at an annual report of the Court of Auditors of the EU would reveal that in practice there are dozens of problems relating to the budget. Here the focus is simply on some of the major issues. Four major problems have affected the EU budget over the past 20 years: budgetary procedure, an alleged imbalance between budgetary appropriations, concern about the adequacy of the budget, and the redistributive aspect of the budget.

Budgetary procedure

Prior to 1975, power over the budget was vested solely in the Council of Ministers. This avoided conflict between the various institutions of the EEC. In 1975, under Article 203 of the Treaty of Rome, budgetary power was shared between the Council and the European Parliament. Parliament was given the right to reject the draft budget, and to have the last say, subject to a constraint, on non-compulsory expenditure. Expenditure was divided between 'compulsory' expenditure and 'non-compulsory' expenditure. The former consisted of 'expenditure necessarily resulting from the Treaty' and related mainly to agricultural expenditure and expenditure on third countries; the latter principally covered the structural funds. Parliament had the authority to increase non-compulsory expenditure by up to one half of the 'maximum rate'. This 'maximum rate' was the arithmetic mean of: (*a*) the trend of GNP of EU countries; (*b*) the average rise in member states' budgets; (*c*) the trend in the cost of living.

The years from 1975 to 1988 were marked by conflicts between Parliament and the Council. However, the Brussels Inter-Institutional Agreement of 1988 secured a financial perspective for the period 1988–1992 between Parliament, the Council and the Commission. Expenditure ceilings established in the perspective were agreed as binding. However, Section B.8 of the perspective states that 'any revision of the compulsory expenditure figure will not cause the amount of non-compulsory expenditure to be reduced'.

At the Edinburgh European Council of December 1992, ceilings were placed on expenditures between 1993 and 1999. Such ceilings related not only to commitments but also to payments. They applied not only to the total budget, but also to particular funds for the major policies of the EU. The financial perspective 1993–1999 gives much more detail than was hitherto customary. Doubtless, in so doing an attempt has been made to secure the budget against revisions. The success of this strategy can only be judged with hindsight.

Imbalance of expenditure on EU policies

A glance at the detail of EU policies would reveal that appropriations were allocated to a considerable number of schemes, with many of which the lay person may not be familiar. There is, for instance, the Ouverture scheme to assist local authorities in less favoured areas of the EU to establish contacts and exchange information and experience with countries in Central and Eastern Europe. There are also various schemes such as Retex, which is a EU initiative to assist the conversion of areas affected by decline in the textile industry, and a variety of programmes and policies with acronyms such as TEMPUS, COMETT, IMPS and NOW which indicate that the EU seems to be willing to finance an endless stream of projects. But for the most part, the EU's expenditure is concerned with agriculture and the structural funds. It is the balance of expenditure between these two funds which is usually in question.

The structural funds are taken to embrace the EAGGF (Guidance) Fund, the European Social Fund (ESF) and the European Regional Development Fund (ERDF). Since 1993 the Cohesion fund has usually been included among them. The SEA pointed towards a need to revise the structural funds and this was undertaken in 1988, in Brussels, at a meeting of the European Council. This Brussels Agreement, as it is often called, proved to be a major development in the budgetary procedures of the EU. Five objectives were targeted in these reforms. These were to:

1.   promote the development of regions whose development is lagging behind;

2.   assist areas in industrial decline;

3.   combat long-term unemployment;

4.   facilitate occupational integration;

5.   speed up the adjustment and development of rural areas.

Certainly this targeting of objectives was one of the reasons for the shift in the balance of budgetary expenditure. There were, however, other reasons. The appearance of a budget which was in the 1980s so heavily biased towards agricultural expenditure, especially EAGGF (Guarantee) expenditure, gave an overt indication that in essence the EU was primarily about agricultural protection. Reduced emphasis on agricultural expenditure would help to make the EU a more acceptable world partner. Futhermore, the excess of agricultural output, which in the EU was principally a consequence of the financing of agricultural policy, was not an acceptable outcome in the long run.

Additionally, there is and was a need for the EU to address the principal macro-economic problem facing members in the late 1980s, namely the problem of recession. It is to some of the consequences of the recession that the structural funds are directed, and hence it was quite natural to seek their expansion. Again, partly as a consequence of the Maastricht Treaty and the provisions for monetary integration contained therein, assistance towards the convergence of the four poorest members of the EU was provided and indicated in the financial perspective agreed by the European Council at the Edinburgh summit in 1992.

Included in the financial perspective of 1993 at the level of ECU 1500 m., the Cohesion Fund is to expand to ECU 2600 m. by 1999. Greece, Ireland, Portugal and Spain are the beneficiaries of the fund, which became operational only after the Maastricht Treaty was ratified. The fund, which is conditional in use, has been introduced to provide a financial contribution to projects in the field of trans-European networks, especially transport infrastructure. The balance of the budget arising from the Brussels inter-institutional agreement of 1988, and also from the provisions of the Edinburgh decisions on the financial perspective of 1992, is given in Table 6.2.

Table 6.2 Balance of EU Budget 1987–1999[1] (ECU m.)

	1987	1988	1989	1990	1991	1993	1994	1995	1996	1997	1998	1999
EAGGF (Guarantee)	2 2951.8	2 6389.6	2 4460.4	2 4979.5	3 1527.8	3 5230	3 5095	3 5722	3 6364	3 7023	3 7697	3 8389
% of total	65	63.9	59.5	57.7	58.6	53.5	52.4	51.7	51.0	49.7	48.8	47.9
Structural funds[2]	6 449.0	7 101.8	8 501.4	10 368.11	3 857.72	12 77	21 885	23 480	24 990	26 526	28 240	30 000
% of total	18.3	17.2	20.7	23.9	25.8	32.2	32.6	33.9	35.0	35.6	36.5	37.4
Grand total budget	35 324.4	41 279	41 131	43 324.8	53 796.6	65 908	67 036	69 150	71 290	74 491	77 249	80 114

[1]   1987–1991 Annual payments (Official Journal C330 Annual Report covering Financial Year 1991)
      1993–1999 Financial perspective (Edinburgh European Council December 1992)
[2]   After 1993 includes the Cohesion Funds

The adequacy of the budget

Prior to 1987 successive overruns in the budget occurred largely because EAGGF (Guarantee) expenditure ran ahead of agricultural appropriations. Indeed, in each year from 1983 to 1987, actual expenditure exceeded the estimates. However, the growth in total expenditure was not solely the result of these agricultural excesses. The expansion of the structural funds, the introduction of new policies (research, fisheries, the Integrated Mediterranean Programme (IMP)) and the introduction of new members in the 1980s placed additional calls on expenditure. Since 1987 expenditure has kept within the budget. A major contributory factor has been the strengthening of the US dollar, which raised the non-dollar prices of agricultural output and reduced the amount by which agricultural stocks had to be depreciated to make them competitive in world markets. However, the agreements made in the European Council meeting in Brussels in 1988 also had an effect on the containment of agricultural expenditure (Shackleton 1990).

The EU has introduced a variety of measures on the revenue side of the budget to meet the growing demand for funds, not only because of the growth of policies under the EU umbrella, but also because of the expansion of funding required for existing policies.

Before 1971, contributions to the EU budget were based on relative GDP. In 1971 the 'own resources' system of earmarking specific taxes was adopted. Indeed, the meaning of 'own resources' has changed somewhat since the early attempts to identify tax bases appropriate for EU usage. Originally tax revenues which were identified more with EU as opposed to national policies were earmarked for EU use. Hence customs duties and agricultural and sugar levies were transferred to the EU. The customs duty source of revenue arose from the adoption of the CET. Agricultural levies arose from the adoption of the CAP. Revenue from VAT limited to a 1 per cent rate of VAT on a common base was also transferred to the EU. The VAT was pre-eminently an EU tax, and new members were obliged to adopt this particular indirect tax. However, as intra-EU trade in manufactures expanded relative to extra-trade, and as tariff rates were reduced under the auspices of GATT, and because the EEC moved towards self-sufficiency in agricultural products, revenue from customs duties and agricultural levies was hardly buoyant. Unfortunately, shrinkage of revenue from these sources was not compensated by growth of revenue from the notional 1 per cent VAT on a common base, because consumption expenditure accounted for a declining share of the GNP of the EU.

It has been claimed that 'the budgetary problem of the Community arose because there was a ceiling on income but not expenditure' (Hill 1984). A number of proposals at both the unofficial and the official level were made to overcome the shortage of finance. As the issue of changes in tax bases and tax rates is by no means over, it appears appropriate to comment on some of the principal proposals.

Proposals have been made which relate to earmarking all, or a proportion of revenue from specific consumption goods (e.g. Denton 1983). Taxes on cigarettes or alcohol or even oil imports have been proposed. Inter-country contributions to revenue based on this kind of proposal would seem to be somewhat arbitary and based on inter-country differences in smoking and drinking. An EU-wide tax on oil imports would obviously favour the UK. Another proposal suggested relating budgetary contributions to the degree to which countries contributed to agricultural surpluses. This was not pursued when it was realised that quite small countries such as Ireland could become significant contributors. A further proposal relating to the expenditure side of the budget came from the Centre of Economic Policy Studies (Spaventa 1986). This was to segment the budget into a EAGF (Guarantee section) part and another part. Resources available for the guarantee were to be strictly limited, with the rest of the budget insulated from imbalance in the agricultural budget.

However, at Stuttgart in 1983 the so-called Stuttgart Mandate was issued calling for a brake on agricultural expenditure. Later in the year, however, a programme for the 'rationalisation of agriculture' was put forward by the Commission containing proposals for the extension of the guarantee threshold principle, supplementary levies, and a product approach to price fixing.

It was at Fontainebleau in 1984 that agreement was reached by the Council of Ministers to expand the resources available to the EU by enhancing the traditional 'own resources'. This was to be done by raising the VAT ceiling from 1 per cent to 1.4 per cent. In prospect at that time was a further enhancement of the ceiling to 1.6 per cent about the year 1988. This prospect was not to materialise. At Brussels in 1988 problems connected with the shortage of financial resources and the need to inject financial discipline into the budget resulted in a series of new measures. A ceiling was set on revenue between 1988 and 1992. This was established at 1.2 per cent of Community GNP by 1992, with intermediate ceilings prior to 1992. To keep below this ceiling it was agreed that the rate of growth of agricultural expenditure should be set at 74 per cent of the rate of growth of Community GNP. While agricultural production and agricultural expenditure are not always contained by regulations of this nature, attempts were made to stabilise agricultural expenditure by introducing production thresholds for produce within which the price guarantees apply. However, beyond these thresholds extra co-responsibility levies are introduced to avoid breaching of the expenditure targets set in the budget. If this does not result in the meeting of expenditure targets, then a cut of 3 per cent is applied to the minimum guaranteed price the following year. As the amounts devoted to agricultural appropriations shrink as a proportion of the total budget between 1993 and 1999 (see Table 6.2), it is to be expected that these agricultural stabilisers will be extended to ensure the realisation of objectives.

Additionally in agriculture, a 'set-aside' scheme was instituted whereby farmers received compensation for taking arable land out of production. Finally, outside the normal budgetary provision a reserve was to be established to finance agricultural expenditure resulting from a significant and unexpected fall in the value of the dollar. The reserve is formally called the 'EAGGF monetary reserve'. To contend with the consequences for financing the CAP when the US dollar depreciates in terms of the ECU, a provisional appropriation of ECU 1000 m. is entered. Introduced by the European Council at Brussels in 1988, the scheme for this monetary reserve was continued at Edinburgh in 1993. Here is an attempt to insulate the rest of the agricultural budget from that aspect of it which occasions expenditure largely beyond the control of the EU itself.

There is no doubt that the Brussels Agreement provided for a significant 25 per cent expansion in the resources available to the EU. Probably a notional VAT contribution of around 1.9 per cent would have been required to produce an equivalent rise in resources. It is unlikely that this rate would have been acceptable to all members.

The Edinburgh European Council of December 1992 reduced the own-resources ceiling prepared by the Commission, the so-called 'Delors II package', from 1.22 per cent of Community GNP to 1.20 per cent in 1993. The reduction for 1997 was from 1.37 per cent to 1.24 per cent, but by 1999 the limit stands at 1.27 per cent of GNP (Shackleton 1993).

To meet any deficiency of traditional own resources below the specified ceiling, a new category of revenue (a fourth resource) was introduced in 1988. This was based on the relationship between a member's GNP and the combined GNPs of all the member countries.

There appears to be little enthusiasm for the introduction of a fifth resource at the present time, in either the Council or the Commission. However, the Select Committee of the House of Lords on the European Communities 1992 reports the European Parliament's proposal of a Community Tax 'to free the Community from its paralysing dependency on national Member States' revenue'.

In 1989 the description attached to own resources was changed. They are regarded as 'tax revenue allocated once and for all to the Community to finance its budget and accruing to it automatically without the need for any subsequent decision by the national authorities' (Commission EC 1989b). In fact this implies that any tax base may be used as part of own resources. The structure of own resources implied by 'once and for all' appears to resolve the future flexibility of revenue to meet changing circumstances, although it opens up considerable potential for dispute, as it implies that part of the revenue from income tax, for instance, could be designated as 'own resources'.

The redistributive aspect of the budget

Given that the EU is committed to economic convergence, it would seem inconsistent if economic divergence was reinforced rather than reduced as a result of the operation of the budget. Initially almost the entire focus of the budget was on matters of resource allocation. Equity was not an issue that was given serious consideration. However, it was realised that on the accession of the UK to the EU a disproportionate financing burden would fall on that country.

For the UK throughout the 1970s gross contributions were high relative to economic prosperity. There were three reasons for this. Firstly, the UK's extra-EU import trade was high and hence dutiable imports were high. Secondly, extra-EU agricultural imports were also relatively high. Thirdly, UK contributions coming from the application of the 1 per cent VAT rate were also large, because of the significance of consumption expenditure to GNP within the UK.

In 1975 a 'financial mechanism' was introduced providing for refunds of excessive gross contributions. The conditions established as a qualification for a refund were somewhat restrictive, however, and no refund was secured through this mechanism prior to 1980. The situation for the UK would have been rendered more acceptable if high gross contributions had been offset by high gross receipts. This was not the case for the UK, where the amount of agricultural production qualifying for EAGGF (Guarantee) expenditure was relatively small. Hence high contributions were only partly offset because receipts were comparatively low.

The effect was to make the UK the second largest net contributor to the budget in the 1980s. Agreements to secure refunds were obtained covering the years 1981–1983, but a more permanent solution was sought. However, the UK was given a larger budget share in the Regional and Social Funds. Hence the emphasis was on an expenditure solution to the UK's budgetary problems. Given the limited nature of the regional and social funds relative to the agricultural budget, the benefits could not be substantial.

In an attempt to resolve the problem of equity and efficiency, the Spinelli Report, commissioned by the European Parliament, was published in 1980. The report proposed that a progressive element could be applied to contributions. One part would be based on GDP per capita relative to the EC average; the other part would be based on an index of population. Countries with relatively low per capita incomes and also relatively low populations would benefit. Although the report did not propose radical changes in contributions, it was never adopted. There is no doubt that there are common features in the Spinelli Report and the Brussels Agreement which was adopted eight years later.

The Fontainebleau Agreement of 1984, in addition to enhancing the resources of the EU by increasing the VAT ceiling to 1.4 per cent, addressed the issue of equity in relation to the UK's net contribution (see Denton 1983). Here it is useful to distinguish between the 'allocated' expenditure of the EU budget and the 'non-allocated' expenditure. Allocated expenditure is that which can be identified as being used for the benefit of a particular country within the EU. Conversely, non-allocated expenditure cannot be identified as earmarked for the use of a particular member. The EAGGF Guarantee and Guidance expenditure can be allocated, but administrative expenditure on the institutions of the EU, or aid to Third World countries cannot be allocated to particular EU members. Hence the net contribution that a country makes to the EU budget is simply the difference between total financial contributions and total allocated expenditure. Thus it is possible to compare a country's relative contribution to the EU budget with its share in allocated expenditures. The introduction of a mechanism for refunding the UK for the gap which existed between payments by the UK of own resources to the EU budget and allocated receipts was an innovation of Fontainebleau. It was to be financed by those countries that received more from the budget than they paid into it. In the event the gap was not measured by relative own resources and allocated EU expenditures, but by relative VAT payments and allocated EU expenditures. This had the effect of reducing the gap for the UK.

The significance of omitting levies in respect of trade with third countries under CAP and customs duties from the calculation of the UK abatement can be evaluated with reference to Table 6.3. In both cases, the UK is towards the top of the rankings. Had the full complement of own resources been included in the evaluation of the amount to be allocated to the UK for abatement, the UK abatement would have been larger.

Table 6.3 Levies paid under CAP and customs duties 1992

Country	Agricultural levies		Customs duties	
	Payment (ECU m.)	Rank	Payment (ECU m.)	Rank
Belgium	60.0	7	976.0	6
Denmark	5.5	10	300.0	8
France	67.0	8	1 838.0	3
Germany	163.4	4	4 501.4	1
Greece	19.0	9	239.6	9
Ireland	1.5	11	176.3	10
Italy	276.0	1	1 300.0	5
Luxembourg	–	12	16.6	12
Netherlands	132.2	6	1 600.0	4
Portugal	160.0	5	169.1	11
Spain	200.0	2	744.2	7
United Kingdom	170.0	3	2 720.0	2

Source : Official Journal of the European Communities; Legislation L31 Vol. 36, 8 February 1993

Two-thirds of the gap was to be refunded to the UK. The adjustment mechanism was a lowering of the VAT-based payment for the UK, but in order to finance this an upward adjustment in VAT payments from the net beneficiaries was proposed. However, the main contributor to the EU budget, Germany, was unwilling to finance a full contribution towards the adjustment for the UK. Germany was therefore given a one-third reduction towards the compensation necessary for the UK. *Ad hoc* arrangements of this nature are far from a rational approach to planning an appropriate budget.

The figures of net contributions to the EU cannot be accepted without question. There are three basic reasons why these figures should not be used without qualification. Two of the reasons cast doubt on the significance of figures in the budget, while the third throws suspicion on the use of the budget as the sole appropriate measure of burden or benefit.

Firstly there is the so-called 'Rotterdam–Antwerp effect'. Goods imported into EU countries other than the Netherlands and Belgium are often imported through the ports of Rotterdam and Antwerp. Import duties collected by the Netherlands and Belgium are counted as part of their gross contribution. The burden of the import duty is of course borne by the consumer of the tariff-laden import. If this is in a country other than the Netherlands and Belgium then the burden borne by its consumers is not reflected in its gross contributions. This implies that the gross contributions of the Netherlands and Belgium overstate the financial burden while the gross contribution of Germany, for example, understates the financial burden.

Secondly, an effect may arise in the recording of gross receipts to the EU budget. Under the CAP, export subsidies are given to bring EU prices down to world prices. But produce may be routed through an EU country other than that where it was produced and the export rebate claimed in the second country. The refund is counted as part of the gross receipts of the second country even though it is the first country that benefits. This is sometimes described as the reverse Rotterdam–Antwerp effect. There is no mechanism to ensure that the benefit will exactly offset the losses for any particular country. Certain countries will be net gainers, others net losers, while others such as the UK will hardly be touched by these two effects.

Thirdly, there are gains and losses that arise outside the budget. These occur because of the existence of EU policies. Consider, for instance, EU countries that export agricultural produce to other EU countries. They do so at prices fixed under CAP. These are normally above world prices. If such exports went outside the EU they would receive funds from the EU budget. None the less, there is a benefit to those countries that are not exporters of agricultural produce to other EU countries. The benefit arises because the price of agricultural products is artificially raised by the effects of the CAP. The consumers of agricultural produce in net importing countries finance this benefit. In relation to agriculture one could draw up an 'economic' budget. The cost or benefit is the volume of net imports or exports multiplied by the difference between EU prices and world prices. Member states such as France, Denmark, the Netherlands and Ireland make significant trading gains, whereas the UK is in significant deficit on intra-EU trade in agriculture, and therefore suffers losses from this trade in agricultural produce.

It is also alleged that those countries that are in surplus in relation to intra-EU trade in manufactures have also gained from the customs union effect. Hence a manufacturing budget and an agricultural budget can be devised and used in conjunction with a financial budget. As the market in manufactures enjoys less protection than the market in agricultural produce, it does not appear unreasonable to focus on intra-EU trade in agricultural produce when a financial budget and an economic budget are considered. At an official level however it is solely the financial budget which is at issue in the determination of the net amount to be assigned to gainers or losers.

The Brussels Agreement of 1988 (Commission EC 1989a and b) marked the next stage in the reorganisation of the EU finances. Recall that a ceiling rising in 1992 to 1.2 per cent of total Community GDP was established. This measure provided in part the financial discipline which was lacking in the budgets of earlier years. It certainly permits a rise of almost 100 per cent in the structural funds, and should especially benefit the Southern European members of the EU. With regard to the redistributive mechanism, the VAT contribution rate of 1.4 per cent was sustained. To assist those countries whose consumption proportion in GNP tended to be high, the VAT base was to be capped at 55 per cent of the GNP (at market prices). It was the introduction of the new fourth resource that clearly injected the principle of ability to pay across all countries. Where traditional own resources are inadequate to meet the new expenditure ceiling, the fourth resource comes into operation. It is a variable topping-up resource to meet the expenditure ceiling. It is levied on countries in the proportion that their GNP bears to EU GNP. It is thus not linked to any specific existing tax within the EU. In 1989, for instance, extra revenue equivalent to 0.0675 per cent of total Community GNP was financed in this way. While this is a further step in the direction of equity, it does not of itself avoid the inequities arising from the payment of other own resources, and consequently rebates for the UK are still needed. Because the UK clearly benefited from the capping of VAT and the introduction of the new fourth resource, the basic amount to which the UK was entitled was to be adjusted to a 'reference compensation amount'. This is basically the difference in the amounts payable under the new budgetary arrangements and under the old scheme. Under the new scheme the UK received a smaller adjustment than under the earlier scheme.

The Edinburgh Council in December 1992 also addressed the issue of the UK abatement. Although it was unanimously approved when introduced at the Fontainebleau summit in 1984, there is certainly evidence of opposition to the British view that the EU budget placed an undue burden on the UK. Hence Møller (1982) claimed 'that if each individual country wanted a "*juste retour*", any attempt to work together in the Community system would be impossible'. Several years later the EU countries are still working together. However, opposition to the UK abatement in 1992 was registered by six member countries of the EU at the Edinburgh European Council. The value of the abatement to the UK was around £2 bn. An attempt to reduce the size of the abatement was discussed by the Commission.

It had been suggested that payments to the Cohesion Fund by the UK should be withdrawn from the calculation of the UK abatement. Additionally, a Commission proposal that in all cases qualified majority voting should apply to all proposals of the Council was put forward. However, the UK Prime Minister, John Major, assumed the Presidency of the Council in 1992. Approval was not secured for these proposals. Unanimity is still required for budgetary changes within the EU.

The meeting of the Edinburgh Council nevertheless introduced some important changes in the way the EU was to be financed. The attempt to make the own-resources system less regressive merits particular attention. The issue of contributive capacity was highlighted especially in two measures which affected the VAT-based resource. Firstly, the notional VAT base was capped at 50 per cent of GNP rather than 55 per cent of GNP. Secondly, the uniform VAT rate applying was reduced from 1.4 per cent to 1 per cent, with increased reliance placed on the new fourth resource. It was claimed that these changes would reduce the VAT element from 55 per cent to 35 per cent of own resources. While some richer as well as poorer members of the EU are likely to benefit from these proposals, the UK was precluded from benefiting from this switch as part of the abatement agreement.

Agreements secured at Brussels in 1988 and at Edinburgh in 1992 are milestones in the development of the EU budget, but these developments are hardly final. There are several factors which support a belief that structural adjustments in the EU budget are likely to continue. Firstly, a focus on net contributions to the EU budget reveals that the UK is not the only country with a problem (Table 6.4). The method used to calculate payments to member states changed between 1990 and 1991, making it difficult to effect a clear intertemporal comparison of payments made. The focus here is on the year 1990. A casual glance at Table 6.4 reveals that there is no close link between relative prosperity and net budgetary receipts.

Table 6.4 Budgetary receipts, payments and net contributions 1990 (ECU m.)

Country	Payments to member states	%	Rank order	Total own resources	%	Rank order	Net contribution (−) or net receipt (+)	Rank order
Belgium	989.8	2.7	11	1 726.7	4.1	7	−736.9	4
Denmark	1 197.6	3.2	9	855.8	2.0	8	+341.8	8
France	6 284.6	16.9	1	8 368.8	19.9	2	−2 084.2	3
Germany	4 807.0	12.9	4	10 949.2	26.0	1	−6142.0	1
Greece	3 033.8	8.1	6	551.3	1.3	9	+2 482.5	12
Ireland	2 260.7	6.1	8	363.6	0.9	11	+1 897.1	10
Italy	5 681.0	15.2	2	6 338.7	15.0	4	−657.7	5
Luxembourg	14.5	0.0	12	68.4	0.2	12	−53.9	6
Netherlands	2 983.6	8.0	7	2 652.1	6.3	6	+331.5	7
Portugal	1 103.2	3.0	10	499.2	1.2	10	+604.0	9
Spain	5 382.7	14.4	3	3 364.5	8.0	5	+2 018.2	11
UK	3 147.0	8.4	5	6 421.4	15.2	3	−3 274.0	2
EUR12	37 277.5	100		42 159.7	100			

Source: Official Journal of the European Communities C324 Vol. 34, 13 December 1991 (Diagram 11B, Payments to member states; Diagram 2, Total own resources)

Significantly, the two poorest members of the EU, namely Greece and Portugal, are not the countries that receive the largest amounts from the budget when net payments or receipts are evaluated on a per capita basis (see Table 6.5). Ireland, on a per capita basis, receives from the budget considerably more than Portugal, the poorest member of the EU. Further attempts to relate the budget more closely to ability to pay are to be expected in the future.

Table 6.5 Per capita national budgetary contributions to or receipts from the EU budget (negative amounts, net recipients; positive amounts, net contributors)

Country	Per capita amount (ECU)	Rank order
Belgium	−74.1	3
Denmark	+34.35	8
Germany	−77.635	2
Greece	+247.0	11
Spain	+51.8	9
France	−36.838	5
Ireland	+541.02	12
Italy	+11.42	6
Luxembourg	−142.0	1
Netherlands	+22.26	7
Portugal	+61.14	10
United Kingdom	−57.11	4

Source : Calculated from 1991 Basic Statistics of the EC

Secondly, the prospect for an increase in the size of the EU will have ramifications for the budget. The entry of some former EFTA members, who will inevitably be net contributors to the budget, may ultimately be followed by some Eastern European countries who will certainly be net beneficiaries. Thirdly, the progress of monetary integration in the EU and the consequential limitation on autonomous national macro-economic policies will undoubtedly give rise to more pressure for an enhancement of the structural funds compared to the EAGGF (Guarantee Fund).

Fourthly and finally, the Court of Auditors of the EU issues an annual report which draws attention to errors and irregularities in the management of Union finances. It is to be hoped that these will be effectively and adequately addressed especially as the size and complexity of the EU's operations expand. Additional appropriations are urgently required by the Court to permit it to undertake its duties effectively.

Conclusion

It is a feature of the financial perspective attached to the Brussels Agreement of 1988–1992 and the Edinburgh Council of 1992–1999 that more detailed control over expenditure has been secured. Additionally, the reorientation of EU policies should assist in the development of a more appropriate balance between budgetary appropriations. The finance of expenditure has moved more towards an ability-to-pay criterion, but the inequities that continue to exist await a more permanent solution.

References and further reading

Coleman D 1983 *Realities of Agricultural Policy*, Paper presented to Manchester Statistical Society.

Commission EC 1987 *Making a Success of the Single Act: a New Frontier for Europe*, COM (87), Brussels.

Commission EC 1989a *Community Public Finance – the Principal Reference Documents of the 1988 Financial Reform*, Office for the Official Publications of the EC, Luxembourg.

Commission EC 1989b *Community Public Finance – the European Budget after the 1988 Reform*, Part 3, Chapter 13, Community Revenue (1A), Office for the Official Publications of the EC, Luxembourg.

Commission EC 1992 Commission Communication, *The Communities' Finances between now and 1997*, 5201/2 COM (92) 2001 final, Brussels.

Commission EC 1989 *The Community Budget: the Facts in Figures*, Office for the Official Publications of the EC, Luxembourg.

Denton G 1983 *Budgetary Problems and Refund Mechanisms in Reform of CAP and Restructuring the EEC Budget*, UACES Secretariat.

Hill B E 1984 *Reform of the Common Agricultural Policy*, Methuen, London, EEC Series.

House of Lords 1992, Select Committee on the European Communities, *Commissions' Proposals for Community Finances 1992*, HMSO, London.

Official Journal of the European Communities C330, Vol. 35, 15 December 1992, Court of Auditors Annual Report concerning the Financial Year 1991.

Official Journal of the European Communities, Legislation L31, Vol. 36, 8 February 1993.

Møller O J 1982 *Member States and the European Community Budget*, Samfundsvidenskabeliet Forlae, Copenhagen.

Padoa-Schioppa T 1989 *Efficiency, Stability and Equity*, Oxford University Press.

Shackleton M 1990 *Financing the European Community*, Pinter, London.

Shackleton M 1993 *The European Community Budget*, Paper given at UACES Annual Conference.

Spaventa L 1986 *The Future of Community Finance*, Centre for European Policy Studies, Paper No. 30, Brussels.

Thompson I 1993 The European Community Budget, *European Access*, February.

Zangl P 1993 The Financing of the European Community after the Edinburgh European Council, *Intereconomics*, Vol. 28, No 3.

CHAPTER 7

The competition policy of the European Union

John Kemp

Introduction

This chapter surveys the status and workings of UK competition policy and explores the implications arising from the creation of the SEM. Initially, an economic rationale is presented for intervention in private industry, whether this is seen, primarily, as a policy to promote competition or as a corrective to monopoly abuse. The next section provides a brief discussion of the alternative policy approaches and the subsequent section provides a review of the development of UK legislation and policy. This is followed by a section outlining current European Union policy. Finally, an assessment is made of the effectiveness of current policy and, with the creation of the SEM, the important implications arising from the Treaty of Rome are considered in relation to the future direction of British policy and proposals for change.

An economic rationale for intervention

Democratic nations, whether they have governments of the right or the left, usually have well articulated policies towards intervention in private industry. Such policies are designed to promote the efficient allocation of resources through the encouragement of competition, which is seen as the active progenitor of economic efficiency and welfare. They are, likewise, employed to limit the losses in efficiency that can arise from the presence of elements of monopoly. It might be thought that such policies spring from a desire, on the one hand, to ensure the free flowering of individual enterprise and, on the other, to guard against the tyrannies of 'big business'. However, there is a clear underpinning economic rationale and consequently the broad thrust of policy is rarely ideologically contentious. Thus, where disagreement does arise it is usually of degree rather than of substance, and is more likely to concern the detailed application of policy as opposed to general principles. It is currently fashionable to talk of 'competition policy' where one formerly talked of 'monopoly' or 'anti-monopoly policy'. The fact that this is partly a semantic change reflects the existence of an underlying consensus. We turn now to examine the basis for this consensus.

Gains from trade

It is self-evident that when buyers and sellers come together in trade there is a gain to both parties. If this were not the case, there would simply be no reason for trade to take place. Economists have developed concepts for analysing these gains, which prove useful in assessing the relative efficiency of competitive and monopolistic situations.

Using these concepts, we initially identify the gains that arise from trade when a perfectly competitive market is in equilibrium, as illustrated in Figure 7.1. Here the intersection of supply and demand determines the quantity sold (Q) and the price paid (P). The total benefit is the sum of consumer and producer surpluses DAC of which APC goes to consumers and DPC to producers. Hence, there is a readily identifiable gain to both parties.

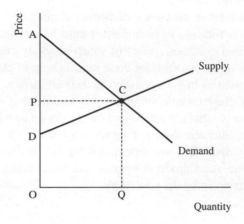

Figure 7.1 Surplus under perfect competition

Now there are many qualifications and points of fine detail surrounding the interpretation and use of these concepts of surplus, and these we have omitted from the foregoing argument.[1] For our purposes, it is sufficient to note that for the majority of economists, the use of these concepts of surplus is a legitimate way of analysing the benefits (and losses) that arise under differing competitive conditions. In the next sub-section we employ these tools to analyse the comparative efficiency of perfect competition and pure monopoly.

The relative efficiency of competition and monopoly

Before deriving the results of this section it is necessary to state clearly a number of underlying assumptions. If any one of these does not hold, then the results cannot be upheld. Hence, the propositions of this section apply only under the highly restrictive conditions now enumerated. Firstly, it is assumed that consumers are utility maximisers and, perhaps more contentiously, that producers are profit maximisers. It is assumed that the price paid and received does represent the value of the marginal unit traded both to the buyer and to the seller. Further, it is assumed that units of consumers' and producers' surplus can be added and subtracted, i.e. a unit of surplus represents the same quantity of benefit irrespective of whether it accrues to the buyer or seller.

Superscript numbers refer to notes that appear at the end of the chapter.

It is now assumed that the objective of policy is to maximise economic welfare, where economic welfare is equated with total surplus. Thus, in comparing alternative economic structures, the most efficient is defined as the one that generates the greatest total surplus, where that total surplus is the sum of consumers' and producers' surplus. It will be noted that this ignores altogether the important question of income distribution. As far as economic efficiency is concerned it is irrelevant whether surplus accrues to consumers or to producers. If a situation is deemed to be inequitable, then it is in principle possible to redistribute income according to some appropriate canon of equity. In other words if we 'bake the biggest cake' it should be possible to provide greater shares for all.[2] This is not to deny that questions of income distribution are important, but they do not concern us here, and so we restrict ourselves to 'baking the biggest cake'.

We now compare the relative efficiency of perfect competition and pure monopoly and demonstrate the inherent inefficiency of monopoly. It must be stressed that these represent two highly abstract and idealised extremes, neither of which remotely exists within the real world. However, the results that are generated from these models help to clarify our interpretation of real world markets, and assist us in the evaluation of their efficiency.

Purely for reasons of diagrammatic simplicity we assume that the perfectly competitive industry supply curve (Sc) is infinitely elastic and can be drawn as a horizontal straight line as in Figure 7.2a. This simplification does not in any way affect the qualitative nature of the results. Price (Pc) and output (Qc) are determined by the intersection of the supply and demand curves at C. There is no producer surplus, and total surplus is composed entirely of consumer surplus which is given by the area ACPc.

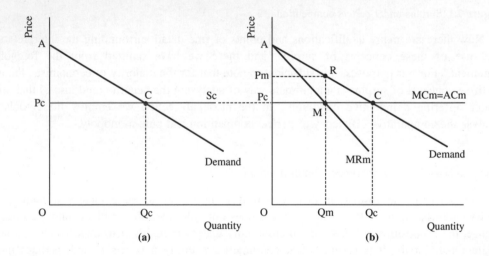

Figure 7.2 (a) Perfect competition, (b) pure monopoly

Suppose the industry is now monopolised with (unrealistically) no change in costs. That is, all productive units are merged into a single firm without any change in their numbers or their costs of production and, further, this newly created firm acts solely as a costless decision-making and coordinating mechanism for the activities of what were formerly the independent units. It follows that the supply curve (Sc) of Figure 7.2a becomes identical to the marginal cost curve (MCm) of the monopoly firm. As such it can be read horizontally across to Figure 7.2b. A consequence of the assumption of constant costs is that the monopolist's marginal costs are equal to average costs (ACm) as shown. There is no reason for consumers' tastes to have changed, and so the demand curve is unaffected. In Figure 7.2b we can observe the changes due to monopolisation. Faced with the downward sloping market demand curve, the monopoly producer will maximise profits by producing where marginal cost is equal to marginal revenue at M, output will be cut back to Qm and price will be raised to Pm. Consumer surplus is now reduced to area ARPm. Surplus of PmRMPc has been transferred from consumers to producers and total surplus has fallen to ARMPc. There is, therefore, a net loss of surplus of RCM. Thus, economic welfare has unambiguously been reduced. With the important proviso, 'other things equal', monopoly inevitably distorts resource allocation and is inefficient *vis-à-vis* perfect competition. This is the heart of the case against monopoly. It is not so much that those buyers who actually consume the Qm units are having to pay the higher price Pm for them, since the higher price represents the value to them of the marginal unit bought. Rather, it is that there exist people willing to pay prices lower than Pm, but which are in excess of the marginal costs of providing additional units. The existence of monopoly denies them that opportunity, and this is manifest in the inevitable reduction in total surplus. It is in this sense that monopoly is said to be economically inefficient, and to misallocate resources through the restriction of output. Economic welfare could be increased if more resources were channelled into this industry and production increased up to Qc with a consequent lowering of prices.

Now this is a very powerful result. It means that we can state quite categorically that the effect of monopolisation *per se* is to reduce economic welfare. We do not even need to be able to measure the somewhat esoteric concept of surplus, since it is always a one-way reduction. The qualitative effect is apparently unambiguous.

Unfortunately, things are never this simple. The result depends critically on the caveat that 'other things are equal'. This is seldom the case. In particular, following monopolisation costs are unlikely to remain unchanged, as we have so far assumed. Indeed, the argument is often advanced that mergers bring benefits through reducing costs of production because of the attainment of economies of scale. It is undeniable that large-scale production can be technically more efficient, and so following an analysis detailed by Williamson (1968) we need to consider how the previous result is affected if, after monopolisation, production takes place with lower costs.

In Figure 7.3 price and output under perfect competition are, as before, at Pc and Qc. Suppose now that under monopoly costs are lower, i.e. the supply curve of competition (Sc) shifts downwards to form the monopolist's marginal cost curve (MCm). The monopoly equilibrium now occurs where the MR curve intersects this lower MC curve at E (as opposed to M). Thus monopoly price and output become Pe and Qe. Output has fallen and price risen, but not by as much as in the case depicted in Figure 7.2. We can now evaluate the effects of this change in terms of the alteration in surplus.

Total surplus is now equal to AREG, of which ARPe is consumer surplus and PeREG is producer surplus. Compared with the competitive surplus of ACPc this change has been brought about by a loss of RCK, due to output restriction (i.e. monopolisation *per se*) and a creation of additional producer surplus of PcKEG, due to the ability of the enlarged monopolised firm to achieve lower costs. Area PeRKPc is simply a transfer from consumers to

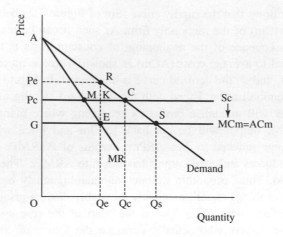

Figure 7.3 Pure economies of scale

producers and can therefore be ignored. Thus, whether or not total surplus under monopoly (AREG) is greater or less than (ACPc) under perfect competition depends on whether the gain (PcKEG) is greater than the loss (RCK). There is no *a priori* justification for stating which will be the dominant effect. On this matter economic theory is silent. The net effect will vary according to the cost conditions within the particular industry under consideration, and within the real world we might expect considerable variation from one industry to another. Indeed, empirical evidence on economies of scale across a large number of British industries suggests considerable diversity in their extent (e.g. Pratten 1971, Silberston 1972, HMSO 1978). Thus, on the basis of empirical evidence about the nature of costs it is not possible to make a definitive statement of the effects of monopoly. It should however be noted that while the analysis in this paragraph cautions against outright condemnation of monopoly and merger, the case against restrictive practices and collusive agreements is not weakened. This is because after agreements, unlike mergers, individual firms maintain their separate existence. It is therefore difficult to envisage how, under these circumstances, offsetting economies of scale could be attained without any rationalisation of productive units.

The analysis in the preceding paragraphs suggests that there is no theoretical justification for condemning monopoly and/or merger outright, since the ill-effects of output restriction could be more than offset by reductions in costs. Under such circumstances monopolisation would result in an increase in total surplus. Therefore, the policy suggestion that arises from theory is that in seeking to determine the effects of monopolisation it is necessary to weigh carefully the costs against the benefits, to examine the trade-off of one against the other. However, this raises an important practical issue. Earlier we noted that, in the absence of cost changes, it was not necessary to be able to actually measure the abstract concept of surplus in order to form the conclusion that monopoly would bring about a reduction in it. If now, with changes in costs, it is possible that surplus will be either increased or decreased, then it becomes of crucial importance to have some means of measurement. Clearly this might not be a task that can be undertaken with any great degree of precision. Yet if we are to pronounce on the desirability or otherwise of individual monopoly situations, or proposed mergers, this is clearly what is required to provide an unambiguous policy recommendation.

Some qualifications to the theoretical results

We have seen above that economic theory suggests, other things being equal, that monopoly leads to an inefficient allocation of resources in the sense that the level of output is restricted. There are a number of qualifications to this prediction, apart from the possibility of economies of scale discussed above. These are particularly important when considering the likely effects in the real world.

Firstly, the analysis is entirely static, ignoring changes that may take place over time. Thus, any demonstrated effects on surpluses may be exacerbated or ameliorated as the industry progresses, and so welfare losses which occur over time may cancel out immediate gains or vice versa. Further, this static analysis is cast in terms of certainty. Real firms have to make decisions within a climate of uncertainty, and market outcomes will differ according to their attitudes to risk.

Secondly, the competition of economic theory is cast solely in terms of price competition and narrowly defined profit maximisation. The foregoing analysis neglects the effects of firms' other competitive variables such as product quality, product range and product differentiation. Furthermore, if firms pursue objectives other than profit maximisation then the picture becomes even less clear-cut.[3] This is not the place to explore the many alternative theories of the firm, but it might be worth noting that, for example, the theory of sales revenue maximisation (Baumol 1959) assumes that managers pursue the objective of maximising revenue rather than profits. As a consequence, higher levels of output are predicted than under profit maximisation. The implication of this is that any policy proposal for a particular industry can be made only after an investigation of not only the structure of the industry, but also the objectives and conduct of the firms within it.

Thirdly, in economic theory it is presumed that any level of output is always produced at the lowest technically feasible cost. For the economist, inefficiency arises because the wrong level of output is produced. However, in the real world there is an additional concept of efficiency, which takes cognisance of the fact that real firms are never as technically efficient as the theorists' firm. This type of inefficiency arises because workers and management are often ill-equipped or lacking in motivation and so do not perform to the best of their abilities. Inefficiency of this sort, which involves a given level of output being produced at a cost which is higher than the theoretical minimum, is termed X-inefficiency. It is what management and business schools try to eradicate through education and training. It is what the average person understands by 'inefficiency'. Clearly such inefficiency is incompatible with perfect competition where the competitive threat would be sufficient to remove any less efficient firm. However, in monopoly markets X-inefficiency could arise, because of the absence of competitive discipline. This would seem to strengthen the case against monopoly, for now there is reason to believe that a movement towards monopoly could lead to higher costs through the creation of X-inefficiency. This would offset, to some extent, any cost reductions due to economies of scale. The net effect on costs is therefore unclear, for the picture is now becoming highly complex. It is, however, evident that it would be necessary to weigh carefully all the costs and benefits before any categoric policy recommendation could be made.[4]

Fourthly, the theoretical proscription of monopoly has been arrived at by comparing the two theoretical extremes of perfect competition and pure monopoly. In the real world there is never a movement from one to the other, and it is correspondingly less clear what the implications for both allocative and X-efficiency are. For example, if a merger takes place between two firms in an industry of ten firms, so moving the industry apparently closer to monopoly, it is not at all apparent, *a priori* (even in the absence of any economies of scale), what the effects on either type of efficiency will be. Again, it would seem that this matter could only be resolved after a detailed investigation of the particular industry in question.

Fifthly, even if there are undisputed economies of scale so that there is a net increase in surplus, it can still be argued that there is a social opportunity loss. Surplus could be increased further if the monopoly firm were required to produce where its marginal cost was equal to price. Thus in Figure 7.3 an administered move from equilibrium at E to S would lead to an output of Qs and price of G, with a further increase in total surplus to ASG.

Sixthly, and most importantly, the theoretical analysis that we have undertaken is entirely partial. That is, in considering the effects on one industry in isolation we have ignored any repercussions throughout industry as a whole. Thus, an individual merger might be seen to be totally innocuous, but if it is just one more merger among a spate, then the overall trend towards the monopolisation of industry in general may be worrying. It is rather like the problem of litter louts: one dropped piece of paper is harmless in itself, but the problem involves the total volume of litter!

Seventhly, Baumol *et al.* (1982) have argued that resources will be allocated efficiently (in the sense that prices will be equal to marginal costs) in industries which are perfectly contestable and that this result holds irrespective of the number of firms in the industry.[5] A perfectly contestable industry is one which, in addition to free entry, is characterised by completely free exit. Thus, in the absence of any costs of leaving the industry, there will always be the incentive to enter, compete any profits away and then get out quickly without cost. The only protection against this potential threat of competition is afforded by firms charging prices equal to marginal costs and earning only normal profit. The implication of all this is that large numbers of firms are not necessary to achieve economic efficiency, and so it is equally possible for oligopolies to attain an efficient allocation of resources. Thus, in this view, attention should be focused on the freeing of conditions of exit, rather than solely on encouraging actual competition from increasing numbers of firms. It is not possible to enter into this debate here, for as yet these ideas have not gained universal acceptance. However, we do need to note that they are posing an important challenge to the conventional wisdom on the circumstances of resource misallocation. They should therefore caution us against being overly dogmatic.

Finally, the Austrian school of economics puts a different interpretation on the existence of profit. Competition is seen as a process, with profit representing both the spur and the reward of enterprise. Thus profit is a symbol of success, encouraging innovation and progressiveness, rather than being symptomatic of resource misallocation. Accordingly, this requires recognition of the dynamics of industrial change, which are often obscured by reference solely to comparative theoretical equilibria, as in the neoclassical tradition. Consequently, subscribers to the Austrian tradition would be somewhat less inclined to an actively pro-interventionist stance.[6]

Ideally, all the above qualifications would need to be taken into account in any attempt to prescribe policy. The predictions of economic theory are not sufficiently clear-cut to permit us to proscribe monopoly outright. Theory does point to a clear suspicion that a lack of competition can, most certainly, lead to inefficiencies, but it also identifies possible benefits from the attainment of lower-cost production. An unambiguous policy recommendation would require evaluation of all these costs and benefits. Yet, given the qualifications noted above this is clearly a daunting task. There have been a number of attempts to establish empirically whether any general conclusions can be drawn on the extent of welfare losses throughout the economy due to the presence of monopoly. If these could be found to be overwhelmingly large or small then the results could be of use in the framing of policy. However, and not surprisingly, no general consensus has emerged and the conclusions are no less disparate than those of theory.[7]

Empirical evidence of monopoly welfare losses

A number of attempts have been made to estimate the magnitude of the losses due to the presence of monopoly in the economy as a whole. If a clear picture emerges, then this can be of assistance to policy makers. Unfortunately, as we shall see, the evidence is no less ambiguous than theory. In order to highlight the nature of the difficulties, we shall briefly consider some of these studies.

An early attempt was undertaken by Harberger (1954), who calculated that, for US manufacturing industry, the resultant welfare losses were only of the order of 0.1 per cent of GNP. This is clearly very small, and if it were generally representative then it would call into question the necessity for constructing any elaborate and costly policy to oversee monopoly, since the benefits gained would be unlikely to justify the costs of implementation. The way in which these estimates were obtained can be seen by reference to Figure 7.4.

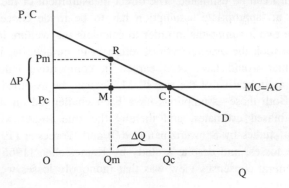

Figure 7.4 Welfare loss due to monopoly

In this figure the welfare loss is equivalent to the triangular area RCM. Thus, the size of this is given by:

$$D = \tfrac{1}{2}\Delta P \Delta Q \qquad\qquad [1]$$

where ΔP is the difference between Pc and Pm, and ΔQ is the difference between Qc and Qm. The distortion of the monopoly price from the competitive price or the price cost margin (M) is defined as

$$M = (Pm - Mc)/Pm \qquad\qquad [2]$$

but, since under perfect competition $P = MC$, equation [2] can be written as

$$M = (Pm - Pc)/Pm = \Delta P/Pm \qquad\qquad [2*]$$

The elasticity of demand at R is defined as

$$E = (\Delta Q/Qm)/(\Delta P/Pm) \qquad [3]$$

which on rearrangement gives

$$\Delta Q = (E/Pm)\Delta PQm \qquad [3*]$$

On substitution of equation [3*] into equation [1] and multiplication of the right-hand side by Pm/Pm (i.e. by unity)

$$D = \tfrac{1}{2}(\Delta P/Pm)^2 PmQmE \qquad [4]$$

or

$$D = \tfrac{1}{2}M^2 SE \qquad [4*]$$

which is negative (a loss), since with a downward sloping demand curve the elasticity of demand (E) is negative. Thus, the welfare losses are now computable in terms of (i) the level of sales revenue, S (i.e. PmQm); (ii) the rate of return M (i.e. $\Delta P/Pm$), which is the monopoly mark-up expressed as a ratio of the monopoly price; (iii) the elasticity of demand E. In principle, these are estimable magnitudes. The level of sales revenue is readily obtainable. Given constant average costs (for which there is considerable supportive evidence in manufacturing), it follows that marginal and average costs are equal. Hence, ΔP is the difference between price and average costs, since under perfect competition Pc = MC. Thus, industry rates of return can be estimated. The direct measurement of the elasticity of demand is not easy, and so an appropriate assumption has to be made concerning its magnitude. Harberger then made two assumptions in order to calculate the welfare losses for a sample of 2,046 firms. First, he took the *average* rate of return in manufacturing industry as typical of the rate of return that would have been earned in competitive industry, and then took deviations from this as indicative of the size of M. Second, he assumed that the elasticity of demand was unity. Both these assumptions have been challenged on the grounds that they create downwardly biased estimates, and thereby the true losses would be understated. However, subsequent studies by Schwartzman (1960) and Worcester (1973) also showed low estimates of welfare losses, and despite a study by Kamerschen (1966) showing somewhat higher losses, the general consensus view was that monopoly losses were typically not very high for the US economy.

More recently, as a result of further studies of both the US and the UK economies, this consensus has been challenged. Posner (1975) has suggested that in situations that are not perfectly competitive, firms engage in promotional activities and in attempts to create barriers to entry. To the extent that these activities raise firms' costs, it can be argued that they are wasteful and thus should be included as further elements of losses due to monopoly. If this is done then, clearly, much higher estimates of losses are obtained than those of Harberger. A difficulty is now apparent in that there is no clear criterion available for deciding everything that should or should not be included as elements of welfare loss. Inevitably decisions on what to include and what to leave out are based on the value judgements of the researcher, and on practical considerations involving the limitations of available data. Consequently, it should not be surprising to find disparate estimates. More recently, Cowling and Mueller (1978) have produced estimates based on UK as well as US data, which suggest that welfare losses amount to as much as one half of monopoly profits.

Consider equation [2*]:

$$M = (Pm - Pc)/Pm = \Delta P/Pm \qquad [2*]$$

With constant costs Pc = AC = MC, and on the assumption that firms maximise profits, it follows that firms equate MC and MR. Thus, MR can be substituted for Pc. Thus from [2*]

$$M = \Delta P/Pm = (Pm - MR)/Pm \qquad [5]$$

Further, it can be shown that

$$MR = P[1 + (1/E)] \qquad [6]$$

and on substitution of this into [5] and rearranging, we obtain

$$\Delta P/Pm = [Pm - Pm[1 + (1/E)]]/Pm \qquad [7]$$

which gives

$$\Delta P/Pm = 1/E \qquad [8]$$

and rearranging again

$$\Delta P = Pm/E \qquad [9]$$

Substitution of the elasticity of demand (equation [3]) into equation [9] gives

$$\Delta P = Pm[(\Delta Q/Qm)(\Delta P/Pm)] \qquad [10]$$

Whence, on substitution of equation [10] into equation [1] and cancelling terms, an expression for welfare loss is obtained

$$D = \tfrac{1}{2}\Delta PQm \qquad [11]$$

Equation [11] is Cowling and Mueller's expression for welfare loss. In equation [11] ΔPQm is the level of monopoly profit, and so according to them losses are equal to one half of monopoly profits. These losses appear to be around 10 per cent and 4 per cent of manufacturing output for the UK and the USA respectively, figures which are much higher than earlier estimates.

Cowling and Mueller's methodology has been criticised by Littlechild (1981), and their estimates may, arguably, be biased upwards. However, their results along with Posner's have helped to dispel the previously held consensus view that monopoly losses were generally relatively small. It seems that not only is theory ambiguous on the general effects of monopoly, but so is the empirical evidence. This lack of any general conclusion from both theory and empiricism gives support to the piecemeal or cost–benefit approach to monopoly policy, whereby individual industries are evaluated on their merits. However, even this has not been a view acceptable to all, as is discussed in the following section.

Alternative policy approaches

In the light of this ambiguity in the theoretical predictions, allied with a lack of any clear empirical consensus on the extent of these losses and benefits, the question arises as to what form a pro-competition or anti-monopoly policy should take. The clear implication would appear to be that an individual cost–benefit approach is appropriate, with each monopoly situation being judged on its own merits only after a careful weighing of the gains and losses. Such an approach comes closest to the spirit of the pragmatic investigatory stance taken within the UK, where the Monopolies and Mergers Commission and the Restrictive Practices Court pronounce on individual cases. However, this *ad hoc* procedure has not been without its critics, largely because of doubts about whether it is possible to perform the exercise with sufficient precision to arrive at a clear-cut evaluation.[8]

During the 1970s there was a vigorous debate surrounding the alternative approaches to UK policy. The issues raised are no less relevant to the formation of an appropriate EU policy, and so they are reviewed here. The main discussion and disagreements have centred around the appropriate policy for dealing with mergers. In the case of restrictive practices there is less contention. They are generally seen as anti-competitive and necessitating legislation to proscribe them, since they almost invariably create the detrimental effects of monopoly without engendering the benefits. In the case of single or dominant firm monopolies, while it is accepted that these may behave detrimentally to the public interest at large, few democratic governments have had, or are likely to have, the political will to intervene directly in their operation, particularly where their market positions have been legitimately attained and their activities are not overtly illegal. Usually the most that governments have been prepared to do has been to publicise their activities and/or to seek voluntary undertakings. Whether or not governments should take greater powers to break up already existing monopolies is an issue which is as much political as economic, for it involves issues of the freedom of the individual and the state. However, where attempts have been made to build up monopoly by merger there has been a heightened awareness of the inherent dangers, and governments have been more willing to take direct action to prohibit them. In the light of this, rules and *laissez-faire* approaches to mergers are now briefly considered as alternatives to that of pragmatic cost–benefit.

Those who strongly doubt whether the cost–benefit exercise can be adequately performed are more inclined to a rules-based or structural approach. The major proponents of a rules-based approach in the UK have been Crew and Rowley (1970, 1971). They argue that it is simply not possible to quantify all the costs and benefits involved, so any judgement must inevitably be inadequately based. In support of this they indicate that there have been worries about the ability of the Monopolies Commission to maintain consistency across its investigations. Thus, they claim a climate of uncertainty is created which militates against the decision-taking ability of firms. On the other hand they are not prepared to countenance the complete free rein of market forces, since the dangers of monopoly are well known. Consequently, they propose a policy more akin to that of the USA and based on rules which would automatically forbid mergers above a given size. This would remove the uncertainty and leave firms free to operate unconstrained within the legally created framework. They recognise that such arbitrary rules would result in some beneficial mergers being stopped, but argue that this sacrifice would be offset by the improvements in X-efficiency. In support of this approach they claim (contentiously) that economies of scale are, in general, only moderate, and also (on the basis of scant evidence) that the association between monopoly and X-efficiency is strong. Thus they contend that losses resulting from the automatic prohibition of mergers above a certain size are unlikely to be substantial, and are more than likely to be offset by the benefits arising from the creation of a climate of greater certainty and competition.

A *laissez-faire* approach of non-intervention has had few adherents in the past, since most economists have accepted that theory and evidence do suggest that matters cannot be left entirely to the market. However, Beacham and Jones (1971) came close to taking this line on the grounds that it is not possible to perform the cost–benefit exercise well enough to obtain a soundly based conclusion. On the other hand they could see little merit in a policy based on a rules approach, since rules are inevitably arbitrary and lacking in any underlying economic logic. As a result they have considerable doubts about the validity of the case for the control of mergers. More recently George (1989) has re-examined this approach, pointed out its drawbacks and concluded that the balance of theory and evidence does suggest that there is a need for a mergers policy. In contrast, economists of the Austrian tradition (e.g. Littlechild 1981, 1989) have come closer to the *laissez-faire* view, partly as a consequence of their different interpretation of profit. It is possible that they had some influence on the government of the UK during the 1980s, which was markedly less disposed to intervene directly in industry than its predecessors. However, most economists (and possibly politicians) accept that some form of control is required, and that this has to be exercised within one of the alternative frameworks.

It is the lack of clear and unambiguous predictions from both theory and evidence that is the source of the dispute over the nature of the approach to monopoly policy. However, on balance a majority of UK economists have appeared to favour the discretionary cost–benefit approach or have thought the rules approach too dogmatic (see e.g. Sutherland 1970, Howe 1972, Utton 1975, Fleming and Swann 1989, George 1989), and have tended to argue for a continuation of the present investigatory policy with some considerable strengthening of procedures. Thus, UK policy continues to retain the character of discretionary intervention rather than moving towards that of North American rules-based approaches. In its overall approach to competition, EU policy is much closer in spirit to UK policy than it is to any of the alternatives discussed above, although there are some important differences of detail which are considered later. This in itself presents a powerful argument against change, for it is clearly desirable that national and EU policies should be broadly similar if only because this is less confusing to the business community.

UK policy

Member states of the EU are free to determine their own policies towards competition within their national boundaries. However, in the case of matters affecting intra-Community trade EU policy necessarily takes precedence. UK and EU policies have developed separately, largely in isolation and over a different time scale. So with the creation of the SEM it is clearly desirable that there should be the greatest degree of harmonisation, without removing altogether the independence of national governments to deal with matters of internal trade. In order to elucidate the relationships between UK and EU policy it is helpful, firstly, to outline the current framework of UK policy before discussing that of the EU.

In stark contrast to the USA where legislation stems from the latter part of the nineteenth century, anti-monopoly or competition policy was virtually non-existent within the UK prior to 1948. Shortly after the First World War tentative steps towards the implementation of a monopoly policy were being considered. However, these were soon overshadowed by the need to deal with the problems of the general decline of demand during the Great Depression. Thus it was not until after the Second World War that governments seriously embarked on the task of introducing legislation to control monopoly. The extension of policy since the passing of the initial Monopolies and Restrictive Practices (Inquiry and Control) Act of 1948 can be seen as part of a gradual and continuous process, which has led, in what might be described as an eclectic or *ad hoc* manner, to the complex pattern of current legislation, culminating in the Competition Act of 1980. There are differences between the way in which competition policy operates in the UK and in the EU. However, official UK proposals for reform currently exist, particularly towards restrictive practices, which will ultimately bring the respective policies into closer alignment, and so reduce the likelihood of inconsistencies in treatment.

There are three major strands of policy. These are the treatment of dominant firm monopolies, restrictive practices and mergers. In 1973 the Fair Trading Act brought these together within the purview of a single body, the newly created Office of Fair Trading, to be overseen by a civil servant, the Director General of Fair Trading.

Dominant firm monopoly

Where a firm or a group of firms acting collectively accounts for 25 per cent of the market or more, the Director General of Fair Trading can refer the industry to the Monopolies and Mergers Commission for investigation. This body is then charged with providing a general report on the operation of the industry, and making recommendations for change where the public interest is seen to be compromised. The Secretary of State at the Department of Trade and Industry then has complete liberty to accept or reject these recommendations, and to decide whether, and how, they should be acted on. It is interesting to contrast this statutory definition of monopoly of 'one quarter' with that of economic theory where monopoly refers to the existence of a single firm. Real world monopoly is a much less precise concept than that of theory.

Since the 1980 Competition Act it is also possible for the Director General of Fair Trading to refer a particular practice of an individual firm to the Commission, where complaints have been received from supposedly injured parties, or the practice is suspected of limiting competition. In such cases a quick cost–benefit type appraisal and recommendation can be made. Where the practice is found to be anti-competitive the Minister can then accept voluntary undertakings from the firm to modify its practice or invoke extensive powers to proscribe the practice.

During its early years the Commission was given a wide range of briefs, and considerable information and understanding was gained about the nature of the competitive processes that existed within British industry. In particular, in a report on collective discrimination it was shown that restrictive practices in the form of agreements between firms were widespread throughout industry, and generally tended to operate against the public interest. The publication of this report led directly to legislation to control them.

Restrictive practices

Restrictive practices, in the form of formal agreements between firms, are presumed to operate against the public interest. Hence they are pronounced illegal unless the parties to an agreement can set aside the presumption by 'proving' to the satisfaction of the Restrictive Practices Court that the agreement operates in the public interest. All agreements have to be registered with the Office of Fair Trading, where it is decided at what stage a registered agreement should be brought before the Court. The arguments that can be employed to defend an agreement are tightly drawn and defined in a series of 'gateways'. If an agreement successfully passes one or more of these gateways the defendants still have to demonstrate that it passes a more general gateway or 'tailpiece' by conferring substantial benefits to the public interest, with the demonstrated benefits outweighing any detriments.

There is an important distinction between the approach to restrictive practices and that towards dominant firms and mergers. Restrictive practices policy is non-discretionary and purely legalistic, with issues to be resolved within the courts, as opposed to ministerial judgements made on the basis of administrative recommendations. The element of political discretion has been removed.

There is one particular practice that has been singled out for special treatment, namely resale price maintenance. It had become clear that resale price enforcement by suppliers was an important barrier to the attainment of efficiency in the distributive sector. Thus, the legislation was extended to prohibit a supplier from imposing any contractual requirement on a reseller to maintain prices, or from refusing to supply resellers where the basis for such refusal is that the resellers have been cutting prices. The prohibition can be contested in the Court, but the overall result has been the widespread abandonment of resale price maintenance[9] and a fundamental change in the pattern of retail distribution, as new types of outlet developed and replaced the older, small, independent, specialist stores.[10]

The impact of the restrictive practices legislation has been such that many agreements were abandoned as firms were unwilling to incur the costs of defending an agreement within the Court, and also as firms gradually came to recognise the difficulties of overturning the presumption that an agreement operated against the public interest. Information agreements have been brought within the scope of the legislation because many firms circumvented the intentions of the legislation by forming agreements to swap information on, for example, proposed price changes. Clearly if firms are predisposed to behave in mutually acceptable ways then such cooperation can be achieved simply through the dissemination of information and without the necessity to make a formal agreement. A major problem with the operation of restrictive practices legislation is that it is often difficult to capture secret or verbal agreements between firms. Also, because penalties in the UK, as opposed to the EU, have never been severe, firms have had contempt for the legislation. The whole procedure by 1988 was officially seen as no longer dealing adequately with the issues, as inflexible, slow, costly and in need of review (see Department of Trade and Industry 1988c). This has led to proposals for a move to an EU type approach, which is discussed later.

Mergers

If a proposed merger is likely to lead to the merged firms having a market share greater than one quarter or alternatively involves assets in excess of £30 million, then it may be referred to the Monopolies and Mergers Commission. This must then, within six months, carry out an investigation of the costs and benefits to determine whether the merger is contrary to the public interest. If the Minister accepts the report he then has the power to prohibit a contrary merger from taking place. However, there is an important distinction to be made here, and this is that unlike restrictive practices, judgements about mergers possess an essentially political dimension. The appropriate minister retains complete discretion on whether or not to refer a merger to the Commission, and whether or not to accept any recommendation. In the past ministers have been charged with failing to refer mergers which might have been politically sensitive, despite claims that a strong economic case existed for referral. As long as this element of political discretion remains there is a potential source of dispute.

Throughout the whole of competition policy there is a presumption that intervention is justified in order to preserve the public interest. This creates a difficulty in the operation of competition policy, no less in Europe than in the UK. It is not always clear what the public interest is or what serves it. Who are the public? Are they producers, consumers, or both and more importantly what exactly is in their interest? The definition had been left somewhat vague in the legislation, although it was intended to embrace all relevant matters. Such imprecision creates the greatest problems within a legalistic approach to restrictive practices, where courts faced by inadequate definition have had to develop their own interpretations. However, in the 1973 Act the interests of consumers are stressed, and explicit reference is made, for the first time, to the necessity of 'maintaining and promoting effective competition'. Thus competition is singled out for the first time as the chosen mechanism for ensuring the public interest.[11] Further informal articulation of this was provided by the 1984 'Tebbit guidelines', which indicated that in future greater attention would be given to competition aspects when deciding whether to make a merger reference. Thus, in the 1973 Act and in legislation since, it seems that the public interest almost becomes whatever it is that competition promotes. From this time on there was a shift in emphasis in official discussions from 'anti-monopoly' to 'pro-competition' policy. This was not entirely a semantic shift, and was to foreshadow a much wider change in attitude to the relationship between the state and the economy, which was to be felt throughout the 1980s.

Up to 1980 UK policy had been framed with scant reference to EEC legislation. However, since then there have been further reviews and proposals which have had to take some cognisance of the creation of the single market.

European Union competition policy

In the section on alternative policy approaches, an economic rationale was shown to underpin monopoly and competition policies. This same rationale applies no less to trade between the states that comprise the EU than to trade within an individual state. Thus, the worries about the nature of resource misallocation which have been instrumental in influencing national policies have also been important in determining the shape of EU policy. Therefore, the EU has sought to develop a policy designed to secure the benefits that arise from a competitive market, since as national barriers to inter-state competition are removed there is a danger that these can be replaced by privately erected barriers. The competition policy of the EU stems from the Treaty of Rome and is mainly embodied in Articles 85 and 86. These were designed to ensure free competition within the EU, with the European Commission being charged with the responsibility for applying the legislation. In the process of this the Commission has to work closely with national governments, and so it is clearly desirable that domestic and EU law should be mutually consistent. Individual states still retain the right to develop their own distinct policies on competition where trade is contained within their national boundaries. Therefore, even after the completion of the SEM, the provisions of UK competition policy remain unaffected, inasmuch as they concern internal UK trade. However, in terms of trade between member states, national legislation becomes subordinate to EU legislation.

Article 85 is concerned with the operation of restrictive practices, where they affect trade between member states. Thus, article 85(1) prohibits agreements '...which may affect trade between Member States and which have as their object or effect the prevention, restriction or distortion of competition within the common market...', and continues by listing specific types of agreement that are prohibited. The sort of agreements which the legislation is designed to catch is precisely the same as those which the UK legislation is aimed at, namely price fixing, market sharing, restrictions on supply, etc. There is with Article 85(3) provision for the granting of exemptions by the Commission in the case of beneficial agreements '...which contribute to improving the production or distribution of goods or to promoting technical or economic progress, while allowing consumers a fair share of the resulting benefit...', provided that such agreements do not impose any indispensable restrictions or provide the possibility of eliminating competition. These exemptions may be granted either as block exemptions for certain categories of agreement (e.g. cooperative research and development, exclusive distribution, exclusive purchasing) or on a case-by-case basis. While there is a clear similarity between the intentions of Article 85 and of UK restrictive practices legislation, in operation and emphasis the two approaches differ markedly. In the European legislation the emphasis is on the *effects* of a restriction, rather than the *form* of it as in the UK. That is, in the UK the requirement to register an agreement is based on the precise legal form of an agreement and not on its effects on competition. As a result many inconsequential or even pro-competitive agreements are caught up, while others that have anti-competitive effects may be drafted in a way designed to avoid the law. By contrast, within EU law, it is the object or effect of an agreement that determines whether or not it is subject to the law. For example, in *dyestuffs*, the manufacturers did not admit to having formed an agreement but it was still possible to find them guilty of operating a concerted practice. On a number of occasions dyestuff producers had been observed to make simultaneous and similar price revisions. The producers did not admit that they were engaged in a concerted practice, but argued that the parallel price changes were simply a natural consequence of oligopolistic competition. Irrespective of this, their behaviour in making parallel price changes was found to have the *effect* of limiting competition, and consequently enabled the EU to find them guilty of operating a concerted practice for which they were substantially fined.[12] Such an effects-based approach is seen as being more efficient in that it is likely to capture for investigation a greater number of anti-competitive agreements and fewer of those that are innocuous.

Agreements that fall within the ambit of Article 85 are investigated by the Commission on the receipt of a complaint and/or request for exemption. The appropriate body within a member state (e.g. DTI and/or OFT within the UK) is then consulted and assists in an advisory capacity, following which the Commission delivers judgement. Unlike the UK, where the Court on declaring an agreement 'contrary to the public interest' then has little power to impose effective penalties against offending firms, the Commission has considerable powers of enforcement and can fine firms up to 10 per cent of their turnover for operating an anti-competitive practice. Firms then have the right of appeal to the European Court of First Instance, and ultimately to the European Court of Justice. The Commission's record on attacking cartels and concerted practices is impressive, as it has vigorously pursued and successfully secured the termination of a substantial number and variety of concerted practices. In particular, it has taken a strong line against price fixing (e.g. dyestuffs, glass containers) and market sharing or quantity agreements (e.g. cement) to the extent that such practices are now unlikely ever to be granted an exemption.

In the *glass containers* case of 1974, producers within five European countries were found to subscribe to an agreement to notify each other immediately of price changes, and also to align export prices with the domestic prices of the price leader within the importing country. The anti-competitive features of this practice are obvious and the Commission accordingly declared the system illegal.

The practice of exclusive dealing has also been the subject of investigation. If manufacturers appoint exclusive dealerships, then this could facilitate the division of the European market into sub-markets with restricted competition between and within them. In 1964 the *Grundig Consten* case highlighted this problem. The German manufacturer gave exclusive distribution rights to Consten for the sales of Grundig products within France, and forbade its non-French distributors from exporting into France. The effect of this policy was that prices in France were 20 to 50 per cent above those in West Germany. The Commission accordingly found this an infringement of Article 85.

Article 86 is concerned with the behaviour of dominant firm or near-monopoly situations and bans the abuse of a dominant position where it affects trade between member states through the imposition of 'unfair' trading conditions. A non-exclusive list of examples of such abuses is provided:

(a) directly or indirectly imposing unfair purchase or selling prices or other unfair trading conditions

(b) limiting production, markets or technical development to the prejudice of consumers

(c) applying dissimilar conditions to equivalent transactions with other trading parties, thereby placing them at a competitive disadvantage

(d) making the conclusion of contracts subject to acceptance by the other parties of supplementary obligations which, by their nature or according to commercial usage, have no connection with the subject of such contracts.

For Article 86 to be invoked there has to be an effect on trade, as it is not dominance itself that is contrary to Article 86, but the abuse of that dominance. Within the article there is no definition of what comprises dominance in terms either of market share or of other criteria. This differs from, for example, the position in the UK legislation where dominance is arbitrarily equated with possession of a market share of 25 per cent or more. To some extent, this lack of guidance provides greater flexibility on the part of the authorities, who are not constrained by a requirement to satisfy some precisely defined criterion of dominance as a precondition for investigation. So, the conditions of dominance can vary from case to case. If an abuse is found to exist then, almost by definition, there must be some element of dominance, otherwise there would be no basis for that abuse. Indeed, it has been argued (Fairburn, *et al.* 1986) that the authorities, having found an abuse, have then adopted the device of contriving to define the market in such a way that the discovered abuse then becomes an abuse of a dominant position. Thus, dominance can be seen to arise where a firm has the power to behave independently of its competitors and customers, and this may result from a combination of a number of factors, none of which separately would necessarily imply dominance. This was the situation in the case involving the *United Brands Company*. The company was found to have abused its dominant position in the market for bananas within the Community in four ways: (i) distributors and ripeners were prohibited from reselling green bananas, (ii) it refused supplies to distributors or ripeners who had participated in advertising campaigns for rival brands, (iii) different prices were charged according to the buyer's country, although there was no ostensible reason for this, (iv) unfair prices were charged in Germany, Denmark and the Benelux countries. The Commission fined the company and ordered it to cease the practices. The first three of these are clearly anti-competitive. However, it is not as easy to be objective about what are or are not 'unfair' prices, and on appeal to the European Court of Justice this charge was overturned for lack of proof.

The procedure for investigation and possible sanctions follows the same pattern as outlined earlier for matters dealt with under Article 85. Under Article 86, the Commission has successfully dealt with a number of abuses such as the granting of loyalty rebates (e.g. Hoffman-la Roche), refusals to supply (e.g. Commercial Solvents), and price discrimination (Chiquita) among others.

In the case of *Hoffman-la Roche* the Commission found that the practice of offering major buyers loyalty rebates in return for taking all their requirements from Hoffman-la Roche was an abuse of a dominant position, and thus incompatible with Article 86. The practice had the effect of restricting the buyers' freedom to take up alternative supplies and also acted as an entry barrier by making it difficult for new products to secure outlets.

The Commission held that refusal to supply, in order to eliminate competition, was contrary to Article 86 in the decision on *Commercial Solvents*. ZOJA, a major manufacturer of drugs for tuberculosis had been the subject of a failed takeover bid. In response to this, the United States Solvents Corporation and its Italian subsidiary, Institutio Chemioterapico Italiano, decided to refuse ZOJA supplies of essential intermediate products for which they held a world monopoly. Additional steps were then taken to ensure that ZOJA could not obtain supplies anywhere else on the world market. In the face of this attempt to eliminate it from the market, ZOJA complained. The Commission imposed fines and ordered the companies to resume supplies.

It is important to emphasise again that it is not dominance in itself which is contrary to Article 86, but the abuse of that dominance. This, combined with the greater flexibility in defining dominance, leads to a European approach based more on the effects of, rather than on the formal structure of monopoly, as distinct from the situation in the UK where structural criteria have to be satisfied before investigation can proceed.

Until recently there was no specific European legislation to deal with mergers. The only avenue for EU control was through the application of Article 85 and/or Article 86, which was only open to those cases involving the operation of restrictive practices and/or the abuse of a dominant position. Thus, if a merger was to lead to the creation of a dominant position and a consequent restriction of competition, this could arguably be classed as an abuse under Article 86. This procedural approach was successfully established by the Commission in the *Continental Can* case, where the merger further enhanced existing dominance: following the take over of Dutch and German metal container firms by a Belgian subsidiary of Continental Can, the Commission sought to invoke Article 86. This challenge was subsequently overturned at the European Court of Justice in 1973, because the Commission had not demonstrated that competition had been sufficiently restricted. However, the important general principle that Article 86 could be applied to mergers that restricted competition was accepted, although this power was weakened by the fact that the article could only be applied to mergers *ex post*, that is to mergers already completed. Later, in the *Philip Morris* case of 1987 it was demonstrated that Article 85 had a relevance for merger control and could be applied where a firm acquired an influential shareholding in a competitor. However, given the growth of international competition and the emergence of the multinational enterprise, control of mergers through Articles 85 and 86 came to be widely recognised as too weak, particularly as leading up to 1992 the numbers of all types of mergers including cross-border mergers were increasing, although cross-border mergers do not appear to represent a rising proportion of the total (see Geroski and Vlassopoulos 1993). Thus, 'at best the existing rules were limited and technically inadequate for a proper merger control policy' (Brittan 1992).

After a long period of drafting and redrafting, a European Merger Control Regulation (Council Regulation 4064/89) finally came into force on 21 September 1990. This now enables the Commission to investigate and control those 'concentrations' (i.e. mergers and takeovers) which have a 'Union dimension', while those mergers not having a Union dimension remain subject to domestic policies. Mergers with a Union dimension are defined as those where the parties have an aggregate turnover in excess of ECU 5 bn, and where at least two of those parties have a Union turnover greater than ECU 250 m. If, however, each of the enterprises achieves more than two thirds of its turnover within the same single member state, then the merger does not come under the Regulation. Special criteria apply for mergers between financial institutions. Mergers that are found to possess an EU dimension must be notified to the European Commission which then carries out an investigation to determine whether they are 'compatible with the common market'. Within a period of one month the Commission will decide whether there are any 'serious doubts' as to the merger creating or strengthening a dominant position to the likely detriment of effective competition. In the absence of such doubts the merger is permitted to proceed. If such doubts exist then an investigation is carried out over a maximum of four months to determine whether the merger should be prohibited or not.[13]

By the end of March 1993 the Commission had examined some 140 merger proposals. Of these, by far the majority were found to raise 'no serious doubts', but in eleven notifications 'serious doubts' were raised, and so were referred for detailed investigation. 'Of these, two were allowed to proceed without conditions, six were allowed to proceed with conditions imposed upon the companies, two were awaiting judgement, and only in the case of Aerospatiale/Alenia/DeHaviland was a merger prohibited. Thus, in only 5 per cent of mergers referred to it did the Commission find that some form of control was necessary. Whether this rate is indicative of the future remains to be seen.[14] In the next paragraphs some of the different types of decision the Commission has made are reviewed.

The proposed acquisition of *Alfa-Laval* by *Tetrapak* is an example of a notification where initial 'serious doubts' were expressed, but which was then approved following the subsequent detailed investigation. Alfa-Laval was a major manufacturer of milk and juice processing machines, whereas Tetrapak had a dominant position in liquid packaging machinery. First indications were that the merger could create or enhance a dominant position. However, in the subsequent enquiry the markets for packaging and processing machines were found to be distinct, and so there would be no extension of dominance. Accordingly, the takeover was allowed to proceed unconditionally.

In the case of *Aerospatiale/MBB*, the proposed merger was seen to lead to a high market share in civilian helicopters. However, because of competition on the international market from manufacturers in the USA, such as Sikorsky and Bell, the Commission did not feel that the merged firm would attain a dominant position. No serious doubt was raised, and no further investigation was required.

However, this was not so in the disallowed merger of *Aerospatiale/Alenia/DeHaviland*. ATR was the leading manufacturer of turbo-prop aircraft on the world market, and was jointly owned by Aerospatiale and Alenia. DeHaviland was the second major producer of turbo-prop aircraft, and Aerospatiale and Alenia were seeking to purchase it. Such acquisition would have led to the creation of a firm with in excess of 50 per cent of the world market in turbo props, and in some sub-market categories considerably more than this. On examination the Commission found that there was unlikely to be any competitive threat from other small-scale suppliers of turbo-props, and that exit from the market was more likely than any new entry. In this situation the Commission found against the merger.

In a number of instances where original merger proposals have been unacceptable, firms have had the choice of abandoning them or negotiating conditions for acceptance with the Commission. Typically, this has involved some divestment of existing activities. Thus, in *Accor/Wagons-Lits*, the Commission found that the combined firms would account for 89 per cent of motorway catering and 69 per cent of light meals. Also, the merged firm would have been some 18 times larger than its nearest rival in light meals, and any new entrants would face very high entry barriers. The market would have been clearly dominated by a single firm, and so approval was given only on condition that Accor divest itself completely of Wagons-Lits operations in France.

The future of EU and UK competition policy

In recent years there have been a number of wide ranging official reviews of most aspects of UK competition policy, which have involved widespread consultations with academia, business and other interested parties. This consultative process has led to the publication of government White Papers setting out new proposals for change. While still maintaining an independent domestic policy towards competition within the UK, these proposals will have the effect of bringing that policy into greater alignment with the approach under EU policy. In the case of restrictive practices, the new proposals represent a major shift towards a European-type approach. However, in the case of mergers the proposed changes are largely procedural, and no significant reorientation of present policy is envisaged. Policy towards dominant firm monopoly and anti-competitive practices is currently under review and at the consultative stage.[15]

Despite the early successes of restrictive practices legislation in combating collusive agreements, there is now a belief that within the present business climate the legislation possesses fundamental weaknesses. This belief was articulated within the official review of restrictive practices policy (Department of Trade and Industry 1988c). The main problem is that the policy approach that has evolved is no longer seen as efficient. In particular the deterrent effect is weak since the penalties for operating an illegal cartel are inadequate, and the Director General of Fair Trading has few powers to intervene and initiate investigations in situations where there is a suspicion that a secret cartel is in operation. A further difficulty is that the current legislation provides no means for combating the growth of the tacit or informal collusion which has come to replace the formal agreements of earlier years. In an attempt to deal with these inadequacies the new proposals (Department of Trade and Industry 1989) represent a change from the present *form*-based approach to an *effects*-based approach, and involve almost the wholesale adoption of the principles and form of Article 85. In general, restrictive practices are to be banned. As in Article 85 an illustrative list of prohibited practices is to be published, which will include such specific practices as price fixing or any other practices which may be expected to have that effect. Collusive tendering, market sharing and collective refusals to supply are also to be included. There will be, again as under Article 85, a facility for the block exemption of certain practices which are not seen as anti-competitive. In addition, the legislation will be strengthened by granting powers to enable the Director General of Fair Trading to initiate investigations where there is a suspicion that prohibitions are being breached. It will become a criminal offence not to comply fully with any investigations, and it will be possible to impose substantial financial penalties, not only on the companies operating a prohibited agreement, but also on those directors found responsible for negotiating or operating such an agreement. The effect of these changes should be to create a more relevant and effective policy, not only by creating greater harmonisation with EU restrictive practices policy, but also by strengthening domestic policy through the adoption of an approach designed to combat any practice which has the effect of restricting competition, as opposed to one that emphasises the form of an agreement, sometimes to the neglect of that effect. Despite all this it appears that the proposals currently have a low priority in the Government's legislative programme.

For many years there have been worries over the increasing monopolisation of British industry, as evidenced by increased levels of both aggregate and market concentration, and of which there is little doubt that merger activity has, at times, been a major causal factor (see e.g. HMSO 1978, Hughes 1993). It is also clear that current merger policy has been somewhat permissive, for while it has been effective in preventing a limited number of individually important mergers, it has had little impact on the level of merger activity as a whole. An important reason for this is that it is an entirely partial approach as explained in the section discussing qualifications to the theoretical results, also, such a case-by-case approach is never capable of examining anything other than a small minority of all mergers. This is seen as particularly worrying by some commentators, since there is evidence (e.g. Meeks 1977) that post-merger profitability has tended to decline. The implication of this is that many mergers can be regarded as failures in the sense that they do not attain the gains in efficiency claimed as their justification. These sorts of issues have led to calls for the strengthening of merger policy.

However, in the case of mergers there are no official proposals to change the orientation of policy, despite the concerns which have been expressed about the operation of present policy. This largely stems from the current Government's reluctance to intervene in the workings of the market, because

> intervention by public authorities in lawful commercial transactions should be kept to a minimum, since broadly speaking the free commercial decisions of private decision-makers result in the most desirable outcomes for the economy as a whole. This broad principle applies as much to transactions involving the sale and purchase of productive assets (and shares representing them) as to other commercial transactions.[16]

This of course is a value judgement which a government is entitled to make, but it is one which some economists would argue is not fully justified by the evidence, on the basis of which there have been calls for much more stringent control. The main arguments for a tightening up of merger policy, along with suggestions as to how this could be achieved, are considered by George (1989). One suggestion that is favoured by a number of commentators is to alter the onus of proof. At present the Monopolies and Mergers Commission is charged with determining whether a proposed merger is contrary to the public interest. This means that many mergers for which there have been no demonstrable advantages, but which have not been found to be overtly anti-competitive, have been allowed through, and thus contributed to the general increase in industrial concentration. This consequence of existing policy is particularly important in periods of high merger activity when there is a bandwagon effect with more and more firms seeking to engage in takeover activity. In view of this, a frequently canvassed suggestion has been that in referred mergers the onus should be placed on the firms to demonstrate that the proposed merger would directly confer benefits to the public interest. In support of this it can be asked, if the proposers of a merger cannot demonstrate such benefits then who can? Such a change should have the effect of reducing the number of apparently aimless mergers among large firms, and this in itself might help to ameliorate the bandwagon effect on all firms during merger waves. However, in the latest proposals (Department of Trade and Industry 1988b) these calls have largely remained unanswered, apparently because the official doctrinal position is that

> Government should not normally intervene in the market's decisions about the use to which assets should be put, since private decision-makers will usually seek (and are usually the best placed to achieve) the most profitable employment for their assets, and in competitive markets this will generally lead to the most efficient use of those assets, for the benefit of both their owners and the economy as a whole.[17]

Again this is not a view which has been endorsed by all, but it does provide an explanation as to why the government's proposed reforms are largely confined to measures concerned with speeding up the investigatory process and making existing policy more efficient. The current official view is therefore that mergers are part and parcel of the competitive process, as opposed to restrictive practices which impede that process.

The newly introduced EU policy on mergers outlined in the previous section is similar in intent and approach to that of the UK. However, there is at least one important distinction. Within the UK it remains, and will continue to remain, ultimately the prerogative of a politically accountable minister to decide, acting on the advice of the bureaucracy, whether to permit or to forbid a particular merger. By contrast, within EU policy the element of political discretion is much less, since the decision to permit or to forbid an investigated merger is a matter for the administration. Whether political or administrative accountability is the more desirable depends on one's view about the relationships that should exist between State and society, but it is more likely that where decisions are made by political appointees there will be greater uncertainty, for such decisions then embody both a political and an economic dimension. For this reason EU merger policy *ought* to display less arbitrariness than has been the case within the UK. However, following the first takeover to be disallowed (Aerospatiale/Alenia/DeHaviland), some doubts have been expressed over the abilities of Commissioners to submerge their national interests and remain free from political pressures. The potential for such conflict arises from the differing perspectives of industrial and competition policy. Some see 1992 as providing the opportunity for the restructuring of industry and the attainment of international competitiveness, while others see it as providing the opportunity to achieve efficiency by the creation of competitive conditions throughout the EU.[18]

The legislation on anti-competitive and exploitative behaviour is currently the subject of a consultative green paper, in which the Government 'consider that there may be benefit in aligning this aspect of UK competition law with EU law' (Department of Trade and Industry 1992). Three alternative proposals for strengthening policy are canvassed. In brief, these are: (i) some extension of powers within the existing legislative framework; (ii) the substitution of a prohibition system for the existing UK legislation, i.e. the adoption of an approach similar to that under Article 86 of the EU; (iii) the introduction of a prohibition system for anti-competitive practices, but with the retention of the procedures for the investigation of dominant firm monopolies. Of these, the first alternative would be the weakest in its effects. Only the second and third go any way towards the harmonisation of domestic and Union policy, while also enabling the necessary extension of control. It remains to be seen what system the Government will propose, but if, as has been argued in this chapter, there are benefits from the harmonisation of policy, then it clearly might be sensible to adopt an approach similar to that of Article 86.

Thus, EU and UK competition policy are moving closer together. This is to be welcomed, for with greater harmonisation of policies industry will be able to operate more efficiently through being able to plan within an environment of greater certainty, and will be more secure in the knowledge that its domestic and international operations are likely to receive compatible treatment from the respective authorities.

Notes

1. The interested reader is referred to any standard intermediate micro-economic theory text, e.g. Laidler and Estrin (1989).
2. The reader might note some similarity to the Thatcherite 'trickle down' argument. However, implicit in that view is a 'belief', nowhere clearly articulated, that somehow there will be an automatic mechanism that will ensure that the larger the cake, the more for *all*. No such assumption is made here. Ultimately questions of income distribution and equity have to be confronted head-on.
3. For a discussion of alternative theories of the firm, see e.g. Sawyer (1979).
4. For a more detailed treatment of the problem of X-efficiency within this context, see Rowley (1973).
5. Strictly speaking, for a market to be perfectly contestable requires a minimum of two firms. However, as pure monopoly is extremely rare in the real world, for our purposes this distinction is largely academic. For a readable and non-technical discussion of the nature of contestability and its implications for public policy, see Button (1985).
6. UK policy towards industry under the Thatcher administration was partly influenced by arguments outside the mainstream of the Anglo-Saxon tradition. These stem from the Austrian approach and have found sympathy in a Conservative ideology which has favoured a move towards privatisation, deregulation and a less interventionist stance.
7. For accessible surveys of the evidence and arguments see e.g. Clarke (1985) or Hay and Morris (1991).

8. It is possible to review only briefly the issues here. Those who wish to explore them more fully are referred to the interchange between Crew and Rowley (1970, 1971) and Howe (1971), and to the survey by Howe (1972).

9. Only two commodities remain subject to RPM – books and proprietary medicaments. In 1962 the net book agreement was successfully defended under the 1956 Act, and later, individual RPM on books was deemed not to be against the public interest under the 1964 Act. Currently, claims are being made from some quarters for another look at books, and some major resellers appear to be squaring up for a challenge to publishers. In 1970 the case of medicaments was successfully defended under the 1964 Act.

10. It is legal and widespread in practice for suppliers to publish maximum or recommended prices. However, resellers cannot legally be prevented from cutting these prices, although in some trades suppliers have found ways to 'encourage' compliance.

11. In terms of the technical discussion of the economic rationale for intervention, this can be thought of as equating the public interest with total surplus, and thus embracing both producer and consumer surplus. In the 1973 Act the stress placed on consumers' interests represents a value judgement that consumers' surplus should be weighted more heavily.

12. For a discussion of this and other EC cases, see e.g. Jacquemin and de Jong (1977) and Swann (1983, 1988).

13. For a fuller critical evaluation of the European Merger Control Regulation see Bishop (1993). For a review from the standpoint of a leading Commissioner see Brittan (1992).

14. For a detailed breakdown of merger decisions and a comprehensive survey and critique of the operation of EU merger policy since 1989 see Neven *et al.* (1993).

15. On restrictive practices: consultative green papers (HMSO 1979, Department of Trade and Industry 1988c) and white papers (Department of Trade and Industry 1988a, 1989). On mergers: green paper (HMSO 1978) and white paper (Department of Trade and Industry 1988a), with the latest statement of policy to be found in Department of Trade and Industry (1988b). For a more detailed discussion of the proposals with reference to the EU see Fleming and Swann (1989). On dominant firms and anti-competitive practices see green paper (Department of Trade and Industry 1992).

16. Department of Trade and Industry (1988b), p. 6, paras 2.8–2.9.

17. Department of Trade and Industry (1988b), p. 6, para 2.9.

18. For some discussion of these issues see Chapter 8.

References and further reading

Baumol W J 1959 *Business Behaviour Value and Growth*, Macmillan, New York.

Baumol W J, Panzar, J C and **Willig R D** 1982 *Contestable Markets and the Theory of Industry Structure*, Harcourt Brace Jovanovich, New York.

Beacham A and **Jones J C H** 1971 Merger criteria and policy in Great Britain and Canada, *Journal of Industrial Economics*, 19, pp. 97–117.

Bishop M 1993 European or National? The Community's New Merger Regulation, in Bishop M and Kay J A (eds), *European Mergers and Merger Policy*, Oxford University Press.

Bishop M and **Kay J A** (eds) 1993 *European Mergers and Merger Policy*, Oxford University Press.

Brittan L 1992 *European Competitive Policy*, Brassey's, London.

Button K J 1985 New approaches to the regulation of industry, *Royal Bank of Scotland Review*, 148, December, pp. 18–34.

Clarke R 1985 *Industrial Economics*, Blackwell, Oxford.

Cowling K and **Mueller D C** 1978 The Social Costs of Monopoly Power, *Economic Journal*, 88, 77–87.

Crew M A and **Rowley C K** 1970 Anti-trust policy: economics versus management science, *Moorgate and Wall Street Journal*, Autumn, pp. 19–34.

Crew M A and **Rowley C K** 1971 Anti-trust policy: the application of rules, *Moorgate and Wall Street Journal*, Autumn, pp. 37–50.

Department of Trade and Industry 1988a *DTI – Department for Enterprise*, White Paper Cmnd 278, HMSO, London.

Department of Trade and Industry 1988b *A Department of Trade and Industry Paper on the Policy and Procedures of Merger Control*, Department of Trade and Industry, London.

Department of Trade and Industry 1988c *Review of Restrictive Trade Practices Policy*, Green Paper Cmnd 331, HMSO, London.

Department of Trade and Industry 1989 *Opening New Markets: New Policy on Restrictive Trade Practices*, White Paper Cmnd 727, HMSO, London.

Department of Trade and Industry 1992 *Abuse of Market Power*, Green Paper Cm 2100, HMSO, London.

Fairburn J A and **Kay J A** (eds) 1989 *Mergers and Merger Policy*, Oxford University Press.

Fairburn J A, Kay J A and **Sharpe T A E** 1986 The economics of Article 86, in Hall G (ed.) *European Industrial Policy*, Croom Helm, London.

Fleming M and **Swann D** 1989 Competition policy – The pace quickens and 1992 approaches, *Royal Bank of Scotland Review*, 162, June, pp. 47–61.

George K 1989 Do we need a merger policy? in Fairburn J A and Kay J (eds), *Mergers and Merger Policy*, Oxford University Press.

Geroski P and **Vlassopoulos A** 1993 Recent Patterns of European Merger Activity, in Bishop M and Kay J A (eds), *European Mergers and Merger Policy*, Oxford University Press.

Harberger A C 1954 Monopoly and Resource Allocation, *American Economic Review*, 44, 77–87.

Hay D A and **Morris D J** 1991, *Industrial Economics and Organization Theory and Evidence*, 2nd edn, Oxford University Press.

HMSO 1978 *A Review of Monopoly and Mergers Policy*, Green Paper Cmnd 7198, HMSO, London.

HMSO 1979 *A Review of Restrictive Trade Practices Policy*, Green Paper Cmnd 7512, HMSO, London.

Howe M 1971 Anti-trust policy: rules or discretionary intervention? *Moorgate and Wall Street Journal*, Spring, pp. 59–68.

Howe M 1972 British merger policy proposals and American experience, *Scottish Journal of Political Economy*, February.

Hughes A 1993 Mergers and Economic Performance in the UK: a Survey of the Empirical Evidence 1950–1990, in Bishop M and Kay J A (eds), *European Mergers and Merger Policy*, Oxford University Press.

Jacquemin A P and **de Jong H W** 1977 *European Industrial Organization*, Macmillan, London.

Kamerschen D R 1966 An Estimation of the Welfare Losses from Monopoly in the American Economy, *Western Economic Journal*, 4, 221–36.

Laidler D and **Estrin S** 1989 *Introduction to Microeconomics*, 3rd edn, Philip Allan, London.

Littlechild S C 1981 Misleading calculations of the social costs of monopoly, *Economic Journal*, 91, pp. 348–63.

Littlechild S 1989 Myths and merger policy, in Fairburn J A and Kay J (eds), *Mergers and Merger Policy*, Oxford University Press.

Meeks G 1977 *Disappointing Marriage: a Study of the Gains from Merger*, Cambridge University Press.

Neven D, Nuttall R and **Seabright P** 1993 *Merger in Daylight, the Economics and Politics of European Merger Control*, Centre for Economic Policy Research, London.

Posner M E 1975 The Social Costs of Monopoly and Regulation, *Journal of Political Economy*, 83, 807–27.

Pratten C F 1971 *Economies of Scale in Manufacturing Industry*, Cambridge University Press.

Rowley C K 1973 *Anti-trust and Economic Efficiency*, Macmillan, London.

Sawyer M C 1979 *Theories of the Firm*, Weidenfeld and Nicholson, London.

Schwartzman D 1960 The Burden of Monopoly, *Journal of Political Economy*, 68, 627–30.

Silberston A 1972 Economies of scale in theory and practice, *Economic Journal*, supplement, 82, pp. 369–391.

Sutherland A 1970 The management of mergers policy, in Cairncross A K (ed.), *The Managed Economy*, pp. 106–134, Blackwell, Oxford.

Swann D 1983 *Competition and Industrial Policy in the European Community*, Methuen, London.

Swann D 1988 *The Economics of the Common Market*, 6th edn, Penguin, London.

Utton M A 1975 British merger policy, in George K D and Joll C (eds), *Competition Policy in the U.K. and E.E.C.*, Cambridge University Press.

Williamson O E 1968 Economies as an anti-trust defence: the welfare trade-offs, *American Economic Review*, 58, pp. 18–36.

Worcester D A 1973 New Estimates of the Welfare Loss to Monopoly, United States: 1956–69, *Southern Economic Journal*, 40, 234–45.

CHAPTER 8

Industrial policy in the EU

Frank McDonald and Margaret Potton

Introduction

The 21st Report on Competition Policy of the EC (1991) defines industrial policy thus: 'Industrial Policy concerns the effective and coherent implementation of all those policies which impinge on the structural adjustment of industry with a view to promoting competitiveness. The provision of a horizontal framework in which industry can develop and prosper by remedying structural deficiencies and addressing areas where the market mechanism alone fails to provide the conditions necessary for success is the principal means by which the Community applies its industrial policy.'

This definition of industrial policy clearly demonstrates its wide ranging nature. Indeed, this definition appears to include competition policy (to maintain a competitive environment), deregulation policies (to remove legal impediments that prohibit or limit competitive markets) and a wide range of social, regional and R&D programmes (to correct market failures). The EU has been active in all these areas. However, in the case of the EU it is not clear if these policies and programmes constitute an effective and/or coherent approach to industrial policy. Further, in some areas it is not clear that the EU is the appropriate agency to take the lead in industrial policy. The EU is hampered in devising a coherent industrial policy because of the very diverse approaches that the member states have adopted towards their national industrial policies (see Beije *et al.* 1987).

Rationale for industrial policy

Three main approaches to industrial policy can be identified:

1. market-based or negative industrial policy;

2. interventionist or positive industrial policy;

3. selective intervention or strategic industrial policy.

Market-based industrial policy is founded on the view that market mechanisms are on the whole effective in generating an efficient and vibrant industrial structure. This approach requires intervention only where there are significant cases of market failure. Thus, if externalities lead to under-provision of R&D expenditures or training for labour there may be a case for government intervention to correct these market failures. However, most of the advocates of this view have reservations about the ability of governments to correct market failures of this type successfully, and some argue that government intervention to correct for market failure often leads to a worse outcome than that which arises from the 'imperfect market process'. In other words, government intervention leads to greater inefficiencies than does market failure (see Buchanan 1978). Therefore, in the market-based approach industrial policy is mainly negative, i.e. the prevention of abuse of market power and the removal of legal impediments to free trade. Hence competition policy, the removal of state aids to promote competitive markets and deregulation programmes are regarded as the cornerstones of industrial policy.

Interventionist industrial policy is based on the view that market failure in areas such as R&D and labour training are important obstacles to the development of a dynamic industrial base. Social and regional considerations are also considered to be important factors in devising a 'good' industrial policy. Such social and regional factors are often considered to have important economic effects due to loss of productive potential and high public expenditures that arise from unemployment. Positive action and financial support by governments to ensure adequate R&D and training expenditures and to provide aid to poorer groups and regions is considered to be an essential part of industrial policy. This approach tends to see a need for intervention in a wide range of industries and sectors covering both declining and rising industries.

The selective interventionist approach to industrial policy takes a more strategic view of industrial policy. In this approach the main role for industrial policy is to aid the growth of rising industries to replace those that are in decline. The need for such a strategic approach arises from the imperfect nature of the competitive environment, in particular in cases where there exist strong economies of scale and learning effects. In these cases selective help by use of state aids can give competitive advantages to companies by allowing them to enter the market first and thereby reap the benefits of economies of scale and/or learning effects. State aids can also be used to help companies to 'catch up' on foreign competitors that are established in the market. The theoretical benefits of this approach have been put forward by Krugman (1991). However, Krugman is somewhat reluctant to advocate such an approach to industrial policy because of the risks of retaliation from competitors and also because it is very difficult for governments to gather and assess the appropriate information that would allow them to choose potential 'winners'. However, the benefits of such strategic approaches seem to have been accepted by some American economists (Tyson 1992) and the economic rationale for projects such as the European Airbus rest on strategic interventionist arguments. The arguments for and against an interventionist policy in the EU, in the light of the globalisation of economic activity, are examined in Nicolaides (1993).

Most countries take a somewhat eclectic view of industrial policy. Although the USA and the UK tend to a market-based approach and France and Italy to a more interventionist view of industrial policy, these countries have elements of both these approaches in their industrial policies. However, in many countries there has been a pronounced shift towards a more market-based approach to industrial policy. This movement can be seen in the deregulation programmes in areas such as transport services, telecommunications services and airlines. The growth of privatisation programmes also bears witness to the move towards market-based industrial policies. Nevertheless, the large-scale protection of declining industries and the widespread used of state aids by many countries provides evidence that interventionist industrial policies are still a potent force in many economies. Many countries also make significant use of state help for strategic purposes, particularly in the R&D area.

The EU has also taken an eclectic approach to industrial policy. In historical terms the EU began with a significant interventionist approach in the areas of coal and steel with the Treaty of Paris which founded the ECSC. However, the EEC was more concerned with establishing free movement of goods, services, capital and labour and the development of a strong competition policy. As the EU has developed more interventionist and strategic approaches to industrial policy have arisen, for example the growth of R&D programmes and polices to aid declining industries and poorer regions. Nevertheless, the EU has also engaged in significant deregulation programmes. For instance, a large part of the SEM programme was largely concerned with deregulation and the Union has embarked on significant deregulation programmes in the telecommunication services and airline industries. The Commission is also encouraging the privatisation programmes that are taking place in many of the member states.

The need for a positive EU industrial policy has become an important issue due to the growth of Union policies and programmes that affect industry and because of the concept of subsidiarity. In order for externality arguments to be a valid rationale for a common industrial policy for the EU, the member states of the Union would have to encompass most of the spill-over effects of R&D and training programmes. Given the lack of labour mobility in the EU, it is hard to see a pronounced externality effect in labour training within the member states. The position with regard to R&D programmes is less clear. However, given the increasing globalisation of business activities it is not obvious that the EU is the appropriate agency to provide a coherent and effective R&D policy. The attractiveness of the EU as an effective agency for the provision of industrial policies to promote 'economic and social cohesion' would depend on the acceptance of this as an important goal for the Union, and also on whether this goal could be better met by promoting free movement in a predominantly market-based system.

The role of the EU in negative industrial polices arises from the key economic integration programmes of the Union. The conditions that will allow the free movement of goods, services, capital and labour require deregulation of national rules that prohibit or restrict free movement and the creation and maintenance of a competitive environment. One of the major problems with regard to the development of a common industrial policy for the EU is to decide on the level of positive measures that are required for an effective free movement area. Another problem area is connected to the need for political and/or economic reasons for an industrial policy that promotes 'economic and social cohesion'.

Industrial policy as laid down in the Treaties

First it is important to look at what provisions for industrial policy are laid down in the Treaties. The European Coal and Steel Community Treaty, signed on 18 April 1951 in Paris, includes Articles 54, 55 and 56 relating to investment and financial aid. Article 54 is on investment programmes and loans. The High Authority may 'facilitate the carrying out of investment programmes by granting loans to undertakings or by guaranteeing other loans'. It may also 'assist the financing of works and installations which contribute directly and primarily to increasing production' (Article 54). It can also ban loans if they are contrary to the Treaty. Article 55 says that the 'High Authority shall promote technical and economic research into the production and increased use of coal and steel'. The High Authority may 'initiate and facilitate such research'.

The High Authority also has in its power provisions in the Treaty to effect production (Article 58) if the community 'is confronted with a period of manifest crisis'. It can establish a system of production quotas subject to Article 74. Article 46 establishes that the High Authority shall 'periodically lay down general objectives for modernisation, long-term planning of manufacture and expansion of productive capacity'. Thus the Treaty of Paris is quite *dirigiste*.

The Treaty of Rome, signed on 25 March 1957, hardly mentions industrial policy. Aids granted by member states are mentioned in Articles 92 and 93.

Article 92 states that 'aid to promote the economic development of areas where the standard of living is abnormally low or where there is serious unemployment' is compatible with the Common Market, as is 'aid to promote the execution of an important project of common European interest or to remedy a serious disturbance in the economy of a Member State' and 'other categories of aid as may be specified by decision of the Council acting by a qualified majority on a proposal from the Commission.' Article 93 is on the organisation of State aid. Section 1 says 'the commission shall, in cooperation with member states, keep under constant review all systems of aid existing in those states. It shall propose to the latter any appropriate measures required by the progressive development or by the functioning of the common market.' The Commission has means of controlling state aid which is not compatible with the Common Market (Article 93) and ways of enforcing it through the ECJ.

At the time of the signing of the Treaty of Rome the industrial policies of France and Germany, which were the two dominant member countries at the time, were very difficult to align as they were very different. The French government believed in a *dirigiste* policy. There was a need in France for the government to have a strong influence on industrial development, if not to plan it centrally as in the then Eastern bloc. In Germany, on the other hand, there was and still is a reliance on a *laissez-faire* regime wedded to untrammelled market forces.

In 1957 intervention in industry was not really an issue. The main aim was to set up a common market based on competition and a healthy industrial structure was expected to follow.

In the Euratom Treaty, signed in Rome on 25 March 1957, there are provisions in Article 70 for investment in mining for minerals.

Thus, up to the SEA there was not much specifically laid down in the Treaties concerning industrial policy apart from the above-mentioned provisions in the Treaty of Paris regarding coal and steel. Article 23 of the SEA, however, modified the Treaty of Rome by adding Title V on economic and social cohesion which includes Article 130c on the ERDF, which 'is intended to help redress the principal regional imbalances in the Community through participating in the development and structural adjustment of regions whose development is lagging behind and *in the conversion of declining industrial regions*' (our italics). This is where regional policy definitely overlaps with industrial policy. Regional policy will be mentioned later in this chapter. Title VI, which was also added to the Treaty of Rome by Article 24 of the Single European Act, is about research and technological development. Article 130f stipulates that the 'Community's aim shall be to strengthen the scientific and technological basis of European industry and to encourage it to become more competitive at international level'.

Thus research, technological development and demonstration programmes were to be implemented by promoting cooperation with undertakings, research centres and universities.

Member states were to coordinate their R&D policies and programmes and the Commission could take any useful initiative to promote such coordination (Article 130h). The Community was to adopt a multi-annual framework programme setting out all its activities. Thus strong guidelines for policy in research and technological development which were to become very important in later years were laid down in 1986 in the SEA.

It is not until we come to the Treaty on European Union, signed in Maastricht on 7 February 1992, that the Treaty of Rome is amended to include a section on industry, Title XIII, Article 130 which we shall quote in full.

Article 130

1. The Community and the member states shall ensure that the conditions necessary for the competitiveness of the Community's industry exist.

   For that purpose, in accordance with a system of open and competitive markets, their action shall be aimed at

   ● speeding up the adjustment of industry to structural changes

   ● encouraging an environment favourable to initiative and to the development of under-takings throughout the Community, particularly small and medium-sized undertakings

   ● encouraging an environment favourable to cooperation between undertakings

   ● fostering better exploitation of the industrial potential of policies of innovation, research and technological development.

2. The member states shall consult each other in liaison with the Commission and, when necessary, shall coordinate their action. The Commission may take any useful initiative to promote such coordination.

3. The Community shall contribute to the achievement of the objectives set out in paragraph 1 through the policies and activities it pursues under other provisions of this Treaty. The Council, acting unanimously on a proposal from the Commission, after consulting the European Parliament and the Economic and Social Committee, may decide on specific measures in support of action taken in member states to achieve the objectives set out in paragraph 1.

The Title shall not provide a basis for the introduction by the Community of any measure which could lead to a distortion of competition.

There is also a section in the part of the Maastricht Treaty on amendments to the Rome Treaty called Title XV on Research and Technological Development which is an essential part of EU Industrial Policy as it is today. Article 130f of Title XV says that 'The Community shall have the objective of strengthening the scientific and technological bases of Community industry and encouraging it to become more competitive at international level, while promoting all the research activities deemed necessary by virtue of other chapters of this

Treaty.' The Community is to encourage firms, research centres and universities in research and technological development activities, aiming to enable firms to 'exploit the internal market potential to the full' especially through the 'opening up of national public contracts, the definition of common standards and the removal of legal and fiscal obstacles to that cooperation'. The Community shall encourage all aspects of research and cooperation between member states in the technological field. A multi-annual framework shall be set up in this field. 'At the beginning of each year the Commission shall send a report to the European Parliament and Council. The report shall include information on research and technological development activities and the dissemination of results during the previous year, and the work programme for the current year' (Article 130p).

Thus, a very thorough programme for research and technological development (RTD) is laid down in the Maastricht Treaty. Hence it was first with the SEA and then most definitely with the Treaty on European Union (1992) that Community Industrial Policy was mapped out in the treaties.

A short history of Union industrial policy

Industrial policy has gradually evolved during the years through reports from commissioners, summit communiqués, EU documents and draft directives since its fragile start in the Treaty of Paris in 1951. Progress has finally been crystallised in the Maastricht Treaty after 40-odd years of piecemeal development, which we now trace.

Articles 92–94 of the Treaty of Rome on aid granted by member states were written so that state aids did not distort competition. In the 1960s state intervention was in the realm of regional aid. Therefore the initial priority was to get member states to agree to guidelines on regional aid. Between 1968 and 1971 regional policy, which was the first of the EC's common policies not to be based on the Treaty of Rome, was conceived. Different types of region were classified, aid 'ceilings' were established for different categories of region, and there were methods of ensuring that information and notification about regional aid were given to the Commission.

The Community's slow progress in technological development was recognised as early as 1967 when the EEC Medium Term Economic Committee set up a Working Party for Scientific and Technical Research Policy, or PREST. In this year it completed a report which proposed some ideas for encouraging research and innovation in the member states and in the Community. The first Council of Science Ministers was held in 1967 and it made some resolutions. It noted that Europe needed to catch up with the USA and announced that the Community would establish a legal and tax framework that would encourage research. It furthered collaboration in the seven areas mentioned by the PREST working party, i.e. data-processing, pollution, telecommunications, meteorology, transport, the metallurgical industries and oceanography.

A new Directorate General XII for Research, Science and Education was founded at the Commission after the First Council of Science Ministers. Also, a new Directorate General III was established for industrial affairs in 1967.

In 1970 the Council of Ministers established a forum called COST, i.e. European Cooperation on Scientific and Technical Research. Through this the Community collaborated with some non-member states.

The 1960s and early 1970s were good years, and the Commission got member states to keep their aid within limits and guidelines. Investment aid to new industries and mergers were approved. At this time the main thrust of industrial policy was the aim to complete the internal market. Stress was put on the importance of eliminating non-tariff barriers to trade, reducing national preferences in government purchasing and creating a harmonised tax, monetary and legal background for European industry. Industrial policy was primarily at this time a weakening of state intervention.

In the early 1970s, however, the EC increased in size. Recession, inflation, low growth and high rates of unemployment followed the doubling of the price of oil. The internal market was not completed by the mid-1970s and the common market was under threat from subsidisation and non-tariff barriers (often in the guise of technical barriers).

By 1969, the 12 year transition period culminating in the completion of the customs union had ended and the Community could give its attention to new goals. Among these was industrial policy. In 1970 Guido Colonna, the Commissioner for D.G. IV, produced a 'Memorandum on Industrial Policy in the Communities' otherwise known as the Colonna Report. It expressed the need to create a single European industrial system by enabling firms to function on a Community-wide basis and by creating a single European market. It stressed how important it was for companies to organise themselves on a European level. This would necessitate the provision of a European Company Statute, the harmonisation of company laws of member states and the setting up of laws in member states relating to corporate groups and possibly new kinds of business networks. There was a need to eradicate taxation of cross-frontier mergers, which was unfavourable as against mergers carried out within a country. The Commission perceived the transnational firm as a means to facilitate progress in technology. The concept of development contracts, which were to be given primarily to firms that were prepared to carry out technological development internationally, was originated. New kinds of industry based on technology were to be established to compensate for old industries which were declining. The need for mobility of labour and the use of the ESF in coping with declining industries was mentioned. In time the management of the vicissitudes of industries in decline was to become a main pillar of EU industrial policy. Most of the measures mentioned in the Colonna report were adopted by the Heads of State at the Paris Summit in 1972.

In 1973 an action programme on industrial and technical policy was put forward by the Commission under the influence of the Paris Summit communiqué. It was a subdued version of the Colonna report. Two suggestions were made – firstly the harmonisation of company law in the member states and secondly the creation of a European company statute.

Also in 1973 a Commission memorandum establishing a scientific and technology policy programme was published. In the first part of 1974 a programme of action on this subject was adopted by the Council of Ministers, mentioning the need for cooperation in science and technology, a free exchange of scientific and technological information, collaboration on projects of EU interest, the founding of an umbrella organisational structure, and forecasting about science and technology. As a result of this the EU spent a certain amount on research and technological development, but not enough to close the technological gap. This was later rethought in 1986 under the aegis of the SEA, as has been mentioned above.

Also in 1973 a draft discussion on merger control was put forward. France and Britain especially queried the Commission's objectivity in making decisions on these matters, especially on mergers involving complicated technical issues. Not until 1989 was an agreement arrived at whereby the vetting of intended mergers in member states was carried out by the Commission. Details on this Merger Control Regulation are provided in Chapter 7.

In 1975 the Colonna report proposal for a European Company Statute was embodied in the 'Proposal for a Council Regulation on the statute for European Companies' (Commission EC 1975). This was a development from the *Proposal for a Council Regulation Embodying a Statute for European Companies* (Commission EC 1970b). The European Company Statute has not yet been adopted at the time of writing in June 1994. It originally ran up against the problem of 'Mitbestimmung' (the question of workers' participation in decision-making) in German companies not being accepted throughout the Community and the problem of to what extent the European company should come under the aegis of the ECJ. The statute for a European company was still being discussed in the Council in Autumn 1993, and the UK government was against it largely on the grounds of worker participation problems and the fact that it would necessitate a change to English national law in the form of changing the structure of companies. Gradual harmonisation of the national laws of member states concerning companies has also been very slow.

The early 1970s was a very busy time for the development of industrial policy. Again as a result of the Colonna report's advocation of cross-frontier cooperation, there was a *Proposal for a Regulation by the Council on the European Cooperation Grouping (ECG)* (Commission EC 1974)

In 1972 the Business Liaison Office, as it was then known (now the Business Cooperation Office (BCO)) was founded by the Commission originally on a temporary basis for three years. It now provides a permanent service to companies on fiscal and economic problems in cross-frontier cooperation. It also facilitates the 'twinning' of SMEs and small banks.

Also around this time the Community published two international patent conventions – the Munich Convention for the Grant of European Patents of 1973, i.e. the European Patent Convention in conjunction with non-member states, and the Luxembourg Convention for the European Patent for the Common Market of 1975, i.e. the Common Market Patent Convention, in conjunction with member states. This was in accordance with the free movement of goods principle of the Rome Treaty, as there were now no patent barriers to trade.

Problem industries

The recession in the mid-1970s in the aftermath of the doubling of the price of oil led to an intensification of the problems of Europe's older industries. This led to a policy in the Community of helping declining industries (as had been mentioned in the Colonna Report) specifically through the use of the ESF. However, since then a variety of programmes have been established to help declining industries – RECHAR, RENAVAL, RESIDER and RETEX. The industries which were in decline at this time and were showing structural problems were textiles, steel and shipbuilding. More recently the European petrochemical industry has faced problems of declining sales and overcapacity.

Textiles

In 1971 the Commission produced a policy document on the rules for member states giving aid to the textile industry – *Framework for Aid to the Textile Industry* (Commission EC 1971a). It said that state aids should improve competitiveness and improve structure in the industry, and not simply fund inefficiency. As the industry consisted of a very large number of small-scale enterprises, this was difficult to supervise.

The late 1970s and early 1980s saw the Commission in conflict with the governments of member states, especially Italy. The Commission took a more protectionist point of view in the renegotiations of the MFA in 1977 (lasting until 1981) and a system was developed whereby market quotas were guaranteed for developing countries.

In 1985 DGIII, the Directorate General for industrial and technological affairs, established production quotas within the member states to cut out excess capacity. DGIV, the Directorate for Competition, said that this was in conflict with Article 85 of the Treaty of Rome on competition.

The difficulties of the industry seemed to have eased by the mid 1980s and the policy of the Commission progressed from regulating aid from the member states to its elimination through modernisation and technical progress in the industry. This policy was continued with the establishment in 1992 of RETEX, a scheme to help regions with a high dependence on textiles and clothing industries. This programme is aimed at improving the quality, design and marketing of textile products and at helping with the retraining and redeployment of redundant staff.

The need to modernise and rationalise this industry has been further strengthened by the Uruguay agreement whereby GATT will seek to progressively remove the protectionist effects of the MFA. This liberalisation of trade in textiles and clothing could lead to some problems for European-based textile companies, and it may increase the social and economic costs of the necessary rationalisation of this industry.

Steel

Under the 1951 ECSC Treaty the policies for steel have been more *dirigiste*. In 1975 the effects of the recession first hit the industry. Output had decreased by 20 per cent by 1977 and the industry was functioning on only 60 per cent of its capacity. A system of voluntary production quotas was started. Anti-dumping duties were fixed for steel imports under GATT rules and minimum prices were imposed.

The decline, however, continued. In 1980 a state of crisis was recognised. The production quotas were made obligatory. The Davignon Plan, called after the Commissioner for DGIII, was conceived and a scheme for compulsorily reducing capacity was started. During the early 1980s quotas were rigidly adhered to. Pressure on imports was kept up and the Commission made VER agreements with 15 non-EC countries affecting 75 per cent of the EC's imports.

By 1988 the crisis had subsided. The Commission had calmed squabbles between member states. Collective bargaining power as exemplified by the Commission had a more incisive effect on the policies and prices of competing overseas countries than the member states could have sustained separately. Steel quotas were finally abolished in 1990.

However, by the early 1990s there was once again a crisis in the European steel industry. Considerable overcapacity exists and the growth of imports from the NICs and Central and Eastern Europe have made this problem even more severe. The EU has instituted quotas against steel imports from Central and Eastern Europe and has had disputes with the USA over state aids to parts of the European steel industry.

The decision in February 1994 to fine 17 steel companies for breaches of Article 85 has lead to strong criticism of the Commission. The 17 steel companies claim that the practices they were accused of (price fixing and market sharing) stopped in 1992 and that they were largely instigated by the Commission in attempts to deal with the crisis of the late 1980s. The Commission has also been attacked for its failure to reduce the level of state aids that are given by the Italian, German and Spanish governments. The 17 companies that were fined were particularly aggrieved by this, as they have no or very few state aids. These companies are also unwilling to cut back production, in accordance with the plans of the Commission, until these state aids are eliminated. The Commission therefore faces considerable difficulties with its policy towards steel, and the *dirigiste* approach that the Commission and some member states have taken towards the steel industry has contributed to these difficulties.

The EU established the RESIDER programme in 1988 to help in the process of combating the social and economic costs of steel plant closures in the poorer regions of the Community. RESIDER is limited to a 55 per cent share of the costs of job creation schemes and 50 per cent for projects to improve the infrastructure of regions affected by the closure of steel plants. The EU may have to expand the RESIDER programme if it is to succeed in convincing some member states to close low productivity steel plants. Such rationalisation appears to be essential if the EU is to overcome the large overcapacity in the Community.

Shipbuilding

In 1969 there was a directive to harmonise all aid being given by the governments of member states to the shipbuilding sector. This was done to keep distortion of competition within the EC to the lowest possible level. The ultimate objective was to eradicate all state aids in the long run.

The oil crisis in the early 1970s resulted in 40 per cent less tonnage of ships being produced in Community shipyards by 1976. A directive in 1978 subjected state aids to shipbuilding to two tests: (*a*) state aids should increase the efficiency of the shipyards; (*b*) state aids should maintain or decrease capacity rather than increasing it.

In 1979 the Commission tried to encourage ministers to accept a policy whereby two tons of old ships would be scrapped for every one ton of new ships built. Thus total capacity would decrease and employment would increase. This policy was not adopted. In 1986 there was a new directive to modernise the industry and to aim to eradicate state aids totally. In all there have been six directives up to 1992 attempting to restrict state aid to shipbuilding. By 1990 aid was restricted to 20 per cent of the selling price of a ship.

In 1988 the EU began the RENAVAL programme to provide aid to regions affected by the decline in shipbuilding and ship repair activities. RENAVAL has similar objectives and conditions for applicability as RESIDER.

Petrochemicals

The European petrochemicals industry has entered a period of decline in the 1990s due to the saturation of markets for basic chemicals, environmental factors that have reduced consumption of pesticides and herbicides, the introduction of new materials that have reduced the demand for traditional oil-based materials, and the growth of import penetration from the NICs and Central and Eastern Europe. The EU has responded to this decline by restricting imports from Central and Eastern Europe and by encouraging rationalisation by the large petrochemical companies. So far this policy has not been very successful in reducing the overcapacity in this industry.

The EU has not yet established a new programme to help ease the social and economic costs of the necessary rationalisation of this industry. However, pressure to set up a new programme to ease the difficulties caused by this problem may grow because some of the least viable petrochemical plants are situated in the poorer regions of the EU. The problems facing this industry may also lead some member states to institute new state aids programmes to help keep their petrochemical industries competitive. The EU is therefore likely to face considerable pressures to develop a policy to deal with these problems.

The list of problem industries in the EU has grown in the 1980s and 1990s. These industries have some common features: static or declining markets, significant import penetration and, in some cases, low productivity compared to the NICs and high levels of state aids. The EU has generally adopted the view that these industries have to rationalise, modernise and move to higher added-value activities.

Nevertheless, the EU has resorted to protectionist measures (particularly against Central and Eastern Europe) and it has allowed some member states to continue to provide significant state aids to these industries. The Commission has also been active (in the steel and petrochemical industries) in promoting collaborative arrangements between companies to achieve reductions in capacity in efforts to boost prices. However, the Commission has not always been careful to ensure that such reductions in capacity are based on economic criteria such as closure of high cost plants.

This reluctance to take a tough stance seems to be partly based on regional policy and 'economic and social cohesion' considerations. However, reluctance to tackle the problems caused by state aids and capitulation to powerful interest groups may explain why the Commission appears to have an aversion to allowing market forces to achieve rationalisation of these declining industries.

Research and technological development

Research and technological development has already been mentioned in this chapter in connection with the provisions laid down for it in the SEA and in the Maastricht Treaty of 1992. In addition, the early years of research and technological development were mentioned in the historical account of industrial policy – PREST (1967), COST (1971) and the first Council of Science Ministers of 1967 which led to the founding of a Directorate General (XII) for Research, Science and Education, also in 1967, were important features. The Colonna Report (1970) also mentioned the importance of technology as an important development to encourage new industries to offset those in decline. As mentioned previously, a *Memorandum concerning Overall Community Action in Scientific and Technological Research and Development* (Commission EC 1971b) was published in 1971. This was produced by the new Directorate General XII, which deals with science research and development. This report was principally concerned with the fact that many Community bodies were concerned with research and development. It was proposed that CERD, a European Research and Development Committee, should be inaugurated. This committee would comprise the senior civil servants responsible for research and development policy in the Community countries. Its agenda would include setting up areas of research in the Community in this field. The Joint Research Centre (JRC) had been established as the Joint Nuclear Research Centre under the Euratom Treaty of 1957. In 1971, after member states had withdrawn their nuclear energy programmes and it had gone into decline, the JRC widened its brief to include all research. Today the JRC is concerned with new energy sources (e.g. solar power), the environment and its protection, and the working of major installations. It is still responsible today for such things as nuclear safety and nuclear measurement. In 1973 the JRC once again had a multi-annual programme and funds given to it by the Community.

The Community can therefore work directly through R&D done through the Community organisation – the JRC – or it can work indirectly by giving research contracts to the research groups and laboratories of its member states. In this way the Community pays half the cost and those running the contracts in Community countries pay the other half. The Community also carries out coordination of national research, and the costs are limited to the coordination costs.

During the 1970s and early 1980s there was a great multiplication of Community organisations wearing a large number of acronyms which made the R&D field more and more bewildering, for example BRIDGE (Biotechnology Research for Innovation, Development and Growth in Europe), BRITE (Basic Research in Industrial Technologies for Europe), DELTA (Developing European Learning through Technological Advance), ESPRIT (European Strategic Programme for Research and Development in Information Technology), EUREKA (European Research Coordination Agency), RACE (Research and Development Programme in Advanced Communications Technologies for Europe), STEP (Science and Technology for Environmental Protection) and STRIDE (Science and Technology for Regional Innovation and Development in Europe). A great many more R&D programmes were begun in the 1980s. The Community could not be accused of failing to generate R&D programmes.

The SEA rationalised all this and encouraged the EU to underpin the scientific and technological basis of its industry with a multinational framework. Thus in 1986 a framework was set up for action in this field in the quinquennium from 1987–1991. Some 7.7 bn. ECU was devoted to its budget and eight areas of activity were chosen, of which the principal ones were the exploitation of marine resources, energy, biotechnology, telecommunications and information technology.

The most recent policy document in the field of science and technology at the time of writing is the Second Commission Working Document concerning RTD Policy in the Community and the Fourth Framework Programme (1994–1998) of Community RTD activities. This was prepared after the signing of the Maastricht Treaty on 7 February 1992 and after guidelines were issued at the Edinburgh European Council in December 1992. Its object is to secure agreement between the three institutions on the broad lines of the Fourth Framework Programme by mid-1993 and to facilitate the proposal in this field which the Commission puts to the Council and Parliament on the ratification of the Maastricht Treaty. 'A very significant point which emerged from the discussions was the emphasis placed on the important role of research with a view to improving the quality of life and *strengthening the competitiveness of industry in the Community*' (from the 'Second Commission Working Document concerning RTD Policy in the Community and the Fourth Framework Programme

(1994–98) of Community RTD Activities' – our italics). Some 13.1 bn. ECU (current prices) is earmarked for the Fourth Framework Programme (1994–1998).

The European Council stressed that 'Community support for Research and Development should continue to focus on generic, precompetitive research and be of multi-sectoral application..... Improving the dissemination of results amongst enterprises, particularly small and medium-sized businesses, cost-effectiveness and coordination between national programmes should be priorities for Community action.'

The European Council also called on the Commission 'to bring forward proposals for improving the management and efficiency of research funded by the Community to achieve better economic effectiveness. ...it should be ensured that Community activities contribute the most value added possible to efforts already under way in member states.' The framework should empower the Community, using appropriate means, to respond rapidly to scientific and technological change. It should be allocated enough financial resources to pursue the objectives set by the Maastricht Treaty.

The concept of subsidiarity is mentioned in the document. 'The Community should take action on research only if the objectives can be better achieved by the Community than by member states acting on their own.' National policies on research and community policy should be mutually consistent. This is based on the fact that less than 4 per cent of all government research and technological development by the member states is on joint action under a Community policy. The activities focused on by the Fourth Framework are information and communications technologies; developing the information and communications infrastructure; industrial technologies; environment, life sciences and technologies; energy, research for a European transport policy; and targeted socio-economic research.

The Fourth Framework Programme has been adopted and ought to appear in the Official Journal in late May, early June 1994.

Industrial policy in the EU in the 1990s

The most up-to-date Commission documents on industrial policy as such at the time of writing are Commission EC (1990, 1991a, 1991b) (see References). The IT industry is one of the new industries the EU is investing in as part of its new approach to industrial policy. In Commission EC (1990) a policy in favour of following positive adjustment policies including a technological development policy is advocated. It is useful to employ this approach to the Community's electronics and information technology (IT) industries, which are currently afflicted with serious structural adjustment problems. It is a strategic industry because of its 'enabling' nature and its value-added effects on the economy as a whole.

These industries have three main products – components, computers (i.e. hardware, printers, software and optic and industrial automation applications), and consumer electronics. These are the industries with which the report on the IT industry (Commission 1991a) deals. They had a worldwide turnover in 1990 of 700 bn. ECU and a turnover in the Community of 175 bn. ECU. Their market is expanding rapidly, represents 5 per cent of GDP and it is expected to rise to 10 per cent by the year 2000. Because of their 'enabling' nature these industries are very important, as they provide the hardware, software and application systems now used in practically all economic and social sectors. It is calculated that 60–65 per cent of workers in the population are affected in some way by these technologies and their applications.

Commission EC (1991a) does two things:

1. it examines the relative industrial and technological conditions of the EU's electronics and IT industries;

2. it establishes, together with Commission EC (1990), a number of measures which the EU and member states would be prepared to implement.

American and Japanese firms have cornered significantly more of the world market. Facing up to difficulties at the moment, European companies are busy restructuring – they are trying to reduce costs, to increase productivity and to be more responsive to rapid changes in demand. These restructuring exercises are expensive and involve job-shedding.

The Community industry has a limited presence in certain key sectors – semiconductors, peripherals and consumer electronics – and it is in a difficult situation with computers. Thus it has to import components from its competitors, and the increased demand for IT products and services in Europe is only partly being met from European companies. This imbalance has contributed to the trade deficits of many of the member states with Japan and the USA.

Much change is currently taking place in the EU – industrial research and technological development work and many restructuring activities have been pursued, major technological programmes have been set up in member states, EU intervention has increased through several community programmes. EUREKA is a programme set up on the initiative of France in 1985 uniting 19 European countries – the EUR12, EFTA and Turkey – and the Commission to strengthen cooperation between industry and research institutes in the field of advanced technology and public works projects (Gondrand 1992). ESPRIT is another important programme. It was formed after the Commission investigated industries in which the EU was falling behind Japan and the USA. Information technology was deemed to be such an industry. Thus in 1984 a ten year programme was launched under the acronym ESPRIT. It combined 12 major European companies, many research centres and universities and very many SMEs. The first plan, lasting five years, cost 1500 m. ECU with the Community contributing half of the budget. For the second phase of ESPRIT the budget has risen to some 3200 m. ECU. RACE, yet another IT connected programme, was set up in 1985. It is developing the technology base for a network of integrated broad-based telecommunications systems using optical fibres.

Commission EC (1991a) provides five proposals for action.

1. *Regarding demand*, trans-European networks are to be created incorporating harmonised telecommunication services, and this will stimulate the demand for IT and electronic equipment.

2. *Technology*: The EU is to consider launching a second generation of RTD programmes, ranging from projects at the pre-competitive stage to projects geared more closely to the market.

3. *Training*: The Union needs to train research scientists and engineers capable of developing and making the best use of the new information technology.

4. *External relations*: The Union is to sustain a competitive Union electronics and IT industry by adopting a trade policy based on the following six objectives:

'(i)   the maintenance of an open, multilateral trade system

(ii)   the improvement of access to the markets of the main trading partners in electronics and IT (notably the USA, Japan and South Korea)

(iii) the establishment of fair competition in international markets

(iv)   support for scientific, technological, industrial and commercial cooperation in the international sphere

(v)   continuing integration of European markets by means of new agreements with EFTA and East European countries

(vi)   economic restructuring aid for the East European countries.'

5. *The Business environment*: There is a need to improve financing systems. It is important to finance systems for firms which are capital intensive and require higher RTD expenditure. 'The public authorities should hold discussions with banks and financial institutions on ways in which such capital could be employed in conjunction with taxation measures.' There should be faster standardisation and integration of standards into products (hardware and software).

Biotechnology is another important fast-developing industry. The paper (Commission EC 1991b) says 'The recent commission communication on industrial policy stressed that *only those industries in the forefront of [the] technological process can maintain and improve competitiveness in the European economic system as a whole*' (our italics). This is why the biotechnology industries are crucial to industrial policy. It is therefore of prime importance that the public authorities at national and community level provide clear and predictable conditions for the industry.

In 1985 world sales of biology-derived products (excluding fermented foods and drinks) were roughly ECU 7.5 bn. For the year 2000 industry estimates vary between ECU 26 bn. and ECU 41 bn. Thus even the lower estimate provides for a threefold increase in sales. Biotechnology is a strategic industry affecting the major challenges in the world: food, health, environment and population growth. An outline of the biotechnology industries in Europe is given in Marks (1993).

New vaccines developed through biotechnological techniques have already saved lives and improved the quality of life for humans and animals. There is ongoing development of drought-resistant plants, of great interest to many developing countries, and other plants are being rendered unattractive to their predators, thus reducing the need for pesticides. Biotechnology is also being applied to food production and this has important implications for the EU's agricultural policy.

However, anxieties have been expressed about dangers inherent in biotechnological techniques and their implications for human and animal health. It is suggested that advice should be available to the Commission in the area of ethics in biotechnology.

In biotechnology the time required for innovations to reach the market is very great because of the time required for registration. This cost in time as well as money makes research in this sector particularly important. It is therefore the role of government to encourage industrial development of biotechnology while ensuring that a satisfactory ethical and safety-orientated framework exists. The purpose of the paper (Commission EC 1991b) is to examine the future perspectives for competitive biotechnology in the EU.

Within the EU it is the pharmaceutical, agrochemical, food and drink sectors which have been the most active in developing the industrial applications of biotechnology. Uses of biotechnology such as energy, metal extraction, waste treatment, chemical products and bioelectronics are relatively underdeveloped as yet.

A significant number of firms in the EU that are active in biotechnology are chemical and pharmaceutical multinationals which provide a broad industrial base for research and development as they have significant technological and financial capacity. The current community average for employment in the sector is 19.8 per cent, i.e. approximately 15 million jobs.

Two factors will affect the competitiveness of the biotechnology industries, namely international policy strategies and intellectual property rights. Other factors affecting competitiveness of countries involved in biotechnology are 'financing and tax incentives for firms, government funding of basic and applied research, personnel availability and training, the legislative framework, intellectual property law, university–industry relationships, anti-trust law, international technology transfer, investment and trade, government targeting policies in biotechnology, public perception and consumer choice.'

The economic importance attached to the protection of intellectual property in this field should not be underestimated, since firms will invest in long-term high risk projects only if they are assured of adequate patents for the results of their research. Trade barriers resulting from different levels of protection should be avoided. These principles were negotiated by the EU in GATT and new rules in this area were established in the Uruguay agreement.

The Commission and the governments of member states are responsible for ensuring that the regulatory and industrial frameworks relating to biotechnology which exist within the Union are conducive to the competitive development of the industries involved. It is therefore the role of these authorities to promote a single market for biotechnology, to achieve a competitive position insofar as the protection of intellectual property is concerned, to provide the necessary framework for encouraging research and development, and to ensure protection of human, animal and plant health and the environment. It is important to industry to have a harmonised and transparent approach to regulation because of the high investment cost of research in biotechnology.

The completion of the SEM for biotechnology will depend mainly on the application of two tools at Union level: the legal framework for product authorization and the industrial use of standards. The regulatory system, based on scientific analysis and evaluation covers worker protection and product legislation based on the three criteria of safety, quality and efficiency, which are also applied when assessing whether a product can be authorised for distribution on the open market.

Regarding standards – in industrial areas other than biotechnology, the regulatory approach of the Commission complements the self-regulatory activities of industry. In the different issues raised by biotechnology the industry has an interest in the legislator indicating from the beginning the scope and orientations for standardisation in order that confusion be avoided. In connection with the protection of intellectual property the Commission has proposed two measures to ensure that the Union's industries and agricultural producers are in a position to be competitive at an international level – firstly the legal protection of biotechnological inventions to ensure harmonisation within the Union, and secondly plant variety rights to assure plant breeders that, through a single decision, they may acquire direct and uniform protection throughout the whole Union as opposed to the existing fragmented approach.

Simultaneously there is a need for greater international harmonisation on issues such as burden of proof, 'grace periods', 'first to invent versus first to file' and access to deposited strains. The Union sees the need for research, development and innovation in this field. The SEA has provided new impetus towards a strategy for research and competitiveness in the biotechnology industries.

Further action must be taken in the development of the legal framework, the use of standards, the protection of intellectual property and financial support for research and development. Ethical issues raised by biotechnology must be addressed. Further consideration will have to be given to the risk assessment of biological agents and to implementing existing EU legislation on worker protection, health, safety and the environment. The impact on consumer information and choice needs to be taken into account.

The Commission intends to pursue a dialogue with CEN, the European Committee for Standardisation about standards, to draw up a clear mandate for CEN's activities in biotechnology and to identify those aspects that can best be developed by CEN.

Regarding research, development, innovation and investment, the Union must remain attractive for investment in biotechnology. The Union will continue the development and implementation of a policy for research and development in biotechnology. It will be verified that state aid encourages and does not inhibit competitiveness. State aid will be rigorously examined and controlled. More near-market research and perhaps less pure research should be encouraged by the Commission. The Commission is developing an approach to stimulate the formation and growth of small companies in biotechnology.

In the area of intellectual property, the Union must maintain a strong system of patent protection if investment in biotechnology is to be encouraged. With respect to ethics, recent debate has centred on ethical aspects of human genome analysis, of human embryo research, of environmental research, of animal welfare and of intellectual property law. The Union collaborates with important Council of Europe work in this field. The Commission thinks it desirable that the Union should have an advisory structure on ethics and biotechnology. The Union has established a working group on human embryos and research.

Regarding the legislation framework, new biotechnology products involving gene manipulation may need to be reviewed and assessed. The Commission foresees that a number of biotechnology products, such as new products involving gene manipulation, will have to be regulated under existing Union sectoral legislation.

The general position of the EU with regard to industrial policy has been outlined in the report – *Industrial Policy in an Open and Competitive Environment* (Commission EC 1990). This report provides an analysis of industrial policy for the EU in the 1990s. With the completion of the SEM and the further liberalisation of world trade, European industry is at a turning point in the mid-1990s. What role should public authorities play in industry's new situation? That is the Commission's main question in this document and it sets out to answer it. Guidelines are laid down for the development of industrial policy in the EU.

The main issue is 'which conditions need to be present in order to strengthen the optimal allocation of resources by market forces, towards accelerating structural adjustment and towards improving industrial competitiveness and the industrial and particularly technological long-term framework' (Commission EC 1990). Public authorities are at the same time catalysts and innovators. The main thrust for competitiveness should come from the firms themselves, but they should be sure of the conditions set by the public authorities.

A number of emerging technologies are very important – advanced materials, advanced electronics and information systems, integrated manufacturing systems, and life-science applications.

Macro-economic conditions are more difficult because of problems of low growth and unemployment, the requirement to improve environmental standards, the need to rebuild strong and competitive economies in Central and Eastern Europe and the challenge of coping with an ageing population in member states. These problems make it difficult to achieve stable macro-economic conditions in the EU. However, the report regards stable macro-economic conditions as being crucial for the development of a strong industrial base.

Technological innovation is very important to industrial policy. The report states that 'the impact of technology is not limited to a few high technology sectors but affects the whole economy, both in terms of products and production methods. Thus, the mastery of generic technologies such as flexible manufacturing systems and information technology, new materials and biotechnology possess great importance for the competitiveness of European firms' (Commission EC 1990).

The paper says that Union industrial policy should be established around the following considerations.

'(i) Laying down stable and long-term conditions for an efficiently functioning market economy; maintenance of a competitive economic environment, as well as a high level of educational attainment and of social cohesion.

(ii) Providing the main catalysts for structural adjustment. In this respect the completion of the internal market has a strategic role to play. The principles on which the internal market programme are based, built around the harmonisation of essential items and the mutual recognition of member states' own systems, also provide optimal opportunities for industrial development.

(iii) Developing the instruments to accelerate structural adjustment and to enhance competitiveness.'

Conclusion

The EU has clearly developed a treaty basis for a limited role in positive industrial polices. So far it has had more economic impact on industrial structures by its negative industrial polices such as the creation of a CU and the SEM and the development of a common competition policy. The deregulation of the telecommunications services and airline industries is another area where the EU is significantly affecting the industrial structures of the Union by use of negative industrial polices. The role of the EU in positive industrial polices has been significantly less influential. Nevertheless, the EU plays an important role in the speed of adjustment of the declining industries of the Union. The social and economic cost of this adjustment is also influenced by Union policies and programmes. It is clear that the

Commission would like a greater role in positive industrial polices to correct for market failure, and for strategic reasons. However, whether the EU should have such a role is a question to which there appears to be no clear answer. If the EU is regarded as an economic agency with primarily political objectives, the case for a common interventionist industrial policy is quite strong. If, however, the Union is considered to be an economic agency with primarily economic objectives, the case for a common industrial policy is less clear.

References and further reading

Beije P R, Groenewegen I, Kostoulas I, Paelinck J and **van Paridon C** (eds) 1987 *A Competitive Future for Europe? Towards a New Industrial Policy*, Croom Helm, London.

Buchanan J M 1978 *The Economics of Politics*, Institute of Politics, Institute of Economic Affairs, London.

Commission EC 1970a Memorandum on the Community's Industrial Policy, or The Colonna Report, *Bulletin of the European Community, Supplement 4/70*, Luxembourg.

Commission EC 1970b Proposal for a Council Regulation embodying a statute for European companies, *Bulletin of the European Communities, Supplement 8/70*, Luxembourg.

Commission EC 1971a Framework for Aid to the Textile Industry, Communication from the Commission (SEC (71) 253).

Commission EC 1971b Memorandum concerning overall Community Action in Scientific and Technological Research and Development, *Bulletin of the European Community 1/71*, Luxembourg.

Commission EC 1973a Towards the Establishment of a European Industrial Base, *Bulletin of the European Communities, Supplement 7/73*, Luxembourg.

Commission EC 1973b Scientific and Technological Policy Programme, *Bulletin of the European Communities, Supplement 13/73*.

Commission EC 1973c Draft convention on the International Merger of Sociétés Anonymes, *Bulletin of the European Communities, Supplement 13/73*, Luxembourg.

Commission EC 1974 Proposal for a Regulation by the Council on the European Cooperation Grouping (E.C.G.) *C14/30, Official Journal*, 15 February.

Commission EC 1975 Proposal for a Council Regulation on the Statute for European Companies, *Bulletin of the European Communities, Supplement 4/75*, Luxembourg.

Commission EC 1987 Towards a dynamic European economy, *Green Paper on the Development of the Common Market for Telecommunication Services and Equipment*.

Commission EC 1990 *Industrial policy in an Open and Competitive Environment: Guidelines for a Community Approach*, Communication of the Commission to the Council and to the European Parliament (COM (90) 556).

Commission EC 1991a *The European Electronics and Information Technology Industry: State of Play, Issues at Stake and Proposals for Action*, Communication from the Commission (SEC (91) 565).

Commission EC 1991b *Promoting the Competitive Environment for the Industrial Activities based on Biotechnology within the Community*, Communication of the Commission to the Council and to the European Parliament (SEC (91) 629).

Commission EC 1993 *Second Commission Working Document concerning R.T.D. Policy in the Community and the Fourth Framework Programme (1994–98) of Community R.T.D. Activities*.

de Jong H W (ed.) 1988 *The Structure of European Industry*, Kluwer Academic, London.

Gondrand F 1992 *Eurospeak, a User's Guide. A Dictionary of the Single Market*, Nicholas Brealey, London.

Hall G (ed) 1986 *European Industrial Policy*, Croom Helm, London.

Hodges M 1983 Industrial Policy: Hard Times or Great Expectations? in Wallace H, Wallace W and Webb C, *Policy-Making in the European Community*, Wiley, London.

James S 1991 Industrial Policy after 1992: making the most of the internal market, in Gowland D and James S (eds), *Economic Policy after 1992*, Dartmouth, Aldershot.

Krugman P 1991 *International Economics, Theory and Policy*, Harper Collins, New York.

Marks E 1993 Biotechnology, in Johnson P (ed.), *European Industries*, Edward Elgar, Aldershot.

Nevin E 1990 *The Economics of Europe*, Macmillan Education, London.

Nicolaides P (ed) 1993 *Industrial Policy in the European Community: A Necessary Response to Economic Integration*, Martinus Nijhoff, Dordrecht.

Price V C 1981 *Industrial Policies in the European Community*, Macmillan, London.

Price V C 1990 Industrial policy in El-Agraa, *The Economics of the European Community*, Philip Allan, London.

Swann D 1983 *Competition and Industrial Policy in the European Community*, Methuen and Co. Ltd., London.

Swann D 1992 *The Economics of the Common Market* (7th edn), Penguin, London.

Tyson L 1992 *Who's Bashing Whom? Trade conflict in high-technology industries*, Longman, London.

Ungerer H 1990 *Telecommunications in Europe*, Office for Official Publications of the EC, Luxembourg.

CHAPTER 9

Social policy

Stephen Dearden

Introduction

This chapter outlines the evolution of the EU's social policy beginning with the 'social clauses' of the Treaty of Rome, which included the establishment of the European Social Fund. Although a number of Directives were adopted in the 1970s on various aspects of employees' rights, it is the passage of the Single European Act which has given new impetus to the evolution of EU social policies, an impetus continued with the Social Charter and the Maastricht Treaty on European Union. However, central to these developments has been the debate as to whether action should extend beyond the immediate needs of the establishment of an internal market. Concern has been voiced that an unregulated internal labour market will undermine the competitive position of those member states that have relatively high wages and social security, and that the additional stresses of the structural transformation required by the Single European Market (SEM), both for individual employees and for industries, requires an explicit commitment to the policies necessary to maintain 'social cohesion'. This debate as to the nature of social policy within the EU has brought into sharp focus the ideological conflict between those who support an interventionist or corporatist approach to economic and social policy and those who argue for the primacy of market forces and minimal government intervention. This conflict will be a recurring theme throughout this chapter. But first we need to ask what are the major characteristics of the European labour market.

In 1991, of the 328.7 m. population of the EU, 148.1 m. were economically active, either employed or unemployed. The overall labour force activity rate of 55 per cent has remained constant for 30 years. However, trends in the activity rates of men and women have differed significantly. While male activity rates have fallen steadily from 82 per cent in 1960 to 69 per cent in 1990, female activity rates have risen over the same period from 32 per cent to 42 per cent.

The structure of employment has seen a steady shift out of agriculture (23 per cent 1960; 6.2 per cent 1991) and manufacturing (40 per cent 1960; 31.3 per cent 1991) towards the service sector (37 per cent 1960; 62.3 per cent 1991). However, at the same time unemployment has risen dramatically across Europe, especially after 1980. Thus in 1970 EU12 unemployment was only 2.4 per cent, but by 1993 it had reached 10.6 per cent (Figures 9.1 and 9.2). High unemployment has also been particularly concentrated among the younger

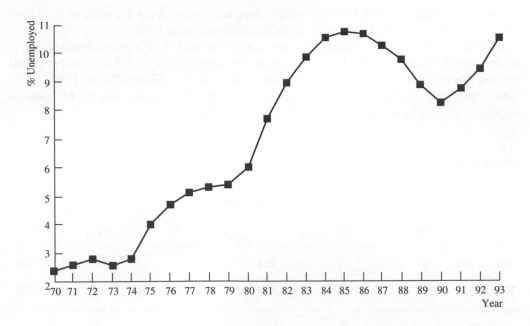

Figure 9.1 EU unemployment rate

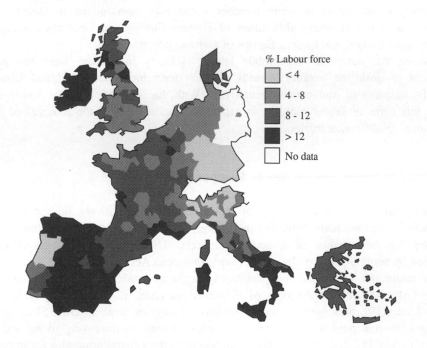

Figure 9.2 Unemployment rates 1991

age group (Figures 9.3 and 9.4). These deteriorating labour market conditions have stimulated renewed interest in the development of an active European Social Policy.

How far the EU can be regarded as a common labour market, or will develop into one in the foreseeable future, remains an open question. Between 1980 and 1985 the number of EU workers employed in another member state remained relatively constant (2.1 m. 1980; 1.9 m. 1985). The only exception to this experience was the 30 per cent fall in EU migrant employees in West Germany, from 732,000 to 520,000 (Table 9.1).

Table 9.1 EU migrant employees

						(thousands)						
	_B_	_DK_	_D_	_GR_	_E_	_F_	_IRL_	_I_	_L_	_NL_	_P_	_UK_
1980	159	11	732	5	–	653	–	–	–	84	–	466
1985	144	12	520	6	–	640	17	14	50	76	–	398

Source : Eurostat

The Commission does not expect any dramatic changes in this pattern, except for an increase in the currently low activity rates of women accompanying migrant male workers. The demographic ageing in some member states may also induce increased migration, especially with the economic difficulties of Eastern Europe and Germany's acceptance of migrants from Central and Eastern Europe of German origin.

However, the nature of the mobile labour is likely to change, from the permanent movement of unskilled workers towards the temporary movement of skilled labour, often under the auspices of multinational employers. With the completion of the Single European Market this form of labour mobility is expected to increase with the removal of legal and professional qualification barriers.

The Treaty of Rome and the Single European Act

The social provisions of the Treaty of Rome (1957) are relatively limited and scattered throughout its various parts. None the less it does extend its concern beyond those conditions necessary for the creation of a common market. This broader social commitment was reinforced by some of the Articles of the Single European Act (SEA) (1987).

Thus under the Treaty binding provisions sought to establish freedom of movement of workers (Arts 48 and 49), freedom of establishment (Arts 52–58), equal pay for men and women (Art. 119), and rights to social security of migrant workers (Art. 51). Non-binding provisions covered paid holidays (Art. 120), commitments to improving living and working conditions (Arts 117 and 118), and the laying down of the general principles for implementing a common vocational training policy (Art. 128). In addition it established the European Social Fund (Arts 123–128).

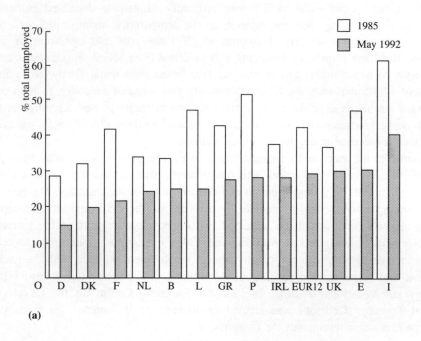

(a)

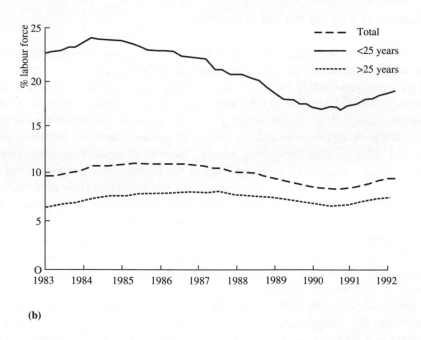

(b)

Figure 9.3 (a) Young people (<25 years) as a percentage of the unemployed in EUR12 in 1985 and May 1992; (b) unemployment rates in EUR12 1983 to May 1992

The European Social Fund (ESF) was originally limited to localised retraining and resettlement, to providing financial support to the temporarily unemployed, and to issues associated with migrant workers. However, in 1971 the role and operation of the Fund underwent significant reform. Its financing was switched from levies on member states to the Community's own resources, and it was set two broad objectives: firstly, to facilitate the employment adjustment resulting from Community policies, and secondly, to help overcome the structural problems experienced by certain regions or target groups, i.e. migrant workers, young job-seekers, women and the handicapped. To achieve these objectives 90 per cent of the Fund's resources were allocated to vocational training.

In response to the increase in unemployment in Europe, rising from 2.6 m. in 1974 to 6.5 m. in 1980, the ESF was quadrupled. This rise in unemployment and the lack of a clear set of objectives led in 1983 to a simplification and concentration of its activities. The new problem of youth unemployment was to receive 75 per cent of the ESF, and 40 per cent of the remaining general fund was to be allocated to the depressed regions of the Community – Greece, Northern Ireland, Ireland, Mezzogiorno. Other employment measures adopted during the 1970s included attempts to coordinate national employment policies, with the exchange of information and research, and resolutions on training schemes for the young, information technology and vocational training. In 1975 the European Centre for the Development of Vocational Training (Cedefop) was created to disseminate information on training, and to promote good practice throughout the Community.

Harmonisation of working conditions

Although the remit of the Treaty of Rome was relatively narrow in this area a number of directives were adopted covering collective redundancies (1975); employee rights in the event of company takeovers (1977) or insolvency (1980); equal pay (1975); equal access to employment, vocational training (1976) and social security (1986). In 1974 an Advisory Committee on Safety, Hygiene and Health Protection at Work was established leading to a series of Safety at Work Directives, and in 1975 a European Foundation for the Improvement of Living and Working Conditions was created. As with Cedefop it is administered by a quadripartite board composed of representatives of the Commission, employers, workers and member governments. Non-binding recommendations for the introduction of a 40 hour week and a minimum four weeks' paid holiday (1975) were also adopted, together with a call for the examination of the potential for reorganising working time through early retirement and reductions in overtime working. But the generally deteriorating economic situation, widening internal differences following the second enlargement of the Community and changes in government (especially in the UK) led to a period between 1981 and 1984 of inactivity in the development of a Community social policy.

With the passage of the SEA much broader social issues were addressed, with a commitment to the harmonisation of national provisions in regard to health, safety, environmental and consumer protection (Arts 100a and 118a), and to policies fostering 'the economic and social cohesion of the Community' (Arts 130a–130e). Although Art. 110a introduced Qualified Majority Voting (QMV)[1] to overcome the blocking power of individual member states, this is confined to those measures essential for the establishment of the SEM, i.e., health and safety legislation. Thus proposals relating to the free movement of people and employees' rights remain subject to individual member state veto. Article 118a also qualifies proposed legislation in that it requires it to take into account existing national conditions and regulations, and ensures that it does not impose administrative and financial burdens on enterprises. Article 118b also committed the Community to the encouragement of a 'social dialogue' between management and labour, i.e. the creation of a European dimension to industrial relations. This non-binding provision has, as we will see, yielded little success, and underlines the significantly greater difficulty in achieving progress in those social areas beyond those minimum conditions essential to the completion of the single market.

The Single European Market

With the commitment to the completion of the SEM by 1992, and the passage of the Single European Act, interest was rekindled in the social implications of evolving EU policies.

The movement towards the SEM was recognised as having implications for employment throughout the Community. Changes in costs and relative prices, stimulation of new technology and the general level of economic growth, were all factors which would determine the employment consequences of the Single Market. Econometric studies, although based upon some heroic assumptions, suggested a positive effect upon most EU macroeconomic measures. However the consequences for employment remained the most ambiguous, especially in the absence of a comprehensive external trade policy. Nonetheless a study by DG

Table 9.2 Sectors vulnerable to potential restructuring, 1986
(Industrial restructuring as a result of opening up public contracts in sectors where State purchases are predominant)

	Community market (in ECUm.)	Current capacity utilisation rate	Intra-EU Trade	Number of EU producers	Number of US producers	Reduction in costs*
Boilers	2 000	20%	very low	12	6	20%
Turbine generators	2 000	60%	very low	10	2	12%
Locomotives	100	50–80%	very low	16	2	20%
Central computers	10 000	80%	30–100%	5	9	5%
Telephone exchanges	1 000 –5 000	70%	15–45%	11	4	20%
Telephones	5 000	90%	very low	12	17	–
Lasers	500	50%	very high	1 000+	1 000+	–

* The reduction of costs represents economies of scale resulting from a doubling of production
Source: Atkins (Study of the costs of non-Europe/public contracts)

II (Social Europe 1988) does allow us to isolate the characteristics of those industries and regions most likely to be affected by the completion of the SEM (Table 9.2). Five indicators were utilised to identify the vulnerable sectors – the level of non-tariff barriers; the spread of real productivity and pre-tax prices across the Community; the proportion of member states' demand met by Community imports; and the proportion of a sector's turnover accounted for by small businesses.

These variables allowed the identification of two industrial sectors where the impact of the SEM was likely to induce considerable restructuring. Firstly, where there currently exist high levels of intra-EU imports but significant non-tariff barriers: this sector is dominated by large firms and characterised by state involvement, either as owner or as principal customer, and includes telecommunication equipment, computers and office equipment. The opening up of public procurement would profoundly affect this sector, encouraging the emergence of integrated European firms. This was expected to have uncertain consequences for employment, a situation reinforced by the impact of new technology. The second vulnerable industrial sector identified in the study was also characterised by high non-tariff barriers, but had very little intra-EU trade. Again these industries – shipbuilding, railway equipment, iron and steel, pharmaceuticals – are usually principally suppliers to government agencies or are state owned. The creation of these national standard-bearers has produced particularly fragmented industries, with large price and productivity differences. Again the opening up of public procurement procedures would result in a significant increase in intra-EU trade and industry restructuring.

In the tertiary sector, particularly financial services, the development of a single financial market may have important employment consequences. Although banking is already internationalised, considerable variations continue to exist in charges, and insurance remains fragmented and subject to national protection, except in the United Kingdom and the Netherlands. Again the employment consequences of enhanced competition were uncertain in a sector which was subject to considerable technological change.

The second, and complementary element to analysing the impact of the SEM was the regional dimension (see Chapter 10). The expected enhancement of economic growth would not benefit all regions equally, and even before the structural changes arising from enhanced economic integration, regional disparities within Europe had increased. This resulted from both the general deterioration in employment conditions since the mid-1970s and the second enlargement. A region's competitiveness is likely to be influenced by a number of factors. Firstly, the qualifications and skill mix of the labour force, which might be undermined by outward migration. Secondly, the infrastructure, estimated to be 40–60 per cent below the EU average standard in some regions. Finally, labour costs: differences in labour productivity are often greater than differences in wage levels, and the levelling-up of wage levels with economic integration would undermine the competitive position of some regions. Two types of area were therefore identified as being particularly vulnerable to structural problems: the underdeveloped mainly rural areas, and the regions where there was a concentration of declining heavy industries.

However, concern has also been expressed that particular social problems would emerge from the completion of the SEM across all of the EU. These arguments have focused on two issues – social dumping and illicit work (moonlighting).

Social dumping

Social dumping expresses the concern that employment will be lost in those states whose higher social standards are reflected in higher average labour costs. Faced with loss of market shares and firm relocation, there will be downward pressure on social conditions (wages, social security, minimum labour standards, etc.). This fear has led to demands for minimum wage levels, social security provisions and minimum health and safety guarantees, to avoid competitive pressures reducing standards to unacceptably low levels. However, it has been argued that concern about social dumping is misplaced. It is pointed out that it is not a new phenomenon but predates the completion of the SEM. Wage costs are not the only determinant of competitiveness, but must be considered within the context of relative productivity, with human and physical capital allowing high wage sectors to maintain their comparative advantage.

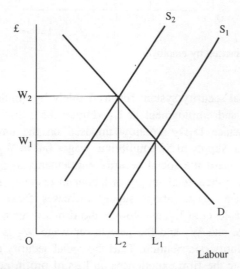

Figure 9.4 Social security financed by employees

It can also be shown that high levels of social security contributions, by either employer or employee, need have no effect on competitiveness. Consider in Figure 9.4 the situation where all the social security benefits are financed by payroll contributions by the employee. With employment at L_1 and wages at W_1 the imposition of a payroll contribution on employees is equivalent to a reduction in the net wage offered – i.e. equivalent to the vertical distance S_1S_2. However, this fall in the net wage shifts the supply curves of labour from S_1 to S_2. The equilibrium wage paid by employers now increases to W_2 and employment falls to L_2. But if workers regard the social security benefits that they now receive as part of their total wage package, and this is fully taken into account in their labour supply decision, then the supply curve will shift back to S_1, wages and employment returning to their original level. Of course not all social security benefits may be regarded as part of the remuneration package – e.g. maternity benefits to a single man – in which case the labour supply curve will shift only part of the way back to its original position. But the more inelastic the initial labour supply curve, the less impact this disregard of social security benefits will have on employment and wages.

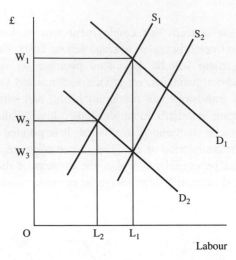

Figure 9.5 Social security financed by employers

Turning now to a social security system financed solely by employers, we begin with an equilibrium wage at W_1 and employment at L_1 (Figure 9.5). Social security contributions equal to the vertical distance D_1D_2 are now imposed on the employer, reducing labour demand to D_2. With labour supply at S_1 equilibrium wages fall to W_2 and employment to L_2. But again, if employees regard the social security entitlements as part of their total wages, they will respond by raising their total supply of labour in response to the increased value of their remuneration package – i.e. labour supply increases from S_1 to S_2. This returns employment to its previous level at L_1, and lowers the firm's wage rate to W_3. The difference between the original wage rate W_1 and the new lower wage W_3 is equal to the cost to the employer of the social security contribution. Thus the social security tax has been shifted onto the employee, and therefore the firm experiences no loss of profit, no increase in total labour costs and no change in its relative competitive position.

The only problem arises in a situation where wages are not downwardly flexible. Studies (Coe and Gagliardi 1985, Dearden 1993) have suggested that European labour markets tend to be characterised by a relatively high degree of real wage rigidity, and that this inflexibility has increased in the 1980s, despite increasing levels of unemployment. However, increasing economic integration induced by the SEM is expected by the Commission to enhance wage flexibility, as more competitive product markets increase the elasticity of firm's demand for labour. But economic integration and monetary union may also increase workers' awareness of comparative rates of pay and conditions of employment across the Community. There is already some evidence that workers' expectations are rising in Spain, Greece and Ireland (Commission EC 1991), while Portugal's 1991 'social pact' links wage increases to the ECU value of the escudo and to the relative performance of productivity.

However real wage flexibility can also be achieved by increases in national price levels while money wages remain constant, but this will affect international competitiveness unless it is possible to undertake a devaluation of the currency. As the EU moves towards a full monetary union, with narrow band exchange rates and then the adoption of a common currency, such adjustments will finally become impossible, and employment may shift to the low cost regions of the EU, creating a competitive downward pressure upon all wages in the Union. This argument has been challenged on a number of grounds. It is argued that the relative unit labour costs, which also reflect variations in the productivity of labour, are more significant. Wage costs alone are unlikely to be the major factor in location decisions, except in the case of labour-intensive industries. It has also been pointed out that this very process of relocation to low wage areas is the market adjustment mechanism for spreading the benefits of economic growth throughout the EU.

Critics of the 'market forces' approach have also warned of the possibility of cumulative economic divergence as the poorer regions, especially in the Southern member states, find themselves specialising in labour-intensive, low wage, low productivity industries where they already face intense competition from the Asian NICs.

The differences in labour costs faced by firms operating across the EU arise not only from differences in member states' social security systems, but also from the variation in other elements of the fixed labour costs. These costs include the extent of paid holidays, paid sick leave, benefits in kind (e.g. subsidised mortgages, canteens, sports facilities, cars) and redundancy pay. These emerge from collective bargaining, and express employees' preferences, and reflect the influence of such factors as the adequacy of state schemes, the structure of the national tax system and the cultural characteristics of countries.

In 1990, non-wage labour costs in manufacturing were 30 per cent of total labour costs in France, Italy and Belgium, 25 per cent in Portugal and 26 per cent in Spain and the Netherlands. By contrast they were only 13 per cent in the United Kingdom and 3 per cent in Denmark. High fixed labour costs create competitive pressures to substitute part-time workers when some of these fixed costs can be avoided. This has already been observed in the Northern member states of the EU. By 1990, 43 per cent of the women who were employed in the UK were working part-time and 59 per cent in the Netherlands. However, female part-time working remains less than 10 per cent in Italy, Spain and Greece, and has not increased in recent years. Overall in the Community 28 per cent of women are employed part-time, in contrast to 4 per cent of men. To eliminate these 'distortions to competition' and casualisation of part of the labour force, the Commission has prepared a number of 'atypical workers' Directives, extending to employees on short-term and part-time contracts the same entitlements to holiday pay, redundancy pay, etc. as full-time workers.

Illicit work is work outside the formal labour market's tax and social security system and is most frequent among those who are already employed. It is thought to be concentrated among the professions, in domestic services, in agricultural work and vehicle repairs and among skilled manual workers in building and public works. It is also estimated to be twice as prevalent among the southern states of the Union, reflecting differences in the structure of the local economies, levels of taxation, cultural attitudes and the effectiveness of official controls. It is of concern within the single market since it distorts the operation of the labour market and competitiveness. Those firms within the Union which employ labour illicitly will reduce their labour costs and gain a competitive advantage in production. Thus they will displace those firms that finance the social security systems, and will undermine established safety regulations. Therefore the Commission has taken a number of actions to attempt to minimise its occurrence. It has sought effective compliance in public contracts to national and EU standards, close attention to subcontracting arrangements and monitoring of cross-frontier activities. The Commission has also pursued the adoption of common administrative 'standards' for taxation and social security contributions across regions and forms of employment (e.g. part-time, temporary workers).

EU policy

The Union's policy in the social area may be seen as seeking to fulfil three broad roles. Firstly, harmonisation of national policies, especially in areas where it offers obvious advantages, e.g. labour mobility. Secondly, encouraging convergence, through both its own discussions and encouragement of inter-state cooperation. This approach is likely to be most appropriate where states are faced by similar problems, e.g. the impact of demographic changes on social security systems. Finally, the Commission can act as a focal point for the spreading of innovatory experience throughout the Union. With the commitment to the completion of the SEM added urgency was given to the Commission's 'watchdog' role in anticipating the social consequences of restructuring. But the Commission is also a direct participant in fostering the necessary adaptability in the labour market. Thus the following sections will outline the broad areas of Commission activity, ranging from the more passive information role to its more controversial attempts at harmonisation through the Social Charter and European company laws.

Although the Treaty of Rome had laid down the fundamental freedom of movement of workers (Arts 48–51) and the right of establishment in any economic activity across all member states, a succession of secondary legislation has been required to give concrete form to these principles. EU nationals may now reside in any member state to seek or take up employment, accompanied by their families (Directive 68/360/EC), establish firms or provide services (73/148) and remain in that territory after having been employed in that state (70/1251, 72/194). In addition, workers and their families should receive equal treatment in respect of social security, housing, access to education and training, etc., to any domestic national. Indeed the Union has sought coordination of national social security legislation to facilitate mobility through Regulations 71/1408 and 72/574. These Regulations establish three basic principles: firstly, the application of a single body of legislation in each case; secondly, retention of all accumulated rights and entitlements (i.e. transferability); thirdly, equal treatment between domestic nationals and citizens of other member states.

But some problems remain unresolved or unaddressed. Frontier workers, commuting from a country of residence to employment in another state, have a number of established rights, e.g. to social security benefits, but specific difficulties remain, particularly in regard to taxation. EU nationals seeking public sector employment in other member states have faced restrictions. Although discrimination in employment is allowed on grounds of 'public policy, security or health, and exercise of public authority' this has been narrowly interpreted by the Court of Justice. The Commission therefore decided to take action to eliminate employment restrictions in the public utilities, health services, teaching and non-military research. The rights so far described are focused specifically on the needs of workers and their dependents. Those who are not economically active continue to face residence restrictions, usually a test of 'adequate means' for intending migrants. To facilitate labour adjustment the Commission has proposed the transferability of unemployment benefit while workers seek employment in other member states. Although a proposed Directive granting a general 'right of residence' throughout the Union for students and the retired and other non-employed people faced substantial opposition from several member states, the Maastricht Treaty on European Union created citizenship of the Union, with the right to freedom of movement and residence. However, the necessary measures for its realisation will still require unanimous agreement.

The Commission has also pursued a number of general policies aimed at enhancing worker mobility. In particular it established comparability of vocational qualifications beginning with hotel and catering, motor vehicle repairs, construction, electrical, agricultural and textile trades. Minimum skill requirements are being defined for training qualifications, with the assistance of Cedefop, but this work is unlikely to be completed until 1996. The Commission has also been given responsibility for developing a broad Union-recognised vocational training pass, but this will have to be built on current activity in this area. However faster progress is being achieved via the mechanism of mutual recognition. Directives have already established mutual recognition of diplomas for doctors (1975), nurses (1977), dental practitioners (1978), veterinary surgeons (1978), pharmacists (1986), and architects (1985). Further, the Commission sought a general system of recognition of diplomas, subject to a minimum three years' post-secondary training. This was finally agreed to commence in 1991, although subject to the requirement of either a period of adaptation or an aptitude test for those professions where there are substantial national differences, e.g. lawyers and accountants.

The Union also established Sedoc (Regulation 68/1612), a European system of employment information exchange, but this remains inadequate and little used, with only 1000 job applications processed annually. But the Commission continues to foster a programme of exchanges and cooperation between national employment services focusing on such topics as the frontier labour market, organisation of employment services and labour market management.

The need to establish minimum European standards for health and safety has been accepted as essential to fair competition within the SEM. A good example of the approach now being taken is that of the proposed Machines Directive, which covers over half of the total production of the European mechanical engineering industry. This proposal, based on a Council resolution of May 1985, is innovative in that it defines only basic requirements, leaving detailed specifications to the individual standardisation bodies. The Commission also invited representatives from industry, trade unions, European standardisation bodies (CEN and Cenelec) and member governments to be involved from the beginning. The European Trade Union Confederation (ETUC) requested a tripartite structure of employers, trade unions and the Commission to be created to oversee its practical implementation. This proposal was accepted, and is likely to be followed in the drafting of other safety directives. As part of the new working programme following from the SEA, the Commission is also preparing framework Directives to establish minimum health and safety standards at work. Again both sides of industry are closely involved in their preparation, and in addition the Commission believes that trade unions should be 'properly consulted in preparation of standardisation measures, and in the management of these Directives'.

In defining the role of the Structural Funds in facilitating the changes required by the accelerated economic integration of the SEM, the Commission followed two broad principles. Restructuring must coincide with the broader Union objectives, and Union funds must be matched by national funds. The Structural Funds – ERDF and ESF – have been supplemented by sectoral programmes aimed at restructuring the shipbuilding and steel industries. But these *ad hoc* measures have created unnecessary complexity. In response the Commission had proposed reform of the Structural Funds in a draft regulation (COM (87) 376 final/2) adopted in June 1988, based on four principles:

1. concentration on five objectives
    (a) promoting the development and structural adjustment of the less developed regions
    (b) converting the areas seriously affected by industrial decline
    (c) combating long-term unemployment
    (d) facilitating the occupational integration of young people
    (e) promoting the development of rural areas

2. precise definition of the tasks of the structural funds in relation to these objectives

3. an increase in resources

4. rationalisation of both assistance and management methods.

In February 1988 the Heads of State accepted the proposed reform of the Structural Funds and doubled their appropriation, in real terms, from ECU 7 bn. in 1987 to ECU 14 bn. in 1993. The ERDF will focus on support for productive investment, modernisation of infrastructure, and studies of the potential for physical planning at the Union level (see Chapter 10). The ESF will concentrate on assisting young people and the long-term unemployed, expanding general employment, and providing workers with vocational skills. Between 1989 and 1993 ECU 20 bn. was allocated to the ESF; 90 per cent of these funds will be spent on vocational training in the less developed regions of the Union (those with a GDP less than 75 per cent of the EC average).

Ensuring the provision of adequate training of the labour force will be essential for the structural adjustment necessary for the successful completion of the SEM. The process of creating the SEM required both new types of training, i.e. corporate planning for small and medium sized firms and the general expansion of education and training to create a European pool of skilled labour. The Commission ought to develop a strategy building on discussions with both sides of industry, and focusing on its three roles. Firstly, the training of young people, building on a Council Decision (December 1987) calling for the setting-up of a system giving all young people the right to up to two years' basic training. Secondly, the Commission may seek to improve comparability between national training systems. Finally, the Commission can foster recognition of the importance of continuing and further training of the labour force by both industry and the state. These general principles have been given expression in the further development of a vocational policy required by Article 128 of the Treaty of Rome. The White Paper on the completion of the internal market built on this, calling for comparability of qualifications (Council Resolution July 1985), a general system of recognition of higher education diplomas and the introduction of a vocational training pass. Two programmes, ERASMUS (1987) and YES (1988) encourage increased student mobility and youth exchanges respectively, while the LINGUA (1989) programme aims to foster students' knowledge of Union languages. A Council Resolution in December 1986 recommended measures for the training of young people, the in-service training of employees and the training of women. This was supplemented by a Council Decision in December 1987 on an action programme on vocational training for young people to commence from January 1988. Finally, the Commission is preparing a programme of action on adult continuing training within the context of the agreed joint policy on vocational training.

A central feature of the proposals for a European company law has been the desire to encourage worker participation, since the Commission believes this to be an important factor in firms' economic success. A number of proposals addressing this issue have been considered including the 'Fifth Directive' concerning company structures and the powers and duties of governing bodies. There has also been a Regulation on the status of the European Limited Liability Company, first drafted in 1970, and the 'Vredeling Directive' (1980). The latter proposal specifically sets out to be a piece of social legislation, being concerned with information provision to, and consultation with, the workforce in large companies, especially multinational companies. This directive has, however, been 'frozen' in the face of opposition from employers.

In June 1988 the Commission returned to this issue and submitted a new memorandum on the creation of a European Company statute. It proposed a simpler statute abandoning many aspects of the previous draft, and it would be optional. Firms could choose to operate under the new statute or retain their existing national corporate existence. In terms of worker participation three alternative options are available to a European Company: a German model with workers represented on the management bodies; the Franco-Italian system of a works council separate from the management board; and the Swedish model, under which individual firms establish an agreement on participation with the workers. However, various safeguards are proposed. Prior agreement with the workforce on representation will be required before a European Company can be incorporated, with a 'fallback' national standard model specified should there be a failure to reach an agreement. Any member state may also restrict the choice of model available. All three options will require quarterly reports on the company to the employees, and prior consultation with the workforce on decisions relevant to them. Despite the increased flexibility, these proposals have continued to face the implacable opposition of the European employers (UNICE, Union of Industrial and Employers' Confederations of Europe) as part of their general hostility to the emergence of any European level of collective bargaining. None the less the Commission intends to press ahead with a draft Directive under the Social Protocol (see below) which excludes the UK. This would require the establishment of Works Councils in those businesses employing 1,000 workers in the EU, and with at least 100 employees in two member states.

Some concrete progress has however been made with the Regulation on the European Economic Interest Group (EEIG). Although its scope is narrow, applying to firms employing fewer than 500 people, it is both flexible and innovative in that it allows the formation of a corporate body constituted under European, as opposed to national, law. It is intended to overcome the difficulties smaller enterprises face in cooperating across member state frontiers. Firms from two or more member states can form an EEIG in any area where cooperation appears useful – e.g. purchasing, research and development, marketing or tendering – and registration confers full legal capacity to operate throughout the Union.

Social cohesion

The negotiations leading to the adoption of the Community Charter of Fundamental Social Rights at the Strasbourg summit in December 1989 brought into sharp focus the fundamental divisions between those advocating an interventionist regulatory role for the Community in the social area, and those who argue for the primacy of market forces and a *laissez-faire* approach.[2] The latter were most clearly represented by the UK government, which failed to support the adoption of the Social Charter and two years later demanded an opt-out from the

Social Protocol at Maastricht. However, the European employers' organisation (UNICE) has also maintained its opposition to an extension of labour market regulation beyond that necessary to ensure fair competition under the SEM.

Proponents of unregulated labour markets, with freely negotiated labour contracts, regard them as providing both economic efficiency in allocating labour and a wide variety of pay and conditions to meet individual workers' preferences. Attempts to impose uniform conditions (minimum wages, holiday entitlements, redundancy protection, etc.) will impose additional costs on firms. In response, companies will substitute capital, part-time workers, or more skilled workers for their low productivity unskilled employees whose employment costs have now risen, and whom such regulation was principally intended to benefit.

An alternative view is that such attempts at regulation will encourage the emergence of dual labour markets; a regulated high wage high productivity sector, and an unregulated low wage unskilled sector offering unstable employment. This 'insider–outsider' problem is already found in many member states. In Spain and Greece high levels of youth unemployment, and the increase in the amount of part-time employment, are blamed on the existence of tightly regulated procedures for the recruitment and dismissal of full-time workers. Regulation in the EU will thus benefit only existing workers, at the expense of those wishing to enter the labour market.

The emergence of dual labour markets will in turn become a major problem for ensuring fair competition across the Union, especially as member states already vary in their ability and willingness to enforce EU, and even national, regulations. It has been estimated that 25 per cent of Spain's labour force already works in its informal or 'black' economy, 30 per cent in Greece, 18–28 per cent in Portugal and 25 per cent in France. But it has been argued that these developments have actually been encouraged by the shift to deregulation across Europe in the face of the enhanced competitive environment of the 1980s.

The simple 'social dumping' argument of differential social security provisions leading firms to relocate to the lower cost regions of the Union can also be seen as a variant of the 'insider–outsider' phenomenon, as both employers and employees in the high cost member states such as Germany attempt to defend their existing conditions from competition. However it has already been observed that increasing economic integration, far from encouraging such relocation to underdeveloped low cost regions, may actually reinforce the advantages of the high productivity areas. Under these conditions of 'cumulative divergence' an interventionist social policy is more easily justified. It might be argued that such intervention should confine itself to the supply-side policy of enhancing vocational training, but the general conditions of employment that an employee faces are likely to influence the decision as to whether to invest in human capital. Improving conditions through EU regulation may raise employee morale and therefore productivity, but it is also likely to reduce staff turnover. High turnover imposes substantial recruitment and training costs on firms, and firms will be unwilling to incur any additional costs by further investment in their employees unless there is an expectation of a long-term commitment by their labour force. Thus imposing improved employment conditions may complement, rather than inhibit, the transformation of the low productivity industries and regions of the Community.

Certainly the Commission views the creation of social cohesion as essential to realising the benefits of an integrated European economy. The Social Charter represents a broad statement of the principles that were to achieve this objective.

The Social Charter

Building on the objective of improving the living and working conditions embodied in the Treaty of Rome and consolidated in the SEA, both the Economic and Social Committee and the European Parliament called for an explicit political commitment to fundamental social rights. Existing international agreements, such as the ILO Convention, have not been fully ratified by all member states, and are regarded as inadequate in providing for the needs of the successful creation of the SEM. Thus the Social Charter addressed both the conditions necessary for the completion of the SEM, and attempted to create the social guarantees that the Commission regarded as essential to maintain broad political support for these developments.

The Social Charter includes the following commitments:

1. Improvements in living and working conditions.'The development of a single European labour market must result in an improvement in the living and working conditions of workers within the EC'. To avoid downward pressure on these conditions a number of issues must be addressed, including the form of employment contracts (e.g. temporary, seasonal, part-time) and the organisation of working hours. There is a specific call for the establishment of a maximum working week. In addition procedures relating to collective redundancies and bankruptcies should be addressed.

2. The right to freedom of movement. The establishment of the right to equal treatment with any other EU national in regard to the practice of any trade or occupation, access to training, rights to social security and residence.

3. Employment and remuneration. All employment must be fairly remunerated, established either through law or collective agreement, with particular attention to those workers not subject to the 'normal' employment contract of indefinite duration. Wages may not be withheld, except in conformity with national regulations, but 'in no case may an employed person be deprived of the means necessary for subsistence'.

4. The right to social protection. 'Subject to the arrangements proper to each member state, any citizen of the EC is entitled to adequate social protection' (i.e. social security or a minimum wage).

5. The right to freedom of association and collective bargaining. 'Every employer and every worker has the right to belong freely to the professional and trade union organisation of their choice.' This entails the right to choose whether or not to belong to a trade union and the right to strike. Procedures for conciliation and mediation between the two sides of industry should be encouraged, and contractual relations established at the European level if this is deemed desirable.

6. The right to vocational training. 'Every worker has the right to continue his vocational training throughout his working life.' Both public and private bodies should establish continuing and permanent training schemes and provide leave for training purposes.

7. The right of men and women to equal treatment.

8. The right to information, consultation and worker participation. To be developed 'along appropriate lines and in such a way as to take into account the legal provisions, contractual agreements and practices in force in the member states.'

9. The right to health protection and safety at work.

10. The protection of children and adolescents. The minimum working age must be set at 16 years, and those over this age shall receive fair remuneration, and for a period of two years shall be entitled to vocational training in working hours.

11. Elderly persons shall receive an income that guarantees a decent standard of living.

12. To ensure the fullest possible integration of disabled persons in working life, measures must be taken in respect of training, integration and rehabilitation, complemented by action to improve accessibility, mobility, transport and housing.

It should be noted that the Social Charter has no legal status, and many of the rights outlined above are qualified so as to accommodate existing national practices. This must weaken the force of any commitment to it by member states. None the less the Social Charter is important in that it provides the underpinning for the implementation of a 47 point Social Action Programme (SAP)(COM(89) 568). But of these 47 proposals only 20 will involve binding Directives or Regulations, and by the end of 1992 only eight had been approved by the Council of Ministers.

Many of these measures are merely a continuation of existing developments aimed at fostering worker mobility within the Union, enhancing training provision and establishing common health and safety requirements. However, some proposals are more controversial, and face strong opposition from the UK government and the European employers. These include three 'atypical worker' Directives, extending to part-time and fixed-term workers the same entitlements as enjoyed by full-time workers; a Directive establishing minimum employment conditions for young people; three Directives on collective redundancies, written contracts of employment and restrictions on working hours (48 hour week maximum); and a Directive establishing minimum paid maternity leave. The Commission has made progress with the working hours, maternity and young workers Directives by a broad interpretation of the Health and Safety Articles of the SEA (Art. 118a), allowing qualified majority voting to overcome UK opposition. Similarly the Commission has employed Art. 100a – actions necessary for completion of the single market – to further the Directive extending entitlements to atypical workers. But in some cases this is being challenged before the European Court.

In the case of the most controversial aspects of the Social Charter the Commission is proposing only non-binding opinions and recommendations. Thus under the SAP the right to freedom of association, collective bargaining and the right to strike have been compromised by being made subject to national 'traditions' (EIRR 1990). Similarly the discussion about the introduction of an EU-wide minimum wage has been replaced by reference to a Commission opinion as to 'fair wages' – i.e. a wage sufficient to maintain a satisfactory standard of living. Although it is anticipated that the Commission will continue to pursue SAP measures under the existing powers of the Treaty and the SEA, the Social Protocol negotiated at Maastricht offers substantial advantages in ensuring progress. The Protocol 11, excluding the UK, extended QMV to measures covering working conditions, information and consultation of workers, equality and the integration of the unemployed. Unanimity is still required for measures affecting social security and social protection, redundancy, trade unions, and immigrant workers. Legislation under the Social Protocol will not have the status of EU law since it is technically outside the Treaty on European Union. However, its influence is unlikely to be confined to the Protocol 11, as a failure by the UK government to match 'Social Protocol' standards may be challenged as a distortion of competition under the existing SEA. There must therefore be serious doubt as to how long the UK will be able to sustain its opt-out in practice.

The social dialogue

The SAP associated with the Social Charter also seeks the 'continuation and development of dialogue with the social partners' and consideration of the need for collective agreements at the European level. But is there a need to establish a European framework of industrial relations?

As before there is a conflict between the 'corporatists' who see it as an important dimension in the creation of 'social cohesion' at the European level, and the neo-liberals who see it as a threat to the economic efficiency of free labour markets. For the latter, efficiency demands flexibility for management in the determination of pay, employment contracts and hiring and firing, i.e. 'the right to manage'. UNICE has sought to defend this flexibility by opposing any EU measure which encourages the emergence of a European dimension to collective bargaining. In addition it has emphasised the substantial obstacles that the EU faces in this area, given the substantial variation in collective bargaining traditions across the member states. In particular the frameworks of industrial relations in the member states vary in their emphasis on rights embodied in legislation or acquired through collective bargaining. Thus in the UK the existing legal framework is limited to immunities, not specific rights. With the loss of trade union membership and consequent weakening of collective bargaining, a highly 'flexible' labour market has been created. By contrast German industrial relations have remained 'corporatist', and in Italy large firms continue to face substantial legal constraints on their hiring and firing activities.

However, both sides of industry have been involved in the development of Community social policy from its inception. Thus the Economic and Social Committee was established under the Treaty of Rome, but its influence to date has been limited as it covers perhaps too broad an area. Since 1972 the 189 member Committee has had the right to draw up opinions on all questions relating to the Community, but it remains advisory. None the less it is able to call on independent experts and is often therefore a source of technical expertise, and has occasionally, as in the Beretta Report on the social aspects of the SEM, made a significant contribution. Two further groups of Committees bring together employers and employees. The Advisory Committees deliver opinions before the Commission adopts a position. These Committees cover vocational training, freedom of movement of workers, social security for workers, safety, hygiene and health protection, etc. The second group is composed of Sectoral Joint Committees and informal groups, covering industries such as railways, sea fishing, road and maritime transport

The ETUC had begun to press the need for the development of an active social policy in the late 1960s, and in response the first Quadripartite Conference, involving representatives of the Commission, Ministers of Labour, employers and employees, was held in Luxembourg in 1970. This led in turn to the creation of the Standing Committee on Employment, composed of representatives of the Commission, Council, employers and trade unions. From 1974 until 1978 conferences were held annually, but at the 1978 meeting the ETUC expressed its concern at the lack of evidence of any positive results from the meetings. Although the Commission drew up proposals, adopted by the Council in June 1980, no conferences have been held since. But the Standing Committee on Employment continues to survive. Its deliberations precede decisions by the competent institutions, and it provides a forum for consultation and discussion between the Council, the Commission and the two sides of industry. Until 1974 it focused on reform of the ESF, but its agenda has now widened to include unemployment, reorganisation of working time and youth unemployment. Since 1980 it has also considered new technology and long-term unemployment. None the less the Committee remains purely consultative, and it has been unable to create the initial momentum for the creation of a comprehensive social policy.

By the early 1980s the ETUC was expressing increasing dissatisfaction at this lack of progress, and the relationship between the employers and trade unions reached its lowest ebb when employers' opposition ensured the freezing by the Council of the 'Vredeling Directive' on worker consultation in 1986. This Directive had already been substantially revised in response to the comments of the European Parliament and the Economic and Social Committee, and had begun its fruitless journey six years before.

An attempt was made to overcome this impasse by Jacques Delors, who presented an action plan, including the commitment to the completion of the SEM, at the 1984 Fontainebleau Summit. To revive the 'social dialogue' a meeting was held in November 1985 at Val Duchesse, which led to the establishment of two working parties, examining macro- and micro-economic issues. However, the momentum was not maintained.

There has been an attempt to revive the Vredeling Directive under the guise of a draft Directive on European Works Councils (EWC). This would require companies operating in at least two member states, and with at least 1000 employees, to negotiate with workers' representatives the establishment of a Works Council. This would provide only a limited forum for discussion of changes in employment and the introduction of new work practices. None the less, even in this diluted form it continues to be rejected by UNICE, who remain concerned about the development of any form of pan-European collective bargaining.

Under the influence of French national legislation, French multinational companies (MNCs) have been experimenting with EWCs (e.g. B.S.N., Thompson, Elf Aquitaine). This has been emulated by other European MNCs such as Volkswagen, Grundig and Volvo. These consultation arrangements have, in turn, enhanced the role of the European trade union bodies. In some cases European company networks have emerged (e.g. Ford of Europe Workers' Committee), while in others more formal international bodies such as the European Metalworkers' Federation and the European Confederation of Chemical and General Workers' Unions have been formed. Meanwhile the ETUC has been strengthened as the number of affiliated trade unions has grown, especially among those for 'white collar' workers. In October 1990 the first genuine European trade union was created by the merger of the 12 national airline pilots' associations.

More recently some dissent has emerged among the national associations within UNICE as to its uniformly hostile approach to EU attempts at fostering a 'social dialogue'. Belgium, Dutch and Italian employers have argued that an active involvement in European social policy-making would be more productive than outright hostility, especially when faced with the threat of Directives being imposed. As a result UNICE appears to have shifted its policy stance, and in November 1991 it reached agreement with the ETUC that they should participate in consultations over any proposal emerging from the Social Protocol. If the EU decides to legislate, then UNICE and the ETUC will seek a nine month period in which to negotiate a draft Directive for approval by the Council of Ministers. However, some national employers' associations, such as the British CBI, have rejected this agreement. It must also be recognised that the disagreement within UNICE may lie more in the means than in the ends, the ends being to ensure 'strict limits on the scope of EU intervention in this area, whether by law or agreement' (Secretary General of UNICE, *Financial Times*, November 1991).

Conclusion

Three general problems face the EU in the establishment of effective legislation and these problems are particularly acute in the social area. Firstly, the relationship of EU to national legislation. With the wide variety of national labour laws and collective bargaining traditions, mutual recognition may offer advantages over harmonisation. However, in the relatively simple case of labour mobility, ensuring mutual recognition of qualifications has proved a major task. Alternatively, greater use might be made of Regulations, which do not require translation into national legislation by the individual member states, but are enforced directly by the national Courts.

Secondly, there is the issue of whether progress in the social area is best achieved by legislation or the fostering of the 'social dialogue'. European collective agreements would overcome the problems of imposing EU legislation across disparate national labour markets and, as we have seen, there is some limited acceptance of this approach by UNICE. However, achieving social policy objectives by collective agreements in turn raises a number of difficulties. There is the problem of employees who are not trade union members, and the possibility of de-recognition of trade unions by employers who wish to avoid their obligations. There is also the danger of a combination of collective agreements and legislation creating a confusion and complexity that will inhibit effective monitoring and enforcement. Belgium has offered an interesting way forward. Drawing upon its own industrial relations experience it has suggested 'law by collective agreement'. In this approach, framework agreements would be negotiated at the European level between the employers and employees' representatives and these would be implemented through national collective agreements or legislation. Only if there were a failure to reach agreement at the European level would the Commission propose legislation.

The final problem in social policy formation is related to the question of subsidiarity. Subsidiarity has moved centre stage with the Maastricht agreement, and has led to a debate as to the appropriate institutional arrangements to address social issues. Rulings on the limits of the Commission's competence with subsidiarity are most likely to be undertaken by the European Court of Justice (ECJ), but the European Parliament feels that social legislation requires special arrangements, and has proposed the creation of a European Labour Court within the ECJ.

However, progress in EU social policy depends on the political commitment of the individual member states and of the partners in the 'social dialogue'; and yet even more so than in many other areas of EU policy, social legislation remains controversial. As Rhodes (1992) concludes, 'the future of the "social dimension" remains uncertain as Euro-liberalism and Euro-corporatism continue to contest the regulatory terrain, at both member state and Community levels.'

Notes

1. Qualified Majority Voting consists of 54 votes out of a possible total of 76 in the Council of Ministers. These votes are weighted as follows: Belgium 5, Denmark 3, France 10, Germany 10, Greece 5, Ireland 3, Italy 10, Luxembourg 2, Netherlands 5, Portugal 5, Spain 8, United Kingdom 10.
2. For a presentation of the contrasting views of those advocating interventionist and free-market approaches to labour market policy, see Addison and Siebert (1993) and Rhodes (1992).

References and further reading

Addison J and **Siebert W** 1993 The EC Social Charter: the nature of the beast, *The National Westminster Bank Quarterly Review*, February.

Coe DT and **Gagliardi F** 1985 Nominal Wage Determination in Ten OECD Countries, *OECD Economics and Statistics Working Papers*, 19.

Commission EC 1988 *Social Europe, the Social Dimension of the Internal Market.*

Commission EC 1989 Employment in Europe, *COM* (89)399.

Commission EC 1990–1991 *The Social Dimension*, Periodical 2/1990.

Commission EC 1991 Developments in the labour market in the Community: results of a survey covering employers and employees, *European Economy*, Vol. 47, March.

Dearden S 1993 *Wage Flexibility in the European Community*, Manchester Polytechnic, mimeo.

EIRR 1990 Social Charter: action programme released, *European Industrial Relations Review*, No. 192.

Gold M 1992 Social Policy: the UK and Maastricht, *National Institute Economic Review*, 95–103.

Gordon I and **Thirlwall A** 1989 *European Factor Mobility, Trends and consequences*, Macmillan, London.

Hart R *et al.* 1988 *Trends in Non-wage Labour Costs and their Effect on Employment*, Commission of the European Communities.

Laffan B 1983 Policy implementation in the European community; the European social fund as a case study, *Journal of Common Market Studies*, Vol. XXI, June.

Molle W and **Mourik A V** 1988 International movements under conditions of economic integration: the case of western Europe, *Journal of Common Market Studies,* Vol. XXVI, March.

OECD 1988 *Employment Outlook*, September.

Overturf S 1986 *The Economic Principles of European Integration,* Praeger, New York.

Read R 1991 The Single European Market, Does European mobility matter? *International Journal of Manpower*, Vol. 12, No. 2, pp. 36–41.

Rhodes M 1992 The future of the social dimension: labour market regulation in post-1992 Europe, *Journal of Common Market Studies*, Vol. XXX, March.

Venturini P 1989 *1992: The European Social Dimension*, Commission of the European Communities.

Warner H 1984 EC social policy in practice: community action on behalf of women and its impact on member states, *Journal of Common Market Studies*, Vol. XXIII, December.

CHAPTER 10

Regional policy

Judith Tomkins and Jim Twomey

The emergence and persistence of regional disparities

There are very few features that are common to nations at differing stages of economic development. But there is one feature that is prevalent in every nation at each stage of development, i.e. the existence of spatial disparities in economic performance. It appears to be an inescapable fact that regardless of whether a nation is developing, developed or experiencing economic decline, the indigenous population will experience differing degrees of economic prosperity depending on their particular location in the economy.

There are many reasons why such spatial differences within nations emerge and are maintained. In terms of geography, there may be a simple explanation such as a relatively poor endowment of natural resources which prevents exploitation of the land and inhibits economic development. On the other hand, other regions may well be in a position to benefit from the discovery of natural resource stocks such as oil and gas. Also important in terms of geography, however, is the issue of peripherality. Regions can be disadvantaged by their distance from population or production centres. This distance may therefore result, *inter alia*, in above-average transport costs, restricted access to large urban conglomerations with a concomitant reduction in the capacity to develop service activities, and an inferior transport infrastructure.

One of the major economic reasons why certain areas perform better than others will lie in the differing natures of respective industrial structures. At any time certain industries or sectors of an economy may be experiencing some degree of growth while others experience some degree of decline. It is clear, therefore, that the economic fortune of any one region will tend to reflect the distribution of economic activity within that region. Many areas in Europe have historically tended to specialise in a narrow range of industries such as coal, steel and shipbuilding. In the face of changes in patterns of demand, output and competition in the mid-to late twentieth century these industries have experienced something of a decline. In less than 40 years, European coalfields have lost 57 per cent of their production and 82 per cent of their workforce, while the iron and steel industry has lost 60 per cent of its workers. The same regions that once benefited from growth in these industries have, subsequently, suffered economic decline and depression.

Many other economic factors might be viewed as contributing to the emergence of spatial disparities in economic prosperity. Evidence from the UK suggests that the peripherality of certain areas is often manifestly displayed by substantial differences in the levels of innovation, the rate of new firm formation and the extent of external control between regional economies. In addition, the important research and development activities of many technologically advanced industries often tend to be concentrated in 'core' as opposed to peripheral economies, with the latter frequently assuming a 'branch-plant' nature.

As far as standard neo-classical economic theory is concerned, it is of no real consequence why regional disparities emerge since there are mechanisms in an economy which will ensure that they will prove to be only a temporary phenomenon. Provided that labour and capital are perfectly mobile, that factors of production are fully employed and that there exists free competition, then it is argued that market forces will ensure the removal of spatial disparities. In practice, however, these conditions are met on so few occasions that one might conclude that spatial differences in economic potential are unlikely ever to be equalised. Indeed, it is possible to imagine circumstances in which regional disparities are not reduced but further extended. Cumulative causation theories provide a strong theoretical rationale for widening regional prosperity.[1] The basis of these theories lies in recognition of the fact that, because of the impact of differing levels of productivity or the existence of internal and external[2] economies of scale, it is perfectly feasible that economic benefits begin to accumulate in particular regions of an economy and become self-perpetuating.

In such circumstances, market forces may actually come to reinforce this development and contribute to unbalanced regional growth.

Defining the Union's regional problem

Any attempt to assess the nature and magnitude of the regional problem in the Union is a complex task. Union members represent a series of very diverse and heterogeneous economies at different stages of development and with differing structural problems. The task is further complicated by the fact that the collection of regional data for the EU is not only a vast undertaking but often produces output that is of more doubtful reliability than the national counterpart. This latter aspect of regional data should become less of a problem with the progress of time and the development of administrative mechanisms directed at greater accuracy, but it does indicate caution when comparisons are made with early regional statistics of the Union.

Another problem connected with analysis of the regional problem in the EU relates to the precise definition of a region. It is often the case that the definition of administrative regions within countries tends to reflect certain historical and institutional processes which, although they might have produced some degree of spatial cohesion, do not necessarily accord with what one might view as appropriate for economic scrutiny. This point is noted in the First Periodic Report on the social and economic situation in the regions (1981). The report considers which level of geographical unit is most suited to analysing regional problems in the Union from the three levels defined in the mid-1970s and subsumed under the French acronym NUTS levels I, II and III.[3] It decided that the level II regions or standard 'administrative base units' were appropriate for consideration. In the UK, the counties are regarded as the level II regions, while the traditional regions are viewed as level I. However, the countries of Ireland, Luxembourg and Denmark are defined as both level I and level II regions within the Union.

The use of level II regions for analysis of regional disparities was perfectly understandable in light of the fact that there already existed in many countries an administrative structure which was in a position to provide relevant statistical information. The problems and criticism that arose from this decision, however, reflected the varying sizes of the administrative units. For example, certain German regions (notably Hamburg, Bremen and West Berlin) were little more than cities and quite small relative to the large British and French regions. This criticism was to some extent pre-empted in the report by recognition of such difficulties and there has been a movement in recent years to a further disaggregation of the relevant geographical unit.

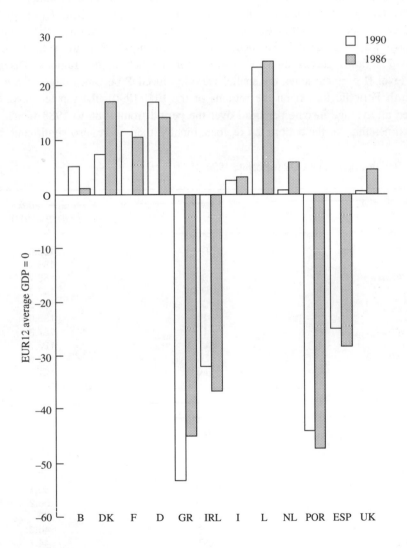

Figure 10.1 GDP per capita: national deviations from EUR12 average (GDP at market prices converted into PPSs; EUR12 = 0)
Source : Regional Trends, Eurostat

In terms of the statistics directly employed to assess regional economic performance, by far the widest exposure tends to be given to measurements of regional per capita GDP. The Gross Domestic Product of a region represents the total sum of the value added in that region minus the input of factors of production located or employed outside the region. The convention is to measure regional GDP at market prices and to value it in purchasing power standards (PPSs) to permit inter-country comparisons of living standards.

At a national level, per capita GDP differentials measured in this manner vary substantially. Indexing the average of the 12 members at 100, the 1990 national distribution of per capita GDP in PPSs ranged from 123.7 in Luxembourg and 117 in Germany to 47.1 in Greece and 56.2 in Portugal (Figure 10.1). In terms of level I administrative regional units, the disparities are even greater, ranging from a very high value for Hamburg (183.5), in Germany to 44.6 in Nisia, Greece, as shown in Table 10.1 and Figure 10.2. The population of the top ten regions in fact enjoyed an average level of income in 1990 (using GDP as the measure of income) which was 2.3 times greater than the average for the bottom ten regions. Disaggregating further to level II regional units, the spatial variation in GDP becomes larger again. As noted in the Fourth Periodic Report on the regions of the EU (1990), the top ten level II regions experienced an average income per head over the period from 1986 to 1988 which was more than three times that for the bottom ten regions. Finally, there were also significant differences

Table 10.1 Regions ranked by GDP per capita 1990

Top ten level I regions	Country	GDP index (EUR12 = 100)
Hamburg	D	183.5
Ile de France	F	166.4
Region Bruxelloise	B	165.7
Bremen	D	147.7
Hessen	D	135.3
Lombardia	I	135.0
Emilia-Romagna	I	127.3
Luxembourg	L	123.7
Baden-Wurttemberg	D	123.5
South East	UK	121.3
Bottom ten level I regions		
Ireland	IRL	68.2
Sicilia	I	66.3
Noroeste	ESP	62.7
Centro	ESP	62.3
Sur	ESP	59.1
Portugal	POR	56.2
Attiki	GR	50.4
Voreia Ellada	GR	46.2
Kentriki Ellada	GR	44.7
Nisia	GR	44.6

Note : Excluding regions of former East Germany
Source : Regional Trends, 1993

in the spatial variations in GDP within the EU nations themselves. For example, the wealthiest region in Greece in 1990 is recorded as having a GDP per capita at 50.4 per cent of the EU average, only 5.8 percentage points above its worst region. At the other extreme, the range in Belgium for that same year extends from 165.7 to 84.6. Dunford (1993) in fact provides much

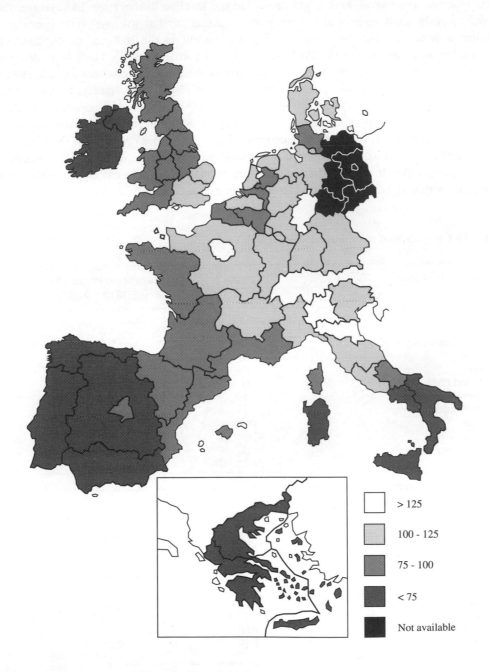

Figure 10.2 GDP per capita 1990 (EUR12 = 100)
Source : Regional Trends

detailed evidence to show how inequality increases with territorial disaggregation, and how the degree of regional imbalance within member states differs, with Italy exhibiting the most deep-rooted disparities.

That such differences exist indicates the wide variety of economic prosperity within the EU. Whereas some areas have a per capita income level well above the EU average, there simultaneously exist areas which have just a fraction of that average. It is important to recognise, however, that the degree of disparity evident in the statistics in the late 1980s reflects the accession of Greece (1981) and Spain and Portugal (1986). There is no doubt that the enlargement of the Union via the introduction of these nations considerably added to the nature of the Union regional problem. Padoa-Schioppa (1987) notes that as a result of their accession, Greece, Spain and Portugal increased EU GDP by 10 per cent, population by 22 per cent and employment in agriculture by 57 per cent. In addition, the same source reports that the population living in areas whose per capita GDP is less than 25 per cent of the EU average has virtually doubled as a consequence of the expansion. These statistics should, however, be kept in perspective. It remains the case that approximately 50 per cent of all regions in the Union lie within 15 per cent of the EU average per capita GDP.

Table 10.2 Regions ranked by unemployment (April 1992)

Top 10 level I regions	Country	Unemployment rate (%) (EUR12 = 9.4%)
Luxembourg	L	1.8
Baden-Wurttemberg	D	2.9
Bayern	D	3.0
Hessen	D	3.7
Rheinland-Pfalz	D	3.7
Lombardia	I	4.2
Emilia-Romagna	I	4.5
Portugal	POR	4.5
Nord Est	I	4.6
Schleswig-Holstein	D	4.7
Bottom 10 level I regions		
Sud	I	16.4
Noroeste	ESP	16.6
Northern Ireland	UK	16.7
Ireland	IRL	17.6
Centro	ESP	18.5
Sardegna	I	18.7
Campania	I	21.3
Sicilia	I	21.8
Canarias	ESP	24.8
Sur	ESP	25.9

Source : Eurostat, 1993

Per capita regional GDP is only one way of viewing the spatial disparities within the EU. One might also consider looking at the range of employment/unemployment experience, labour market participation and activity rates, although international comparisons of unemployment are notoriously difficult given the variation in definitions and data collection. Table 10.2 and Figure 10.3 show patterns of unemployment across the EU in 1990 and 1992. It is evident from the data that the divergence in unemployment rates is even greater than that for GDP per capita. The Sur region of Spain in 1992 experienced 25.9 per cent unemployment, nearly three times the EU average, whereas the rate in Luxembourg was only 1.8 per cent. However, low recorded unemployment is not necessarily evidence of high levels of per capita income, since at the national level both Portugal and Greece have below average unemployment rates, and yet income levels are only half the EU average. The EU has at various stages attempted to devise summary indicators of regional performance as a guide to the magnitude of the regional problem. In the Second Periodic Report on the development of the regions (1984), for example, a 'synthetic index' based on both GDP and unemployment was calculated. In the Third Periodic Report (1987) the index was amended to take account of labour force growth. In the case of the latter report, this illustrated that the 'least favoured regions' were almost exclusively large agricultural areas on the periphery of the Union in contrast to the 'most favoured' regions which were characterised either by being large administrative/service centres or by containing large industrial concentrations.

Table 10.3 Employment in the EUR12

	% Unemployment		% Employed in agriculture	
	1990	1986	1990	1986
Belgium	7.3	11.8	2.7	2.9
Denmark	8.0	5.8	5.7	6.2
France	8.7	10.4	6.0	7.3
Germany	4.9	6.6	4.2	5.3
Greece	7.0	8.3	22.2	28.5
Ireland	14.2	18.3	14.0	15.8
Italy	9.8	10.5	8.5	10.9
Luxembourg	1.6	2.6	3.5	4.0
Netherlands	7.4	10.3	4.4	4.8
Portugal	4.2	8.3	17.4	21.9
Spain	16.4	21.2	10.9	16.1
UK	6.9	11.5	2.3	2.6
EUR12	8.3	10.5	6.4	8.3

Source : Regional Trends, 1993; Eurostat

That there is still a close relationship between economic prosperity and the relative size of the agricultural sector is evident from Table 10.3 and Figure 10.1. Spain, Greece, Portugal and Ireland have the largest percentage of their workforce in the agricultural sector and the lowest per capita incomes. Thus there are a variety of perspectives on regional economic performance. The Fourth Periodic Report (1990c), however, notes that GDP per capita is probably the best available measure for regional comparisons of economic activity.

As for changes over time in spatial disparities within the EU, other than those generated by the accession of new members, there is some evidence of a long-run convergence in economic performance arising from the increased integration of national economies, as predicted by neo-classical economic theory (Barro and Sala-i-Martin, 1991; 1992).[4] Similarly, Boltho

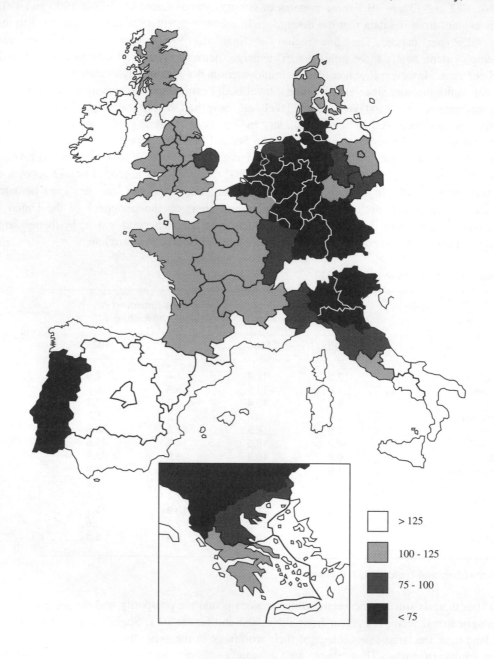

Figure 10.3 Unemployment 1992 (EUR12 average = 9.4% = 100)
Source : Eurostat

(1989) demonstrates that from 1950 onwards there has been some reduction in the degree of regional income imbalance. It appears that equalisation tended to be more pronounced in the 1950s with the relative decline of the role of agriculture, extensive postwar migration and the implementation of extensive welfare programmes. In the 1960s there is evidence that the process of equalisation began to slow down somewhat and statistics suggest that the first oil shock of 1973 actually reversed the trend altogether, with disparities tending to widen, although the temporary acceleration of economic growth in the late 1980s inhibited this process. The phenomenon of convergence occurring during periods of faster growth in the EU would not come as a surprise to regional economists. It is a common observation that spatial disparities tend to be reduced when national economies as a whole experience growth and vice versa. In fact, Boltho points out that the greater part of the equalisation that has occurred in the EU since the 1950s is due to greater inter-country equality rather than greater intra-country equality, i.e. disparities have been reduced as nations as a whole have converged rather than regions within nations moving closer together. More recently, Cardoso (1993) presented a similar view, arguing that the convergence of national economies has been achieved by particular regions within countries bearing the burden of this adjustment, so that regional imbalances at the sub-national level have in some instances increased.

It is by no means obvious, therefore, that regional disparities within the EU will reduce over time. The forces of convergence, such as factor mobility, are seen to be weak, to operate only in the long run and to be subject to significant disturbance by short-run phenomena such as recession. As is evident from Figure 10.1, the four countries with per capita GDP well above the EU average in 1986 also held similar positions in 1990. Likewise, the four countries which were well below the EU average in 1986 were also the least wealthy in 1990, although three of these (Spain, Portugal and Ireland) showed a marginal improvement, and only one (Greece) became relatively worse off. It is argued in the Fourth Periodic Report (1990c) that such persistent disparities are the result of long-term characteristics in the various economies and their regions, relating to factors such as levels of education, training, research and development. Consequently, it is only in the long term that such differences may be eliminated, if at all. For example, although as a group Spain, Portugal, Ireland and Greece grew faster than the rest of the EU from 1986 to 1990, a growth rate 1.25 per cent higher than the rest of the EU would need to be sustained for 20 years before they could attain 90 per cent of the EU average GDP per capita. It is clearly the case, therefore, that the forces of convergence are relatively weak, and that the implementation of active regional policy has a vital part to play in helping to reduce regional disparities in economic performance.

The evolution of regional policy

Regional policy did not emerge in the EU until 1975, but prior to this time there was embodied in the Treaty of Rome an implicit concern for regional disparities. In the preamble to the Treaty, the objective of 'reducing both the differences existing between the various regions and the backwardness of the less favoured regions' clearly signals this concern. However, it was also recognised in the Treaty that EU policies such as CAP could themselves have a significant differential regional impact. It was accepted that member states would operate their own national regional assistance instruments and that the EU's preoccupation would be to ensure that national aid did not conflict with its competition policy. This was to be achieved by providing protection for domestic industries under the guise of regional aid. Thus Article 92 provided for aid by member states 'to promote the economic development of areas where the standard of living is abnormally low, or where there is serious underemployment' provided that such aid did not 'adversely affect trading conditions'. Assistance was to be generally 'selective' and 'exceptional', contributing to investment rather than running costs.

As regional policy at the national and EU level has evolved over the years and in order to ensure that national assistance does not conflict with the pursuit of competition and free trade, the EU has defined criteria for determining aid eligibility (usually on the basis of GDP per capita and/or unemployment rates). Restrictions have been placed on the percentage of a nation's population which may be covered by aid, and ceilings have been imposed on the level of support measures. Not surprisingly, such actions by the EU have been fiercely contested by individual states at various times, particularly when the EU sought to reduce the extent of any nation's regional assistance measures.

The Treaty also established mechanisms through which regional assistance could be directed, if desired. In discussions prior to the final draft of the Treaty of Rome, for example, the concept of a specific regional fund was considered but rejected in favour of the European Investment Bank (EIB) which would provide finance for a range of activities including regional development activity. The European Social Fund (ESF) was not, on the other hand, specifically charged in the Treaty with providing regional assistance. Nevertheless, its overall responsibility to increase the geographical and occupational mobility of labour within the Union has meant that, in practice, a lot of its funds have been channelled towards the relatively less prosperous areas.

Moves towards a more active and coherent Union regional policy gradually gathered momentum throughout the 1960s. In its first report on regional policy in 1965 the Commission called for EU policy to be integrated with national policy. The post of Director General for regional policy was established in 1968, and the next year saw proposals by the Commission for the creation of regional aid instruments. Although these proposals were not accepted, they represented the forerunners of the policy which was to emerge in the 1970s. An additional urgency was injected into the moves towards a coherent regional policy by the emergence of the debate on economic and monetary union in the 1970s. It was felt at the time that regional disparities would inhibit commitment by member states to such integration. Thus the Paris Summit in 1972 produced a clear statement that a high priority should be given to correcting regional imbalances which would otherwise interfere with the realisation of economic and monetary union. In this light, a commitment was also made to the creation of a regional fund.

The problem of the enlargement of the Union, which would inevitably cause a widening of regional inequalities, also gave impetus to the regional policy debate. In particular, a mechanism was required to channel funds to the UK as compensation for the effects of CAP, from which other member states benefited disproportionately. The basis of future regional policy and its instruments was eventually to be found in the Thompson Report (EEC 1973) on the regional problems of the enlarged Union, which reaffirmed the view that in the long term, monetary union was not possible without an effective regional policy.

Regional policy 1975–1985

The European Regional Development Fund (ERDF) was finally established in 1975, together with general agreement on the definition of a region, on the criteria for determining eligibility for assistance and on the general characteristics that policies should possess. In particular, to qualify for national assistance (and hence EU assistance) a region would need to exhibit one of the following: a per capita income level below the EU average, more than 20 per cent of the population engaged in agriculture, unemployment more than 20 per cent above the EU average, or particularly high levels of migration. A limit had already been placed on the extent of national assistance two years earlier to prevent member states from engaging in self-defeating competitive bidding to attract mobile investment, and also in recognition of the basic idea of the Treaty of Rome that there should be a single market with free competition.

The ERDF initially had a small budget, with the facility to provide investment grants and loans for specific projects. Grants were available up to 20 per cent of capital costs or 50 per cent of the aid supplied nationally, and loans were available through funds directed via the EIB at reduced rates of interest (3 percentage points below the market rate). Projects were therefore not in themselves initiated by the ERDF; member states put forward projects to receive assistance and the limited funds available were allocated on the basis of predetermined national quotas. Italy and the UK received the largest allocations (40 per cent and 28 per cent respectively), indicative of their relatively less prosperous state compared to other members.

It was not long before these arrangements came under review. In 1977, the Commission felt it necessary to reconsider EU regional policy in view of the fact that its operation had highlighted certain difficulties. The economic experience of the 1970s had exacerbated existing regional problems as well as giving rise to new ones. Firstly, the EU's role in policy was essentially passive under the existing arrangements in that any regional dimension to the aid available was largely determined by member states themselves. Secondly, there was the emergence of what was to be a continuing question for EU policy, namely the issue of 'additionality'. It was argued that ERDF resources did not in fact represent truly additional aid for problem regions if such aid merely replaced expenditure that national governments would otherwise have incurred themselves.

As a first step towards dealing with these two questions, the 1977 review proposed that EU policy should increasingly be concerned with problems arising from peripherality, particularly where more than one nation was involved, or from the consequences of other EU policies, such as CAP. In 1979, therefore, the Council amended the structure of the ERDF to allow a proportion of the fund to be allocated for 'specific regional development measures' which were not nationally allocated. This non-quota section to the ERDF is interesting for a number of reasons. It represented an attempt by the EU, albeit in a small way, to address the problem of additionality, to take the initiative in regional matters and to introduce 'programme'[5] financing into its regional policy – a mechanism which was to become more important subsequently. In the event, however, the Commission could obtain agreement for only 5 per cent of the ERDF budget to be non-quota, and very little interest was expressed in these funds by member states.

The suggestion of the 1977 review that a comprehensive system of periodic review, analysis and assessment of regional policy should be instigated was upheld, leading to the First Periodic Report (1981). This initiated a process of regularly updating the regional policy of the EU together with a programme of regional impact assessment to evaluate the regional effect of other EU policies. The outcome of the Report and the debate which this generated was a new ERDF Regulation which came into force on 1 January 1985. Although a

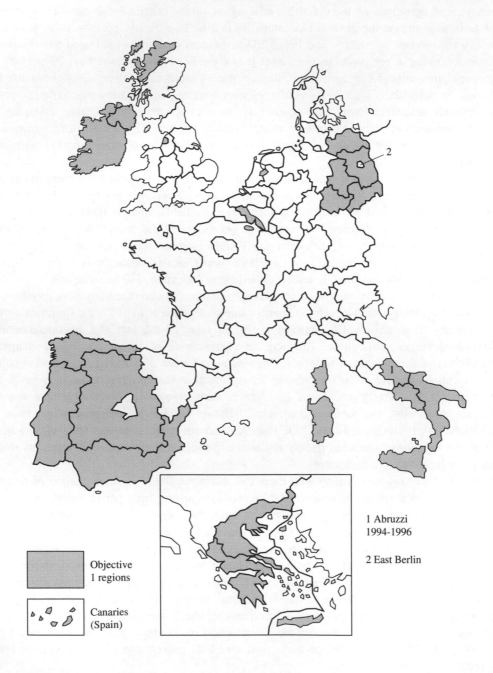

Figure 10.4 Objective 1 regions 1994–1999
Source : Commission EC

compromise, it contained substantial revisions. The principal objectives of EU policy were to provide aid to areas of industrial decline or slow development with a simple criterion for aid eligibility. This consisted of an index (with a score of 75 or below) which combined relative per capita income and relative unemployment levels, and was an attempt to redefine the assisted areas more narrowly so as to direct funds to those areas most in need. This was necessary since 40 per cent of the EU's population lived in areas which were eligible for assistance (including 37 per cent of West Germany's population). There was to be greater emphasis on actions to promote indigenous growth using local resources, rather than a reliance on large-scale investments by private and public sectors. It was also the intention to increase the share of the fund directed at service industries, such as tourism, from the existing 14 per cent to 30 per cent. The Commission was attempting by these measures to reduce the past bias towards spending on large infrastructure projects favoured by national governments.[6] Finally, the programme approach was to be extended over the whole Fund, with National Programmes of Community Interest, Community Programmes and Integrated Development Programmes[7], so that at least 20 per cent of the budget would be directed towards programme expenditure. Individual projects were still considered for fund assistance up to a maximum of 50 per cent of expenditure, but programmes could receive up to 70 per cent. The advantages to the Commission of programme financing arose from the long-term nature of such a plan for regional development, which required agreement on financing arrangements in advance from all the concerned parties down to the local government level. There was therefore a degree of assurance about the 'additionality' of EU funds. This was even more so for the special programmes developed by the Union, such as the Integrated Mediterranean Programmes which were established to enable the southern regions of France, Italy and Greece to adjust to the accession of Spain and Portugal into the EU.[8]

With the provision for periodic review, the basic framework for future regional policy was now in place. Nevertheless, the commitment by the EU in terms of actual resources was still extremely small; ERDF expenditure in 1984, for example, constituted only 0.08 per cent of the EU's GDP. Set alongside the regional impact of other EU policies, notably CAP, the ability of the regional funds to make progress towards correcting spatial disparities was severely restricted. The CAP, the largest component of the EU's budget, by providing assistance on the basis of output and type of product, was not regionally directed and often worked in the opposite direction to regional policy. In 1985, the wealthier northern regions of the EU received 25 per cent above the average of budgetary expenditure per person employed in agriculture, whereas the regions in the southern periphery received 25 per cent below the average, and even less in some instances. Thus the regional assistance provided by the EU could be viewed as a rather weak attack on a problem which the Union had itself exacerbated.

In terms of the form (rather than the scale) of policy, there was still the problem of 'additionality' as a cause for concern. Not only were many projects already under way before ERDF resources were committed, but member states were free to add ERDF aid to the national aid for the project (individual additionality) or to add such aid to national regional expenditure as a whole (global additionality). The latter option was more frequently adopted, so that it became very difficult to evaluate the contribution, if any, that ERDF expenditure might have made to economic development. While a new regulation in 1985 ruled out the option of global additionality, the question of individual additionality remained for the future.

With the accession of Spain and Portugal in 1986, and the resulting shift in regional disparities within the Union, the argument for a further enhancement of regional policy was strengthened. Evidence of this was already to be seen in the Integrated Mediterranean Programmes. But perhaps more importantly, the Single European Act (SEA) of 1986 added an urgency to the search for a more effective regional policy. Indeed, anticipation of the possible unequal distribution of the benefits of greater competition meant that reform of the Structural Funds, i.e. the ERDF, the ESF and the EAGGF Guidance Section, became an essential condition within some member states for agreement to proceed towards completion of the SEM.

The Single European Act: the reform of the Structural Funds 1989–1993

The SEA was the most important development within the EU after the Rome Treaty. Chapter 2 discusses in some detail the implications of the SEA for EU integration, and the potential aggregate economic benefits that might accrue over the long term. The concern here, however, is not so much that of the level of such benefits but their spatial distribution. As noted above, the Rome Treaty did not explicitly incorporate any regional dimension, but it did recognise that EU policies might well have a differential spatial impact. It was generally the case, nevertheless, that in the 30 years following the signing of the Treaty, EU policies were only rarely developed in a framework which explicitly evaluated the spatial impact of those policies.[9] Indeed, the EU was frequently more concerned with the question of whether national aid programmes contravened its competition policy rather than whether its competition policy might have any adverse consequences for the regions of member nations.

As part of the process towards implementation of the SEA, an agreement was reached in early 1988 to double the size of the Structural Funds in real terms by 1992. The mechanisms for distributing the Funds were also subject to major revisions and became effective on 1 January 1989. The reforms provided a clear statement of the five main objectives of EC regional policy (Table 10.4), the means by which policy would be implemented and the role of each of the Structural Funds in meeting these objectives. The Structural Fund allocations under each objective, totalling over ECU 60 bn., are also given in Table 10.4.[10] Overall, the former, rather piecemeal, approach to regional policy was replaced by a more coordinated strategy with emphasis on three key features – the concentration of resources directed at particular problems and areas, the partnership between the Commission and regional authorities, and programme-rather than project-based regional assistance.

Concentration of resources was to be achieved through definition of the objectives which became the basis for identifying the regions eligible for aid, and through the allocation of the major share (approximately 70 per cent) of the Structural Funds to Objective 1 areas. Such regions were to be designated for a period of five years and were specifically defined to be those areas (NUTS Level II) where per capita GDP in PPSs was less than 75 per cent of the Community average. On this basis, all of Greece, Ireland and Portugal, most of Spain, Southern Italy, the French Overseas Departments and Northern Ireland (a special case) qualified for Objective 1 funding at this time, and the percentage of Objective 1 funding allocated to each is given in Table 10.5. Priority was in this way accorded to the least prosperous regions and countries of the Union, partly due to the expectation that these areas might benefit least from the SEM.

Table 10.4 Objective regions of the EU and allocation of Structural Funds 1989–1993 (ECU m., 1989 prices)

Objective region	Fund	CSFs	Community initiatives	Total
1. Development of structurally backward regions	ERDF, ESF, EAGGF Guidance	36 200	2 100	38 300
2. Reconverting regions in industrial decline	ERDF, ESF	6 705	500	7 205
3. Combating long-term and 4. youth unemployment	ESF	7 233	217	7 450
5(a). Adjustment of agricultural structures (related to reform of CAP)	EAGGF Guidance			3 415
5(b). Development of rural areas	ERDF,ESF, EAGGF Guidance	2 607	188	2 795

Source : Commission of the EC

Designated Objective 2 regions presented more of a problem for the Union in terms of reaching agreement on the specific criteria for the definition of industrial decline, and hence upon the particular regions to be assisted. In the end, areas were originally selected for three years (at NUTS Level III) according to such conditions as unemployment rates significantly higher than the EU average during the previous three years, and industrial employment as a percentage of total employment greater than the EU average in every year of the previous fifteen years. Areas suffering substantial job losses in specific industries could also be considered; for example, in late 1990 certain coal-mining areas were incorporated into the list of Objective 2 regions. In 1991, recognising that the problems of Objective 2 regions were invariably of a long-term nature, the period of eligibility was extended to 5 years.

Table 10.5 Objective 1 allocations 1989–1993

	ECU bn. (1989 prices)	Per capita (eligible population)	% of total
Spain	9.78	433	27.0
Italy	7.44	354	20.6
Portugal	6.96	705	19.2
Greece	6.67	653	18.4
UK	0.88	554	2.4
Ireland	3.67	1 048	10.1
France	0.88	572	2.4
Total	36.28	516	100.0

Source : Commission of the EC

The problems in selecting Objective 2 regions are well illustrated by the UK case, where the final list of Objective 2 regions during this period contained anomalies in that some areas became eligible for EC but not national assistance, despite the fact that ERDF monies were required to be additional to national expenditure and could not therefore constitute 100 per cent of any assistance measure.[11] Also, in the context of industrial decline, the UK argued for the inclusion of some inner city areas under Objective 2. In the event, such areas were excluded but there was agreement by the Commission to consider other means of assistance for urban areas until the next review of regional policy in 1993, when the issue would be re-examined.[12]

A further factor in the debate surrounding Objective 2 centred on the type and proportion of aid to be granted under this heading. As has already been stated, infrastructure spending previously constituted a large percentage of EU aid to member states. However, under the new regulations spending on infrastructure projects in Objective 2 regions was limited to those projects which directly provided 'the basis for the creation or development of economic activity' of the area concerned. This represented a much tighter definition than under Objective 1. Furthermore, aid to industry had to be demonstrably 'additional' to national expenditures, and overall assistance was limited to a maximum of 50 per cent of total expenditure.

Overall, while the UK was the main beneficiary under Objective 2, the fact that the UK was excluded from Objective 1 assistance (with the exception of Northern Ireland) meant that access to the vast bulk of the Structural Funds was denied. As the UK (and other more prosperous countries) moved up the league table of relative prosperity with the accession of new member states, it is not surprising that assistance under Objective 2 was fiercely debated, and that ultimately a significant degree of political influence also became a relevant factor in the selection procedure.[13] Of 900 areas proposed by member states, 60 were ultimately designated under Objective 2.

Objectives 3 and 4 were not in themselves regionally restricted, although the new priorities for ESF funding had a regional dimension. For instance, more resources were to be directed to the long-term unemployed, particularly among young people, in the Objective 2 and 5(b) regions.

Finally, Objectives 5(a) and 5(b) differed somewhat from the previous four in not being concerned with industrialisation as such, but with rural restructuring and development. The regional dimension is principally to be found in 5(b), which represented an addition to the previously stated objectives of the EAGGF Guidance Section – to improve productivity in the agricultural sector, to assist in the provision of infrastructure and in the promotion of structural change among farms in rural areas. Aid was now to be granted to measures which promoted diversification into other activities such as tourism and craft industries. While such rural development in non-agricultural activity was also made eligible for aid from the ERDF and ESF, the overall level of funding in this area was set at a relatively low level in relation to the other Objectives and in comparison to the budget allocated to the CAP. Again as with Objective 2, there was much debate on the areas eligible for aid under 5(b). The criteria for determining selection were a high percentage of total employment in agriculture and a low level of agricultural income and socio-economic development. Additionally, peripheral areas experiencing depopulation, environmental pressures or other unfavourable characteristics inhibiting development, such as the size structure of farms, could be considered.

Thus, via these five Objectives, but principally through 1, 2 and 5(b), it was hoped to provide a more focused strategy for the reduction of regional disparities and the promotion of balanced development in the SEM.

The main mechanism for the coordination and implementation of policy was to be the Community Support Framework (CSF). Arguably the most significant element in the Structural Fund reforms, the CSF is representative of the shift from project to programme assistance and the greater element of partnership between the Commission and the regional and local authorities. A CSF is an amalgamation of a regional plan drawn up by the individual member state and the Commission's own priorities for assistance in the relevant area. Since funds are likely to be limited in relation to the demand for them, the Commission's own priorities become important in deciding where and how to intervene. In this way the CSF provides both a statement on the objectives for the particular region in question, and also a programme of intervention measures to be pursued, together with the sources of necessary funds, thereby achieving a greater coordination between the Structural Funds and other Union instruments.[14]

Lastly, to operate alongside the CSFs and Integrated Development Operations were a number of Community Initiatives, undertaken by the Commission to address directly particular problems in certain areas not felt to be adequately covered by the CSFs.[15] In particular, a number of initiatives emerged with the primary purpose of providing assistance for those regions at a disadvantage with respect to the SEM (mainly, but not exclusively, Objective 1 regions).[16]

Through the above reforms, it was intended to create a more effective Union regional policy to cope with the additional stresses facing some regions as a result of adjustments to the SEM. Policy was to operate through a partnership of local, regional, national and EU authorities in the pursuit of common policy objectives. By engaging in some instances in direct dialogue with local and regional authorities and by-passing national governments, the Commission hoped to be able to coordinate the allocation of the Structural Funds and direct aid more effectively to the problem areas, thereby also implicitly weakening the influence of national government upon the use of EU funding. Central to the whole process was the CSF, the latest stage in the trend towards programme rather than project intervention. Overall, the reforms (particularly the CSFs) represented a further attempt to move away from the passive form of EU regional aid, whereby EU expenditure was simply added to nationally determined projects and regional policy was therefore little more than a system of budgetary transfers.

The overall effect of the above measures was to shift the future direction of assistance towards the poorer regions. Existing member states such as the UK were to receive relatively less in terms of regional aid than previously, although this could in part be compensated by the general increase in the size of the Structural Funds. Despite this increase in the size of these funds, and the fact that regional aid could contribute a significant input of resources to any particular area, it remained the case that the extent of EU regional assistance was small, amounting to approximately 28 per cent of the total EU budget by 1992.

The Maastricht Treaty and the Structural Funds 1994–1999

The termination of the Structural Fund Regulations agreed in 1989 coincided in 1993 with the ratification of the Maastricht Treaty. Not surprisingly, therefore, the future direction and magnitude of regional policy has been formulated against this background of debate on the moves towards greater political, economic and monetary union.[17] Article 2 of the Treaty expresses a fundamental commitment to economic and social cohesion within the Union and a reduction in regional disparities is recognised to be part of the process of cohesion. Indeed, without progress towards such cohesion, economic and monetary union is unlikely to be achieved (Begg and Mayes 1993). The need for an active regional policy, acknowledged in the adoption of the SEA, has thus been reinforced.

In recognition of this fact, the Maastricht Treaty made provision for a new Cohesion Fund to provide assistance for the poorer member states,[18] while at the Edinburgh Summit in 1992 the Structural Funds (including the Cohesion Fund) were increased to account for over 35 per cent of the Union Budget by 1999 (Table 10.6). Thus the Structural Funds have doubled in relative terms since 1987, when they constituted only 17.8 per cent of the total budget. Also agreed at the Edinburgh Summit was the introduction of a new European Investment Fund (EIF), a Union instrument to promote the EU's Growth Initiative. The Fund is designed to guarantee loans for large infrastructure projects relating to trans-European networks, and to assist investment by small and medium-sized enterprises, especially in areas designated for regional aid. Although not directly spatially defined, the Fund's assistance is expected to benefit the peripheral regions of the Union.

Table 10.6 Budget for structural action 1993–1999

	Structural Funds	Cohesion Fund	Total ECUm. (1992 prices)	Objective 1
1993	19 777	1 500	21 277	62.3%
1994	20 135	1 750	21 885	65.7%
1995	21 480	2 000	23 480	66.6%
1996	22 740	2 250	24 990	67.4%
1997	24 026	2 500	26 526	68.2%
1998	25 690	2 550	28 240	69.4%
1999	27 400	2 600	30 000	70.4%
Total	161 248	15 150	176 398	67.4%

Source : Commission of the EC

In terms of the policy framework, the basic principles underlying the reforms of 1989 have been retained, namely the focus on lagging (Objective 1) regions and on programmes, partnership and additionality.[19] It is still the case, for example, that as much as 70 per cent of the enlarged Structural Funds will be allocated to the lagging regions. These areas, agreed as Objective 1 regions in 1993, are shown in Figure 10.4, where it can be seen that the inclusion of former East Germany, one region each in Belgium and the Netherlands, and parts of mainland France and the UK has extended the list of lagging regions, and hence population coverage, in comparison to the previous planning period.[20] Objective 2 and 5(b) regions are expected to receive a 14 per cent increase in funding by 1999, and although the total extent of such Objective 2 regions in population terms remains broadly the same at approximately 15 per cent, an expansion in the Objective 5(b) regions is anticipated to reflect the continuing difficulties of peripheral rural areas and their further problems arising from the reform of the CAP.[21] A new Objective 6 was initially proposed to assist in structural adjustments in the fisheries, but in the end assistance to regions which are suffering the consequences of decline in fishing and fish processing are to be incorporated within the existing framework, particularly under 5(a).[22] Finally, the non-spatially restricted Objectives 3 and 4 have been integrated into a single Objective 3, with totally new definition for Objective 4 concerned with the adaptation of the workforce to industrial change and new production techniques.

Community Initiatives continue to operate alongside CSFs, and over the 1994–1999 programming period are scheduled to absorb some 9 per cent of the Structural Funds.[23] In the light of the proliferation of such programmes in the previous period, and various problems identified (such as overlap with CSFs), a review of such Initiatives is intended to produce a separate Regulation during 1994, providing a more coherent and focused approach for these particular instruments.

Additionality continues to be of some concern, and it appears to be more difficult for some countries, such as the UK, to demonstrate that EU regional expenditures are truly additional resources, and are not simply replacing national expenditures. However, member states in the future must be able to account transparently for their receipts from the Structural Funds under each Objective, or risk losing some of these Funds. In a similar vein, countries which are severely budget-constrained find it difficult to provide the matching funds necessary to qualify for Union assistance. Over the period 1994 to 1999, therefore, the levels of EU participation in terms of their percentage contribution are likely to increase in some cases, particularly in the Cohesion countries. Finally, simpler decision-making procedures for programme planning are to be accompanied by more effective monitoring and evaluation. The general appraisal of policy is to be strengthened, such that a mid-term review of performance could potentially reallocate resources from member states whose programmes were performing badly to those making better use of EU finance.

To conclude, it can be seen that regional policy has progressed since 1975 in accordance with growing perceptions of the need to deal with actual and potential regional disparities arising from both the enlargement of the Union and the drive towards greater economic integration. Whether the magnitude, direction and effectiveness of such policy is adequate in relation to the extent of the problem is, however, debatable. The economic theory which predicts significant gains from integration largely ignores the distributional implications, but as Begg and Mayes (1993) state, 'the reality of the EC is that the division of costs and benefits is central to the political agreements needed to proceed with integration'.

Economic integration and regional policy: the Single European Market

The Single European Act (1986), which launched the process of further economic integration, was designed to create a Single European Market (SEM) in all goods, services, capital and labour, and contained a commitment to strengthen economic and social cohesion through a reduction of the disparities in the development of the Community's regions. However, exactly how the achievement of the SEM will ultimately affect regional economies throughout the Union is, on the whole, rather vague. Indeed, in the extensive assessment of the economic potential of the SEM undertaken by the Commission[24] there was little in the way of spatial analysis. The report states that estimation of the benefit distribution by country, let alone region, would be an enormously complex task and accordingly does not attempt to examine in any detail the spatial dimension. The hope seems to have been that the SEM itself would promote convergence in economic performance through forces such as greater factor mobility and the 'trickle-down' effect to all regions of economic growth in the aggregate. As Begg (1989) pointed out, 'the emphasis in much of the analysis of "1992" seems to be that, provided the macroeconomic gains for the Community as a whole are realised, questions about the spatial impact of the single market are of secondary importance'. This view is reinforced by the fact that where studies were carried out on behalf of the Commission, the general conclusions pointed to a greater concentration of economic activity rather than convergence (e.g. P A Cambridge Economic Consultants 1988). In fact, it is difficult to escape the conclusion that the SEA was adopted for the anticipated aggregate benefits, with little regard for the distribution of those benefits. The major concern at the time seemed to be that regional differences should not stand in the way of further integration.

Despite the rhetoric on cohesion and convergence, therefore, the actual extent of the EU's commitment to reducing the range in economic prosperity within its boundaries must be questioned. The Structural Funds provide a compensatory mechanism of sorts for potential 'losers', and over time have become increasingly focused on the promotion of indigenous development in the backward regions. Nevertheless, the increases in the regional funds which have occurred over time must be placed in perspective, as the resources available are small in relation to the problems they are designed to address. Although the SEA *was* accepted on the basis of the 100 per cent increase in the Structural Funds, it could be argued that some areas/nations suffered from an 'underselling' of their position. In relative terms the weight of the Structural Funds in the EU budget increased from 20 per cent to approximately 28 per cent, and yet at the same time CAP accounted for more than 60 per cent of the budget, principally to the benefit of the developed regions. By 1999, it is intended that 35 per cent of the EU budget will be regionally directed (Structural plus Cohesion Funds), but the sums involved will represent only approximately 0.4 per cent of GNP in the Union. The major share of the budget is still *not* regionally focused, so that the overall effect of Union expenditure on the less developed regions can be expected to be largely neutral (Franzmeyer *et al.*, 1991). Furthermore, some of this expansion in funding is directed towards former East Germany, which is expected to receive some 14 bn Ecu under Objective 1 for the period 1994–99. Allowing for this, the expansion of the Structural Funds relative to the EU budget as a whole is much more modest, and reflects a 'wider' rather than a 'deeper' attack on regional problems. The extent of the real increase in per capita funding for Objective 1 regions is therefore not as great as might be anticipated. As is apparent from Table 10.5, there were large differences in per capita funding for the Objective 1 regions in the previous programming period 1989–1993, with Ireland receiving 2.4 times as much as Spain. For the period 1994–1999, this imbalance is addressed through an increase in the Objective 1 allocation to Spain (estimated to receive approximately 40 per cent of all such funds), but to some extent this simply represents a redistribution, occurring at the expense of a relative decline in Objective 1 funding for other areas such as Italy and Ireland.

In comparison to the magnitude of regional aid described above, the economic growth resulting from the internal market programme was estimated to be of much greater significance, at approximately 6 per cent of GNP.[25] The questions that appear not to have been officially asked are what proportion of these projected gains will accrue to areas already experiencing relative prosperity; to what extent will such gains occur at the expense of reductions in the prosperity of already disadvantaged and underdeveloped regions; and whether the regional assistance is adequate to ease the adjustment process to any significant degree.

It is clear that at the heart of these issues is the question of whether greater economic integration and any subsequent economic growth will exacerbate or reduce existing regional disparities. The answer to this question is rather uncertain, dependent as it is on an understanding of the complex processes of economic development both spatially and sectorally. However, what is apparent from the discussion below is that there is little evidence, if any, that underdeveloped regions will benefit to a greater extent than other areas from greater economic integration.

Already in this chapter there has been a discussion of the forces which appear to contribute to varying regional prosperity, and the ultimate outcome of the SEM will be the result of a series of different processes interacting with these existing forces. There will be immediate or direct effects arising from the removal of non-tariff barriers, and more long-term or indirect effects involving the rationalisation, restructuring and relocation of industry as a consequence of a more competitive environment. In the case of the former, all regions may benefit to some extent from the cost reductions arising from the removal of non-tariff barriers. However, there may be job losses in particular areas associated with the closure of customs offices, or with the emergence of competition in the area of public procurement. In the case of the latter, many peripheral areas of Europe are to some extent sustained economically by public procurements placed to industries within those regions. A more open market in public procurement will place these industries and therefore regions in some jeopardy. Although the costs of favouring domestic public procurement are significant (estimated to be in the region of 0.5 per cent of Union GDP), the removal of this practice may itself impose costs on the already disadvantaged regions.

In the longer term, a large proportion of the projected benefits resulting from the SEM programme are expected to emerge from the exploitation of scale economies (Cecchini 1988). If such economies are to be achieved then two possible scenarios present themselves: either existing product markets will be serviced by fewer firms or they will expand to a level consistent with greater output levels (Begg 1989). If the expansion in demand is insufficient to accommodate the increased productive potential of the Union then the relevant scale economies may well be achieved by some rationalisation of existing production units.

The extent to which this impacts on various regions in any economy will obviously reflect the spatial concentration and nature of those industries/sectors that experience such restructuring. If British evidence is anything to go by, large and relatively dated production units often tend to be the first to close in periods of rationalisation. These units are typically located in peripheral regional economies (Tomkins and Twomey 1990). It should be noted, however, that the spatial impact of scale economies will be ameliorated to some extent if the relevant industry/sector is already integrated to a relatively high level within Europe. In this case the potential economies will be somewhat low and the impact of their realisation minimal.

Discussion concerning the potential impact of scale economies, in terms of restructuring, does not finish with consideration of the peripheral economies. If the concentration of production and distribution units becomes a major force in the transition to the SEM, there will be an inevitable tendency for that concentration to occur in the core regions which will probably not only contain relevant headquarters and production units, but also guarantee proximity to markets and immediate access to a range of supporting service functions.[26] Apart from the potential loss of economic activity from more peripheral areas, it is not necessarily the case that such further concentration in core regional economies should be viewed as in any way desirable. Several core economies in the centre of Europe are already relatively congested. Further demands on such areas may actually begin to produce diseconomies in the form of increased congestion and 'overheating'. These potential costs are not considered in the background research to the SEA. They may significantly reduce the projected gains of closer European integration.

To the extent that completion of the SEM will encourage production activities to become more mobile, there are a series of factors which will also come to determine choice of location. In the same way that rationalisation may encourage centralisation towards core economies, proximity to major market centres and abundance of supporting service activities may be expected to draw 'footloose' production and distribution units towards central areas of an economy. This effect will be reinforced if the infrastructure of peripheral areas appears inadequate. Surveys of the determinants of business location choice frequently point to the availability of suitable premises and labour, access to air transport, access to motorway networks, etc. as important factors influencing the location of new business units.[27] Therefore while the emphasis on infrastructure projects within EU regional aid has in general been much reduced, there must still be a strong case for maintaining such aid to peripheral areas.

Another element that might be expected to influence location of economic activity will be the extent of differentials in factor costs.[28] It is the case, for example, that there exist wide disparities in labour costs between nations in Europe. Hourly wages in Greece, Spain and Northern Ireland in 1990 were less than 75 per cent of the EU average, whereas parts of Germany and Denmark exhibited rates at least 25 per cent above the average (Ernst and Young 1990). Consideration of such data alone is, of course, misleading because no account is taken of differentials in productivity between nations, which can substantially alter unit labour costs. At the sub-national level, the peripheral/least favoured regions might be expected to exhibit lower labour costs than the core regions. But again this is not necessarily the case, since the nature of national and local labour markets and their degree of integration within national or collective bargaining frameworks might well produce a relatively even spatial distribution of wage rates.

Recent research supports many of these conclusions. Camagni (1992) argues that the lagging (Objective 1) regions will not only benefit less from the SEM, but will directly suffer as a consequence of the abandonment of preferential public purchasing policies and other traditional assistance measures. Furthermore, they are also likely to lose their advantage in unit labour costs through harmonisation regulations and the general moves towards enhanced integration. Quevit (1992) also concludes that lagging regions are particularly sensitive to the effects of the SEM. Out of 120 industrial sectors, 40 have been identified to be significantly affected by the removal of non-tariff barriers and the potential for economies of scale (Buiges *et al.*, 1990). The lagging regions typically contain a higher than average share of such sectors, with the notable exception of Italy. In Greece, for example, more than 75 per cent of manufacturing employment occurs in these industrial sectors. However, the generally weak economic structure in the lagging regions means that there are few opportunities for generating economies of scale. Similarly, the traditional industrial regions, according to Quevit, will suffer particularly from the liberalisation of public procurement and from the long-term impact of the SEM because of their relatively low research and development capacity, making them less dynamic and adaptable to change.

On the other hand, the main beneficiaries of the SEM are seen to be the already successful regions. Dunford (1993) finds evidence of positive correlations at various regional levels between per capita GDP and rates of growth in per capita GDP, supporting the cumulative causation theories of widening regional disparities. Amin *et al.* (1992) contend that, despite the emphasis in EU regional policy on indigenous economic development, existing large firms remain a major influence on the underdeveloped regions. Focusing on pharmaceuticals and telecommunications equipment, the rationalisation and restructuring within such firms as they respond to the SEM tends to reinforce rather than reduce existing comparative advantage in the successful regions. Begg (1992) draws similar conclusions for the financial services sector, where response to the SEM provides the existing financial centres with the largest share of the benefits. However, both studies sound a note of caution for the most successful regions and urban centres in that competition from other centres is likely to intensify. This view is shared be Steinle (1992), who suggests that the well-established centres and regions are showing signs of saturation and congestion, as argued above. By defining a measure of 'regional competitiveness', those areas of the Union with a greater capacity to adapt to change and restructuring are identified. In general, they are not the most successful areas nor are they the less developed, peripheral regions. Thus it is proposed that certain intermediate areas possessing a high degree of dynamic competitiveness are in the position to benefit most from the SEM.

It is apparent from the preceding discussion that there are inherent conflicts between the pursuit of greater competition and equity in the regional distribution of the benefits of a more competitive market. EU regional assistance measures in this sense serve two purposes; to redistribute resources to the less favoured regions and to overcome the impediments to indigenous long-term growth. To prevent national regional assistance from going beyond these functions and giving an 'unfair advantage' to their assisted areas, the Commission has always been concerned to examine the nature of national regional policy instruments for signs of domestic protectionism. New schemes or amendments to existing schemes within member states require Union approval and must demonstrate 'regional' relevance. Over the years, the Commission has recommended abolition of state aid schemes in apparent conflict with its competition policy. The Commission has also applied continuing pressure, particularly to the Northern European member states, to reduce their national aid expenditure and the extent of their assisted areas, so as to create a 'level playing field' for regional aid within the EU. In addition to these pressures emanating from the Union as a whole, there has been a reorientation of national regional assistance since the 1980s towards a more focused and selective approach, particularly in Northern Europe. Public expenditure constraints at the national level have also played a part in determining changes in the level and form of national regional assistance measures, with a distinct North–South divide evident (Bachter and Michie 1993). Denmark, for example, removed all regional development aid in 1991, and assisted area coverage has been significantly reduced in the UK, Belgium, Denmark, former West Germany and the Netherlands, a trend which began in the UK in 1984. As Bachter and Michie (1993) also note, in all North European member states with the exception of Germany, national regional aid expenditure has declined between 1985 and 1990. In France, for example, the fall was over 57 per cent. In comparison, such expenditures in Southern Europe and Ireland either increased or remained constant over this period, while in the cases of Ireland and Spain the extent of the assisted areas has actually increased. Yet despite these trends, national *per capita* expenditure on regional assistance exhibits substantial differences. Between 1986 and 1988, the average per capita expenditure on the population in the assisted areas in peripheral regions was ECU 16, compared to ECU 90 in the central regions of the Union. Thus the shortage of funds at a national level places the less advanced countries and regions at a further disadvantage.

In conclusion, while traditional neo-classical theory predicts long-run convergence in economic performance as a result of increased integration, at an empirical level the forces at work to produce this effect appear extremely weak. Furthermore, it is by no means evident that the shock of the SEM will reinforce this trend to convergence – in fact the opposite is more likely so that EU regional policy is therefore an essential and complementary policy to counteract the adverse spatial consequences of the SEM. As the previous discussion demonstrated, there are many reasons to suppose that the difficulties of underdeveloped regions, peripheral regions and declining industries will worsen as many of the structural adjustments to the SEM take place. Whether the magnitude and direction of regional aid is adequate for the task is debatable.[29] What is also clear is that the drive for monetary union will compound this problem, and place further stresses and responsibilities at the door of EU regional policy.

Monetary union: the regional dimension

Just as the impact of the SEA may have a series of implications for the spatial distribution of economic activity and prosperity within the EU, monetary union may also impart a number of effects which will modify regional fortunes. It is important, first of all, to note that monetary union will effectively alter the status of member nations within the EU to that of regions within the union. Chapter 4 discusses the overall macro-economic issues in more detail, for example the extent to which monetary union might produce faster growth, but the principal concern here is with the spatial implications. In this context, if there are differences in the unit cost and therefore the competitiveness of nations which are *not* connected in a customs or monetary union, then attempts to eliminate such differences (reflected in associated balance of payments positions) can potentially be made via trade restrictions or movements in relative exchange rates, although the effectiveness of the latter policy is by no means certain. In fact, Stevens (1991) argues that it is because devaluation does not work as an instrument of economic policy that the argument for a single currency is made more powerful. What remains true, however, is that with the removal of trade barriers and the emergence of complete monetary union, the member nations of the EU will confront precisely the same issues that confronted regions within those nations prior to the union. The fundamental issues of balanced growth, peripherality and the problems facing areas of industrial decline or delayed development will become difficulties which not only regions, but member nations as a whole, may have to address within the EU.

As one might expect from the discussion elsewhere in this chapter, there are a variety of reasons why adjustments to monetary union, and any aggregate economic gains, are not likely to be evenly distributed across all regions, nor are there any purely economic arguments for the existence of redistributive policies to counteract such trends. As Begg and Mayes (1993) point out, using the example of German unification, a monetary union can function satisfactorily in the presence of significant regional disparities. It is the political acceptability of such imbalances and the extent of redistribution which is often more problematic.

In terms of adjustments to monetary union, therefore, any 'uncompetitive' region (i.e. nation) of the union that does not undertake and succeed in reducing differential unit (and particularly labour) costs will experience pressures commensurate with a current account deficit. If this is not accommodated by capital inflows there will be downward pressure on income levels and subsequently increased unemployment. If the rise in the numbers of jobless does not encourage a decline in unit costs then the deficit region/nation will continue to experience an underemployment of resources. The President of the Commission recognised this potential outcome when he stated that 'with the reduction of exchange rate variability, it is important for the wage system to become more responsive to considerations of competitiveness'.[30] In the same report another contributor commented, 'for EMU to be sustainable, the economies of countries forming the union must be similarly competitive or else some countries would be faced with the equivalent of a constant balance of payments deficit which, in EMU, would be reflected in terms of stagnation and unemployment.'[31]

In the absence of exchange rate changes, therefore, adjustments in the labour market become crucial in restoring or maintaining an economy's competitive position. It is argued by the Commission[32] that wage flexibility in response to employment conditions may increase with monetary union and that there is already evidence of this for those economies participating in the ERM prior to suspension. Such an effect is dependent on wage bargaining procedures taking account of the implications of monetary union, and it remains to be seen whether this will continue to be the case in the longer term. However, there is no reason to suppose that regions within countries will experience increased wage flexibility in either the short or the long term.

Thus, in the absence of increased or sufficient flexibility in wage formation within the 'uncompetitive' member economies, it is probably the case that these economies will be forced to suffer periods of unemployment with the onset of monetary union. If these economies are also those with existing substantial disparities in regional prosperity, then the transition to monetary union may well serve to aggravate the relative position of the latter, in that any reduction in national income arising from the processes outlined above is itself likely to have a disproportionately large effect on the disadvantaged regions of those countries.

Another response to spatial differences in unemployment might lie in labour mobility. In this sense, monetary union presents another potential source of imposed spatial depression on certain areas in the EU. Following the establishment of the union there might well emerge a tendency for money wage rates to converge between member nations given a degree of labour mobility. The problem that this might create lies in the fact that many peripheral areas within nations tend to have lower productivity levels than the core areas. Equalisation of money wage rates would, in this scenario, raise the unit costs of production in peripheral areas, thereby reducing competitiveness and contributing to further decline.[33] Equalisation of wage rates or attempts to impose common conditions in labour markets through mechanisms such as the Social Chapter might have the same effect (see Chapter 9).

One further implication of monetary union stems from both the above observations. A well-known rationale for regional policy interventions is that countries with extensive regional imbalances in economic activity appear more prone to suffer inflationary pressures, and to suffer them sooner, than more spatially balanced nations. Any increase in aggregate demand in such an economy will hit a capacity constraint in the successful regions long before this happens in the disadvantaged areas, leading to inflationary pressure in the former. If monetary union widens the disparities within nations, the removal of exchange rate policy options in such circumstances may necessitate other conventional policies, for example, a reduction in aggregate demand, to reduce inflation. It is probably the case that the weaker areas of the relevant nations will lose most from this action, since regional disparities tend to widen when aggregate demand falls and narrow when demand rises. Indeed, it is ironic that the weaker regions of a country tend to 'catch up' most in times of expansion, and yet it is partly because of the regional differences that inflationary pressures emerge and induce policies which prevent further gains. Furthermore, the pressure for convergence in inflation rates, and the requirement for more coordinated fiscal policy within the EU, which is implied by monetary union, may therefore impose greater constraints upon the spatially imbalanced countries.

The success of monetary union in promoting a more balanced development within the EU rests ultimately on factors such as the degree of wage flexibility and the mobility of capital in response to differential labour costs, versus the advantages of centralisation and agglomeration. It is thus difficult to predict the precise spatial outcome of establishing a monetary union within the EU. While the benefits of faster growth may spread throughout the EU, it cannot be assumed that this will occur in a balanced manner. There is as noted above a real risk that the process will aggravate the degree of imbalance that presently exists. The policy implications are to some extent summarised in the contribution of the Bundesbank President to the Delors report:

> within the monetary union, balance-of-payments policy is replaced by regional policy, with the latter helping to finance inter-regional differences in current account imbalances through transfer payments. The differences in the level of economic development of individual member countries of the Community suggest that extremely large funds would be needed to finance the necessary fiscal compensation. Only through a very effective regional policy could these differences perhaps be reduced to an extent that would be compatible with the existence of a monetary union.[34]

This comment suggests that certain areas of the EU may well experience substantial dislocation from the process leading to monetary union. It is not stated but it is also probably true that the greater the haste for union, the greater will be the potential dislocation.

There is, however, a danger that like the discussion of the SEM noted above, the details of the spatial impact of this process below the level of the nation state will simply be obscured by considerations of the aggregate impact on member countries. While accepting the possibility that the effects of monetary union may create greater shocks for the less favoured regions/countries, particularly those whose economies are initially very distorted,[35] the general belief expressed by the Commission is nevertheless that growth in the EU as a whole will be accompanied by a narrowing of regional disparities, and that 'comprehensive regime change is the key for the convergence of lagging countries and regions'.[36] The same criticism can potentially be levelled at the discussions of monetary union as is made above regarding the SEM, i.e. that EU politicians are proceeding to adopt policies which are very vague in their analysis of spatial considerations. In terms of the specific funding for regional development, it is debatable whether the increases connected with the implementation of the SEM programme and the Maastricht Treaty will be sufficient to deal with the spatial problems that arise from the former programme, let alone those which stem from monetary union.

Conclusion

It is widely accepted, if not empirically demonstrated, that the prospect of widening regional imbalances poses a threat to economic and monetary union. Therefore in the pursuit of such a union, EU Regional Policy must be effective in promoting balanced development. While the changes implemented since 1989 go some way towards creating a more effective regional policy in that the dispersion of funds has shifted towards the poorer regions, given the gulf between the rhetoric of the commitment to balanced development and the extent of subsequent policy action it is difficult to escape the conclusion that the issue of space and the impact of EU policies over space are but a minimal consideration in the design of a greater vision.

Notes

1. See for example Perroux (1950); Myrdal (1957); Hirschman (1958); Kaldor (1970); Dixon and Thirlwall (1975).
2. That is localisation and urbanisation economies; see Armstrong and Taylor (1993).
3. NUTS – Nomenclature of Territorial Units. There are 71 NUTS level I regions, 176 level II regions and 829 level III regions.
4. Regional disparities within the EU are, however, nearly twice as great as those observed in the US. The process of convergence is predicted to occur through factor mobility. For example, diminishing returns to capital imply that less developed regions will have higher returns to capital, encouraging investment.
5. Programmes are the combined application of different measures covering several years.
6. By 1985, of 26,000 investment projects supported by ERDF, 19,000 were related to infrastructure spending, notably roads.
7. Integrated development operations (IDO) were programmes which combined national resources with funds from ERDF and other Community instruments, to address a particular problem in a particular area. The first Community integrated operations were launched in 1980/81 in Naples and Belfast.
8. Other programmes: the STAR Programme was developed to improve access to advanced telecommunications by the less developed regions. VALOREN was designed to exploit the indigenous energy potential of regions, reducing oil dependency as well as improving energy efficiency.
9. Regional Impact Assessment (RIA) schemes represented one notable exception.
10. This total was fixed before the unification of Germany, which increased the population of the EU by 16 million. An additional sum of ECU 3m. was made available for the period 1991–1993 in order to assist in the restructuring of the five new regions (Lander) of former East Germany in its transition to a market economy. The area, and hence the appropriation, was not divided by Objective, because of a lack of suitable data with which to do so.
11. This problem also applied to 5(b) areas. Thus two types of Objective 2 and 5(b) areas were created – those that were also designated for national regional assistance (approved by the Commission under its competition policy rules) and those that were not. It was intended, however, that more coherence should be developed over time in terms of the area map showing eligibility for aid under both Union competition and regional policy regulations.
12. It was agreed to finance two projects in London and Marseilles out of the 5 per cent non-regionally restricted component of the ERDF, focusing on job creation, economic development in general and the analysis of typical inner city problems. A third project was approved for Rotterdam in 1991, for the promotion of small businesses. It is the intention to build up a series of specific urban projects which analyse different aspects of urban areas, but which are capable of generalisation to other similar areas.
13. This was also true for 5(b) regions.
14. For the CSF for Northern Ireland up to 1993, 45 per cent of expenditure was provided by the Structural Funds, 32 per cent by the UK public sector and 23 per cent from the private sector, with

the aid of loans from the EIB. There were in total throughout the EU 110 CSFs amounting to nearly ECU 47bn. from 1989 to 1993.

15. Examples: RESIDER for steel closure areas; RENAVAL for shipbuilding areas; RECHAR for coal mining areas; ENVIREG for areas with environmental problems leading to delayed social and economic development; STRIDE for regional research and technological development, directed mostly to Objective 1 regions; POSEIDON for the Canary Islands, the Azores, Madeira and French overseas departments, to aid in adjustment to the Single Market; REGIS for support to very peripheral regions in terms of infrastructure spending.

16. 1990: INTEREG to aid development in border areas of nations or the Community as a whole (cross-frontier cooperation); REGEN to aid diversification of regional energy supplies to industry and to promote energy efficiency; PRISMA to assist firms in disadvantaged regions to cope with job losses arising directly from the Single Market, e.g. competition in public procurement; LEADER to aid rural development by grants to agencies which promote tourism, small firm growth, vocational training, and marketing of local output; TELEMATIQUE (the next phase of STAR) to promote the use of advanced telecommunications in small and medium-sized enterprises. The total allocation for all Community Initiatives 1989–1993 was ECU 3800m.

17. The principle of subsidiarity in the Maastricht Treaty may be interpreted as an intention to give greater priority to the regions, rather than nations, of Europe. The Treaty in fact established a 'Committee of the Regions' to advise both the Commission and the European Council. Meanwhile, the concept of eight 'super-regions' which transcend national boundaries had already been introduced in 1991 by the Commission. Gripaios and Mangles (1993) provide a discussion of the economic integrity of these super-regions.

18. ECU 15,150m. 1993–99 with indicative allocations: Spain 52–58 per cent, Greece 16–20 per cent, Portugal 16–20 per cent, Ireland 7–10 per cent.

19. There are some, relatively marginal, changes concerning eligibility criteria, programming periods and administrative procedures. For example, the programming time horizon for the Structural Funds is extended to six years, and regions under Objectives 1, 3, 5(a) and 5(b), because of the long-term nature of the problems involved, are defined for the whole period. Objectives 2 and 4 have two three-year programming periods. There is also a greater degree of flexibility than previously in the designation of Objective 2 regions, to include, for example, urban areas with particularly severe problems.

20. A more flexible interpretation of the eligibility criteria has permitted regions with slightly more than 75 per cent of EUR12 average GDP per capita to be included within Objective 1.

21. By the end of 1993 Objective 2 regions had been determined, with London becoming the first capital city to receive such assistance for parts of the inner city. The UK and France are likely to be the major beneficiaries overall because of high levels of industrial unemployment, urban decay and the decline of traditional industries. 31 per cent of UK and 26 per cent of French citizens are covered by Objective 2 funds, which is well above the 15 per cent average for the EU as a whole.

22. Additionally, a new financial instrument for fisheries guidance (FIFG) has been created.

23. There are also a number of new initiatives such as KONVER for the conversion of areas previously dependent on defence-related industries.

24. Commission EC (1988).

25. Cecchini (1988).

26. At a more general level it is probable that increased integration will also produce some horizontal and vertical integration by dominant firms. The resulting increase in merger and acquisition activity opens the potential that existing headquarter functions might themselves be relocated from their existing sites (Begg 1989).

27. See for example, Department of Trade and Industry (1983), and Ernst and Young (1990).

28. Twomey and Taylor (1985); Taylor and Twomey (1988).

29. Amin *et. al.* (1992), for example, are quite pessimistic about the capacity of *any* regional policy instrument to generate the necessary conditions for successful and sustainable indigenous growth.

30. Delors (1989).
31. Doyle (1989).
32. Commission EC (1990b) p. 149.
33. The Third Periodic Report (1987) points out that, in general, high labour costs areas also tend to be high productivity areas and vice versa. Indeed, regional (i.e. intra-national) differences in labour costs are shown to be significantly smaller than those in labour productivity.
34. Pohl (1989).
35. Commission EC (1990b) p. 223.
36. Commission EC (1990b) p. 225.

References and further reading

Amin A, Charles D R and **Howells J** 1992 Corporate restructuring and cohesion in the new Europe, *Regional Studies*, Vol. 26 No. 4, pp. 319–331.

Armstrong H and **Taylor J** 1993 *Regional Economics and Policy*, Harvester Wheatsheaf, Hemel Hempstead.

Bachter J and **Michie R** 1993 The restructuring of regional policy in the European Community, *Regional Studies*, Vol. 27 No. 8, pp. 719–725.

Barro R J and **Sala-i-Martin** 1991 Convergence across states and regions, *Brooking Papers*, pp. 107–172.

Barro R J and **Sala-i-Martin** 1992 Convergence, *Journal of Political Economy*, Vol. 100, 223–251.

Begg I 1989 The regional dimension of the 1992 proposals, *Regional Studies*, Vol. 23, No. 4, pp. 368–376.

Begg I 1990 European integration and regional policy, *Oxford Review of Economic Policy*, Vol. 5, No. 2, pp. 90–104.

Begg I 1992 The spatial impact of completion of the EC internal market for financial services, *Regional Studies*, Vol. 26, No. 4, pp. 333–347.

Begg I and **Mayes D** 1993 Cohesion, convergence and economic and monetary union in Europe, *Regional Studies*, Vol. 27, pp. 149–155.

Boltho A 1989 European and United States regional differences: a note, *Oxford Review of Economic Policy*, Vol. 5, No. 2, pp. 105–115.

Buiges P, Ilkovitz F and **Lebrun J-F** 1990 The sectoral impact of the Internal Market, *European Economy* (Social Europe, special issue), CEC, Brussels.

Camagni R P 1992 Development scenarios and policy guidelines for the lagging regions in the 1990s, *Regional Studies*, Vol. 26, No. 4, pp. 361–374.

Cardoso A R 1993 Regional inequalities in Europe – have they really been decreasing? *Applied Economics*, Vol. 25, pp. 1093–1100.

Cecchini P 1988 *The European Challenge: 1992, the Benefits of a Single Market*, Wildwood House, London.

CEE 1961 *Documents de la Conférence sur les Economies Régionales*, 2 vols, Brussels.

CEE 1964 *Rapports de groupes d'experts sur la politique régionale dans la CEE*, 3 vols, Brussels.

CEE 1965 *Première communications de la Commission sur la politique régionale dans la CEE*, Brussels.

Commission EC 1981 *The regions of Europe, First Periodic Report on the social and economic situation of the regions of the Community,* EEC, Brussels.

Commission EC 1984 *The regions of Europe, Second Periodic Report on the social and economic situation of the Regions of the Community*, EEC, Brussels.

Commission EC 1985 *Completing the internal market*, White Paper from the Commission to the European Council, COM(85), 310, final, EEC, Brussels.

Commission EC 1987 *The regions of the enlarged community, Third Periodic Report on the social and economic situation and development of the Regions*, EEC, Brussels.

Commission EC, 1988 The economics of 1992, *European Economy*, No. 35, Brussels.

Commission EC, 1990a *Economics and monetary union*, Sec(90), 1695 final, Brussels.

Commission EC 1990b One market, one money, *European Economy*, No. 44, Brussels.

Commision EC 1990c *The Regions in the 1990s: Fourth Periodic Report on the Social and Economic Situation and Development of the Regions of the Community*, Brussels–Luxembourg.

Commision EC 1991 *Europe 2000: Outlook for the Development of the Community's Territory*, CEC, Brussels.

Delors J 1989 *Regional implications of economic and monetary union*, Report on Economic and Monetary Union in the EC, CEC's Office for Official Publications, Luxembourg.

Department of Trade and Industry 1983 *Regional Industrial Policy: Some Economic Issues*, DTI, London.

Dixon R J and **Thirlwall A P** 1975 A model of regional growth rate differentials along Kaldorian lines, *Oxford Economic Papers*, 27, pp. 201–14.

Doyle M F 1989 Regional policy and European economic integration, in Delors (1989).

Dunford M 1993 Regional disparities in the European Community: evidence from the REGIO databank, *Regional Studies*, Vol 27, No. 8, pp. 727–743.

EEC 1973 *Report on the regional problems in the enlarged Community*, Brussels.

EEC 1977 Guidelines for community regional policy, *Bulletin of European Communities*, Supplement 2/77.

Ernst and Young 1990 *The Regions of Europe*, Milton Keynes.

Franzmeyer F, Hrubesch P and **Seidel B** 1991 *The Regional Impact of Community Policies*, Office for Official Publications of the European Community, Luxembourg.

Gripaios P and **Mangles T** 1993 An analysis of European super regions, *Regional Studies*, Vol. 27, No. 8, pp. 745–750.

Hirschman A O 1958 *The Strategy of Economic Development*, Yale University Press.

Kaldor N 1970 The case for regional policies, *Scottish Journal of Political Economy*, Vol. 27, pp. 337–347.

Magnifico G 1985 *Regional Imbalances and National Economic Performance*, Office for Official Publications of the European Communities, Luxembourg.

Myrdal G 1957 *Economic Theory and Underdeveloped Regions*, Duckworth, London.

P A Cambridge Economic Consultants 1988 *The regional impact of policies implemented in the context of completing the Community's internal market by 1992*, Final Report, DG XVI, Commission of the European Communities, Brussels.

Padoa-Schioppa T 1987 *Efficiency, Stability and Equity*, Oxford University Press.

Perroux F 1950 Economic space: theory and applications, *Quarterly Journal of Economics*, pp. 64, 90–97.

Pohl K O 1989 A further development of the European monetary system, in Delors (1989).

Quevit M 1992 The regional impact of the internal market: a comparative analysis of traditional industrial regions and lagging regions, *Regional Studies*, Vol. 26, No. 4, pp. 349–360.

Steinle W J 1992 Regional competitiveness and the Single Market, *Regional Studies*, Vol 26, No. 4, pp. 307–318.

Stevens J 1991 The politics of British participation in European monetary union, *National Westminster Bank Quarterly Review*, May.

Taylor J and **Twomey J** 1988 The movement of manufacturing industry in Great Britain: an inter-county analysis 1972–1981, *Urban Studies*, Vol. 25, pp. 228–242.

Tomkins J and **Twomey J** 1990 The changing spatial structure of manufacturing plant in Great Britain 1976–1987, *Environment and Planning*, A 22, pp. 385–398.

Twomey J and **Taylor J** (1985) Regional policy and the interregional movement of manufacturing industry in Great Britain, *Scottish Journal of Political Economy*, pp. 257–277.

CHAPTER 11

Environment policy

John Hassan

Introduction

The Treaty of Rome made no provision for a Community environment policy. When it became apparent from the early 1970s, however, that environmental difficulties were capable of disrupting the economic life of the Community, the necd to take some action in this field was recognised. This Chapter will focus on selected aspects of environment policy: those affecting waste management, water and atmospheric pollution. Noise pollution, protection of fauna and nuclear safety are considered to be less central to the theme of economic integration explored in this book.

During the 1960s there was growing awareness of environmental degradation, for example the smogs of Los Angeles and the progressive pollution of the River Rhine. Such events were viewed as localised pollution problems. The international dimension became more apparent during the following decade, dominated by the two oil shocks of 1973 and 1979. This led to the price of energy increasing tenfold, and the finite nature of the supply of resources on which economic growth depended became more widely appreciated. A boost was given to energy conservation. In the OECD region overall energy use per unit of GDP fell by some 25 per cent between 1973 and 1985.

Environmentally, however, progress was limited. Acid deposition emerged as a major problem. In Scandinavia it was noted that lakes were becoming incapable of supporting life and forests were dying back. Acid rain is caused by emissions of sulphur dioxide (SO_2) and nitrogen oxides (NO_x) into the atmosphere, particularly from coal-fired generating stations and motor vehicle exhausts. At first few believed in any connection between transboundary pollutants and environmental damage, but subsequently acid rain was accepted as an international problem. Faced with a rapid increase in Waldsterben (forest damage), West Germany in the late 1970s and early 1980s abandoned its earlier opposition to international action and became a leading advocate of strong emission controls in the EU. Meanwhile concern over the deteriorating quality of the River Rhine, a major source of drinking water in Holland, led to a Decision being adopted by the Community in 1977 to protect the river against chemical pollution. The approach which characterized policy-making in the 1970s was of perceiving pollution as a localised, sectoral problem. The EU adopted policies on waste management and water pollution in 1975–1976. 'Framework' Directives were followed by

'Daughter' Directives which prescribed detailed procedures or standards in narrowly defined fields of environmental management and in specified economic sectors.

With environmental degradation assuming global dimensions and even apparently threatening the very existence of some animal, if not the human, species, some reconsideration in the 1980s of this reactive and sectoral approach was inevitable.

The depletion of the ozone layer is caused by emissions into the atmosphere of chlorofluorocarbon (CFC) gases. CFCs are used in aerosols, refrigeration chemicals and the manufacture of plastics. The depletion of the planet's protective ozone shield could, it is feared, cause an increase in human and animal cancers and a disruption of the ocean's food chain.

Emissions of CFC gases also contribute to global warming, but about two-thirds of its cause is thought to be an increase in CO_2 emissions. The burning of fossil fuels and the loss of vegetative cover leads to an accumulation of CO_2 and other greenhouse gases in the atmosphere. Re-radiation of heat is thereby inhibited, causing a 'greenhouse effect' through the closing of the earth's 'atmospheric window'. Major climatic changes, flooding of populated lands and disruption of ecosystems may ensue if this process continues unchecked, according to some analysts.

Consequently in the late 1980s Community and other international efforts were channelled into addressing these global pollution problems. At the beginning of the 1990s there had also been renewed focus on waste management and water pollution control in the EU, one however which recognised the cross-sectoral implications of these tasks.

Statements adopted by the ministerial councils of supranational bodies such as the EU and OECD suggested a sea-change had occurred; compared to limited action in the past the possibility of concrete progress being achieved in environmental policy was indicated. Such a shift can partly be explained as a response to the growing environmental awareness of the public and the politicisation of green issues. More fundamentally it can be interpreted as the outcome of an acceptance of the view that environmental protection and economic growth are not conflicting, but are in fact mutually supporting, objectives. Most clearly articulated in the influential *Brundtland Report* (World Commission) of 1987, this approach emphasises the interdependence of ecological and economic imperatives, and stresses the need to integrate environmental protection into other policy areas so as to achieve sustainable economic growth. Such principles are now embodied in the EU environmental policy.

Briefly, the aims of the policy are to protect the environment of Western Europe and to achieve an integrated approach to its implementation so as to assist the formation of an internal market. This chapter examines the case for an EU policy and assesses to what extent its objectives have been realised.

The need for an EU environment policy

The threat of ecological disaster justifies the adoption of more rigorous action on the environment. With pollution manifesting itself as a trans-frontier problem there is also clearly a role for a supranational body like the EU to coordinate European action in the field.

The case for an EU environment policy can also be argued in simple economic terms. If environmental degradation continues unchecked it may well impose varying external costs on firms and create disparities between member states. Particularly in the context of attempts to achieve a SEM there is, therefore, unequal competition between partners. This may also arise where member states pursue different environmental policies. A harmonisation of environmental standards, and of the definition, handling and transportation of dangerous and toxic substances, and common labelling of consumer goods, appears to be required for the creation of a genuine SEM with no frontier controls. Environmental protection was formally regarded as a component of the legislation on the internal market. Under Article 100A of the SEA harmonisation of product legislation to promote a 'high level of protection' on matters concerning health, safety, the environment and consumer protection was stipulated. The environmental problem can be described in economic terms as the outcome of the wishes of the people and firms to minimise what they pay for the use of resources. If firms can employ the earth's atmosphere or waters at very low cost, i.e. as a common sewer, such firms would maximise profits at output levels which take account of their own private costs and revenues, but which largely ignore the external environmental costs imposed on others.

Economists' solutions to this problem include the proposal that property rights for all resources should be assigned to corporations and individuals. With competitive markets being established each person or enterprise pursuing their own interests would unwittingly (through the action of the invisible hand) promote the common good. Property rights in the ownership of finite or natural resources would be established. So, if a timber company is assigned property rights to a restricted area of forest, it will be in its interest to log and reafforest selectively. Thereby deforestation will be reduced. Unfortunately, as Mishan (1990) argues, in many cases the property rights solution is a non-starter in the real world. To take an extreme but very relevant case, there is no way that global oceans and atmosphere can be parcelled out to private undertakings which would be responsible for their maintenance.

Given the problems of internalising external pollution costs, practice in the European Union has relied on the imposition of common environmental standards. Misgivings over the unwieldy character of regulatory instruments has, however, led to increased discussion of the use of economic incentives such as pollution taxes or tradeable permits to encourage polluters to take less environmentally damaging decisions. A carbon tax has been promoted by the Commission. It exhibits a characteristic that both environmentalists and advocates of a market approach would welcome: a device which penalises polluters and contributes to the integration of environmental costs and risks. The carbon tax particularly makes sense in terms of the Community's 1990 agreement to restrain the growth in CO_2 emissions. In November 1991 environmental ministers welcomed the plan. The tax would be introduced in stages, the equivalent of $3 a barrel of oil in 1993, rising to $10 by the year 2000. The proposal soon, however, ran into political difficulties. Ultimately it foundered on the rock of British resistance: Britain in April 1993 refused to accept the need for a Community energy tax.

Current Union environment policy stresses the need to develop economic instruments and there is extensive literature on the issue. The fact is, nevertheless, that actual application of this approach has been negligible. A minor exception are the tax differentials which encourage the use of lead-free petrol. Some European countries have imposed water pollution charges, but their clear intention is to raise revenue. They do not represent an attempt to equate the marginal benefits and costs of pollution control, charges generally being set too low to achieve this aim. Up to the present, lack of data on which to base alternative methods of pollution control and concerns over the administrative costs have held back their implementation. There is, however, considerable interest in the use of the market mechanism to promote environmental objectives and widespread application may occur in due course.

In the meantime the SEM process poses several implications for the environmental standards approach. To illustrate this let us assume that prior to the creation of a common market a country A (e.g. Germany) has high environmental standards. This imposes higher costs on firms (in, for example, being required to restrict polluting emissions). They, however, can be protected from overseas competition through tariffs or other non-tariff barriers. Country B (e.g. a country in the Mediterranean south) may traditionally accept much lower environmental standards. With the creation of a common market barriers to trade are removed, and let us assume that common environmental standards are adopted. But at what level?

For country B, D = domestic demand, PMC = private marginal costs in the production of product Q; SMC(B) and SMC(A) are defined as PMC plus external marginal costs (it being assumed that they include only environmental costs) in countries B and A respectively (see Figure 11.1). Assuming the environmental standards of country B are virtually non-existent and are adopted in the common market, where a world market price of P_0 prevails, it produces product Q at output level q_1 and exports $q_1 - q_2$ to country A. Country B acquires a competitive advantage by ignoring the marginal environmental costs represented by the shaded triangle, selling Q at less than its 'true' costs of production. This, McDonald (1989) explains, can be defined as a type of social dumping. This follows from country B overproducing Q because it takes no account of environmental costs of producing Q. If it took account of these environmental costs it would produce at q_4.

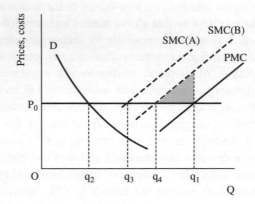

Figure 11.1 Equal output and price for product Q in country B

Where the (high) environmental standards of country A are adopted in the common market, however (a situation analogous to Germany persuading the EU to adopt its emission control standards), country B experiences losses. It is forced to produce at a non-optimal point q_3, with exports reduced to $q_3 - q_1$.

As it is very difficult to estimate true environmental costs it would be almost impossible to adopt an optimal solution where each country produces where its SMC = P. Consequently the EU may impose either too high or too low emission standards, leading to the problem described above. However, as McDonald explains, the situation may not be so serious in practice. As countries with traditionally low environmental standards may also be those with lower productivities and therefore higher PMCs than countries like country A, this limits the scope for the former's firms to penetrate the markets of countries with high environmental standards. It seems probable that a system of common environmental standards can be established which is not too disadvantageous to either type of country, but which permits progress to be made towards the goals of an EU environmental policy. As the SEA explicitly permits member states to adopt more stringent measures than EU standards, however, there is acknowledgement that non-identical standards will exist. Acceptance of incomplete harmonisation is a contradictory position, however, and is likely to be a source of difficulty for the EU environmental policy.

The desirability of environmental policy is demonstrated by studies which underline the low costs of implementation and the high costs of non-action. Tentative estimates in a Commission EC (1987) report suggested that the damage to forests caused by acid deposition was around ECU 300 m. per year, while lost agricultural production from the same cause approached ECU 1 bn. Without preventive environmental policies, damage and replacement costs must be borne by industry. Corrosive emissions attack plants, damaging their lifespan and effectiveness. The bulk of impacts, however, fall more widely on the economy. Pollutants damage buildings, soil fertility and infrastructures, creating additional repair and maintenance costs and ill-health among workers. It has been estimated that in OECD countries public spending on the environment amounts to 1.2 per cent of GDP on average, yet the costs of repair and damage to the environment are equivalent to an estimated 3.5 per cent of GDP. Furthermore, adoption of effective waste management measures reduces waste and waste disposal costs, and has beneficial consequences for the balance of trade.

Such studies help to strengthen the argument that environmental protection rather than conflicting with the goals of economic growth, in the long run is absolutely essential to it, by conserving finite resources, reducing waste, reducing repair and maintenance expenditures, and by improving the health and productivity of the labour force.

EU actions

For many years the environment hardly figured at all in EU thinking. It was not until 1971 that the Commission made its first detailed communication to the Council on the need for an EU policy. Soon the oil crisis and growing pressure from environmentalists created a situation which led to the Heads of State's meeting in Paris in 1972 to agree to the adoption of an environment policy. An Environmental and Protection Service with responsibility in the field was established. The Treaty of Rome made no mention of environmental matters, and for a long time the development of an environment policy rested on a rather liberal interpretation of the application of the omnibus clause, Article 235, to environmental issues. Any legislation deriving from the latter required unanimity of agreement among ministers, which restricted the amount of progress which could be made. Further the Environmental and Protection Service was not elevated to full DG status within the Commission until 1981, which made it, in principle, a rather weak division in the Commission compared to fields like agriculture or energy.

The 1972 Paris Summit led to agreement on the first Environmental Action Programme (EAP). It covered the period 1973–1977 and identified general principles appropriate to an environmental policy. The latter contained aims with which it was hard to disagree, such as the desirability of protecting, and achieving international cooperation on, the environment. The second EAP(1977–1981) essentially extended and updated the first. With the third EAP(1982–1986) there was some reorientation of approach.

Important principles were adopted for the EU environmental policy in the first EAP, which remain key characteristics today, in particular the polluter pays principle, an emphasis on preventive rather than remedial action, and the need to take account in decision-making of all environmental impacts. Despite these stated principles, Community actions on the environment in the 1970s were, as previously stated, reactive and sectoral. By the early 1980s, with a growing appreciation of the interdependent nature of the environmental problems facing the globe's economies, an attempt was made to pursue a more integrative and preventive approach. The limitations of 1970s actions, concentrating on remedial interventions in industrial sectors where urgent action was needed, were recognised. It was realised that full account should be taken of the interaction of sources of emissions, pollutants themselves and environments which receive pollution, and of the transfer of pollutants from one part of the environment to another. In the third EAP (1982–1986) environmental protection was viewed as a key development in many fields, not as a self-contained sphere. An overall framework for policy development was established, and the need to integrate the environmental dimension with planning activities in other areas such as energy, industry and tourism was emphasised.

To secure a truly preventive environmental policy, not one of just crisis management, required a system of Environment Impact Assessment (EIA). Such a system had been in existence since 1969. It was not proposed in the EU until 1980. As they feared some sacrifice of national sovereignty was involved, it took a further five years to persuade governments to accept the proposal. Finally, a 1985 Directive made EIA obligatory for certain public and private projects.

The Directive requires member states to carry out assessments of the likely environmental effects of planned major industrial or infrastructure projects before planning consents are given. Applicants for consent have to provide information on the nature of the project, its probable polluting effects, and impacts on wildlife, natural resources and the cultural and archaeological heritage. In special cases certain projects can be exempted, and the Directive does not apply at all to projects authorised by specific national legislation like the Channel Tunnel. Furthermore, it merely requires environmental factors to be taken into account in project planning, and in no way constrains the planning authorities to act in any particular way. Nevertheless, the Commission believed the EIA Directive would be a crucial factor in leading to environmental considerations being incorporated into project planning in the future.

The growing importance of environmental policy in the EU was given formal recognition in the SEM legislation. The SEA is extremely significant for the development of Community environmental policy. Firstly, it explicitly affirms the Community's competence to concern itself with environmental protection, thus filling the gap in the 1957 Treaty of Rome. Under the SEA, the Council of Ministers could take decisions by qualified majority on environmental measures which benefit from the free circulation of goods. Article 130 establishes the legal basis for all actions on the environment (unanimity being the rule under Article 130, though qualified majority voting can be adopted if the Council so decides). The Article sets out the objectives of environmental policy, restating goals such as 'the polluter pays' and preventive principles.

Secondly, it is fundamentally stated in the Act (clause 130R(2)) that 'environmental protection requirements shall be a component of the Community's other policies'. This represents a stage forward in environmental policy, building on the EIA Directive. The latter obliges individual projects to take account of environmental impacts. The new legislation, however, requires that other Community policies evaluate the environmental dimension, thus establishing the basis of a truly integrative environmental policy. It is the only area of Community policy imposing such a requirement. If properly enforced it would have far-reaching implications for other policy areas, such as agriculture and transport.

The completion of the SEM has many environmental implications, including the effects of removing border controls on, for example, the transport of radioactive or other toxic wastes. The additional growth generated by the single market may make environmental issues more acute. The requirements of product harmonisation have led to a great deal of technical work being undertaken in a variety of fields in preparation for the elimination of border controls. The technical implications of the SEM may be illustrated by reference to the attempts to develop legislation designed to ensure the smooth functioning of the common market in batteries, their accumulators, and their safe disposal. To achieve conformity of approach considerable adjustment to national practice was implied, and extensive technical negotiations on the legislation to achieve this objective were undertaken.

The fourth EAP (1987–1992) continued established principles but also incorporated the recent emphasis on integration in Community action. It stressed that action was urgently required in the use of agrochemicals, treatment of agricultural wastes, conservation of species, product standards and the completion of the SEM. The Commission, within this framework, drafted proposals to lay down new standards to control the pollution of ground-waters by nitrates, and new measures to adapt existing legislation to new or newly understood aspects of such problems.

The SEM programme as well as having static economic effects such as the suppression of border controls requiring technical harmonisation measures to be developed, will also have dynamic economic effects. These include the probability of increased economic growth. Acknowledging that in practice it is extremely difficult to distinguish environmental impacts associated with this additional growth, a Commission 'Task Force' (1990) appointed to review the environmental dimensions of 1992 registered one particular concern. This was that a potential dynamic consequence of the Single Market would be increased air pollution associated with increased activity in the transport and electricity generation sectors. Economic incentives, supplementing regulatory instruments, were recommended to address the environmental implications of the increasingly liberalised economic environment which the SEM will create.

Attempts have been made to adopt measures which reinforce the current thrust of the EU's integrative and preventive environmental policy. In 1990 the European Environment Agency was established. Initially its main activities were concerned with data collection and publication, promoting the exchange of environmental information, seeking to achieve the harmonisation and comparability of EU environmental data, and producing a three-yearly report on the state of the environment. Pressure from the European Parliament for the agency to be given powers to enforce EU law and to execute EIAs on EU-funded projects led only to the concession that after two years the agency's role would be reviewed.

In March 1992 the fifth EAP was adopted for the years 1993–2000. Allegedly it is less reactive and more proactive in the strategies it puts forward, it places emphasis on sustainable development and gives priority to action in such fields as integrated pollution control and waste management. The three-volume document, however, is purely an advisory and analytical series of suggestions of actions the Commission might propose, without any legal status whatsoever. Similarly it is difficult to discern what the involvement of the Community as a full participant at the June 1992 Rio de Janeiro environment conference may have in the long term on the practical development of the Union's environment policy. More significantly, the Maastricht Treaty had been signed. It confirmed the effect of the SEA in conferring on the Union explicit authority to act in the environment field. The Treaty largely reaffirmed the recent thrust of policy, including the objective of integrating environmental protection priorities into other Union policies.

Summary of EU environmental legislation

Measures in three important areas of environmental legislation can be summarized as follows.

Waste management

The focus of the Community's approach has been to promote the safe disposal of hazardous substances. Framework Directive 75/442 represented the EU's first measure in the field, and required member states to ensure that waste disposal does not harm human health and the environment and to designate competent authorities to manage waste disposal. Since 1975 a proliferation of Directives, building on the Framework Directive, specified more explicitly the substances to be controlled and the processes to be followed. Directives cover the disposal of products such as polychlorinated biphenyls and terphenyls, waste oils, liquid containers, sewage sludge and other toxic or dangerous substances.

Outside waste disposal it seems fair for McArthy (1989) to imply that the other strands of EU waste management policy on the recycling and re-utilisation of waste have, until recently, done little more than piously extol good practice. The urgency of achieving concrete progress has increased with the single market because the disappearance of national borders in 1992 removed the means of policing cross-frontier transfers of hazardous wastes. In March 1990 the Commission's paper 'A Community Strategy for Waste Management' was approved by a Council Resolution. The Commission clearly hopes to secure more effective measures which focus on prevention and recycling, thereby both exploiting waste as a 'secondary natural resource', and diminishing the pollution threat which untreated waste represents. Environmental handling, improvement of practice regarding waste incineration and dumping, and updating EU rules on trans-frontier waste movements are some areas for which proposals have been made in response to the imperatives which face the Union in the 1990s.

Water pollution

Measures to control water pollution have been considered 'the jewel in the crown of the EC's environment policy' (Economist Intelligence Unit 1989), many measures to combat water pollution having been agreed to. The objective of Framework Directive 76/464 was to compel member states to take action to prevent the entry of dangerous substances into ground water. Two lists of substances are covered by EU legislation. 'Grey list' substances should not exceed emission standards set by reference to water quality objectives. It was intended that 'black list' effluents should be subject to stricter control, that absolute emission limits should apply, and that 129 substances should form the basis of EU action. To obtain agreement on the measures it was necessary to concede that water quality objectives could be employed as an alternative control method, and that individual Directives would be necessary to install each substance on the 'black list'. Until recently, only six, including mercury, were on it.

In 1991 two additional water Directives were agreed. The urban wastewater directive will require urban sewage authorities to raise the quality of their effluent discharges progressively over the next ten years. A Directive was also agreed on the reduction of river and coastal pollution by nitrates leached from natural and chemical fertilisers.

The bulk of EU water Directives define quality standards for certain types of water, including drinking and bathing water, shellfish waters and freshwaters for fish. The Directive relating to the quality of bathing-beach waters, for example, was adopted in 1976. Much-publicised legal action has been taken by the Commission against member states, including the UK, for failing to comply with the bathing and drinking water Directives. Negatively, this illustrates the dilatory and variable way the member states have applied agreements they were party to. Positively, enforcement proceedings are evidence of the Commission's greater determination to have environment policy implemented.

Atmospheric pollution

There were significant achievements in the late 1980s in securing member states' agreement on measures to reduce air pollution: significant in that such agreements were obtained despite enormous difficulties in the form of opposition from sectional and national interests, and in that they address the worldwide problems of acid rain and global warming. EU Directive 88/609 was the first major attempt to tackle the problem of acid rain. It is an agreement to reduce emission discharges into the air of SO_2, NO_x and dust from new power stations. Targets for reducing such emissions from existing power stations were also agreed, in stages up to a total 60 per cent reduction for the year 2003 in relation to the 1980 level. The Directive implies that costly discharge abatement investment programmes (approaching £1 b. in the UK) will be necessary in the electricity supply industries.

In October 1990 the Community agreed to stabilise CO_2 emissions in the year 2000 at their 1990 levels. In 1991 agreement was reached in a Directive to reduce emissions of pollutants from heavy goods diesel vehicles.

EU legislation obliges car manufacturers to produce cars capable of running on lead-free petrol. Also, member states agreed to emission limits for cars for carbon monoxide, NO_x and hydrocarbons. This Directive, 89/458, effectively gave the car industry until 1992 to fit three-way catalytic converters to new cars with engines under 1.4 litres. It was hoped that voluntary limits in larger cars would be converted into mandatory standards in due course. The Community has also been party to international agreements to combat ozone depletion, and in March 1989 the Council passed a resolution agreeing to ban most CFCs by 2000.

Assessment

Environment policy is often regarded as one of the EU's major successes. Despite the lack of an explicit legal basis, and unanimous voting tending to apply, there existed by 1986 about a hundred Community texts in the field of the environment. By 1990 the policy had moved away from a reactive stance to a more preventive, integrative approach. The SEA gave an important boost to environmental protection, whereby it acquired full policy status. By June 1989 the number of environmental measures agreed to by the Council of Ministers had risen to 160. Compared to the results achieved in such fields as transport, which had long enjoyed an explicit legal basis, this may be viewed as a remarkable success. There is a tendency in the literature, however, to qualify this assessment strongly. Questions are asked as to why in the 1980s the real environment had improved so little in the wake of so much environmental legislation (see Klatte 1986).

Evidence on trends in atmospheric pollution revealed a mixed pattern. On the one hand emissions of smoke and SO_2 in the 1980s showed declines in almost all areas, which were unlikely, however, to prevent further environmental damage. On the other hand emissions of CO_2 and NO_x continued to rise, and fears existed that they would continue to increase in the future (Weidner 1987). Some improvement in the quality of inland waters could be reported; levels of chloride, ammonium and detergents tended to decline. But unacceptably high levels of dangerous substances still occurred in many inland waters. Evidence indicated that nitrogen and nitrate levels increased in some EU countries in the 1980s. While in 1987 the Commission claimed to detect an overall improvement in inland water quality, it did not venture that EU environmental measures were the prime causal factor at work (Weidner 1987). Furthermore, the marine environment witnessed loss of habitats, dumping in coastal zones, and the gathering of a variety of pollutants in the seas, contributing to a complex range of difficulties.

There is the question of whether the EU is the most appropriate body for international action on the environment, given the trans-continental nature of pollution. Some international agreements have been tougher than those proposed by the EU. The 1979 Geneva Convention on transboundary air pollution led to a number of states forming the 30 per cent club. They committed themselves to reducing by 30 per cent total annual SO_2 emissions or their trans-boundary fluxes by 1993 (base year 1980). Up to the late 1980s compared to these obligations the impact of EU Directives on transboundary pollutants was limited.

The EU, however, has subsequently made more progress in the area. It has effectively negotiated with international agencies on transboundary pollution. It has been an active participant in the Geneva Convention deliberations and in international initiatives to combat ozone depletion. The latter process culminated in the worldwide June 1990 agreement to phase out CFC and other ozone-depleting chemicals altogether by 2000.

The fifth EAP itself admits that the legislative approach has failed to reverse recent adverse environmental trends. In order to understand the patchy and contradictory progress apparently achieved in the field of EU environmental policy, it is necessary to appreciate the limitations of the legislative measures which have been employed to develop the policy.

Of the various forms of action available to the EU it has been Directives which have been mainly employed for environmental policy. They are binding as to the result achieved, but leave to national authorities the choice of form and methods. The absence of centralised coercion emerges in other components of the EU's environmental policy. EIAs are compulsory but their conclusions are not binding. The Commission's EAPs are merely 'noted' by the Council, not formally adopted.

The most serious flaw in the policy, however, and the point where any explanation of the contrast between the mass of legislation passed and the state of the real environment must start, lies with the variable implementation of Directives. Their provisions are generally, observes Klatte (1986), implemented badly, incorrectly, or not at all by member states. Directives should normally be implemented within two years of official notification, yet virtually every member state is guilty of quite frequently violating these procedures, for several reasons.

Under Directives every member state must pass the appropriate legislation, and then apply and enforce the national legislation. In complying with Directives member states will tend to seek to minimise the degree of change in their existing procedures, and to interpret the text of the Directives in this context. Experience has shown that these processes allow considerable scope for distorting, misinterpreting or delaying the implementation of Directives.

Haigh (1987) has noted the contrasting perspectives on environmental management in local and regional implementing authorities. For example, English water authorities (or companies) and German Lander may have different views on their obligations from their national governments, let alone the European Commission, and may even actively oppose Directives.

Legislation is often imprecise, containing too many discretionary elements and subject to diverse interpretations. The most notorious example, perhaps, was the Bathing Water Directive's employment of the vague definition of Bathing Waters as those where bathing is 'traditionally practised by a large number of bathers'. In France the number of designated bathing beaches was 3000, but there were only 14 in Germany and 27 in the UK. Different criteria were applied in different countries.

Insufficient resources are made available to implement environment policy. Environmental protection's share of the EC budget has been very small, rising from only 0.02 per cent of the general budget in 1978 to 0.06 in 1986. Given the small staff concerned with this field the Commission has left the initiation of complaints against those who contravene EU Directives to individual persons or organisations.

A more fundamental difficulty is that the objectives of EU policies occasionally conflict with one another. Environmental protection may, for example, conflict with free trade tenets. In a case relating to Danish environmental law permitting only returnable containers, the European Court of Justice agreed with the Commission that this Danish law discriminated against imported drinks. Nevertheless it held that this was justified, as the imperative of environmental protection may limit the application of free trade. Doubts arise over the Commission's commitment to environmental protection, as despite this judgement it is pursuing a similar case against a compulsory bottle deposit scheme operating in Germany.

A number of contradictory positions, therefore, are adopted within the Union. The 'balanced pursuit of environmental and energy policy objectives' has, in particular, been identified as of 'special importance'. This follows logically from the incorporation of the concepts of 'sustainable development' and 'integration' into the EU environmental policy. Certainly, if environmental objectives are integrated into all fields of economic activity at every stage, the possible conflict between economic growth and environmental protection will be averted, and sustainable development will be achieved. Owens and Hope (1989), however, are sceptical as to whether such a reconciliation between environmental and economic growth objectives is likely to be achieved in the foreseeable future.

Sometimes the objectives of environmental and energy policy are in harmony, particularly the goal of improving energy efficiency. But sometimes they conflict. The EU energy policy has sought to improve energy security by increasing indigenous energy production and also by expanding nuclear power. An increase in energy production and consumption conflicts with the enforcement of strict pollution control standards and protection of the biosphere. Also, most environmentalists believe that a commitment to increase nuclear power conflicts with environmental objectives.

Owens and Hope contrast the rather weak DG XI (with responsibilities in the environmental area) with the powerful, long-established Energy DG XVII. They suggest that the environment will always play second fiddle to the dictates of economic growth, and that environmental implications are destined to be considered only after the formulation of energy policy.

Their analysis, however, does not explain the paradox of the success of a weak environmental DG in securing so much legislation, in contrast with the well-known failures experienced by a strong Energy DG in articulating a Union energy policy. It also may underestimate the post-Chernobyl reassessment of nuclear power's role in the Union.

Conclusions

Some of the weaknesses of Union environmental policy are shared by other Union policies. Policy implementation which relies on Directives is vulnerable to a certain amount of national reinterpretation in any sphere of Union action. Where contradiction or conflicts exist between the fields of the environment, energy, economic growth or trade liberalization, there will be bound to be some problems in the practical implementation of environmental policies.

Some governments have employed foot-dragging tactics and industrial interest groups may resist the EU policy-making process. The goals of environment policy may, however, be promoted by green consumerism or environmental pressure groups. Market trends may encourage business to develop more environment-friendly products and manufacturing processes in advance of regulative requirements. It has been estimated that the potential world market for environment-friendly products and technologies is £100–£150 bn. (Cornelius 1989). Various polls testify to an increased interest among consumers in purchasing environment-friendly products.

Some of the criticisms noted above concerning EU environment policy implementation failures or lack of rigour in the measures may already be out of date. Much current criticism of EU policy is that it is too rigorous. The drinking water Directive in particular is criticised as setting excessively high water quality standards in relation to the questionable benefits and heavy costs of complying with the measure. The agreements reached in 1988 and 1989 on atmospheric emission reductions were measures with bite. Effective implementation of Union legislation, if necessary through employment of the legal enforcement mechanism, is now repeatedly stressed as an objective in Commission papers on environmental policy, 'enforcement' having emerged as a new and important theme in the fourth EAP of 1987–1992. Arrangements are being made to establish processes which will facilitate the development of environmental policy in the Union, including the EIA requirement and the European Environmental Agency.

EU environment policy now assumes a position of great importance in Western Europe. It can be demonstrated that significant past or contemporary investment expenditures in the chemical, energy, water or car manufacturing industries have been, or are being, influenced substantially by the need to comply with EU environment directives.

The EU environmental policy is currently shaping the way Western Europe's environment will evolve. The policy's two major themes are to assist the SEM process and to contribute to the realisation of sustainable growth, in particular by integrating environmental considerations into policy and project development more widely. There is no uniformity of view over the best choice of instruments for the realisation of these ambitious objectives. How far they will be realised depends on the relative importance that the Union and member states are prepared to attach to environmental protection in comparison with more short-term objectives.

References

Commission EC 1987 *The State of the Environment in the European Community 1986*, Office for Official Publications of the European Communities, Luxembourg.

Cornelius A 1989 The new revolution is set to check the bad habits of European industry, *The Guardian*, 24 June, p. 9.

Economist Intelligence Unit 1989 *European Trends 1988–89*, p. 52, London.

Haigh N 1987 Assessing EC environmental policy, *European Environment Review*, Vol. 1, No. 2, pp. 38–41.

Klatte E 1986 The past and future of European environmental policy, *European Environment Review*, Vol. 1, No. 1, pp. 32–37.

McArthy E 1989 *The European Community and the Environment*, PNL Press, London.

McDonald F 1989 European Environmental Standards: the effects on the UK, *British Economic Survey*, Vol. 19, No.1, pp. 51–54.

Mishan E J 1990 European and political obstacles to environmental sanity, *National Westminster Bank Quarterly Review*, May, 25–42.

Owens S and **Hope C W** 1989 Energy and the environment: the challenge of integrating European policies, *Energy Policy*, Vol. 17, No. 2, pp. 97–102.

Task Force 1990 *1992 and the Environment: Challenges and Opportunities*, Independent report required by the Commission of the European Communities, Brussels.

Weidner H 1987 *Clean Air Policy in Europe: a survey of seventeen countries*, Internationales Institut für Umwelt und Gesellschaft, Berlin.

World Commission on Environment and Development 1987 *Our Common Future*, Oxford University Press (also described as the *Brundtland Report*, after the Chairman's name).

CHAPTER 12

Transport policy

Stephen Dearden

Introduction

Transport, together with agriculture and external trade, was one of the few areas specified in the Treaty of Rome where the Commission was specifically required to develop a common policy (Arts 3, 74–84). A Common Transport Policy (CTP) was expected both to contribute to European economic integration and to enhance economic development.

The adoption of a CTP was restricted to road, rail and waterways, but could be extended to marine shipping and aviation if the Council of Ministers so decides (Art. 84). The CTP requires common rules for all cross-border traffic (Art. 75), forbids discrimination in transport charges (Art. 79) and calls for reductions in the costs of crossing frontiers (Art. 81). However, while prohibiting general subsidies to transport undertakings, the Treaty permits state subsidies for the coordination of transport or for public service obligations (Art. 77), or as part of regional assistance (Art. 80). Art. 78 also states that any measures concerning transport rates and conditions 'shall take account of the economic circumstances of the carriers'.

Thus from its beginnings transport policy has been an uneasy amalgam of two approaches:

1. the establishment of non-discriminatory competitive conditions in the European transport market;

2. the adoption of an interventionist and regulatory approach, based on the view that efficient transport is central to the functioning of modern economies and to the process of economic integration in the EU.

Given that individual member states gave a different priority to these two approaches, conflict and policy inertia were the inevitable outcome.

The first attempt to establish the general principles of a CTP was offered by the Schaus Memorandum (Commission EC 1961) and embodied in an Action Programme which was to be implemented in the period up to 1970. Three alternative policy approaches were considered in the Memorandum: a policy focusing on fostering competition, on establishing a Community market in transport, or on an active interventionist approach. Although the last would seek to ensure that all transport modes faced harmonised conditions of competition, with a fair allocation of infrastructure costs, it was intended that capacity controls should be established to avoid the emergence of unstable market conditions. Regulations should also take into account the wider social and regional objectives of the Community.

The Council of Transport Ministers failed to reach consensus on either the Memorandum or the Action Programme. The Commission therefore prepared proposals in four areas. Firstly, the control of road and inland waterway transport capacity with the establishment of common rules for entry into the industry. In particular, the Commission proposed the introduction of Community quotas of authorisation for interstate road haulage. Secondly, the adoption of a 'forked tariff' setting upper and lower tariff limits to avoid operators exploiting dominant positions and to avoid creating destabilising cut-throat competition. Thirdly, to harmonise member state technical, tax and subsidy regimes in transport. Finally, to coordinate investment in transport infrastructure and to ensure that each mode of transport contributes fairly to the infrastructure costs that it imposes.

However, because of opposition from the member states very little progress was made until a Council Decision in December 1967 established a timetable for implementing these proposals. Over the next few years a 'forked tariff' regime was introduced in road haulage, together with common driving hour regulations; common competition rules were established; and criteria were agreed for controlling rail subsidies. But overall the development of a CTP had remained a hesitant affair. The entry of Denmark, Ireland and the UK in 1973 deepened the paralysis as disagreements emerged over adjusting the Community's road haulage quotas to accommodate the new member states, and over attempts to introduce new weight and dimension limits for commercial vehicles.

The Commission attempted to stimulate development of the CTP by the publication of a policy statement and Action Programme in 1973. This was mainly a restatement of the 1961 Memorandum, with an emphasis on establishing the right to the freedom of Community transport operators to provide services throughout the EU and on the creation of a harmonised competitive transport market across the Community. However, it also turned attention away from operational controls through quotas and regulated tariffs towards the planning and financing of an integrated Community transport network. This approach was reflected in the four priority areas selected in the Action Plan:

1. the creation of a Community network transport plan

2. the development of criteria for the allocation of infrastructure costs between modes of transport

3. addressing the role of railways in the Community's transport plan

4. planning the development of the inland transport market.

Once more resistance by the Council ensured that by the end of the 1970s little progress had been made in developing the CTP. Although the number of Community quotas for interstate road haulage had risen over the years, they still represented only 5 per cent of all road haulage within the EU. Meanwhile, difficulties remained in implementing Community regulations on road haulage drivers' hours. However, pressure from the new member states, and a ruling by the European Court in 1974, extended the authority of the Treaty to marine and aviation transport.

In a further attempt to rouse the Council of Transport Ministers from their lethargy, the Commission, in October 1980, presented a list of 35 proposals for action over the next three years. The failure of the Council to respond to these proposals led the European Parliament to instigate action against the Council of Ministers in the European Court of Justice (ECJ) under Art. 175 of the Treaty. It accused the Council of failing to establish a CTP as required by Arts 3 and 74 of the Treaty. In May 1985 the ECJ ruled that the Council had indeed infringed the Treaty of Rome by 'failing to ensure freedom to provide services of international transport and to lay down the conditions under which non-resident carriers may operate transport services in a member state (13/83).'

This judgement, together with the accession to the presidency of the Commission in 1985 of Jacques Delors, who was committed to the establishment of the SEM, gave new impetus to the development of a CTP. Not only is the transport industry a significant part of the European economy, but its efficiency is essential to the achievement of a successful SEM. Subsequently in Articles 129b–129d of the Treaty on European Union the Community specifically committed itself to an active role in the development of trans-European transport networks. To achieve this objective it will foster harmonisation of technical standards and contribute, through feasibility studies, loan guarantees and interest rate subsidies, to national programmes of common interest. Transport infrastructure projects will also be eligible for support from the Cohesion Fund that the Treaty established.

To review these more recent developments in EU transport policy, the major areas of the Community's activities will be examined. These include infrastructure, railways, road freight, inland waterways, air and maritime transport.

Infrastructure

Transport infrastructure is the fixed capital of any transport system and includes the provision of ports, airports, roads and railway lines. There are three aspects of Union interest in regard to transport infrastructure: pricing, finance and the coordination of investment.

A correct pricing regime for the use of infrastructure is essential to ensure that users make the economically optimum choice of transport mode. To establish such a pricing regime, and to secure a Community transport market that was fair and competitive, it was also necessary to ensure that state aids were clearly identified and subject to Community controls. To this end, in 1970, a Regulation was introduced establishing a standard system of accounting for expenditure on transport infrastructure and, in 1971, a Memorandum was published containing the Commission's views on a suitable pricing regime. This was the result of six years of studies of infrastructure costs and benefits.

Economic theory suggests that charging for the use of infrastructure should reflect the equilibrium outcome in a perfectly competitive market, i.e. price should equal marginal cost. But it also suggests that pricing should take account of any additional social costs that the market is failing to identify. These social costs or externalities might include accidents, air pollution and noise pollution. The Commission therefore argued that charges should reflect the marginal social costs that an additional vehicle would impose. But they also specifically recognised that congestion costs are an important externality. One additional vehicle on a congested road slows all other vehicles, increasing their travel time and therefore imposing a significant social cost. Thus in cases where congestion exists the Commission argues for a fixed 'congestion tax'. This is explained in Figure 12.1.

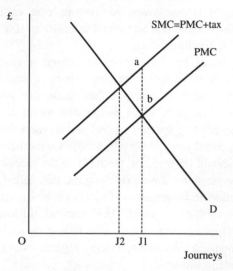

Figure 12.1 Transport pricing with congestion costs

Drivers are faced with private marginal costs (PMC, including wear and tear, petrol and travel time) which increase as the volume of traffic rises and congestion slows the journey. Faced with these costs, J1 journeys will be made. However, this represents over use of this resource since the private costs faced by each driver are failing to reflect the full social costs they are imposing: each additional vehicle not only experiences a slower journey, but slows all other vehicles on the congested road, imposing social costs. The imposition of a tax (ab) equal to these congestion costs reduces the volume of traffic to the optimum J2.

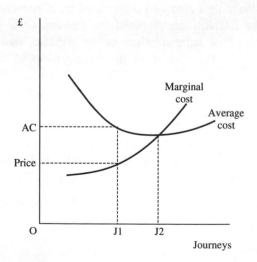

Figure 12.2 Average cost pricing

However, charging each user the marginal social cost that he or she imposes can result in insufficient revenue being raised to cover the costs of provision of the infrastructure. If the number of journeys being made (J1, Figure 12.2) is less than the optimum capacity of a road (J2), marginal cost pricing will not cover the average cost of each journey. Again the Commission recognised this problem and advocated imposition of a 'balancing charge' (AC − price) to cover any remaining funding deficit.

Infrastructure charging based on these proposals raised a number of serious practical problems. For the inland waterways such a pricing regime would substantially raise freight rates since, historically, this mode of transport has made the smallest contribution to its infrastructure costs. For road transport, where the greatest social costs in terms of congestion and pollution are occurring, existing systems of fuel and motor vehicle taxes are incapable of reflecting the true marginal social costs. Although a 1968 Council Directive had suggested that commercial road vehicles should be taxed on the basis of the marginal costs they imposed on the road network, as determined by their axle weights, this failed to take into account the wider externalities of pollution and congestion. To reflect marginal social costs, more complex systems of road pricing would be required. The practical difficulties of adopting such a system, together with the reluctance of member states to lose control of an important source of tax revenue (which a harmonised Community pricing regime would imply) have ensured that little progress has been made in this area.

It was recognised in the 1961 Memorandum that the Community had an important interest in the coordination of infrastructure investment, since investment decisions by member states were likely to reflect only national priorities. With increased intra-EU traffic it was essential that infrastructure projects were also assessed in their wider Community context, and if necessary funded by Community resources. The inadequacies of national transport planning were confirmed by studies in 1964. Thus in 1965 the Commission proposed a programme of infrastructure work focusing on harmonising rail electrification schemes, identifying a strategic European road network, improving links between seaports and their hinterlands and establishing links between the European waterway systems. In 1966 the Council instigated a system of Community consultation on transport infrastructure projects, but resistance by the member states to the erosion of their autonomy undermined the effectiveness of this procedure.

However, in 1978 the Commission proposed the creation of a Transport Infrastructure Committee (TIC) composed of representatives of the member states to consider national infrastructure programmes in the context of the development of a Community transport network. Meanwhile, the Commission continued the work begun in 1973 to identify the likely future transport needs of the EU up to the turn of the century. But the Council continued to resist the development of a more active role for the Community in planning, evaluation and financing of projects of Community interest.

Having identified projects with an important Community benefit the issue of Community finance was clearly crucial. In 1976 the Commission published a Memorandum identifying four categories of projects that were to receive financial support. These were:

1. projects within a member state designed to eliminate bottlenecks in EU traffic

2. cross-frontier projects

3. projects fulfilling broad Community objectives

4. projects which standardise the EU transport network.

These were translated into a more detailed list of short- and long-term objectives, including the upgrading of intercity rail links (eg. Amsterdam/Brussels/Strasbourg), links with peripheral areas (e.g. Dublin/Cork/Galway, East Anglia, Mezzogiorno), routes overcoming natural obstacles (e.g. Channel Tunnel, Apenine crossings) and bridging 'missing links' between transport networks (e.g. inland waterway link between Belgium and France). Qualifying projects should have been eligible for all forms of EU financial assistance, including EIB, ERDF and, since 1979, New Community Instrument loans.

In response to this Memorandum the Council, in 1981, asked the Commission to evaluate the Community 'interest' in a limited number of specific projects. Subsequently the Commission presented a list of projects to form an experimental programme selected from submissions by the member states. The total cost to the EU budget was to be ECU 968 m. to be dispersed over the years 1984–1986, and the project was to offer a maximum support of 20 per cent of the cost of each project. Of the total, ECU 250 m. was to be spent on rail projects and ECU 550 m. on roads.

The European Parliament was critical of this road bias, and advocated instead an intermodal approach, and a greater attention to the needs of the inland waterways, ports and airports. In response, in 1983, the Commission published a 'multi-annual transport infrastructure programme' (MTIP) to continue until the Council finally responded to the 1976 Memorandum. The MTIP would have provided a maximum of 70 per cent support for eligible projects which could have been combined with other sources of Community assistance. In addition to the experimental programme and the MTIP the Commission proposed support for a number of minor projects to be funded from the 1982 budget. At a cost of ECU 10 m., this involved a contribution to modernising transalpine rail links and to preparatory studies for the Channel Tunnel.

The MTIP was not realised, but the concerns of the European Parliament were reflected in the shift of priorities expressed in the 1986 Medium Term Transport Infrastructure policy. Priorities were now to be:

1.   improvements in land–sea corridors

2.   links to peripheral regions

3.   construction of a high speed rail network

4.   reductions in transit traffic costs, including development of combined transport (road/rail).

The modernisation of ports and airports was specifically identified as an important part of infrastructure policy, as were the demands created by the accession of Greece, Spain and Portugal to the EC. Reducing transit costs raised the question of the role of non-EU countries in the transport network of the Community, particularly that of Austria and Switzerland. Austria's imposition of a transit tax in 1978, and a Swiss 28 tonne heavy goods vehicle (HGV) limit, had highlighted third-country transit problems. In response the EU had entered into transport agreements with these countries, and in 1980 the Commission had set a precedent by recommending a financial contribution to the Pyhrn motorway in Austria.

The 1986 document also attempted to clarify the complex financial sourcing of infrastructure projects. It proposed concentrating funding under Specific Transport Instruments (STC). However, the Council has resisted the establishment of a specific fund for transport.

But the Commission has been successful in its advocacy of the use of private capital in major transport projects such as the Channel Tunnel. This was inevitable given the huge sums necessary to finance such projects, estimated at ECU 20 bn. up to the end of the century.

Although the attempts by the Commission to establish a clearly assigned Transport Infrastructure Fund have been unsuccessful, substantial EU expenditure has been undertaken through other EU Funds and the EIB. Up to 1982 the European Investment Bank had expended ECU 4.6 bn. on transport projects (20 per cent of its Community financing). Of this, 35 per cent financed road projects, 29 per cent gas and oil pipelines and 10 per cent rail schemes. Another significant contributor to transport infrastructure financing has been the European Regional Development Fund, which together with the EIB expended ECU 5.8 bn. between 1981 and 1985 on such projects. In the UK this included support for developments at Birmingham and Manchester airports, the Tyne and Wear Metro, Irish Sea ferries and work at the ports of Ramsgate and Harwich.

The railways

Across Europe the share of freight carried on the railways has been falling. In 1970 31.4 per cent of freight was carried by rail and 54.9 per cent by road, and by 1980 the relative shares had changed to 23.2 per cent and 65.8 per cent respectively. In 1990 the railways' share had fallen further to 17.4 per cent, while Europe's roads now carried 74 per cent of all freight. Similarly, by 1990 in none of the countries of the EU did the railways carry more than 9 per cent of passenger traffic.

Table 12.1 Share of rail transport

	Route (km) (1983)	Freight ('000 m.t.m.km) (1989)	%	Passenger ('000 m.p.km) (1990)	%
Germany	28 130	61.1	21	40.4	6
Belgium	3 860	8.0	18	6.5	7
Denmark	2 350	1.7	15	4.9	7
France	34 627	53.3	27	64.0	9
Ireland	1 987	0.6	9	1.2	
Italy	16 148	20.6	10	45.5	7
Netherlands	2 892	3.1	5	10.8	7
Portugal		1.72	14	5.7	7
Spain	2 461	12.0	7	16.7	8
United Kingdom	17 435	17.3	11	33.5	5

Source: European Conference of Ministers of Transport, Annual Reports
Notes: m.t.km, million tonne kilometres; m.p.km, million passenger kilometres; %, percentage share of total freight/passenger transport.

None the less the railway systems of the EU vary considerably in their extent and importance in national transport (Table 12.1) Although these characteristics are determined in

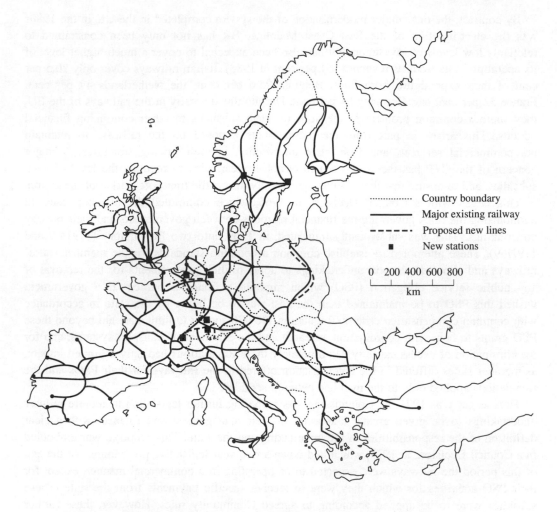

Figure 12.3 Europe's railways

part by the economic geography of each member state, they also reflect the transport policies pursued by the individual governments. Thus in both Germany and France there was discrimination against road haulage for freight traffic beyond 150 km. These two countries, together with Italy, also share a commitment to the development of new high-speed rail lines, of which the French Trains à Grande Vitesse (TGVs) are the most well known. Over the years 1976 to 1982 German railways invested ECU 9,000 m., French railways ECU 4,500 m., and British Rail (BR) ECU 3,000 m. In 1985 the German government approved a ten year investment programme of ECU 17,500 m., with a doubling of their high-speed network to 2,000 km by the end of the century. In France, the completion of the South-East TGV to Marseilles and Switzerland was followed, in 1983, by the decision to develop the TGV Atlantique to the South-West at a cost of ECU 1,900 m. In Italy, a new line is being constructed from Rome to Florence at a cost of ECU 2,270 m.

By contrast, the only major modernisation of the system completed in the UK in the 1980s was the electrification of the East Coast Mainline. BR has not only been constrained to relatively low levels of investment but has also been expected to cover a much higher level of its operating costs from its revenues (64 per cent in 1983). Italian railways cover only 20.5 per cent of their expenditure from fares, Belgium 25.6 per cent, the Netherlands 49 per cent, France 52 per cent and Germany 56 per cent. Despite this diversity in the railways of the EU, they share a common problem in the need for state subsidies to cover continuing financial deficits. This arises in part from the requirements imposed on the railways to maintain non-commercial services, and from state intervention in their pricing structures. A major concern of the CTP has therefore been to establish clear rules to regulate the level of such subsidies, and to ensure that they do not significantly distort the transport market of the Union.

This began with a Council Decision, in 1965, which committed the member states to harmonising the rules governing the financial relations between governments and their railway undertakings. This was subsequently translated, in 1969, into two Regulations (1191/69 and 1192/69). These attempted to establish common accounting standards for the member states' railways and allowed transport undertakings to apply to their governments for the removal of any public service obligation (PSO) which imposed a financial burden. If a government wished this PSO to be maintained then the cost was to be borne by the state in accordance with common compensation criteria. Regulation 1107/70 sought to limit state aid beyond these PSO grants to help with coordination, research and development of transport systems, and for the elimination of excess capacity. Unfortunately these Regulations had only a limited impact, as member states differed in the compensation offered to the railways for their PSOs and the Regulations applied only to the mainline network services.

Thus as early as 1971 the Commission was preparing further legislation to require railway undertakings to be given greater autonomy in their management and finance, with a clear definition of the responsibilities of the undertaking and the state. This proposal was embodied in a Council Decision, in 1975, which laid down a five-year legislative programme. At the end of this period the railways were expected to be operating in a commercial manner, except for their PSO activities for which they were to receive specific payments from the state. These subsidies were to be applied according to agreed Community rules. However, these further attempts to restrict the level of member state subsidies continued to be frustrated by the vagueness of existing EU Regulations and the difficulties of assigning railway costs.

In December 1989 the Commission again returned to these problems with a proposal for new PSO rules. Under the resulting 1991 Regulation the existing systems of PSO grants were required to be replaced by a system of public service contracts agreed between the states and the railways. These grants can be retained for urban, suburban and regional services. The 1989 Commission proposals also raised again the issue of the separation of infrastructure management from service provision, and under Directive 91/440 separate accounts are now required for infrastructure and train operations. The Commission, as has already been described, has attempted to remove distortions in the transport market by establishing clear common criteria for the allocation of infrastructure costs. In the case of the railways it is argued that equality of treatment with the public road network would require the state to accept the financial responsibility for the infrastructure, with individual services being charged their marginal cost. This appears to offer an attractive means of alleviating the recurring financial deficits of railway undertakings. However, where marginal cost pricing is inadequate to cover average costs, additional charges must be made. Generally governments receive more in road taxes than is spent on road construction and maintenance, but overall railway revenues fail to cover their infrastructure costs. A transfer of responsibility for the infrastructure from the railways to the state would merely result in a reassignment of the underlying deficits. The core problem remains that of the nature of railways, with their high fixed costs and economies of scale which result in falling average costs as the volume of traffic increases. A more fruitful approach to improving the financial performance of the railways is likely to be found in focusing on matching capacity to demand and to achieving the potential productivity gains in their operation.

The Commission also has responsibility for assisting in the integration of the Community's national railway systems. Although most of the rail systems of the EU share a common track gauge (with the exception of Spain and Portugal) and the Berne loading gauge (with the exception of the UK), their power and signalling systems often differ. Thus the Channel Tunnel requires locomotives which can operate under three different electric power systems, with the smaller rolling stock compatible with UK railways. However, there is a long history of cooperation between the railways of Europe through a variety of institutions, especially the Union Internationale des Chemins de Fer (UIC). Their European Infrastructure Plan, adopted in 1973, has identified those lines whose development is necessary to the establishment of an integrated European network. As we have already seen, the Commission has also given priority in its infrastructure proposals to the development of a Community high-speed rail network. In 1990 the Commission submitted a plan, based on national intentions, for such a network to meet the needs of passenger traffic up to the year 2010. Subsequently a working group has been established to examine the issues of funding and technical harmonisation.

The plan identified 14 key rail links: one of these, and the most significant from a UK perspective, is the Channel Tunnel. Having opened in 1994, planning began in 1985, with substantial finance provided by 210 commercial banks and the EIB. At a total cost of ECU 12.5 bn., it is expected to carry 30 million passengers and 14 million tonnes (mt) of freight in its opening year. This is anticipated to rise to between 26 mt and 38 mt of freight by 2013. Of this freight traffic, slightly more than half is expected to use the Shuttle trains, as compared with the through freight services. The problem of developing a high-speed rail link from London to the Tunnel remains unresolved. The preference of the current UK government for private finance, and their intention to privatise and fragment BR, are likely to create additional obstacles. Thus the existing UK rail network will have to accommodate the additional Channel Tunnel traffic for at least 15 years. Given this problem, and the competition from air services for passengers travelling beyond London–Brussels–Paris, the Tunnel is likely to be of greater significance for rail freight than passenger services.

Combined transport

The Channel Tunnel will be of importance in the development of combined transport within the EU. Combined transport is the carriage of goods that involves more than one mode of transport. It includes containers and 'piggyback' road/rail systems. Of these, containerisation is the most well established. Intercontainer, a consortium of 23 railway companies, carried 904,803 TEUs (twenty foot containers) in 1985. Traffic is concentrated on Marseilles-Fos and Rotterdam, and is particularly important for German and French railways. The carriage of road vehicles or swapbodies by rail is less developed, and in 1985 463,138 consignments were carried by this means. Germany has the largest volume of piggyback traffic for internal freight transport, and Italy for international trade.

Combined transport can be cost-effective over longer distances (450–500 km), and offers environmental benefits if it can divert freight traffic from road to rail. It is also hoped that it may contribute to improving the financial performance of the railways. For these reasons the Community has been encouraging its development since 1975, when a Directive freed HGVs from all restrictions if the trunk haul was by rail. In 1982 these exemptions were extended to road haulage combined with inland waterway carriage, and a scheme was adopted to reduce vehicle excise duties for HGVs for that part of journeys undertaken by rail. The Community has also offered financial assistance for the development of combined transport terminals, and recommended the adoption of competitive tariff structures that encourage combined transport.

A study by the Kearney Group of consultants for the Commission, completed in 1990, confirmed the economic advantages of combined transport and predicted a tripling of such traffic by 2005. It suggested that further improvements were possible through standardisation of equipment and organisational changes. In October 1990 a working party was formed with the specific remit of identifying those measures necessary for the establishment of a European combined transport network. In 1991 a Directive further liberalised controls of the road element of combined transport, including allowing non-resident hauliers to carry out the road legs of the journeys, and exempted the road trip elements from any domestic tariff regulations. Recently Directive 92/106 extended the existing concessions for combined transport to all multi-mode unitised freight transport, and Regulation 3578/92 renewed the existing provisions for state aid for another three years.

Road haulage

The EU has had a far greater impact on the operational environment of the road haulage industry than that of the railways. It has consistently pursued its objective of establishing a common competitive market in road transport, and to this end has sought the harmonisation of national regulations and the removal of restrictions. Road haulage has been subject to licensing in all of the member states at some time, restricting entry to the industry or the business for which road haulage can compete with rail. In the UK these controls were abandoned in 1968, and in Belgium in 1960, but in the rest of the Community restrictions remained. Complementing these domestic restrictions were licensing regimes for controlling road haulage between the member states. But these clearly conflicted with the Treaty commitment to establishing the free provision of services (Art. 52).

The Commission recognised that transitional arrangements would be necessary, and sought to achieve this by introducing a Community quota of licences for intra-EU haulage. A hesitant start was made in 1968 with an experimental three-year scheme, which was applicable only to cross-border traffic; solely domestic haulage still required a national licence. These EEC permits were shared between each of the member states and this allocation was to become a source of considerable acrimony. A succession of Regulations extended the scheme, but by 1983 only 5 per cent of all road haulage was under a Community licence. In 1984 the Council decided to increase the EU quotas by 30 per cent in 1985 from their current 4,038, and subsequently by 15 per cent in each of the following four years. The commitment to the SEM increased the pace of deregulation. In 1988 agreement was reached to increase the EU quota by 40 per cent for two years and, more significantly, to abolish all permit requirements by January 1993.

Linked to the issue of intra-state road haulage has been the restrictions on cabotage – the carriage of goods for customers at any stage of a journey between member states. This involves the opening up of the road haulage business of every member state to any EU operator. Article 75 of the Treaty requires the Council to determine the conditions under which non-resident operators may provide services within a member state other than their own. Despite a 1985 ECJ ruling, little progress was made on this sensitive issue until 1989 when Regulation (4059/89) created an EU quota of 15,000 cabotage permits. These were valid for two months, but could be converted by member states into double the number of one-month permits. The UK chose to do this, allocating 2,214 permits. These arrangements are intended to be only temporary until a definitive cabotage regime can be agreed.

Similar liberalisation has been taking place in the road passenger industry. The EU has concentrated its attention on international coach and bus services, leaving national services to be regulated by individual member states. Although there were existing international regulations on which the EU could build, it was a judgement of the ECJ in 1987 that forced the pace of liberalisation. It was not until 1992 that the Council finally agreed a Regulation abolishing licensing. They also agreed to allow cabotage on 'closed-door' tours, where the same group of passengers stays with the same coach. The question of extending cabotage to scheduled bus services will be the subject of a Commmission report by 1995.

The liberalisation of the entry of operators into member states' road transport markets has been complemented by the deregulation of tariff controls. As has already been described, the issue of tariff controls illustrated the clear conflict of philosophy between those member states advocating the primacy of market forces and those attempting to avoid instability or the abuse of market power by maintaining regulation. The compromise that finally emerged in 1968 was the 'forked tariff', setting compulsory maximum and minimum rates. This 'forked tariff' was to apply only to international road freight traffic, and the rates were to be set by agreements between the relevant member states. This system was never adopted by Denmark, the UK and Ireland. In 1977 it was watered down by the introduction of an alternative voluntary system of reference tariffs. Again the choice was to be determined by mutual agreement between the member states concerned with a particular traffic. This system clearly failed to establish a uniform Community common market in road freight traffic, and with the movement towards the SEM it was finally agreed that from 1 June 1990 all tariff controls would be abolished. However, a truly fair and competitive transport market would also require a common vehicle taxing regime. In 1988 the Commission proposed harmonisation of HGV taxation on the basis of a common method of infrastructure charging. Vehicles would still be taxed in their country of registration, but on the basis of their use of the total road network of the Community. So far no agreement on this issue has proved possible.

Differing vehicle technical specifications with regard to weight and overall dimensions were also viewed as an obstacle to the efficient operation of HGVs, and to the development of the European vehicle manufacturing industry. These differences had arisen from the various national assessments of the trade-off between vehicle operating efficiency and environmental damage. Axle weights in particular are crucial in determining the level of road damage that a vehicle can inflict, e.g. a 10 tonne axle weight does 17 times more damage than a 5 tonne axle. Attempts to arrive at a Community consensus proved extremely difficult.

It took ten years to achieve agreement amongst the original six members for a maximum axle weight of 11 tonnes and 40 tonnes overall. Unfortunately, this was rejected by the new member states, Denmark, Ireland and the UK. In 1985 a compromise was finally reached with a maximum 44 tonne limit, and 11.5 tonnes for driving axles. However, a derogation was given to the UK and Ireland to continue with their lower limits of 32 tonnes. Following the Armitage Inquiry in 1980, the UK government had raised the weight limit to 38 tonnes (see Dearden 1990). Despite continuing public concern, the Government has recently announced its intention to allow 44 tonne lorries to operate to railheads, as part of combined transport. As there is no requirement that this should be the nearest railhead, and insurmountable problems of enforcing this restriction are anticipated, this is seen as a final capitulation to the UK's road haulage lobby, and the pressures to harmonise with the EU. These EU maxima apply only to international transport, and each country, while conforming to these limits, may also allow domestic operation of vehicles in excess of these limits. As the EU seeks harmonisation across both international and national transport markets, further pressure to raise the EU maximum to the highest current national limit (46 tonnes) is likely.

Fair competition and road safety considerations have led to a series of social measures controlling the working conditions of drivers. As early as 1969 a Regulation establishing controls over driving hours was introduced. This was to be enforced through personnel log books, but the inadequacy of this method quickly led to a Regulation (1463/70) requiring the installation by January 1976 of automatic recording equipment (tachographs). The UK rejected this Regulation, but legal proceedings by the Commission forced compliance, and it was applied in the UK from January 1982. However, the EU recognised that the existing Regulations were too restrictive and, in 1986, revisions were made extending driving hours and increasing their flexibility. But at the same time there was concern at the failure of all member states to fully enforce the Regulations. Consequently in 1989 common enforcement standards were prescribed by a further Directive.

Inland waterways

The inland waterway network is an important mode of transport in continental Europe. It joins the Mediterranean to the North Sea, and extends from the Channel into Central and Eastern Europe. There is 6,500 km of navigable waterway in Europe, centred on two systems: the Meuse/Scheldt linking Belgium, France and the Netherlands, and the Rhine/Main/Danube. Of these the Rhine is the more significant, carrying 57 per cent of Europe's 50 bn. tonne-kilometres of waterborne freight. However, it is an industry that has seen its share of freight traffic fall from 13.7 per cent in 1970 to only 8 per cent in 1990. It has consistently suffered from over-capacity, resulting in low returns to capital with a consequent failure to invest in modern vessels. This problem has been exacerbated by competition from Eastern European boats operating at artificially low prices.

The Rhine navigation is governed by the long established Mannheim Convention (1848), and this has inhibited EU intervention in the inland waterways industry. None the less, the EU has harmonised the technical specification of vessels (82/714) and established mutual recognition of navigation licences (76/135). In 1983 the Commission submitted five proposals to the Council, concerning entry to the industry, working conditions, introduction of a voluntary set of reference tariffs, cabotage, and access to the Rhine navigation. The

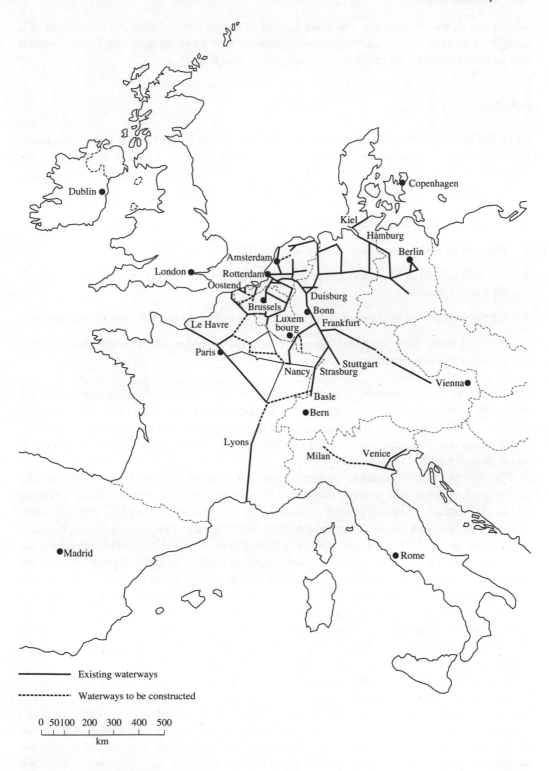

Figure 12.4 Europe's waterways

subsequent Action Programme was more limited in scope, but included the preparation of a compensation scheme for scrapping vessels combined with a ban on state aids for new vessels and an examination of the problems of infrastructure charging.

Aviation

Of all the modes of transport, aviation is the most highly regulated. The EU has to develop its policies within the context of well-established international and bilateral agreements. The foundations for the postwar system of international civil aviation were laid with the Chicago Convention of 1944. The Convention identified five air freedoms:

1.   the right to overfly states' territories;

2.   the right to land for technical reasons e.g. refuelling;

3.   the right to land to disembark passengers and cargo travelling from the country of an airline's registration;

4.   the right to pick up passengers and cargo for journeys to the country of an airline's registration;

5.   the right to transport goods and passengers between two countries other than the country of registration (cabotage).

Signatories to the Convention granted the first two rights to all other signatories, but the remaining rights were determined by bilateral agreements (e.g. the 1946 Bermuda Agreement between the UK and the USA). Complementing the Convention was the creation of IATA (the International Air Transport Association) in 1945, which organises a series of conferences at which fares are agreed for scheduled services.

The European civil aviation industry was characterised by relatively small, usually state-owned, national flag carriers. Scheduled services between states were usually restricted to the flag carriers, who were often entitled to 50 per cent of the traffic, with a revenue sharing pool. In 1989, of the 750 non-stop short-haul flights in Europe 71 per cent had only one carrier and a further 24 per cent only two (Pryke 1991). Fares were agreed by the regulatory bodies of the two states. The high operating costs of many European airlines were sustained by this regime, producing fares 45–75 per cent above those in the USA (McGowan and Trengove 1986). None the less during the 1980s scheduled domestic air traffic increased by 65 per cent and intra-European traffic by 31 per cent. Domestic flights account for approximately 11 per cent of European airlines' total revenue passenger kilometres (RPKs) and intra-European flights a further 20 per cent, with only three airlines (Air France, British Airways and Lufthansa) accounting for 46 per cent of Europe's total RPKs.

Despite this highly regulated environment, one of the earliest actions in the European aviation industry was an attempt to establish a European Civil Aviation Community. In 1958 Sabena, Lufthansa, Air France, KLM and Alitalia had discussed an agreement to foster cooperation and possibly a merger. The principal objective was to standardise their aircraft fleets, coordinate ground control and pool traffic rights. Negotiations soon moved beyond the companies to involve their respective governments. In 1962 the companies and their governments signed an Air Union pact. Until 1965 inter-governmental negotiations continued between all the original six member states, but outside the aegis of the EEC. Meanwhile the Commission attacked these activities as incompatible with the Treaty, and called for the development of a Community-based air transport policy.

In 1972 the Commission proposed action on air transport covering three main areas – improving regional scheduled services, developing a common approach to negotiations within IATA and on air links with non-Community countries. But progress was not really made until 1979 with the Commission's Civil Aviation Memorandum No. 1. Although this document suggested that freedom of entry into the industry was only a long-term prospect, it also represented the first clear commitment to the goal of establishing a competitive market environment. This shift had been encouraged by ECJ rulings in 1974 and 1978 that the competition requirements of the Treaty (Arts 85, 86 and 90) also applied to air transport. It was also recognised that the move to a competitive environment would require a clear Community policy regulating the level of state aids to their national airlines. But the endeavours of the Commission to establish a more liberal regime were frustrated by the Council, including its attempts to deregulate regional air services. Meanwhile Lord Bethell's action before the ECJ to force the Commission to intervene against the fare-setting arrangements in the industry failed.

However, the movement towards deregulation that had begun in the USA in the mid-1970s was beginning to influence the tenor of international negotiations. The apparently rigid regulatory regime of the Chicago Convention/IATA had always offered some scope for flexibility. The Convention had always excluded non-scheduled services from its ambit, and hence the considerable growth of the charter market in Europe, encouraged by those states that wished to develop their tourist industry. By 1990 65 per cent of European air traffic (passenger kilometres) was charters. Most charter airlines are based in the UK and some are comparable to national airlines. Britannia Airways flew 14.1 bn. RPKs in 1991, compared with Aer Lingus 4.1 bn., Alitalia 19.1 bn. and SAS 16.5 bn. Also, the international regulatory controls had never applied to domestic flights, and offered considerable scope for liberalising bilateral agreements. Thus, in 1984, the UK and the Netherlands opened access on all their bilateral routes to all their national airlines. Fare controls were removed unless both governments disapproved (double disapproval). Subsequently the UK extended such liberalising agreements to flights to Germany, Belgium and Ireland. This reflected the commitment of the UK to a liberal market environment in air transport and followed the US government's radical experiment in domestic deregulation begun in 1978. The USA applied its deregulatory zeal not only to its domestic air transport market, but also to its bilateral agreements and its dealings with IATA, assisted by the competitive pressures from S.E. Asian airlines, which had remained outside the system. The beneficial results for passengers of the US experience increased the pressure on the EU to curtail its protectionist regime.

Discussions within the Community moved slowly forward in 1984 with the Civil Aviation Memorandum No. 2. It introduced the concept of 'zones of flexibility' into fare-setting. Governments would determine a reference tariff and a 'zone of reasonableness' in bilateral agreements. Within this zone airlines would be free to set fare levels, subject to country of origin approval or 'double disapproval,' i.e. vetoes by both governments. The dominance of national flag carriers remained relatively unchallenged, although 50:50 traffic-sharing deals would be allowed to vary to 75:25. In return for this limited increase in flexibility the Commission was prepared to exempt fare setting, capacity-sharing and revenue pools from the application of the competition rules of the EU for a period of seven years.

This proposal was overtaken by another landmark judgement by the ECJ in the Nouvelles Frontieres case of 1985. This involved an attempt by the French regulatory authorities to prevent a travel agent from offering cut-price air tickets. Although the ECJ had already ruled on the applicability of the EU's competition rules, the 1985 judgement opened the way for parties to a dispute to force reference by national courts to the Commission's ruling on any restrictive agreement.

This judgement forced the hand of the Council and the result was the first positive step towards deregulation. The 1987 Regulation explicitly confirmed the authority of the Commission to apply the EU's competition rules. However, it also allowed the Commission to give block exemptions until 1991 to three categories of airline agreements:

1.   those concerning planning of capacity, revenue-sharing and consultation on tariffs;

2.   those concerned with computer reservation systems;

3.   those covering ground handling services.

These exemptions seriously undermined the immediate impact of the Regulation but, being under the control of the Commission, created leverage in forcing the transition to a more competitive environment. This was indeed what was to occur.

The Council also accepted a Directive which significantly reduced the ability of individual member states to control air fares. Although a government might still reject a proposed fare to prevent 'dumping' or predatory pricing, it was unable to reject fares on the grounds that they were lower than those currently offered. The Directive also specifically established the discounting of fares, within a broad range, as an automatic right. These arrangements were to apply for three years, after which further liberalisation was to take place. Similarly, greater access was to be allowed to new airlines, but in stages. Over the next three years member states were to allow traffic shares to move from 50:50 to 60:40, to accept additional airlines on routes (on a bilateral basis), and to introduce limited fifth freedom rights (cabotage).

The Second Aviation Package (1991) extended the right of the Commission to give block exemptions to airline agreements until the end of 1992, but it also committed the member states to ending the capacity-sharing arrangements from January 1993. From that date scheduled fares were also to be allowed to match non-scheduled fare levels. This process of liberalisation was completed in the Third Aviation Package of three Regulations, which were also to apply from 1993. The Licensing Regulation introduced uniform criteria for the issue of an air transport operator's licence, to be recognised by all member states. The Market Access Regulation opens all EU routes to all licensed operators. Limited cabotage continues until April 1997, after which full cabotage becomes available. Finally, the Fares and Rates Regulation removes all controls on fare levels, subject only to safeguards against excessive tariffs. All remaining restrictions on non-scheduled services are also removed. These three Regulations will finally establish a single competitive air transport market within the EU. These conditions were extended to Norway and Sweden in an agreement signed in June 1992, and it is expected that they will also be adopted within the European Economic Area.

However, the final deregulation of the air transport market is by no means the end of the story. The problem of distortions arising from state subsidies and from the potential abuse of monopoly power remains. Indeed, European airlines have quickly responded to the changing transport environment by seeking partners. Following the US experience, it is expected that only a few major airlines will dominate the market by the turn of the century. British Airways has made no secret of its global ambitions, and has swallowed British Caledonian (in 1988) and Dan Air (in 1992), and taken minority stakes in TAT (a French regional carrier), Delta Air (a German regional airline renamed Deutsche BA), US Air and Quantas (the Australian national airline). Meanwhile Air France has taken over UTA and Air Inter, and taken a 37 per cent stake in Belgium's Sabena Airlines; Lufthansa has acquired a 26 per cent stake in Lauda Air (Austria); and KLM has invested in Air UK, Transavia (Holland), Air Littoral (France) and Northwest (USA).

But airlines have also followed the US companies in attempting to develop hub and spoke route networks. Domination of central hub airports creates the potential for the control of take-off and landing slots. The Commission has identified this problem, and in 1990 submitted proposals seeking to establish explicit rules for slot allocation, with half of unused or under-utilised slots being offered to new entrants. In addition the proposals would allow, under certain circumstances, the reallocation of incumbent airlines slots to new entrants.

There is also the possibility of adopting a system of slot auctioning to ensure efficient rationing. The Commission has taken action against Lufthansa and Aer Lingus for their attempts to place restrictions on 'interlining', where passengers may exchange tickets between airlines serving the same route. Problems may emerge with the ownership of Computer Reservation Systems (CRSs) by airlines. Such systems, used by travel agents, not only allow the owning airline to give priority to its own services, but also provide it with information on the bookings of any other airline using the system. These CRSs are likely to be closely monitored by the Commission, with the threat that the block exemption under the 1987 Package could be ended. Similar problems may emerge with the use of code-sharing by airlines for through flights, or with agreements for sharing marketing, customer services or ground services.

The EU also has an important role in the rationalisation of the highly fragmented system of air traffic control (ATC). In 1991 there were 44 control centres with 31 separate operating systems; three-quarters of these centres were reported as having significant deficiencies. It has been estimated that inadequacies in Europe's ATC cost $4 m. in 1988 (AEA 1990) and that Europe's airways could accommodate 30 per cent more traffic with an integrated system. In 1992 EU Transport Ministers agreed to move towards such integration but, as it will involve the loss of states' control of their national airspace, political opposition can be expected.

The transition from a regulated to a competitive air transport market environment in the EU has begun in earnest. The response of the airline companies will require careful monitoring by the Commission under its Art. 86 powers. The Commission will have the difficult task of ensuring that a balance is maintained between the achievement of economies of scale in operation through merger and the potential abuse of monopoly power. It is too early to say whether the consumer will experience the same gains in lower fares and improved services that were experienced with US deregulation. The existence of competition from charter airlines and from the high-speed rail network may already have provided a stimulus to efficiency. But the major obstacle to realisation of a competitive common air transport market in the EU remains the existence of state subsidies. Only British Airways is wholly within the private sector, and with the state-owned airlines making substantial losses it is not surprising that current EU regulations continue to allow state aid.

Maritime transport

The EU accounts for approximately 20 per cent of world trade, and 95 per cent of this trade is sea-borne. Although declining, in 1983 the merchant fleet of the Community was still 23 per cent of the world total, earning $9 bn. None the less, like aviation, maritime transport was initially excluded from consideration under the CTP. This arose from the 'continental' orientation of the original six member states, between whom sea transport was of little importance, and from the complexities of attempting to apply the Treaty within the context of a substantial number of existing international agreements.

In 1970 the Bodson report had first called for the development of a coherent Community approach to shipping under the powers of Art. 84(2) of the Treaty. It identified a number of issues which needed to be addressed i.e. agreements with non-EU states on cargo reservations and action on discrimination, a common approach to international negotiations, harmonisation of state aid and of crew conditions. Although supported by the Parliament, action under Art. 84(2) required unanimity, and French opposition ensured that no progress was made until the 1974 ECJ judgement. This found that the competition rules of the EU also applied to air and sea transport, and arose from an action against France for maintaining rules which discriminated against non-French seamen. This judgement coincided with increasing concern in the UK, Netherlands and Germany about unfair competition from COMECON fleets, and from the French about the dangers of oil spillages. Thus from 1974 the Commission was to focus on four issues – relations with the COMECON countries; organisation of liner shipping, and in particular the United Nations Conference on Trade and Development (UNCTAD) code of conduct; the application of the EU's competition rules; marine pollution and safety at sea.

By 1976 the COMECON fleet accounted for 64 per cent of bilateral trade with the UK, 75 per cent with Germany and 95 per cent with the Netherlands. In the international market it was also capturing an increasing share, with 25 per cent of North Atlantic trade. In 1978 the EU asked member states to monitor the freight liner trade (regular scheduled shipping services) with East Africa, Central America and the Far East, where competition with COMECON shipping was thought to be most acute. Member states could then apply to the Council for permission to instigate counter-measures against countries where they believed unfair competitive practices were taking place.

More controversial was the debate within the EU on the ratification of the UNCTAD Convention on a Code of Conduct for Liner Conferences signed in 1974. This had arisen from the political pressure from the developing countries for a greater share of the shipping between themselves and the industrialised world. Liner Conferences are composed of the shipping companies involved in a particular trade, and determine shipping rates and market shares. The crucial feature of the Code was the adoption of a 40/40/20 rule for participation in a trade. The national shipping companies of the two countries in the trade would each be reserved 40 per cent of the traffic, with 20 per cent open to 'cross-traders'. The USA was opposed to a further reinforcement of these shipping cartels. In the EU Denmark and the UK, with their established fleets, also opposed ratification, while France, Belgium and Germany supported the Code. Disagreement focused on two issues: the share to be allocated to non-EU OECD countries, and the treatment of non-EU non-OECD carriers. The final compromise Regulation (954/79) that allowed ratification confined the 40/40/20 rule to those Conferences involving developing countries. Elsewhere commercial criteria were to apply in determining the shares of cargo traffic. The Code finally came into force in 1983.

Although, contrary to expectations, the ratification of the Code did not require adaption of the EU's competition rules in relation to Liner Conference agreements, the Commission remained concerned that they were compromising the Treaty. First submitted in 1981, a proposed Regulation sought to empower the Commission to enforce Art. 85 against restrictive agreements, and Art. 86 against abuse of dominant positions in sea transport. Exemptions were to be given to the Liner Conference agreements, subject to certain conditions (e.g. consultation with users) since these were seen as contributing to a stable market environment. However, it was not until 1986 that this extension of the powers of the Commission was agreed under Regulation 4056/86. This was one of a package of four Regulations accepted by the Council to realise its commitment to establishing free and fair competitive conditions in shipping. A complimentary Regulation (4055) prevented discrimination by a member state against the shipping companies of other EU members in any of its trades. Existing unilateral cargo reservations were to be phased out by 1993. Similarly, cargo-sharing agreements with third countries are now only allowed in exceptional circumstances. Attempts by third countries to impose such agreements can be met by counter-measures from the Union under Regulation 4058. Finally, Regulation 4057 empowers the EU to impose compensatory duties on non-EU ship owners found to be engaging in unfair pricing practices. This Regulation is of particular relevance to the problem of competition from Central and Eastern European fleets.

These four Regulations create the foundations for a Common Shipping policy, and commit the EU to concerted action to combat protectionism by non-EU countries. They represent a significant transfer of power from individual member states to the Union. The EU, by combining the individual influence of the member states, will have a much greater impact on the international negotiations that will determine the shape of this industry.

The Commission is now turning its attention to the harmonisation and improvement of the operating conditions of EU shipping. One proposal to emerge is for the creation of an EU shipping registry (EUROS) under an EU flag, but this is likely to face opposition, especially from the UK government. None the less, it might contribute to meeting the concerns of some member states about operating standards and the threat of marine pollution. Concern had focused on this issue in 1978 after the Amoco Cadiz oil spillage on the Brittany coast. In response to a Council request the Commission had proposed a programme of action for the control of oil pollution, and also for Directives requiring member states to ratify a series of outstanding international agreements. These included the 1974 International Convention for the Safety of Life at Sea (Solas), the 1973 International Convention for the Prevention of Pollution from Ships (Marpol), and the ILO Convention 147 concerning minimum standards on merchant ships. Although the Council authorised a series of technical studies it declined to impose ratification on all member states, instead it merely agreed a Recommendation.

However, the Council did agree Directives on pilotage in the English Channel and North Sea, and for compulsory notification of potential marine hazards from oil tankers using Community ports. This failed to satisfy the European Parliament, which prepared its own critical report on what it regarded as the Council's inadequate response. In 1985 the Commission had reviewed its progress to date and outlined its future policy (COM(85)90). Although 'support for international efforts to maintain and improve maritime safety' had been identified as an important objective, so had the need to 'improve the commercial competitiveness of Community shipping.' The problem of the need to operate within the context of international agreements, combined with the reluctance of some member states to impose additional operating costs on their merchant fleets, has tended to inhibit progress in this area.

Conclusion

As can be seen from this review, the Common Transport Policy differs fundamentally from the EU's two other common policies for agriculture and external trade. In contrast to external trade policy it has both an external and internal dimension, and unlike agriculture there has been no inclination to develop a highly interventionist regulatory regime. Indeed, the history of transport policy has been one of the gradual erosion of the influence of those member states attempting to sustain, at the Community level, their national interventionist traditions. However, the differing views as to the nature of a CTP, and the political debate about the appropriate boundaries for 'subsidiarity', ensured an impasse in its evolution for the first two decades of the Community. As in other areas of policy, it was the commitment to the establishment of the SEM by 1993 that broke the log-jam of policy development.

The success of the transport dimension of the SEM initiative has had a major impact on the internal transport market of the EU, laying the foundations for fair and competitive market conditions. However, the greatest weakness of the CTP as it has evolved is its failure to establish a clear system of infrastructure pricing that can take account of the social and environmental costs that each mode of transport imposes. Until this is achieved significant distortions will remain, imposing substantial economic costs. However, since no member state has found this an easy issue to address at the national level, it would be harsh to condemn the Union for the lack of progress that it has made.

References and further reading

Abbati C 1986 Transport and European integration, *European Perspectives*, CEC.

AEA 1990 *Association of European Airlines Yearbook*, Brussels.

Button K and **Swann D** 1989 European Community airlines, deregulation and its problems, *Journal of Common Market Studies*, Vol. XVII, June.

Commission EC 1961 *Memorandum on the General Lines of a Common Transport Policy*.

Dearden S 1990 Road freight transport, social cost and market efficiency, *Royal Bank of Scotland Review*, No. 168, December.

Erdmenger J 1983 *The European Community Transport Policy*, Gower, Aldershot.

McGowan F and **Trengove C** 1986 *European aviation, a common market*? Institute of Fiscal Studies, London.

Papaioannou R and **Stasinopoulos D** 1991 The road transport policy of the European Community, *Journal of Transport Economics and Policy*, Vol 25, May.

Pryke R 1991 American Deregulation and European Liberalisation, in Banister D and Button K, *Transport in a Free Market*, Macmillan, London.

Stasinopoulos D 1991 The Second Aviation Package of the European Community, *Journal of Transport Economics and Policy*, Vol. 25, January.

Whitelegg J 1988 *Transport Policy in the EEC*, Routledge, London.

CHAPTER 13

The Common Agricultural Policy

John Gibbons

Introduction

There was a time when agriculture in Western Europe was most affected by the changing seasons, the whims of climate and disease and the odd warring tribe. In recent times European farmers have tended to reflect on a host of other forces affecting their occupation. These include consumer and environmental lobbies, the closure of lucrative Middle-East markets through war and instability, increasing competition from producers outside the EU, the low earning potential of small holdings, the reform proposals of EU officials and the criticisms of GATT negotiators. But the picture is not altogether as bleak as it is sometimes painted, particularly for Europe's large farmers who have basked in the privilege of large supports from the EU since the 1960s based on a regime of price guarantees. This has ensured that while all farmers gained something, the large farmers gained most of all.

When the EEC was established in 1957 memories of food shortages were still fresh from the experience of the Second World War. Article 39 of the Treaty of Rome thus prominently declared the objectives of a Common Agricultural Policy (CAP) as follows:

(a) to increase agricultural productivity

(b) to ensure a fair standard of living for the agricultural community

(c) to stabilise markets

(d) to assure the availability of supplies

(e) to ensure that supplies reach consumers at reasonable prices.

To achieve these objectives the member states set up the European Agricultural Guidance and Guarantee Fund (EAGGF) to finance a price support system and the development of the structure of European agriculture. The Price Guarantee Section has operated by a series of target and intervention prices aimed at market stability. This is achieved by an annual price review, and by creating market intervention systems which vary from product to product. The Guarantee Section has also provided subsidies in the form of export refunds when the price of EU farm goods set by the CAP is higher than world market prices. The Guidance Section of the EAGGF has funded improvements in rural infrastructure to help individual farmers and regions within the EU attain the goals set out in the CAP. The question arises as to why a common agricultural policy which is expensive and complex to operate was created, and why it is sustained in the face of strong criticism. Embodied in the objectives of the CAP were elements of the agricultural policies which already existed at national level in a number of member states. Agricultural protectionism had been established in many countries since the 1930s. The tradition of support for agriculture in Europe was also in part a recognition of the special problems of that sector. These included the impact of the vagaries of climate on planned levels of agricultural production, leading in a free agricultural market to extreme fluctuations between scarcity and over-supply, and consequent price fluctuations. These factors may be illustrated by Figure 13.1.

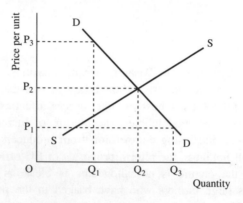

Figure 13.1 Supply and demand in agriculture

High price levels represented by P_3 occur as a result of shortages due to low production levels Q_1, such as those that result from poor weather conditions. Exceptional farming conditions generate high production levels Q_3 and low prices P_1. Equilibrium occurs at production levels Q_2 and price levels P_2. However, price will fluctuate around this equilibrium level. The more price-inelastic the demand curve, the greater will be the magnitude of these fluctuations. Agricultural products are also susceptible to price fluctuations arising from the fact that output cannot be immediately adjusted to current market prices: this can give rise to cobweb-type cycles. Other problems of the agricultural sector in Western Europe have included the low income elasticity of demand for agricultural products relative to many industrial sectors. Thus as incomes have risen generally in Western Europe, demand for agricultural products has not increased at the same rate and accordingly the proportion of income spent on food has declined. Technological advances affecting output have increased the supply of agricultural goods, but because of decreasing returns to scale in agriculture, and the relative inflexibility of farm sizes, the rate of increase has been less than that experienced in manufacturing industry. The result of these and other economic problems which are peculiar to agriculture has been that most governments, encouraged by agricultural pressure groups and in some cases fearful of the electoral revenge of the farming community, have intervened with agricultural support measures. By one means or another these have been aimed at maintaining a constant supply of agricultural goods at stable prices and protecting farm incomes from severe decline.

How the CAP works

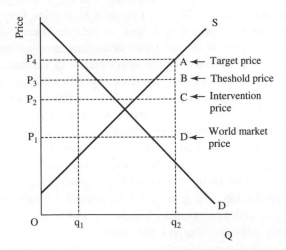

Figure 13.2 The CAP pricing system

A stylised version of the CAP pricing support system can be illustrated using Figure 13.2. This example is based on the market for wheat. The market for other agricultural products is somewhat different, but the general principles used here can be applied to many of the products which the CAP covers. A target price is set on a yearly basis to achieve a desired wholesale price in the city of Duisburg in Germany. As Duisburg is faced with poor levels of local supply of wheat, the price in Duisburg is likely to be higher than the EU average. This price is shown as P_4 in Figure 13.2. A threshold price is then calculated by allowing for transport and distribution costs of wheat from the port of Rotterdam. This is shown as the price P_3 in the figure. To ensure that imported wheat does not enter the EU at a price less than the threshold price, a variable import levy is imposed. This is equal to BD in Figure 13.2, i.e. the difference between the world market price P_1 and the threshold price P_3. In Figure 13.2 the target price results in excess supply of the amount q_1–q_2. To keep the market price close to the target price the authorities must remove this excess supply from the market. This is achieved by setting an intervention price, usually some 10 to 15 per cent below the target price. In Figure 13.2 this is given by the price P_2. If the market price of wheat falls to P_2 the authorities will enter the market and buy wheat to support the price. If the target price, supported by the import levy, is consistently above the equilibrium price, the authorities will have to buy wheat regularly to support the market price. This is the origin of the large stocks of foodstuffs which are associated with the CAP, and is the source of the large budgetary costs of operating the system. An easy way to reduce these stocks of foodstuffs would be to export them. However, this cannot be done without an export subsidy to bring the price down from the intervention price to the world market price. An export subsidy of CD is required in order for it to be possible to export this good. The use of such export subsidies by the EU has resulted in conflict with countries who are major exporters of agricultural goods, as they have rightly claimed that this is an unfair trading practice.

Problems with the CAP and possible solutions

While the objectives of the CAP were formulated mainly in recognition of the special problems in the agricultural sectors in Western European economies, they also took account of an additional political question, which was how to balance the national interests of the members of the EEC. In the case of the two major economies involved in the establishment of the EEC, West Germany was attracted by the opportunities of an industrial free trade area, while France saw market advantages for its relatively efficient agricultural industry. The establishment of the CAP brought about price levels in agriculture which were significantly higher than those prevailing in most member states before the CAP. Under pressure from an electorally significant farm lobby the German government refused to open its borders to a free community agricultural market unless common prices for cereals were set at levels favourable to its own farmers. This set in motion a high-price policy in the CAP. It is perhaps not surprising therefore that a major factor in European agriculture since the early 1960s has been the steady increase in production, which in time went beyond self-sufficiency in many sectors and created an export potential. For example, in the early 1980s the EC became an exporter of beef and cereals, having been previously a net importer.[1] From 1964, when common price levels for cereals were set at German price levels, the CAP has provided farmers with a strong incentive for expanding production.[2] Through the EAGGF it has also absorbed much of the EU budget in support of those prices. This has generated debate outside the agricultural sector about the equity of such high levels of subsidisation for Europe's farmers.

There are theoretical solutions to these problems. If it is accepted that some sort of support for farmers is required because of the factors outlined above, and because of the strategic importance of food supply, then three possible solutions may be considered: a modified CAP system, a direct subsidy system and a direct income support system.

Assuming that there is a perfectly competitive market for agricultural products, and that the EU cannot affect the world market price of these products, and considering only the partial equilibrium effects, then Figure 13.3 can be used to illustrate the effects of these three possible systems.

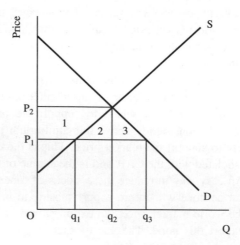

Figure 13.3 Alternative systems for supporting farmers

The world market price of P_1 would result in domestic demand of q_3 and domestic production of q_1 the difference $q_3 - q_1$ would be imports from the rest of the world. The modified CAP system would operate by setting a target price of P_2, thereby eliminating the burden of intervention buying and the need to use exports subsidies to dump agricultural goods on the world market. This would be done by setting the import levy to $P_2 - P_1$, implying zero imports. The welfare effects of this can be examined by use of the loss of consumer surplus resulting from adopting this policy. As the price rises from P_1 to P_2 there is a loss of consumer surplus shown by the areas $1 + 2 + 3$. Of this the area 1 is simply a transfer from consumers to farmers, not a net welfare loss. Area 2 is the cost of the resources used to produce the extra domestic production (i.e. q_1-q_2). This is a net welfare loss as these costs involve the use of resources which could have been used elsewhere in the economy. The area 3 represents the loss of consumer surplus which follows from the fall in domestic demand from q_3 to q_2, resulting from the rise in the price of the good. This is also a net welfare loss. Therefore this CAP type system would lead to net losses equal to areas $2 + 3$. If this system were to have an import levy which allowed for some positive level of imports, the net welfare losses would not change in character, but there would be a transfer from consumers to the government of the importing country. In the EU such revenues are transferred to the budget of the Union. It is left to the reader to work out the details of the welfare effects of such a policy.

A direct subsidy system would operate by granting a subsidy to farmers of P_1-P_2 times $0-q_2$. With this subsidy domestic farmers would increase output to q_2. Domestic consumers would still be faced with a price of P_1, therefore, domestic demand would remain at q_3, but imports would fall to q_2-q_3. Farmers would receive a transfer of income equal to areas $1 + 2$. Of this transfer, the area 1 is simply a transfer from the government to farmers. Area 2 is the same as the area 2 in the modified CAP system outlined above, and is therefore a net welfare loss. Therefore, the direct subsidy system appears to have fewer welfare losses than the modified CAP system, as there is no loss of the area 3 in the subsidy system. This, however, depends on the taxes necessary to finance the subsidies not themselves imposing welfare losses. Economic theory suggests that nearly all taxes will have net welfare losses attached to them. In order for the direct subsidy system to have lower net welfare losses than the modified CAP system, it would be necessary for the welfare losses associated with the taxes to be less than the area 3.

The direct income support system would not affect the price or quantities represented in Figure 13.3. The EU would simply transfer income to farmers to keep them involved in agricultural production. The welfare effects of this would depend on the size of the welfare losses associated with the taxes used to finance these income support schemes. If these losses are less than areas $1 + 2 + 3$, then the income support system would have advantages over the other two systems.

Economic theory, in this very simple example, suggests that the direct income support system is the least-cost method of providing support to farmers. As is outlined below, the EU approach to agricultural support has begun to move in this direction. This change is linked to the various pressures which are being brought to bear on the CAP system.

The pressures to reform the CAP

Some agriculturalists respond to criticism of the CAP by blaming much of its high costs on the failure of the EU to achieve progress in integration in the other sectors of economic activity, and the absence of full economic and monetary union. Thus it is suggested that the links between the production, processing and marketing of agricultural products have not been helped by failings in transport policy and the absence of a common policy on food processing and of common efforts to improve the marketing of agricultural products.[3] Currency differences between member states in the absence of monetary union have also led to the system of expensive subsidies and levies called Monetary Compensative Amounts (MCAs). The CAP has, however, not been immune to change. In order to explore some of the dimensions of this change, three issues are given particular attention:

1.   the international pressure for change which has been notably channelled through the Uruguay Round of GATT negotiations

2.   an internal momentum which has come from within the EC for reform of the CAP, especially during the 1980s and early 1990s

3.   the impact of the SEM, which has particular effects on animal and plant health regulations, and which also offers the potential for the industry to reorganise.

In addition, the system of MCAs is examined below.

The global backdrop to change

The process of integration in European agricultural policy is taking place against the backdrop of a global impetus for change.[4] The impact of the Uruguay Round of GATT negotiations on agricultural trade is perhaps the most important factor. Agriculture has been at the top of the Uruguay Round of GATT negotiations, and has posed a major challenge to the CAP. Previous GATT Rounds achieved multilateral tariff cuts for industrial goods, but were less successful in dealing with agricultural goods. From 1986, when the Uruguay Round began, the USA and the 'Cairns Group' of agricultural exporters sought to bring about changes in international levels of agricultural support.[5] Attention was focused particularly on the high subsidies given to European farmers through the CAP. It has been argued that these subsidies have led to high prices, which in turn have encouraged expansion in agricultural production. This has transformed the EU from a major importer of agricultural goods into a major exporter in recent years. Particular opprobrium has been directed at the EU regime of export refunds for agricultural exporters which ensure the competitiveness of high-priced EU agricultural goods on international markets. This has led to unfair competition and lower prices for other countries who export agricultural products. At the beginning of the Uruguay Round, the USA backed by the Cairns Group first demanded the 'zero option', i.e. the abolition of all supports within ten years, and the introduction of international free trade in agricultural goods. It then revised this proposal to a demand for 90 per cent cuts in export subsidies, and 75 per cent cuts in other supports. The EU argued that free trade in agriculture would lead to violent market movements, damaging to both farmers and consumers. It proposed an international policy of production quotas, and the setting aside of farmland from production. Furthermore, proposals for 'zones of influence' divided among agricultural exporting countries were suggested as a means of stabilising prices and reducing subsidies.

As the GATT talks continued unresolved into the 1990s it became clear that the size of the gap between the EU negotiating stance and that of the USA–Cairns Group on the question of reform of agricultural support in the EU was matched by the size of some of the divisions that were appearing between EU member states on this subject. Eventually after seven attempts to find agreement among the Trade and Agriculture Ministers of the EU on the issue of farm subsidies, an offer was made at the GATT meeting in Brussels in October 1990 of 30 per cent cuts in subsidies backdated to 1986 (a year in which support levels and rates peaked because of poor international market prices). This was equivalent to an offer of a reduction of support for farmers of 15 per cent between 1991 and 1995. In order to achieve agreement between the Trade and Agriculture Ministers of the EU on this negotiating position for the GATT meeting, various safeguards had to be included. These involved, at French insistence, protective measures against the dumping of products such as cereal substitutes on the EU market, and at German insistence a formula to allow almost limitless direct income aid to be paid to rural dwellers. The various negotiating positions of member states in their attempts to reach a common position for GATT were affected by the strengths of their respective agricultural lobbies (e.g. the formidable German lobby led by the German Farmers Union (Deutscher Bauernverland) resisted policies that would adversely affect small farmers) and by the importance of different agricultural product sectors in their agricultural economies (e.g. cereals in France and the UK, beef and milk in Ireland).

The negotiating positions of those participating in the GATT talks were influenced by the different levels and forms of support for agriculture which operated in their countries and trading blocs. Thus, countries such as Australia and New Zealand, with generally low levels of support, strongly advocated reducing the trade barriers to agricultural exports. By contrast the USA and EU, with similar levels of agricultural support, disagreed about what were acceptable forms of support because of variations in their own policy mechanisms. In the case of wheat and maize, for example, 76 and 91 per cent respectively of the support in the EU came from 'market price support' (through minimum import and intervention prices), while in the USA only 17 per cent for wheat, and zero in the case of maize, came from this source. The USA had put much heavier reliance on direct payments to farmers. The bottom line for the USA in its GATT negotiations was that:

> the US [wished] to open up the European Community and Japanese agricultural markets to competition from their low cost supplies of various products and at the same time to eliminate subsidised exports from the EC to third countries.... The EC and Japan however without the same pressures of the US trade deficit were inclined to try to maintain their traditional protectionism for agriculture subject to the dictates of internal budgetary discipline.[6]

The suspension of the GATT talks in Brussels on 7 December 1990 was evidence of the large gap that existed between the EU negotiators and those of the USA and the Cairns Group. Despite the resumption of discussions in February 1991, the persistence of an atmosphere of brinkmanship in the negotiations was a constant reminder of the fragility of the Uruguay Round of trade talks.

The renewal of talks after the suspension was partly a consequence of developments in the EU when new CAP reform proposals, which included the abolition and reduction of some export refunds (notably cereals) began to emerge. These are discussed in more detail below. However, it can be stated at this point that 'the unwillingness of the EU to concede significant reform of the CAP was widely seen as a block to a successful outcome' of the Uruguay Round'.[7] That the European Commission was aware of this perception of EU policy abroad was revealed in the text of its CAP reform proposals of 1991 when it noted that 'our trading partners are becoming decreasingly tolerant of a CAP whose surplus products weigh even more heavily on world markets'.[8]

From July 1991, the EC moved to discuss specific cuts in the three main areas of agricultural protection: export subsidies, support for farmers' incomes and market access. During the remainder of 1991 and the first half of 1992 the Community also undertook what was declared to be a major reform of the CAP.[9] The effect of these changes in the GATT talks was to offer a renewed possibility of overcoming the particular impasse between the USA and the EC on agriculture which was the biggest stumbling block in the way of concluding the Uruguay Round.

However, major obstacles remained. Firstly, there were differences of substance. For example, in December 1991 the then GATT Secretary General, Arthur Dunkel, tabled a set of recommendations covering the main areas of dispute between the USA and the EU on agriculture. One of these recommendations was for a phased reduction in the volume of subsidized agricultural exports of 36 per cent over the years 1993–1999. This was strongly rejected by the EC, as was a revised proposal for a 24 per cent reduction over the same period which the USA presented as its minimum negotiating position.[10]

Secondly, the negotiations during 1992 took place in a highly charged political atmosphere in the EC and the USA. For example, the French referendum on the Maastricht Treaty on European Union in Autumn 1992 ruled out acceptance by France of any deal that could be interpreted by anti-Maastricht campaigners as 'selling out' its agricultural interest and what some regarded as its unique rural way of life. Also, the US Presidential race which climaxed towards the end of 1992 meant that the USA could not entertain second thoughts about its minimum position of the 24 per cent phased reduction in the EU volume of subsidised exports.[11]

Finally, there were the frequent if more minor setbacks which seemed to cloud the main attention of the negotiations. For instance, the whole EU negotiating position seemed to be thrown into disarray when its then Farm Commissioner, Mr McSharry, resigned as Joint EU GATT Negotiator in protest against reported interferences by Jacques Delors, the President of the EC Commission, during talks in Chicago. Only after what seemed to be a humiliating climbdown by Mr Delors did McSharry resume his role in the negotiations.[12]

Despite all these obstacles, a breakthrough seemed apparent in November 1992 when the EU and US negotiators struck a 'deal' aimed at ironing out their particular differences on the issue of agricultural support in the GATT talks. Known as the Blair House Agreement, after the venue in Washington where the deal was struck, compromise was reached on a number of issues including the vexed question of the volume of subsidised exports from the EU when a phased reduction of 21 per cent was agreed.[13]

Selling such a deal in Europe proved more difficult than could have been anticipated by the negotiators. National political interests again threw themselves in the way of an agreed EU position based on the Blair House deal. The French government moved to the political high ground, arguing that this USA–EU deal was not compatible with CAP reforms agreed in May 1992 and that the EU negotiators in Washington had gone beyond the mandate set by the Council of EU ministers.[14] A general election in France in early 1993 produced a colourful rhetoric of opposition to the deal in defence of French national interests and demand for its renegotiation. French farmers took to the streets to air their opposition to the deal. Threats of US sanctions against EU products (including French wines) were turning the conflict into a card game with high stakes.[15]

The brinkmanship continued until early December 1993, just over a week before the deadline of 15 December for the GATT as a whole, by which time the French had gained a considerable number of concessions both in the CAP, during the negotiations on the annual price review (e.g. through extra direct income payments of cereal producers) and in the EU–USA negotiations after the Blair House Agreement (e.g. on the timing of the phased-in reductions on agricultural supports).

The effect these developments had on the efforts to reform the CAP, a process which had begun as a consequence of many internal criticisms before the Uruguay Round of GATT began in 1986, is now examined.

The climate of change in the European Union

In 1987 the Commission described what it saw as the positive achievements of the CAP. It claimed that there had been:

(a) a spectacular growth in agricultural production and efficiency

(b) the security of supply of agricultural products

(c) reasonable prices compared with food prices in other non-EC industrial countries

(d) the protection of farm incomes from fluctuations in world market prices

(e) a contribution to European external trade by encouraging exports.[16]

Critics of the CAP focused particularly on the budgetary cost of the policy, which rose from ECU 4.7 bn. in 1976 to an estimated ECU 32.9 bn. in 1991. They also centred attention on the way in which the budgetary cost of the CAP had been shared out between member states, with the UK in 1979 claiming compensation for what it saw as inequalities in the system of financing the Community Budget (see Chapter 6). Other criticisms have included over-production leading to food surpluses, evidence of illegal and legal abuses of food subsidies, and damage to the environment. Most important, in terms of the direction in which the CAP is now moving, have been the criticisms about the way in which subsidies have been distributed among farmers. The CAP has tended to benefit large farmers much more than small farmers, through a price guarantee system which has ensured that the biggest windfalls from price increases have gone to the biggest producers. This policy has helped to reproduce a pattern within each of the Union states whereby agricultural 'output is dominated by a minority of farmers who have large farms, the remaining majority having small farms and consistently low incomes'.[17]

Arising from such criticisms, some policy changes emerged during the 1980s. The dispute over Britain's budgetary contribution led to the publication of a number of Commission reports on the policy, which eventually led to a notable policy reform in 1984. Production quotas, which have been central to the common sugar market regime since its inception, were introduced to curb milk production in that year. They supplemented co-responsibility levies which were applied to milk from 1977, and were aimed at sharing the cost of surpluses in the sector between producers and the EU.[18] In February 1988 the Council decided, in what is referred to as the Stabiliser Agreement, that the annual growth rate of EAGGF guarantee expenditure should not exceed 70–80 per cent of the annual growth rate of the GNP of the EU. Increases in cereals and oil seed surpluses generated a system of 'agricultural stabilisers' (a policy favoured by the UK government) whereby farmers were penalised by price cuts for excessive production, and the curbing of access to the intervention system of guaranteed prices. Other policies have been introduced since 1988, such as diversifying farms into rural tourism or the craft industries, and the arable 'set-aside' policy whereby farmers have been given direct area compensation payments to leave land fallow and offered large subsidies to encourage them to turn their land area to woodland. Since 1992 this has been emphasised as farmers have been given a new role as stewards of the countryside.[19] In spite of these changes there is still a trend of continuing surpluses and large budgetary costs. In January 1991, in response to the long-term pressures for change from within the EU, and against the backdrop of the suspended GATT negotiations, the Commission approved a 'Communication' (discussion document) by its Agricultural Commissioner, Mr McSharry. In the 'Communication' proposals were made to cut agricultural subsidies radically and reduce quotas. In July 1991, a radical restructuring of the CAP was announced in a detailed plan from the Commission (the so-called McSharry Plan).[20] Significant reductions in support for cereals in particular were anticipated. Most controversial were the proposals to create a two-tier EU farm policy that would mostly favour small and medium-sized farmers. Critics of the plan argued that it placed a burden on efficient EU farmers to bale out 'inefficient small-holders'.[21] Moreover, the growth of third country food imports worried larger EU farmers who were having their production cut back as a result of EU quota restrictions. Criticisms of the proposals stemmed mostly from Britain, Denmark and the Netherlands, who are considered to have larger and more effective farm units. These divisions underlined the difficulty in forging a way ahead, but what seemed clear as proposals to reform the CAP were debated in 1991 was a trend away from production-linked subsidies to income support paid directly to farmers.

The McSharry Plan was for the most part accepted by the Council of Ministers in May 1992, although proposed discriminatory measures between large and small cereals farmers were softened in response to the objections of large farmers. The main emphasis was on cereals for which measures were phased in from 1993. These included area aids introduced to compensate farmers for losses in sales revenue for the cereals they were no longer producing in 'set aside' land. Price reductions of 29 per cent for 1995/96 were also agreed with the expectation that by 1995 export refunds might no longer be required in this sector due to possible parity between EU intervention prices and world market prices.[22] Such an anticipated outcome responded to the demands of the USA–Cairns Group GATT negotiators as well as critics of the cost of the CAP budget.

The EU Farm Price Agreement of 1991/92 had reflected the onset of this era of retrenchment and stocktaking of the CAP. Every year the Commission presents a proposal for agricultural support prices and related measures for the coming marketing year. The Council of Agriculture Ministers is supposed to make a decision before the end of March, but in 1991 agreement was slow to emerge, requiring five sessions of talks between February and May. In order to hasten a decision the Commission invoked a clause of the 1988 Stabiliser Agreement, which states that where there is a danger of a budget overrun the Council of Agriculture Ministers must take a decision on the Commission's proposals within two months. The bitter pill of budgetary restraint was hard for some member states to take. While agriculture ministers from ten member states, led by France, lobbied to raise the agricultural budget ceiling, the Commission, supported by agriculture ministers from the UK and the Netherlands, rejected their arguments. On 24 May 1991 a budget was produced which, although not as severe as originally proposed, maintained expenditure below the overall budget guidelines and prepared the ground for the more fundamental reform of the CAP promised by the Commission in the McSharry Plan. Part of the cause of the budget problem in 1991 was the weakness of the dollar and the cost to the EC of supporting huge surpluses in beef (nearly at record levels), milk and sugar. Another factor was the cost to the CAP of the re-unification of Germany (see Chapter 18).

In 1990 this added to the pressures for change in the CAP, particularly in the hard-hit beef and milk sectors. At a time when the Commission had been trying to find ways of reducing the cost of the CAP there was a necessity for increased reliance on 'safety net' intervention in the beef sector, with the EC accepting all tenders of beef. The loss of important markets in the Middle East due to the Gulf Crisis, the disease scares of 1989/90 and the general decline in consumer preference for beef products also hit the sector badly in 1990/91. In an attempt to gain hard currency many Eastern European countries dramatically increased exports of beef to the EC. In Eastern Germany producers were forced to sell half a million cows because of milk quota restrictions, thus adding to market and policy uncertainties.

By the time of the 1993 price review the situation was just as critical, for different reasons. The new farm commissioner Mr Rene Steinchen warned that there was no extra money to meet the wish-lists of European farm organisations. Yearly price cuts arising from the McSharry Plan over the next three years were foreshadowed, although with compensation for farmers in the form of direct income payments. Despite this, the CAP was set to cost ECU 35.1 bn., up by over ECU 3 bn. on 1992. The capacity of EC farm ministers to override Commission recommendations for political reasons was blamed for continuing increases in the CAP, despite reform attempts.[23]

A number of trends are evident in the CAP in the early to mid-1990s. In the first place the EC agriculture support package is being gradually reformed if not quite reduced in its cost. Secondly, farmers are to be assisted in adjusting to the new climate by a number of accompanying measures, for example direct income subsidies.[24] Thirdly, the reform process in the CAP increasingly dances in time to the sounds emerging from the Uruguay Round of the GATT negotiations, affecting farmers accordingly. Farmers are also being affected by the SEM developments.

The impact of the single market

The main pre-Single European Market business in the agricultural sector has been completed since mid-December 1992, just two weeks before the deadline and after a global agreement on a package of measures ranging from the future agrimonetary regime to the new EU system for the banana market.[25] Agriculture in the EU and its related industries are also changing in many ways in response to the SEM generally. The elimination of physical barriers to trade simplifies intra-Union transport of agricultural products, the elimination of technical barriers to trade increases competition between member states for food products; and the elimination of fiscal-related barriers to trade affects farm input costs such as farm machinery, fertilisers and feeding stuffs. While farmers can in general expect cheaper input prices as a consequence of competition between input suppliers and manufactures, they can also expect greater intra-EU competition to exert downward pressure on product prices. The harmonisation of health and other regulations, the restructuring of the food industry and the abolition of MCAs affect increasingly the market conditions in which farmers operate. Some are affected more than others, and changes in regional policy resulting from the SEA also have an impact on the farmers of the Union.

Harmonisation affecting the agriculture and food industries

The EU has adopted legislation covering methods of producing, processing and marketing agricultural products and foodstuffs. In 1970 it laid down the conditions which additives to animal feeding stuffs must meet to be authorised in the EEC. In 1976 EEC legislation laid down maximum levels for pesticide residues on and in agricultural products. A Directive was adopted in 1981 governing residues of veterinary medicinal products in foodstuffs.[26] The impetus for change in this area has been hastened by the SEM. This is indicated by the fact that 74 of the 300 measures envisaged in the 1985 White Paper 'Completing the Internal Market' concerned animal, plant health and veterinary regulations. The main objective of the Commission has been to ensure that all member states harmonise their approaches to animal and plant health to ensure free trade within the EU.

   The main threat perceived by agricultural producers and traders in the member states has been that the abandonment of border controls will increase the risk of infection as live animals move freely from one part of the EU to another. Fears on this issue arose in 1989/90, when the UK had to accept a ban on exports to other parts of the EU of some of its livestock because of fears about the spread of bovine spongiform encephalopathy (BSE or 'mad cow disease').[27] Division has also existed among member states over the Commission's plans to end the vaccination of live animals against foot and mouth disease, and to introduce instead an EU-wide policy of compulsory slaughter in the event of an outbreak of the disease. But the achievement of these objectives has important trade implications for the EU as a whole, which are used to justify their introduction. Important overseas customers for the EU's $1 bn. of pigmeat exports, such as the USA, Japan and other countries of the Pacific, will accept only meat which comes from non-vaccinated areas (e.g. UK, Denmark and Ireland). The creation of a Single Market which includes vaccinated areas has raised concern that valuable sales outside the Union might be lost.[28] Animal health directives have therefore been aimed at raising standards to the highest level rather than lowering them to the lowest common denominator. They have been supplemented by a variety of emergency plans to notify each member state about the outbreak of disease. The use of hormonal growth promoters in livestock was banned by EU legislation, and levels of antibiotic residue were controlled. In addition, a plant 'passport' system for EU-wide sale of plants was introduced.[29] The difficulties involved in implementing these policies and ensuring compliance in all member states by producers and processors have given rise to some cause for concern and bad feeling between member states.[30] In November 1990 Britain faced investigation by the Commission for refusing to let animals go for slaughter in Spain and Portugal because of animal welfare concerns. Also in that year France imposed a temporary ban on imports of Belgian pigs. New, if exotic, surveillance techniques were promised as the European Commission funded 'spy in the sky' techniques to monitor farming activities in the SEM, which offers the interesting prospect of European integration policy enforcement by advanced technology. Sceptics point to failures to stamp out fraud in the CAP as evidence that a major problem for the SEM will be the enforcement of its rules and regulations. The EU has adopted legislation aimed at a unified policy for the EU in relation to food, covering areas such as additives, materials in contact with foodstuffs, labelling and the official inspection of foodstuffs in retail outlets. This will affect the cost of preparing agricultural products for the market, and ultimately demand for those products. The relationship between food processing and agricultural production is also being affected by SEM changes governing the movement of capital and companies across frontiers. These changes will affect the bargaining position of farmers in the increasingly deregulated market environment.

Free trade and the food industry

To understand the implications of the SEM for the restructuring of the food industry it is important first to disentangle and discuss some aspects of the relationship between food and drink processing and agricultural production. Apart from the obvious relationship of having much of their raw material supplied by the agricultural industry, the food and drinks processing and distribution sectors are linked to agriculture by the operations of the CAP. Intervention storage, disposal subsidies, regulations governing additives and labelling, the MCA system, export refunds and import tariffs all tend to involve food and drink processors at first hand and farmers only in a secondary role.[31] This angers some critics who point out that 85 per cent of the CAP budget goes to food traders rather than farmers because farmers generally do not operate on a large enough scale to meet EU requirements to be classified as suppliers. Because of the high price policy of the CAP, and with the EU market protected to some extent from third country competition, intra-EU trade has increasingly attracted the attention of European food-processing companies. By the standards of the food-processing industries in the US the food-processing sector in the EU is relatively fragmented. Of the top 45 food companies based in the EU, only 10 are present in all of the five largest EU countries.[32] About half of the top 45 food companies are present in only one or two of the largest member states. In general, with a few exceptions such as Unilever, EU food companies have mainly focused on their home country markets. The impact of the SEM on company merger policy is likely to change this, bringing about a consolidation of the EU food-processing industry into fewer and larger firms, and with these firms operating in several EU countries.

The effects of this are likely to be felt by farmers whose bargaining positions will be eroded. In 1990 the five largest retailers in the UK – Sainsburys, Tesco, Argyll, Asda and Gateway – controlled 61 per cent of the total grocery market.[33] The likelihood is that farmers will attempt to protect themselves against such powerful forces by moving closer to the market, establishing their own marketing organisations and thereby attempting to maintain prices in the market-place. The system of MCAs, i.e. border taxes or subsidies on agricultural products, has also affected the input costs of the food industry.

MCAs and the SEM

The system of MCAs in effect has divided the EU into 12 national markets. It was introduced in 1969 when the French franc and the German mark were devalued and re-valued respectively. The MCAs were created to ensure that French consumers and German producers were not penalised by the effects of the exchange rate changes on agricultural prices, and by speculators moving produce from one member state to another to gain advantage from exchange rate windfalls. Farm prices, levy and subsidy rates have been fixed in Brussels in ECUs but have been converted into national currencies by the Commission at fixed exchange rates called 'green rates'.[34] Where the 'green rates' have been lower than the market exchange rates, MCAs have been charged as a levy on imports and a subsidy on exports, and where 'green rates' have been higher than the market exchange rates, MCAs have been charged as a subsidy on imports and a levy on exports. The system has applied to trade in most agricultural products. In recent years there has been a gradual trend towards the dismantling of the MCA system. This has been propelled by moves towards monetary union since the establishment of EMS in 1979, and the subsequent stabilisation of exchange rate fluctuations. In 1984 the process of eliminating the system was advanced by a new method of calculating MCAs. This included the creation of a device called 'switchover' mainly directed at helping German farmers. 'Switchover' ensured that if a strong currency (usually the D-mark) climbed within the ERM against the ECU the effect was not a revaluation of Germany's green rate but a devaluation of everyone else's. The result was 'that German prices expressed in D-marks, would remain constant instead of falling. And prices expressed in all other national currencies would rise.'[35] In July 1988, the Council of Agriculture Ministers and the European Commission declared that they intended to dismantle the remaining vestiges of the system by the end of 1992 and return CAP pricing to a 'real ECU' basis. In July 1990 it was reported that practically all British MCAs had been eliminated by the strength of sterling.[36] The Farm Price Agreement of May 1991 formalised this when it was decided to dismantle UK monetary gaps entirely. Only Greece, Portugal and Spain in July 1991 still had green rates which were not perfectly aligned with market rates.[37] In the eyes of critics, what remained of MCAs was an important obstacle to the idea of a single market in agricultural products. However, it was expected that the success of the EMS and progress towards EMU would eventually eliminate this obstacle to an SEM throughout the EU.

The crisis that befell the ERM in the autumn of 1992 (see Chapter 4) showed how premature were such expectations, undermining as it did the project of EMU. None the less, the EU maintained its commitment to the goal of abolishing MCAs on 1 January 1993. It duly did so, but declared that it would retain the 'switchover' mechanism 'for at least a further two years'.[38] This was a costly decision taken by farm ministers for political reasons (with the main benefits going to German farmers) contrary to the recommendations of the Commission. The mechanism had led to price rises for most farmers of over 20 per cent since its inception in 1984, and with the currency turbulence it was estimated that the cost to the agricultural budget of this single item would be ECU 1.5 bn. leaving little room for manoeuvre in meeting additional demands such as those being made by the French government in their campaign against the Blair House agreement in the GATT Round discussed already in this chapter.[39]

The near-collapse of the ERM in August 1993 led to further crisis and the consideration of further options to save the CAP pricing structure, but possibilities for action were limited. The availability of options was reduced on the one hand by commitments being entered into in the

Uruguay Round of GATT negotiations to cut subsidies to farmers in the EU, and on the other hand by the EU's own guideline on farm spending as a proportion of the total EU budget. By early 1994 the commitment to stay within the agriculture guideline on spending was weakening as, amongst other factors, the cost of maintaining the inflationary switchover mechanism continued to spiral.

Agriculture and regional and social policy

Although overshadowed by the market and farm-price supporting system of the EAGGF (Guarantee Section), the Guidance Section of the EAGGF has expanded in an *ad hoc* way since 1964, when it was agreed to make Guidance Section grants for up to 25 per cent of the cost of approved projects which would serve to improve farm structures.[40] In 1972, three further directives of relevance to farming were adopted. They covered the modernisation of farms, early retirement for farmers and training and advice.[41] These policies were inspired by the 'Mansholt Plan' of 1969 through which the Commission attempted to set out its long-term objectives for EEC agriculture. In 1975 the policies were expanded by directives on 'Mountain and Hill Farming and Farming in Certain Less Favoured Areas'. Other initiatives such as the Mediterranean Policy of 1977 were aimed at farm structures in areas like the Mezzogiorno and Corsica, and in 1981 there was an expansion of EAGGF support for Mediterranean regions and the West of Ireland.[42]

During the 1980s the trend has been towards integrated regional development where improvement of farm structures is seen as part of a wider policy of reshaping the socio-economic environment of poorer regions. The initiative of the SEM took place against this backdrop. If the SEM were implemented in the absence of policies for the poorer regions, the already advantageous position of the strong central economies would be further consolidated. To help the poorer peripheral regions, which include many rural areas, the Structural Funds were revamped to act as a form of compensation to disadvantaged areas through directly transferred resources. There are three components of the Structural Fund: the ERDF, the ESF, and the Guidance Section of the EAGGF. They are intended to help make the idea of the SEM more palatable to the member states in which poorer regions are situated, and to help those regions compete in the new conditions. The inclusion of regional policy in the SEA under the title 'Economic and Social Cohesion' implies that the fundamental objective of the EU is the creation not just of a large free-trade area, but also of genuine European economic integration. At the EU Summit meeting of February 1988 a milestone was reached in the development of the EU in that agreement was achieved on a number of interrelated issues, namely, the financing of the overall EU Budget for the next five years, the CAP budget for the next five years, and the doubling of the Structural Funds by 1993. The Maastricht Agreement, with its provision for a Cohesion Fund and a Committee of Regions, reinforced this trend towards greater emphasis on regional investment (see Chapter 4).[43]

Conclusion

Major forces for change in EU agriculture have emerged from the Uruguay Round of GATT negotiations, the internal pressure for reform of the CAP and the creation of the SEM. They are shaping an industry which is increasingly open to world market competition, which is supported less by EU production-linked subsidies and more by direct income support. Increasingly the industry will have to respond to the demands of the environmental and consumer lobbies. There is also a tendency towards fewer but larger farms, and a corresponding exodus from the land of many smaller producers. As a result of the GATT talks the reduction of export refunds for exporters of agricultural products is making the highly priced products of EU farmers less competitive in world markets. The gradual lowering of EU import thresholds is also enabling more agricultural imports from other countries to compete with EU farmers.

In the CAP the freezing or reduction of common prices for agricultural products has gradually moved EU agricultural prices closer to world price levels, and combined with the 'set-aside' schemes, agricultural stabilisers and quotas, may reduce the budgetary cost of the CAP, but may also have the effect of reducing EU farmers' share of the European market in agricultural goods. The growing emphasis of EU policy-makers on direct income support, however, maintains the principle that EU farmers should be protected. This may also be the method of protecting farmers which has the lowest budgetary cost. The efforts by policy-makers to placate environmentalists by paying some farmers to be guardians of the countryside also offers a way of keeping some farmers in gainful employment. With the creation of the SEM the harmonisation of production, processing and marketing standards is leading to more market integration, which may marginally lower farmers' input costs, but certainly puts increased competitive pressures on the market for agricultural products and processed goods.

Finally, the inexorable exodus from the countryside continues, despite the protests by many farmers' organisations across the EU, and the demands for assistance from the national governments of member states. With membership of the EC, member states handed over most agricultural policy-making to Brussels, and are now unwilling, or unable, to step in again. The livelihood and way of life of many farmers meanwhile is disappearing, leaving the land of rural Europe to an agricultural elite of large producers.

Notes

1. **Commission EC** 1987 Twenty years of European Agriculture, *Green Europe*, Brussels, p. 45.
2. **Hill B** 1984 *The Common Agricultural Policy: Past, Present and Future,* Methuen, London, pp. 22–23.
3. **Commission EC** 1983 Implications for the agricultural sector of the lack of matching degree of integration in the other areas of Community Policy, *Green Europe*, Brussels, pp. 5–7.
4. **Matthews A** 1988 *The Challenge of 1992 for the Rural Economy*, TEAGASC–AFDA Conference Paper, Dublin, p. 12. This paper identifies the background factors which affected USA/EU relations over agricultural matters such as the Third World debt crisis and U.S. interest rates.
5. The Cairns Group consists of largely agricultural export-oriented countries which have joined together since 1986 to present common positions on the GATT farm talks. Its members are Australia, Argentina, Brazil, Canada, Chile, Colombia, Fiji, Hungary, Indonesia, Malaysia, New Zealand, Philippines, Thailand and Uruguay.
6. **Coleman D** 1990 *GATT Negotiations and their Likely Effect on British Agriculture*, Manchester University, p. 4.

7. **Swinbank A** 1993 CAP reform, *Journal of Common Market Studies*, Vol. 31, No. 3 September, p. 360.

8 *Agra Europe*, February 1991, Green Europe Supplement, London, p. 17.

9. **Commission EC** 1991 *The Week in Europe*, p. 1.

10. *Agra Europe*, 3 July 1992, p. 2.

11. *Agra Europe*, 10 July 1992, p. 3.

12. *Agra Europe*, 6 November 1992, p. 3; 13 November 1992, p. 1 (supplement E).

13. *Financial Times*, 21 November 1993, p. 1.

14. *Financial Times*, 18 March 1993, p. 32.

15. *Financial Times*, 16 September 1993, p. 6; 21 September 1993, p. 1.

16. **Commission EC** 1987 The Common Agricultural Policy and its Reform, *European Documentation*, Brussels, pp. 64–68.

17. **Hill B** 1993 Agriculture, in Johnson P (ed.) *European Industries*, Edward Elgar, Aldershot, p. 28.

18. **Hill B** 1984 pp. 121–122.

19. **Swinbank A** 1993 p. 363.

20. *Green Europe*, January 1991, p. 15; Communication of the Commission to the European Parliament – The development and future of the CAP, July 1991.

21. *The Independent*, 5 February 1991, p. 10.

22. **Swinbank A** 1993 pp. 361–362.

23. *Financial Times*, 4 February 1993, p. 30.

24. *Agra Europe*, December 1990, Green Europe Supplement, p. 13.

25. *Agra Europe*, 18 December 1992, p. 1 (Supplement E).

26. **Commission EC** 1990 *From the Farmer to the Consumer*, pp. 16–19.

27. *Agra Europe*, February 1990, Green Europe Supplement, p. 20.

28. *Financial Times*, 24 January 1993, p. 26.

29. Com(88) final OJ 81, 10 April 1989.

30. *European Parliament News*, 2 April 1990, Dublin, p. 4.

31. **Coleman D** 1989 *Changes in UK Agriculture caused by joining the EEC*, Manchester University Press.

32. **Irish Farmers Association** 1988 *Guide to the Single Market*, IFA, Dublin, p. 13.

33. *Farmers Guardian*, 15 February 1990, p. 8.

34. *Agra Europe*, January 1991, CAP Monitor, p. 201.

35. *The Economist*, 25 September 1993, p. 54.

36. *Irish Farmers Journal*, 4 July 1990, p. 9.

37. *Agra Europe*, June 1991, Green Europe Supplement, p. 29.

38. *Agra Europe*, 27 November 1993, p. 16.

39. *Financial Times*, 4 February 1993, p. 30.

40. Regulation EEC No. 17/64.

41. Directives 72/159/EEC and 72/161/EEC.

42. For example, Regulation EEC Nos 1362/78 and 1820/80.

43. ISEC B25/92, 29 September 1993, p. 6.

CHAPTER 14

External trade policy

Keith Penketh

Introduction

The commitment of the EU to free multilateral trade is shown by the membership of all its member states of GATT. GATT was established in 1948 in an attempt to avoid the adoption of trade restrictions which had characterised much of trade in the 1930s. A key principle of GATT is that there should be no trade discrimination against members of the organisation. This implies that the most efficient producer should supply the market regardless of the country of origin of the good or service. This principle has not been attained among the GATT members, and the EU operates on the basis of discriminating against non-members by the operation of the CET. GATT has therefore had to adapt or develop rules to take account of trading blocs such as the EU. Regional trading blocs such as the EU are not therefore illegal under GATT rules, but they are against the spirit of the GATT principles. In 1962 the Council of Ministers gave the Commission the power to institute and operate a common external policy. Relations between GATT and the member states of the Union are therefore mainly the responsibility of the Commission, which in turn takes its general stance on international trade matters from the Council of Ministers. Negotiations on the various trade rounds of GATT are conducted by the Commission on behalf of the Union, and as the EU is the largest trading bloc in the world this gives it a major influence at GATT rounds. The EU also has many trade agreements with non-members. These include Associate Membership agreements and preferential trade arrangements such as those with the African, Caribbean and Pacific countries (ACP agreements) carried out under the auspices of the Lome conventions, and the Commission also negotiates on trade in clothing and textiles between the developed and developing countries in the Multi Fibre Arrangement (MFA). The fact that the EU is the largest exporter and importer in the world also means that any disputes about world trade will normally involve it. The EU is often involved in disputes with major trading nations such as the USA and Japan over trading practices. Many of these disputes are about the trading practices of the EU, particularly concerning the operation of the CAP and other Union restrictions on trade. Other disputes are about practices of the USA or Japan which allegedly inhibit imports into these countries. Moves to liberalise trade in services and to open up public procurement contracts to international tendering are also heavily influenced by the policies of the EU, which is therefore an active participant in all the key issues affecting world trade. Consequently the common external policy of the EU plays a major role in the operation and development of the world trading system.

The Common Commercial Policy

The Common Commercial Policy (CCP) of the EU is to be distinguished from other international relations of the Union. Externally at a political level the EU attempts to present a European dimension to the outside world on those extra-EU issues which lie outside the confines of the CCP. The EU has fostered European political cooperation, and has also assumed an implicit external interest on such matters as the environment, law of the sea, Middle Eastern and South African affairs. Many other political issues are also jointly discussed.

With reference to external trade policy, Article 3 of the Treaty of Rome specifies that the activities of the EU shall include a common customs tariff and a common commercial policy with third countries. Commercial policy is further detailed in the Treaty in Articles 110 to 116. Examples of what are included in CCP are given in Article 113. This includes changes in tariff rates, trade agreements, cooperation agreements, export policy and measures to protect fair trade. In practice, commercial policy relates to any measure affecting the flow of trade between the EU and the rest of the world. It is normally taken to cover trade in services in addition to goods. The EU's powers under the CCP are exclusive, and are not subject to unilateral action by individual countries (Bourgeois 1987).

The significance of commercial policy has diminished since the original six formed the EEC. The reasons for this are twofold. Firstly, the formation of the customs union has naturally fostered the growth of internal trade relative to extra-trade. Secondly, the expansion of the EU from six to twelve members has had the effect of internalising what was originally external trade. In 1955, intra-EU trade of the original six was just under 35 per cent of total trade. By 1990 intra-EU trade had risen to 60 per cent of visible trade. These figures do, however, conceal considerable inter-country difference between intra- and extra-trade proportions. At one end of the scale was the UK, with the highest proportion of extra-EU trade at 47 per cent, while Belgium/Luxembourg had 27 per cent extra-EU trade. The shrinkage of extra-EU trade in these terms should not conceal the importance of the extra-trade for the EU. The EU is the world's largest trading bloc. In 1990 extra-EU trade was 20.7 per cent of world trade compared to 16.8 per cent for the USA and 9.7 per cent for Japan. The share of EU trade in goods and services (exports and imports) as a proportion of GDP stands at 25 per cent. In these terms extra-EU trade is not insignificant.

EU trade is obviously important to the prosperity of her trading partners. While the USA is still the largest single exporter to the EU, the cumulative growth of trade from China and Japan over the past ten years is exceptional (see Table 14.1).

The significance of commonality with regard to the CCP requires some explanation. Commonality does not mean that all traded goods are treated equally: indeed, whole commodity sectors are specially protected. Nor does it imply that there is no difference in the treatment of third countries. A primary objective of the CCP is to secure uniformity of treatment by EU members in trade relations with third countries. It is uniformity of treatment across internal members in relation to third parties which is important, and which gives commercial policy its commonality. Unfortunately it cannot be claimed that even this fairly modest objective has been attained. Some aspects of commercial policy bear differently across EU members in relation to commodities or countries. The doctrine of the 'level playing field' in matters of external trade relations has not yet been attained. There are certain aspects of commercial policy where there are no inter-country differences. The cornerstone of

Table 14.1 Top trading partners of the Community: imports

Country	ECUm. 1990	Share in total imports 1990 (%)	Cumulative growth 1980–1990 (%)
USA	85 182	18.4	78.4
Japan	46 224	10.0	230.9
Switzerland	34 338	7.4	118.1
Austria	20 989	4.5	194.1
Sweden	19 296	4.2	61.9
former Soviet Union	16 749	3.6	47.2
Norway	16 465	3.6	98.3
China	10 603	2.3	437.1
Finland	10 438	2.3	125.5
Canada	9 409	2.0	47.2

Adapted from Table 83, European Economy No. 52 Eurostat

commercial policy, namely the CET, is common to all participants. It is in aspects of the 'new protectionism' that a lack of commonality arises. In what follows the focus is firstly on the aims of the CCP as formally described by the Treaties. These aims can be evaluated in the light of trading practices which have arisen. Secondly, the nature of discrimination with regard to the extra-trade of the EU is described. Here the emphasis is not only on sectoral discrimination but also on third country relations which are discriminatory. The nature of agreements possible with third countries within the EU's treaty-making powers is discussed. To complete this section legitimate measures of protection which may be used against unfair or illicit trade are examined. Thirdly, the implications for the EU's external market, given the completion of the SEM, are discussed. Finally, the difficulties of completing the Uruguay Round negotiations and the effects of this on the external trade policy of the EU are examined.

Aims of the CCP

The CU aspect of the EU is the establishment of a discriminatory trading area. It is perhaps surprising to observe that the aim of the CCP as outlined in Article 110 of the Treaty of Rome is to progressively abolish restrictions on international trade and to lower tariff barriers.

Certainly the EU had with other countries in GATT succeeded in lowering duties against third countries. The EU participated in the various GATT rounds, namely the Kennedy, Tokyo and Uruguay rounds. It is estimated that in 1988, tariffs on the main industrial goods had declined to an average of 4.7 per cent. There are obviously individual product variations from this average: for instance, the tariff on imported cars stands at 11 per cent. However, this decline in protectionism has been countered by an increase in protection. Protectionism is distinguished from protection by the fact that it is an attempt to protect domestic industries from fair external trade practices, whereas protection is a legitimate aspect of commercial policy because it attempts to shield industries against unfair trade practices. It would appear to be the case that currently the EU exhibits a rise in protection, if only manifested by the number of anti-dumping duties levied against specific imports into the EU.

Leon Brittan, Vice President of the Commission of the EU, distinguished between free trade and open trade: 'Open trade is not free trade. Free trade is possible within the Community because the rules guaranteeing a level playing field are strong and are firmly in force. However we cannot yet do away with the old instruments of trade protection: safeguard actions, anti-dumping and countervailing duties where subsidies have been granted contrary to international standards' (Brittan 1993).

Some would question whether this rise in protection represents a legitimate defence of European industry (Hindley 1989). Hindley argues that a liberal estimation of the dumping margin makes it easy to claim that certain imports have been dumped.

The objective of abolishing restrictions progressively on trade with the outside world may appear perverse. It implies that the EU born of the customs union participates in the demise of that very institution which originally formed its foundation. This would doubtless be interpreted by some as weakening the EU. Perhaps expansion in the number of participating countries, the adoption of common policies, and other integration measures are the essence of cohesion in the EU today. Trade discrimination may no longer be of major significance. There is little doubt, however, that some countries both inside and outside the EU do not view commercial policy in this light: here are three examples.

1. In October 1989 the US Secretary of Commerce protested against the proposal by the Commission to pursue a policy of promoting a non-EU broadcasting content in the EU of less than 50 per cent. His allegation pointed to a rise in protectionism and a growth of 'Fortress Europe' (Riddell 1989).

2. In the early part of the 1980s a memorandum submitted by the French government to the European Council linked industrial policy in the EU to lowering internal barriers but raising external barriers. New products were alleged to require a secure domestic market to stimulate development and to enable Europe to reconquer its own domestic market (Pearce and Sutton 1986).

3. More recently Jerome (1992) pointed to a number of trade issues that have caused friction, for example subsidies for the European airbus, prohibitions on the use of meat hormones, and new regulations for slaughterhouse inspections.

However, trade officials within the Commission deny that the EU could become a trade fortress, saying rather that there would be 'an unprecedented wave of liberalism' (Montagnon 1989).

A further aim of the CCP is to assist the Third World and enhance its economic development. Here aid may be in the form of grants to provide assistance when emergencies arise, or more commonly concessions are made in trading relations between EU and Third World countries.

Discrimination by the EU in external trade policy

The external trade policy of the EU has been influenced by various changes that have affected the development of the CCP. Firstly, the establishing of the SEM led to the disappearance, for trade in goods, of internal frontiers. This means that the negotiation of trade policy by the EU with the rest of the world is absolutely vital. Negotiations by the member states are meaningless in a Union with no frontiers with respect to the movement of goods. Secondly, the countries which have adopted the Maastricht Treaty and also envisage monetary union can hardly anticipate the development of unilateral trading policies under irrevocable fixed exchange rates or a common currency. Thirdly, an important principle in the analysis of the international economy is to illustrate that in a 'first-best' world free trade results in gains to the countries participating in trade. Where, however, the world is not first best, but is beset with imperfections, rigidities and immobilities, the introduction of free trade may do more harm than good. Rather than plunge immediately into free trade, a gradual approach may be adopted which allows a phased and careful adaptation towards a wholly open economy with measured shifts in resource allocation taking place. Social and political issues may be paramount. If, for instance, the production of an imported good is based on 'sweated labour', a country may ban the import of such a good in order to discourage unacceptable labour practices. Such social or political gains must be set against the economic cost of these actions. Given that exchange rates do not necessarily respond to the flow of trade, potentially comparatively advantaged industries may be hindered by the failure of the exchange rates to adjust to the dictates of trade. This can occur as relative interest rates and expectations exert powerful influences on exchange rates occasioning industrial dislocation. If the exchange rate mechanism places an industry at a comparative disadvantage, then the short-term reaction will be industrial shrinkage and rising unemployment. However, the long-term future for this industry may not be insecure. If a country does not adhere to a fixed exchange rate regime, then a selective use of external trade policy can offer transitory protection.

The CET is, for the EU, the best known example of a discriminatory trading practice. This measure is reinforced by other measures designed to protect EU industries. Indeed, in its Trade Policy Review of the European Communities, GATT asserts that the CET is not the decisive measure in regulating trade flows. Other protective measures include import prohibitions, non-automatic licensing, import quotas, variable levies, minimum price regulations and export restraint agreements. Such measures are especially applied to what may be termed 'sensitive' industries, in particular agriculture, textiles and clothing, steel, and the car industry.

Additionally, the commercial policy of the EU does not apply with full force to all countries. A considerable number of countries are granted trade preferences. Under the terms of these agreements such countries are less discriminated against than those countries which have not been granted preferential treatment. First, however, let us turn to the sectoral exceptions.

Departures from the principle of free trade in agriculture are well known and discussed further in Chapter 13. Steel is regulated by the European Coal and Steel Community and, as a result of the Davignon Plan (1977), overcapacity and measures to protect the industry from foreign competition were introduced. These measures involved both subsidising domestic industry and the regulation of imports. Indeed, to shield the European steel industry from competition, agreements on minimum prices are made with major suppliers.

Most attention, however, is directed towards the agreement restricting trade in textiles and fibres. There are a variety of reasons for highlighting this sector. Firstly, it is the route by which most developing countries choose to industrialise. Secondly, discriminatory arrangements affecting this sector go back a long time. Britain had negotiated import limitations as far back as 1959 when agreements were reached on cotton textile imports from Hong Kong, Pakistan and India. Thirdly, these industries are often located in the less prosperous parts of a given country. The first MFA covering cotton, man-made fibres and wool was signed in 1974. Initially an annual 6 per cent growth in domestic quotas was agreed, but a very limited growth in domestic consumption arose. In fact consumption of these products within the EU rose by only 1 per cent. In consequence the MFA was renegotiated and the 6 per cent figure for growth in quotas was reduced. Under MFA IV, which was renegotiated for the period 1986–1991, the EU concluded bilateral agreements to limit imports into the EU by use of VERs. Textile exporters were allowed to transfer up to 20 per cent of an unused regional quota to another country. Although a considerable displacement of labour in the textile sector of the EU has already occurred, it seems likely that some kind of special protection for this industry will continue to exist after 1992. Discussions on the MFA in the context of the recent 'Uruguay Round' confirm the view that a version of the MFA is likely to continue into the 1990s. For instance, the proposal of India that current quotas should be frozen and then phased out by 1996 was rejected by the EU. Additionally, the proposal by the EU that the USA should phase out tariffs on textile imports was rejected by the USA on the grounds that the USA was honouring demands by developing countries to phase out quotas.

Among other traded goods discriminated against, imports of automobiles and electronic products are to the fore. Voluntary Export Restraints have been negotiated at both a national and a Community level to reduce imports of these two particular goods. Since the coming of the SEM, however, bilateral national agreements are somewhat redundant and such agreements are now made at EU level.

The principle of non-discrimination in trade enshrined by GATT is further breached by measures taken by the EU which are discriminatory with regard to third countries. Under GATT the 'Rule of Non-Discrimination' is intended to prevent countries from discriminating against trading partners. However, the EU does practice measures which are discriminatory in a third country sense. They arise directly out of the treaty-making powers of the EU. Quite a large number of these trading agreements are linked to Third World countries (Ludlow 1989). A hierarchy of regimes can be distinguished (see Commission EC 1993).

It has been estimated that 60 per cent of the imports that enter the EU are covered by preferential agreements to which the EU is signatory (GATT 1991). Such agreements, however, do not give *carte blanche* to countries to export to the EU duty-free whatever they wish. Exceptions to the full rigours of the CCP are specified. The grantees are required to conduct their trade within the limits of the indicated specifications. Nevertheless, the EU trade agreements with third countries are an important part of the common commercial policy. Unless indicated, the agreements apply without exception to all countries within the EU. It cannot be claimed, however, that the incidence of the agreements is the same among the 12 constituent countries. For example, an agreement which liberalises the importation of textiles into the EU will have a much greater impact on a country where textile production is relatively significant. Thus the textile industry in Portugal is much more important in terms of production and employment than the textile industry in the Netherlands. In these terms, while this aspect of the CCP is common, it is certainly not equitable. In cases where the industrial structure of those countries granted preferential treatment closely resembles the industrial structure of the less prosperous members of the EU, these poorer EU countries shoulder the main burden of granting trade preferences. Yet another argument for an appropriate allocation of the Structural Funds of the EU budget!

Agreements have been made with the following.

1. *African, Caribbean and Pacific countries (ACP)*. Generally these embrace the former colonies of the EU countries. They are the most liberal agreements that the EU has been signatory to. The agreements are contained under the Lomé Convention. Quota limits are waived for industrial goods, and imports are almost duty-free. Imports of agricultural products receive reductions in variable levies but there are some quantitative limits. However, the granting of preferential treatment for some products can mean that restrictions are imposed against imports to the EU from outside ACP. A recent dispute involving the preference given to bananas from some of the ACP countries highlights this issue. This agreement leads to restrictions on the export of bananas to the EU from non-ACP countries. Germany, the leading consumer of bananas in the EU, has protested about paying higher prices for bananas from ACP countries when cheaper supplies are available elsewhere. France and the UK support this preference agreement and wish to uphold the agreement with the ACP countries.

2. *Mediterranean countries*. Agreements which are not identical in their preferences have been made with southern Europe (Cyprus, Malta, Turkey and Yugoslavia), southern Mediterranean countries (Algeria, Egypt, Morocco and Tunisia) and eastern Mediterranean countries (Israel, Jordan, Lebanon and Syria). The agreements made have usually taken the form of trade and cooperation agreements, and for those countries that aspire to join the Union, association agreements are normally made. Both agricultural and industrial preferences are less than given under the Lomé Convention. For instance, tariff quotas are often used to define quantities subject to duty-free entry.

3. *The General System of Preferences (GSP)*. For some less developed countries outside Lomé, the EU has granted GSP status. Formal agreements are not made and reciprocity is not a feature of these preferences. The concessions are revised annually, but they are not as favourable as those under Lomé and the Mediterranean agreements. Korea and Taiwan do not enjoy the benefits of the GSP.

Forms of agreement

Agreements, when they are made, can take various forms. For countries aspiring to subsequent membership of the EU they may take the form of an Association Agreement which will normally aim to secure full participation of the country concerned in the customs union of the EU. Normally, a staged approach is adopted, the transition to full participation possibly taking several years. There is no guarantee that full membership of the EU will eventually be secured. Although agreements between the EU and Malta, Cyprus and Turkey are of this type, there appears to be little immediate prospect of membership for these countries.

Trade and cooperation agreements grant concessions on trade and also provide for technical cooperation and/or financial aid. Agreements with the EFTA countries were initially of this type. These types of agreements may be reciprocal or non-reciprocal. Agreements with EFTA were reciprocal, but agreements with the Maghreb countries (Algeria, Morocco and Tunisia) and the Mashreq countries (Egypt, Jordan, the Lebanon and Syria) were non-reciprocal, simply conferring MFN status by EU countries. It is not that EU countries would not prefer reciprocation, it is simply often politically inexpedient to insist on reciprocation. The USA has made it clear to the EU that retaliatory measures would ensue if the EU insisted on reciprocation in all markets. The possible loss of US exports to countries to which the EU has granted trade concessions has encouraged the USA to take an active interest in the EU's external policy.

Finally, there are simply cooperation agreements which have no direct implication for trade. Thus the agreement between the EU and the Gulf Cooperation Council signed in 1986 for an unlimited period was a cooperation agreement. Cooperation and joint ventures in a number of fields were envisaged.

Mention should be made of the so-called 'Europe Agreements'. These are in essence association agreements and apply to the former collectivised countries of Central and Eastern Europe. Poland, Hungary, the Czech and Slovak Republics, Bulgaria and Romania have concluded such agreements with the EU. The agreements involve reciprocation, but free access will be granted to the EU market in five years, whereas ten years is needed to secure full reciprocation. However, for certain commodities which are regarded as sensitive within the EU protection is to remain in force. Such sectors are agriculture, food processing, textiles, clothing, ores and metals, and chemicals.

It has been argued that these exclusions are wrong-minded, and that free trade should proceed on a broader front (Rollo and Smith 1993). Furthermore, it is reported (Economist Intelligence Unit 1993) that the Commission believes the original timetable for dismantling tariffs and quotas should be dropped and the whole process speeded up.

Protection or protectionism by the EU?

A variety of measures can legitimately be used by EU member countries against unfair trading practices by third countries. Unfairness is defined in terms of the nature of the practice. No attempt is made to provide an invariant standard against which unfairness in a specific case can be measured The following methods of protection may be adopted to inhibit a free, but allegedly unfair, flow of trade:

(i)   anti-dumping duties

(ii) countervailing duties

(iii) safeguard measures

(iv) surveillance measures

(v)   trade deflection measures

(vi) the new commercial policy instrument

(vii) counterfeit goods measures.

It is not normally at the behest of an individual EU member country to impose a protective measure, but rather on the receipt of complaint the Commission has the power of investigation, and subsequently the Council of Ministers may order the imposition of the precise measure. It is, however, often claimed that when these protective devices are used to manage trade they are used to shield 'sensitive' products. The nature of specific practices and related measures is discussed below. An interesting legal view of the measures described is given in Van Bael and Bellis (1990).

Dumping

To qualify for protection by the imposition of an anti-dumping duty an imported commodity must satisfy two conditions. These are firstly that the good must be 'dumped', and secondly that the import must threaten material injury to an established domestic producer (GATT Article 6). Economists have not always been wholly condemnatory of the practice of dumping. Viner, for instance alleged that dumping was harmful if it was not continuous. Continuous dumping could produce consumer gains which exceeded producer losses. Sporadic dumping could displace domestic firms, and after displacement, continue the exports of the good at a relatively high price. There is no time schedule within the policy of the EU to distinguish whether the dumped imports are continuous or sporadic. It is sufficient to establish that the good has been imported below the 'normal' price.

Usually representations are made to the Commission by the relevant trade association of the industry harmed by the dumped import. If the import is found to have been 'dumped', then an anti-dumping duty may be imposed. The rate of duty may be quite high. For instance, in 1988 a 21.9 per cent anti-dumping duty was imposed on imports of video-cassette tapes from Hong Kong. However, anti-dumping duties are usually producer-specific. They are subject to the so called 'sunset clause', i.e. they lapse five years after their imposition.

An exporter whose goods are subject to an anti-dumping duty may have an interest in circumventing the duty. Thus it may attempt to divert part of the manufacture of the good to a third country outside the EU, or indeed to a country within the EU. To meet this contingency the EU has devised Anti-Circumvention Measures. Basically they consist of establishing the conditions under which origin attributable to a particular good may be defined. The so called 'screwdriver plants' in the EU, where the final assembly of a good takes place, are subject to a value added proportion to avoid the incidence of an anti-dumping duty. For instance, if a good has more than 40 per cent local content then anti-dumping duties are not levied. There is however no uniformity of practice. The rules that exist today derive from Regulation 802 of 1968 which defines a product's origin in terms of where 'the last substantial process or operation was performed...resulting in the manufacture of a new product'. In other words, a change in the commodity's Standard International Trade Classification category was necessary. The regulations are, however, often more specific and relate to particular products; for instance on the import of video-cassette recorders from five companies in South Korea and Japan, a 45 per cent local content was defined to confer appropriate origin.

In practice it is not easy to secure the imposition of anti-dumping duties on products assembled within the EU (Commission EC 1989). Conditions which must be satisfied have been designed to reduce overt interference with the inflow of foreign direct investment. Positive action against circumvention is likely to arise only if:

(a) there is an anti-dumping duty in force on imports of the finished product

(b) the assembly operation has to be carried out by a party which is related to or associated with the manufacture of the finished product

(c) the value of parts originating in the country of assembly of the finished product has to exceed by 50 per cent the value of all other parts and materials used

(d) account must be taken of the extent of research and development carried out by the assembler.

These conditions, taken together, are very restrictive. They make action to secure redress against 'screwdriver plants' unlikely, except in a minority of cases. Here, there is the potential for friction within the EU both at an intra-industry and at an inter-country level. Notwithstanding the above, there are those who claim that anti-dumping duties go far beyond use in special cases, but are the principal EU instruments of protection against imports from Japan and east Asia (Hindley 1992).

Countervailing duties

The practice by governments of subsidising the production of goods or/and the export of goods is widespread. The subsidy may be direct (given for reasons of trade) or indirect (not specifically related to trade), but if it causes injury within the EU it is regarded as an unfair trading practice and may have a countervailing duty imposed on imports of it into the EU. The duty is subject to the approval of the Council of Ministers. A restrictive interpretation of the definition of subsidised imports has been used by the Commission, presumably because the practice of subsidisation is widespread within the EU itself. The subsidised imports must satisfy the condition of specificity. This means that the subsidy must be peculiar to that industry. Presumably the small number of countervailing proceedings initiated between 1977 and 1988 (only 12 cases) results from a restrictive interpretation of this regulation. However, difficulties surrounding the calculation of the exact amount of subsidy given may be an additional reason why the regulation is scantily used. When they are used, the duties are country-specific and not company-specific. However, in agriculture for wine, certain fruits and vegetables and fishery products, countervailing charges are imposed if exporters do not comply with established reference prices.

Safeguard measures

An exception to the principle of not imposing quantitative restrictions on imports occurs where imports threaten to cause serious injury to domestic producers. If this is accepted by the Commission then safeguard measures can be imposed consisting of quotas. They may for instance take the form of VERs. Before 1985 it was possible for member states to adopt interim protective measures. Interim protective measures cannot now be imposed unless a safeguard clause is contained in a bilateral agreement between the member state and third country. This principle of 'serious injury' was used to justify bilateral national VERs between a member state and a third country. Today if the Commission recognises damage to EU producers, quantitative restrictions may be imposed for a three year period. Textiles, steel, electronics and cars are all examples of restricted commodities.

Surveillance

Unilateral action can be taken in matters of surveillance. Evidence may be gathered prior to the establishment of a case for Safeguard Measures. Import licences may be required on the importation of certain imports under surveillance which nonetheless are not subject to limitation. They merely provide the evidence from which to pursue where appropriate, a redress to the alleged damage inflicted on the domestic industry. Evidence in support of the EU adopting a more open trade policy since the coming of the SEM is provided by the significant decline in surveillance measures. These were reduced from 1300 in 1990 to 184 in 1991.

Trade deflection measures

Where imported goods are subject to quotas (eg textiles and related products under MFA), an exporter subject to a restriction may attempt to gain access to an EU country through the unprotected market of another. Restrictions on deflected imports require application to the Commission and also authorization. Textiles are held to be most subject to Article 115 authorizations which stipulate that 'the Commission shall authorise Member States to take the necessary protective measures, the conditions and details of which it shall determine'. Here is a case where Article 115 was used to prevent trade deflection through the importation of a restricted commodity through another member state. However, since the coming of the SEM with open internal borders for intra-trade, national restrictions hardly make sense and in consequence Community wide restrictions are imposed. Footwear is a case in point.

New commercial policy instrument

Unfair trading practices are seen to relate not only to imports but also to unfair competition with EU exports in third markets. Illicit commercial practices used by third countries were the reason why the CCP was extended in this direction. The Commission adopts an investigatory role but the Council of Ministers decides on the nature of retaliation. Measures can be quite wide in scope. They range from quantitative controls on the country's imports to import tariffs and the withdrawal of concessions granted in a trade agreement.

Counterfeit goods

Responsibility for action is here left with the national government. Where evidence is positive the goods may be disposed of or other measures of equivalent effect taken. It is worth noting that threatened domestic industries often react by claiming that imports are in fact counterfeit.

Fortress Europe or an open playing field?

The so-called playing field of the EU not only has a level dimension but also an open one. Fears that the EU with an SEM will move towards a 'Fortress Europe' cannot be discounted. The fear has not only been expressed by official representatives of larger third countries with which the EU trades, but also directly by industrialists especially in the Far East. Secretary of

Commerce for the USA, Mr Mosbacher, is quoted as saying 'I'm very disturbed about signs of protectionism or "Fortress Europe" that are beginning to appear.' A Hong Kong industrialist, Mr Tien, who is vice-chairman of the Hong Kong Committee on Anti-Dumping Proceedings, believed that the SEM would bring with it a 'Fortress Europe' mentality. Another source claims that the term 'Fortress Europe' is on close examination one of the sillier slogans of the time (Montagnon 1989). Nevertheless, there are real fears that the completion of the SEM has led to a further movement away from free trade as far as the external trade of the EU is concerned.

The likelihood of more, or less, external protectionism requires careful analysis. Certainly there is evidence from official sources that leads to the belief that there is a distinct possibility of greater external protectionism. For example, in the early 1980s President Mitterand of France deplored the penetration of the EU market in high-technology goods. His solution to enable Europe to reconquer its domestic market was to lower internal barriers and raise external barriers. Also in the early 1980s M. Thorn, then President of the Commission, asserted that Europe needed external protection for its advanced technology industries to enable them to reach international levels of competitiveness. However, times change and in the late 1980s a senior Commission trade official, Mr Johannes-Friedrich Besseler, is reported to have stated that the development of the SEM would release a wave of liberalism, and that the EU could not become a trade fortress even if it wanted to. The SEA does not directly address issues which relate to the CCP. Therefore we must infer from likely developments in the SEM what the probable consequences are for the external market. To enable us to do so it is useful to distinguish between measures which are the automatic consequence of enhancing the SEM, and measures which are discretionary in their external application. The final effect on external trade depends on the balance of the two sets of measures.

There is little doubt that the effect of strengthening the SEM is to encourage the growth of intra-trade at the expense of extra-trade. As is indicated in Chapter 2, the barriers to internal trade are numerous and complex. But whatever the nature of the internal barriers, whether physical, resulting from a lack of standardisation, or a barrier to public procurement, their removal will increase the competitiveness of intra-European trade. Assuming for the time being that the 'status quo' prevails in the rest of the world, the creation of the SEM produces effects which are both trade creating and diverting in the Vinerian sense (see Chapter 1). Certainly some of the increased imports from EU partner countries will replace higher cost domestic production and in consequence will be trade creating. Other intra-EU imports will be trade diverting. This follows from the displacement of third country exports to the EU by intra-EU trade induced by the discriminatory effects of the SEM. It is to be expected that the balance of trade will improve for EU countries but worsen for the rest of the world. Substantial effects on the balance of trade of the EU's principal trading partners are forecast. Bird and Zeller (1989) forecast an eventual worsening of the current accounts of the USA and Japan by $18 bn. and by $10 bn. respectively. Certainly these are not small amounts. Obviously the effects on external trade will be influenced by elasticities of demand and supply. However, other developments are relevant. The growth of positive trade balances in EU countries will inject into them extra demand and therefore output growth. The SEM will initially strengthen the trading balance of the EU with the rest of the world, and hence the trading balance of the rest of the world with the EU will deteriorate. Therefore, the SEM will enhance the growth of EU income but will have a deflationary impact on incomes in countries outside the EU. This relative income effect will stimulate imports into the EU from outside, but will also depress EU exports to the rest of the world. The expectation is that the trade balance of the EU will first improve but ultimately deteriorate. Which of these two forces is likely to dominate depends on the relative size of price and income elasticities of demand. The size of the change in income is of course also relevant. A careful exposition of the analytics of the case was undertaken by Johnson (1961). Bird and Zeller, in their analysis, emphasise the price effect in predicting the outcome of events.

A second influence which is automatic, and which occurs because barriers on intra-trade are eliminated, results from the disappearance of Article 115 of the Rome Treaty. This article is in part intended to prevent deflection of trade and enforce residual restrictions under the so-called 'GATT hard core waiver clause'. The abandonment of internal frontier controls will make it difficult to monitor intra-EU trade. Therefore, it is possible that regional quotas allocated to Member States under the MFA or under the GSP will disappear (O'Cleireacain 1990). However, judging from the discussions at the Uruguay Round it seems unlikely that the MFA will be abandoned. Rather, EU-wide quotas will replace national quotas, but it is difficult to say in advance whether they will be more or less restrictive than existing agreements. However, in 1989 a change took place in the GSP system of the EU. Sub-divisions of EU quotas into national quotas were abolished.

There are indeed areas of EU extra-trade which under the Uruguay Round proposals were due to be liberalised. For the first time, intellectual property, services and agriculture have been placed on the agenda. To date progress appears limited. However, with regard to agriculture Cooper (1989) believes that there will simply be a switch from one form of protection to another. In the SEM he foresees the abandonment of green rates of exchange and monetary compensatory amounts. When a country's exchange rate appreciates against the ECU, and as a result support prices in local currency decline, he believes there will be considerable pressure to raise agricultural support prices and hence offset the improved access to the EU market which exchange rate appreciation would provide. The adjustment in support prices would, however, represent a net increase in protectionism. A country with a depreciating currency is doubly protected. Both the exchange rate mechanism and the higher support price help to protect the domestic producer.

Dornbusch (1990) asserts that the greatest threat to an 'open Europe world partner' is the social dimension of 1992. He states that the possible harmonisation of labour market arrangements, from job security to wages and social security benefits, without proper regard to productivity differentials will make some countries uncompetitive especially in relation to the world outside. The effect will be to produce calls for protection. As the claim for protection is likely to be persistent, and to come from the less prosperous members of the EU, it is probable that calls for protection will be translated into additional levels of protection.

In contrast to aspects of commerce which emphasise a possible protective side to future EU trade relations with third countries, there are features of the present situation which emphasise a growth of liberalisation in trade relations. Not least among these considerations is the reduced significance of extra-trade to the EU. Not only will there be the relative growth of intra-EU trade, as greater freedom is introduced by the growth of the SEM, but there is also the possibility of enlargement of the EU. With this enlargement, there will be growth in intra-EU trade. By definition, extra-trade will not be as large a problem as hitherto. Consequently, the pressures to resist trade liberalisation evident in the Uruguay Round could well recede as the EU experiences both broadening and deepening of the integration process.

Areas in which some countries of the EU have been found to be uncompetitive in, for example, clothing and consumer electronics are those where reorganisation has taken place and/or expenditure on R&D has been undertaken at both a national and an EU-wide level. Sensitivity here should not be as pronounced in the future as it was in the past. Nevin (1990) claimed that the rest of the world could only lose as a consequence of the SEM, largely as a result of trade diversion increasing as the SEM is established. In consequence he suggested that the CET should be reduced as the EU moves towards the SEM.

There is the danger that increased penetration of markets from inside the EU may incline some members to attempt to compensate by reducing the freedom of access of third countries. Such protective practices are less transparent, and less open *vis-à-vis* the world outside than within the EU. It is, however, encouraging to note that a recent GATT report (GATT 1991) states that many national import restrictions have been scrapped.

To summarise, the effects on extra-trade of the development of the SEM are threefold:

1. the amount of trade diversion occasioned by the reduction of non-tariff barriers, and the consequent decline in extra-EU trade

2. the extent to which EU economies grow and the consequent stimulation of extra-EU trade

3. the changes in external barriers which arise as a consequence of these effects.

For countries outside the EU, and indeed outside the trade preferences of the EU, the full rigour of external discrimination applies. Here countries look to the outcome of the protracted Uruguay Round of GATT which commenced in 1986 and was completed in December 1993. The so-called 'Quad Trade Agreement', between Canada, Japan, the USA and the EU gave a push to the lagging round, but it is not clear if this agreement can be successfully adopted by the remaining countries of GATT. Problems remain which have not yet been resolved, for instance reaching a multilateral steel agreement, securing a liberalisation of trade in services, and opening up Japan and Korea to imports of certain agricultural products. Reports from GATT draw attention to the frequent usage of instruments such as anti-dumping duties which are allegedly used for purposes of protection but are, because of their use in practice, better defined as protectionism.

Conclusion

The CCP of the EU has important implications for the world trading system. The growing integration of the member states and the possible enlargement of the EU can only increase the importance of the Union in world trading issues. The following chapters examine the relationship of the EU with the Third World, the rest of Europe and within the Triad.

References and further reading

Bird R and **Zeller S** 1989 Global effects of Europe 1992, Paper presented to the *27th Applied Econometrics International Conference on International Trade*, University of Montreal.

Bourgeois J H J 1987 The common commercial policy – scope and nature of the powers. In Volker E L M (ed.) *Protectionism and the European Community*, 2nd edn, Kluwer, London.

Brittan L 1993 Shaping a framework for global trade: the challenge for the European Community, Jean Monnet Regional Lecture, *European Access*, No. 3.

Commission EC 1989 *Sixth annual report of the Commission on the Community's anti-dumping and anti-subsidy activities*, Office For Official Publications of the EC, Luxembourg.

Commission EC 1991 *Agreements and other related commitments linking the Communities with non-member states*, DG for External Relations, Office for the Official Publications of the EC, Luxembourg.

Commission EC 1993 The European Community as a World Trade Partner, *European Economy*, No. 52, Office for the Official Publications of the EC, Luxembourg.

Cooper R N 1989 *Brookings Papers on Economic Activity*, No. 2.

Curzon G and **Curzon V** 1987 Follies in European trade relations with Japan, *World Economy*, Vol. 10, pp. 155–176.

Dornbusch R 1990 *Brookings Papers on Economic Activity*, No. 2.

Economist Intelligence Unit 1993 External Relations, *European Trends*, 2nd quarter.

GATT 1991 Trade Policy Review of the European Communities, Vol. 1.

Hindley B 1989 The Design of Fortress Europe, *Financial Times*, 24 July.

Hindley B 1992 Anti-Dumping Policy After 1992, paper presented to CREDIT Conference, *European Trade Policy After 1992*, April.

Jerome R W (ed.) 1992 *World Trade at the Crossroads*, University Press of America, New York.

Johnson H E 1961 *International Trade and Economic Growth: Studies in Pure Theory*, Harvard University Press, Cambridge, Mass.

Johnson H G 1958 Economic Expansion and International Trade, *International Trade and Economic Growth*, Allen Unwin, London.

Ludlow P 1989 *Beyond 1992 – Europe and its Western Partners*, Centre for European Policy Studies, Paper No. 38.

Montagnon P 1989 EC could not become a trade fortress, *Financial Times*, 24 July.

Nevin D J 1990 EEC Integration Towards 1992 – Economic Policy European Forum, Vol. 10, pp. 13–62.

News of the Uruguay Round of MTN, November 1989 NUR, No. 32.

O'Cleireacain S 1990 Gaps in the EC's CCP, *Journal of Common Market Studies*, Vol. 28, No. 3, pp. 201–217.

Pearce J and **Sutton J** 1986 *Protectionism and Industrial Policy in Europe*, Routledge and Kegan Paul, London.

Riddell P 1989 Fears of Fortress Europe, *Financial Times*, 18 October.

Rollo J and **Smith A** 1993 The Political Economy of Eastern European Trade with the European Community: Why so sensitive? *Economic Policy*, No. 16.

Van Bael I and **Bellis J F** 1990 *Anti Dumping and other Trade Protection Laws of the EC*, 3rd edn, CCH Editions, Bicester.

CHAPTER 15

The European Union and the Third World

Stephen Dearden

Introduction

The economic relationship between the EU and the developing world has been heavily influenced by the colonial histories of many of its member states. From the inception of the Community France required the inclusion of its overseas territories in the customs union, and special arrangements for Morocco and Tunisia, while Italy sought similar concessions for Libya. Thus under Articles 131–136 of the Treaty of Rome there was provision for 'association' status for non-European countries that had a 'special relation' with Community members.

But some 30 years after decolonisation, does 'dependence' still characterise the economic relationship of the Third World to the EU? Do these countries remain exporters of primary products and importers of European manufactures? For trade remains central to the long-term sustained economic development of less developed countries (LDCs), and is a barometer of the degree of their past success in achieving the necessary structural transformation of their economies. Given this pivotal role of trade to LDCs it is necessary to examine the agreements regulating LDC–EU trade.

Trade preferences

The Lomé Conventions

The first Lomé Convention was signed in 1975, and replaced the Yaounde Conventions which began in 1964 and had mainly benefited the ex-French colonies. Lomé was a response to the entry of the UK and the problem of preserving Commonwealth LDC trade preferences. Although it excluded many of the Asian Commonwealth countries, the number of associated states benefiting from Lomé now totals 69 – the ACP group (Africa, Caribbean and Pacific). Each Convention lasts for five years and has both an aid and a trade component. Lomé offers duty-free access for ACP exports of manufactures and most non-CAP agricultural products. However, subsequent economic pressures have led to the EU imposing selective forms of protection, e.g. textiles. It must also be noted that 70 per cent of ACP exports would have entered the EU duty-free without the Lomé Conventions. The greatest benefit to the ACPs from Lomé arises with products that otherwise face substantial tariffs, and therefore command artificially high prices within the European market. Unfortunately these comprise the smallest category of ACP exports to the EU. In return for these tariff preferences the Community only requires non-preferential and non-discriminatory most-favoured-nation treatment.

The General System of Preferences

For those LDCs excluded from the Lomé Conventions, the General System of Preferences (GSP) is significant. Originally conceived as a worldwide scheme, it was intended to offer duty-free access to developed country markets for LDC manufactured exports. The EU's GSP was instituted in 1971, but the Community's overriding commitment to the ACPs compromised the emergence of any comprehensive concession to LDCs.

Over its history the EU's GSP has become increasingly discriminatory, both by product and by country of origin. Thus from 1986 the GSP was withdrawn from the products of those countries where income per capita was greater than $2000, and where the country's share of EU imports of those products exceeded 20 per cent; in the case of textiles the share limit is 10 per cent. Brazil, Hong Kong, China, South Korea and Singapore have all experienced the withdrawal of some GSP concessions, and some authors have concluded that GSP benefits have been withdrawn from most LDCs' manufactured products that have penetrated EU markets to any significant degree. In addition about 140 sensitive products, including textiles and clothing, are subject to tariff quotas or volume limits under the GSP. Once exports reach their tariff quota, further sales are subject to the higher 'most-favoured-nation'(MFN) tariff arrangements. These tariff quotas or volume limits are often applied by individual EU member states.

Thus the pattern of trade preferences faced by exporters to the EU is a complex one. Seven categories of trade preferences can be identified, as follows.

1.   Tariff-free trade. Trade between member states, and trade in manufactures and processed agricultural products with EFTA and Israel.

2.   Lomé–ACP associated states. Duty-free access for manufactured goods and most non-CAP agricultural products.

3.   'Super GSP', offering duty-free access on a limited range of products; available to the poorest LDCs and, on a temporary basis, to Bolivia, Colombia, Ecuador and Peru from 1990 and Central American countries from 1992 (for agricultural products). These temporary agreements will expire at the end of 1994.

4.   14 Mediterranean countries and Eastern European States. These agreements, which are bilateral, began with a comprehensive Mediterranean Policy agreed by the Council of Ministers in 1972, providing duty-free access for most manufactured goods and tariff reductions for agricultural products, in exchange for MFN treatment for EU exports. However, minimum import prices for agricultural imports were maintained, and subsequent economic pressures have led the EU to impose restrictions on imports of particular products, e.g. textiles.

5.   Non-ACP LDCs qualifying for the GSP, e.g. ASEAN countries.

6.   Other GATT signatories that qualify for MFN status, i.e. Western industrialised countries outside EFTA.

7.   Least favoured: Vietnam, Cambodia, North Korea, Albania and Taiwan.

Patterns of trade

In 1991 the EU imported goods to a value of ECU 150,318 m. from LDCs, of which ECU 19,134 m. was from the ACP countries. In the same year exports to the LDCs as a whole totalled ECU 142.672 m., and of this ECU 15,937 m. went to the ACPs. These figures underline the importance of the EU as both an export market and as a source of imports for LDCs. However, to evaluate the contribution of both Lomé and the GSP to fostering LDC exports we must take a longer-term perspective and examine relative trade performance.

Table 15.1 EU10 Import growth in real terms (in 1980 ECU m.)*

	1958	1970	1980	1984
Intra-EU	40 380	157 094	252 693	279 310
Extra-EU	79 110	161 727	272 899	278 905
LDC	35 370	59 308	116 691	98 588
Other DC	39 300	90 700	133 798	152 108
	in indices (1980 = 100)			
Intra-EU	16.0	62.0	100	110.5
Extra-EU	29.0	59.3	100	102.2
LDC	30.3	50.8	100	84.4
Other DC	29.4	67.8	100	113.7

Source : Eurostat, *Trade Statistical Yearbook,* Luxembourg, 1985
    *Nominal imports deflated by EU10 import unit value

Table 15.2 OECD manufactured imports from LDCs ($bn.)

	Total OECD	USA	Japan	EU	OECD imports from LDCs as % of total import of manufactures	Annual change in volume (%)
1979	60.5	25.7	6.3	21.5	10.1	
1980	69.7	29.4	6.3	25.9	10.3	6.0
1981	75.5	35.3	7.1	24.2	11.5	9.4
1982	76.9	37.6	6.8	23.3	12.0	10.8
1983	86.0	46.4	6.6	23.6	13.1	16.2
1984	108.8	62.6	8.7	25.6	14.5	30.0

Source: OECD Observer, March 1986

In real terms LDC exports have increased dramatically since the inception of the EU. Especially in the 1970s LDC export performance was impressive, growing faster than either developed countries' exports or intra-EU trade (Table 15.1). However, in the 1980s the position dramatically reversed, with the LDCs alone experiencing a reduction in their value of exports. In the year 1979/80 the LDCs accounted for 21.5 per cent of the EU member states' imports, but by 1988/89 their share had fallen to 11.4 per cent. This deterioration in export performance can be accounted for by two factors: the switch in oil imports away from LDCs and the fall in primary commodity prices. LDC exports susbsequently recovered, but it is notable that the ACP share of LDC exports to the EU has shown little improvement despite their tariff advantages under Lomé (Table 15.3).

Table 15.3 EU imports by source, 1985–1992 (US$bn.)

	1985	1986	1987	1988	1989	1990	1991	1992[1]
Total imports	315	335	441	467	515	597	617	691
Imports from ACP	23	10	17	19	20	24	24	24
Imports from other developing countries	122	125	144	158	177	215	229	255
ACP share (%)	7.1	3.1	4.0	4.0	3.9	4.1	3.9	3.5

[1]Estimate
Source: IMF, Direction of World Trade Statistics (1992)

But of more long-term concern is the trend in manufactured exports. Although primary products dominate LDC exports, accounting for two-thirds of the total, it is the trend in manufactured products that would be expected to reflect the process of sustained economic development in LDCs. As can be seen from Table 15.2, the value of LDC manufactured exports has stagnated since 1980, and this is in sharp contrast to the dramatic increase in their exports to the USA.

This might be explained by lower levels of economic activity and growth in demand in the EU. Table 15.4 illustrates LDCs' share of total EU imports for particular product groups. Although for manufactures this shows a slight rise to 17.9 per cent in 1987, for the first half of the 1980s the share was static at 14 per cent. It can also be seen from this table that the share of the ACP countries in manufactured exports to the EU showed a dramatic deterioration over this period, while the Asian NICs – Taiwan, Thailand, Singapore, Hong Kong and South Korea – showed equally dramatic gains, despite receiving only GSP preferences. In 1980 the NICs accounted for 15 per cent of all the EU's imports from the LDCs; by 1990 their share had risen to 32.4 per cent, 90 per cent of these imports were manufactures. Worldwide the NICs' share of the trade in manufactured goods was 21 per cent, which is comparable to the EU's 26 per cent and 24 per cent for Japan.

If we also examine the overall share of the ACPs in EU imports it suggests there has been little apparent benefit from the preferences given under Lomé, with import shares almost halving between 1975 and 1987. Similarly, studies of the impact of the GSP on non-ACP LDCs (Langhammer and Sapir 1987, Davenport 1986) suggest that it has been of very limited value in stimulating exports, because of the small preference margins, quantitative limits and problems associated with rules of origin. Rules of origin specify the minimum level of

Table 15.4 Developing countries' shares in EU imports, 1962–1987 (%)

	1962	1970	1975	1980	1985	1987
Food, beverages **SITC 0+1**						
ACP (66)	11.4	13.4	14.4	16.7	18.9	17.2
Mediterranean countries (12)	12.3	9.2	6.1	6.9	7.7	8.4
NICs (4)	0.3	1.0	1.1	1.1	0.8	1.0
Raw materials **SITC* 2**						
ACP (66)	12.6	12.4	11.8	9.5	9.7	8.8
Mediterranean countries (12)	6.6	5.7	6.0	5.0	6.0	5.1
NICs (4)	0.7	0.6	0.4	1.0	0.7	0.7
Mineral fuels **SITC 3**						
ACP (66)	3.1	6.0	7.5	10.1	12.8	7.8
Mediterranean countries (12)	15.0	31.8	14.2	16.1	24.3	21.7
NICs (4)	0.00	0.0	0.0	0.1	0.1	0.3
Manufactured Goods **SITC 6+7+8**						
ACP (66)	6.6	6.5	2.8	1.9	1.6	1.5
Mediterranean countries (12)	2.1	2.7	3.2	3.8	5.0	5.6
NICs (4)	1.7	2.1	3.8	8.6	8.1	10.8
	10.4	11.3	9.8	14.3	14.7	17.9
Total extra-EU Imports						
ACP (66)	8.8	8.9	7.3	7.3	7.5	4.8
Mediterranean countries (12)	8.0	9.4	7.5	8.3	10.9	8.6
NICs (4)	0.9	1.5	2.4	3.5	3.5	6.0

Source : Eurostat, compiled by Bourrinet (1989)
*Standard International Trade Classification

domestic value added for a product to qualify as originating from a given LDC and therefore to receive the appropriate trade concessions. However, Davenport suggests that trade preferences may have been useful in establishing particular export industries in certain LDCs, e.g. plywood from Brazil, South Korea and Indonesia; capacitors from Malaysia and Singapore. These industries, once established, have sufficient comparative advantage to overcome any subsequent loss of tariff preferences.

Table 15.5 Import shares and growth in imports of crude tropical products, 1978/79 to 1986/87 (tonnes)

	EU import ECU m. 1986/87	Import 1986/87	Share	Average growth 1978/9–1986/7		ACP tariff preference margin
		LDC	ACP	LDC	ACP	
Bananas, fresh	1 266.1	100.0	23.4	1.6	3.4	20
Pineapples	121.9	99.1	92.6	9.0	8.8	9
Coffee beans	5 364.0	99.2	41.4	3.4	4.7	4.5
Tea	489.0	88.5	44.9	0.2	3.4	0
Cocoa beans	1 506.2	100.0	85.0	4.5	3.7	3
Tobacco	1 745.2	50.4	15.9	0.4	7.0	7.5
Palm nuts/kernels	17.8	97.4	92.3	−3.4	−2.9	0
Palmoil	392.3	99.8	24.1	4.9	6.3	5.5
Oilcake, meal	112.8	99.8	8.6	14.1	−3.1	0
Raw sugar	674.2	99.6	81.7	−0.0	1.2	L
Crude rubber	768.0	99.6	15.8	27.4	6.9	0
Sisal etc.	29.6	99.5	39.4	−1.0	−7.6	0
Wood, rough	744.7	81.3	78.4	−2.9	−2.1	0
Weighted averages[1]						
all products	–	75.7	34.0	4.0	3.9	–
crude products	–	91.2	44.7	3.8	4.3	–

Source :   Comext

Notes :   ([1]) Averages are weighted by 1986/87 total EU imports.

L: Levy on on-ACP imports. The major ACP sugar producers have specific quantities of imports guaranteed at Community sugar prices.

Although Lomé appears of limited value from the perspective of the overall performance of the ACPs, it may have been significant in fostering and protecting exports of particular products. But this is difficult to demonstrate, as can be seen from Table 15.5. Here a comparison of ACP and total LDC shares in the growth of tropical products suggests a very mixed pattern. In the case of coffee, tobacco and palm oil, where there are significant ACP preferences, these countries have gained market share relative to other LDCs. But similar gains have occurred with tea, where there is no ACP preference. None the less, the ACP countries dominate in the supply of certain tropical products to the EU, including pineapples, cocoa beans, palm nuts, raw sugar and wood.

For some non-traditional non-primary products McQueen and Stevens (1989) have suggested that the foundations have been laid for significant export growth. Although the absolute value of these exports is small, totalling only 6.9 per cent of non-fuel ACP exports to the EU in 1987, they have shown sustained growth. These products are based on processing raw materials, increasing the value added of previously exported primary commodities. They include wood and leather products, cotton yarns, fabrics, clothing and canned tuna. In some cases, such as man-made yarns and veneers, this export growth has been associated with substantial ACP preferences over other LDC exporters, but this advantage has failed to produce gains in market shares in other products, e.g. tinned pineapples, wooden furniture.

Causes of failure

Thus in certain commodities the ACP countries in particular, and the LDCs in general, have achieved an increased market share in EU imports. Despite this, the provisions of the Lomé Conventions and the GSP have not led to strong overall export growth to the EU. Since 1980 the stagnation in the export performance of the LDCs has become more pronounced, with some loss of market share even in traditional primary exports. Several factors might account for this.

Firstly, it has been suggested that it reflects a deterioration in LDCs' internal supply conditions, and therefore their international competitiveness. Overvalued exchange rates, rising wage costs, or capital shortages lowering productivity, could undermine competitiveness. However, this does not explain the contrasting experience of LDC exports to the USA and EU (Table 15.2). Whereas the value of EU imports has risen by only $4.1 bn. over the period 1979 to 1989, US imports from LDCs increased by $36.9 bn.

Secondly, it is argued that technological change is undermining LDCs' comparative advantage. Automation and the micro-chip revolution are challenging the advantage LDCs have held in low labour costs for product assembly. Without this advantage production plants will tend to be located near their main markets, where design, marketing and production can be more easily integrated, and production made more responsive to changing market conditions. The new automated methods of production, essential to the new sophisticated products, also require the specialist support industries found only in the developed world. Although this may be a long-term phenomenon which may challenge the competitive position of LDCs in the export of manufactures, it is unlikely to explain the short-term deterioration in their export performance, and again is unable to explain their differential experience in the USA and the EU.

Finally, one may seek an explanation not in the LDCs, but in the increase in protectionism by the EU itself. Isolating the trends in the degree of protectionism by the EU presents a number of serious difficulties. These arise from the significance of non-tariff barriers to LDC exports, which take many forms, are often cumulative for particular products, and for which information is difficult to obtain. They have also applied both at the national and the EU level.

Tariffs faced by the LDCs rarely appear to have presented serious obstacles to most of their exports since the Tokyo Round of tariff reductions (1973–1979) – e.g. the non-agricultural 'most favoured nation' tariff is only 4.7 per cent. However certain products do face significant duties, such as textiles with a 10–20 per cent levy and clothing with 16 per cent, and for agricultural products under the CAP regime tariffs are often greater than 100 per cent.

In terms of the non-tariff instruments eight categories can be isolated – industry subsidies, public procurement, technical regulations, minimum import prices (under CAP), voluntary export restraints (VER), quotas, anti-dumping duties and surveillance. Public procurement policy, industry subsidies and technical regulations have also distorted intra-EU trade and hence have become a focus for harmonisation and EU control. Industry subsidies in particular have often inhibited LDC export growth, given their use in those very labour intensive industries where LDCs might be expected to demonstrate a comparative advantage. Here we shall concentrate on the five remaining non-tariff 'trade instruments' and their inter-relationships.

Turning first to quotas (applied under Regulations 288/82 and 3240/83), it was only in 1982 that member states began to publish a general list of quotas. Interpretation of their impact is difficult given the level of aggregation, both by product and geographically, as some member states apply quotas to individual countries, others to 'zones' of 30–50 countries. Further, some quotas are not necessarily enforced, although they remain available. Given these considerable qualifications there is still no evidence to suggest that the application of quotas has increased in recent years, although in 1993 120 still remained in force, principally applied by Italy and France to imports of a wide variety of manufactured goods.

However, the volume limits on LDC exports are more likely to arise under the more extensive VERs. There are two broad categories to consider – Multi Fibre Arrangement (MFA) and non-MFA VERs. The MFAs, first established in 1974, run for four years and currently involve VERs negotiated with 25 countries. Successive MFAs became increasingly restrictive until the mid-1980s, with both more LDCs and more products being subject to 'quotas'. By 1986 60 per cent of LDC textile exports and 78 per cent of clothing exports were facing non-tariff barriers in developed country markets. A review of non-MFA VERs is more problematic, but Pelkman (1987) concludes that they became popular in the late 1970s, and even more extensively employed in the early 1980s.

Short of VERs, member states or the EU may undertake surveillance of particular imports – i.e. the accelerated processing of statistical information. This is not as innocuous a process as it might at first appear. It may require prior import documentation, which may be refused, or it may be used to inhibit LDC exports by threatening the imposition of other 'safeguards' should they exceed informally notified growth rate limits. Surveillance is central to triggering the MFAs' 'safeguard options', and it occurs with all 159 'sensitive' products in Benelux, France, Italy and the UK, but only to a very limited extent in Germany and Greece, and not at all in Denmark. Pelkman suggests that the extent of surveillance increased over the period 1975–1985, but since the early 1980s the Commission has attempted to reduce the number of approvals, requiring member states to make a more substantial case.

In contrast to the *ad hoc* approach taken to quotas and VERs, the EU has subscribed to the Anti-Dumping Code of GATT since 1980. Dumping is identified where the prices charged in export markets diverge from those charged for the product in the country's home market, i.e. a form of international price discrimination. Where there is evidence of dumping, and of a resultant 'material injury', an anti-dumping duty can be imposed. Although the EU subscribes to the GATT Code, the determination of 'normal prices' and the 'injury test' have led to accusations of hidden protectionism. The mere threat of investigation is often sufficient to ensure small LDC producers accept 'price undertakings', i.e. raise their export prices. Over the period 1980–1989 the Commission received 449 complaints of dumping. In 21 per cent of the cases anti-dumping duties were imposed and in 41 per cent price undertakings were obtained from the exporting countries. The countries most frequently involved in complaints were Japan, COMECON countries and the NICs.

In general, over the decade 1975–1985, Pelkman suggests that tariff liberalisation in the Tokyo Round, and some concessions on the GSP and Lomé, have been more than offset by the increased protectionism of the MFA and *ad hoc* VERs. This conclusion is supported by the evidence of increased protectionism among all OECD countries in the early 1980s found by Balassa and Balassa (1984) and Page (1985). In particular, trade restraints may have been targeted at a particular group of LDCs, the NICs – Taiwan, South Korea, Hong Kong, Brazil and Singapore; and they have certainly focused on a particular group of 'sensitive' products, i.e. textiles, clothing, footwear, consumer electronics and steel.

Finally, it must not be forgotten that the CAP continues to represent a serious obstacle to the development of LDC agricultural exports; not only to the EU itself, but also through the competition on world markets presented by subsidised EU exports of surplus produce. During the 1980s EU food exports grew by 50 per cent and by 1990 accounted for 17 cent of the world total. It is estimated that the EU's dumping of food on the world's markets had depressed prices by 13 per cent, while US dumping had depressed prices by a further 10 per cent. The major losers from the CAP among the LDCs include Argentina and Brazil, efficient producers of cereals, meat and sugar; Turkey, fruit and vegetables; and the Philippines and West Indies, sugar. None the less, in 1987 LDC food exports to the EU still totalled $22 bn., almost half the value of their non-oil primary exports.

The trend towards increased agriculture protectionism has been challenged through the pressure of the 13 nation Cairns Group, which includes both developed countries (Australia, Canada and New Zealand) and developing countries (Brazil, Chile, Philippines, Malaysia). This group pressed for the inclusion of agricultural products in the GATT Uruguay round of trade negotiations, a position supported by the USA but opposed by the EU. Through the reduction in agricultural protectionism the Cairns Group sought the eventual elimination of EU agricultural subsidies and the movement towards free trade, which would benefit not only efficient LDC and developed country agricultural exporters, but also EU consumers.

The reduction in agricultural subsidies was to be one of the major areas of contention between the US and EU in the GATT negotiations. The final compromise to emerge requires the EU to cut its agricultural export subsidies by 21 per cent over the six years from 1994 and to substantially reduce import tariffs on agricultural products.

Aid

Of the total world aid flow of $56 bn. in 1991, 75 per cent was bilateral and 25 per cent multilateral, with a quarter of this multilateral aid provided by the EU. In addition to its contributions through the EU, each of the Community's member states contributed to other multilateral agencies (e.g. World Bank) and funded national bilateral aid budgets. Only France and Germany had bilateral aid budgets larger than the EU budget. In 1989/90 France's total net aid was $7.6 bn., Germany's $2.1 bn., Italy's $3.2 bn., the UK's $2.4 bn., the Netherlands' $2.1 bn., Denmark's $0.9 bn., Belgium's $0.7 bn. and Spain's $0.6 bn. The EU's aid is targeted at the ACP countries under the Lomé Conventions. As a result two-thirds of EU aid is allocated to sub-Saharan Africa, with 10 per cent received by both the Americas and South Asia.

Union aid is principally administered through the European Development Fund (EDF) which had been established under the Treaty. Subsequently a separate EDF became associated with each Lomé Convention. Thus Lomé III, commencing in 1986, is associated with the sixth European Development Fund (EDF6), disbursing ECU 7.4 bn. There is no requirement that the funds must be disbursed within the period of any given Lomé Convention. Thus by May 1989, 74 per cent of Lomé III funds had been committed, but only 11 per cent disbursed. In addition the European Investment Bank will make available to the ACPs ECU 1.1 bn. Eighty per cent of EDF6 funds are allocated to conventional aid projects (programmable), and 20 per cent to Stabex and emergency aid. Stabex began with Lomé I and provides partial compensation to the ACPs for falls in agricultural export earnings, either from a decline in commodity prices or from a fall in output; 48 'soft' commodities are now covered. Similar earnings support is offered to states dependent on mineral exports under Sysmin, created under Lomé II. There is also provision under Article 188 of the Treaty for assistance with the financing of imports during structural adjustment.

The programmable aid is divided, at the commencement of the convention, into shares for each region and state. Each ACP government then negotiates a National Indicative Programme (NIP), setting out in broad terms the framework within which the aid will be spent. Within this framework specific projects are then planned.

Lomé IV

Although the economic situation of many ACP countries has deteriorated throughout the period of the conventions, this deterioration became more marked during the period of Lomé III. Falling commodity prices, rising world interest rates and substantial borrowings have resulted in a serious debt problem for many LDCs, especially in Africa where ACP countries' debt has risen from $56 bn. in 1980 to $128 bn. in 1987.

Two major issues began to be addressed during Lomé III, and have been a major focus of debate in the negotiations for Lomé IV: trade versus aid, and structural adjustment in the ACPs.

In regard to trade the Northern member states of the EU have sought a further extension of trade preferences on temperate agricultural goods to ACPs rather than further increases in the volume of EU aid. However, they have faced opposition from the Southern member states whose produce would face the enhanced competition. The relative importance of trade compared to aid flows can be seen in Table 15.6. For 12 of the 25 largest recipients of EU aid, the value of this aid represented less than 10 per cent of the value of their exports to the EU.

Table 15.6 The relative importance of aid and trade

	Aid from EU 1990/1991 ($m.)	Total exports to EU1990 ($m.)	EU aid as % of exports to EU
Egypt	176.7	2 589.8	6.8
Côte d'Ivoire	138.2	1 889.5	7.3
Cameroon	134.9	1 554.1	8.7
Turkey	115.7	6 692.8	1.7
Ethiopia	109.2	145.0	75.3
Sudan	106.0	180.5	58.7
Jordan	99.6	103.5	96.3
Mozambique	96.4	71.2	135.4
Bangladesh	83.6	564.7	14.8
India	73.9	5 119.2	1.4
Tanzania	48.2	199.6	24.1
Mali	48.2	88.0	54.8
Burundi	48.2	84.1	57.3
Malawi	45.0	150.8	29.8
Guinea	41.8	344.5	12.1
Kenya	41.8	585.7	7.1

Sources : OECD, *Development Co-operation*, 1992.
       Eurostat, *Monthly EEC external trade (combined nomenclature)*, 10/1992.

The second major focus of debate within the EU has been the degree to which aid should be directed towards countries undertaking 'structural adjustment' policies, that is economic reforms involving cuts in government expenditure, removal of price controls, devaluation and privatisation. Initially under the conventions the ACPs were left with substantial freedom in deciding their aid priorities, but with Lomé III an attempt was made to influence ACP development strategies by stating EU preferences, for example development of the food sectors, including drought and desertification control. Thus three-quarters of funds allocated under the NIPs were focused on rural development, and the EU succeeded in establishing a 'policy dialogue' with each ACP government, asking it to indicate the range of policy measures it would take to support these priorities.

None the less, in the negotiations over Lomé IV some member states, especially the UK and the Netherlands, wished the ACPs to focus even more clearly on structural adjustment policies by re-allocating a greater proportion of EU aid funds away from conventional projects. The EU influence over the ACPs is clearly greater the larger is the proportion of Lomé IV funds that have not been pre-allocated to countries under their NIPs. A further constraint on the ACPs arises with the issue of coordination of Lomé aid with IMF/World Bank funding. Again the greater the proportion of Lomé aid dispersed under 'special structural adjustment' funds, the greater is the potential for such coordination.

A structural fund had been established under Lomé III of ECU 500 m. during 1988 to provide import support for the poorest African states in response to the Stabex fund becoming overdrawn. The eligibility criterion to draw from this fund was that each LDC must have introduced appropriate economic policies; agreements with the IMF/World Bank are taken as evidence of this. Thus ACPs that have obtained a World Bank structural or sectoral adjustment loan (SAL/SECAL) may then apply for EU funding for a general import support programme. About half of the ACPs have sought adjustment credits from the World Bank; without World Bank support the EU will make its own assessment as to a specific sectoral import support programme. However, fundamental disagreement with the IMF/World Bank may create difficulties for ACPs then applying to the EU.

Lomé IV was finally signed in December 1989, and unlike previous conventions will run for ten years until the year 2000. The financial resources allocated to the first five years of the Convention total ECU 12 bn., a 20 per cent increase in real terms over Lomé III (Table 15.7). Of the total, ECU 10.8 bn. will be disbursed through EDF VII, and the remaining ECU 1.2 bn. through the EIB. In recognition of the increasing financial difficulties of the ACP countries, more of the assistance will be in the form of grants rather than loans, and EIB loans will themselves be at lower interest rates (3–6 per cent) than under Lomé III. Of the EDF funds, ECU 1.25 bn. is set aside for assisting regional cooperation among the ACPs themselves, and ECU 1.15 bn. has been allocated specifically to structural adjustment support (SAS). The Commission had proposed an SAS fund of ECU 2 bn., and in view of the smaller sums allocated anticipates that only 30 to 35 ACP countries will benefit. These are most likely to be those already receiving IMF/World Bank approval. Thus Lomé IV SAS may be regarded as merely complementary to IMF/World Bank funding.

In terms of trade concessions there is a reduction in restrictions on 40 agricultural products. The value of these concessions varies considerably. In the case of rum all restrictions will be abolished after 1995, but with other products concessions have been limited. For example, the ACPs sought an increase of 30,000 tonnes in EU imports of rice and received an increase of only one-tenth of that. Critics suggest that the concessions fail to provide the ACPs with the

Table 15.7 Volume of aid for the first five years of Lomé IV in comparison with Lomé III

	Lomé III		Lomé IV	
	Value (million ECU[1])	%	Value (million ECU)	%
Aid	4 790	64.54%	6 845[2]	63.38%
Risk capital	635	8.58%	825	7.64%
Stabex	925	12.50%	1 500	13.89%
Sysmin	415	5.61%	480	4.44%
Structural adjustment support (SAS)	–	–	1 150	10.65%
Soft loans	635	8.58%	–	–
Total EDF	7 400	100%	10 800	100%
EIB	1 100		1 200	
Total resources	8 500		12 000	

[1] 1 ECU = approximately £0.7 or 69 French francs (February 1990).
[2] Part of it can be used for SAS.

transparent trading regime for agricultural products that they need, but these agreements must be seen within the context of the wider GATT negotiations, and their demands for fundamental reform of the CAP. However, wider concessions under GATT undermine the privileged access enjoyed by the ACP countries under Lomé.

Stabex and Sysmin have both been expanded and revised under Lomé IV. Stabex funding has been increased by 62 per cent to ECU 1.5 bn in the face of falling commodity prices, and the threshold for assistance has been lowered from a product contributing 6 per cent of an ACP country's total export earnings to a contribution of 5 per cent. Also, Stabex transfers will no longer be repayable, but the EU will have greater control of the use of the funds, directing them particularly towards greater diversification.

Sysmin has been increased to ECU 480 m., and has also moved from loans to grants. It will now also cover uranium and gold, as well as copper, cobalt, phosphates, manganese, bauxite and alumina, tin and iron ore. Any ACP where 20 per cent of export earnings is derived from these minerals can now seek assistance.

Finally, Lomé IV has offered a crucial concession on the issue of rules of origin. These are intended to prevent access to the EU of exports from LDCs that embody only a small amount of local value added, unless the inputs are from other ACP countries or the EU itself. It has been argued that these restrictions undermine the LDCs' attempts to initiate the early stages of industrialisation or limit the countries with whom they might develop economic relationships. Under Lome IV if at least 45 per cent of the value added of a product can be shown to have been created within an ACP it may be imported into the EU duty-free (as compared with 60 per cent under Lomé III), 'as long as no market disturbance is entailed'. Although Lomé IV contains promises to restrict the use of this measure, this qualification may prove significant.

Lomé IV also emphasises the role of private sector development within ACPs. This is to be encouraged with the provision of risk capital through the EIB, technical assistance and investment protection. It also provides for the environmental assessment of development projects, encouragement of 'micro-projects' with non-governmental organisations, and the encouragement of active population policies. Whether Lomé IV 'retains the long term development aims of Lomé III while containing measures to help arrest the economic crisis' (*Europe Information* 1990), or whether it marks 'a further step away from . . . the political ambition of being a model for relations between rich and poor countries' (Stichele 1990) remains to be seen.

The impact of the single market

The movement towards a single market was perhaps the most important development in EU–LDC relations. Although it is not an issue that has been addressed by the Commission, a number of authors have attempted to evaluate its impact (e.g. Davenport 1990), and it is best considered in terms of trade creation and trade diversion.

The Cecchini report suggests a 4.5 to 7 per cent enhancement of the EU's growth rate as a result of economic integration, and this in turn will increase demand for LDC exports. Matthews and McAleese (1990), assuming an extra 5 per cent growth of GDP for the EU, calculated that this would increase LDC exports by 6 per cent ($5.5 bn.), although 75 per cent of this increase will be oil. For other products, especially manufactures, the efficiency gains of the EU's own producers arising from the single market, such as economies of scale, will lead to enhanced competition for LDC exports. The extent of this trade diversion will vary from product to product, and will be expected to be most severe for LDCs where EU producers experience the greatest efficiency gains. Thus LDC exports of steel and chemicals might be particularly adversely affected.

Although Davenport (1990) believes that on plausible assumptions trade creation for LDCs' manufactured goods will be approximately offset by trade diversion, Langhammer (1990) suggests a one-off reduction in EU demand for LDC manufactures of $2.3 bn. However, any estimate must be highly tentative, as it depends on the response of the European producers to the opportunities of the single market, and to the Union's detailed policies.

In particular for the LDCs, the existing national preferential arrangements for their exports were often inconsistent with the 1992 programme, and many member state quotas, VERs, etc. needed to be replaced by EU arrangements. Thus under Article 115 of the Treaty of Rome member states were allowed to suspend imports of goods from other member states where third countries were attempting to circumvent quotas through trans-shipment. With the ending of border controls recourse to Article 115 was no longer available. Article 115 restrictions required the approval of the Commission, and have proved the most reliable indicator of the extent of the application of quotas. During the 1980s the number of such restrictions has halved. However, VERs are of more significance in limiting the volume of LDC exports and these have survived 1992 on a Union basis. For although the Commission generally believes that many industries should be able to withstand import competition after the restructuring following from economic integration, footwear, consumer electronics and ceramic tableware continued to face quotas.

But the most significant VER is the MFA. Although MFA IV introduced a new mechanism whereby unused individual member state quotas could be transferred to other member states, in practice the total EU quota limit on LDC exports remained under-utilised. The elimination of individual member state VER quotas, as required by the SEM, offers potential benefits to LDC exporters. For the LDCs as a whole, Davenport estimated that these benefits were likely to be modest, and less than the growth in exports in recent years (e.g. 5.4 per cent p.a. 1981–1987). However, for those LDCs that substantially under-used their quotas – Brazil, Thailand, Sri Lanka, Philippines and Peru – the gains could be significant. By contrast, LDC exports that were previously quota-free would now become constrained by the new EU quotas, and the Commission may prove more effective in the enforcement of any quota arrangement than existing national agencies. However, the future of MFA IV was bound up with the Uruguay Round. The Textile Negotiating Group has been successful in bringing clothing and textile trade back under GATT arrangements. As part of the agreement the MFA is to be phased out over the next ten years, with quotas on clothes imports being replaced by tariffs.

A particular problem arises with imports of bananas. Half of the Union's imports originate from the ACPs and are an extremely important source of export earnings, especially to the island economies (e.g. St Vincent, St Lucia). However, they are in competition in EU markets with exports of 'dollar' bananas from Central and South America, where large plantations have a cost advantage. Special arrangements had therefore been made to preserve their traditional markets in the UK, France and Italy. But these arrangements were incompatible with the abolition of Article 115 restrictions on intra-Community trade. The Commission had proposed imposing an import quota on non-ACP bananas (COM(92)359), but the GATT negotiations were seeking the abolition of non-tariff barriers to the trade in agricultural products. Thus the new Banana Protocol, commencing from July 1993, established a tariff quota of 2 million tonnes for non-ACP banana imports. Up to this limit a duty of ECU 100 per tonne is imposed, this increases to ECU 850 per tonne on any additional imports; an effective tariff of 170 per cent. ACP banana imports continue to be duty-free, but the CAP was extended to include support for EU banana production. However, the Banana Protocol has been challenged and found inconsistent with the GATT Treaty. This may have profound implications for the whole Lomé Convention.

Exports from the LDCs may also be affected by changes to national tax regimes resulting from the single market programme. It has been proposed that all member states should set their VAT and excise duties within common bands, with excise duties limited to alcohol, tobacco and petroleum products. If adopted this will have important implications for LDC exports of coffee, cocoa, and tobacco. Currently coffee is subject to excise duties in many member states, e.g. Germany 41 per cent, Denmark 15 per cent. Abolition of these duties is expected to raise the value of EU imports by ECU 466 m. (3 per cent), the main beneficiaries being Brazil, Colombia and the Ivory Coast. Similarly, the abolition of excise duties on cocoa, and a 5 per cent VAT rate, would increase LDC exports by ECU 50 m. By contrast, an upward harmonisation of excise duties on tobacco within the EU would produce a 40 per cent price rise, with a consequent 10–15 per cent fall in LDC exports, worth ECU 50–80 m. Here the major losers would be Brazil, Zimbabwe, India and Malawi. However, measures to harmonise these taxes have been postponed until at least 1996.

The progressive adoption of common technical standards within the EU need not disadvantage LDCs. The creation of minimum common standards mainly concerns manufactured goods and services, which are not significant for many LDCs. The mutual recognition of certification implies that any LDC export need only satisfy the conditions for any one member state, but certification may in some cases be required only for non-EU producers, which may create opportunities for discrimination. The close involvement of EU industries in setting Union technical standards may also offer further opportunities for deterring non-EU competition.

EU standards have existed for some time in relation to the health of plant and animal product imports. Since 1993 all inspections are carried out at the first port of entry, or in the exporting country, and Union-wide clearance given. This may result in tighter standards being applied to achieve uniformity, with adverse consequences for particular LDC exports, such as planting materials and cut flowers. A Directive for meat products requires Union licensing of both slaughterhouses and processing plants for all non-EU suppliers, presenting problems for some African exporters. Another Directive setting standards of water quality may pose a threat to south-east Asian shellfish exports.

Some aspects of EU–LDC trade relations were unaffected by the 1992 programme. For example, the national export credit agencies continued to operate independently. Similarly, 58 per cent of member states' bilateral aid has continued to be tied to purchases from the donor countries, despite a Commission proposal in November 1991 to open up bilateral aid to procurement from any member state of the EU. This widening of the LDC recipients' choice of suppliers would significantly increase the real value of the aid, as enhanced competition should reduce prices. But if the advantages to national donors of bilateral aid programmes are reduced, it must be questioned whether the existing volumes of aid will be maintained.

However, aid might be replaced to some degree by commercial investment in LDCs. It is open to question whether this has been encouraged or discouraged by the creation of the single market. In the 1950s the USA had already begun to shift its focus of investment away from LDCs towards developed countries, and this trend was followed in the 1970s by the UK and in the 1980s by Japan. By the 1980s most EU countries had already re-orientated their investment, and France and West Germany were directing only between 10 and 20 per cent of their overseas investment to the LDCs. By 1983 direct investment in LDCs had fallen dramatically to only $9 bn. from $14 bn. in 1981. There has been a considerable recovery in the past few years, with investment averaging $25 bn. at the beginning of the 1990s. Part of this has been attributed by the IMF to debt equity-swaps in Latin America and to an increase in Japanese investment in Asia. Six of the EU's member states account for the bulk of the Union's foreign investment (France, Germany, Italy, the Netherlands, Spain and the UK). In the mid 1980s their annual investment in the LDCs was averaging $4.5 bn.; by 1989 this had increased to $10 bn.. However, this investment has been concentrated in the NICs (35% in 1988/89) and Latin America (38%). In 1990 this outflow fell significantly. Although this may be explained as a response to the Kuwait crisis and to the onset of recession in Europe, it is also possible that the advent of the single market has had an adverse impact.

Molle and Morsink (1990) have suggested that there is a huge potential for intra-EU direct investment as the internal barriers are removed. To fully exploit economies of scale, cost reductions, market opportunities and the enhanced income growth of the single market, substantial restructuring and investment will occur throughout European industry. In addition, developments in Central and Eastern Europe have generated substantial demands for investment, and both historical ties and commercial advantage are likely to produce a positive response from the Western European countries. The Union has responded by initiating the foundation of the European Bank for Reconstruction and Development, with a capital of ECU 10 bn., one of whose principal aims will be to act as a catalyst for private sector investment in Eastern Europe.

Finally, mention might be made of the impact on immigration control policy of the creation of the SEM and the Treaty on European Union (TEU). So far our discussion has focused solely on the movement of goods and capital. However, for some LDCs, especially those of North Africa, the EU has been a significant destination for emigration. Emigration has made some contribution to reducing the pressures of rapidly increasing populations but limited employment creation, while remittances have been an important source of income. The creation of the single internal market entails free movement of labour and removal or minimising of border controls. In turn this implies the need for the development of a common immigration control policy. Despite the increasing average age of Europe's population, labour shortages are more likely to be met by Eastern European migration and more capital-intensive modes of production than by relaxation of EU controls on LDC immigration. Indeed, political pressure is likely to ensure that those countries that have traditionally adopted more liberal immigration controls, such as Italy, bring their policies into line with the more restrictive approach increasingly followed by the Northern member states. The TEU singles out immigration control as an area for a 'twin-track' approach, with a Treaty of Rome procedure for establishing common EU visa requirements by June 1996 as well as cooperation provisions for the harmonisation of asylum policies and immigration controls. The draft Regulation on visa requirements, based on the policies agreed by the Schengen group of EU countries, will require visas for most visitors from Third World countries.

Conclusion

In Table 15.8 Davenport estimated that the overall effect on LDCs of the EU's economic integration, and its enhanced growth, would be a 4 per cent (ECU 4.6 bn.) increase in exports, but ECU 3.3 bn. of this increase would be in oil. For the poorer LDCs the major benefits would arise from enhanced cocoa and coffee exports. In manufactures the impact on LDC trade appeared likely to be minimal, as trade creation is offset by trade diversion in the single market. The movement from national to Community textile quotas would produce a 3–5 per cent increase in LDC exports, and renegotiation of the MFA would significantly enhance their long-term prospects. However, VERs on other products, especially consumer electronics and shoes, were likely to emerge at the Community level, targeted initially at the Asian NICs.

Table 15.8 Impact of 1992 on major LDC exports

	EU imports from LDCs (1987)	ECU m. %LDC share in EU imports	1992 Impact
Textiles	10 571	50.4	846
Shoes	975	56.7	−259
Cocoa	1 645	98.1	50
Coffee	4 123	99.1	466
Bananas	1 392	100.0	−
Tobacco	1 969	54.2	−65
Primary commodities	60 417	11.5	3 550

Source : ODI (1989)

The existing Lomé and GSP trade preferences for LDCs have proved ineffective in encouraging LDC exports, and they have been severely compromised by the increased use of non-tariff barriers, especially VERs. But protectionist measures are always difficult to remove once they are established, as powerful vested interest groups are created, including those LDCs that currently enjoy privileged access to EU markets. Further, with the structural adjustments required for the economic integration of the Union, internal pressures for restrictions on imports are likely to become more acute. The Commission has shown its willingness to instigate safeguard investigations, and apply anti-dumping duties or VERs, and in negotiations with LDCs has stressed the need for reciprocity of access for EU exports to their markets. But as important for the prospects for LDC trade with the EU is the outcome of the long delayed Uruguay Round of the GATT. This will see an average reduction in tariffs of 50 per cent and the phasing out of non-tariff barriers, such as the VERs. Such general tariff reductions might be seen as undermining the tariff preferences enjoyed by the ACPs, but these preferences are already being challenged under the existing GATT agreement. Estimates by Davenport (1992) suggest that the loss of these tariff advantages will have only a minor impact on their share of trade. However, the reductions in agricultural subsidies in the developed countries will raise world food prices, and it is estimated that this will cost sub-Saharan Africa and the Maghreb countries an extra $7 bn. Indeed, the general benefits from a new GATT agreement will be received principally by the developed world. The OECD estimates that of the $250 bn. increase in world trade over a decade, three-quarters will accrue to the developed countries. In the developing world the consequences will be mixed. The Asian NICs are expected to gain $7.1 bn.; $3.3 bn. from farm liberalisation, $1.8 bn. from textile trade and $1.1 bn. from services. India is expected to gain $4.6 bn. and South America $8.0 bn., but Africa as a whole is expected to lose $2.6 bn.

Given these likely loses to the least developed countries it is suggested that the EU should take advantage of the mid-term review of Lomé IV to extend trade preferences to additional products for these particular countries. Overall recent changes in EU trade policy have been criticised as being inconsistent with the Maastricht Treaty commitment to 'a smooth and gradual integration of the developing countries into the world economy' (Art. 130u) and unrelated to the EU's other development policies.

The EU should recognise that without internal economic change the LDCs will derive little benefit from their relative trade advantages, and that therefore the EU should concentrate its aid programme on technical assistance, education and support for the development of diversified export-oriented strategies. Aid needs to be untied from individual donor countries, and the requirement of open competition for public contracts under the SEM may force this change on the member states. However, critics have gone further and have argued for a significant shift in the balance of aid from bilateral aid, offered by individual member states, to multilateral aid administered by the EU. With the EU taking responsibility for project aid, advantages can be obtained from better coordination and economies of scale in administration. Too often member state bilateral aid is competitive and motivated by the demands of export promotion. But to fully realise the development benefits of the EU's aid, a clearer statement of the EU's development priorities is required. The current pattern of aid merely reflects the historical links of the EU countries or current political considerations. The 1992 policy statement by the EU's Development Council (Horizon 2000) fails to provide this coherent framework, i.e. to identify the criteria for assistance and the EU's overall development strategy. Until this central weakness is addressed the arguments for placing the EU at centre stage in the administration of Europe's aid to the developing countries may remain unheeded.

References and further reading

Balassa B and **Balassa C** 1984 Industrial protection in the developing countries, *The World Economy,* Vol. 7, No. 2, June.

Baldwin Edwards M 1991 Immigration after 1992, *Policy and Politics*, Special Edition, July.

Bourrinet J 1989 The implications of 1992 per group of less developed countries, Paper presented at a meeting organised by the Netherlands Ministry of Foreign Affairs, October.

Commission EC 1990 Lomé IV, *Europe Information*.

Commision EC 1992 *Proposal for a Council Regulation (EEC) on the Common Organisation of the Market in Bananas*, com (92) 359.

Davenport M 1986 *Trade Policy, Protectionism and the Third World*, Croom Helm, London.

Davenport M 1990 The external policy of the Community and its effects on the manufactured goods of the developing countries, *Journal of Common Market Studies*, December.

Davenport M 1992 Africa and the unimportance of being preferred, *Journal of Common Market Studies*, June.

Davenport M and **Page S** 1989 *Regional Trading Agreements, The impact of the implementation of the Single European Market on developing countries*, ODI Report, October.

Davenport M and **Page S** 1991 *1992 and the developing world*, ODI Report.

Langhammer R 1990 Fuelling a new engine of growth or separating Europe from non-Europe, *Journal of Common Market Studies*, December.

Langhammer R and **Sapir A** 1987 *The Economic Impact of Generalised Tariff Preferences: Thames Essays 49*, Gower, London.

Matthews A and **McAleese D** 1990 LDC primary exports to the EC, Prospects post 1992, *Journal of Common Market Studies*, Vol. 29, No. 2, December.

McQueen M and **Stevens C** 1989 Trade Preferences and Lomé IV; Non-traditional ACP exports to the EC, *Development Policy Review*, September.

Molle W and **Morsink R** 1990 European direct investment in Europe: an explanatory model of intra-EC flows, in Burgenmeier B and Muichielli J, *Multinational and Europe 1992*, Routledge, London.

Overseas Development Institute 1989 *The Developing Countries and 1992*, Briefing Paper, November.

Overseas Development Institute 1989 *Negotiating the Fourth Lomé Convention*, Briefing Paper, October.

Page S 1985 *The Costs and Benefits of Protection*, OECD.

Pelkman J 1987 The European Community's trade policy towards developing countries, *Europe and the International Division of Labour*, Stevens C. (ed.), Hodder & Stoughton, Sevenoaks.

Stichele M 1990 *Lomé Briefing No. 14*, Liaison committee of development non-governmental organisations to the EC.

CHAPTER 16

The European Union and the rest of Europe

Frank McDonald, Andrei Kuznetsov and Keith Penketh

Introduction

The term 'Europe' is often taken to mean Western Europe and is often used as another term for the EU. However, this narrow focus on Western Europe is changing because of the end of the Cold War, the collapse of communism in Central and Eastern Europe and the demise of the Soviet Union. The Warsaw Pact and COMECON have disappeared from the European economic and political scene and organisations such as NATO and EFTA are of less importance in European affairs. New European economic and political structures are emerging and the EU is at the heart of this process. In economic matters the EU is without doubt the most important European agency. Even in foreign policy and security/defence issues the EU is becoming an agency of some importance. The agreement in the Maastricht Treaty to increase cooperation between the member states in foreign policy and security/defence issues holds the prospect of greater EU involvement in such fields. The EU is therefore a most important player in the process of creating new economic and political structures in Europe.

The importance of the EU in the process of reconstructing European economic and political structures can be gathered by the attempts of many countries either to join the EU or to establish close relationships to it. Austria, Finland, Iceland, Norway and Sweden have joined with the EU in establishing a European Economic Area (EEA), and all these countries have also applied for membership. Switzerland has also applied for membership but problems have arisen because of a referendum, held in 1992, which rejected the concept of membership of the EEA. Many of the countries of Central and Eastern Europe have also made it clear that they wish to join the EU, and Turkey, Malta and Cyprus have been waiting for some time for their applications for full membership to be considered by the member states of the EU. In spite of the many problems which the EU faces in developing its integration programmes and in defining a political structure acceptable to its members, it seems that most European countries regard the EU as the key to the future development of Europe.

EFTA and the EU

The EFTA countries are important to the EU for geographic, historic and economic reasons. Firstly, there is the geographic dimension. The EFTA countries are not only part of Europe, but are of course part of Western Europe and hence they are close to existing members of the EU. Although all current members of the EU are located in Western Europe, membership of the EU is not restricted to Western European countries but simply to European countries. Secondly, in a historical sense they have been associated with the development of the EU. At one time it was common to describe Europe as being at 'sixes and sevens'. Today it is appropriate to describe Europe as divided into 'twelves and sevens'. While the EU has expanded in numbers, EFTA has changed its composition. It has shed three members to the EU, namely the UK, Denmark and more recently Portugal, but gained three new members, namely Finland, Iceland and Liechtenstein. The other members of EFTA are Austria, Norway, Sweden and Switzerland. The countries of EFTA can be split into two groups, namely the Nordic countries, and the Alpine countries. Thirdly, there are the economic ties between EFTA and the EU. As a group, EFTA is a most important market for EU exports. However, the relative significance of EFTA to the EU has fallen since the EU was formed (Table 16.1), although EFTA has maintained her lead as a significant supplier of EU imports. Trade dependence is thus reciprocal. Because of the fall in the significance of EFTA as a market for EU exports, the interdependence of the two regional trading blocs is approximately in balance today.

Table 16.1 Share of EU imports from and exports to third countries (%)

	1958	1980	1992
Imports by origin from:			
Western industrial countries (excluding EUR 12)	31	23	24
EFTA	9	9	9
USA	11	9	7
Japan	0.7	3	4
Central and Eastern Europe	3	4	3
Exports to:			
Western industrial countries (excluding EUR 12)	30	22	21
EFTA	12	11	9
USA	8	6	7
Japan	1	2	3
Central and Eastern Europe	3	3	3

Shares relate to both intra- and extra-trade of the EU.
Source : Eurostat External Trade Statistical Yearbook 1993

This reciprocal trade dependence is also evident at a disaggregated level. Taking the five most important countries of EFTA in terms of commodity trade, it is possible to compare the rank order of individual EFTA countries as suppliers of extra-EU imports and purchasers of extra-EU exports.

Table 16.2 EFTA countries as suppliers and purchasers of extra-EU imports and exports (%)

	Norway	Sweden	Finland	Switzerland	Austria
Extra-EU imports					
1958	3.0	6.0	1.4	4.7	2.7
1980	3.0	5.9	1.9	8.8	5.4
1992	2.6	5.7	2.9	9.7	7.5
Extra–EU exports					
1958	1.9	5.3	1.9	3.6	2.3
1980	6.2	7.3	2.6	7.3	4.5
1992	5.4	7.2	2.9	8.9	6.7

Source : Eurostat International Trade Statistical Yearbook 1993

Table 16.2 illustrates how prominently EFTA countries figure in trade with the EU. Spatially this may not evoke surprise, but in terms of population size it is perhaps remarkable that these countries figure so prominently in the trade of the EU. The most populated of the EFTA countries, Sweden, has a population of just under 8 million. Collectively the EFTA countries have less than half the population of Germany and have fewer people than Poland. In 1992 these five EFTA countries supplied over 28 per cent of the EU's extra-imports and absorbed over 31 per cent of the EU's extra-exports. The growth over the past 35 years of Switzerland and Austria as sources of supply of EU imports is quite pronounced. While doubtless numerous demand and supply factors can confer comparative advantage in trade, both the spatial aspect and the trade discrimination aspect spring to mind to account for the prominence of EFTA countries in the trade of the EU.

In contrast to significant EFTA/EU trade, trade between EFTA countries is not of a high order. Moreover, this trade has declined over time. Intra-trade is higher for the Nordic EFTA members than for the Alpine members. Nevertheless, the significance of the home market has declined, and the significance of the EU has increased in the trade of EFTA countries.

Not only is the EU of interest to EFTA countries because of the relative high amount of commodity trade with the EU, but the state of the trading balance occasions some concern in EFTA. As a group of countries EFTA has never been in surplus with the EU in commodity trade. There are, however, country exceptions to this general rule. Norway has always managed to maintain a balance of trade surplus with the EU, and in 1988 Sweden managed to turn round a long standing deficit with the EU into a small surplus. Switzerland and Austria have been and remain in significant deficit with EU countries (Table 16.3).

Finally, it is not merely in matters of trade but also in direct investment that the EU is assuming increasing significance for EFTA. In Sweden, for instance, companies such as Stora, Tetra-Pak, IKEA, Ericsson and Volvo have all enhanced their manufacturing facilities in the EU. In the past seven years Swedish direct investment in the EU has risen more than tenfold. Compared to the 1960s, the share of EFTA in outward foreign direct investment flows has doubled. Moreover, 80 per cent of this flow is attributable to Sweden and Switzerland. The EU is the principal recipient of this outward flow. The outward share to the EU is around two-thirds of total EFTA direct investment. It is argued by Leskelä and Parviänen (1990) that as EFTA countries have experienced relatively high employment, the traditional implications of

Table 16.3 EFTA countries trade balance with the EU 1991 ($US m.)

Country	Trade balance (+ = surplus)
Austria	−7 341
Finland	+ 1 581
Iceland	+138
Norway	+10 241
Sweden	+3 065
Switzerland	−10 490
EFTA	−2 808

Source : EFTA Trade in 1991, Economic Affairs Department, EFTA

foreign direct investment for domestic labour simply do not arise. It is alleged that investment at home would require the importation of labour, which is unnecessary when such investment is directed overseas.

The historical development of EFTA

In 1990 EFTA reached the age of 30: an age which was described as an 'age of maturity and of all dangers' (*EFTA Bulletin* 1990). The position of EFTA in relation to the EU is best understood by a brief survey of the evolution of EFTA to date. Formed in 1960, EFTA is the younger brother or sister of the EU. It was founded two years later than the EEC by those countries that felt they were unable to digest the supranationality aspect of the EEC, or the CET, or both. However, there was a desire to remove trade barriers and promote closer economic cooperation between themselves and other members of the OECD (including the EU). The Stockholm Convention was adopted by seven founding members of EFTA on 4 January 1960. Twelve years later, in 1972, and after much vacillation, two of the founding members of EFTA, the UK and Denmark, joined the EEC.

An important step, in 1972, was the development of free trade between the remaining EFTA countries and the EEC. Bilateral free-trade Agreements were concluded between the EEC and the individual EFTA countries. The area of free trade embraced by the Agreements was known as the European Economic System (EES). With minor exceptions the Agreements covered trade in industrial goods. Most tariffs between the EEC and EFTA were abolished on industrial (non-agricultural) goods by 1977, but 1983 marked the culmination of the process whereby all non-agricultural trade could be described as tariff-free. The extension of tariff-free trade for non-agricultural commodities to the EFTA countries may be regarded as an act of magnanimity by the EEC to the smaller countries of EFTA. Although per capita incomes in EFTA were above the average for the EEC, the size of the market in the EEC measured by the size of the population was more than 12 times that of EFTA. Hence it may be claimed that reciprocal tariff cuts, even when measured in effective and not nominal terms, were not reciprocal swaps of opportunity as the size of the respective markets was so different. The EFTA countries had been given much richer pickings in terms of market size than the countries of the EEC. Indeed, countries like the UK which made net budgetary contributions to the budget of the EEC but did not embrace some of the policies of the EEC such as the CAP, could claim that EFTA countries obtained the principal advantage of membership – namely free trade – but avoided some of the costs of membership. This argument, which does have an initial appeal, is subject to question. While it is true that EFTA countries were offered the prospect of the larger EEC market, their ability to exploit that market was constrained. The industrial sector of the EEC was much larger than in EFTA and hence the potential of the EEC to compete in EFTA markets was much greater.

Non-tariff barriers in EFTA–EU trade

While trade in non-agricultural goods was tariff-free by 1984, it would not be correct to assert that trade was NTB free. The impediments to internal trade listed in the Cecchini Report (1988) also applied to third countries. A particular NTB relates to the rules of origin. These are used to determine whether goods imported into the EU from EFTA, or into EFTA from the EU, qualify for duty-free treatment. For example, a country with a low external tariff may attempt to import goods from overseas and then export them tariff-free into an EU country. To safeguard against possible trade deflection, rules of origin exist to prevent countries being swamped by non-eligible imports. The members of EFTA claimed, however, that the origin system adopted was particularly constricting for them. Not only had domestic value added to exceed specified requirements, but goods destined for subsequent importation into the EU had to change their Common Customs Classification. In other words, they became goods of a separate and distinct identity. Moreover, in contrast to members of the EU, members of EFTA cannot accumulate value added between themselves. Obviously border controls are necessary to ascertain that the regulations with regard to origin are satisfied. It has been suggested that the high compliance costs of the rules of origin resulted in their non-use. One quarter of industrial trade in the early 1980s between EFTA and the EU was not traded duty-free but at the CET (Herin 1986).

The next landmark in the development of EU/EFTA relations was the first ministerial meeting held in Luxembourg in April 1984. The meeting resulted in the 'Luxembourg Declaration' and laid a foundation for the development of an EU/EFTA infrastructure. It looked towards an EES of 19 nations. Cooperation between the two groups was to go beyond the strict confines of commodity trade, and extend to such matters as education, state aids, technical standards and intellectual property. A 'High-Level Contact Group' meets twice a year to review progress and define priorities.

Progress has certainly been made in the development of some of the objectives laid down in the Luxembourg Declaration. In 1985, for instance, five of the EFTA countries participated with the EU in Eureka and subsequently in COMETT. In 1988, EFTA signed the Lugano and Tampere Conventions on the jurisdiction and enforcement of civil and commercial judgements. Rules of origin and competition policy were defined as priority areas. Some limited progress has been made which has facilitated the removal of technical barriers to trade. In part this arises from EFTA countries' participation in CEN and CENELEC in establishing European standards. In the same year the single administrative document (SAD) was introduced in the EU for customs clearance. However, it was not confined to intra-EU trade but was also designed for use for trade between the EU and EFTA. Following the issue of the White Paper on the Internal Market in 1985, and the passing of the SEA in 1988, the agenda for discussion of the High-Level Contact Group was expanded to include considerations relating to free trade not only in commodities but also in services, capital movements, and population mobility. However, difficulties emerged as work progressed. Numerous issues had not been resolved by 1988, and the EU found difficulties in dealing with EFTA when national views diverged within EFTA and the Association could not speak with one voice.

Subsequent to the passage of the SEA, Jacques Delors, President of the Commission, proposed 'a more structured partnership going beyond the current association agreements . . . some sort of osmosis between the Community and EFTA to ensure that EFTA's interests are taken into account . . . but this must stop short of joint decision making, as this would imply Community membership' (1989).

A new environment for EFTA

There is little doubt that the competitive position of EFTA countries is likely to decline following the implementation of the SEA. Norman (1989) points to various effects of the SEM: lower real trade costs resulting from the elimination of non-tariff barriers to trade, more aggressive competition, and lower unit production costs arising from high-cost producers losing market shares to lower cost producers. It is not only in EU markets that the trade of EFTA is likely to decline, since EFTA will experience increased competition in third markets as well as home markets. However, given the high proportion of EFTA trade undertaken with the EU this is the most important area of concern. It is not surprising that the EU should seek to ameliorate some of these disadvantages. A study by Schmitt (1990) examines in detail the trade effects that the SEM will have on the EFTA countries. Schmitt considers them to be disadvantageous. There is a view that the EFTA countries should either desire to shape the EES while remaining members of EFTA or apply for membership of the EU and depart from EFTA. There is evidence of movement on both fronts.

In July 1989, Austria formally submitted an application for membership of the EU. To some this was surprising, because a view had been taken that the continued neutrality of a country effectively precluded its membership. Panattoni (1978) quotes Verdoss (1956): 'a permanently neutral state cannot join a multilateral economic group such as the Common Market because such an organisation aims at the fusion of the national economies concerned, and to this end it delegates authority to a central organ to follow a united policy which is binding on member states.' In opposition to this view, Rack (1990) asserts that Article 237 of the Treaty of Rome does not exclude neutral states and that the neutrality of Austria can give the Community a 'sense of balance'. A further point in favour of a neutral country such as Austria securing membership was the existing composition of the EU. The EU already has a neutral country as a member, i.e. Ireland. However, the fact that in 1986 over 69 per cent of Austria's exports went to the EU indicates that her trade dependence on the EU is far greater than that of many existing members.

In the event, the Commission was unwilling to consider further applications for membership until January 1993. This did not, however, inhibit Sweden from declaring an interest in joining the list of countries seeking membership of the EU. Towards the end of 1990 the Social Democratic government signalled its intention to join the EU. The other route to developing closer links between the EU and EFTA, by the creation of the European Economic Area (EEA), came into effect on 1 January 1994. Formal negotiations began in June

1990 with the objective, according to Frans Andriessen, external affairs commissioner, 'of giving EFTA a say in the shaping but not in the final taking of future Community decisions'. It is claimed that the strength of the case for EFTA lies not only in the extent to which the two blocs are integrated in trade, but also in the fact that EFTA holds ECU 10 bn. direct investment in the EU (Lugon 1990). Additionally there is extensive scientific and technical cooperation. By way of further example, Switzerland is estimated to provide work for 600,000 EU nationals inside its boundaries, and through Swiss investment in the EU a further 400,000 are employed. These figures exclude seasonal workers (Blankart 1989, *Financial Times* 1990).

The decision to establish the EEA on 1 January 1994 means that a free trade area for most goods, services, capital and labour exists between 17 countries of Western Europe (i.e. the 12 member states and Austria, Finland, Iceland, Norway and Sweden). The EEA has a combined population of nearly 380 million and it accounts for approximately 40 per cent of world trade.

In the negotiations to set up the EEA there were difficulties relating to Norwegian fisheries quotas, transit licences for goods through Austria and Switzerland and EFTA countries' contributions to the structural funds of the Union to aid in the development of its poorer Southern European members. Agreement was reached on all these matters, but Switzerland was unable to join the EEA because a referendum held in 1992 rejected the proposal that Switzerland should accept the conditions for membership of the EEA. Liechtenstein was therefore unable to join the EEA because of its special trading relationships with Switzerland. However, Liechtenstein has indicated that it wishes to join the EEA when solutions have been found to the problems caused by the Swiss rejection of the EEA.

The EFTA countries that are members of the EEA will adopt Union rules on company law, consumer protection and education, and they will also accept the R&D policies and programmes and the social and environmental policies of the EU. The competition policy of the EU relating to anti-trust matters, abuse of dominant position, mergers, state aids and public procurement will apply to those EFTA countries that are members of the EEA. The agreement covers free movement of labour, the mutual recognition of professional qualifications, and free movement of capital except for some types of real estate and foreign direct investment into EFTA countries. The EFTA members of the EEA will not adopt the CET and there may still be some frontier checks between EU and EFTA countries. There is no commitment for EFTA members of the EEA to adopt EU harmonisation on taxation matters, and the CAP will not operate in the EEA and therefore agricultural goods will not be included in the free movement scheme. To ensure the free movement of goods, rules of origin will have to be developed to allow for the identification of goods deemed to be eligible for inclusion within the EEA. Special arrangements will also be necessary for food products and fish (because of the CAP and fisheries policy) and energy, coal and steel (because of the ECSC).

The EEA seems to be a halfway house to full membership of the EU. The EFTA countries will have no voting rights on new Union legislation and there is considerable potential for disputes over existing EU rules and regulations. The new joint court could be faced with a large number of disputes as Union laws on competition and social issues are applied to EFTA countries when they do not have much influence on the decision-making systems of the EU. Moves towards EMU and political union will also impinge on the EFTA countries, and the pressures for them to become full members that can exercise full rights in the decision-making processes are likely to grow. The exemptions to free movement for some commodities and rules of origin conditions will also hamper the development of economic integration in Western Europe, and in order to overcome these problems full membership would seem to be necessary.

Some issues pertaining to membership

It is appropriate to pause to outline some of the particular issues impinging on participation in the EEA, and on membership of the EU. The EEA is perceived as the extension of the SEM to include EFTA. This implies that goods and services pass not only duty-free between the two trading blocs, but also non-tariff barrier-free. Failure to participate in the EEA would mean that the EU countries under the SEM would secure a competitive edge over other competitors in EU domestic markets. Hence non-participating countries' imports would be displaced. The reduction in trade costs and increased competitiveness for EU-based companies may also displace production and sales in third markets.

Additionally, some would argue that a threat would exist to the maintenance of the capital stock in EFTA countries, as plants in EFTA were relocated in the more buoyant markets of the EU. However, membership of the EEA is not costless, although financial contributions are quite small and this has been viewed as compensation for the exclusion of aspects of economic life in EFTA from the rigours of an open market (e.g. EFTA's fishing grounds).

Some further reasons for extending the Agreements to encompass actual membership of the EU are given by Baldwin (1992). These range from securing a say in the development of the *acquis communautaire*, without which EFTA countries can feel dangerously exposed to securing the benefits of the EU's more protective political muscle when participating in international negotiations such as those that relate to GATT.

Whether, for EFTA countries, joining the EU represents a move towards freer trade (compared to the EEA) is not simple to evaluate. On the one hand the CET is slightly higher than the average of existing external EFTA tariffs, and the EU's protective measures (anti-dumping duties) now apply to new members. On the other hand NTBs between participants would disappear, and the special relationships which are guaranteed by the treaty to third countries have also to be guaranteed by new entrants to third parties.

The primary gain to the EU of countries passing from the EEA to full membership of the EU is budgetary. The EFTA countries, which are relatively prosperous, will, under VAT related payments and the new fourth resource, make relatively significant payments. It is also anticipated that the EU will be able to reduce its agricultural surpluses through trade with EFTA.

The 'widening and deepening' argument

There is no doubt that countries such as the UK and Denmark, that are opposed to some aspects of the further deepening of the EU, welcome the accession of new members from EFTA. While EFTA members strengthen the representation of the north as opposed to the south within the EU, the increase in numbers is seen as a factor which in itself impedes the deepening process. However, Gardner (1993) reports that the probability remains that enlargement will gradually reinforce the power of the Union. To support this view he adds that all four applicants are supportive of EMU, and also urge more progress on social policy and the environment. Additionally he asserts that they are enthusiastic for more majority voting on industrial policy, common foreign policy and security policy. Such policy views will hardly be welcome to those that had hoped to inject into the EU a staunch anti-federalist bloc.

The Swiss position

Although Switzerland sees economic advantages to EU membership, the increasing focus of the EU on political union is viewed by many in Switzerland as something to be avoided. Swiss democracy requires not only a nation-wide referendum, but also a referendum in all the cantons before such membership could take place. The ECJ, which has the ultimate jurisdiction in matters of EU law, is viewed as an institution that would usurp Switzerland's democracy. Nevertheless, the Swiss government recently announced that it would be seeking full membership and that measures to allow for such an outcome would be implemented as soon as possible.

In December 1992 a national referendum was held in Switzerland on joining the EEA. By a small majority the Swiss voters rejected the government proposals. A more positive rejection was given by the Swiss cantons, 16 out of 23 rejecting the treaty. This was taken by the President of the Commission, Jacques Delors, to represent not only a rejection of the EEA but also a rejection of the idea of EU membership for the Swiss.

The developing situation

Although four EFTA countries have ratified the EEA Treaty, it was not possible to bring the Treaty into effect early in 1993 as had been hoped. Spain did not undertake ratification until late 1993. Needless to say, the Treaty did not come into effect until all countries had ratified it. In the meantime four EFTA countries, Austria, Finland, Sweden and Norway are pursuing their applications for membership of the EU, which it is hoped will occur in 1995. Membership by all four countries is by no means a foregone conclusion because the applications are to go to referenda in the applicant countries in 1994. However, in June 1994 the referendum in Austria produced a decisive 'Yes' verdict.

The Turkish position

Turkey has had an Association Agreement with the EU since 1963. Separate consideration of the country is justified because Turkey certainly does not come within the discussions which relate to EFTA, or Central and Eastern Europe, or the Third World. In 1989 Turkey had its application to join the EU turned down. A reason given by the EU was that it could not digest additional members until the SEM was complete in 1993. This is an aspect of the broadening versus deepening issue where broadening is alleged to be prejudicial to deepening the EU.

Mention is also made in the Commission's report to differences with Greece over Cyprus. The implication is that Turkish entry would depend on a resolution of these differences with Greece. The Turks take great exception to this part of the report. However, Turkey has other suspicions about rejection. One factor is religion. Turkey is an Islamic country whereas all existing members of the EU have a predominantly Christian tradition. The Treaty of Rome, however, does not confine membership to fundamentally Christian countries. Certainly the economic problems that Turkey confronts are not likely to engage the sympathies of existing Union members. The population of Turkey at 52 million is five times that of Greece or Portugal. Turkey has a positive balance of trade with the EU. However, Turkey is relatively underdeveloped, with 55 per cent of its workforce in agriculture, and a level of per capita income which is only two-thirds that of Portugal. Its population is growing very rapidly, and is expected to reach 68 million by the year 2000.

The accession of Turkey to the EU would certainly not be without cost to the EU budget. There would be increased expenditure under the CAP to absorb surpluses of citrus products, dairy produce and olive oil. Contribution to the budget would be low, principally because of low VAT payments. Moreover, substantial regional development funds would be needed to raise living standards. There is no doubt that Turkey would be a net beneficiary from the EU budget. Additionally, free movement of Turkish labour would not commend itself to Germany and some of the other EU countries. If Turkey eventually succeeds in its desire for membership it will probably be conditional on restrictions on free movement of labour. The signs certainly do not look encouraging for Turkey with EFTA and Central and East European countries also waiting on the sidelines.

However, it would be difficult to reject the Turkish application as a matter of principle. In 1991 Turkey supported the allied powers in the conduct of the Gulf War. Certainly there are significant political as well as economic issues underlying the application of Turkey. The Iraqi oil pipeline through Turkey makes the country particularly sensitive to developments in Iraq. It is also argued that continued rejection of the Turkish application would strengthen the power of the Islamic fundamentalists in the country. Clearly the issue is a complex of both economic and political matters which makes it difficult to foresee an early resolution of the Turkish application for membership of the EU.

Eastern Europe

The countries of Central and Eastern Europe share many similar features and face many similar problems. This situation arose from certain common factors which influenced their postwar development, including their political system (based on communism) and their economic system (based on central planning) and the domination of the Soviet Union.

The rise to power of Gorbachev in 1985, and the introduction of *perestroika* and *glasnost* movements, finally allowed Eastern European countries to escape from their Stalinist legacy. In the late 1980s a cascade of democratic revolutions opened the way for radical political and economic reforms. The collapse of communist rule in Central and Eastern Europe has triggered a very intensive process of economic restructuring in the ex-socialist countries. Post-communist regimes have generally demonstrated a willingness to break away from centrally-planned models of economic development in favour of models in which market mechanisms are to play a prominent, if not a leading, role.

Fulfilling this ambition has proved to be a task of the utmost complexity. Long before the initiation of reforms, the European socialist countries experienced a protracted economic crisis. It existed mainly in repressed and hidden forms owing to an overwhelming state control of nearly all aspects of economic and political life. Its visible features were declining rates of economic growth, wasteful use of resources including labour and capital, a widening technological gap with advanced countries, persistent shortages on the supply-side and serious financial imbalances. The actual scale of deficiencies had not been clear until the change of political regime and elimination of central planning helped to establish the truth. The economies of Romania, Bulgaria, Eastern Germany, Poland, the former USSR and to a lesser degree the former Czechoslovakia were revealed to be suffering from serious structural problems, badly managed, uncompetitive and non-responsive to technological innovation.

The old central planning system has been analysed by Kornai (1986) using the concept of the 'soft budget constraint'. According to Kornai, the planning system sought to maximise desired output, and financial considerations were secondary to this. Efficiency in allocating resources could therefore not be achieved by financial criteria such as profit, as few prices were determined by market conditions, and differences between costs and the value of sales were covered by taxes and subsidies. There was also little effective competition between enterprises, and costs and revenues were determined in an arbitrary way by administrative discretion. Consequently, enterprises had little incentive to use resources efficiently, as they faced few financial pressures, i.e. soft budget constraints. Indeed, the incentive was for the enterprise to acquire the maximum amount of resources possible in order to produce as much output as possible. This resulted in low productivity, and a tendency to make poor quality goods. A secondary effect is that enterprise managers have little experience in setting prices, marketing and selling products, and financial control procedures.

These problems have been exacerbated by the control of foreign trade by the planning authorities. The linking of national economies to the world economy increases competition by extending sources of supply. The transfer of technical developments is also closely connected to the openness of an economy to direct foreign investments, joint-ventures, and licensing and patenting agreements. In Western economies the benefits of these factors have been acknowledged. In Eastern European countries under communism, the costs of such a system were considered to be greater than the benefits. Trade and other economic transactions with the West were also hindered by the inconvertibility of currencies, and the nature of the exchange rates. Most exchange rates were administratively determined, and had little relationship to the true value of the currency. Eastern European countries also found difficulties in exporting to the West because of trade restrictions imposed on them, and problems in penetrating Western markets because of the poor quality of their manufactured goods. The countries of Eastern Europe therefore have a legacy of poor integration into the markets of the West.

While the exact size of macro-economic imbalances inherited by democratic regimes in Eastern Europe is debatable, it is clear that they were serious enough to provoke, at a certain point, an economic crisis. Hidden inflation in Poland, which existed in the form of a price gap between an official and a 'black' market, had already become hyperinflation under the last communist government, while in Romania stagnation and decay became evident in the early 1980s. However, the squeeze in the economies of Central and Eastern Europe in the 1990s would not have been so pronounced had there not been some important external shocks.

The ruinous impact of the decline in trade between the European ex-socialist countries must be placed first in the list of such shocks. Intra-COMECON trade was responsible for 40–50 per cent of their industrial exports. As COMECON collapsed at the beginning of the 1990s East European producers, due to the low competitiveness of their goods and also because of trade barriers imposed by the EC, failed to increase their share of Western markets quickly enough to compensate for the shrinkage in their traditional markets. Another consequence of the collapse of COMECON was the erosion of the financial position of ex-socialist countries which for years had benefited from implicit trade subsidies from the Soviet Union. Partly for political reasons and partly owing to inefficiency of the price mechanism, the Soviet Union sold its energy and non-food raw materials to Eastern Europe at prices below prevailing world market prices and bought manufactured goods from Eastern Europe at prices above world prices. Experts estimate the sum of transfer in dozens of billion dollars (Marrese and Vanous 1988). Finally, the Gulf War of early 1991 should be mentioned. It not only disrupted trade with some Arab countries but also inflated world oil prices, thus aggravating the economic situation in Central and Eastern European countries, all of which depended heavily on imported oil.

Political changes in Eastern Europe have triggered the process of marketisation, i.e. the process of dismantling a Soviet-style economic mechanism and the restoration or, in some cases, the construction of a capitalist economy, with dominant private property and market-based allocation of resources providing the basis for economic activity. This task has proved to be extremely challenging owing to the precarious state of the European ex-socialist economies and the difference between the two economic models. Problems range from technical deficiencies, such as lack of functional capital markets and credit systems required for efficient capital formation and resource allocation, to a more general issue of changing prevailing behavioural patterns at all levels of society. They also involve finding the shortest ways towards creating jobs with high value added and wealth generating capacities, improving labour productivity, and providing sustained technological innovation in order to increase national competitiveness in the face of the growing importance of international markets. What makes a systematic change of European Soviet-style economies particularly challenging is the fact that reformers cannot rely on any of the elements of the existing economic mechanism as being adequate to the standards of a market-based system. Their task is to redesign this mechanism but at the same time to avoid a complete economic breakdown following from the progressive disintegration of their economic and political systems.

Although economies in the countries of Central and Eastern Europe basically imitated a Soviet pattern, starting economic conditions for marketisation were not equal across the region (see Table 16.4). Two countries, Hungary and Yugoslavia, had made some advance towards a decentralised open economy, while others had stuck to a conventional rigid central planning model. National peculiarities and in particular political constraints, which were different in the different countries of the region, conditioned short-term policy choice and to a lesser degree long-term strategies. At the same time, there appears to have been no great difference in opinions in the former socialist countries as well as in the West as to the nature of the essential stages of transition towards a market-type economy.

The first necessary stage is *economic stabilization*, which implies the initial adaptation of the existing economic mechanism (prices, credit, money supply, wages) to the standards of the capitalist system. Macro-economic stabilization is essential in order to eliminate the most dangerous financial imbalances inherited from central planning (monetary overhang and fiscal deficit) and to kick-start the price mechanism which, under the market economy, facilitates the allocation of resources.

The second element or stage is a radical *institutional reform* aimed essentially at the restoration of private property and competition. Privatisation in the broadest sense is meant to eliminate the indeterminacy of capital ownership in the former socialist state, which was one of the main reasons for inefficient employment of capital assets in the period of the command economy. Privatisation is also expected to induce changes in entrepreneurial behaviour and to make enterprises profit-motivated (under central planning they were output maximizers). Micro-economic reform is also necessary to create a market relationship between the owner of

Table 16.4 Basic indicators for Eastern European countries

Indicator	Soviet Union	Bulgaria	Czecho-slovakia	German Democratic Republic	Hungary	Poland	Romania	OECD
Population (million, 1988)	286.4	9.0	15.6	16.6	10.6	38.0	23.0	824.8
GDP (billion USD, 1988)	1 590.0	50.7	118.6	155.4	68.8	207.2	94.7	12 073.0
GDP per capita (USD)	5 552.0	5 633.0	7 603.0	9 361.0	6 491.0	5 453.0	4 117.0	14 637.0
Annual growth of GDP (%)								
1981–85	1.7	0.8	1.2	1.9	0.7	0.6	–0.1	2.5
1986–88	2.3	1.9	1.5	1.7	1.5	1.0	0.1	3.5
Living standards(1987):								
Cars per 1 000 inhabitants	50.0	127.0	182.0	206.0	153.0	74.0	11.0	385.0
Telephones per 1 000 inhabitants	124.0	248.0	246.0	233.0	152.0	122.0	111.0	542.0
Share of workforce in agriculture (%)	21.7	19.5	12.1	10.2	18.4	28.2	28.5	8.0
Gross domestic investment/GDP (%)	33.2	32.7	24.7	29.2	28.5	36.5	37.1	20.6
Share of private enterprise in GDP (%)	2.5	8.9	3.1	3.5	14.6	14.7	2.5	70–80
Workers with secondary education (%)	27.3	n.a	29.4	n.a.	33.8	28.9	n.a.	61.0
Exports of goods as % of GDP (1988)	6.8	23.0	19.7	13.7	14.7	6.4	11.2	14.4
Exports of manufactured goods as share of exports to non-socialist countries	63.0	59.3	72.4	77.3	79.6	63.4	50.6	81.8
Change of share of OECD markets (%, 1979–89)	–26.0	–18.5	–44.0	–25.2	–7.8	–32.3	–46.3	–

n.a. = not available
Source : OECD

the capital and the manager of the firm which is more conducive to better performance by enterprises. This presupposes the adoption of new laws (for example, bankruptcy legislation), but no less important is the creation of an appropriate institutional environment including investment banks, capital exchanges, auditing and consulting firms and other types of business services. These types of services were non-existent under socialism. Another important issue is to put an end to the monopolistic position of producers in the market by the direct break-up of large enterprises and through new business formation.

The third element, which is closely linked to the second, is *capacity restructuring*, i.e., the shift of capital and labour from primary and machine-building industries to those producing consumer goods and high-tech products, and from industrial production to services. Integration of the ex-socialist economies in the international market is normally regarded as an important component of such a restructuring.

The immediate consequences of marketisation have proved to be quite disappointing. From the outset a temporary deterioration of performance was regarded as an inevitable cost of transition. Indeed, marketisation in Central and Eastern Europe may be accurately described as a transition from one system of development and a related set of priorities and ruling principles, institutions and regulatory mechanisms to a completely different, if not an opposite, system with its own priorities, institutions and regulatory mechanisms. Such a profound qualitative change could not but provoke some drastic adjustments. However, the actual scale and persistence of the crisis vastly exceeded expectations, as a decrease in national output, growing inflation and unemployment, and financial imbalances have proved to be general attributes of the initial stage of transition (see Table 16.5). As the economic improvement expected from market reforms had been late to materialise, increasing scepticism with respect to the validity of the chosen strategy of change became noticeable by the middle of 1992. Characteristically, the UN Economic Survey of Europe in 1991–1992 analysed the economic situation in Eastern and Central Europe with the heading 'Reform results to date: more pain than gain?'.

In 1993 a degree of optimism was apparent because the data demonstrated that at least one country, Poland, appeared to have turned the corner. Most importantly, in the third quarter of 1992, industrial production in Poland showed growth over the previous period for the first time since 1989, although in absolute figures this brought Poland to the volume of industrial output it had in the mid-1980s. There was also a decrease in the inflation rate, and growth of hard-currency exports and a trade surplus were recorded. The Czech Republic and Hungary are expected to follow Poland in this upward swing within one or two years. However, prudent commentators talk about years of uncertain transition ahead, pointing at the fact that countries involved have increasingly become areas of socio-political tension. For Bulgaria, Romania, Albania and the former Soviet republics the results of reforms, despite some progress, were at most modest. In any case, with an overhang of state-owned enterprises in some countries and unclear results of mass privatisation in others, it still appears to be premature to claim that the most difficult stage is over.

Strategies of reforms

The complexity of the process of reforms and its ambiguous results so far have made the choice of reform strategy crucial. It could be either a 'big-bang', 'shock therapy' type of

Table 16.5 Key indicators: European transition countries 1983–1992 (percentage change since same time in previous year)

Country	Rate of economic growth					Industrial production		
	1983–88	1989	1990	1991*	1992†	1990	1991	1992‡
Albania	–	–	–13.1	–30.0	–	–7.6	–42.5	–
Bulgaria	1.4	–0.4	–17.5	–25.7	–20.0	–12.6	–23..3	–20
Czechoslovakia	1.8	–0.7	–1.5	–25.7	–17.5	–3.5	–21.3	–18.0
Hungary	1.4	–0.2	–3.3	–10.2	–	–4.5	–19.1	–19.6
Poland	4.2	–0.2	–11.6	–7	–	–24.2	–11.9	–0.8
Romania	2.9	–5.8	–9.9	–13.7	–	–19.0	–22.7	–22.9
Yugoslavia	0.9	–6.6	–8.4	–15	–	–10.3	–19.0	–
Ex-GDR Länder	2.1	–	–14.7	–33.9	1.8	–28.1	–28.1	–3.1

	Unemployment rate§				Inflation rate		
	1990	1991	1992†		1990	1991	1992†
Bulgaria	1.6	10	14		65	400	80
Czechoslovakia	1.0	8	7		10	15	9
Hungary	1.7	10	12		30	38	20
Poland	6.1	10	14		250	80	50
Romania	1.3	4	7		40	200	130
Yugoslavia	13.6	15	–		583	150	–

*January–June
†Estimate
‡January–August
§End of the year

Sources : Based on East European Statistics Service, December 1992, No. 197, p. 12; Nuti 1992, Table 2; Welfens 1992, p. 13; PlanEcon Report, 1992, No. 38–42; *The Economist*, 19 December 1992, p. 28.

approach, as in Poland, or a more gradual one, as in Hungary. Both approaches have their merits and demerits. As it happens, the Polish model of macro-economic adjustment has set, by and large, the pattern for Eastern and Central Europe.[1]

The terms 'shock therapy' and 'big bang' are ambiguous and are sometimes used loosely. They often refer to any programmes having as their conspicuous feature a drastic and massive change in key economic parameters.[2] However, it is important to keep in mind that Polish-style reform programmes suggest different tactics at different stages of transition. The institutional reform was conceived as taking a long time in order to develop an effective legal and organisational framework and also to retrain administrators. Thus, the contrast between the two approaches in question was not so sharp as it might seem, and mainly concerned the phase of stabilisation.

The main (theoretical) arguments for gradualism were: (*a*) gradual reforms may be better prepared and (*b*) cautious reforms would be easier for the population to accept, thus diminishing the threat of negative social reaction to transition. For some time it seemed that Hungarian experience gave enough justification for these beliefs. In Hungary market-oriented reforms were initiated in 1968. Although they developed at a very slow pace, by the end of the 1980s the economic mechanism employed in the country had become much closer to Western standards than anywhere else in Central and Eastern Europe. However, major success failed to come: industrial production fell throughout the early 1990s while unemployment and inflation were on the rise. As a result, the government was forced to contemplate speeding up economic reforms, while in politics the ruling Democratic Forum had to face disappointed voters and the rise of nationalist extremism. Consequently, Hungary has lost many of its credentials as a success story.

Although other Eastern and Central European countries have not followed the Hungarian approach to reform, this was probably not because the results were discouraging but because the situation they found themselves in prompted a different choice. Most importantly, the external and internal imbalances these countries faced in 1990 were far more critical than those faced by Hungary in 1968 when 'crawling' economic reforms were launched. These new challenges, including devastating hyperinflation, growing shortages and deteriorating foreign debt position, required immediate action. This took the form of monetary and fiscal restrictions, price liberalization, the devaluation of domestic currencies and wage guidelines. This approach was already used in some developing countries. What made the difference was the speed of applying these measures and the fact that they were introduced for the first time in a non-capitalist economy characterised by the absence of a comprehensive banking system, labour and capital markets and developed taxation. Unlike most developing countries, in Central and Eastern Europe stabilization took place in a situation of social accord as a new polity was enjoying an enormous credit of public confidence, permitting reformers to realise some very daring projects. This 'social pact' was based on the assumption that reforms would produce a swift output in the form of amelioration of living conditions of the majority of the population. The Polish experience has demonstrated that 'shock therapy' was effective in eliminating pervasive shortages of consumer goods. At the same time the extent of poverty has not diminished, and may have grown while a relatively small group of people with very high incomes has been emerging.

After three years of reforms, one can see that a group of three Eastern European countries has the best prospects for recovery in the future. These are Poland, Hungary and the Czech Republic. This may be interpreted as suggesting that there are no generally valid recipes for success without reference to country-specific conditions. Another consideration is that nowhere in the countries of Central and Eastern Europe was the course of economic austerity implemented consistently enough to endorse the claim that 'shock therapy' was fully applied. The actual practice of reforms, due mainly to social pressures, has been characterised by opportunism and manoeuvring not provided for by theoretical schemes. The more it became clear that the transformation was going to split the nation into losers and winners, the more important became the social and political dimensions of reforms. Governments were tempted to postpone unpopular decisions, introducing last minute changes in already accepted policies, or, in contrast, to rush into measures favourable to particular interest groups. This often distorted the contemplated effects of reforms and made the process of transformation more uncertain in terms of results.

Challenges of marketisation

Stabilisation plans pursued, in the early 1990s, in Poland, the former Czech and Slovak Federal Republic, Bulgaria and Romania were largely similar. In Poland, for example, the plan included drastic price and trade liberalisation, targeting the real money supply and real interest rates, large devaluations and internal convertibility allowing the residents of the country to trade the zloty for foreign currencies in the national exchange market, extreme fiscal pressure on the state sector, rigid budget policy, wage restrictions, and, in the longer run, large-scale privatisation.

There are some very strong arguments in favour of a price adjustment at an early stage of reform. First, there can be no market allocation leading to internal and external adjustment in the absence of reliable price signals but, if administered prices and market prices 'coexist', price indicators such as enterprise profits do not convey much meaning. Second, market-clearing prices are necessary to determine the real value of fixed assets which under central planning were often given arbitrary evaluations, in order to help resume a normal investment process.

The problem with price liberalisation is that in order not to allow a switch to market prices to translate into sustained hyper-inflation it is necessary to enact very firm anti-inflationary measures which carry the risk of inducing recession. Stabilisation reforms succeeded mainly in establishing more realistic prices and exchange rates, the elimination of queuing, and improving the quality of goods and services as a result of increasing foreign competition. None the less, inflation was not curbed. A sharp price-rise during the initial stage of stabilisation had been expected. However, many countries found themselves stuck in this stage for much longer than had been foreseen. Persistent double- to triple-digit inflation became a fact of life in most Central and Eastern European countries (with the exception of former Czechoslovakia) in the early 1990s.

Tight monetary, credit, fiscal and wage policies forced a collapse in demand which led to major problems for nationalised industries in transitional countries. In Poland, Bulgaria, Romania and former Czechoslovakia real wages dropped by 25–30 per cent and at the end of 1992, after over two years of reforms, they were still below pre-reform levels. A rapidly shrinking economy drove up unemployment, which undermined demand even further. The shrinking economy implied falling tax revenues, while rising unemployment inflated social expenditures thus pushing the government budget deficit to record levels. The deep and persistent fall in output was widely acknowledged as the main setback of the stabilisation stage.

The troublesome coexistence of sky-rocketing inflation and a devastating industrial slump has become characteristic of Bulgaria, Romania and the former Soviet republics. Unfortunately for these economies, they seem not to have been able to find a way out of this trap.

The privatisation of a huge public property is universally regarded as another big issue of a post-communist transition. In Eastern Germany the public sector included 8,000 firms, in Poland about 7,500, in former Czechoslovakia 4,800, in Romania 4,000, in Hungary 2,500 and in Bulgaria 5,000. The public sector accounted in each case for not less than 80 per cent of national value added.[3] For comparison, in the UK the much-heralded privatisation programme of the first Thatcher government involved only about 20 firms, accounting for a mere five per cent of value added.

Unlike stabilization programmes, from the very beginning there was little unanimity at a government level as to a conceptual framework for privatisation. All these countries agreed on the need for a privatisation programme, but questions arose as to how to privatise, to what extent and how to treat the state sector in the meantime.

Former Czechoslovakia provided a good example of the differences in approach to privatisation. While in the Czech Republic the political leadership put all its trust in the invisible hand of the market and started a large-scale privatisation programme, in Slovakia the government was much more prudent in its approach and showed a willingness to preserve a considerable state presence in industry. It is clear that this latter approach was pre-determined by the fact that industrialisation in Slovakia took place in the postwar period and was implemented according to a socialist doctrine giving priority to large and very large enterprises with a bias towards heavy industry.

In fact, high concentration of production and employment in big enterprises was a general feature of socialist economies. In 1990, the share of enterprises employing more than 500 people in industry was 43 per cent in Czechoslovakia, 86.9 per cent in Poland, 74.5 per cent in Romania and 72.1 per cent in Bulgaria. Also, the enterprises were more narrowly specialized than is usual in the West: there was often just one national producer of a particular product. The gigantic scale of many state-owned companies aside, it was typical of state enterprises to be overmanned and to have a vast array of supporting productions and social services, including kindergartens, medical centres, holiday homes and other types of service unrelated to the main business of the enterprise. It was obvious that they could not survive unchanged under any other conditions than those of a centrally planned economy. The economic recession of 1990–1992 has made things worse as enterprises have lost markets, reduced production, accumulated debt and discontinued their normal investment processes. As a result, many enterprises seemed to be unsaleable unless a prior streamlining and financial restructuring was undertaken. However, the dominating belief has been that if big enterprises remained in state ownership they would not adapt to market conditions.

Already at the early stage of the stabilisation process public enterprises found themselves deprived of traditional state subsidies, while the clear provisions of how the state sector was to be financed were generally missing. It was assumed that the enterprises would try to adjust to hard budget constraints by cutting costs. The actual reaction was different: they started raising prices and accumulating debt between companies, thus demonstrating that macro-economic measures alone were not sufficient to bring about desirable responses at the enterprise level. This made the need for privatisation even more urgent.

There are two principal ways of handling this problem in the former socialist countries. One reflects the perception that the duty of the government is to speed up the process while a market mechanism is to be entrusted with the task of restructuring the national property. According to the other, micro-economic restructuring should precede or accompany the privatisation of state companies in order to increase their value and attractiveness as an asset and then to submit them for public sale.

The Czech Republic has chosen the first approach. There the voucher scheme has proved the most intriguing part of a large-scale privatisation programme. Each adult citizen was entitled, almost for free, to a voucher booklet allowing him or her to bid for the shares of privatised entities at public auctions. Over eight million persons became owners of vouchers. In the first round of auctions, in 1992, corporate assets with a 'net book value' of about $9.3 bn. were distributed to millions of new shareholders.[4]

Nobody has yet had a chance to evaluate the impact of voucher privatisation on the economy, but the implications of the scheme raise general scepticism outside the Czech Republic.[5] Probably the main problem with this scheme is that it does not provide any visible evidence that the change in ownership will promote profit maximisation and business efficiency. No new capital or expertise will be introduced into troubled companies. Furthermore, the individuals receiving a share in privatised enterprises, if ownership is broadly spread, will not have any influence over the specific competitiveness of the companies they come to own. Since, with so little information available, the acquisition of assets will entail a considerable element of chance, new owners may soon discover their property to be uncompetitive and unprofitable. In other cases enterprises which are competitive in their operations may fall into the hands of incompetent individuals who lack the necessary entrepreneurial skills and could ruin the business. As a result business conditions in the country may become even more precarious.

In Romania some 17.5 million people have received voucher booklets for assets estimated to be worth leu 1,500 bn. However, the Romanian mass privatisation programme does not copy the Czech one. Two-thirds of property will be sold by conventional methods (auctions and sell-offs) and the 30 per cent intended for voucher owners are to be put in five private ownership funds with the object of maximising their value.

The idea of prior restructuring of most enterprises is implicit in the privatisation programmes of Poland, Hungary and Bulgaria. However, financial and organisational restructuring takes time and money, and extends the period of a transition during which public bodies continue to interfere with economic processes. To many this seems unacceptable. The authorities of Poland and Hungary are reported to be considering a Czech-style voucher scheme. In the meantime, the desire to speed up the privatisation programmes dominates the decision-making process in these countries. Hungary has paved the way by adopting, in January 1992, a new bankruptcy law which made it possible for creditors to force companies into bankruptcy if they do not pay their debts within 90 days. Such enterprises or their assets may then be bought for bargain prices. This law was inspired by an understandable desire to liberate the economy (and the budget) from inefficient enterprises and, moreover, to do so in the best traditions of neo-liberalism, leaving the market to decide winners and losers. As a result, more than 17,000 firms, producing about one-third of the country's exports, went bust between January 1992 and April 1993.

Only Germany provides an example of privatisation based on prior comprehensive micro-economic restructuring. In July 1990, 10,500 East German enterprises, employing four million people, were put in the care of a government agency called the Treuhandanstalt. The Treuhandanstalt was entrusted with a mandate to maximise the returns on the sales of state assets while ensuring optimum employment. Its stated policy is to privatise quickly. However, if a company cannot be sold, the Treuhandanstalt's policy is to attempt to restructure it to salvage at least the core business or any other viable part. By June 1992, 4,803 companies had been privatised, 1,209 closed down and 5,435 were still owned by the Treuhandanstalt.[6] Few

Central and Eastern European governments will be able to spare the resources and expertise that the Treuhandanstalt can lavish on state property. The apparent dilemma of privatisation programmes is that case-by-case privatisation by a central agency cannot accomplish much, given the resources available to be applied to this end. However, speedy mass privatisation may prove to be a shaky alternative. In 1993, as in 1990, most analysts accepted the proposition that in order to be effective privatisation must be rapid, but they still did not agree on how to achieve this objective.

The reconstruction of Eastern Europe and the EU

As mentioned above, international factors have had a great impact on the dynamics of post-communist transition. The collapse of the intra-COMECON market in 1989–1990 was responsible for much of the decline of industrial and agricultural output in the area. Foreign debt was and still is another major issue. The communist governments of Eastern and Central Europe received loans from the West in the 1970s totalling $49.8 bn. These resources were generally misallocated and did not generate the flow of income in hard currency sufficient to repay them. As a result, in 1988 the area had a cumulative debt of $103.1 bn., putting a great strain on the economy, with Poland and Yugoslavia being in particular difficulties.

Unfolding marketisation boosted demand for foreign capital. Transitional countries sought financial credits to support structural adjustments and foreign direct investments to start up privatisation and modernisation of nationalised industries, and to make up for the chronic undercapitalisation which was typical of centrally planned economies.

This situation has given Western political governmental structures, international organisations and multinational corporations considerable leverage over Eastern and Central European governments. Relations between the EU and Eastern Europe were not good until 1988, when COMECON and the EU signed an agreement on mutual recognition of the two organisations. Prior to this agreement, COMECON countries did not formally recognise the EU, because of Soviet apprehension about the role of the EU in East–West relations and because of the insistence of the EU on dealing with individual Eastern European countries rather than with COMECON. The EU adopted this stance as it regarded COMECON as being unable to negotiate on trade matters on behalf of its members, while clearly the EU was able to do this. This stalemate continued until 1988 in spite of the obvious desire of reformers in Eastern Europe to forge closer links with the EU. With the launch of the *perestroika* programme in 1985, the scene was clearly set for COMECON to formally recognise the EU and to allow each Eastern European country to negotiate with the EU. As COMECON collapsed, the EU insisted on measures leading to accelerated opening of the markets of the ex-socialist countries to Western products.[7] The argument was that an end must be put to a situation in which Central and Eastern European countries were protected from competitive pressure of international trade which, in market economies, provided a strong incentive to improve efficiency. Transitional economies were called on to lift or restrict foreign trade control and facilitate access to foreign exchange resources for the residents by introducing internal convertibility of the national currency.

As a result, at the initial stage of transition the post-communist economies made a great stride towards openness when the industrial slump was at its deepest. Furthermore, although export to the West increased, it could not compensate for the collapse of intra-COMECON trade because Western governments were not ready to open Western markets to Eastern European goods. When Poland volunteered to drop all import restrictions the EU did not reciprocate. Now Poland has one of the lowest tariff regimes in the world, but half of Poland's exports to the EU confront some kind of restraint. The most Poland, Hungary and former Czechoslovakia obtained was the arrangement of associated status with the EU amounting largely to a promise of a ten-year transition to free trade. In the meantime the steel lobby has ensured that the EU has set an extremely low ceiling on East European imports – one per cent of total EU raw steel capacity. The EU has also refused to relax restrictions on imports of food, textiles, clothing and chemicals. Together with iron and steel, these are the most competitive industries (they account for 33–46 per cent of exports to the EU from former Czechoslovakia, Poland and Hungary) and are suffering from the collapse in their markets due to a rapid decline in intra-COMECON trade. Many of the potential markets for Eastern Europe are likely to be in low value added manufactured goods. These industries are often located in the poorer regions of the EU, therefore trade liberalisation could well worsen the regional problems of the EU. These problems as well as the problems with agricultural products are limiting the access of Central and Eastern European economies to the markets of the EU.

The West appears to be putting more emphasis on the restoration of trade within Central and Eastern Europe. The immediate challenge, however, is not to let it collapse even further. To stimulate intra-regional trade an infusion of financial resources is necessary. The G-24 countries and international institutions have made commitments to the Eastern and Central European countries amounting to $100 bn. including food and medical aid, economic restructuring and technical assistance, export credit and investment guarantees, debt relief, and balance-of-payments support.[8] However, only a meagre share of what the West promised has actually been delivered. Besides, just a fraction of these funds was in grant form, the rest was loans and credit guarantees. As a result, according to the Institute for East–West Studies, levels of disbursement were disappointingly low, from 3 to 27 per cent, as recipient governments were reluctant to place an extra financial burden on their countries.

The EU has recognised that Central and Eastern European countries face serious problems in the transition to market economies. In the long run the EU has much to gain from aiding this reconstruction process. The countries of Central and Eastern Europe have the potential for rapid growth as they make this transition. The demand for goods, services, capital and 'know-how' will be very large. The EU is well placed to benefit from this growth in demand. The consumer market is also potentially very large, especially for consumer durables such as cars. Central and Eastern Europe may also provide a useful production base for many European firms seeking to supply this growing market, and for exports to Western Europe. Already many European car firms have reached agreements to produce cars in Central and Eastern Europe to supply the growing demand there and, if trade liberalisation is successful, to export to Western Europe.

Direct help by Western companies in the form of selling equipment and providing 'know-how' is a quick way of helping in the reconstruction process. Most Central and Eastern European countries welcome joint-venture enterprises. Some encourage direct investment either by buying existing enterprises or by establishing new enterprises. The privatisation programme could provide a quick method for Western companies to gain production plants in Central and Eastern Europe. Such companies could then transfer technology and processes at a very fast rate. This would greatly assist the transition process.

However, the troublesome heritage of centrally planned economies indicates that a great many long-term problems need to be solved before Central and Eastern Europe becomes an attractive area for many Western firms to operate in. The inflow of private capital has been below expectations and far below levels that policy makers consider desirable. The largest amount of foreign investment has been recorded in Hungary, where by the end of 1992 foreigners owned three per cent of productive assets, far below the planned 20–25 per cent. Private investors were mainly discouraged by high political and policy risks. In turn, the barriers to the export of products to the EU were important deterrents to some foreign investors, including firms from North America and the Far East, which would like to exploit location and cost advantages of ex-socialist countries to compete in Western European markets.

Some experts within and outside Central and Eastern Europe accuse the EU of providing an example of protectionism undermining liberal economic reforms in the post-communist European countries. The Institute for East–West Studies Task Force on Western Assistance to Transition[9] has summarised an agenda for Western governments: (*a*) abandon the use of tied assistance to Central Europe, particularly in the form of export credits; (*b*) provide a higher proportion of assistance in grants as opposed to loans; (*c*) open markets progressively to Central Europe; (*d*) provide incentives for private investment in Central Europe.

The EU has developed a four-point programme to help Eastern Europe:

1. trade liberalisation to establish a free trade area with Eastern Europe

2. industrial, technical and scientific cooperation

3. a programme of financial assistance

4. the creation of a system of political dialogue.

The trade liberalisation programme will proceed on the basis of the EU removing tariffs and quotas as reforms are implemented in Eastern Europe. The Czech Republic, Slovakia, Hungary and Poland are keen to join with the EU and EFTA to establish an area of free movement of goods and services. The long-term objective of these countries, however, is full membership of the EU.

Industrial, technical and scientific aid is given to improve the infrastructure of Eastern Europe, and to help transfer Western technology and 'know-how'. The PHARE and TEMPUS programmes of the EU form part of this help. The PHARE programme, initially to help Hungary and Poland to develop in the areas of agriculture, industry and the environment has been extended to cover most of Central and Eastern Europe. Help is given especially to train people to implement reconstruction programmes. The TEMPUS programme is to aid staff exchanges and training programmes between institutions of higher education in the EU and Eastern Europe. Financial assistance to reconstruct the economies of Eastern Europe is provided by the EIB and EBRD. The latter bank was set up by the G24 industrialised countries, with the EU as the lead partner. It is based in London and provides funds to assist developments in Eastern Europe. At present the objective is to provide limited funds linked to specific projects. Calls for a Marshall Aid-type programme of a general package of aid have so far been rejected in favour of selective aid to improve the infrastructure, and to help in the transfer of Western technology. The EU has also provided food aid to the former Soviet

Union, and Germany has provided more general aid and loans, particularly to the former Soviet Union. The amount and type of financial aid is a matter of some dispute within the EU. Germany has called for large-scale unspecified aid in order to encourage reform in Eastern Europe, especially for the former Soviet Union. The UK has opposed this, arguing that specific aid connected to the transition process would be more effective. There is a fear that large-scale general aid could provide some Eastern European countries with the means to delay reform. However, the need to provide more financial help as well as trade concessions and technical help is being increasingly stated.

The system of political dialogue has been established to help and encourage the move towards democracy, and to provide a forum for discussing problems and worries connected to the reconstruction process.

Hungary, Poland, the Czech Republic and Slovakia have special access to the political processes of the EU because of their associate membership status.

There can be no doubt that the EU is greatly involved in the reconstruction of Eastern Europe, and is the key link between Eastern Europe and the West. A free trade area in goods including some Eastern European countries seems possible in the future. According to the Commission, full membership for Hungary, Poland and the Czech Republic is possible by the year 2000. For the rest of Eastern Europe the problems of reconstruction would seem to make the position less clear. The large-scale reconstruction necessary to make the transition to democratic, market-based economies is likely to be a long process in Eastern Europe. The adjustment to integration with the EU is also likely to be a long and, for Eastern Europe, painful process of change.

The EU faces some problems in arriving at joint agreement on Eastern European matters, as member states have different perceptions about Eastern Europe. For Germany, relations with Eastern European countries have high priority, while for countries like the UK relations with Eastern Europe are not as high in their priorities for the EU. It is also clear that the EU is more important economically for Eastern Europe than vice versa.

Given these differences in perceptions, and in the economic importance of Eastern Europe, it is not easy for the EU to reach agreement on developing relations with Eastern Europe. However, whatever the differences and disputes within the EU over Eastern Europe it is obvious that the two are increasingly being drawn closer together.

The EU and Russia

A major effort to modernise the Russian economy can be traced back to 1985, when President Gorbachev inaugurated a programme of economic 'acceleration'. It proved to be ill-conceived and it was ineptly implemented. It has contributed to dramatising the deficiencies of a command economy rather than remedying them. A critical breakthrough in terms of economic reform came in early 1992 when the Yeltsin/Gaidar government introduced a set of austerity measures intended to facilitate a quick shift to a market-regulated system.

The reform strategy of the Russian government included four major objectives. Firstly, the liberalisation of almost all prices in tandem with a firm budget policy and a very restricted monetary expansion to curb inflation. Secondly, the provision of maximum liberty to all forms of business activities. A great stride towards economic openness was to be made in order to make the internal market more competitive. This was expected to help stabilize prices and markets after the initial inflationary jerk. The rouble was to become internally convertible. Its exchange rate, due to the policy of economic austerity and the support of the stabilisation fund supplied by the IMF, was to start to appreciate. Thirdly, an active social policy was envisaged in order to compensate for the inflationary shock and the social consequences of mass redundancies. Fourthly, there was to be a vast institutional reform incorporating privatisation and denationalisation of state-owned enterprises. The turnaround in economic performance and the first improvements in the living conditions of the population were forecast to start within one year after the initiation of reforms.

Table 16.6 The concept and realities of Russian reforms

	Official prognoses 1992		Actual figures	
	January–February	July	January–March 1992	1992 compared with 1991*
Inflation per year (%)	up to 500	up to 500	620	2700–800
Budget deficit (% of GNP)	0–1	10	15	22–25
Increase of money flow (M2) (%)	50–129	470	43	730–800
GNP (% to 1991)	92	88	86	78–80
Industrial output (% to 1991)	92	88	87	80
Gross investment in fixed capital (% to 1991)	74	55	56	50
Unemployment by the end of 1992 (millions)	10.5	10.5	–	0.6

*Preliminary figures

Source : *Svobodnaia mysl*, 1993, No. 1 p. 40, 42

Contrast between intentions and actual results of the reforms is apparent from the data presented in Table 16.6. Trends revealed in 1991–92 persisted in 1993: inflation has become uncontrollable; the rouble has collapsed; industrial production has entered a state of free-fall with no sign as yet that this is about to end; new investments in 1992 barely reached a half of the pre-1991 level; state-owned enterprises persist in preserving an unexpectedly high level of labour retention.

This initial stage of the Russian economic reforms had a bias towards monetary stabilisation. However, state-owned enterprises failed to adjust spontaneously to a new price, monetary and fiscal policy by cutting capital and labour costs and restructuring their production. Instead they engaged in stalling growth and delaying the 'supply response', increasing prices and wages, accumulating inter-enterprise debts and retaining redundant labour. As a result, inflation persisted while production was further squeezed, making prospects for recovery ever more distant.

In late 1992, the emphasis of reforms was moved onto an institutional axis. The government has been seeking to achieve a shift from 'soft' to 'hard' budget constraints through privatisation of state owned firms. From a neo-classical perspective this appears to be the only way to make managers behave as profit maximisers. However, given the limitations to privatisation as conditioned by current legislation and the socio-political situation in the country, it is difficult to expect this policy to produce significant and fast changes in enterprise behaviour. The current privatisation programme leaves too much discretionary power in the hands of central authorities and branch ministries (actually, about 80 per cent of state-owned enterprises may go private only with the permission of supervising bodies), while in other cases this power rests with workers of privatising enterprises. In both events one may hardly expect a swift behavioural shift to materialise. Besides, it is still not certain that a change in ownership will be sufficient to produce positive effects given the technological structure of Russian industry and the fact that the internal market is likely to remain relatively closed to foreign competition. In any case, large-scale privatisation programmes need to overcome many practical difficulties that make this a very protracted process (despite the efforts of the government, Russian privatisation slowed down in the first quarter of 1993 in comparison to the previous period).

In their plans, Russian reformers allocate an important role to foreign investments, which are considered to be essential for renovating the country's ailing industry and also as a major source of privatisation funds. Joint-ventures already play a noticeable role in Russia's industrial structure. At the beginning of 1992, they employed 130,000 persons and had a volume of sales of more than eleven billion roubles. In some branches their presence was quite substantial: by the middle of 1991, their share in telephone production was 10 per cent, in computers 7 per cent, in textile equipment 4 per cent and in footwear output over 2 per cent.[10] However, according to widespread opinion, joint-ventures have failed as an attempt to induce foreign capital to participate more actively in restructuring and modernising Russia's industrial structures. Major firms with solid reputations, modern technology and large amounts of capital have so far shown no particular interest in participating in joint-ventures. Foreign partners prefer to invest in services than in industrial production. With few exceptions they have been keen to extract short-term profit instead of embarking on long-term projects as was initially hoped. Foreign firms have also brought with them a sophisticated technique of disguised transmission of profits abroad. Therefore, shortly after the green light was given in the Soviet Union for the creation of joint-ventures with the participation of foreign firms, a search started for additional instruments to induce the inflow of production assets from abroad. Free economic zones may become the next major step towards the opening-up of the national economy and the intensification of foreign investment in the country. In the meantime, the authorities have been quick to pass decisions legalising free economic zones in the country. In summer 1992, the Russian President signed an extensive decree on some measures promoting the development of free economic zones. Similar legislation was endorsed in the Ukraine, Belarus and Kazakhstan.

At present, on paper at least, Russia is probably second only to China in the spread of free economic zones. Twelve officially proclaimed zones cover a territory of 1.2 million square kilometres with 18 million inhabitants, making up 12 per cent of the population of Russia. At the same time, the performance of these zones in terms of attracting foreign capital has been negligible. This contradiction deserves attention. Clearly, the investment climate in modern

Russia leaves much to be desired. Both political and policy risks remain high. None the less, some progress has been made leading to the construction of what may be considered as a good foundation for the future. One result appears to be particularly important from the point of view of the foreign investor: the acknowledgement of the principle that foreign investors deserve encouragement and remuneration for the risks they run in supplying their capital to a foreign country has penetrated the juridical system of the country and to an extent, through publicity given to discussions on foreign investment, the social mentality. Equally important have been the legal rights of basic guarantees protecting foreign property and the right to expatriate profits. The apparent progress in the updating of other juridical norms dealing with different aspects of business and property relations in the country will undoubtedly also have a favourable effect on capital inflow. All this must eventually eliminate many of the contradictions which still erode the organisational structure of the Russian economy. Overall, it is important to see that, despite all fluctuations, the principal line of development of a foreign investment policy has been oriented towards a more liberal and open approach.

The relationship of the EU with the countries of the former Soviet Union will be very difficult to establish. The Baltic States have already made clear their intention to follow the Czech Republic, Slovakia, Hungary and Poland by seeking associate and then full membership of the EU. The intentions of the larger countries such as the Russian Federation and Ukraine are less clear. These countries pose great problems for the EU due to their size in terms of both population and production (see Table 16.7) and their links to the underdeveloped Asian republics of the former Soviet Union. Bringing such countries to close relationship with the EU would mean that areas with very different economic, political and cultural characteristics would be drawn towards the Union. It is clear that the level of economic integration of the former Soviet Union requires some sort of agreement between these countries if economic disaster is to be avoided. Only the Russian Federation, and perhaps the Ukraine, appear to be sufficiently large and economically independent to isolate themselves from the rest of the former Soviet Union (see Table 16.7). Even the Russian Federation would find it difficult without some firm arrangements between the countries on conducting trade. This follows from the deliberate policy, adopted by central planners, of obtaining intermediate products from many different republics, thus making the production processes highly interdependent. Therefore, attempts by these countries to immediately cut themselves off from each other are doomed to failure, while their immediate impact on the economy is quite devastating. Only in the long run when these countries have reconstructed their economic and political systems would it be possible for them to establish close economic links with the EU. Given the nature of the economic and political crisis which faces the former Soviet Union, this is likely to take a considerable amount of reconstruction of all aspects of their societies. Compared to the former Soviet Union the countries of Central and Eastern Europe face a relatively easy task in integrating into the European economy. The policy of not granting the former Soviet Union large-scale financial assistance may also have to be reconsidered as the magnitude of the problems facing these countries becomes clearer. The former Soviet Union may have to construct some kind of economic community among these countries, perhaps on the lines of the EU, to facilitate trade and currency relations between themselves. However, many of these countries wish to be strongly connected to the heartland of Europe, and this means close links to the EU. Any new economic community in the former Soviet Union would also press for close links to the EU. The demands which this will place on the EU could well be one of the most troublesome policy areas in the late 1990s.

Table 16.7 Population and production in the former Soviet Union

Republic	Population (million)	Share of NMP(%)	Share of exports that is inter-republic trade (%)
Russian Federation	148.0	61.1	18.0
Ukraine	51.8	16.2	39.1
Uzbekistan	20.3	3.3	43.2
Kazakhstan	16.7	4.3	30.9
Belorussia	10.3	4.2	69.6
Azerbaijan	7.1	1.7	58.7
Georgia	5.5	1.6	53.7
Tadjikstan	5.2	0.8	41.8
Moldavia	4.4	1.2	62.1
Kirghizia	4.4	0.8	50.2
Lithuania	3.7	1.4	60.9
Turkmenistan	3.6	0.8	50.7
Armenia	3.3	0.9	63.7
Latvia	2.7	1.1	64.1
Estonia	1.6	0.6	66.5

Notes : NMP = Net Material Product (the Soviet version of GNP).
Source : *British Economic Survey,* Vol. 21, 1991

Issues connected to the enlargement of the EU

Most countries in Europe are seeking membership or close economic and political links with the EU. This raises at least four major problems with regard to the future development of the EU:

1. the effects on trade patterns

2. the implications for monetary integration

3. the impact on the budget of the EU

4. the consequences for the political and institutional structures of the EU.

If the EU extends membership to include most of the countries of Europe, or enlarges the EEA to create a free movement area for goods, services, capital and labour covering most of Europe, there would be significant changes in trade patterns. In particular, there would be growth in the share of intra-European trade and a consequent decline in extra-European trade. If such a change led to large-scale trade diversion, the enlargement could result in net welfare losses. Trade diversion is most likely to arise in cases where the tariffs and NTBs of prospective members are high and where they have low levels of trade with the EU. In these circumstances it is likely that the removal of barriers to trade will induce shifts in trade flows from lower cost non-EU suppliers. The potential for prospective members to benefit from the dynamic effects of an enlargement of the EU would be largely dependent on their ability to integrate into the economic heartland of the EU. Economies that can be easily linked to the main centres of economic activity in the EU are most likely to reap the dynamic benefits that would arise from any enlargement of the EU. Countries with high productivity, good infrastructures and developed business systems are probably best suited to reap the benefits of rationalisation and also of the introduction of new technologies and management/production systems that would emerge to take advantage of the new market opportunities that would arise from an enlargement of the EU. Countries with low productivity, poor infrastructures and underdeveloped business systems are likely to find it difficult to compete in an enlarged EU, and they may find themselves in direct competition with the some of the NICs and the more vibrant developing countries. On the whole it would appear that the EFTA countries are likely to benefit from the changes in trading patterns that would arise from an enlargement of the EU. The situation with regard to Central and Eastern Europe and Turkey is more problematical. Nevertheless, such economies could benefit from closer links to the EU as this might provide a stimulus for them to boost their levels of productivity. They may also be attractive sites for some types of foreign direct investment, in particular for assembly plants for goods to be sold in the richer parts of the EU.

The ability of prospective members of the EU to adjust to the monetary integration schemes of the EU varies considerably. Most of the currencies of EFTA countries are already closely linked to the Deutschmark, and their levels of economic development and the structure of their economies are fairly similar to those EU countries that are most likely to develop monetary integration, especially the move towards monetary union. Countries such as Austria, Norway, Sweden and Switzerland probably pose fewer economic problems for monetary union than, for example, Greece or Portugal. However, because of the economic and monetary situation of the countries of Central and Eastern Europe and Turkey, significant problems would arise if they were to seek to join in the move towards monetary union in the EU.

Enlargement could lead to considerable problems for the budget of the EU. Some prospective members would find it difficult to compete in the EU, and if the Structural and Cohesion Funds were to be expanded to help them adjust to membership the problems of financing the budget could become very difficult. This factor probably counts heavily against early membership for the countries of Central and Eastern Europe and Turkey. However, the EFTA countries cause no problems in this area as they would be net contributors to the budget.

The EU is already experiencing difficulties in developing the political and institutional structures of the Union to allow it to govern itself effectively. Heated debates are taking place on the issues of subsidiarity and on whether the EU should develop into some type of federal system with strong political and social objectives or into a more inter-governmental arrangement that would be mainly concerned with trading issues. Significant enlargement may give rise to increasing pressure to make the EU a more inter-governmental organisation. Enlargement would also put great pressure on the institutional structures of the EU. The institutional structures are already considered to be hampered by the cumbersome practices and procedures that are used to make and implement EU laws, and the monitoring and enforcing of these laws is also putting strain on the Commission and the ECJ. Enlarging the EU would make the task of effectively governing the EU even more difficult. A fundamental reconstruction of the institutional structure and some kind of agreement as to the type of Union that should be built seem to be essential if the EU is to expand to encompass the many countries seeking membership.

In spite of these difficulties, the problems caused by allowing the EFTA countries to join seem to be fairly minor. This is mainly due to their relatively small size and their level of economic development. However, the countries of Central and Eastern Europe and Turkey present a series of problems that will be more difficult to overcome. Indeed the case for early membership for these countries would seem to be largely political, i.e. attempts to stabilise Central and Eastern Europe. A further political objective, at least for some member states, may be to make it more difficult for the EU to move towards monetary union and to make attempts to development a federal EU a very difficult, if not impossible, task.

Notes

1. See *UN Economic Commission for Europe* 1992; Fry and Nuti, 1992.
2. *UN Economic Commission for Europe* 1992, p. 41.
3. *The Economist*, 21 September 1991, Survey on Eastern Europe, p. 10.
4. The firms most popular with voucher holders were almost exclusively banks, hotels, breweries, ceramics works, and foreign trading companies (*Transition, the Newsletter about Reforming Economies*, Vol. 3, No. 7, July–August 1992, p. 11).
5. See for discussion Lang F, Short-run effects of economic reforms in Eastern economies, *Intereconomics*, September/October 1991, pp. 223–229; *The Economist*, 21 September 1991, Survey on Eastern Europe, pp. 17–18; *Newsweek*, 16 March 1992, pp. 40–41; *The Economist,* 16 May 1992, pp 91–92.
6. *East European Markets*, 26 June 1992, p. 15.
7. As the disappointing results of reforms piled up, the IMF, in the person of its executive director, was compelled to accept that under certain conditions 'it might not be as heretical as it looks to maintain import tariffs, keep production in some sectors under government control . . ., implement a rigorous income policy, and avoid massive price increases . . . ' (*External Economic Relations of the Central and East European Countries, NATO Colloquium 1992*, Brussels, NATO, p. 69).
8. *Transition, the Newsletter about Reforming Economies,* Vol. 3, No. 7, July–August 1992, p. 12.
9. *Ibid.*
10. *Ekonomika o zhizn'*, 1992, No. 5, p. 13.

References and further reading

Baldwin R 1992 *The economic logic of EFTA countries joining the EEA and the EC*, EFTA Occasional Paper.
Blankart F *Financial Times*, 6 November 1989.
Calvo GA and **Coricelli F** 1992 Stabilizing a previously centrally planned economy: Poland 1990, *Economic Policy*, No. 14, pp. 175–208.
Cecchini P 1988 *The European Challenge 1992*, Wildwood House, Aldershot.
Church C 1990 EFTA and Nordic countries responses to the EC in the early 1990s, *Journal of Common Market Studies*, Vol. 28, No. 4, pp. 63–75.
Dabrowski P 1991 East European trade (Part 1): The loss of the Soviet market, RFE/RL Research Institute, *Research on Eastern Europe*, Vol. 2, No. 40.
Dahlstrom G 1989 EFTA/EC relations as seen by the Swedish trade unions, *EFTA Bulletin*.
De Groote J 1992 Economic transition and western assistance to Central and Eastern Europe, *External Economic Relations of the Central and East European Countries, NATO Colloqium 1992*, pp. 59–78, Brussels.
Delors J 1989 *Introduction to Commission's Programme for 1990*, European Commission, Brussels.

EFTA Bulletin, January 1990, Editorial.

The Economist, 11–17 August 1990.

Ellman M 1993 General aspects of transition, in Admiral PH (ed.), *Economic Transition in Eastern Europe*, Blackwell, Oxford.

Financial Times, 27 April 1990.

Fry M and **Nuti DM** 1992 Monetary and exchange rate policies during Eastern Europe's transition: some lessons from further east, *Oxford Review of Economic Policy*, Vol. 8, No. 1, pp. 27–44.

Gardner D *Financial Times*, 11 June 1993.

Gowan P 1991 Old medicine, new bottles: Western policy toward East Central Europe, *World Policy Journal*, Vol. 9, No. 1, pp. 1–34.

Herin J 1986 *Rules of origin and differences between tariff levels in EFTA and the EEC*, EFTA Occasional Paper, No. 13.

IMF, The World Bank, OECD, EBRD, 1990, *The Economy of the USSR: Summary and Recommendations*, The World Bank, Washington, DC.

Kornai J 1986 The soft budget constraint, *Kylas*, Vol. 39, pp. 27–39.

Leskelä J and **Parviänen S** 1990 *EFTA countries' foreign direct investments*, EFTA Occasional Paper, No. 34.

Lugon J 1990 The EFTA dimension widening the Community circle, *UACES Conference*, University of Kent, Canterbury, 25/26 June.

Marrese M and **Vanous J** 1988 *Soviet subsidisation of trade with Eastern Europe. A Soviet Perspective*, University of California, Berkeley.

Norman V 1989 EFTA and the Internal European Market Economic Policy: A European Forum, *Economic Policy: A European Forum*, Cambridge University Press, Cambridge.

Nuti DM 1992 Economic inertia in the transitional economies of Eastern Europe, paper presented at the conference *Impediments to the Transition: The East European Countries and the Policies of the European Community*, European University Institute, Florence, 24–25 January 1992, (mimeo).

Panattoni JL 1978 *Treaty relations and European integration*, PhD thesis, University of Washington.

Pinto B, Belka M and **Krajewski S** 1993 *Transforming State Enterprises in Poland. Microeconomic Evidence on Adjustment*, Policy Research Working Papers: Transition and Macro-adjustment, Poland Resident Mission, WPS 1101, World Bank, Washington.

Rack R 1990 The Austrian application widening the Community circle, *UACES Conference*, University of Kent, Canterbury, 25/26 June.

Rosati D 1992 The CMEA demise, trade restructuring and trade destruction in Central and Eastern Europe, *Oxford Review of Economic Policy*, Vol. 8, No. 1, pp. 58–81.

Schmitt N 1990 New international trade theories and Europe 1992: some results relevant for EFTA countries, *Journal of Common Market Studies*, Vol. 29, No. 1, pp. 62–73.

UN Economic Commission for Europe 1992 *Economic Survey of Europe in 1991–1992*, UN, New York.

Verdoss A 1956 Austria's permanent neutrality and the UNO, *American Journal of International Law*, 50, 1, 61–8.

Wallace H and **Wessels W** 1989 *Towards a new partnership: the EC and EFTA in the wider Western Europe*, EFTA Occasional Paper, No. 28.

Welfens PJJ 1992 *Market-oriented systematic transformations in Eastern Europe*, Springer-Verlag, Berlin.

CHAPTER 17

The Triad and the NICs

Frank McDonald

Introduction

The EU generally regards relations with the USA, Japan and the NICs as less important than relations with EFTA. This relative lack of interest may be because EFTA is a larger trading partner of the EU than is the USA, Japan or the NICs, and Central and Eastern Europe is nearly as important for EU trade as Japan. However, much of the trade with Japan involves sensitive products such as cars and consumer electronic equipment. The strategic nature of these sectors is perceived to be of great importance by many of the governments and companies of the member states of the EU. The rapid growth of Japanese exports to the EU, combined with a persistent balance of payments surplus with the EU and accusations of deliberate restriction on imports to Japan, have increased tension in trade matters. Trade in agricultural products is a major source of friction between the EU and the USA (see Chapter 13). The passing of the Omnibus Trade Act in 1988 by the USA has the potential to provoke trade disputes between the EU and the USA. The Super 301 provisions of this Act require the US government to take retaliatory action against countries that are deemed to discriminate against the USA in trade matters.

The role of the USA and Japan in providing DFI in the EU also increases the importance of relations with them, especially as some member states regard DFI as a way around necessary protection of European-owned companies. This is connected to the so called 'screwdriver plant' problem. Some member states claim that Japanese companies simply assemble products within the EU from kits exported from Japan, thereby escaping the protectionary measures implemented by the EU. The creation of the SEM seems to have increased the activities of Japanese firms in setting up production plants within the EU. Some member states regard this DFI as a welcome contribution to boosting productivity and the quality of products. Others regard it as a threat to the future of existing European-based companies. Another argument arises over the high technology nature of some of the DFI. It is claimed that this results in the domination of European high technology industries by foreign-owned companies, leading to Europe becoming no more than a site for US and Japanese assembly plants. The computer and information technology equipment sectors in Europe are dominated by US and Japanese companies. This has raised the question of whether such foreign-owned firms should be allowed to participate in EU research and development programmes such as ESPRIT.

The member states of the EU face growing penetration of their markets from the NICs.

Many markets in Europe are experiencing increasing competition from companies based in Taiwan, South Korea and Hong Kong. The countries of ASEAN (Brunei Darussalam, Malaysia, Philippines, Singapore and Thailand) are also seeking new markets in Europe. In many respects these countries are following the Japanese path. They have very fast growing economies and they base their expansion on export-led growth. The first markets they have targeted are steel, shipbuilding, low value-added manufactured goods and chemicals. They have had considerable success in these markets and they are now turning to other, more high-technology sectors. Already companies such as Hyundai and Samsung are experiencing success in penetrating the European markets for cars and consumer electronics. US and European multinationals have also established production plants in these NICs and they are increasingly supplying the European market from these plants. The rapid growth of China holds out the prospect of this large economy becoming an NIC. If this happens the penetration of EU markets by the NICs will undoubtedly rise.

The Triad

The relationship between the USA, Japan and Europe is often referred to as 'the Triad': this term was popularised by Ohmae (1985). The Triad is often regarded as the most important group of countries in the world. One of the reasons for the importance of the Triad arises from the size of the combined output from these counties. The countries of the Triad are in effect the engine of the world economy. As they grow they tend to pull the rest of the world along with them; conversely, if they enter recession they drag the rest of the world into recession. Consequently, relationships between the members of the Triad have a strong impact on the transmission of booms and slumps across the world economy. The mechanisms which link these economies in the economic cycle are not clearly understood, but the trading and DFI links certainly play a key role in the process. Equally important, or perhaps more important, are the links created by the international financial markets. The centres of these international financial markets are in the USA (New York and Chicago), Japan (Tokyo) and Europe (London). Changes in stock, futures and exchange rate markets in one of these centres are quickly picked up by the other centres, and funds flow freely between these markets in response to these changes. This process is of great importance in the transmission of cyclical changes in economic activity.

Another reason for the importance of the Triad is that most of the large multinational companies have their base in the USA, Japan or Europe. Many of these companies are also world leaders in their fields. In telecommunications equipment, for example, there are AT&T and Tie Communications (USA), Alcatel and Siemens (Europe), NEC and Fujitsu (Japan). The large vehicle manufacturing companies are also based in the Triad: Ford and General Motors in the USA, Toyota, Honda and Nissan in Japan and Volkswagen and Daimler Benz in Germany. In some industries Japanese companies are not important relative to US and European companies, for example the food processing industry – Nestlé, Unilever and BSN in Europe and Kelloggs, Campbells and Coca-Cola in the USA.

There is little doubt that, of the members of the Triad, the USA has the strongest economy. The USA has the largest economy in terms of absolute and per capita GDP and it is also the home base of many of the largest multinational companies. In many sectors US companies are among the world leaders in terms of market share and technological development. Generally,

US companies have a strong presence in a wide range of industries, for example information technology and computing equipment/software (IBM, Hewlett Packard, Dell and Microsoft), vehicle production (Ford and General Motors), food processing (Coca-Cola, Heinz, Mars, Philip Morris), aerospace equipment (Boeing and McDonnel Douglas), chemicals (Dupont and Union Carbide) and personal hygiene products (Proctor & Gamble and Colgate-Palmolive). The Europeans and the Japanese have a strong presence in some of these industries but not in all of them. The Europeans have few world leaders but they are fairly strong in a number of sectors, e.g. telecommunications equipment (Alcatel, Siemens and Ericsson), food processing (Nestlé, Unilever, Cadbury-Schweppes and BSN), consumer electrical goods (Philips and Electrolux), vehicle production (Volkswagen, Renault and Fiat) and chemicals (BASF, Holest, Rhône Poulenc and ICI). The Japanese have many world class companies but they tend to be concentrated in a smaller number of sectors. The Japanese tend to excel in vehicle production (Toyota, Honda and Nissan), information technology and computing equipment (NEC, Hitachi and Fujitsu) and consumer electronics (Panasonic, Sony and Toshiba).

The dominance of the USA in terms of economic size, world class companies and technological leadership is often overlooked in discussions on the Triad. The rise of Japanese companies and their successful penetration of the US market, particularly the car market, has led to a view that the USA is in a period of relative decline and needs to restructure its economic base fundamentally in order to survive as a major economic power. This case is argued, with some force, by Thurow (1992). There is also a school of thought which is pushing for new policies based on government intervention to help US companies improve their productivity. This school also calls for the management of foreign trade and DFI to compensate for unfair competitive advantages enjoyed by the Europeans, but especially by the Japanese. One of the leading advocates of this policy is Laura Tyson, who has been appointed as a senior economic advisor to President Clinton (see Tyson 1991).

This view of US decline is probably greatly overstated. As indicated above, the Americans are still the major players in many of the fastest growing markets in the world. There is also evidence that the USA is still the most productive nation in the world. A study by the McKinsey Global Institute (1993) discovered that, on average, the Japanese were 83 per cent as productive as the Americans and the Germans (the most productive European country) were 79 per cent as productive. In some industries the Japanese are more productive than the Americans (cars and car parts, consumer electronics, metalworking and steel), while the Germans do not have higher productivity in any major sector and could match the Americans only in steel and metalworking. The USA has a decisive lead over the Germans in computers, cars and car parts, consumer electronics, soaps and detergents, beer and food processing. They have a clear lead over the Japanese in soaps and detergents, beer and food processing. Perhaps the main problem of the US and European economies is that they are best in areas where they do not have strong exports to Japan, while the Japanese are best in areas where they do have strong exports to the USA and Europe.

The economies of the Triad have trading, technological and financial links. However, the development of economic integration in Europe and the creation of the North American Free Trade Area (NAFTA) between the USA, Canada and Mexico have led to fears that the Triad may evolve into three relatively closed trading groups based on NAFTA, a 'Fortress Europe' and Japan (possibly with close links to the NICs of south east Asia). If such evolution were to take place there might well be potential for conflict and trade wars between the members of the Triad. Such conflict would raise serious difficulties for the world economy. Theory suggests that in such circumstances cooperation can result in mutually beneficial outcomes, whereas conflict can lead to all parties suffering losses. However, these theories also suggest that cooperation between such parties can be very difficult to achieve and maintain.

Cooperation or conflict?

The issue of cooperation versus conflict can be analysed by using game theory. This theory is useful for analysing international relations as it provides a relatively straightforward method of investigating cooperative and non-cooperative behaviour between nations (see Nicholson 1989). The key to this analysis is the pay-off matrix. Suppose that the EU and Japan are considering whether or not to grant trade concessions by easing or eliminating barriers to trade imposed on foreign firms.

EU

		A	B
	A	2,2	0,3
Japan			
	B	3,0	1,1

A = policy of granting trade concessions

B = policy of not granting trade concessions

If both parties adopt A the outcome is a pay-off of 2 each. If they both choose B, the outcome is a pay-off of 1 each. If the EU chooses A, and Japan B, the pay-off becomes 0 for the EU and 3 for Japan (vice versa if the EU chooses B and Japan adopts A). This is the classic prisoner's dilemma game, where the outcome for a player depends on the choice of policy of the other player. Obviously, the best aggregate outcome is for both to choose trade concessions and adopt policy A. However, if one player chooses B and the other player chooses A the pay-off is 3 for the player who opts for B and 0 for the player who chooses A. There is therefore an incentive for both players to choose policy B, as by doing this the minimum pay-off is 1 and the maximum is 3, as opposed to a minimum pay-off of 0 and a maximum of 2 if policy A is adopted. In these circumstances a non-cooperative, or conflict, outcome prevails, even though the cooperative outcome yields the greater aggregated benefits.

   The simple nature of these games tends to conceal some of the problems of directly using such models to explain real world behaviour. Firstly, traditional economic theory suggests that unilateral trade concessions are better than no trade concessions. This follows from the gains to consumers of reducing trade barriers which leads to lower prices and higher outputs. In these circumstances it is not clear why the policy of not reducing trade barriers confers benefits to either party in the game. In the real world, however, trade concessions are often denied unless there is a reciprocal granting of concessions. Indeed, this principle of reciprocity seems to be replacing the more liberal MFN treatment which characterises the GATT rules in the trade in goods and services. The MFN clause requires no discrimination against any GATT member with regard to trade concessions which have been conceded, and that this should apply even if there is no reciprocal granting of concessions. In the granting of trade concessions in services and on the rights of foreign companies to establish subsidiaries, both the EU and the USA lay some stress on reciprocity. Hence, in trade liberalisation other than in goods, reciprocity is becoming an important consideration. Even in the granting of trade concessions on goods, agreement on trade liberalisation packages in GATT are often dependent on reciprocal agreements to reduce barriers. The rationale for these actions may be based on placing consumer interests on a lower level than producer interests. It is also possible to provide a theoretical justification for this behaviour, as some of the new theories of international trade suggest that unilateral trade concessions are not necessarily beneficial. In a world of increasing returns to scale and imperfectly competitive market structures there can be a sound economic case for providing strategic protection to allow domestic industries to reap advantage from economies of scale and to benefit from the learning effects of expanding domestic production. However, the advocates of these new theories (see Krugman 1991) maintain that it is probably not possible to pursue such policies efficiently, and that the objective of free trade is on balance the best policy. Nevertheless, to engage in unilateral free trade while your trading partners are implementing strategic protection policies is likely to harm your economy. This suggests that the implementing of free trade policies is best done by negotiations on some kind of reciprocal basis. It is therefore possible that pay-off matrices such as the above are a reasonable, though simplified, characterisation of real world behaviour.

A second problem with the use of such models is the assumption that players act with certain knowledge of the content of the pay-off matrix. In practice the size of benefits will be very uncertain, but game theory does not require accurate valuations. What is necessary is to know the ordering of benefits. It is not unreasonable to expect the ordering of benefits to be known by players. A more serious problem arises if only one player chooses the policy. Obviously, different views exist within a country about the ordering of benefits from trade policy. A political decision must be made on this issue, thereby allowing the government to act as one player. Changes in the political system within the country could radically alter the orderings in the pay-off matrix. In the case of the EU this is further complicated by the Union acting for a number of member states. Quite often the member states take different views on these matters. The current UK government is in favour of a liberal attitude towards granting trade concessions, and regards the principle of reciprocity with some suspicion. The French government however, tends to take a more conservative line on trade concessions, and regards reciprocity as very important. Consequently, the EU has more problems than single countries in arriving at a ranking of benefits. This might make the playing of such games rather difficult for the EU.

A third problem is the assumption that the games are played in isolation from each other, which implies that the players do not learn. If the non-cooperative solution emerges from several games, it might be expected that the players would learn how to make arrangements to allow for cooperative outcomes to be achieved. This can be analysed using the theory of supergames, where the same game is repeated a large number of times. The problems of playing supergames in international trade relations are discussed by Keohane (see Guerrier and Padoan 1988). In such games problems arise with free riding, when some players in the game reap benefits from cooperative solutions without themselves granting concessions. This results in a sub-optional outcome in the sense that the maximum possible benefits to the system as a whole are not reaped. It might be argued that Japan has done this by benefiting from trade concessions which have opened up the markets of the USA and the EU to foreign competition, without much in the way of liberalisation of the controls on entry to Japanese markets. The solution to this problem revolves around various forms of reciprocity. In this respect the insistence by the EU and the USA on using the principle of reciprocity may be wise. This does not mean that the way in which the EU is using this principle is useful in achieving a cooperative outcome. Indeed Ishikawa (1990) maintains that the EU is adopting too rigid a concept of reciprocity in dealing with Japan and the USA. The main problem is the attempt by the EU to obtain 'mirror image' treatment. This involves the granting of exactly the same concessions by all parties, and presents problems in areas such as financial services where laws and regulations govern access to the market. In the past the EU has insisted that in order for Japanese or US firms to gain equal access to the European financial services market, EU firms must face the same conditions in the Japanese or the US market. This is basically asking Japan and the USA to adopt in their home markets the emerging EU rules and regulations governing access to a single European financial services market. This hard form of reciprocity is unlikely to succeed. The principle of equivalent but not identical access would seem to be useful in order to achieve a cooperative solution to this problem. The EU seems to have moderated its view on this issue in talks with the Americans, and seems to be adopting an approach based on equivalent access.

It would appear to be important for the EU, Japan and the USA to find ways of playing these supergames which allow for cooperative solutions to be found. This requires mechanisms to control free riding by utilising loose forms of reciprocity. Systems to reduce cheating and non-fulfilment of agreements are also needed. Keohane sees international institutional innovations as playing an important role in this process. Institutions can monitor and publish data to identify, and therefore deter, cheating and free riding behaviour. These institutional forums can also be used to forge issue linkages. This involves linking separate issues in order to reach agreement, so that, for example, the EU could grant access to US firms to the European financial services market in return for American concessions on the CAP problem. Hence institutional forums and agencies could play a key role in allowing cooperative outcomes to emerge. The Uruguay Agreement to liberalise trade and to create a new international agency, the World Trade Organisation (WTO), could play an important role in monitoring and policing trading relations between the members of the Triad. In the case of the EU, Japan, and the USA, the existing institutional frameworks could hamper such developments. International agencies such as the IMF, G7 and the OECD have representation from member states rather than from the EU. Only in GATT does the EU represent all member states. With the growing importance of EU–Japanese–US relations, it might help to achieve cooperation if the EU rather than the member states were the prime negotiator. The creation of the SEM has added impetus to the role of the EU in these agencies. The moves towards EMU within the EU would seem to indicate that the role of the EU in the main international monetary agencies must grow. In the future not only trade issues but international monetary issues are likely to be within the competence of the EU, rather than the member states. In these circumstances good relations between the members of the Triad could become very important. This implies a need to change international institutional arrangements to allow the EU a greater role. Such institutional change has dramatic implications for political arrangements within the EU. What seems to be necessary is for a decline in the role of some member states in international agencies, with a corresponding growth in the role of the EU. There may be a need in the future to form new international agencies composed of the EU, Japan and the USA. In this respect recent moves to improve contacts between the EU and the USA and Japan could prove to be significant. The presidency of the Commission holds regular meetings with officers of the US presidency and annual meetings with the Japanese government to discuss issues of mutual interest. These meetings provide evidence of the growing importance which the EU attaches to relations with the US and Japanese governments. Three major issues can be highlighted in current relations between the members of the Triad: trading arrangements, the implications of American and Japanese DFI and the problems caused by persistent balance of payments deficits that the USA and the EU have with Japan.

Trading arrangements with the USA

The USA adopted a benign attitude towards the EEC in the 1950s and 1960s. The demise of the Bretton Woods system and the relative decline of the dollar, combined with the rise of the Deutschmark and the increasing industrial power of the EEC, led to a change in American attitudes towards the Community. The prime dispute has been over the CAP (see Chapter 13). The crisis in the world steel industry in the 1970s, 1980s and 1990s also led to some bitter trade disputes. Both parties were heavily involved in helping their steel industries, the Americans by use of import quotas and the EU by a host of policies implemented under the ECSC. This led to both sides accusing each other of unfair trading practices, and to the implementation of a series of trade restrictions. This dispute ended with the increase in the demand for steel in the wake of the boom in world growth in the late 1980s, overcapacity and the restructuring of the steel industry in both the EU and the USA. However, overcapacity in world steel production has led to new problems between the USA and the EU in the 1990s.

The American insistence on trying to apply US law to foreign individuals and companies outside the USA has also caused friction with the EU. This is the so-called extraterritoriality problem. The most famous example of this was the US embargo in 1982 on the use by European firms of some American goods, patents and licences to build the Siberian pipeline. This was a pipeline to carry natural gas from Siberia to Western Europe. The Americans regarded this pipeline as a threat to the independence of Western Europe, and the US government tried to take unilateral action to control the activities of European firms engaged in work for the pipeline. This action was deeply resented in Western Europe, and eventually the embargo was withdrawn. Another extraterritorial issue arose when the USA tried to impose federal taxes on companies on a unified basis even for company profits which had been earned in Europe. This was also resented in the EU, and was never implemented. Ironically, some of the EU proposals on company disclosures, taxation and worker participation could have extraterritorial implications for US companies with subsidiaries in the EU.

By the 1980s relations between the EU and the USA had been soured by these disputes. The passing of the Omnibus Trade Act in 1988 led to a further deterioration in relationships. The Super 301 provisions of this Act require the US government to identify countries using unfair trading practices, and such countries must take action to stop these practices. If they do not the US government unilaterally imposes trade restrictions against them. The EU maintains that such trading conflicts should be resolved by GATT rather than by unilateral action. This Act is perceived by the EU as evidence of the growth of protectionism in the USA. However, the EU also has a range of unilateral devices such as anti-dumping and surveillance procedures (see Chapter 14). In 1994 the USA has threatened to use the Super 301 provisions in its trade disputes with Japan. The many trade disputes that the USA has with the EU may lead to the Americans taking action under the auspices of Super 301.

The potential for trade disputes between the EU and the USA seems to be increasing. Both parties have complaints about the other's trading behaviour. The EU has complained about US policies for public procurement contracts, as a host of federal, state and even local government rules and regulations control public procurement in the USA. Federal and state governments also operate 'Buy American' policies on many public procurement contracts. This makes it very difficult to check US compliance with the GATT rules on public procurement. In 1986 the USA reached agreement with Japan on stabilising prices and exports of semiconductors. As the USA and Japan account for 87 per cent of the world market for semiconductors, this agreement is tantamount to a world price-fixing agreement. Such agreements are obviously harmful for third parties such as the EU. The EU is also concerned with the system of setting and maintaining technical standards in the USA. These standards are issued by a multitude of federal and state authorities, and often pay little regard to international systems of setting standards. This makes it difficult for EU firms to collect information in order to comply with US standards. Meanwhile, the EU is moving to a system of common European standards which will make it relatively easy for US firms to gather information on European standards. In short, the EU regards the US market as one with considerable NTBs against EU firms.

The Americans also have complaints about EU trading practices. The public procurement directives being issued to open up public tendering within the EU tend to discriminate against non-EU firms. For example, if the tenders from EU and non-EU firms are equivalent, then the directives imply that the EU tender should be accepted. If a tender includes 50 per cent or more non-EU content, the contracting body can refuse to accept the tender. These directives are also unclear about the position of foreign subsidiaries which tender for public procurement contracts. As most of these subsidiaries are American owned, this is a matter of some concern for the USA. The Americans also claim that the European telecommunications equipment market is effectively closed to US competition because of differences in standards. There is also concern that the rules and regulations being formed to create the SEM, especially in the financial services sector, will harm the USA as they imply that American banks might be disadvantaged compared to EU banks. This is connected to the reciprocity problem referred to above. A directive issued in 1989 called for most European television broadcasting to be domestically produced. (The Uruguay Round was agreed only after this dispute over broadcasting was dropped from the negotiations. This issue is therefore still unresolved.) This is clearly aimed at reducing American television programmes on European networks. There have also been complaints from the USA about the large subsidies from European governments for the European Airbus. As the USA is the only viable alternative source of such civil aircraft, this is regarded as a protectionist policy against the USA. The CAP provides a perennial source of American complaints about EU trading practices.

This catalogue of complaints about each other's trading practices and behaviour is indicative of the poor relations between the EU and the USA. This would seem to make more urgent the need to avoid conflict, and to work towards cooperative solutions.

Trading arrangements with Japan

The postwar incorporation of Japan into the world trading system has been a rather difficult process. Although Japan applied for membership of GATT in 1952, it was not granted membership until 1955. Even then many West European countries refused to grant Japan MFN treatment, because of claims that Japan engaged in unfair export practices and that the Japanese domestic market was effectively closed to Western exports. Most Western European countries applied quantitative restrictions on some Japanese exports. It was not until the mid-1960s that Japan was granted MFN treatment and admission to the OECD. Consequently, by the time the EU developed the CCP the attitude of Western European countries towards Japan was one of distrust and suspicion.

It is difficult to find rational reasons for this attitude. There was a legacy of bad relations because of the export policies of Japan in the 1930s. In this period the Japanese had practised large-scale dumping of imitation Western products and had frequently ignored trademarks and patents. The experiences of the Second World War resulted in opposition from the UK and the Netherlands to granting Japan full rights in the world trading system, but these explanations seem inadequate to explain the hostile attitude of Western Europe towards Japan in the immediate postwar period. The sharp cultural differences between Japan and Europe, and a marked lack of interest about Japan, may have contributed to this hostility. In this period Europe was preoccupied with the growth of the Cold War, and the early moves towards European Unity. When Europe finally began to take an interest in Japan, the dramatic growth of the Japanese export-led industries led to what might be regarded as a kind of paranoia. There developed a school of thought which regarded Japan as a country engaged in economic warfare to destroy Western industries. The persistent and growing trade surplus of Japan only added to this paranoia, particularly as Japanese exports in the 1960s and 1970s tended to be concentrated in sensitive sectors, such as shipbuilding, steel and textiles. During the 1970s and 1980s the growth of Japanese exports of cars and consumer electronics made further inroads into highly sensitive sectors. In more recent times Japan has become a leading exporter of computers and other information technology equipment. The increasing dominance of Japanese exports in these sensitive areas has led to a continuing hostility towards Japan. This rather sad history of trading relations between Europe and Japan has had a powerful influence on the attitude of the EU towards Japan.

The EU inherited a series of quantitative restrictions which member states had imposed on various Japanese products. Member states have added to these by agreeing a series of VERs with Japan. These VERs became popular in the 1980s, particularly for cars and consumer electronics. The EU has become unhappy with these VERs as they are bilateral arrangements between member states and Japan, and therefore they undermine the CCP. They also required the maintenance of frontier controls within the EU, since without frontier controls Japanese imports could enter the EU by way of a member state that did not have a quantitative restriction, or VER, on that product. Therefore, in order to verify compliance with VERs and quantitative restrictions it is necessary to maintain frontier controls. As the SEM removed frontier controls, bilateral VERs and quantitative restrictions had to be abolished. They were replaced by an EU-wide set of restrictions. In particular a VER agreement has been reached that restricts exports of Japanese cars into the EU to 1.23 million cars. This agreement is due to expire in 1999. However, VERs restrict competition, and they are harmful to consumers. This is illustrated in Figure 17.1.

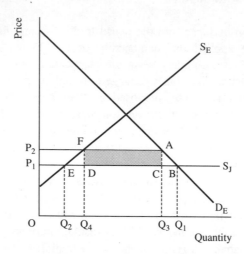

Figure 17.1 Effects of a VER

It is assumed that the EU and Japan are the only sources of supply of this good, and that Japanese supply is perfectly elastic. Both of these assumptions can be dropped, but this complicates the analysis and does not add significantly to the conclusions. Before the VER was agreed, a total quantity of Q_1 would be supplied: Q_2 from the EU, and Q_2Q_1 of imports from Japan. After the VER of Q_4Q_3 is agreed the price rises to P_2, and quantity sold declines to Q_3. Production in the EU rises to Q_4, and Japanese imports fall by Q_3Q_1. This leads to a total consumer surplus loss of P_1P_2AB. Of this loss P_1P_2FE is transferred from EU consumers to EU producers. This follows from the higher price which consumers must pay for the good. The triangle FDE is also transferred from consumers to producers, but this is needed to pay for the resources needed to produce the extra EU output. The triangle ABC is the consumer surplus loss resulting from the reduction in quantity from Q_1 to Q_3. The area FACD is equal to $Q_4Q_3 \times P_2 - P_1$, i.e. the increase in price times the size of the quota imposed by the VER. This is a transfer from EU consumers to the Japanese exporters. This explains why Japanese companies are often willing to accept VERs, as this extra revenue could be greater than the loss of revenue from the fall in Japanese exports. For such an outcome it would be necessary for the good to have a price inelastic demand. This analysis clearly identifies the winners from VERs (Japanese exporters and EU producers), and the losers (EU consumers).

The EU has a variety of complaints about Japan's protection of its domestic market, in particular impenetrable technical rules and regulations, exclusion from public procurement contracts, and heavily bureaucratic import documentation procedures. Ishikawa (1990) argues that these problems are also experienced by Japanese firms seeking to export to the EU. Both parties are maintaining protectionist trading practices. In some ways trading disputes between the EU and Japan have similarities with those between the EU and the USA. Presumably similar solutions based on equivalent reciprocity should be sought for both the USA and Japan.

There are, however, differences in the problems which the EU faces with Japan. Firstly, Japan runs a consistent balance of payments surplus with the EU. Secondly, the export of services to Japan is severely hampered by legal barriers. Thirdly, the Japanese marketing and distribution system is complex and involves close collaboration between Japanese producers and wholesalers and retailers. This makes it difficult for EU firms to sell consumer goods in Japan, unless they have Japanese subsidiaries. The marketing and distribution costs which EU firms face in Japan are therefore likely to be higher than those costs for Japanese firms selling in the EU. It could be argued that the EU suffers (relative to Japan) from less productive manufacturing operations and more efficient distribution systems. The Europeans are therefore suffering from being good retailers but poor producers. Fourthly, Japanese companies have close collaboration with each other under the auspices of the Japanese Ministry of International Trade and Industry (MITI). Much of the collaboration between firms encouraged by MITI would be illegal if carried out in the EU. The EU therefore maintains that this is tantamount to an unfair trading practice. These issues make it more difficult for the EU to reach agreement with Japan, as opposed to the USA. Given that the EU has not achieved significant cooperative solutions with the USA, the prospects for establishing good relations with Japan do not appear to be good.

Trading arrangements with the NICs

Relationships between the EU and the NICs of south east Asia are not as developed as those with the USA and Japan. However, as the NICs have increased their share of the EU market the Union has extended its relationships with these countries in efforts to find solutions to trading problems. In the 1990s there have been several visits by senior members of the Commission to the NICs in attempts to develop dialogue on trading matters. The EU has proposed a new Agreement with ASEAN to replace the one agreed in 1980. The Agreement will be non-preferential in terms of trade barriers, but will seek to promote cooperation to encourage trade.

In the main the EU takes the view that the NICs should be encouraged to liberalise their trading systems to grant companies in the EU easier access to their markets. Thus the Commission has complained about the close relationship between South Korean manufacturers and their subcontractors and distributors. There has also been some concern over the difficulties of tendering for public procurement contracts. The EU claims that these systems act like a series of NTBs and that they are a significant barrier to entering the markets of South Korea. These complaints from the EU and the USA are very similar to those they make about the difficulties of entering the Japanese market because of the system of *keiretsu* (the collaborative relationships that exist between Japanese assemblers, suppliers and distributors, based on close financial links and technical collaboration. These problems have led the EU to embark on a process of seeking to promote 'fairer' market entry conditions and trading arrangements with South Korea. It is likely that the other NICs will also become increasingly subject to such pressures from the Commission.

The Commission has also imposed a number of anti-dumping measures against the NICs, for example on magnetic discs from Japan, Taiwan and China; on electronic weighing scales from Singapore and South Korea; on monosodium glutamate from Indonesia, Taiwan, South Korea and Thailand. Anti-dumping measures on video cassettes from Japan and South Korea and compact-disc players from Taiwan, Singapore and Malaysia expired in 1993, but they could be renewed. The Commission has also imposed a large number of anti-dumping measures against China (see Commission EC (1993) for a review of these). The EU has taken an increasingly tough stance on what it regards as unfair trading practices by the NICs.

The EU is developing dialogue with the NICs of south east Asia. However, this dialogue seems to be mainly concerned with complaining about the trading practices of these NICs. The presence of large-scale Japanese DFI in the NICs and the growing strategic alliances between Japanese and NIC companies have raised fears that Japan will use the NICs as low wage cost bases from which they can attack US and European markets. In general, the NICs are regarded as smaller versions of Japan, but with the added dimension of higher tariff and non-tariff barriers, lower wage costs and even stronger protection of domestic markets because of the nature of their internal economies, i.e. impenetrable distribution, service sector and public procurement systems and close links between suppliers and manufacturers which make it very difficult for European suppliers to be awarded contracts. The main problems between the EU and the NICs are therefore market access for EU companies and accusations of unfair trade restrictions and practices by the NICs.

The Uruguay Agreement of GATT provides a multilateral system of dealing with such complains by use of GATT rules. However, it is not yet clear whether GATT can deliver in these areas. It is also not obvious that the Europeans and the Americans always have a valid case in these areas. In some cases the main problems seem to be that European and US companies do not undertake the necessary modification of their strategies and operations to allow them to penetrate the markets of the NICs successfully and/or to defend their domestic markets successfully against import penetration by the NICs. The EU and the USA are also often keen to promote bilateral solutions to the problems of trading with the Japanese, and this preference for bilateral dealings may well spill over to their dealings with the NICs.

The prospects for good relationships between the EU and the NICs do not appear too good. The main problems seem to arise from the Europeans adopting a fairly hostile approach to the rise of new low cost competitors in EU markets. The arrival of these new competitors has stimulated growing interest by the EU in the trading activities of the NICs. In some ways history is repeating itself, as the EU takes a very similar approach to the NICs to the one it has taken to Japan. The main complaints against the NICs are very similar to those levelled against the Japanese. In essence these complaints are often based on accusations that these economies do not operate on European/American models of company behaviour, and also that the state provides extensive help and protection that make it very difficult for European/US economies to compete on equal terms. The solutions to these problems, according to the Europeans and the Americans, are to be found in transforming Japan and the NICs into economies that are more similar to those of Europe and the USA. In some sectors of Japan and the NICs this view is increasingly being regarded as a type of cultural imperialism that has its roots in the failure of European and American economies to adopt new systems of management and production to enable them to compete successfully. However, pressures have arisen that are forcing some European and US companies to adopt some of the cost saving and quality enhancing procedures of Japanese and NIC production systems. These pressures have been brought to bear by the growing penetration of European and American markets by the Japanese and NICs and by the expansion of Japanese DFI into the USA and Europe. Nevertheless, the Americans and the Europeans still regard the domestic economies of Japan and the NICs as being very difficult to penetrate due to hidden forms of protection and, in the case of the NICs, high tariff barriers. The issues of DFI and policies to obtain greater access to markets are examined below.

Balance of payments problems with Japan

The EU and the USA have had persistent balance of payments problems with Japan in the 1980s and the 1990s. The USA experienced its largest deficit in 1987 ($60 bn.); the EU peaked in 1988 at $29 bn. In spite of an appreciating yen and several attempts by the Japanese to reduce their persistent large surpluses with the USA and the EU, these surpluses continue. According to the Commission, 'this says something about the openness of markets', (Commission EC 1991). The USA has taken an even stronger line, and in 1994 has threatened to apply Super 301 rules against the Japanese if they do not open up their markets.

Both the Americans and the Europeans have therefore taken the view that their deficits with the Japanese are largely due to the 'hidden protection' practised by the Japanese. In particular, they complain about the *keiretsu* system; the role of MITI in promoting systems of collaboration between Japanese companies and that these systems are closed to non-Japanese companies; the 'buy Japanese' practices in public procurement contracts; and the structure of distribution and retailing systems that make it very difficult for non-Japanese companies to sell consumer goods in Japan. The Japanese have established an agency, the Fair Trade Commission (FTC), which is charged with the responsibility of breaking up the anti-competitive practices in the distribution and retailing industries. The FTC is also seeking to liberalise public procurement systems and generally to act against the range of anti-competitive practices that make Japan one of the most expensive markets in the world. The EU has encouraged the Japanese to allow the FTC to liberalise markets as the best way to allow European companies greater access to the Japanese market. The EU has sought to highlight the benefits to Japanese consumers of such liberalisation, and has therefore adopted a rather cautious approach to the question of opening up Japanese markets to foreign competition. The Americans have taken a tougher approach to the question of market access, and have threatened to impose trade sanctions unless the Japanese achieve specified increases in American imports. In effect the Americans have begun to move towards concepts of 'managed trade' in their desire to reduce their balance of payments deficit with Japan. So far the EU has not adopted this approach.

However, economic theory suggests that balance of payments deficits are not caused by problems of market access but that they arise from the macro-economic policies that countries adopt. It is possible to analyse this question by using a simple national income model of an economy.

$$Y = C + I + G + X - M \tag{1}$$

Y = income, C = consumption, I = investment, S = savings, X = exports, M = imports, G = government, T = taxation revenues, G − T = government budget, S − I = private sector loanable funds budget.

Absorption (A) is the amount of national income that is consumed in the economy, given by:

$$A = C + I + G \tag{2}$$

National income is consumed, saved or taxed, and is therefore defined by:

$$Y = C + S + T \tag{3}$$

Substituting equation (3) into equation (1) and rearranging gives

$$(G - T) - (S - I) = (M - X) \tag{4}$$

Equation (4) tells us that the balance of payments $(M - X)$ is determined by the government and private sector loanable funds budgets. Therefore, for example if $S = I$ but $G > T$ a balance of payments deficit must prevail. In these circumstances the absorption of the economy cannot be met without running a balance of payments deficit. Increasing market access or depreciating the currency will not improve a balance of payments deficit unless absorption is decreased. Thus if the Japanese improve market access and/or appreciate the yen in attempts to boost their imports (while the Americans and the Europeans maintain their high absorption rates), balance of payments surpluses with the USA and Europe will persist. The increase in exports to Japan arising from the opening up of their markets and/or appreciation of the yen will boost national income in the USA and Europe. However, this will boost absorption unless steps are taken to reduce budget deficits. Consequently, countries that run persistent budget deficits will experience persistent balance of payments deficits.

The problems the USA and Europe have experienced with regard to persistent balance of payments deficits with Japan have been primarily caused by the fact that the Japanese have operated macro-economic policies that have led to surpluses in their government and private loanable funds budgets, while the Americans, in particular, have run large deficits in their budgets. The best solution to the persistent balance of payments surpluses of Japan are therefore to be found not in market access policies but in macro-economic cooperation. What seems to be required is policies that will end the tendencies of the USA and Europe to have deficits and the Japanese to have surpluses in these budgets. The balance of payments problems that the USA and Europe have with Japan are connected to inappropriate macro-economic policies, not to issues of market access.

This does not mean that policies to encourage the opening up of Japanese markets are of no value. The growth of trade that could follow from the opening up of Japanese markets would lead to benefits to all the members of the Triad. These benefits would arise from the welfare gains from freer trade that would result from the reaping of comparative advantage and from the boost to growth that would follow from the 'supply-side' effects of the increase in competition that greater trade would induce. The opening up of Japanese markets (and also those of the NICs) would have effects similar to those of any liberalisation programme, e.g. the SEM programme. However, measures to resolve incompatible macro-economic policies within the Triad would seem to be a necessary component in any moves to resolve the trading problems caused by persistent Japanese balance of payments surpluses.

Japanese and US DFI in the EU

The EU is already a very large market for non-EU firms. The creation of the SEM and the EEA has resulted in a single market of 365 million consumers. It is therefore not difficult to see why many American and Japanese companies are keen to have access to the EU market. The use of DFI to establish subsidiaries in the EU is only one way of gaining access to this market. Alternative and easier methods exist via exporting and licensing agreements. Both of these activities are undertaken by American and Japanese companies. However, DFI is a growing method of gaining access to the EU market. The USA is the largest source of DFI in the EU, but Japanese DFI has increased dramatically in the past decade. Tables 17.1 and 17.2 provide some illustrative data on DFI inflows into Europe.

Table 17.1 Inflows as percentage of total DFI in Europe (by investing country to recipient country)

Investing country	Receiving country							Total (ECU) bn
	EUR12	EFTA	D	F	I	UK	NL	
USA	85	15	14	8	6	32	11	135.8
Japan	94	6	8	7	2	39	22	43.4
D	83	17	–	16	9	13	11	51.3
F	88	12	8	–	8	13	27	33.5
I	83	17	10	12	–	11	17	32.5
UK	87	13	13	18	7	–	21	39.2
NL	80	20	17	13	2	16	–	36.0

Note : Data for 1990, except for France (1989).
Source : Based on data in Thomsen and Woolcock (1993)

Table 17.2 Inflows of DFI into Western Europe (percentage of stock of DFI in each country or Western Europe as a whole), 1989

Investing country	Receiving country					
	Western Europe	D	F	I	UK	NL
USA	27	30	12	14	41	27
Japan	5	7	6	2	5	4
Europe	60	56	75	80	39	66

Source : Based on data in Thomsen and Woolcock (1993)

Tables 17.1 and 17.2 show that the bulk of DFI into Europe is located in the EU, that the USA is the single largest source of DFI inflows into Europe, but that the greater part of DFI inflows into Europe is intra-European. The UK has the largest DFI inflows from the USA and Japan, with the Netherlands being the second most important location for such DFI. Japan is about as important as Germany as an investor in Europe. The UK receives significantly more of its DFI from outside Europe than do the other member states of the EU. The Netherlands is a significant receiver of DFI from all the major investors in Europe. Of the four large member states Italy appears to be the least popular location for DFI into Europe. It is clear that the UK and the Netherlands have significantly different DFI profiles from those that prevail in the rest of Europe. The main reason for the profile of the Netherlands may be connected to its position as the gateway into the heartland of the EU. The UK position may be partly explained by the relatively large share of the UK's trade which is outside Europe. Indeed, the UK is considerably more involved with non-European countries not only in trade but also in its outflow of portfolio investments and DFI ventures. The UK is the only member of the EU that has more DFI in the USA than in Europe. The UK is also the largest source of DFI outflows from Europe. In this sense the UK is a more international economy than the other countries of Europe.

An obvious reason for DFI is to aid exporting and licensing activity. Hence, banking, insurance and other commercial activities (e.g. establishing marketing and distribution channels) go hand in hand with exporting and licensing activity. Such DFI forms a large part of the inflow into the EU. Increasingly however, Japanese DFI is concerned with establishing production plants in the EU. American companies have a long tradition of establishing production plants in Europe. Many reasons can be put forward to explain such DFI. It can be factor-based to gain benefits from lower labour costs or the exploitation of natural resources, to acquire successful product lines and/or technological developments, and to reap economies of scale. Market-based DFI can occur to allow companies to avail themselves of lower transport costs, and to gain proximity to local markets (location-specific advantages). There can also be a desire to retain market power by controlling brand names and trademarks (ownership-specific advantages). The existence of tariffs and NTBs can also induce DFI, to allow foreign companies to overcome such trade barriers.

A study by Thomsen and Nicolaides (1990) maintained that trade barriers are a major reason for DFI into the EU. Heitger and Stehn (1991) found evidence that Japanese investment into the EU is greatly influenced by a desire to overcome trade barriers. Yannopoulos (1990) identified four incentives for DFI into the EU arising from the creation of the CU and the CM. These incentives are:

1.   rationalisation to take advantage of opportunities to exploit comparative advantage

2.   rationalisation to reap the benefits of cost reductions from economies of scale and lower levels of X-inefficiency

3.   import-substitution to defend market share

4.   import-substitution to gain market share.

The development of the CU and the CM lead to trade creation because as tariffs and NTB are removed this induces product specialisation in order to exploit the benefits of comparative advantage. Multinational companies that are already in Europe will seek to undertake investments to allow them to achieve greater product specialisation in their European operations. Such rationalisation will allow them to take advantage of the trade creation effects. However, the creation of the CU and the CM also leads to trade diversion and suppression (see Chapter 1). These provide an incentive to multinationals that are excluded from the EU market (by such trade diversion and trade suppression) to defend their market share in Europe by investing in import-substitution projects in Europe. The potential to reduce cost arising from the creation of the CU and the CM also induces multinationals to engage in investments in order to reap economies of scale and benefit from lower levels of X-inefficiency. The expansion of the size of markets that follows from the CU and the CM leads to incentives for multinationals to undertake import-substitution investments because the market is now large enough to be supplied from Europe rather than by exports from the home base of the company. The Cecchini Report estimated that the trade diversion effects of the SEM would reduce EU imports by 2 per cent, and when the benefits of cost reductions and economies of scale were added an estimated reduction of 5–7 per cent in EU imports was considered possible. Such reductions in EU imports provide strong incentives for multinationals to increase their import-substitution and rationalisation investments in the EU.

All the above incentives for DFI into the EU arise from location-specific advantages. However, there may also be ownership-specific advantages that encourage multinationals to increase their DFI into the EU. In many areas connected to branded products the defence of trademarks and brand names is a very important objective. The creation of the CU and the CM induces rationalisation of companies that have such objectives, as a result of the opportunities to expand sales and reduce costs. If multinationals wish to retain strong control over their trademarks and brand names they may seek to take advantage of these opportunities by DFI rather than by alternatives such as franchising or licensing. The food processing industry appears to be motivated by such considerations. There have been several major acquisitions by food processing companies in attempts to rationalise production and distribution systems in Europe, e.g. takeovers such as the Nestlé acquisition of Rowntrees and the purchase of Jacobs Suchard by Philip Morris. The French-based food company BSN has also been involved in a series of mergers and acquisitions in Europe. One of the main reasons for such DFI appears to be a desire to acquire ownership of trademarks and brand names that can be marketed throughout the SEM.

The attitude of some member states to Japanese transplants or so-called 'screwdriver plants' may also have contributed to the growth of DFI into the EU. The dispute over the Nissan car plant in the north east of England highlighted this issue. France claimed that these cars should be regarded as Japanese, not European, and therefore they should be subject to the controls that existed on the imports of Japanese cars. The expansion of Japanese car plants in the UK by Toyota and Honda has increased the intensity of this debate. The response from the Commission was to impose a 60 per cent European content rule on such Japanese transplants. Such rules of origin may well lead to incentives for Japanese car companies to increase their DFI into Europe to ensure fulfilment of these rules. However, all Japanese car plants in the UK already fulfil this rule. Further Japanese car plants use procedures such as Just-in Time and Total Quality Management, which require suppliers close to the assembly plants. It is therefore not clear whether the European content rules have any significant effect on DFI. Nevertheless (in terms of the value of content), most Japanese car companies do not fulfil a 60 per cent rule, because many of the engines and transmission systems for Japanese cars (that are assembled in Europe) are imported from Japan. However, most Japanese car companies have or are undertaking investments that will allow them to supply the bulk of their engines from European sources. It is not clear whether this move towards European manufacture of engines arises from commercial considerations or from fears that rules of origin will be modified to force them to use more European-produced engines. Nevertheless, the Japanese experience in the USA suggests that a high local content in transplant car plants is a major objective, and there are no rules of origin obligations in the USA.

The attitude of the Commission to rules of origin for Japanese car transplants reflects the differences that exist among the member states towards Japanese DFI into the EU. Countries such as the UK and the Netherlands are keen to maximise the flow of DFI from the USA and Japan. They tend to see this as an effective and quick method of boosting productivity, acquiring high-technology products and processes and more effective management systems.

Other member states, in particular France, regard such DFI with some apprehension. They are concerned about the possibility of US and Japanese domination of high-technology industries and about the effects of such DFI on existing European industries, notably the car industry. There are also concerns that the EU has not developed a comprehensive policy towards DFI into the EU and that this could result in multinationals exploiting member states by threatening to move locations to those member states that will give them the best deal. Therefore, issues such as state aids, living and working conditions and the characteristics of stock markets and company law could be affected by the power of multinationals to coerce the governments of member states. These concerns stem from a belief that most of DFI into the EU is based on factor-based reasons. i.e. to gain advantages from lower labour costs, higher state aids, etc.

However, Thomsen and Woolcock (1993) in their study of DFI into the EU maintain that most DFI into the EU is market-based and that it stems largely from intra-industry trade and the advantages that result from being close to clusters of high economic activity. Thomsen and Woolcock argue that such DFI plays a crucial role in the integration of markets and in the creation of a more competitive market. Therefore, barriers to DFI are regarded as having the same disadvantageous effects as barriers to the movement of exports and imports. In developed economies the fastest growing area of trade is the intra-industry sector, and DFI plays a significant role in the promotion of such trade. The transfer of new technologies and management systems is also connected to DFI flows. In such circumstances curtailing DFI would harm the long-term objective of encouraging the economic integration of the member states. Thomsen and Woolcock concede that not all DFI into the EU is driven by market-based considerations. Factor-based issues such as labour costs, taxation rates and state aids do influence DFI flows. However, the decision to invest in a particular member state or region is a complex one, and these factors are often minor compared to market-based issues. On the whole Thomsen and Woolcock favour competition among rules by the member states to determine the best regulatory frameworks. Such an outcome would also seem to be in line with the concept of subsidiarity. Nevertheless, there are areas where Union action is required to ensure that markets are competitive and that obstacles are not created that inhibit the creation of effective industrial structures. Therefore, the merger control regulation and Articles 85 and 86 need to be rigorously enforced to prevent the creation of anti-competitive behaviour by multinationals. However, the EU must also ensure that member states do not use their powers to prevent the creation of effective structures in areas such as telecommunications and airline services. In both these areas DFI by US and European companies has an important role to play in the creation of effective European networks. The development of new industries such as biotechnology and the creation of electronic highways could also be hindered if the EU or some of the member states placed undue restraints on DFI in these areas.

It is likely that the governance of DFI will become a important issue in the EU. In principle, there are no good reasons to treat DFI as being significantly different from trade flows. In the past the EU has taken a general position that is in favour of liberalising trade flows. Consequently, it is difficult to argue for a change in this policy with regard to DFI flows. In general DFI flows have similar effects to trade flows, i.e. they boost competition, lower costs and lead to rationalisation of business activities. DFI flows also have added advantages in that they transfer technology and management expertise. However, they lead to winners and losers and the rise and fall of companies. These effects also arise from trade flows. Perhaps the greatest difference between DFI and trade flows is that the former involves ownership rights over economic assets and the consequent right to transfer profits to other countries. Nevertheless, in systems where there is free movement of capital the right to transfer profits exists for national as well as foreign-owned companies. Given that DFI is one of the key mechanisms for conducting international business activities and that Europe is a large investor in the USA and increasingly in Japan, it is difficult to argue that the EU should adopt a restrictive approach towards the development of DFI in the Union.

Prospects for future relations

Relations on economic matters between the EU, the USA and Japan are not particularly good. The creation of the SEM and moves towards EMU make it important for all parties to improve this situation. The development of a coherent EU approach to this issue would seem to be a prerequisite to solving these problems. There is some evidence that the EU is placing a higher priority on relations with the USA and Japan than it has in the past. The implementation of the SEM programme offers the potential to create a more open system of trading relations within the Triad. There are however strong pressures from within the EU to adopt more protectionist policies. Such pressures are also at work in the USA, and in Japan the whole legal and cultural system has a protectionist aspect. Therefore, prospects for a more open trading system may not be very good. The costs of maintaining the current state of affairs, or of increasing conflicts, are quite high. Certainly, the prospects of economic conflicts involving the use of trade restrictions cannot be healthy for the EU, the USA or Japan

All parties have much to gain from creating a more liberal trading environment. Foreign trade is a major part of the economy of the EU, and the Union is the largest trader in the world. A more restrictive world trading environment is therefore likely to be harmful to the long-term interests of the EU. Given that many of the most effective and technologically advanced companies are US or Japanese owned, it would seem to make little sense to place strong restrictions on these companies, whether they are exporting or operating subsidiaries in the EU. One of the main benefits of creating the SEM is the increase in competition that follows from the removal of trade barriers. In principle the opening up of the European market to US, Japanese and NIC competition should add to these benefits. Undoubtedly some European companies would suffer from increased American and/or Japanese/NIC competition, but this would also be true of increased competition from other member states. For a company operating within the EU it would not matter whether the increased competition came from a Japanese or a German source. The increase in competition would be painful for the company, and beneficial for the consumer. Companies that could not adjust to the new competitive environment would have to exit the market, leaving the more effective companies to operate in that market. This gives rise to structural and regional problems as the system adjusts to the new competitive environment. The Union has already accepted the need for such adjustment by agreeing to the creation of the SEM, and may be prepared to accept more structural change resulting from the moves towards EMU. Indeed, these structural changes are deemed beneficial for the economy and citizens of the EU. It is therefore difficult to see why opening up the EU economy to foreign competition, which would have much the same effects, should be deemed harmful to the EU.

If a very pessimistic view is taken of the ability of European companies to compete with the best American, Japanese and NIC companies it might be beneficial to provide some temporary protection for European companies to allow them time to undertake the necessary adjustment, and to ease balance of payments problems. There may also be some strategic reasons to protect high-technology industries from being overwhelmed by US and Japanese companies. The danger with this approach is that 'temporary protection' is often extended to permanent protection, and this is not normally conducive to an efficient and dynamic economy. Generally the EU operates on the basis that competition is beneficial to the long-term interests of all Union citizens, so that to restrict such competition to European sources does not seem to have much of an economic rationale. Only if the EU were to abandon its long-held (and Treaty-backed) commitment to competition would a move towards a 'Fortress Europe' be possible. The only major area where the EU does not adhere to a basically anti-competitive stance is agriculture, which is not a good example of an effective policy and is certainly not beneficial for consumers. Agriculture is also the sector which creates the most problems for the external economic relations of the EU. There seems little chance of the EU extending the degree of protection it gives to agriculture to other sectors of the economy.

The Union would appear to have much to gain from adopting an open approach to the rest of the world, and to the USA and Japan in particular. In a few politically sensitive and strategically important areas it might be necessary for the EU to adopt a protectionist stance, but generally the EU is likely to adopt a fairly pro-competitive approach. However, as was indicated above, there are a host of unresolved problems between the Union and the USA, Japan and the NICs. For negotiations on trade liberalisation to be successful it is important that the USA and Japan do not perceive the current programme of European integration to be harmful to their interests.

There is good reason to think that the USA, Japan and the NICs will not be harmed by the creation of the SEM – indeed they stand to gain from this programme. Although there will be some trade diversion effects from the creation of the SEM, which will tend to reduce exports to the EU, these effects could well be surpassed by the expansionary influence on their exports to the Union caused by the increase to the GDP of the EU resulting from the 1992 programme (see Figure 2.1 in Chapter 2).

The USA is particularly well placed to benefit from growth in the EU, as it already has a strong presence in many of the markets of the EU. This presence is not only in exports, but also in the large number of US subsidiaries which operate in the Union. Many of these subsidiaries are market leaders and could well benefit from the removal of trade barriers within the EU. For example, eight of the ten largest food processors in the EU are American-owned. Many of these American-owned firms are also Pan-European in their operations, such as Ford, General Motors and IBM, while many European firms are more centred in their domestic market. These American-owned firms can also call on the experience of their parent companies in marketing and distributing to a large single market – the USA. These are advantages that many European firms do not have. The USA may also experience growth in its manufactured exports to the EU.

The Americans may have some problems in adjusting to new European standards, and access to public procurement contracts will be important. However, a considerable part of these exports are connected to American subsidiaries in the EU and, providing that these are treated in the same way as EU-owned companies, the USA should be able to maintain and perhaps increase its share in these markets. Some American companies are also forming joint-ventures with European companies in order to ensure access to the European market. The markets of the EU are, however, likely to become more competitive and American companies will have to come to terms with this both in their exports and in the operation of their European subsidiaries. In many areas the main competition could come from the Japanese.

Although the Japanese have a considerably lower base of exports to the EU and subsidiaries in the EU, they are rapidly expanding in some sectors, in particular in cars and consumer and business electronic equipment. In these sectors they are well placed to reap considerable advantages in the European market. The success of the Japanese in producing low cost and high quality cars and electronic equipment should allow them to have a good performance in European markets. Indeed, they have already made considerable progress in penetrating these markets, and the growth of Japanese subsidiaries in the EU is likely to improve their position further. The Japanese are also becoming major players in the computing and information technology markets, and they should perform well in these markets. Perhaps the major problem that the Japanese face is their success, as this tends to worry many politicians and industrialists, and leads to strong calls for protection. As was discussed above, these calls are already strong in some of the member states. Providing that the Japanese can ease these worries, they should benefit from the SEM. Given that the Japanese are world leaders in many of these areas, it should not be difficult to persuade European decision-makers that to shut out the Japanese from these markets is not in the Union's long-term interests.

If the EU makes progress towards EMU a set of new problems will emerge in relations with the USA and Japan. The possibility of a single currency in the EU would mean a new major world currency. Such a currency would have significant implications for the role of the dollar and the yen. It would make more urgent the need to come to new institutional arrangements for the world international monetary system. If this did not occur there could be the possibility of increased instability in the exchange rates of the major currencies of the world. Unless a view is taken that flexible and widely fluctuating exchange rates are not harmful to long-term economic activity, the prospect of increased instability in exchange rates is regarded with considerable alarm. If stable exchange rates are considered to be beneficial, then provided that any new European currency is introduced within the context of a new and effective arrangement with the USA and Japan the prospects for a mutually beneficial outcome should be good.

The prospects for the EU to establish good relations with the USA, Japan and the NICs should not be adversely affected by the creation of the SEM, and provided proper institutional arrangements are made, the moves towards EMU should not damage relationships. Much would seem to depend on the establishment of effective institutional arrangements, and a mutual recognition of the net gains possible to all parties from close cooperation. However, as the discussion above has indicated, there is a series of potential obstacles to achieving such cooperation.

References and further reading

Bridges B 1992 *EC–Japanese relations: in search of a Partnership*, RIIA, London.
Calingaert M 1988 *The 1992 Challenge from Europe*, National Planning Association, Washington DC.
Commission EC 1991 *Trade Policy Review*, Vol. 8, Office for the Official Publications of the EC, Luxembourg.

Commission EC 1993 *Bulletin of the European Communities*, 7/8, Office for the Official Publications of the EC, Luxembourg.

Guerrier P and **Padoan P C** 1988 *The Political Economy of International Co-operation*, Croom Helm, London.

Heitger B and **Stehn J** 1991 Japanese direct investment in the EC – responses to the internal market 1993, *Journal of Common Market Studies*, Vol. 29, No. 1.

Hufbouer G and **Schott J** 1992 *North American Free Trade: Issues, Recommendations and Results*, Longman, London.

Ishikawa K 1990 *Japan and the Challenge of Europe 1992*, RIIA/Pinter, London.

Krugman P R 1991 *International Economics, Theory and Policy*, Harper Collins, New York.

Latter R 1990 *The Interdependent Triad: Japan, the United States and Europe*, HMSO, London.

McKinsey Global Institution 1993, *Manufacturing Productivity*, Report of the McKinsey Global Institution, New York.

Moswood S J 1989 *Japan and Protection*, Routledge/Nissan Institute for Japanese Studies, London.

Nicholson M 1989 *Formal Theories in International Relations*, Cambridge University Press, Cambridge.

Ohmae K 1985 *Triad Power,* The Free Press, New York.

Schott J 1991 *Free Trade Areas and US Trade Policy*, Longman, London.

Smith M and **Woodcock S** 1993 *The United States and the European Community in a Transformed World*, Pinter, London.

Thomsen S and **Woolcock S** 1993 *Direct Investment in European Integration*, Pinter, London.

Thomsen S and **Nicolaides P** 1990 *Foreign Direct Investment : 1992 and Global Markets*, RIIA, Discussion Papers 28, London.

Thurow L 1992 *Head to Head: The Coming Economic Battle Among Japan, Europe and America*, Nicholas Brealey Publishing, London.

Tsoukalis L 1986 *Europe, America and the World Economy*, Basil Blackwell, Oxford.

Tyson L 1991 *Trade Conflict and High Technology Industries*, Longman, London.

Woolcock S 1991 *Market Access in EC–US Relations: Trading Partners or Trading Blows?* Pinter, London.

Woolcock S and **Yamani H** 1993 *EC–Japanese Trade Relations, What are the Rules of the Game?* RIIA, London.

Woronoff J 1992 *Asia's Miracle Economies*, M.E. Sharpe, London.

Yannopoulos G N 1990 Foreign direct investment and European integration: the evidence from the formative years of the European Community, *Journal of Common Market Studies*, Vol. 28, No. 3.

CHAPTER 18

Economic developments in Germany and their impact on Europe

Heinz Josef Tüselmann

Introduction

The high degree of interdependence between the EU countries has resulted in economic developments in one country affecting the economies of its partners and the EU as a whole. Thus, Germany is in a special position owing to the size of its economy and having the Deutschmark as the anchor currency in the ERM. The openness of all EU economies has increased markedly over the past 30 years and for all, except Ireland, Germany is now the main market for exports. With exports being an important component of aggregate demand, an economically stable and growing Germany is of vital importance for the EU countries. The monetary policy of the Bundesbank is primarily geared towards internal economic conditions, with the overriding objective of price stability and the orientation towards the longer term production potential. Combined with Germany's leadership of the ERM, this has influenced policy options in other countries and their realisation of growth potential. Particularly since German unification, which constituted an exogenous shock for the EU economies, the debate on 'German dominance' has intensified. Obviously unification had the most dramatic impact on the former German Democratic Republic (GDR), which overnight obtained a new political, social and economic system, as well as being suddenly exposed to world competition. Significant changes in the western German economic landscape occurred with respect to the business cycle, the monetary situation, inflation, the external balance and the budget. Via direct and indirect spill-over effects, unification also had an impact on Germany's EU partners, although in the analysis of Germany's influence on the collapse of the ERM there seems to be some confusion with respect to cause and effect. In the first part of this chapter, economic developments in the eastern and western parts of Germany will be analysed, as will the policy consequences. There then follows an outline of the supply-side problems as epitomised in the recent debate about Germany's position as a production location. These problems may affect the performance of the German economy in the longer term. The second part of the chapter will illustrate how far developments in Germany have an impact on other EU economies and monetary integration. German unification serves as a good example to demonstrate the magnitude of this impact. Trade effects, the impact of German monetary policy on the partner economies and its contribution to the *de facto* ERM collapse will be discussed.

Germany and Europe in the 1980s

The 1980s was a period characterised by an extraordinarily long business cycle expansion and the globalisation and integration of markets, with strong growth in world trade and Foreign Direct Investments. Particularly in the second half of the 1980s, the EU experienced rapid economic growth, with average rate of GDP increases of 3.2 per cent,[1] although growth rates varied between different countries (see Table 18.1). In 1988 and 1989 growth rates accelerated to 4.1 per cent and 3.4 per cent respectively and were above the longer run potential rate.[2] Germany, the biggest EU economy, with real GDP being over a quarter of the EU combined GDP,[3] had experienced its eighth successive year of growth by 1990. The average growth rate of 2.1 per cent in the 1980s was slightly below the EU average growth performance (see Table 18.1). With high growth rates of 3.7 and 3.4 per cent in 1988 and 1989 respectively, the economy was operating close to its potential output and tendencies towards stagnation began slowly to emerge.[4] However, growth was proceeding within price stability and external balance. Here, as well as with other main economic indicators, Germany outperformed most of its partner countries (see Tables 18.2–18.5). The average unemployment rate of 6 per cent in the 1980s was the lowest within the EU and fell to 4.8 per cent by 1989. The general government deficit was small and manageable, even recording a slight surplus in 1989. The current account, typically in surplus, improved further in the mid–1980s, peaking at 4.8 per cent of GDP in 1989. Reflecting these surpluses, Germany was a classical capital exporter, making contributions to finance the current account deficits of other EU countries. Inflation fell to 1.5 per cent in 1988, although it subsequently increased to 2.6 per cent in 1989. The corresponding EU averages were 4.5 and 5.0 per cent respectively. However, due to the deflationary impact of ERM membership, the rates of the hard core members were progressively coming down to the German level.

Table 18.1 GDP at constant market prices (annual % change)

	1981–1990	1988	1989	1990	1991	1992
(West) Germany	2.1	3.7	3.4	5.1	5.7	1.5
Belgium	2.0	5.0	3.8	3.4	1.9	1.0
Denmark	2.1	1.2	0.8	1.7	1.2	1.0
Greece	1.5	4.1	3.5	−0.1	1.8	1.5
Spain	2.9	5.2	4.8	3.6	2.4	1.2
France	2.2	4.3	3.8	2.2	1.1	1.9
Ireland	3.7	4.9	6.5	8.3	2.5	2.9
Italy	2.2	4.1	2.9	2.2	1.4	1.1
Luxembourg	3.6	5.7	6.7	3.2	3.1	2.2
Netherlands	1.9	2.6	4.7	3.9	2.2	1.3
Portugal	2.7	3.9	5.2	4.4	1.9	1.7
UK	2.6	4.3	2.1	0.5	−2.2	−0.9
EUR 12	2.3	4.1	3.4	2.8	1.4	1.1

Source : European Economy, Annual Economic Report for 1993, No. 54, 1993

Table 18.2 Unemployment rate (% of civilian labour force)

	1981–1990	1988	1989	1990	1991	1992
(West) Germany	6.0	6.3	5.6	4.8	4.2	4.5
Belgium	10.7	10.2	8.6	7.6	7.5	8.2
Denmark	7.6	6.4	7.7	8.1	8.9	9.5
Greece	7.1	7.6	7.4	7.2	7.7	7.7
Spain	18.5	19.3	17.1	16.1	16.3	18.0
France	9.2	9.9	9.4	9.0	9.5	10.1
Ireland	15.7	17.3	15.7	14.5	16.2	17.8
Italy	9.5	10.8	10.6	9.9	10.2	10.2
Luxembourg	2.5	2.0	1.8	1.7	1.6	1.9
Netherlands	10.2	9.3	8.5	7.5	7.0	6.7
Portugal	7.1	5.7	5.0	4.6	4.1	4.8
UK	9.7	8.5	7.1	7.0	9.1	10.8
EUR 12	9.6	9.8	8.9	8.3	8.8	9.5

Source : European Economy, Annual Economic Report for 1993, No. 54, 1993

Table 18.3 Inflation (GDP deflator, % change on preceding year)

	1981–1990	1988	1989	1990	1991	1992
(West) Germany	2.7	1.5	2.6	3.4	4.2	4.5
Belgium	4.6	1.8	4.7	2.7	2.7	3.6
Denmark	5.8	3.4	4.3	2.1	2.9	2.5
Greece	18.4	15.6	12.7	19.3	19.5	15.6
Spain	9.3	5.7	7.0	7.3	6.9	6.3
France	6.4	3.1	3.5	3.1	3.1	2.9
Ireland	7.0	2.9	4.7	−1.6	1.2	2.9
Italy	9.9	6.6	6.2	7.5	7.3	5.2
Luxembourg	5.1	4.0	6.0	2.9	3.0	2.2
Netherlands	2.2	1.2	1.2	2.5	3.0	2.7
Portugal	17.1	11.6	13.0	14.3	14.3	13.1
UK	6.0	6.6	7.1	6.3	6.7	4.6
EUR 12	6.5	4.5	5.0	5.2	5.4	4.7

Source : European Economy, Annual Economic Report for 1993, No. 54, 1993

Table 18.4 Balance of current account (% of GDP)

	1985	1986	1987	1988	1989	1990	1991	1992
Germany	2.6	4.4	4.2	4.3	4.8	3.5	−0.9	−1.4
Belgium	0.3	2.1	1.4	1.7	1.7	0.9	1.7	1.8
Denmark	−4.6	−5.4	−2.9	−1.3	−1.5	0.5	1.4	2.9
Greece	−8.2	−5.3	−3.1	−2.0	−5.0	−6.1	−5.1	−4.4
Spain	1.4	1.6	0.0	−1.1	−3.2	−3.7	−3.8	−3.9
France	0.1	0.5	−0.1	−0.3	−0.4	−0.8	−0.5	0.1
Ireland	−4.0	−2.9	1.3	1.5	0.8	1.3	4.6	5.9
Italy	−0.9	0.5	−0.2	−0.8	−1.4	−1.9	−2.4	−2.4
Netherlands	4.1	2.7	1.4	2.8	3.5	4.0	3.9	3.4
Portugal	0.4	2.4	−0.4	−4.4	−2.3	−2.5	−3.5	−0.3
UK	0.5	−0.9	−2.0	−4.8	−5.4	−4.2	−1.8	−2.0
EUR 12	0.7	1.4	0.8	0.1	−0.1	−0.3	−0.5	−0.6

Note : West Germany before unification and the whole of Germany after unification.
Source: European Economy, Annual Economic Report for 1993, No. 54, 1993

Table 18.5 General government financial balances (% GDP)

	1981–1990	1988	1989	1990	1991	1992
Germany	−2.0	−2.2	0.1	−2.0	−3.2	−3.2
Belgium	−9.1	−6.8	−6.7	−5.8	−6.6	−6.9
Denmark	−2.5	0.6	−0.5	−1.5	−2.2	−2.4
Greece	−12.4	−13.8	−17.7	−18.6	−16.3	−13.8
Spain	−4.6	−3.3	−2.8	−3.9	−5.0	−4.5
France	−2.2	−1.7	−1.3	−1.5	−2.1	−3.9
Ireland	−8.9	−4.8	−1.8	−2.5	−2.3	−2.4
Italy	−11.2	−10.7	−9.9	−10.9	−10.2	−9.5
Netherlands	−5.6	−4.6	−4.7	−4.9	−2.5	−3.3
Portugal	−7.9	−5.4	−3.4	−5.5	−6.4	−5.4
UK	−1.8	1.0	0.9	−1.3	−2.8	−6.2
EUR 12	−4.4	−3.4	−2.7	−4.0	−4.7	−5.1

Source : European Economy, Annual Economic Report for 1993, No. 54, 1993

Germany's position as a low inflation economy was rooted in the Bundesbank's legal commitment towards price stability. Its monetary policy is not primarily understood as anticyclical policy but is geared towards longer term variables such as the growth of the overall production potential. The Bundesbank aims to allow the stock of money in the economy to grow just as quickly as necessary in the medium term to permit the real economy to exhaust its production potential without allowing scope for inflation to emerge. It thereby quasi-automatically triggers disciplinary adjustment constraints if overall demand exceeds the sum of what can be distributed. Through its longer term orientation and commitment to price stability, German monetary policy has encouraged financial structures to emerge where long-term interest rates are of more importance than short-term ones especially for investment decisions. Whereas monetary policy can exercise relatively close control over short-term rates, capital market interest rates can only be influenced indirectly by the Bundesbank via the credibility of its anti-inflationary policies. Given the relative importance of long-term interest rates, German monetary authorities generally see no close link between short-term interest rates, economic growth and full employment.[5]

German monetary leadership within the ERM with the Deutschmark as the anchor currency was based on the anti-inflationary stance of the Bundesbank. This leadership was generally perceived as useful and necessary in the 1980s to achieve price stability throughout the system and coincided with the desire of all members for low inflation. The Deutschmark served as a point of reference for all other currencies and the respective countries' monetary policy, especially for their short-term interest rates as they needed to hold their currencies stable via the Deutschmark within the agreed bands of fluctuation. German interest rates set the nominal interest rate floor within the ERM. Because of perceived risks of inflation and devaluation, investors insisted on a risk premium over the German rates. Since no other country enjoyed as much credibility, arbitrage prevented their interest rates falling below the German level – at least not substantially and permanently (see Table 18.6). However by improving the credibility of their own anti-inflationary policy, countries managed to undercut the existing risk premiums. By following German low-inflation policies, interest rate differentials moved down gradually from 1983 onwards. By the end of the 1980s price and interest rate convergence was achieved to a considerable degree between the hard-core countries of the ERM. Nevertheless, the cost of achieving low inflation relative to Germany was often associated with higher unemployment rates and lower growth rates than there might otherwise have been, and calls for more symmetrical adjustment were occasionally made. However, these seemed to overlook the fact that to safeguard the stability of the ERM system the monetary policy of the anchor country must be geared primarily to ensure price stability at home. For example, a decrease in official German rates as part of a symmetrical interest rate action to defend central parties would increase the risk of inflation in Germany and thus impede the stability of the ERM's anchor currency. Furthermore, due to diversification in the credit sector, the same monetary policy can have different effects in different countries. The structural differences in the credit sector are the result of different inflation experiences in ERM countries. Due to these structural differences, long-term interest rates and long term credits with fixed interest rates are more important in Germany, especially for investments. In other countries with a long history of inflation such as Italy (or the UK, which joined the ERM in 1990), short-term interest rates and long-term credits with variable money market rates are more eminent. Thus, exchange rate-induced high money market interest rates will have a different impact on economic activity in Germany than, say, Italy.

Table 18.6 Nominal short-term rates (%)

	1981–1990	1988	1989	1990	1991	1992
Germany	6.7	4.3	7.1	8.4	9.2	9.5
Belgium	10.2	6.7	8.7	9.8	9.4	9.4
Denmark	11.2	8.3	9.4	10.8	9.5	11.5
Greece	17.4	15.9	18.7	19.9	22.7	24.5
Spain	14.9	11.6	15.0	15.2	13.2	13.3
France	10.8	7.9	9.4	10.3	9.6	10.4
Ireland	12.6	8.1	9.8	11.4	10.4	12.4
Italy	15.0	11.3	12.7	12.3	12.0	14.0
Netherlands	7.0	4.8	7.4	8.7	9.3	9.4
Portugal	17.2	13.0	14.9	16.9	17.7	16.2
UK	11.8	10.3	13.9	14.8	11.5	9.6
EUR 12	10.8	8.2	10.6	11.4	10.8	11.1

Note : West Germany before unification and the whole of Germany after unification
Source : European Economy, Annual Economic Report for 1993, No. 54, 1993

Eastern Germany after unification

German unification as part of the historical transition process in Eastern Europe started with the establishment of the German Economic and Monetary Union (GEMU) in July 1990. In October 1990 the GDR ceased to exist and joined the Federal Republic of Germany (FRG).[6] The transition from 40 years' planned economy into a free market economy exposed the former GDR to a sharp competitive shock. It soon became clear that the transition would be more painful and would take longer than originally anticipated. At the macro level, unification created a large gap between aggregate demand and supply. Whereas economic activity has collapsed since 1989 to nearly 50 per cent of its original level, aggregate demand has increased with the gap being financed mainly from western German transfers (see Table 18.7).

After two years of double digit real GDP decline (16 per cent in 1990 and 31 per cent in 1991), the eastern German economy constituted only 6.6 per cent of all German GDP with its population being 20 per cent of the total population (see Table 18.7). Considering the fact that inflation in the eastern region was considerably higher than in the western part and that western transfers amounted to nearly 70 per cent of the East German GDP, the real contribution to GDP was significantly lower. There were several reasons for the collapse. The initial conversion rate for incomes and wages on a one to one basis constituted a *de facto* appreciation of the Ostmark, since the market exchange rate was in the region of 1:5 to 1:7. [7] This resulted in an increase in real wages above the productivity level. Whereas labour productivity was estimated to be roughly 30 per cent of the western German level, average real wages had risen to 40 per cent of the western level.[8] Unit labour costs were thus above those of western Germany, which already has the highest unit labour costs in the EU.[9]

Resulting from the generous conversion rate and the sudden exposure to world market competition, eastern Germany saw its competitive position deteriorating right from the beginning of the unification process. The problem was grossly exacerbated by the agreements on wage convergence to the western level by 1994. In the light of economic conditions these agreements have been renegotiated, with convergence now to be achieved by 1996 and subsequently lower annual wage increases (although still above productivity growth). Nevertheless, by 1992 average wages were around 60 per cent of the western level, with productivity being only one-third of that in western Germany.[10] Consequently unit labour costs in the early 1990s were nearly twice as high as in the western region. The rapid wage convergence, although difficult to avoid in a common currency area with relatively high labour mobility between the regions, has severely handicapped the eastern German economy, with its products being uncompetitive at the prevailing cost level. Forty years of central planning have left the former GDR with a large, mainly obsolete capital stock. The lack of modern capital stock is a major obstacle to increasing productivity. Oversized industries characterised by low involvement in the international division of labour are undergoing a dramatic but inevitable structural change. Before unification, the manufacturing sector accounted for well above 50 per cent of employment, whereas in most western industrialised countries the share is less than 30 per cent.[11] Many of these industries, being old and uncompetitive, are closing down. Exports virtually collapsed because of the disappearance of the traditional export markets in Eastern Europe, which formerly took over 70 per cent of its total exports[12] and no corresponding establishment of western markets due to the weak competitive position (see Table 18.7). Whereas in 1990 the former GDR's share of total German trade was still 5 per cent, it shrank by 1993 to 2 per cent.[13] Finally, the preference of

East German consumers for western products immediately after unification provides an additional explanation for the decline in eastern German production.

With most of the capital stock being obsolete, only substantial capital spending will permit a gradual overhaul of the capital stock and significantly improve productivity. Investments will therefore be the most important contribution to self-produced income in eastern Germany. Public investments, making up one half of the transfers to East Germany,[14] have already led to a significant improvement of the infrastructure and an environmental clean-up, thereby enhancing the conditions for private investments. Private investments needed to close the capital gap (to bring eastern Germany to the economic level of western Germany) are estimated to be between DM 1,000 bn. and 1,500 bn.[15] In spite of substantial investment incentives, promised western German and foreign investments until 1995 are only DM 113 bn., creating some 700,000 new jobs.[16] In the light of the degree of underemployment (see Table 18.7), these are far from sufficient. Apart from high labour costs, economic slowdown in the west and the breakdown of the traditional export markets, there are further investment impediments. The issue of property rights is not yet satisfactorily resolved and hence is a continuing source of uncertainty. There is still a bottleneck in public administration and long, complicated planning and approval procedures. Also, the East European countries are emerging as low-wage competitors and therefore as investment alternatives. For example, the Czech Republic has the same productivity level as the former GDR but wages are only 10 per cent of the West German level.[17]

After the virtual collapse of the economy in 1990 and 1991, recovery was expected in 1992, but this faltered as GDP grew only by 7.4 per cent (see Table 18.7). Considering that growth started from a very low base and that transfers from the western part constituted over three-fifths of eastern GDP (see Table 18.7), of which one half was absorbed in non-investment activities, a self-sustained upturn has not yet occurred. While construction and the service sector expanded, there was a decline in industrial production, which is exposed to international competition. Industrial production shrank to one-third of its original level.[18] The necessary shrinking of the industrial base seems to have entered a phase of de-industrialisation. On the other hand, one has to qualify the expansion of the non-industrial sectors. It is based heavily on high financial transfers and public orders, with much of the service sector being subject to regional competition only. The dramatic deterioration in eastern German output is reflected in labour market developments. The official unemployment rates grossly underestimate the true extent of underemployment. Taking into account the government-financed employment sustaining measures, retraining, short-time working arrangements and the reduction of the labour force by early retirements, the true unemployment rates were over 40 per cent in 1991 and 1992 (see Table 18.7). The numbers employed in manufacturing declined from their original level of 3 million to 700,000 by the end of 1992.[19]

While output and employment declined dramatically, aggregate demand increased. Real incomes were boosted by the conversion rate and the wage increases that followed. The release of the backlog of demand accumulated during the communist era and new public sector infrastructure programmes also explain why domestic demand since 1991 is twice as high as domestic production.[20] This in effect means that in eastern Germany more is distributed than is produced there. This gap constitutes a trade deficit with the rest of the world (including western Germany) and is mainly financed by transfers from western Germany, of which one half is absorbed in non-investment activities.

Table 18.7 Eastern German economic indicators

	1990 (estimated)	1991	1992
Real GDP (p.a. % change)	−16	−31.4	6.8
Nominal GDP as % of all-German GDP	9.0	6.6	6.9
Exports (p.a. % change)	−7.4	−52.8	−22.5
Unemployed (thousands)		913	1 170
Unemployment rate (% of civilian workforce)		10.9	14.9
Number in employment-sustaining schemes, early retirement, etc. (thousands)		2 565	2 002
Transfers from western Germany (DM bn.)		132.1	156.2
Transfers as % of eastern German GDP		68	63

Sources : Statistisches Bundesamt, Volkswirtschaftliche Gesamtrechnung 1992; March 1993
Statistisches Bundesamt, Außenhandel 1992; 1993
Statistisches Bundesamt, Datenreport 1992; 1992
DIW Wochenbericht 18-19/93, 6 May 1993
Author's calculations

Germany in the 1990s

After two years of rapid growth and entering a third one in 1990, the western German economy was operating close to its potential output, with unification taking place right at the tail-end of the boom. The already high western German demand was further increased by high demand in eastern Germany. With production in the eastern region collapsing and no reduction in western demand, the high eastern German demand was supported by huge transfers, mainly financed by a higher public sector deficit. The large deficit spending programme prolonged the boom, thus delaying the cyclical downturn. One can speak of a Keynesian expansion programme in a non-Keynesian situation. Real GDP growth in western Germany increased to 5.1 per cent in 1990 and 3.7 per cent in 1991 (see Table 18.1). Given the high degree of capacity utilisation in the West and all-German demand outstripping supply, the gap was filled mainly by higher imports. This led to a deterioration in Germany's trade balance and consequently to a turnaround of the current account. The surge of imports reduced the surplus of the trade balance from DM 135 bn. in 1989 to just 22 bn. in 1991, although it improved slightly to 33 bn. in 1992.[21] Given the traditionally high deficits in services and transfers, the current account moved from a surplus of DM 108 bn. in 1989 to a deficit of DM 33 bn. and

DM 40 bn. in 1991 and 1992 respectively.[22] Whereas the current account surplus equalled 4.8 per cent of GDP in 1989, the deficits in 1991 and 1992 amounted to 0.9 per cent and 1.4 per cent of GDP (see Table 18.4). Reflecting the turnaround in the current account, Germany shifted from being a capital exporter to a capital importer. The capital balance changed from a deficit of DM 135 bn. in 1989 to a surplus of DM 107 bn. in 1992.[23] Even though saving ratios of 13 per cent in western Germany and 11 per cent in the eastern region are high,[24] they are not sufficient to cover the growing financial demand in Germany. This was caused by the financing of the high public deficits and increased credit demand for private investments in eastern and western Germany. The unification boom induced a substantial increase in the demand for labour in the western region, reducing unemployment to 4.2 per cent by 1991 (see Table 18.2). The tight labour market conditions pushed up wage settlements. Wage increases of 6.8 per cent in 1991 and 5.0 per cent in 1992 were far above productivity gains, causing a combined increase in unit labour costs of 9.5 per cent in 1991 and 1992.[25] Unit labour costs rose at a steeper rate than those in Germany's main trading partners, resulting in a deterioration of the price-competitive position.

Unification prompted a swing in the public finances. Starting with a slight surplus in 1989, the large transfers to eastern Germany, making up more than 5 per cent of western German GDP per year,[26] led to a sizeable public deficit of 3.1 per cent in 1992 (see Table 18.2), despite savings and various tax increases. With transfers remaining high in the foreseeable future, the financial stance is expected to worsen further. In 1995 the debts of the Treuhand and the GDR Debt Fund will be merged into the Inherited Burden Fund and will be taken on by the federal government. The debts are estimated to be greater than DM 400 bn. and are to be serviced over a period of 30 years.[27] The public deficit is expected to reach 7 per cent by 1995, with accumulated debts being well above 60 per cent of GDP.[28] The costs of servicing the debts will rise strongly. Interest payments on total government expenditure may climb from 11 per cent in 1989 to 16 per cent in 1994 and increase to 23 per cent in 1997.[29] This will severely circumscribe the scope of action for the government expenditure on public investments in the former GDR. Increases in public debts also put pressure on the capital market, thereby impeding private investments. Furthermore, large parts of the transfers are still used for non-investment purposes in eastern Germany. The convergence programme of late 1991 aimed to consolidate the medium-term public finances and led to various increases in taxes and administrative prices. However, it failed to address adequately the question of drastic expenditure cuts.

Unification generated inflationary pressures. With a rate of 2.6 per cent in 1989, inflation did not begin with unification, but rather the combined effect of unification and a booming economy gave an upward twist to inflation. Inflation escalated to 4.2 per cent in 1991 and 4.5 per cent in 1992 (see Table 18.3). Monetary growth significantly overshot the target range. Demand pressures caused by the expansionary effect of fiscal policy, and cost pressures mainly due to high wage settlements, emerged. These led the Bundesbank to tighten monetary policy. After a series of increases in policy controlled interest rates, the discount rate reached an all-time peak of 8.75 per cent by July 1992, while the Lombard rate stood at 9.75 per cent.[30] This led to high short-term rates (see Table 18.6). With fiscal and wage policy on a collision course with the restrictive monetary policy, the upshot was an unbalanced policy mix. The tightening of monetary conditions also led to an inverted yield curve, with higher interest rates applying to short term maturities rather than long-term ones, and this was against the background of relatively high pre-existing capital market rates.

However, the rate of economic growth in western Germany slowed down during the second half of 1992. During the first half of the year the economy grew by 3 per cent,[31] but the annual growth rate amounted to only 1.5 per cent. For 1993 a negative growth rate of 1.9 per cent was recorded.[32] Apart from the delay in the cyclical downturn caused by unification, the recession is attributable to a number of factors. Wage rises above the level of productivity gains and increases in taxation pushed up costs for firms, which because of tight monetary policy and sharp international competition could not be passed on fully to prices. Consequently profits were reduced and investments declined. With profits plunging, the propensity to invest in real capital was further dampened by the increase in interest rates which made financial investments more attractive. Relatively high long-term interest rates increased the cost of borrowing, since 80 per cent of all loans granted are mainly long-term with fixed interest rates.[33] The slowdown of major European and the US economies, along with the strength of the Deutschmark, weakened demand for German exports. Exports account for roughly one-third of western German GDP, of which over one half are intra EU exports.[34] This demonstrates that not only do economic developments in Germany affect other EU economies, but economic growth in its partner countries is also of vital importance for the German economy itself. Unemployment increased to 8.6 per cent in September 1993.[35] The rise in unemployment reduced wage pressure and wage inflation began to moderate, with settlements for 1993 being between 3.3 per cent and 4.0 per cent.[36]

The appreciation of the Deutschmark caused by the ERM turmoil in autumn 1992 was used twice by the Bundesbank to cut the official rates, in September and December 1992. Even though the public deficit and inflation remained high, the tight monetary policy was further gradually relaxed by a series of rate cuts in 1993. By October 1993 the discount rate stood at 5.75 per cent and the Lombard rate at 6.75 per cent.[37] The Bundesbank justified the cuts on the grounds that monetary expansion had flattened and was moving closer to the target range, that inflation had slowly started to decline and that wage settlements were moderate. Additionally, with the widening of the intervention bands after the ERM crisis in summer 1993, further massive interventions on the foreign exchange markets are unlikely. The Deutschmark appreciated relative to ERM and major non-ERM currencies. With the decrease in official rates, the related short-term interest rates came down too. Favourable developments have occurred in the capital market as well. In this case, the downward stabilising effect of the tight monetary policy on inflation expectations led to positive conditions for funding investments. For maturities above one year, the yield curve has returned to normal, with higher interest rates applying to longer term maturities. However, average yield on public bonds decreased to 5.5 per cent in December 1993, the lowest in international and historical comparisons.[38] Firms wishing to invest are now able to fund their projects on more favourable terms.

The recession has also disclosed weaknesses on the supply-side of the economy, questioning Germany's position as one of Europe's prime industrial bases.[39] As well as perceived location advantages such as relative social and political stability, good infrastructure and a highly skilled, functionally flexible and mobile labour force, companies operating in western Germany have to contend with a series of negative factors, especially on the cost side (see Table 18.8), hampering their price competitiveness. Labour productivity, though relatively high, is not sufficient to compensate for extremely high labour costs. This results in high and rising labour unit costs which are above the level of all other western industrialised countries. Even allowing for the strength of the Deutschmark, a substantial part of the 1989–1993

Table 18.8 Location factors

	Western Germany	France	Italy	UK	USA	Japan
Unit labour costs in manufacturing, 1992; western Germany = 100	100	79	76	70	67	80
Unit labour costs: % change 1989–93 on $ basis	39.3	30.7	13.0	14.9	3.4	25.9
(of which exchange rate effect in percentage points)	(21.6)	(19.6)	(–4.0)	(–6.9)	–	(13.0)
Labour costs per hour in manufacturing, 1992 (DM)	41.96	27.75	32.91	22.79	24.79	30.0
(of which non-wage costs in DM)	(19.46)	(13.18)	(10.29)	(6.85)	(6.93)	(7.18)
Effective annual hours of work in manufacturing, 1992	1.519	1.646	1.675	1.660	1.857	2.007
Plant utilisation in manufacturing 1992 (hours per week)	53	69	73	76	n.a.	n.a.
Total tax burden of joint stock companies, 1992 (% of undistributed profits)	66.2 (61.6 in 1994)	52.2	47.8	33.0	45.3	59.2
Environmental expenditure, 1991 (% GDP)	1.7	0.9	n.a.	0.9	1.2	1.0
(% of private expenditure)	(63)	(38)	n.a.	(51)	(59)	(11)
Return on sales (net), 1990	2.0	2.8	2.4	5.0	5.8	2.6

Sources: Institut der deutschen Wirtschaft (IW); Industriestandort Deutschland, 1993
Institut der deutschen Wirtschaft (IW); Argumente zu Unternehmensfragen, No. 8, 1993
Deutsches Institut für Wirtschaftsforschung (DIW), Wochenbericht, 16/93, 22 April 1993

increase was due to the rising domestic cost level. In particular, the non-wage element, comprising statutory, collectively agreed and voluntary payments, has risen sharply and now constitutes 47 per cent of total labour costs. A considerable burden is the generous social security system, to which employers contribute one half. If no radical reform of the system is carried out, contributions can be expected to rise considerably in the future. Furthermore, the centralised collective bargaining system has led to a low degree of wage differentiation between different branches of an industry and different sizes of firms. This puts the smaller and medium-sized enterprise (SME) sector at a disadvantage. Compared to its industrial competitors, Germany has the shortest working hours per week, the most generous holiday provision and high rates of absenteeism, leading to the lowest effective annual working hours. There are relatively inflexible working time provisions because of statutory labour law and collective agreements. This results in a lack of decoupling of working time and plant operating time, producing the lowest plant utilisation time in the EU. The decreasing plant utilisation time has raised the capital costs per unit of output. Notably hit are SMEs, which often operate single shifts.

The density and complexity of government regulations and legislation are another negative factor. For example, the stringent environmental standards induce a significant cost disadvantage, particularly for the large chemical sector. Germany is a high-tax country, even taking into consideration the relatively favourable depreciation and other allowances. Despite the recent company tax reform, cutting the marginal tax rates, the tax burden remains higher than in other countries. In attempting to evaluate the quality of an industrial location by a single indicator, net return on sales tends to bundle the effects of many positive and negative location factors. The comparatively low return points to a diminishing position of Germany in international location competition, with effects on investment, growth and employment prospects.

Trade effects

The importance of the German economy relies on the fact that it is the biggest EU economy, making up approximately a quarter of the Union GDP and with imports equalling a quarter of its GDP, of which over one half are intra-EU imports.[40] Exports account for a substantial part of the GDPs of Germany's EU partners, which to varying degrees also have relatively open economies (see Table 18.9). The smaller countries such as Belgium, the Netherlands and Ireland have an export proportion of GDP of around 50 per cent or more. For the major economies the proportion is roughly one-fifth in the case of France and the UK and one seventh in the case of Italy. Since 1958 all countries have strikingly increased their share of exports to Germany, which now is the main export destination for all EU members except

Table 18.9 Visible trade

	Exports as % GDP 1989–1992	Exports to Germany as % total exports		Exports growth to Germany (p.a. % change)			Export/import ratio in trade with Germany			
		1958	1991	1990	1991	1992	1989	1990	1991	1992
Belgium	58.0	11.6	23.7	12.7	14.4	−2.3	76	83	94	90
Denmark	27.3	20.0	22.4	18.9	21.0	7.0	76	92	108	107
Greece	13.0	20.5	23.9	18.8	11.9	−8.9	53	56	60	49
Spain	12.1	10.2	15.0	24.3	29.2	5.7	48	57	64	62
France	18.9	10.4	20.7	8.2	20.0	−3.4	72	78	90	88
Ireland	56.8	2.2	12.7	7.9	13.9	15.2	147	172	187	209
Italy	15.2	14.1	21.0	17.3	15.4	3.2	76	86	97	94
Netherlands	47.1	19.0	29.3	8.9	10.8	−2.5	95	103	118	110
Portugal	25.4	7.7	19.1	26.7	16.9	4.5	71	79	75	83
UK	18.0	4.2	13.7	15.5	12.2	8.6	58	68	84	84

Sources: Deutsche Bundesbank, Zahlungsbilanzstatistik, June 1993
          Deutsche Bundesbank, Monthly Reports
          Statistisches Bundesamt, Außenhandel 1992; 1993
          Eurostat, Data for Short Term Economic Analysis, November 1993
          European Economy, Annual Economic Report for 1993, No. 54, 1993
          Author's calculations

Ireland. Between roughly one eighth and a quarter of their total exports are going to Germany. The FRG provides an outlet for one-fifth of all French and Italian exports, for nearly one seventh of total UK exports and for a quarter of the exports of the smaller countries such as Belgium and Denmark.

These figures clearly illustrate the highly interwoven nature of the EU economies with Germany, and indicate the magnitude of the effects of economic developments in Germany on partner countries. High rates of economic growth in Germany, for example as a result of fiscal expansion, tend to raise its demand for imports. This will have a beneficial trade effect by boosting aggregate demand and national output of its EU partners via the foreign trade multiplier. Economic slowdown in Germany, with a tendency for import demand to decrease, will subsequently have a detrimental effect on its partners. Thus, a growing German economy is important for growth and employment prospects in all EU countries. Conversely, the high level of interdependence already achieved between the EU economies can also affect Germany, with exports constituting one third of its GDP, of which over one half are intra-EU. Thus, an economic slowdown in other EU members translates into lower exports, with negative effects on growth and employment.

German unification provides a useful case to illustrate the economic influence of Germany on its partners' economies. As discussed before, unification constituted a fiscal shock, resulting in all-German demand outstripping supply with the gap being filled by an increase in imports. With export growth being rather static and import increases of 10 per cent in 1990 and 16 per cent in 1991, the visible trade balance deteriorated.[41] The surge in imports benefited Germany's trading partners and especially the EU countries since German intra-EU imports stood at 50 per cent. The cyclical slowdown that began to emerge in most European countries in 1990 was somewhat moderated by the impulse of German unification, which acted as a demand expansion programme for the EU. All EU countries benefited by the increase in German import demand and were able to step up their exports to the FRG substantially in 1990 and even more in 1991. Spain topped the list, with increases of nearly 25 per cent and 30 per cent in 1990 and 1991 respectively. France expanded its exports to Germany by 8.2 per cent in 1990 and 20 per cent in 1991. The corresponding figures for Italy are 17.3 and 15.4 per cent, and for the UK 15.5 and 12.2 per cent. The beneficial trade effect, raised the GDP in the EU area by an estimated half a percentage point annually in 1990 and 1991.[42]

Individual countries benefited to different degrees depending on the relative openness of their economies and the extent of their trading links with Germany. The largest contribution to growth was experienced by the smaller, more open economies. Belgium profited most from the trade effect which made up 1 per cent of its GDP in 1990 and 2 per cent in 1991.[43] For the UK the stimulus to economic activity was roughly the same as the EU average. The estimated contribution to GDP was under 0.5 per cent in 1990 and under 0.75 per cent in 1991.[44] With export growth in Germany being relatively flat, all countries were able to improve their traditionally negative bilateral trade balance with Germany. The Danish and Dutch balance even turned into a surplus, whilst significant improvements were recorded in the British and Spanish bilateral balances in particular.

In 1992 the beneficial trade effect ran out. The German economy slowed down, particularly during the second half of 1992, and moved into recession by 1993. The high import growth came to an end and imports actually declined by 1 per cent in 1992.[45] Consequently export growth to the FRG slowed down significantly in most EU countries, and in the cases of

Belgium, Greece, France and the Netherlands it was negative. The British, Italian and Spanish export performance to Germany in 1992 partly reflects the weakening of their currencies in relation to the Deutschmark as a result of the September 1992 ERM crisis. With the decrease in import demand in Germany, most countries saw their bilateral trade balance with Germany worsening somewhat compared to 1991. However, the export/import ratios for all countries except Greece were more favourable than in 1989, the year before German unification. German demand for foreign goods was still perceptibly higher than prior to unification. With imports of DM 638 bn. in 1992 compared to DM 507 bn. in 1989,[46] German trade relations continue to support the business activities of its partner countries.

German monetary policy influence

Economic developments in Germany – and the resulting responses of German monetary authorities – were also transmitted onto the partner economies via the operation of the ERM, which is the transmission mechanism between interest rate changes in Germany and the other ERM members. There too, German unification serves as a good example to demonstrate the degree of influence exerted on other members by special German features. Confronted with inflationary pressures from an over-expansive fiscal policy and excessive wage increases, the Bundesbank successively raised official interest rates between 1991 and summer 1992, leading to high and rising short-term interest rates. With Germany's *de facto* leadership of the ERM and the Deutschmark as the anchor currency in the system, the overriding target for the monetary authorities throughout the ERM was the Deutschmark exchange rate of their currencies. Thus the interest rates of the participating countries were linked to the German ones, which set the nominal interest rate flow in the ERM. Higher German interest rates gave rise to short run capital inflow and a demand for deposits denominated in Deutschmark. The increasing demand on the foreign exchange market for the Deutschmark caused it to appreciate relative to other ERM currencies. Because of the ERM commitment to keep exchange rates within the agreed bands of fluctuation, the other countries had to tighten monetary policy to maintain parity with the Deutschmark. To offset the depreciation of their currencies relative to the Deutschmark they had to raise their interest rates. Additionally, as German interest rates rose, the Deutschmark appreciated against the currencies of non-EC countries. As the ERM members had to keep their exchange rates in line with the strengthening Deutschmark, the currencies of the ERM as a group appreciated against those of external trading partners.

Other ERM countries shared the Deutschmark appreciation and faced higher interest rates than would otherwise have been the case. By passing on interest and exchange rate responses to these nations, the tight monetary policy of the Bundesbank exerted deflationary pressures throughout the EU. High interest rates generally increase the cost of borrowing in the economy with detrimental effects on consumption and investment spending. Appreciation reduces price competitiveness to outside countries and tends to decrease net exports, the overall effect being lower economic growth rates. The deflationary impulse the ERM members were receiving as a result of the unbalanced policy mix in Germany was not in line with their domestic policy needs. Business cycle developments in Germany and other EU countries diverged (see Table 18.1). While the western German economy slowed down from the second half of 1992 onwards, the other EU economies were already experiencing low growth rates from 1990 onwards, although the decrease was somewhat moderated initially by the rising German import demand. By 1991, the UK was even undergoing a severe recession. Thus, the deflationary effects of German unification had led to a sharper slowdown of economic activities in its partner countries than might have otherwise occurred.

Despite lower inflation in the other hard-core ERM countries in the post-unification years, they were not able to bring their short-term interest rates below the German level (see Table 18.6), with the exception of marginally lower rates in the Benelux countries in 1992. They had to contend with higher interest rates than might have been justified. German rates continued to set the floor, reflecting not so much actual performance but rather the credibility that the stability-orientated monetary policy had accumulated over a period of years. This led to deeply rooted market expectations that the Deutschmark will never be devalued against other ERM currencies. Furthermore, due to divergencies in the credit sector, high short-term interest rates had a more severe impact in countries such as Italy and the UK where short-term rates are more important for spending decisions than long-term rates. On balance the net effect of German unification appears to be negative. The deflationary effects transmitted to the EU countries seem to have outweighed the beneficial trade effect.

Since September 1992, interest rates have come down gradually in Germany. This started with a relatively small cut in the official rates, a few days before the climax of the 1992 ERM crisis. The peseta was devalued by 5 per cent, with a further devaluation of 6 per cent along with the escudo in November. The lira and the pound sterling were temporarily suspended from the mechanism. The resulting devaluation/depreciation and improvement in price competitiveness relative to ERM countries, along with the interest rate cuts that followed, contributed to supporting economic activity. This needs to be weighed against the requirement for a more restrictive macro-economic policy to counter inflation resulting from price and wage pressures. With the widening of fluctuation bands to ±15 per cent after the August 1993 crisis, the issue of German monetary policy restricting policy options of its partners is at least for the time being obsolete. Other countries are now free to relax monetary policy to suit their domestic needs. However, the adjustment of the operating rules of the ERM has not led to a competitive devaluation race, with the pattern of exchange and interest rates not undergoing significant changes. Reduction in the short-term interest rates in the hard-core countries followed in line with decreases in German interest rates, reflecting the commitment to relatively fixed parities with the Deutschmark. The potential for larger interest rate cuts was not utilised because of the risk of depreciation and resulting inflationary pressures. This would have endangered the degree of price stability achieved after the long period of painful adjustments. The importance of Germany in their foreign trade was probably another motive.

Germany and the ERM crisis

The intervention of central banks in foreign exchange markets during the ERM crisis was dwarfed by the huge speculative movements in member currencies. Underlying these movements were the liberalisation of international capital flows and the deregulation of financial markets, which had occurred progressively over the past decade. This led to a high volume of liquidity in world financial markets which were able to move vast amounts of money quickly and with low transaction costs. Between 1985 and 1992, the daily turnover on the international currency markets grew by approximately 45 per cent to nearly $1,000 bn..[47] However, international reserves held by central banks failed to grow in line with the transaction volume on the international currency markets. This led to a shift of power relations between central banks and the markets, to the advantage of the latter. Furthermore, a shortcoming of the ERM is that there are established rules concerning exchange rate stability, but there are none for the coordination of other policies, especially fiscal policy which also has an impact on exchange rates. Obviously, by relying on relatively fixed exchange rates against the Deutschmark the currencies of other countries can build up a stock of confidence, but only if the resulting stabilisation constraints are fully met by tight monetary, fiscal and wage policy. This interrelationship seemed to be somewhat forgotten in recent years, especially in the light of the fixed exchange rate illusion that emerged after 1987. Fiscal consolidation in many ERM countries remained behind expectations, and the accumulated public debt ratio of over 100 per cent in Italy and Belgium clearly represents an unsustainable fiscal position.[48]

The fixed exchange rate illusion that emerged since the latest realignment in 1987 was further fostered by the EMU prospects. However, the difficulties in ratifying the Maastricht Treaty and the resulting uncertain outlook on monetary integration have destroyed the fixed exchange rate illusion, and triggered speculative attacks on the weaker ERM currencies in September 1992. The pound and lira were suspended, while the peseta and escudo were devalued. The underlying cause for this development was accumulated fundamental divergencies. The cost and price levels in these countries grew faster than in Germany and other hard core countries since the 1987 realignment. The newer ERM members entered the mechanism at excessively high parities which did not reflect their true competitive position.

Without realignment, their currencies were overvalued resulting in a competitive disadvantage, as partly reflected in their current account deficits (see Table 18.4). Despite persistent and fundamental divergencies, the fixed exchange rate illusion led to a paradox whereby investors built up sizeable holdings of weak, high-interest rate currencies, which they regarded as being strong. Temporarily, these currencies were at the upper limit of their fluctuation bands because interest rate differentials overcompensated for their perceived low depreciation potential. Triggered by the Danish referendum on the Maastricht Treaty, the currencies of those countries whose parity no longer reflected their competitive position initially came under pressure. The markets regarded the prevailing central parities as no longer credible. This shows that the attention of those countries' monetary authorities had focused too much on nominal exchange rate stability with the fundamental prerequisites for exchange rate stability being disregarded. For reasons partly connected with national prestige, countries resisted the necessary realignment for too long, despite existing divergencies. Thus, even without the impact of high German interest rates as analysed above, pressure was building up under the surface that would sooner or later have required a realignment.

The unsuccessful defence of the weaker currencies clearly showed the limits of exchange rate stabilisation via the intervention of central banks on the foreign exchange markets. When market expectations change, central banks fight a losing battle. For market participants that betted on depreciation, the risk of loss was small but profit prospects were high. Following the success of 'one way street' speculation in September 1992, individual speculators made massive profits, and the fixed exchange rate illusion was sunk forever. In the period following, hard-core currencies such as the French franc and the Danish crown came under increasing pressure, despite the fundamentals underlying their currencies being reflected realistically in their central parity to the Deutschmark. With inflation and fiscal deficits in many of these countries lower than in post-unification Germany (see Tables 18.3 and 18.5), these fundamentals were even better than the German ones. However, the markets increasingly doubted that the monetary authorities of these countries would be able and willing to defend the prevailing parities.

The deeper reasons for this credibility problem in their monetary policy was the asynchronous development in business cycles between the anchor country and the other member states, resulting in different interest rate requirements. In most EU countries economic slowdown began in 1990, with the UK already undergoing a recession by 1991. In Germany, the boom period was prolonged by the fiscal expansion induced by unification. Economic activities started to slow down in the second half of 1992. The Bundesbank faced with rising inflation, successively increased interest rates. This led to high interest rates throughout the ERM area. High interest rates were anyhow not appropriate for the other hard core countries since they had already achieved a considerable degree of price stability. High German interest rates exerted deflationary pressures at a time when most of its partners were sliding into recession. This combination of high interest rates and recession led to conflicts between the policy options most appropriate for domestic needs and those necessary to maintain exchange rate stability. In order to maintain the value of their currencies in relation to the Deutschmark, high interest rates were required and this conflicted with the need to lower interest rates because of domestic recession. Nevertheless, the room for manoeuvre to cut interest rates was limited. The Deutschmark was no longer underpinned by low inflation, a current account surplus and a small financial deficit. Despite these changes in its underlying fundamentals, it remained the strongest currency in the system. Because of over 30 years of stability orientated, anti-inflationary monetary policy, the Deutschmark had built up a stock of confidence. This led the markets to believe that the problems caused by unification would have no sharper long-term implications. Thus German interest rates continued to set the floor in the ERM. This shows that the problem faced by other ERM members was not so much Germany's temporary weakness as its long-term strength.

The markets noted the incompatibility between external and internal policy objectives of Germany's ERM partners. They questioned whether monetary authorities would give higher priority to maintaining the existing parities than they would to accommodating domestic economic needs by cutting their interest rates, especially in the light of rising unemployment. This led to doubts regarding the credibility of their monetary policy and thus their ability to hold their currencies stable against the Deutschmark. Although German interest rates have come down gradually since September 1992, there was uncertainty about the timing and extent of rate cuts, and the credibility gap that had opened up invited speculation. The crisis moved towards its climax when France unilaterally cut interest rates and incautious remarks were made regarding the franc's potential as the anchor currency. After the franc fell below its intervention level, French authorities failed to raise interest rates. The ERM was finally adjusted with widening bands of fluctuation, since France and other countries lacked the reserves to sustain their parities, the Bundesbank was unwilling to cut interest rates to preserve the system at the prevailing parities and the French were resistant to devaluation. This disguised the *de facto* collapse of the system and the *de facto* devaluation of the franc, although by the end of 1993 the French franc and other currencies such as the Belgian franc moved back to their old band around the Deutschmark. However, they achieved this by keeping interest rates high, despite high unemployment.

The foregoing discussion indicates that holding the Bundesbank unilaterally responsible for the ERM crises is too simplistic. It is legally obliged to give the utmost priority to safeguarding domestic price stability by appropriate monetary policies. The main cause for high German interest rates was the German government's mishandling of the financial aspects of unification. Instead of financing the high cost of unification by either appropriate tax increases or sufficient cuts in expenditure, there was increased borrowing which overheated the economy. The resulting demand and cost pressures forced the Bundesbank to adopt a tight monetary stance. If calls for quicker and larger interest rate cuts had been accepted, it would have undermined the internal price stability, thereby endangering the stability of the anchor currency on which the system relied.

Although high German interest rates undoubtedly were a contributory factor to the September 1992 crisis, the underlying causes were existing divergencies. The resulting devaluations/depreciations seem to reflect much better the economic reality, in that they have corrected the competitive disadvantages of the countries involved. The ERM appears to have worked relatively well as long as there was no fundamental divergency and when business cycles were synchronised. However, when a severe shock occurred in the anchor country, leading to asynchronous business cycles and different policy needs, the narrow bands were unable to accommodate non-conflicting internal and external policy objectives at prevailing central parities. Nevertheless, the Bundesbank realised that the level of German interest rates would prompt policy conflicts in its partner countries and immediately before September 1992 it offered a realignment. This was not taken up by the other member countries. Therefore, with limited margins of fluctuation and no realignment, there was not much room for divergent interest rate development just at a time when relatively high German inflation called for more flexibility in the system.

Conclusion

The economic landscape in Germany has undergone a fundamental change since the turn of the decade, with German unification being the paramount challenge. Aggregate supply collapsed in the eastern region but aggregate demand was buoyant. The resulting gap was filled by transfers which were mainly financed by an increase in government borrowing, leading to overheating in the western economy. Fiscal expansion in an already booming economy caused a deterioration in the current account and increased inflation. In turn, this led to high interest rates. The economy slowed down from the second half of 1992 onwards, inflationary pressures eased, interest rates came down gradually and the current account improved somewhat. The main cause of concern remains the high and rising public deficit. The German economy also faces problems on the supply side, especially on the cost front. With severe international competition, NICs in particular are increasingly able to compete in quality and cost terms in industries which are regarded as German strongholds.

The developments in Germany affected its partner countries mainly in two ways. In the short term, they benefited from the trade effects of German unification. The extent of these benefits has clearly demonstrated the importance of the German economy for the other EU countries. Beyond the short term, high German interest rates exerted deflationary pressures throughout the EU at a time when the economies of member states were sliding into recession. Because of the dominant position of Germany in the ERM, the other members had to accommodate German monetary policy at the prevailing parities, in spite of different domestic priorities. German monetary policy has also contributed to the ERM crises, although the underlying causes leading to the September 1992 crisis lay deeper. High German interest rates were largely due to the German government's mishandling of the financial aspects of unification. Part of the blame must also be put on Germany's ERM partners, because of their lack of flexibility in their rejection of a realignment at a time when inflation had become a problem in the anchor country. With the widening of fluctuation bands, the issue of German dominance in the ERM should have ended. However, countries still attempt to hold their currencies within the old bands, partly because of the importance of Germany as a trading partner, but also to safeguard the degree of price stability achieved.

Once eastern Germany has caught up, and provided the supply-side problems are successfully tackled, the economic weight of Germany will be further boosted. Despite these difficulties, it is German monetary policy that continues to set the scene for its partner countries.

Notes

1. *European Economy*, Annual Economic Report for 1993, No. 54, 1993, p. 12.
2. Ibid.
3. **OECD** 1991 *Historical statistics*, pp. 122–123.
4. **Pugh G T** The economic consequences of German unification for the EC and in particular the UK, *CEREB Conference on Europe in the 1990s*, July 1993, p. 3.
5. See for example **Tietmeyer H** Geldpolitik der Bundesbank und Zinsen, Lecture at Kreditpolitische Tagung der Zeitschrift für das Gesamte Kreditwesen, 27 October, 1993, in: *Deutsche Bundesbank – Auszüge aus Presseartikeln*, 29 October, 1993, pp. 1–6. **Schlesinger H** German monetary policy and the future of European monetary integration, Speech at Harvard University, in: *Deutsche Bundesbank – Auszüge aus Presseartikeln*, 14 April, 1993, pp. 1–4.
6. For details on the unification process and the particulars of the East German economy see **Tüselmann H J** German unification, in McDonald, F. and Dearden, S. (cds), *European Economic Integration*, 1st edn, Longman, London, 1992, pp. 214–218.
7. **Deutsche Bundesbank** Monthly Reports.
8. **Issing O** Gesamtwirtschaftliche Folgen des deutschen Einigungsprozesses, Lecture at Zermatter Symposium, in: *Deutsche Bundesbank – Auszüge aus Presseartikeln*, 11 August, 1993, p. 3.
9. **Institut der deutschen Wirtschaft (IW)** *Industriestandort Deutschland*, 2nd edn, 1993, p. 8.
10. **Schieber H** Wirtschafts – und geldpolitische Probleme in Wiedervereinigten Deutschland, Speech at I. Ostdeutscher Sparkassentag, in: *Deutsche Bundesbank – Auszüge aus Pressartikeln*, 2 September, 1993, p. 3.
11. **Statistisches Bundesamt** *Datenreport 1992* Bundeszentrale für politische Bildung, Bonn, 1992, p. 426.
12. Ibid., p. 286.
13. **Issing O** op. cit., p. 4.
14. **OECD** *Economic Survey – Germany*, 1992, p. 38.
15. **Köhler L** Report presented to Geldpolischen Ausschuß des Vereins für Sozialpolitik, in: *Deutsche Bundesbank – Auszüge aus Presseartikeln*, 1 April, 1991, p. 12.
16. **Institut der deutschen Wirtschaft (IW)** *Wirtschaftswoche*, 13 March, 1992, p. 12.
17. **Hesse H** Speech, in: *Deutsche Bundesbank – Auszüge aus Presseartikeln*, 15 January, 1993, p. 8.
18. **Deutsches Institut für Wirtschaftsforschung (DIW)** *Wochenbericht* 18–19/93, 6 May, 1993, p. 252.

19. *Financial Times*, 26 January, 1993, p. 2.

20. *European Economy*, op. cit., p. 48.

21. **Deutsche Bundesbank** *Zahlungsbilanzstatistik*, June 1993.

22. Ibid.

23. Ibid.

24. **Deutsches Institut für Wirtschaftsforschung (DIW)** op. cit., pp. 268 and 270.

25. **OECD** *Economic Outlook*, No. 52, December 1992, p. 51.

26. **OECD** *Economic Survey – Germany*, 1992, p. 36.

27. *Frankfurter Allgemeine Zeitung*, 4 April, 1993, p. 3.

28. *National Institute Economic Review*, 4/93, November 1993, p. 42.

29. Ibid., p. 41.

30. **Deutsche Bundesbank** Monthly Report.

31. **Scott A** 1993 Developments in the European Community economies, *Journal of Common Market Studies*, Vol. 31, August, p. 98.

32. **Statistisches Bundesamt** 1994 *Erste Ergebnisse der Ihlandsproduktberechtung.*

33. **Jochimsen R** Perspectives on German and European monetary policy in an international context, Seminar at Eesti Pank, Tallinn, in: *Deutsche Bundesbank – Auszüge aus Presseartikeln*, 8 July, 1993, p. 8.

34. **Statistisches Bundesamt**, *Volkswirtschaftliche Gesamtrechnung 1992*, March 1993; *Außenhandel 1992*, May 1993.

35. *National Institute Economic Review*, op. cit., p. 39.

36. **International Labour Office** 1993 *International Labour Review*, Vol. 132, No. 1, p. 13. **The Economist Intelligence Unit** 1993 *Country Report – Germany*, No. 1, p. 19.

37. **Deutsche Bundesbank** Monthly Report.

38. **Deutsche Bundesbank** Monthly Report.

39. For detailed discussions, see for example: **Bundesministerium für Wirtschaft** 1992 *Strategien für den Standort Deutschland: Wirtschaftspolitik für die neunziger Jahre*, BMWi Dokumentation. **Siebert H** 1992 Standortwettbewerb – nicht Industriepolitik, in: *Institut für Weltwirtschaft*, Die Wirtschaftswelt, No. 4. **Schriftenreihe des Rheinisch–Westfälischen Instituts für Wirtschaftsforschung (RWI)** 1992 *Politische Maßhahmen zur Verbesserung der Standortqualität*, No. 53. **Löbbe K** 1991 Standort Deutschland–Internationale Wettbewerbsfähigkeit und Attraktivität für Auslandskapital, in *Landeszentrale für politische Bildung Baden-Würtemberg*, Außenwirtschaftspolitik.

40. The analysis throughout this section refers to visible trade.

41. **Deutsche Bundesbank** *Zahlungsbilanzstatistik*, June 1993.

42. *European Economy*, op. cit., p. 11.

43. Estimates of Deutsche Bundesbank, presented by O. Issing at Zermatter Symposium, in: *Deutsche Bundesbank – Auszüge aus Presseartikeln*, 11 August, 1993, p. 4.

44. Estimates of Deutsche Bundesbank presented by O. Issing at the German Chamber of Industry and Commerce, London, in: *Deutsche Bundesbank – Auszüge aus Presseartikeln*, 2 April, 1993, p. 4.

45. **Statistisches Bundesamt** op.cit.

46. Ibid.

47. **Haller G** Europäische Währungspolitik, Lecture at Bundesverband der Deutschen Industrie (BDI), in: *Deutsche Bundesbank – Auszüge aus Presseartikeln*, 3 December, 1993, p. 14.

48. **OECD** *Economic Outlook*, No. 52, December 1992, p. 216.

INDEX

acid rain, 187
ACP *see* African, Caribbean and Pacific countries
Adonnino Committee, 17
Advisory Committee on Safety, Hygiene and Health
    Protection at Work, 141
African, Caribbean and Pacific countries (ACP),
    trade agreements, 244
    patterns of trade, 255–8
agriculture,
    EU budget, 77, 80, 81–2
    harmonisation affecting food industries, 232–3
    protectionism, 222, 261
    regional employment disparity, 163
aid,
    Eastern Europe, 292–3
    European Union, 261–2
air pollution, 195
air traffic control (ATC), 217
air transport, 214–7
    deregulation, 216
Air Union, 214
airline mergers, 217
airports, 205
Amin, A., 179
Andriessen, Frans, 277
animal health, 232, 267
Armitage Inquiry, 212
Austria,
    application for membership of the EU, 276
automobiles,
    external trade policy, 243
aviation, 214–7

Bachter, J., 179
Balassa, B., xxviii, 8
'Baldwin' effect, 28
Baldwin, R., 28, 278
Banana Protocol, 266
banking,
    cross-border activities, 72–4
    impact of the Single European Market, 142
    Large Exposure Directive, 73
    Own Funds Directive, 73

    Second Banking Coordination Directive, 72–3
    Solvency Ratio Directive, 73
barriers to free movement, 26
Basic Research in Industrial Technologies for Europe
    (BRITE), 127
Baumol, W.J., 96
BCO (Business Cooperation Office), 123
Beacham, A., 101
Begg, I., 175, 179, 180
Bellis, J.F., 246
Belous, R.S., 36
Benelux, xix
Beretta Report, 153
Bilson, G.F.O., 55
biotechnology industry, 130–2
Biotechnology Research for Innovation, Development
    and Growth in Europe (BRIDGE), 127
Bird, R., 249–50
black economy, 145, 150
Blair House Agreement, 228–9
Bodson report, 218
Boltho, A., 164–5
Brainard, W.C., 36
BRIDGE (Biotechnology Research for Innovation,
    Development and Growth in Europe), 127
BRITE (Basic Research in Industrial Technologies for
    Europe), 127
British Airways, 217
Brundtland Report, 188
Brussels Agreement, 79, 82, 84, 86
budget,
    European Union, 77–89
bus services, 211
Business Cooperation Office (BCO), 123
Business Liaison Office, 123

cabotage, 211
Cairns Group, 226–7, 261
Camagni, R.P., 178
CAP *see* Common Agricultural Policy
capital mobility, 21–3, 68, 70–1
carbon tax, 189
Cardoso, A.R., 165